SLOVAK HISTORY
CHRONOLOGY & LEXICON

Július Bartl

Viliam Čičaj

Mária Kohútová

Róbert Letz

Vladimír Segeš

Dušan Škvarna

SLOVAK HISTORY
CHRONOLOGY & LEXICON

BOLCHAZY-CARDUCCI
PUBLISHERS, INC.
WAUCONDA, ILLINOIS, USA

SLOVENSKÉ PEDAGOGICKÉ
NAKLADATEĽSTVO
BRATISLAVA, SLOVAK REPUBLIC

Táto publikácia vyšla s finančnou podporou Britskej medzinárodnej školy Bratislava, ktorá poskytuje vzdelávací program v anglickom jazyku pre deti vo veku od 2 do 16 rokov.

Britská medzinárodná škola Bratislava
Dolinského 1
841 02 Bratislava
tel./fax: 00421 2 643 64 784, 643 66 992
www.bis.sk
e-mail: bis@computel.sk

ISBN 80-08-00400-2

ISBN 0-86516-444-4

Slovenské pedagogické nakladateľstvo

Bolchazy-Carducci Publishers

Library of Congress Cataloging-in-Publication Data

Lexikón slovenských dejín. English.
Slovak history: chronology & lexicon / by Dušan Škvarna ... [et al.];
translation by David P. Daniel.
p.cm.
Includes bibliographical references (p. 337 – 339) and index.
ISBN 0-86516-444-4
1. Slovakia-History-Chronology. 2. Slovakia-History-Lexicon. I. Škvarna, Dušan. II. Title.

DB2744 .L4913 2000
943.73'002'02-dc21

00-028959

Introduction to the English Edition

A t the end of our millennium, historiography has experienced a renaissance. Interest in the past is expressed not just by specialists – historians, cultural workers or students of history – but also by individuals and groups in society whose specialization and work have little in common with history. Moreover, as globalization increases, the social space is becoming smaller. Today, the attention of many is attracted to countries and nations that, not so long ago, still seemed to be far away and in which previously there was little interest.

With the fall of the Soviet imperial political system, the countries of eastern and central Europe, to which Slovakia also belongs, have assumed a new shape. Cultural, political, economic, tourist and personal contacts have increased many times. In many countries a desire to deepen the knowledge and understanding of unknown neighbors and partners can be detected. It is said that the way to the knowledge of the present leads through a knowledge of the past. Thus, works about the history of those nations that were forced to live behind the iron curtain for half a century have appeared in English-speaking countries. However, this is true only to a modest degree for the past of Slovakia and the Slovaks. Until now, basic handbooks, lexicons, and encyclopedias that provide concise surveys of Slovak history as a whole have not been generally available.

This *Slovak History: Chronology and Lexicon* attempts to fill this gap, at least in part. It is made up of two sections. The first section, the calendar, records Slovak history chronologically from the first evidence about human beings on Slovak territory up to the events that took place in 1998. It consists of notations that summarize important historical events and phenomena. In the calendar individual periods are divided by introductory texts that briefly synthesize the characteristics and problems of the respective subsequent era.

The second section is an encyclopedic dictionary. It contains three hundred, alphabeticallyar-ranged entries. These entries characterize the most important concepts, institutions and events, especially those that could not be appropriately incorporated or sufficiently treated in the chronological overview. The content of the chronology is graphically cross-referenced by dates, words or phrases set in bold type. These indicators call attention to dictionary entries or to chronological data that provide additional information on the specific issue and serves to bind together the text of the work. Genealogical tables of the longest reigning dynasties on the Hungarian throne, the Arpáds and the Habsburgs, a list of all rulers and presidents of those states to which the lands of Slovakia belonged (Great Moravia, the Kingdom of Hungary, Austria, Czechoslovakia, Slovakia), a list of recommended literature and a register of names are provided as appendices to the chronology.

Six historians from Bratislava prepared this chronology of Slovak history. The earliest part of the calendar, up to 1458, was compiled by Július Bartl of the Pedagogical Faculty of Comenius University, the period between 1458 and 1614 by Vladimír Segeš, of the Institute for Military History, the section from 1615 to 1780 by Viliam Čičaj of the Institute of Historical Studies of the Slovak Academy of Sciences, the period from 1780 to 1918 by Dušan Škvarna of the Philosophical Faculty of Comenius University, and the period from 1918 until today by Róbert Letz from the Pedagogical Faculty of Comenius University. Mária Kohútová of the Institute for Historical Studies of the Slovak Academy of Sciences also participated in the preparation of the entries. The initials of the respective author follow each entry.

In preparing the *Slovak History: Chronology and Lexicon* the authors used the results not just of Slovak but also Czech, Hungarian, Austrian and German historians. In this work, Slovak history does not play out in an isolated space but within the broad central European context. It follows the path and the peripatetic ascent of civilization in Slovakia, its social and cultural changes, and expressions of state politics on its lands. It also encapsulates the constitutional changes in Slovakia, the roles of rulers and presidents, reformations in the formation of the modern Slovak nation and civil society in Slovakia during the nineteenth and twentieth centuries, the complicated interweaving of a belated modernization and the national suppression of the Slovaks. Naturally, these and further problems do not have a single interpretation. Among historians and the broad cultivated public they continue to elicit debates and new questions. The authors of the Lexicon do not share the same view on all questions of Slovak history. Thus its content not only reflects contemporary knowledge but, to a certain degree, also the value judgements and the viewpoints of the individual authors.

In view of its scope and succinctness, it is clear that the *Slovak History: Chronology and Lexicon* is intended not just for a group of specialists – historians or students of Slavic or Slovak studies – but for all who have an interest in Slovak historical matters. The authors hope that it will help to improve the knowledge of Slovak history and appreciation of the problems, potential and attractiveness of contemporary Slovakia, as well as, even if modestly, contribute to greater understanding among nations.

Dušan Škvarna
Main author

Translator's Preface

The translation of the *Slovak History: Chronology and Lexicon* makes accessible in the English language a handbook containing both a chronology and a short dictionary of Slovak history. The intended audience of the original publication was both secondary and university students as well as the general public. However, the excellent reception of the volume in Slovakia and the difficulty of finding modern treatments of Slovak history in English led to the decision of the Slovak Pedagogical Press to issue an English translation of this handbook in partnership with Bolchazy-Carducci Publishers.

While the translation attempts to replicate faithfully the Slovak text, it is not a literal translation. Differences between English and Slovak academic style and the extensive use of abbreviations frequently made it necessary to restructure, paraphrase or, in a few instances, to modify or elaborate the original text. At the same time, however, an attempt was made to retain the particular style of each of the several authors.

A particularly difficult problem was the translation of place and personal names, specific historical terms, offices and institutions.

Central European towns are blessed or cursed with a multitude of names. On the one hand, the names of many towns and villages changed during the course of history (e.g., Parkan is today's Štúrovo while Brezalauspurc, Pozsony, Pressburg and Bratislava all refer to the town that today is the capital of the Slovak Republic) or varied significantly with the languages used in the region, primarily Latin, Slovak, Hungarian, German (e.g. Novosolensis, Neusohl, Besztercebánya are the Latin, German and Hungarian designations for Banská Bystrica). The problem became acute when the text refers to locations in other countries using the traditional Slovak designation. To make it easier for the reader to locate a town or place in modern atlases, the current standard English name or the name in the language of the country in which a town is located has been used for locations not in Slovakia.

The translation of names of persons became a particularly vexing problem. All personal names in the original text were given using current Slovak orthographic norms. Initially it was considered to use the English equivalents of all personal names. But it seemed anachronistic to refer to Juraj Fándly as George Fándly, Ľudovít Štúr as Louis Štúr. But to retain Slovak forms (e.g. František Jozef II or Ľudovít Kossuth) was equally anachronistic. A uniform usage proved difficult as it finally was decided to retain the use of the first names of individuals mentioned in the text according to Slovak orthography and usage. However, where an individual is clearly a member of a non-Slovak ethnic group, the last name normally was provided in the form of that ethnic-linguistic group. Moreover, unlike the Slovak text, the English translation gives the Slovak names and their English or Hungarian equivalents.

Even more challenging was finding suitable translations for historical terms, offices, and historical institutions. While some terms, such as gold piece (zlatý) can be resolved using a standard synonym (florin or ducat, although these refer to different coins), some terms defy simple translation. For instance, the etymologically correct translation of servienti (servants) or of *dvorníci* (courtiers) would be factually incorrect since the servienti (servants) were actually noble retainers of the king (thus courtiers in English), while the *dvorníci* (courtiers) were servants, that is craftsmen or handworkers in the service of nobles, magnates or the ruler. Likewise, it seemed best to translate the office Country Judge (Krajinský sudca) as chief justice which better conveys the significance of the position. On the other hand, it seemed best to use the term magistrate rather than mayor to translate the office referred to in Slovak as *richtár, šoltys, fojt, vesnik,* depending on the size and legal status of the community. This emphasizes the primarily judicial rather than administrative character of the chief representative office of a community (in Slovak the terms *mešťa-nosta* or *primátor* are used to describe the latter function). The English equivalent of some terms was so imprecise that the use of the original term or an Anglicized version of the original term was used in the translation (e.g. banderium, sandjak, palatine).

Some translations that might have been more precise were, however, discarded in favor of less precise but normally used translations. For instance, the traditional translation of the Slovak term *župan* is count while *župa* is translated as county. However, the specific character of the older office of *župan* (as opposed to its more modern use, c.f. **župa**) is congruent to that of a sheriff in England and a *župa* would thus be roughly equivalent to a shire. English also uses the term county to translate the Slovak *stolica* which literally means *seat* as in the seat of the territorial administration.

Many terms have multiple denotations and connotations. For instance, *tovarišstvo,* from the term *tovariši* or journeymen literally denotes a journeymen's society but connotatively can mean any society. Thus, the title of the Slovenské učené *tovarišstvo* is translated traditionally as the Slovak Learned Society, although the translation Slovak Learned Journeymen does have a certain charm, while older literature uses *Tovarišstvo Ježišovo* for the Society of Jesus (Spoločnosť Ježišova).

Current Slovak orthographic rules require the use of a hyphen in Czecho-Slovakia. This has been retained throughout the text except for those instances where an official name is cited, e.g. the Czechoslovak Republic, the Czechoslovak Communist Party.

I wish to thank in particular Dr. Anton Šteffek and Mária Jakubičková who read the draft translation and made valuable suggestions that corrected or improved the text. However, they should be absolved of any infelicities, which remain the responsibility of the translator. It is my hope that the English version of the *Slovak History: Chronology and Lexicon* will prove to be a useful handbook for those who wish to become acquainted with the history of the Slovaks and Slovakia.

Finally, I wish to acknowledge my debt to Dr. Albert M. Devine for his help in editing the English version and his updates in content, and the other editors at Bolchazy-Carducci Publishers, Inc.

David P. Daniel

Primeval Slovakia

T he oldest and longest period in human history is known as the Paleolithic or Old Stone Age. Archeological research has defined its further internal segmentation, as in the more recent pre-historic eras, and currently seeks to make dating more precise. This is connected not only with the shorter chronological intervals that delineate individual epochs, but with the growing amount of material relics upon which archeological research depends. However, the evidence that archeological finds provide is limited. Even though modern natural and especially physical science research methods (radio-carbon method, dendro-chronological dating using the annual growth rings of very old trees and the like) are used alongside traditional methods of archeological research, the problem of archeological research remains – the so-called absolute chronology of investigated phenomena, how long this or that epoch lasted expressed in a number of years or millennia. Much more precise is a relative chronology that cites mutual temporal relationships between two cultures without expressing them as a number of years.

Therefore, primeval cultures that have several common indicators (settlements, cemeteries, weapons, ornaments, vessels and the like) have great significance for archeological research. Their names are determined according to the characteristic shape of vessels, ornamental motives and according to the territory where scientists discovered and investigated the relics for the first time. Recent eras have received the name of a culture according to the location of important finds. The development of the methods of the natural and especially the physical science is providing more precise data about several cultures that, until now, have neither been researched in detail nor placed chronologically. Archeology is a very dynamic science and sometimes new finds may change the view of a part of a problem or of a whole epoch.

■ **3,000,000 – 1,000,000 BC**
The first phase of human history is the oldest Paleolithic era, represented first and foremost by finds from southern and eastern Africa, e.g. from Kenya, Ethiopia and other sites where today we are seeking the cradle of man (*Homo*). Until now we do not have any confirmed finds from the territory of today's Slovakia.

■ **Ca. 1,000,000 – 250,000 BC**
Characteristic of the oldest phase of the old Paleolithic era is *Homo erectus*, a man with body held upright. Members of this species appeared in several places on the globe including central Europe.
They gathered vegetation by hand, hunted animals and produced simple stone implements by striking together and splitting stones. They lived in groups and so were able to hunt even large animals. They knew fire and built primitive dwellings or, in some cases, used caves and rock overhangs. In addition to stone tools they manufactured wooden and bone implements. The earliest old Paleolithic settlements in Slovakia were situated in the vicinity of Nové Mesto nad Váhom-Mnešice and in Bratislava. Additional finds of stone tools come from Seňa and Poľovo; remnants of hearths were found in Spišské Podhradie and Vyšné Ružbachy. Skeletal remains of human beings from this era have not been found or, like the unique find from Dreveník near Spišské Podhradie, have been destroyed and thus cannot be used for research.

■ **250,000 – 35,000 BC**
The mid-Paleolithic Era stretched from the penultimate Ice Age (Riss), through the last inter-glacial era (Riss – Würm Inter-Glacial Era), up to the start of the last Ice Age (Würm). The periods received their names accordingly from alpine glaciers. Their alternation connoted changes in the climate and likewise in

the living conditions of prehistoric humans. In this era, erect man (*Homo erectus*) was replaced by a new stage in the development of human beings, intelligent man (*Homo sapiens*) that, according to the locations of their discovery, received the names *Homo Steinheimensis*, living during the oldest phase of this era, and *Homo Neanderthalensis*, living in a more recent phase. In the mid-Paleolithic it is already possible to differentiate individual types of tools such as hand wedges, points, scrapers, knives and the like. Burials with offerings express a belief in an after- life. Settlement is denser but individual cultures are markedly differentiated, which is evidence for weak contacts among them. During the last inter-glacial period (Riss-Würm Inter-Glacial Era) and the beginning of the last Ice Age (early and later Würm) settlements appear in Slovakia in the vicinity of thermal springs, on loess terraces and in caves. Among the most important locations of finds belong those at Gánovce, Hôrka – Ondrej, and Beharovce in the Spiš region, Bojnice in the Upper Nitra Valley, Banka and Radošina in the Považie region. Among the finds of human remains of European significance belong the fossilized imprint of the skull of a Neanderthal from Gánovce near Poprad and a fossilized forehead bone of a young Neanderthal woman from Šaľa nad Váhom.

■ 35,000 – 8,200 BC

The era of the younger Paleolithic is characterized by the flourishing of mature hunter/gatherer cultures. Their creator is already modern man, *Homo sapiens sapiens,* who, from a biological viewpoint, is equivalent to contemporary man. This is demonstrated by the development of the brain and vocal organs that were able to create articulate speech. The success of collective hunting, especially for large mammals (mammoths, bison, reindeer, horses and the like), made it possible to establish larger settlements formed by groups of dwellings. Religious life is characterized by ritual skeletal burials with offerings. Wall paintings in caves as well as sculpted forms and other objects document

the spiritual sphere. To the most important cultures on the territory of Slovakia belong the Szeletian, Aurignacian and Gravettian (Dzeravá skala near Plavecký Mikuláš, Ivanovce, Nové Mesto nad Váhom – Mnešice, Trenčín, Vlčkovce, Zamarovce, Čertova pec near Radošiná, Banka, Moravany nad Váhom, Žabokreky nad Nitrou, Spišské Podhradie, Veľký Šariš, Tibava, Barca II, Cejkov etc.). From this period come also the oldest works of art in Cejkov and the sculpted Venus from Moravia that belongs at the apex of younger Paleolithic visual art. Its age is estimated by scientists, with the help of radio-carbon dating, to be more than 22,000 years.

■ 8,200 – 6,000/5,000 BC

The transition from the Paleolithic to the Neolithic, the New Stone Age, constituted the Mesolithic or Middle Stone Age. The glaciers definitively receded and a gradual warming occurred, resulting in the spread of thermophilic flora and fauna throughout the territory of today's Slovakia. This improved possibilities for hunting, the gathering of vegetation and, as confirmed by relics, fishing. The variety of implements and weapons was broadened. The settlements of the people living at that time are found on hills or places with good drainage (on sand and sand dunes). Objects of organic materials, such as those found in the peat bogs of northern Europe, are not preserved in the sandstone strata of Slovakia. By analogy, however, we can presume the use of bows, arrows, skis, sledges, boats hollowed out from a single tree trunk, oars, rods, fishing nets, harpoons and the like. During this period, communities from beyond the Carpathians penetrated northern Slovakia (Veľký Slavkov). In Veľká Mača near Sereď, along the lower Váh River and the Little Danube, archaeologists have uncovered settlements on sand dunes. Small settlements occur also in eastern Slovakia (Barca, Streda nad Bodrogom, Silická Jablonica).

■ 6,000/5,000 – 3,200 BC

The New Stone Age, the Neolithic, is characterized by a transition to a productive mode of agriculture, the tending of cultivated crops, the breeding of domesticated animals, and the production of more effective polished stone implements, but especially by the production of ceramics. The beginning of this era is often characterized as the Neolithic (agricultural) revolution because it brought fundamental changes in the attitude of man towards using nature for his own benefit. People observed regularity in the changing seasons of the year and the biological cycles of the plant and animal worlds. With this ended the dependency of human beings upon nature and the process of its gradual conquest began. During the Neolithic era contacts with the more developed regions of the Near East started, from whence derived the new lifestyle that penetrated the region. The rural mode of life demanded more permanent habitation and the building of stable settlements. The oldest rural agricultural settlements in southwestern and eastern Slovakia are representative of the people of a culture with linear ceramics (the name being derived from the mode of decoration). Settlements were built primarily on terraces of rivers, near streams and, more rarely, on sand dunes. Settlements were comprised of multi-space stake houses, six to seven meters wide and several tens of meters long. Their walls were sometimes decorated with painted ornamentation (Hurbanovo). The basic social units of that time, monogamous families, owned individual parts of the houses with separate fireplaces. Only fragments of the oldest ceramic products are preserved (Bíňa, Hurbanovo, Michalovce, Nitra, Veľký Grob and others). In the proximity of the houses the inhabitants built various agricultural structures, storage pits, in which grains and legumes were stored. Finds of bones confirm that Neolithic man raised beef cattle, pigs, sheep, goats, and the like. Hunting was only a supplemental source of food. Dogs, which became domesticated animals, were used for hunting. Neolithic people buried the dead in doubled-up positions. Society was dominated, perhaps, by a matriarchy; the fertility cult that penetrated the area from the Near East was important. The most

significant cultures on the territory of today's Slovakia during the Middle Neolithic were the Bükk and Želiezovce and, in the Younger Neolithic, the Lengyel and Polgár cultures.

■ 3,200 – 1,900 BC

The Late Stone Age, the Eneolithic, is characterized by several changes in the life of the population. In agriculture this was the plowing of fields with wooden plows drawn by cattle. Fewer people cultivated larger plots of land and produced a surplus of foodstuffs, even if it was not great. In family arrangements appear elements of a patriarchy in which a man becomes the representative of an extended family. The chief of the patriarchal family was, at the same time, the officiant of the cult. Among the most important cultures of this period in Slovakia are the late Lengyel (Brodzany – Nitra, Ludanice), late Polgár (Tiszapolgár, Bodrogkeresztúr, Lažňany) and the Baden cultures which spread into Turiec, Liptov and Spiš. Cultures with cord ceramics and the culture of bell-shaped cups penetrated the border areas of Slovakia. In the Eneolithic, cremation burials or mound-graves occur alongside skeletal burials. The increased productivity of work enabled the further development of production. The working of copper, gold, and the like appear. The exchange of goods developed and, with this, also conflicts among societies of different economic levels.

■ 1,900 – 1,500 BC

The Early Bronze Age is characterized by a strengthening of cultural influences coming from more developed regions to the southeast, the eastern Mediterranean, Anatolia and the Caucasus. Tilling the soil with a wooden plow was the basis of agriculture. Implements were produced from bronze (an alloy of copper and tin) but also continued to be made from stone and wood. The breeding of livestock expanded and horses were used as draft animals. The division of work continued and military activities were added to male functions in agriculture and the raising of livestock. A corps of warriors developed whose role was to defend the others. They played an important role in the organization of society. Changes also occurred in the building of settlements: they began to be built at strategically suitable promontories that, at the same time, were fortified. Some of the fortified settlements had the character of political and economic centers. Open settlements with houses in regular rows divided by streets also existed. A small group of specialists devoted themselves to the working of bronze from which they produced primarily weapons and jewelry. The dead were buried in a doubled-up position, but in some cultures cremation burials with offerings were used. Motifs testifying to a sun cult appear in burials and ornamentation. The territory of Slovakia fulfilled an important role not only as a cross-roads of commercial and cultural paths but also as a producer of copper that was mined in the central Slovak ore area and which contained high degrees of silver, arsenic, antimony and bismuth admixtures. At the beginning of the Bronze Age a unique Nitra group emerged in southwestern Slovakia. Its demise was connected with the entry of people of the Únětice culture from today's Moravia and Austria. In Slovakia it developed into a specific cultural group, the so-called Hurbanovo type. The Hatvan culture settled along the lower Hron River and in the Ipeľ region. During the transition from the Old to the Middle Bronze Age an agricultural Maďarovce culture (from the finds in Maďarovce, today called Santovka) developed in the fertile lowlands of southwestern Slovakia. It was characterized by fortified settlements at strategic places that express a deeper social-economic stratification and by the extensive production of ceramics (pitchers, amphorae, cups, bowls, pots). In a later period of the Early Bronze Age the Otomani culture developed in eastern Slovakia and penetrated up to the foothills of the High Tatras. The exterior organization of the settlements and the material culture betray the influence of Mycenaean civilization (for example, the massive stone citadel of Spišský Štvrtok). From this period comes also the iron handle of a dagger from a cult object in Gá-

novce (1465 +/- 35 BC). It is the oldest instance of iron in central Europe and evidence of contacts with the Chetitian Empire.

■ 1,500 – 1,250 BC

The Middle Bronze Age is characterized by the spread of barrow cultures, and the Carpathian barrow culture had its origins in the Maďarovce culture. For the production of working implements, bone, horn and bronze were processed, while the use of stone almost ceased. In agriculture a unique type of sickle was used, cattle raising developed, and trade took place with domestic bronze products manufactured from ore mined in central Slovakia. Although mound and skeletal burials were on the decline in Europe, in the territory of Slovakia the building of mounds from stone or wooden constructions continued. The area of today's Slovak-Hungarian border was settled by the Piliny culture. Its characteristic was cremation burials. The Kyjatice culture formed from it later in the era.

■ 1,250 – 700 BC

Important social and economic changes took place in the Early and Late Bronze Age that were expressed by the building of strongly-fortified citadels that had a military, administrative, and productive character. The substance of these changes is difficult to elaborate on the basis of archeological material alone. The Lusatian culture is an explicit cultural circle for which cremation burials in urn fields are typical. In opposition to earlier views about the penetration of this region from the north, today's specialists maintain that the Lusatian culture was original to Slovakia. The Čaka culture (named after finds at Čaka) in southwestern Slovakia and Transdanubia is a direct continuation of the Carpathian mound culture. Its large cairns for chiefs are found also in Očkov, Kolta, Dedinka, Lužany and the like. In Moravia and in southwestern Slovakia the Velatice culture developed from an older mound culture. Its continuation is the Podolie culture centered in western Slovakia. During the Early and Late Bronze Age the production of the bronze industry peaked: practical objects and tools for production, for instance, sickles that speeded up harvesting, were manufactured from bronze. The raising of cattle, horses, and sheep for wool spread into the mountain regions. Woodworking developed with more improved carpentry in the construction of dwellings and fortifications. A wagon with wheels from pliable wood was used. The working of bone and horn and the weaving of textiles improved. The greatest technical advance was in the working of metals. Finds of moulds for casting is evidence for work in series. In addition to foundry work other techniques for the working of metals also developed, such as beating, riveting, and the production of wire. Finds of weapons and jewelry in graves of the wealthy confirm the existence of a socially differentiated society.

■ 700 – 400 BC

On the territory of Slovakia the Old Iron Age, called the Hallstatt Era after finds in Hallstatt near Salzburg, began about a century later than in the Mediterranean region, that is, around 600 BC. The new metal arrived in central Europe from the Black Sea and Italian regions. The mining not only of iron but also of lead, gold and salt developed. Through Thracian tribes the attainments of Greek civilization penetrated the territory from the Black Sea region, especially ceramics worked on the potter's wheel. In eastern Slovakia the Kuštanovice culture formed in contact with the south-east and Trans-Carpathian regions. Southwestern Slovakia became a part of the Kalenderberg culture that is characterized by the culmination and final disintegration of a strict geometricism in the visual arts. The mountainous regions of northern Slovakia were already settled during the final phase of the Bronze Age by a people of the Lusatian culture who lived without external influences. There fortified mountain citadels were typical. The Hallstatt era is characterized by continuing social differentiation manifested in grave equipment. In addition to armor, weapons, and jewelry in the graves of the chiefs there are four-wheeled wagons and luxury items

from more developed southern civilizations, including beaten vessels from the eastern Alps, Etruscan beak-shaped containers and, exceptionally, black-figure Attic ceramics. The separation of tribal chieftains from the remainder of the population is seen also in the settlements: central fortified settlements are found encircled by agricultural farmsteads.

■ 400 – 200 BC

The name of an ethnic group living on the territory of today's Slovakia is already known from the New Iron Age – La Tène (named after La Tène in Switzerland). The Celts, whose original homeland was the Alps, eastern France, central Germany and southern Czechia, entered the Carpathian basin around the 400 BC and then, in a second wave, at the end of the fourth century BC. Celtic settlements were concentrated at the bend of the Danube near Vác in Hungary and along the lower reaches of the Ipeľ, Hron, Žitava and Nitra rivers (finds from Veľká Maňa near Vráble). The original population of this region became dependent on the Celts. The remainder of the population of the original Lusatian culture lived in isolation in the valleys and mountain regions of northern Slovakia where they created the independent Púchov culture. This survived until the beginning of the Christian era. They built fortified citadels at elevated places (Liptovská Mara, Havránok).

■ 200 – 60 BC

Another current of Celtic colonization that entered the territory of Slovakia was probably tribes from northern Italy that had been defeated by the Romans and retreated into the Carpathian basin. The Celtic settlement of Slovakia reached its greatest intensity during the first half of the second century BC and during its second half large administrative and production-commercial centers (*oppida*) were developed. The most significant *oppidum* was on the territory of today's Bratislava. Here the Celts began to strike coins with the inscriptions Biatec, Nonnos and the like, these being, perhaps, the names of their rulers. The most frequently discovered coins with the inscription Biatec have given the name *biatecs* to all Celtic coins. Similar fortified Celtic centers are found in Plavecké Podhradie and in Devín, which, after the destruction of the Bratislava *oppidum,* assumed its function. The Celts in western Slovakia probably belonged to the Boii, which were dislodged from the lands of today's Czechia by the Germans infiltrating from the north.

■ 60 BC – beginning of our era

Dacian tribes, concentrated in the basin of the Tisa River, invaded the territory of central Slovakia under the leadership of King Burebista and subjugated the Celtic population. The evidence for this is settlements with mixed Celtic-Dacian populations in the Nitra and Hron river basins. Nitra was probably the center of this territory. The Dacians subdued the Celtic Boii and Tauriska tribes. The Bratislava *oppidum* was probably destroyed in these wars. The remaining Celtic Cotíni stayed in the mountains of central Slovakia, where they took up mining and the working of metals. Together with the original domestic population, they created the Púchov culture that spread into central and northern Slovakia, including Spiš, and penetrated northeastern Moravia and southern Poland. Along the Bodrog River in Zemplín they created Celtic-Dacian settlements which were known for the production of painted ceramics. The Celts contributed to the development of iron-working and the production of iron weapons and implements, the making of ceramics on the potter's wheel and the perfecting of weaving. They invented rotating stones to mill flour. Cremation burials prevailed among them.

■ 9 – 6 BC

The Germanic Marcomani and Quadi tribes, under the leadership of the chieftain Marobud, destroyed the remnant of the Celtic Empire of Boiohemum centered in Czechia. In this period Roman armies advanced from the south and established the province of Noricum in Austria and the province of Pannonia in the western (Transdanubian) lands in Hungary.

■ 6 AD

Under the leadership of the future Emperor Tiberius, Roman legions left Carnuntum (Deutsch Altenburg and Petronell in Austria), crossed the Danube and, for the first time, entered the territory of Slovakia in order to attack Marobud from the east. The Great Pannonian Revolt (6 – 9 AD) compelled them to return.

■ Ca. 19 – 21

Around 19, internal dissension in the Empire of Marobud (instigated by the Romans) led to his fall and, not long afterwards, to the fall also of his successor Katvald (perhaps in 21). Both chieftains, with their entourage, went into exile on Roman territory. Then, as a preventive measure, the Romans settled their followers on the left bank of the Danube, between the Morava and Váh rivers, and installed Vannius as their king. The vassal Kingdom of Vannius was centered in southwestern Slovakia.

■ 50/51

His nephews, Vangio and Sido, whose allies were the Hermundura and Lugia tribes, organized a conspiracy against Vannius. Vannius did not receive the expected support from the Romans and, defeated, fled to the territory of the Roman Empire, where he was allowed to settle near Neusiedler Lake.

■ 69 – 79

During the reign of Emperor Vespasian, Roman garrisons began to ocupy the whole of Pannonia and continued the construction of a fortified Danubian border (*Limes Romanus*).

■ After 93

Roman camps were built within the framework of the *Limes Romanus* as headquarters for four legions: Vindobona (Vienna), Carnuntum (Deutsch Altenburg – Petronell), Brigetio (Szöny to the southeast of Komárno on the right bank of the Danube), and Aquincum (Óbuda – Budapest). Support camps and forts, 30 – 40 kilometers apart, were established between the base camps. Gerulata (Rusovce) was this kind of camp. On the left, unoccupied bank of the Danube, the Romans built forward support camps (Devín, the castle hill in Bratislava and Iža near Komárno, Kelementia). The existence of a Roman base camp near Štúrovo is presumed. The Romans also paid attention to the building of roads on this territory. In this period the Roman army in Pannonia numbered 40 – 50,000 men.

■ 99 – 106
The wars of Emperor Trajan against the Dacians concluded with the defeat of their leader Decebal and the establishment of the new Roman province of Dacia. At the same time Roman building and fortification activities along the Danube increased. In 99, at the beginning of his campaigns against the Dacians, the emperor undertook an inspection tour of the Roman camps along the Danubian border (*limes*).

■ 2nd century
Along with expeditions to punish the „barbarians" north of the Danube, the Romans continued to build forward support camps (for instance the camp in Stupava). Finds of Roman bricks, ceramics and other objects allow the inference that there were other stations and camps that have not yet been uncovered.

■ 166 – 167
The Longobards and other Germanic tribes coming from the north into Pannonia provoked an uprising of the domestic tribes against Rome.

■ 168
From Aquilea in northern Italy, the co-emperors Marcus Aurelius and Lucius Verus undertook expeditions against the insurgents but with little success. The Germani seized Pannonia and invaded northern Italy. The plague that erupted among their forces also complicated the defense of the Romans.

■ 169 – 171
The Romans expelled the Germani from the western provinces of Noricum and Raetia (in southern Germany). After the death of Lucius Verus (169), Marcus Aurelius assumed sole rule.

■ 172
Roman forces under the leadership of Marcus Aurelius pulled out of Carnuntum and occupied southern Slovakia. They gradually penetrated the more northern valleys and eliminated resistance. Here, in a camp somewhere on the lower course of the Hron River, the emperor wrote the first chapter of his *Meditations*.

■ 173
The Romans were victorious over the Marcomani and the Quadi. Connected with this war is the story of the Thundering Legion, a tale about a miraculous rain somewhere in Slovakia. Allegedly a Christian soldier prayed successfully for rain when the Roman army, surrounded by the barbarians, was hardpressed.

■ 179 – 180
The Roman army achieved further victories over the Marcomani and the Quadi in battles north of the Danube. Under the leadership of the legate Valerius Maximianus 855 soldiers of the second legion (II Legio Auxilia) camped in Laugaricio (Trenčín) where they left an inscription documenting their stay. This is a unique written reference to Roman soldiers at the northernmost point of their penetration into central Europe.

■ 180
On 17 March Emperor Marcus Aurelius died in Vindobona (Vienna). His son, Commodus, undertook a retaliatory expedition. It was successfully completed by the end of the summer of 180. Marcus Aurelius apparently wanted to establish two new provinces, Marcomania and Sarmatia. His death did not allow the realization of this grandiose plan, and Commodus concluded a mutually advantageous peace with the Marcomani.

■ **188**

Commodus undertook further expeditions against the Germani north of the Danube.

■ **Before 350**

The increasing number of barbarian raids fostered more intensive building activity along the Roman *limes*. The older camps were repaired and new ones were built even on the lands of the Quadi far from the border (Cífer – Pác, Veľký Kýr). These advance camps con-entrated the opposition of the barbarian tribes.

■ **374**

The Quadi, allied with the Sarmatians, attacked Pannonia. The Emperor Valentinian personally led the Roman army in what was more a demonstration of strength than a military success, as the Quadi avoided open battle and withdrew to the mountain valleys.

■ **375**

Emperor Valentinian died in Brigetio (near Komárno) during negotiations with envoys of the Quadi and the Sarmatians. After his death, the Romans concluded a peace treaty advantageous for both sides. The Roman army never entered the territory of Slovakia again.

The Slavs on the territory of today's Slovakia and the first state entity of the Slovaks

One of the problems that historiography and archaeology has not satisfactorily solved until now is the entry of Slavic tribes into the territory of today's Slovakia. The older view, that the Slavic tribes were autochthonous (native) to the Danubian basin, has been overturned by archaeological research. Also untenable is the theory that the original homeland of the Slavs was the Balkans. From the transition of the 19th to the 20th centuries a view, supported by archaeological research, prevailed that the homeland of the Slavs extended northward from the Carpathians to the territory between the Vistula, Bug, and Dnieper rivers. From there they spread out in all directions. The western Slavs came through the Carpathian passes and the Moravian Gate. Some of them may have crossed the Carpathian passes to reach the Tisa and central Danubian river basins and then entered Slovakia from the south. This process lasted one to two centuries. The names of the Slavic tribes that settled in northern central Europe and in the Balkan peninsula (Lusatian Serbs – Sorbs, White Croatians – Croatians) support the inference that an originally ethnically homogeneous entity was dispersed by the migrations and settled in different regions. In Slovakia, the entry of the Slavs overlapped the later phase of the Púchov culture and the remnant of the Germanic population that remained after most of the Germani moved west. During the first half of the fifth century, the Huns threatened practically all of Europe. They probably had settlements in the middle Danubian basin and did not directly encroach upon the lands of today's Slovakia. Around the mid-sixth century they were displaced by the Avars who, after the defeat of the Gepids and an agreement with the Longobards (568), settled in the central part of the Danubian basin. They came into contact with the Slavs in southern and southwestern Slovakia up to Nitra and around the Devín Gate, in Prša near Lučenec, and in the southern part of Slovak Zemplín (Barca). The Slavs rebelled against Avar hegemony and, under the leadership of the Frankish merchant Samo (623 – 658), they created a supra-tribal unit or league that defended their independence from the Avars and the Frankish Empire in a battle near Vogastisburg (631), the location of which is still unknown.

The center of Empire of Samo may have been in southwestern Slovakia, southern Moravia or in Lower Austria, on the land where, about two hundred years later, the Great Moravian Empire was established. After the fall of Samo's Empire, written evidence about the Slavs disappears.

Western chroniclers and annalists again began to take note of developments in central Europe in connection with the expansion of the Frankish Empire to the east during the reign of Charlemagne and his son Pipin. The break-up of the Avar Empire (*Kaganate*) between 791 and 796 made it possible for the Danubian Slavs to create larger units to defend themselves against their enemies, especially the Frankish Empire.

Two principalities developed in this area, those of Mojmír in Moravia and of Pribina in Nitra. More historical reports are preserved about that of Pribina, especially the unique information that around 828 Adalram, the archbishop of Salzburg, consecrated a church in Nitra. This was the first Christian church not only in central but also in all of eastern Europe whose existence is documented in writing. The conflict between Mojmír and Pribina and the forcible annexation of the Nitra principality by the Moravian principality (833) led to the creation of a strong state, the Great Moravian Empire, that attained its greatest territorial expansion under Svätopluk (871 – 894). Some more recent sources call him a king and refer to the entity as the Empire of Svätopluk. Attempts to defend its independence from the Eastern Frankish Empire, which after the division of the Frankish Empire (843), manifested greater interest in an eastern expansion, especially during the reign of Louis the German (846 – 876), led Rastislav (846 – 870), the ruler of Great Moravia, to seek independence also in the area of spiritual life. After a failure at the papal curia, he turned to the Byzantine Empire for missionaries. The mission of Constantine and Methodius (863) achieved success, despite the intrigues and obstructions of the Frankish clergy who had previously worked in the territory of Slovakia. The demise of Great Moravia halted the already initiated ecclesiastical organization connected with the consecration of Methodius as archbishop and of other bishops. However, it found fruition in the later organization of ecclesiastical administration in Hungary (the establishment of an archbishopric of Esztergom and the renewal of a bishopric of Nitra in the eleventh century).

Because of its brief existence, Great Moravia was not able to achieve an integration of its outlying lands with the center of the empire in southern Moravia and Slovakia. Therefore, after the death of Svätopluk (894) and a power struggle among his sons, Mojmír II and Svätopluk II, the empire collapsed because of the intensifying raids of Magyar nomadic groups. This process took place gradually when, after the death of Svätopluk, the Czech tribes were the first to withdraw and subordinate themselves to Arnulf, the Eastern Frankish ruler (895).

The demise of Great Moravia hastened the Magyar invasion of the Danubian lowlands in 896. Even prior to this, sporadic raids into central Europe had taken place. In 907 a three-day battle between Magyars and the Bavarians took place not far from Bratislava. By then a central power that would have been able to intervene in this war no longer existed in Great Moravia. The inadequacy of written sources makes it impossible to follow the course of the occupation of southern Slovakia by the ancient Magyars. The tribe of the Magyars that gave their name to whole nation occupied the central lands in the region of middle Danube and Pannonia. The Nitra region, which had become the sphere of interest of the Czech prince, Boleslav, was occupied by armed groups of Magyars during the second half of the tenth century. However, until the end of the eleventh century they did not penetrate northern Slovakia.

■ 5th century

The withdrawal of the Roman garrisons from Pannonia was a manifestation of the general demise of the Roman Empire. The ensuing period of the migration of nations was characterized by an extensive population shift. At the beginning of the fifth century the Quadi retreated to the west. Archaeological finds are very rare because the German tribes (Goths, Rugias and Heruls) remained only relatively briefly in the region. During the course of the fifth century, the nomadic Huns invaded the Carpathian basin but did not substantially encroach upon the lands of Slovakia. The historical sources are silent concerning developments in the territory of Slovakia. It is presumed that the first wave of the Slavic settlement in eastern Slovakia took place during the course of the fourth and fifth centuries while the Slavs settled in south-western Slovakia later.

■ **448**
Priscus, the Byzantine author, mentions a meeting with the Slavs, who offered him mead, somewhere in the Carpathian basin while he was on the way to Attila, the king of the Huns.

■ **453**
Attila, the king of the Huns, died. The Gothic historian Jordanes mentions, in connection with the burial ceremonies, the word *strava* (food) that he considered as pan-Slavic.

■ **Beginning of the 6th century**
Archaeological finds confirm the Longobard occupation of western Slovakia (Zohor, Bratislava – Devínska Nová Ves).

■ **512**
The Byzantine historian Procopius reports that the Germanic tribe of the Heruls, passing from Pannonia through the lands of western Slovakia or Moravia on their way north, came into contact with the Slavic population.

■ **Mid 6th century**
The historian Jordanes writes about Slavic settlements from the Vistula to the Balkans and along the Dnieper. The nomadic tribe of the Avars first entered the lower Danube region and the Carpathian basin during the sixth decade of the sixth century. There, they created a strong empire under the leadership of Kagan Bajan.

■ **568**
After 2 April (Easter) the Longobards, confronted by the Avar danger, retreated from Pannonia into northern Italy.

■ **Second half of the 6th century**
The Avars undertook predatory raids in a wide area of eastern and central Europe against the Slavs, Franks, and Longobards, as well as the Byzantine Empire. Sometimes groups of them crossed the Elbe River. They forced the subjugated Slavs to fight in the front ranks of their armies.

■ **Beginning of the 7th century**
Byzantine armies defeated the Avars in front of the walls of Constantinople. This was the signal for the revolt of the Slavic tribes.

■ **623/624**
Under the leadership of the Frankish merchant, Samo, Slavic tribes rebelled against the Avars. Samo was victorious in several battles and the Slavs elected him ruler. The center of the Empire of Samo was located somewhere in the area of southern Moravia, Lower Austria, and western Slovakia.

■ **631/632**
The Slavs robbed and murdered Frankish merchants. Sycharius, the messenger of the Frankish king, Dagobert, demanded compensation and, at the negotiations, offended Samo who refused further talks. Therefore, Dagobert attacked Samo's empire in three columns. Although Dagobert achieved a partial success in a three-day battle near the Vogastisburg, his army was defeated. Samo undertook a campaign to Thuringia in retaliation. The ruler of the Lusatian Sorbs, Dervan, recognized the sovereignty of Samo. The location of the Vogastisburg is not known, but most probably it lay near the Danube or in the area of the Moravian Gate.

■ **658**
Samo died. After his death the empire (rather a tribal league with a military democracy) collapsed. For the next 150 years there are no written reports about life on the territory of Slovakia.

■ **Second half and end of the 7th century**
The Avars, settled in the southern parts of Slo-

vakia northward from the Devín Gate through the Ipeľ valley up to the eastern Slovak lowlands, were pushed northward about the middle of the seventh century. In most of Slovakia the Avars never settled permanently. From many of the burial sites, it is clear that there was an Avar-Slav symbiosis.

■ **791 – 796**
The end of Avar hegemony in the Carpathian basin was brought about at the end of the eighth century by a campaign of the Frankish ruler, Charlemagne, into lower Austria, the Danubian and Carpathian basin. The Avars submitted to Charlemagne, who resettled them between Carnuntum and today's Szombathely on the Magyar-Austrian border region. The remnant merged with the native population. At this time the typical Avar-Slavic (Keszthely) culture declined.

■ **800**
On **25 December** in Rome, Pope Leo III crowned the Frankish ruler Charlemagne as Roman emperor.

■ **805**
Charlemagne issued a prohibition against selling weapons in the lands of the Avars and Slavs.

■ **822**
At the imperial diet in Frankfurt am Main the Avars appeared for the last time as an ethnic group.

■ **828**
The first known prince on the territory of today's Slovakia, Pribina, built a stone church at his seat in Nitra. It was consecrated by Adalram, the archbishop of Salzburg.

■ **831**
Reginhar, the bishop of Passau, baptized the Moravians (probably only the chieftains and their entourages).

■ **833**
Mojmír, the Moravian prince, expelled Pribi-

na from Nitra who, with his retinue (perhaps about 500 men), sought refuge first among the anti-Frankish Bulgarians and then with the Croatians. Finally, he took refuge with Margrave Ratbod, the administrator of the Eastern March subordinated to the Frankish Empire.

■ **843**
August – The Frankish Empire was divided into three parts by the treaty of Verdun. Charles the Bald received the West Frankish Empire (later France). Lothar obtained the middle part (the lands along the Rhine and possessions in Italy). Louis the German obtained the East Frankish Empire (later Germany) and, under his leadership, this empire increased the pressure on the Slavs to the east.

■ **846**
10 January – The East Frankish king, Louis the German, accepted Pribina into his service as a vassal and granted him a fief in the region of Lake Balaton. There Pribina established Blatnohrad and built several churches. The Principality of Pribina extended through the southern part of Transdanubia and into the area of today's Styria and Slovenia.
August – Internal discord developed within the principality of Mojmír. Louis the German intervened and installed as ruler Rastislav, Mojmír's nephew. From this it is clear that the East Frankish Empire considered the Moravian ruler its vassal. The further fate of Mojmír is unknown. Louis the German did not consider it convenient to install Pribina upon the throne of the Moravian principality for he feared internal conflict within the Moravian principality and a worsening of relations with the East Frankish Empire.

■ **847**
12 October – Louis the German confirmed to Pribina all the territory which Pribina had previously received from him.

■ **855**
Louis the German attacked the Great Mora-

vian Empire in retaliation for Rastislav's aid to Margrave Ratbod who had rebelled against Louis. Great Moravia defended itself against this onslaught.

■ 856
Louis the German named his son Karolman as the administrator of the Eastern March.

■ 861
Prior to 6 July – Pribina was probably killed in battle with the Moravians who supported Karolman in the revolt against Louis the German. The son of Pribina, Koceľ, succeeded him in the Balaton principality.
During the course of the year Rastislav requested Pope Nicholas I to send him missionaries who knew the Slavic language. The pope did not comply for he did not want to risk a conflict with the East Frankish sovereign and did not have priests who had mastered this language.

■ 862
Rastislav made a similar request of Michael III, the Byzantine emperor.

■ 863
Summer – The Byzantine mission of Constantine and Methodius with their entourage arrived in Great Moravia. Constantine had previously systematized Slavic writing, **Glagolitic**, and translated some liturgical texts into Old Slavonic. The arrival of both missionaries impaired the missionary activity of the German priests who, until then, had been active in Great Moravia. This was a source of continual conflict.

■ 864
August – Louis the German attacked Great Moravia and besieged but did not take Devín. After a lengthy siege Rastislav had to recognize Frankish sovereignty and provide hostages.

■ 867
Summer – Constantine and Methodius departed for Rome with a group of disciples.

They first stopped in the Balaton principality to visit Prince Koceľ.
Autumn – Koceľ sent with them a group of about fifty pupils. They later paused in Venice where, in public disputations, they defended the use of the Old Slavonic language for divine services against the **trilingualists.**
Christmas – Pope Hadrian II approved the translation of liturgical books into Old Slavonic which, as a symbol of this agreement, were laid upon the altar of the basilica of Santa Maria Maggiore in Rome.

■ 868
During their year-long stay in Rome, Constantine and Methodius ordained several of their disciples as priests. They continued the translation of biblical texts. At the end of the year the ailing Constantine entered a Greek Basilian cloister and adopted the monastic name Cyril.

■ 869
14 February – Constantine, called the Philosopher, died.
June to September – With the consent of Pope Hadrian II, Methodius returned to Koceľ with a commission as a teacher of the church addressed to Rastislav, Svätopluk and Koceľ.
August – The East Frankish Empire attacked the Slavs. One column attacked the Lusatian Sorbs and the Czechs; a second assaulted Nitra administered by Svätopluk's nephew Rastislav; while a third invaded the center of Rastislav's empire. They unsuccessfully besieged the best fortified of Rastislav's castles (probably Devín). After suffering considerable losses, the East Frankish armies withdrew.
End of the year – At the insistence of Koceľ, Methodius returned to Rome in order to obtain higher ecclesiastical promotion and the commission without which it was not possible to continue his mission successfully.

■ 870
Beginning of the year – Pope Hadrian II ordained Methodius and bestowed upon him the dignity of missionary archbishop of Pannonia and papal legate for the region of Pan-

nonia and Moravia. Methodius returned to Great Moravia through the Principality of Koceľ.

– The prince of Nitra, Svätopluk, without the approval of Grand Prince Rastislav, recognized Frankish sovereignty. Rastislav learned of this and wished to punish Svätopluk, who forestalled him by preparing a trap and captured him on a hunt.

Prior to 14 May – Svätopluk handed Rastislav over to Karolman. Rastislav was taken to Regensburg where, at the end of the year, he was sentenced and blinded. He died in unknown circumstances in a Bavarian prison. Karolman's troops invaded Great Moravia, which was entrusted to the administration of Counts Engelschalk and William.

About the end of the year – Upon returning to Great Moravia, Archbishop Methodius was taken prisoner by the Bavarian bishops, arraigned before a court in Regensburg and cast into prison in southern Germany.

■ 871

Svätopluk was accused of disloyalty to the East Frankish Empire and thrown into prison. In the summer of 871 the Moravians rebelled against Frankish hegemony and elected a relative of the Mojmír dynasty, the priest Slavomír, as ruler. Against the uprising, a campaign was led by Svätopluk who, in the meantime, had been pardoned. Svätopluk secretly concluded a pact with the rebels, went over to their side, and defeated the German army. Engelschalk and William, the administrators of Moravia, perished in battle. Svätopluk became an independent ruler (871 – 894).

■ 872

Repeated attacks of East Frankish troops against the Czechs and the Moravians, despite partial success in Czechia, ended at the Danube as the troops of Svätopluk defeated Bavarian troops of the Frankish army.

■ 873

At the command of Pope John VIII, the papal legate, Paul of Ancona, intervened with the Bavarian bishops in order to have Methodius released from prison. Methodius returned to Great Moravia. He had to pledge to the legate that he would not use the liturgical Old Slavonic language and, at least temporarily, would not impair the ecclesiastical jurisdiction of Salzburg and Passau in Transdanubia.

– Preliminary peace negotiations between the envoys of Svätopluk and Louis the German took place.

■ 874

May – Svätopluk's envoy, the priest John of Venice, and Emperor Louis the German concluded a peace at Forchheim in Bavaria. In recognition of his vassalage, Svätopluk was obliged to pay tribute to the East Frankish Empire.

■ 874 – 879

Svätopluk undertook a campaign against the Vistula Principality and temporarily annexed this territory to the Great Moravian Empire.

■ 879

Spring – Svätopluk sent a delegation led by the priest John of Venice to Pope John VIII in Rome. The pope also summoned Archbishop Methodius so that he could be exonerated of the heresy of which he was accused by the Bavarian clergy.

■ 880

Archbishop Methodius arrived in Rome, with the Swabian Benedictine monk Wiching, whom the pope had consecrated as the bishop of Nitra at the request of Svätopluk, in his entourage. The pope established a Moravian ecclesiastical province headed by Methodius. This subordinated even German priests to him.

June – In the bull *Industriae tuae,* Pope John VIII permitted services in Old Slavonic in Great Moravia but with the provision that the Gospel first be read in Latin. At the court of Svätopluk, at his request, the mass could also be said in Latin. The pope took Svätopluk and his people under the protection of the Holy See, and with this his equal status as a Christian ruler in Europe was recognized.

■ 881
In view of the intrigues of Wiching, Methodius divested him of his episcopal office and entrusted him with missionary activity in Visland (Vistula Principality). Methodius left for the court of the Byzantine emperor. On the way, in the region of the Iron Gate of the Danube he met with several Magyar chieftains. Magyar warrior bands had already roamed the Carpathian basin in 862 and then in 881.

■ 881 – 882
During his stay in the Byzantine Empire, Methodius met with the Emperor Basil I and the Patriarch Photius.

■ 882 – 884
In a war with the Bulgarians, Svätopluk conquered the area beyond the Tisa River thus taking control of the Transylvanian salt trade.

■ 883
Svätopluk's forces invaded Pannonia and occupied the former Principality of Pribina and Koceľ, which was already in the hands of Duke Arnulf of Carinthia.

■ 884
Svätopluk conferred with Emperor Charles the Fat near Tullne and promised him that he would not attack his lands. At this discussion Braslav, the lower Pannonian prince, whose original territory stretched between the Drava and Sava rivers, was referred to as a vassal of Charles.

■ 885
Svätopluk was reconciled with Arnulf. Svätopluk became the godfather of Arnulf's illegitimate son Zuentibold. Wiching left for Rome on a diplomatic mission for Svätopluk by which he was virtually rehabilitated.
6 April – Methodius died. On false information from Wiching, the new pope, Stephen V, forbade divine liturgy in Old Slavonic. He allowed it to be used only in sermons and in the exposition of biblical texts. He sent three other papal legates with Wiching to Great Moravia. With this began the persecution of Slavic priests led by Gorazd, who had been designated by Methodius as his successor before his death.

■ 886
The pupils of Methodius were expelled from the country and took refuge in Bulgaria and Czechia.

■ 890
Svätopluk took advantage of the peace with Arnulf, who in 887 became king (from 896 emperor) of the German Empire, to subjugate the Czech lands and probably also Lusatia and Silesia. Between 890 and 894 the **Great Moravian Empire** attained its greatest extent.

■ 891
Wiching deserted Svätopluk and left for the court of Arnulf, who entrusted him to negotiate with Svätopluk.

■ 892
With the assistance of Magyar warrior bands the army of Arnulf devastated the territory of Great Moravia.

■ 894
Summer – Svätopluk died. Mojmír II became ruler and his brother Svätopluk II obtained the Principality of Nitra.

■ 895
June – the Czech princes Spytihněv and Vratislav freed themselves from the Great Moravian Empire and, at the imperial diet in Regensburg, took an oath of vassalage to Arnulf, as the Lusatian Sorbs would do in 897 in Tribur.

■ 896
Magyar nomadic tribes invaded the Danubian lowlands. Emperor Arnulf bestowed upon Braslav, a lower Pannonian prince, the administration of southwestern Transdanubia with its citadel of Blatnohrad, today's Zalavár.

■ 898

Mojmír II petitioned Pope John IX for the renewal of the Moravian ecclesiastical province and the sending of legates. The pope named a new archbishop and three other bishops. Neither their names nor sees are known.

■ 898/899

Internal disagreements between Mojmír and his brother Svätopluk were fostered by Arnulf and his margraves who invaded Great Moravia, liberated Svätopluk from a besieged Nitra and burned it down. They led Svätopluk away to Bavaria.

■ 899 – 901

The Old Magyars devastated and subjugated the lower Pannonian principality of Braslav.

■ 902

The Moravians warded off Magyar attacks upon the core of the Great Moravian Empire.

■ 905

The Raffelstätt toll rate mentions the „markets of the Moravians." It is presumed that, at this time, shipping on the Danube was still free.

■ 906 – 907

Svätopluk probably perished (near Bánhida) during Magyar attacks upon the Great Moravian Empire.

4 – 5 July and **9 August 907** – Three battles took place between the Bavarians and the Magyars near Bratislava ending in a Magyar victory. At that time, or shortly before, Great Moravia ceased to exist. The first written mention of Bratislava (Brezalauspurc) is made in connection with these battles. Around 907 Árpád, the chieftain of the Magyar tribal alliance, died.

■ First half of the 10th century

Nomadic Magyar warriors began to penetrate southern and also, in part, eastern Slovakia, approximately along the line Nitra – Lučenec – Rimavská Sobota – Zemplín. By the second half of the 10th century the Old Magyar population settled further north. After the defeat of the Slovak magnates, Nitra was ruled by Üllö, the son of Árpád. He was succeeded by Tevel and another member of the Árpád dynasty, Taksony. Magyar bands even reached the city of Lerida in Spain. Residues of the Great Moravian Empire in Moravia itself and in Slovakia are mentioned in connection with this. The Magyars devastated southern Slovakia and the lower course of the Morava River.

■ 953

The Magyar chieftains Gyula and Bulcsu (Bölcs) accepted baptism in Constantinople.

■ 955

10 August Emperor Otto I, assisted by Czech auxiliary bands, defeated the Magyars at the Lech River in Bavaria. After this battle the Magyars gradually adopted a settled way of life.

■ Second half of the 10th century

The territory of western Slovakia came for a time under the sovereignty of the Czech Přemyslids. (In connection with this the Moravian bishopric was renewed prior to 976).

■ Around 970 – 997

Géza, the son of Taksony and grandson of Árpád (born around 949), who was originally the Duke of Nitra, united the other Magyar chiefs under his rule and became the ruler of the Transdanubian principality. In Nitra he entrusted the government to his brother Michael whom he later removed, between 976 and 978. Through his marriage to Charlote, the daughter of Gyula, the Transylvanian prince, he also obtained control of Transylvania. He invited Bavarian missionaries into his lands and later St. Adalbert with missionaries from Czechia.

■ 995

Vajk, together with his father Géza, was baptized, took the name Stephen, and became the administrator of the **Nitra Appanage Duchy** (995 – 997).

■ 997

1 February Géza died. His son Stephen became ruler (from 1000 to 1038 he was king). A revolt against Stephen erupted, led by the chieftain Koppány. Stephen subdued it with the help of Slovak magnates in his service.

■ **Last third of the 10th century**
The Benedictine Cloister of St. Hippolytus on Zobor hill was founded and the Church of St. Emmeramus was built at Nitra castle.

Slovakia during the reign of the Árpád dynasty
(11th century – 1301)

The incorporation of Slovakia into the Hungarian state took place gradually from the middle of the 10th to the end of the 12th centuries when the borders of Hungary were definitively fixed at the crests of the Carpathians, approximately along the border recognized today. Under the first king, Stephen (1000 – 1038), state organization and administrative and ecclesiastical institutions were bound to the older Great Moravian tradition, as the continuity of administrative and ecclesiastical sees (Bratislava, Nitra, Esztergom) testifies. Archaeological finds and the first written sources support this. The word stock of Old Hungarian contains lexical borrowings from old Slovak, which is evidence for the adoption of concepts in state administration, social and spiritual life, agriculture and the like.

In Transdanubia, in the foothills of the Matras and in southern Slovakia, where the Magyars settled, assimilation of the original Slovak population occurred. After the death of Stephen, the first Hungarian king, the internal conflict was exploited by the German Empire, which intervened in the struggles. It sent troops into the Kingdom of Hungary, in particular at the middle of the eleventh century when the succession principle that the eldest member of the Árpád dynasty assume the crown led to struggles among the dukes, candidates for the throne, and the rulers. In this unclear situation, an independent status for the Dukes of Nitra was made possible and they even followed an independent foreign policy (for instance, in the relationship of Duke Géza to Byzantium that continued after he became king). This was one reason why Ladislas I, after he ascended the throne, sought to limit the status of the Duchy of Nitra and in fact liquidated this institution (completed under Coloman in 1105).

In its relations with the German Empire, the Kingdom of Hungary had an advantage, in contrast with the Czech principality. It was geographically more distant and had time to consolidate itself during the period when the German Empire was convulsed by internal conflicts and struggles with the papacy over investiture at the end of the 11th century. Therefore, Hungary, maintained its independence and did not become, as did Czechia, a part or vassal of the German Empire.

The remainder of the twelfth century was marked by the aggression of the Kingdom of Hungary against surrounding countries. It penetrated in particular into the Balkans and to the south, where it collided with the interests of the Venetian Republic and Byzantium. Dynastic struggles between King Stephen III (1162 – 1172) and the rival kings, Ladislas II (1162 – 1163) and Stephen IV (1163 – 1165), his paternal uncles, were incited and supported by the Byzantine policy of influencing developments in Hungary. This did not succeed even though a later ruler, Béla III (1173 – 1196), was educated at the Byzantine court and was reckoned the prospective son-in-law of the emperor. But he did not succumb to the pressure of the Byzantines, and after ascending the throne he followed an independent foreign and domestic policy. The Byzantine sojourn and education as well as his second marriage, to a French princess, had an influence upon Béla's policy and cultural orientation (the establishment of a permanent royal chancellery, the preparation of documents, the penetration of Hungary by the Cluniac reform movement and the like).

From the mid-12th century colonizing waves of Germans, Flemish and Italians entered Hungary. These streams were amplified after the invasions by the Tatars in 1241. In the third decade of the 13th century a conflict between Andrew II and the estates broke out which ended with concessions of the ruler and the issue of the Golden Bull (1222). The king bestowed large **grants** that his successor, Béla IV, attempted to halt. At the same time, the first cities endowed with privileges (Trnava 1238, Krupina, Zvolen, Banská Štiavnica, all before the Tatar invasion, Nitra 1248, Košice, Banská Bystrica 1255 and others) developed. This legally completed the development of cities that already had become centers of economic life (market settlements, settlements around fortresses and the like). This colonization activity intensified after the Tatar invasion. Domestic developments were threatened by armed conflicts with the Czech king, Ottokar II Přemysl (1260, 1271, 1273). These concluded with the defeat of the Přemysl king on the Marchfeld in 1278 by an alliance of Hungary with the Austrian duke, Rudolf Habsburg. The end of the century saw the weak ruler Ladislas IV Cuman (1272 – 1290), whose deviation from the Catholic Church and the adoption of Cuman customs elicited the anger of the papal curia, the domestic clergy and nobility. Attempts by the last Árpád, Andrew III (1290 – 1301) to halt the general anarchy and the decline of the kingdom were unsuccessful. From the eighth decade of the 13th century until the first decades of the 14th century Hungary was devastated by internal struggles and feudal anarchy that in 1301, after the death of Andrew III, culminated in a war over the throne.

■ 1000
25 December – The coronation of Stephen as the first king of Hungary took place with the agreement of the German emperor Otto III and Pope Sylvester II. An archbishopric was established in Esztergom. The first archbishop was Dominic, later Astrik or Anastasius, who, as abbot of the Břevnov monastery near Prague, came to Hungary with St. Adalbert before the end of the 10th century.

■ Beginning of the 11th century
The Polish ruler Boleslav the Brave invaded Slovakia around 1001 and expelled the Přemyslids.
The first book of laws of King Stephen was prepared. It was concerned predominantly with criminal law, but also defined the position of the church and the clergy.

■ 1013 – 1015
The work *The Moral Instruction of Prince Imre,* issued with the first book of laws of King Stephen, was written.

■ Around 1018
The Polish king Boleslav the Brave and the Hungarian king Stephen I concluded a peace with the result that Poland withdrew from Slo-

vak territory south of the Carpathians. The **Nitra Appanage Duchy** was administered by Ladislas the Bald, the cousin of Stephen I and a vassal of Boleslav the Brave.

■ Before 1031
The second book of laws of St. Stephen supplemented and amended previous laws. It regulated the payment of the **tenth** (tithe), the construction of churches, questions of inheritance and criminal law.

■ 1031
2 September Imre, the son of Stephen I, died of injuries received while hunting. After the death of Imre, Stephen had his cousin Vazul blinded. After Ladislas the Bald, Vazul was another appanage duke in Nitra.

■ 1032
The Zobor hermit St. Svorad – Andrew died.

■ 1034
Svorad's fellow monk St. Benedict was tortured at Skalka near Trenčín.

■ 1038
15 August Stephen I died. The new king was his nephew Peter Orseolo, the son of the Venetian doge, who had come to Stephen's

court in 1030 and had become the commander of the royal army.

■ 1038 – 1041
The first reign of Peter Orseolo. As a foreigner, he was not popular and was, moreover, under the influence of the German emperor Henry III. In 1041 he was deposed and expelled from the country. He fled to the Austrian duke and then to the German emperor.

■ 1041 – 1043
Samuel Aba, the former palatine of King Stephen, became king of Hungary. He attempted to renew old traditions and to eliminate the influence of foreigners. In 1042 and 1043 battles between the Hungarian and German armies took place. Henry III was supported by the Czech prince, Břetislav I.

■ 1044
June to **July** – Henry III invaded Hungary again and installed his protégé Peter Orseolo on the throne.
5 July – After losing a battle near Ménfö, the followers of Peter assassinated Samuel Aba.

■ 1044 – 1046
The second reign of Peter Orseolo was characterized by a dependency upon the German Empire. Therefore a new insurrection against him led by Vatha, the so-called pagan uprising, erupted. Peter was captured, blinded, and expelled from the country.

■ 1046
September – Andrew I (1046 – 1060) became king of Hungary. He was the great-nephew of Stephen I. During his reign he lived in exile in Poland. Andrew suppressed the followers of Peter and at the same time the pagan uprising against the new feudal order (**feudalism)** and the church.

■ About 1048
The **Nitra Appanage Duchy** was established.

■ Mid 11th century
The first Hungarian chronicle, the so-called

Bratislava Annals, was written. It is preserved in a version from the 12th century. The later chroniclers Simon of Kéza and Mark of Kált used it.

■ 1051
August – The Emperor Henry III invaded Hungary but did not achieve a decisive triumph. He pillaged the left bank of the Danube with the help of Czech forces led by Břetislav.

■ 1052 – 1053
Repeated forays into Hungary by German armies led by Henry III in the summer of 1052 concentrated on besieging Bratislava but were unsuccessful. Henry's ships on the Danube were sunk. After an eight-week siege the adversaries concluded a peace at the beginning of 1053 which was mediated by Pope Leo IX, who personally came to the camp of the emperor.

■ 1057
Andrew I had his son Solomon crowned as king of Hungary. This elicited a conflict between Andrew and his brother Béla, who was the Nitra appanage duke from 1048. In the **Nitra Appanage Duchy**, Béla followed an independent foreign and domestic policy, had his own army, minted his own coins (**denár**), and installed county administrators in each of his 15 counties. After the coronation of Solomon, Béla fled to Poland because he feared for his life.

■ 1060
With the help of Poland, Béla invaded Hungary. Andrew was killed and Béla seized the Hungarian throne.
6 December – Béla I was crowned king in Székesfehérvár. His short reign (1060 – 1063) was characterized by struggles with Solomon as well as by threats from the German Empire.

■ 1063
July to **August** – Béla I died during a military campaign against Henry IV on the western border of Hungary.
At the end of the year – The German emperor

attacked Hungary and placed his protégé Solomon (1063 – 1074) upon the throne. The
reign of Solomon was occupied with inces-
sant warfare with his cousins Géza and Ladislas, the sons of Béla I.

■ 1064
20 January – In Gyor the rival parties concluded an agreement to divide the administration of Hungary. Solomon was recognized as
king, Géza received the duchy of Nitra and
Ladislas obtained Bihar.

■ Around 1064
The **legend** about the hermits Svorad-Andrew
and Benedict developed. Its author was the
bishop of Pécs, Maurus, who previously had
lived in the Benedictine monastery on Zobor
hill.

■ 1068 – 1071
The nomadic Petchen and Cuman tribes invaded the eastern region of the Kingdom of
Hungary. King Solomon halted this invasion
and, when they accepted Christianity, he let
them settle as border guards in western,
northern and eastern Slovakia.

■ 1072 – 1074
Fighting between Solomon and his cousins
Géza and Ladislas broke out again.

■ 1074
14 March – Solomon was defeated in a battle
near Mogyoród. He withdrew to Bratislava
Castle to await help from Emperor Henry IV.
After 14 March – Géza I (1074 – 1077) became king. Although, at the beginning of his
conflict with Solomon, he was supported by
the domestic bishops, the disapproval of the
papal curia prevented his coronation as king.
He maintained good relations with Byzantium
and from there obtained the royal diadem that
makes up the lower part of the Hungarian royal crown.
August to September – The Emperor Henry IV
undertook a campaign into Hungary that was
intended to support Solomon but was unsuccessful.

■ 1075
Géza I established a Benedictine **cloister**
(monastery) in Hronský Beňadik and granted
it extensive property.

■ 1077
25 April – Géza I died. His brother Ladislas
I (1077 – 1095) became king. In 1192 he
was declared a saint. Ladislas administered
the Duchy of Nitra before obtaining the royal
title. He then entrusted the duchy to his
younger brother Lambert.

■ 1078 – 1092
King Ladislas I issued three sets of laws. They
contained the resolutions from the assembly
of the nobility in Pannonhalma dealing with
criminal matters, economic issues, markets,
merchants and the like (second book). The
third book had a similar content. Both were
written around 1078. The decrees of the ecclesiastical Synod of Szabolcs in 1092 comprised the contents of the first book. It regulated the patronage rights of churches, the
status of clergy and monks, marital law,
church holidays, fasts, ceremonies and the
like.

■ 1083
The first Hungarian king, Stephen, his son
Imre and Bishop Gerhard, and the hermits
Svorad-Andrew and Benedict were canonized
as saints. King Ladislas pardoned Solomon
who had to go into exile. He died at Regensburg about 1087/1088.

■ Before 1086
The Nitra bishopric was restored (**bishops**).

■ 1089 – 1091
Ladislas I occupied Croatia and later undertook a campaign in Galicia. Coloman ended
his expansion to the south.

■ 1095
29 July Ladislas I died. His nephew Coloman
(1095 – 1116), originally destined for a career
in the church, became king.

■ **1096**

One column of participants in the first crusade, traversing Slovakia, plundered the region around Nitra. The local population routed the crusaders.

■ **Around 1100**

King Coloman issued edicts regulating public law, property, jurisdictional and economic questions at a synod in Tarcal.
– A chapter headed by a prior (provost) was established in Bratislava.

■ **1102**

Hungarian forces occupied Dalmatia. At Beograd in Dalmatia, Coloman had himself crowned as the Croatian king.

■ **1105**

The younger brother of King Coloman, Duke Álmos sought the help of the Emperor Henry IV of Germany at Passau. Coloman deprived Álmos of the administration of the **Nitra Appanage Duchy.** In consequence the duchy ceased to exist.

■ **1108**

The Emperor Henry V of Germany attacked Hungary, besieged Bratislava and, together with the Czech prince Svätopluk and Duke Álmos, pillaged south-western Slovakia.
Before 4 November – Henry V concluded peace with Coloman.

■ **1111**

Before 1 September – Coloman confirmed an older grant to the Zobor monastery, made by King Stephen I, of one third of the tolls in Nitra, Trenčín and their environs as well as along the entire length of the Váh River.

■ **1113**

After 1 September – Coloman issued another charter favoring the Zobor abbey that delineated its property in southwestern Slovakia, in the basins of the Váh, Nitra, and Hron rivers. Northwards it extended as far as the region of Turiec. Apart from the charter of 1111, it is the oldest preserved original charter in Slovakia documenting the Slovak settlement by geographic and personal names.

■ **Around 1115**

Coloman had his brother Álmos and his son Béla, who was still in his minority, blinded and imprisoned in Dömös abbey.

■ **Before 1116**

The second book of laws of Coloman regulated economic questions and legal acts between Christians and Jews.

■ **1116**

3 February – Coloman died. The new ruler, Stephen II (1116 – 1131) fought the Czech prince Vladislav I at the Olšava River and was defeated. Therefore he had to withdraw from the territory between the White Carpathians and the Olšava, Morava and Velička rivers that henceforth remained part of Moravia.

■ **1118**

Venice occupied the Dalmatian cities that until then had belonged to Hungary.

■ **Before 1131**

Count Lambert from the Hunt-Poznan family founded a Benedictine monastery in Bzovík.

■ **1131**

1 March – King Stephen II died. Because he did not have any male offspring, he designated as his successor his cousin Béla, who had been blinded as a child and had lived in the cloister in Petrovaradin while his father Álmos had fled to Byzantium.
28 April – Béla II (the Blind) was crowned king.

■ **1136**

In a war with the Venetians Béla II acquired the port of Split and the part of Bosnia called Rama.

■ **1141**

13 February – Béla II died. His successor was

his first son Géza (1141 – 1162). During his minority, rule was exercised by his mother Helena and her brother Belos who later became **palatine**.

■ **1146**
Géza II had to repulse the attack of Boris, the unacknowledged son of King Coloman and his second wife. Boris claimed the Hungarian throne. With the help of the Czech prince Vladislav and the Bavarian duke Henry II, he captured Bratislava with its citadel. But shortly thereafter he returned it for compensation.

■ **1147**
Participants in the second crusade traversed Hungary. The Hungarian king recruited some of them, German and French merchants as well as artisans, and let them settle as **guests** in Spiš, around Banská Štiavnica, in Sriema and Transylvania.

■ **1152 – 1155**
In a war with Byzantium, Boris fought for the Byzantines. He fell in battle in 1152. The Byzantines forced Géza to capitulate. During the war his two brothers, Ladislas and Stephen, as well as the palatine Belos, fled to the Byzantine court.

■ **1162**
31 March – King Géza II died.
Mid-year – The son of Géza II became King Stephen III (1162 – 1172). Because he was not yet of age, Géza's brother Ladislas sought to exercise his claim to the throne and, with Byzantine support, he had himself crowned king.
July – Ladislas II (anti-king) was crowned by the archbishop of Kalocsa for which Lukas, the archbishop of Esztergom and papal legate, excommunicated the archbishop.

■ **1163**
14 January – Ladislas II died before it was possible to resolve the power struggle between him and the legal king, Stephen III. The Byzantines intervened in the internal affairs of the kingdom and placed another candidate on the throne.

27 January – Stephen IV (the rival king) was crowned with the active support of the Byzantines. He, too, was only a tool for the Byzantine policy of intervening in Hungarian matters.
– Stephen III, supported by German troops, was victorious over Stephen IV near Székesfehérvár and again assumed power. He sent his maternal uncle, Stephen IV, into exile in Byzantium.

■ **1164**
Byzantine soldiers occupied Dalmatia and Croatia; Stephen III occupied Sriema. In the war against Byzantium, Czech and Bavarian troops helped Stephen. To strengthen his position, the king settled the orders of the Knights of St. John in Székesfehérvár and the Knights Templar in the Croatian castle of Vrana.

■ **1165**
11 April – Stephen IV was poisoned in Zemun in southern Hungary where, after several defeats, he had taken refuge from his nephew Stephen III, who assumed rule over the whole country.

■ **1172**
4 March – King Stephen III died. His successor was his brother Béla, brought up from 1163 at the Byzantine court as the future son-in-law of the Byzantine emperor Manuel. When the emperor fathered a son, the engagement of his daughter to Béla was set aside.

■ **1173**
18 January – After almost a year of interregnum, Béla III (1173 – 1196) was crowned. He ranks as one of the most capable Hungarian rulers. His stay at the court of the Byzantine emperor opened to him broader horizons and he maintained good relations with the Byzantine Empire. Despite this, he attempted to regain the territory that the Byzantines had occupied.

■ **1180 – 1186**
Hungary occupied Croatia, Dalmatia with the harbor fortresses of Zemun, Serbian Belgrade, and Braničevo and devastated the territory up to Sofia in Bulgaria.

■ **1182**
16 May – Béla III had his eight-year old son Imre crowned as king in order to avoid dynastic conflicts.

■ **1185**
The issue of charters for grants of property by the king (**privileges**) marked the beginnings of an organized Hungarian royal chancellery.

■ **Around 1186**
On the occasion of Béla's second marriage to the French princess Marguerite, a list of his revenues was prepared.

■ **1186 – 1190**
Béla III undertook several campaigns in Galicia and temporarily annexed it to Hungary. His younger son Andrew was named the duke of Galicia.

■ **Around 1190**
Boleslav, bishop of Vac, founded a Prémonstratensian monastery in Leles that later became a **credible place**.

■ **1196**
23 April – Béla III died and Imre became king (1196 – 1204). He conducted wars in the Balkans and with domestic opponents led by his younger brother Andrew.

■ **The transition from the 12th to the 13th century**
Prince Coloman founded in Jasov a daughter monastery of the Varadine Prémonstratensian abbey. The Jasov monastery also became a credible place in the 13th century. King Imre founded the Spiš Chapter.

■ **1201**
Imre attacked Serbia and accepted the title King of Serbia. Between 1200 and 1203 he also fought against the **Bogomils** in Bosnia.

■ **1203**
Imre imprisoned his younger brother Andrew,

who was the duke of Dalmatia-Croatia. Andrew was freed by his own followers.

■ **1204**
30 November – Imre died. His minor son Ladislas became king, with his maternal uncle Andrew as his tutor. Queen Constance, in fear of Andrew, fled with her child to Vienna.

■ **1205**
7 May – Ladislas III died. He had been crowned as a child (26 August 1204) by his father Imre shortly before he died.
29 May – Andrew II (1205 – 1235) was crowned. He conducted an expansive foreign policy, undertook seventeen campaigns in Galicia and obtained the title King of Galicia (Lodomeria). He did not achieve permanent success, however, and only drained the royal treasury. He also fended off attacks by the Plavci, Cumans and others.

■ **1213**
28 September – Queen Gertrude, who came from a princely family of Meran, was murdered. The queen had elicited the animosity of the domestic **nobility** by preferring her relatives and foreigners at the royal court. After the report of the murder had reached the king on a campaign in Galicia, he returned to punish the conspirators.

■ **1217**
13 June – The king bestowed **privileges** upon the **guests** in Hronský Beňadik.

■ **1217 – 1218**
Andrew II entertained the idea of obtaining the Byzantine imperial crown and therefore participated in the fifth crusade to Palestine.

■ **1222**
Before 7 May – The king ordered that clerics were not to be judged by secular courts and were not to pay taxes, and that serfs were not to become priests.
Before 29 May – Andrew II, under pressure from the nobility issued the **Golden Bull** containing the fundamental rights of the Hungar-

ian **nobility**. The nobility was to fight only for the defense of the kingdom and was not required to fight outside the country. If a military expedition lasted more than three months, the king was to pay the nobles. He was not allowed to grant whole counties or to bestow property upon foreigners. **Ismaelites** and Jews were not to be appointed county administrators, functionaries of the mint or salt chambers or as tax collectors, and could not be raised to noble estate. The nobility had the right of resistance (*ius resistendi*) if the provisions of the **Golden Bull** were not observed.

■ 1224
James, bishop of Nitra, founded a Benedictine abbey in Skalka near Trenčín.

■ 1226 – 1234
1226 – 2 February 1234 – conflict continued between the serfs of Pannonhalma abbey from Šaľa nad Váhom and the abbot Uriah over the unceasing and excessive increase in feudal dues.

■ 1228 – 1229
The resistance of the serfs in Dvory nad Žitavou, belonging to the abbey of Hronský Beňadik, to an increase of feudal obligations came to a head.

■ 1231
After 3 March – The **Golden Bull,** issued for the second time, anchored the institution of the **credible places** but eliminated the provisions concerning the nobles' right of resistance.

■ 1233
20 August – In the Treaty of Bereg, Andrew II bound himself to respect the privileges of the church in court, tax, and economic matters.

■ 1235
21 September - Andrew II died.
14 October – His son, Béla IV (1235 – 1270) was crowned king. Shortly after his accession to the throne, he tried to force the return of the property granted by the crown. Therefore he ordered the verification of all donations bestowed by Andrew II. As a result of this he lost the support of the nobility.
– A Cistercian nunnery was established in Bratislava.

■ 1238
Béla IV granted **privileges** to the city of Trnava. This is the oldest known grant of urban privileges in Slovakia.
– A Prémonstratensian monastery was established in Šahy. It became a **credible place**.

■ Around 1238
Béla IV bestowed city privileges upon Banská Štiavnica, Zvolen, and Krupina. Although the original charters of privilege were destroyed in the Tatar invasions, they are mentioned in later charters.

■ 1239
Béla IV received the nomadic Cumans who fled in fear of the Tatars. The nobles resented this, as they viewed the Cumans as supporting royal power.

■ 1241
March – The Tatars invaded Hungary.
11 April – In a battle on the Slaná (Sajo) River near Mohi, the Tatars defeated a weaker Hungarian army. The king saved himself by retreating through Gemer, Turiec, Nitra and Bratislava to Austria and the Dalmatian islands.
End of April – A second column of Tatars invaded Slovakia from northern Moravia.

■ 1242
January – The Tatars crossed the frozen Danube near Esztergom and joined forces. They plundered the mid-Danubian lowlands. Only fortified **castles** such as Bratislava, Nitra, Komárno, Fiľakovo and Abovský Novohrad were able to resist.
Summer – After news of the death of the Great Khan Ogotaj reached the Tatars, they quickly withdrew from Hungary.

■ **1243**
7 June – Béla IV granted privileges to the Spiš Lancers.

■ **1245**
Béla IV had his son Stephen (born 1239), still a minor, crowned king.

■ **1245 – 1275**
St. Martin's Cathedral in Spišská Kapitula was built. Here elements of Gothic style intermingle with elements of Romanesque style. This is typical of the architecture of the mid-13th century.

■ **1246**
Béla IV concluded a peace with Danilo, the Galician duke.
15 June – The Austrian duke, Frederick of Babenberg, attacked Hungary. He perished in battle near the Leitha River.

■ **1248**
2 September – Béla IV bestowed a charter of privileges upon Nitra on the model of those of the Székesfehérvár guests.

■ **1249**
13 April – Béla IV granted property and privileges to the guests from Seňa on the model of those of the Košice guests.

■ **Mid-13th century**
After the departure of the Tatars, the fortification of **castles** and urban settlements began throughout Hungary. The king began to bestow **privileges** upon the nobility to a greater degree, although these were usually only modest grants of property dependent upon military service in the **county castles**. Gothic style gradually penetrated the arts. Monuments are relatively few. More of the production of artisans has been preserved and is evidence for the maturity of gold-smithing, metal smelting and foundry work. Orders of friars settled in the cities: **Dominicans** (Banská Štiavnica, Košice, Gelnica); **Franciscans** (Bratislava, Trnava, Nitra, Trenčín); and of the order of nuns, the Poor Clares in Trnava and Bratislava replaced the older Cistercian **foundations.**

■ **1251**
15 June – Béla IV established the Prémonstratensian monastery in Kláštor pod Znievom. In 1252 he granted it more property.
5 December – Béla IV granted a charter of privileges to Jews in Hungary.

■ **1255**
Before 14 October – Béla IV bestowed urban **privileges** upon Banská Bystrica on the model of Banská Štiavnica.

■ **1257**
12 June – Béla IV bestowed privileges upon his serfs from Liptov and Turiec who had fled before the excessive burdens of serf obligations. The king called them back and moderated their obligations.

■ **1258**
Béla IV named his son Stephen the duke of Styria.

■ **1259**
As the young king, Stephen attacked Carinthia. The estates of Austria rebelled and joined with the Czech king, Ottokar II Přemysl.

■ **1260**
12 July – The Czech king Ottokar II Přemysl defeated the Hungarian army in a battle near Kressenbrunn in the Marchfeld. Béla IV had to surrender his claim to Styria.

■ **1262**
As the younger king, Stephen wrested participation in power from Béla IV. After a military struggle they concluded an agreement in Bratislava. Stephen obtained a grant of territory in eastern Hungary, including eastern Slovakia and Spiš.

■ **1265**
17 August – King Béla IV determined the obligations of the serfs on the royal domain in Liptov (repeated in 1266 and 1270).

■ **1267**
Before 7 September – Béla IV confirmed the **Golden Bull** of 1222. At the same time he ordered that two to three representatives of the minor **nobility** from each **county** participate in the diet in Székesfehérvár.

■ **1270**
3 May – Béla IV died.
17 May – The coronation of King Stephen V (1270 – 1272) took place. Shortly after his accession to the throne, Stephen attacked Styria. In reprisal the Czech king Ottokar II Přemysl attacked western Slovakia.

■ **1271**
April – Ottokar II Přemysl captured the fortresses of Devín, Stupava, Bratislava, Sv. Jur, Pezinok, Červený Kameň, Trnava, and Nitra and occupied the territory up to the Hron River.
2 July – Stephen V had to relinquish claims to Styria, Carinthia, Carniola and the Windish March.
25 August – Stephen V bestowed collective privileges upon the Spiš Saxons and exempted them from the jurisdiction of Spiš County.

■ **1272**
6 August – Stephen V died.
3 September – Ladislas IV Cuman (1272 – 1290) was crowned king. Since he was a minor, his mother Elizabeth ruled on his behalf until 1277.

■ **1273**
February – The Cumans invaded Moravia and Austria.
April – The king of Bohemia Ottokar II Přemysl responded with an invasion of western Slovakia. He re-took approximately the same territory that he had taken in April 1271. During the invasion he set fire to the cathedral in Nitra, but a decisive battle did not occur. The Hungarian army avoided combat.
1 October – Rudolf Habsburg was elected German king. Upon receiving this report, Ottokar II Přemysl left Hungary with his army.

■ **1273 – 1274**
A struggle took place between the noble opposition and Queen Elizabeth Cuman who ruled during the minority of her son Ladislas IV. The rebels imprisoned the queen but her supporters freed her in September 1274.

■ **1277**
23 – 30 May – A **diet** of the **Hungarian estates** declared Ladislas IV to be of age. Although he began to rule independently, the nobility formed various power blocs against him and defeated his army several times.

■ **1278**
26 August – A battle took place near Dürnkrut on the Marchfeld between the armies of the Czech king Ottokar II Přemysl and Rudolf Habsburg, who was also supported by Hungarian troops. Ottokar was defeated and killed in the battle.

■ **1285**
January – Ladislas IV called the Tatars to Hungary in order to support him in his struggle against the **nobility**. The Tatars devastated eastern Slovakia.

■ **1286**
The lords of Kysek captured the castle and city of Bratislava. The county of Bratislava was devastated up to Modra and the Dudváh River.

■ **1287**
The Austrian duke Albrecht captured the castle of Bratislava under the pretence of helping Ladislas IV against Ivan of Kysek.
End of the year – With the consent of King Ladislas IV, the Tatars attacked northern Slovakia and pillaged Spiš for the second time.

■ **1289**
The Austrians spread their dominion over western Slovakia to Trnava, the castles of Šaštín, Sv. Jur and Pezinok.

■ **1290**
Beginning of the year – Duke Andrew from

a cadet branch of the house of Árpád came from Venice to Hungary. He was taken prisoner and handed over to the Austrian duke Albrecht. After hearing the report of the murder of King Ladislas IV, Andrew secretly fled to Hungary from Vienna.

10 July – In a chance skirmish in the Cuman camp in the Transtisa region, Ladislas IV was assassinated.

23 July – Andrew III (1290 – 1301), the grandson of Béla IV, was crowned king. He was the first king of Hungary who at his coronation pledged to respect the **privileges** of the **nobility** granted by previous rulers.

■ **1291**
July to **August** – Abraham Červený from Hlohovec took the territory of western Slovakia and Šaštín castle from the Austrians. The Hungarian army led by Matthew Csák attempted to take Bratislava, but was unsuccessful. The army crossed the Danube and defeated Duke Albrecht of Austria near Vienna.

August – Andrew III regulated by law the nomination of the highest dignitaries of the country and the participation of the county nobles in the judgments of the palatine courts in the counties.

26 August – Austria and Hungary concluded a peace in Hainburg, according to which the Austrians would evacuate the territory they had occupied and the cities of Trnava and Bratislava.

2 December – Andrew III granted city **privileges** to Bratislava.

■ **1298**
5 August – Andrew III issued a decree that repeated several provisions of the **Golden Bull**. It regulated the relationships between the king, the **nobility** and the church. The demand for the return of royal property under unauthorized occupation was reiterated. The nobility in the counties were enabled to elect four judges from their ranks to resolve their disputes. These were the constables (*iudices nobilium*) already mentioned in the law of 1291.

■ **1299**
In his citadel in Trenčín, Matthew Csák began to organize his own court with officials like those at the royal court.

■ **1300**
Spring – In the name of the Croatian nobility, the nobleman George Šubič summoned to the throne of Hungary the twelve-year old Charles Robert from the Neapolitan Anjous.

August – Charles Robert landed at Split and advanced into Hungary. His claim to throne was based upon his relationship to the Árpáds: his grandmother was the daughter of Stephen V.

■ **1301**
14 January – King Andrew III died. He probably was poisoned. With him the Árpád dynasty died out.

Era of the culmination of feudalism (1301 – 1526)

The death of Andrew III unleashed a struggle over the Hungarian throne between the Czech king Wenceslas II who wished to have his son Wenceslas (known in Hungary as Ladislas) placed on the throne, Otto of Bavaria and Charles Robert of the Neapolitan Anjou dynasty. In 1307 Charles Robert emerged as the victor in this struggle. Despite this, it took several years for him successfully to subdue the rebellious nobles near Rozhanovce (1312). Until the death of Matthew Csák (1321) the king was not able to occupy his domains. The reigns of both Anjous, Charles Robert (1307 – 1342), and his son Louis I (1342 – 1382) constitute the era of the greatest political, economic and cultural vigor of the kingdom. The Hungarian – Polish personal union (1370 – 1382) contributed to this. During the course of the 14th century older cities flourished and other settlements obtained privileges as cities. Mines sank deeper shafts, as the king encouraged an interest in mining even on secular and ecclesiastical fiefs by proclaiming mining liberties (1327). The decree Louis I issued in 1351 introduced certainty to administrative-judicial practice and a clearer delimitation of the boundaries between the noble, urban and serf estates.

A hiatus occurred after the death of Louis when, after the short reign of Maria (1382 – 1387), her husband Sigismund of Luxemburg ascended the throne. His accession was not easy and it was characterized, on the one hand, by military conflicts among the Anjous (the intervention of Charles the Small and his attempt to usurp the Hungarian throne in 1385 – 1386) and the capture of both queens (1386 – 1387) and, on the other hand, by the intervention of Sigismund in the summer of 1385 and his election as Hungarian king (1387). The arrival of Sigismund changed the foreign policy of Hungary towards the German Empire, which culminated in his election as German king (1411) and later as emperor (1433).

New elements entered the foreign and domestic policy of the Kingdom of Hungary, including war with the Turks, tense relations with Poland, war with Venice and, after the eruption of the Hussite movement, war with the Hussites. Through a treaty of inheritance with the Habsburgs (1402) a new factor permeated Hungarian politics: the claims of the Habsburgs to the Hungarian crown which were manifested in the election of Albrecht Habsburg (1437 – 1439) and his son Ladislas Posthumous (1440 – 1457) as kings of Hungary. Meanwhile, an internal struggle broke out within the country when the Polish king Vladislav (Varnenčík, 1440 – 1444) was elected king almost at the same time as Ladislas Posthumous. Even the death of Vladislav near Varna could not prevent the internal struggle in Slovakia between John Hunyady and John Jiskra of Brandýs who, at least formally, defended the claims of Ladislas Posthumous to the Hungarian throne. At the same time a war with the Brethren took place.

A consolidation began only after the coronation of Matthias Corvinus (1458 – 1490), who suppressed the last remnants of the Brethren, put the state finances in order and founded a university in Bratislava (1467). During his reign the royal court of Hungary was permeated by Italian humanism. Despite the consolidation of the state, the position of the serfs did not improve because they were burdened with new taxes. The weak rule of both Jagiellonians, Vladislav II (1490 – 1516) and Louis II (1516 – 1526) returned Hungary to where it had been during the 1440s, namely a state of anarchy and the disintegration of its finances. The only difference was that open warfare did not occur. The Jagiellonians, who had at their disposal the extensive confederated structures of the Czech and Hungarian kingdoms, were unable to do anything either for the further development of the kingdoms or to resist the Turks.

The older, in particular Marxist, historiography overestimated the influence of Hussite expeditions into Slovakia (1428 – 1434) and of the later movement of the Brethren (1445 – 1467), which developed in parallel with the sojourn of Jiskra in Slovakia and, therefore, are sometimes confused with them. Neither of these movements extensively influenced Slovakia in the spiritual sphere but instead meant the destruction of cultural values and ruin for the serfs and townspeople. The Lutheran Reformation, which reached the cities of Slovakia even before the battle at Mohács, had an influence upon religious life in Slovakia. At the beginning of the 16th century, as a result of a deterioration of the position of the serfs and the hired work force in the mines, the extensive Dózsa uprising (1514) and the revolt of the miners in central Slovakia (1525 – 1526) erupted. The Dózsa uprising only peripherally extended into the lands of eastern Slovakia. It meant, however, a worsening of the position of the serfs throughout all of Hungary and the so-called eternal bondage to the soil that completely forbade the migration of serfs.

During the whole period from the beginning of the 14th to the end of the 15th centuries, cities and towns (*oppida*) increased in number. In 1405 decrees of Sigismund codified and standardized the status of townspeople on royal territory. But they did not resolve the situation of the whole estate of the towns (other than the towns of the landlords) or the representation of the towns at the diet (this can be observed from the 1440s). Even then, the cities were not represented as a true estate, but in fact were only observers in the diets. Their one voice was not able to influence the decisions of the diet.

The Turkish danger, which appeared as a constant threat from the end of the 14th century (the defeat of Sigismund near Nicopolis, 1396), was warded off for a time by the victory of John Hunyady near Belgrade (1456), but was not eliminated. During the course of the 15th century the Turks occupied all of the Balkans and ended the Byzantine Empire (1453). New attacks in the 1520s and the defeat at Mohács in 1526, where King Louis II died, meant the end of medieval Hungary. Its only chance to ward off Turkish aggression after 1526 was within the framework of the Habsburg confederation.

■ 1301

Before 13 May – With the support of Pope Boniface VIII, Gregory, archbishop of Esztergom, crowned Charles Robert in Esztergom. For this purpose a replacement copy of the royal crown had been prepared.

May – The Hungarian diet declared the coronation invalid.

27 August – Wenceslas (1301 – 1305), the son of the Czech king Wenceslas II, was crowned as king of Hungary. Wenceslas had been invited by a group of nobles led by Matthew Csák. The coronation was performed by the archbishop of Kalocsa in Székesfehérvár. However, Wenceslas, who reigned in Hungary as Ladislas, was not able to achieve general recognition.

■ 1302

28 February to the **beginning of March** – For supporting his candidacy for the throne, Wenceslas (Ladislas) bestowed upon Matthew Csák the counties of Trenčín, Nitra and Komárno, with all of the royal properties and the rank of *župan* or administrator of these counties.

September – The troops of Charles Robert besieged Buda, the capital of Wenceslas, but did not capture it. The papal curia supported Charles Robert. Cardinal Bocassin, who had already been sent to Hungary in 1301, excommunicated Wenceslas and his supporters.

■ 1303

Matthew Csák, together with fief-holders in Abov in eastern Slovakia, defected to the side of Charles Robert. Wenceslas lost the support of the most powerful nobles.

■ 1304

June – The Czech king Wenceslas II undertook a military campaign into Hungary to help his son. Seeing his superiority, Charles Robert avoided a battle. The Austrian Habsburgs involved themselves in the struggle on the side of Charles Robert.

Mid-August – Wenceslas II withdrew from Hungary with his son Wenceslas and the crown jewels.

■ 1305

21 June – King Wenceslas II died. His son Wenceslas III became the king of Czechia and Poland (1305 – 1306). He broke his engagement to the Hungarian princess Elizabeth.

9 October – Through an agreement reached in Brno, Wenceslas III transferred his right of succession in Hungary to the Bavarian Duke Otto III, to whom he also handed over the Hungarian crown. Because he was an enemy of the Austrian Habsburgs, Otto came to Hungary secretly.

6 December – Otto III (1305 – 1308) was crowned as king of Hungary. The bishops of Veszprém and Csanád, who crowned him, fell out of favor with the papal curia. The lords of Kysek and a small part of the nobility supported Otto.

■ 1307

18 July – The city council of Košice issued the articles of the furriers' **guild** (brotherhood) and fixed the prices of their products. (The document was probably written in a later period).

Summer – The Transylvanian duke Ladislas Khan lured King Otto III to Transylvania on the pretext that he would give him his daughter as a wife. Instead, he imprisoned him and deprived him of the royal crown.

10 October – At Campo Rákos near Pest, the Hungarian nobility accepted Charles Robert as king of Hungary. The most significant nobles, including Matthew Csák, were absent from the assembly.

End of the year – Otto succeeded in escaping from prison and fled Hungary. (He formally renounced claims to the Hungarian throne in 1308).

■ 1308

30 May – 5 November – Cardinal Gentilis arrived in Hungary in order to place Charles Robert on the throne of Hungary.

27 November – At an assembly held in the Dominican monastery in Pest, the Hungarian nobility again elected and recognized Charles Robert as king. Cardinal Gentilis was also present.

■ 1309

16 June – Charles Robert was crowned with a replacement crown at Buda. The real crown was held by Ladislas Khan who, by imprisoning Otto of Bavaria, helped Charles Robert to the throne although he did not become his ally.

■ 1310

Before 11 June – Charles Robert deprived Matthew Csák of the office of **palatine,** for his unauthorized occupation of royal property.

27 August – In Székesfehérvár, Charles Robert (1308 – 1342) was crowned for the third time (as the only king of Hungary), this time with the real royal crown.

■ 1311

Before 6 July – Matthew Csák attacked and pillaged Nitra.

6 July – Cardinal Gentilis excommunicated Matthew Csák.

First half of September – The citizens of Košice killed Amadeus (Omodej) of the Aba family in a skirmish with his armed entourage. The commission named by the king to investigate this case favored the citizens of Košice. The king ordered the Abas to return Abov and Zemplín counties and they had to pledge that they would not harm the people of Košice.

■ 1312

15 June – At Rozhanovce near Košice, a battle took place between royal troops, reinforced by townsmen from Košice and the Spiš cities, and the Abas and their allies. Reinforcements sent by Matthew Csák also fought on the side of the Abas, who were defeated.

■ 1314

Matthew Csák, fought in Moravia against the Czech king, John of Luxemburg, as an ally of the Austrian duke, Frederick.

■ 1315

May to June – The struggle between Matthew Csák and John of Luxemburg continued with the advance of Csák into Slovakia. Charles Robert used the preoccupation of Matthew Csák and, on 1 May, his troops captured the fortress of Visegrád (above the Danube) that belonged to Csák.

■ 1317

May – Charles Robert took several castles in eastern Slovakia belonging to the Aba family.

Before 29 August – Matthew Csák devastated the city, castle and cathedral in Nitra. Charles Robert began a general attack against the troops of Matthew Csák. The struggle took place on the territory of Nitra County.

3 November – Royal troops took the fortress at Komárno after a two-month siege.

■ 1318

3 March – The bishop of Nitra excommunicated Matthew Csák for the crimes and damage that he had perpetrated.

■ 1318 – 1321

The conflict between the supporters of

Charles Robert and the troops of Matthew Csák continued during which the territory of Matthias gradually was occupied. As previously, the county administrator of Zvolen, Master Donč, played an important role in the struggle against Matthew.

■ 1321
18 March – Matthew Csák died in his castle in Trenčín. Only after his death were royal troops able to settle the lands he had occupied.

■ 1323 – 1338
Charles Robert implemented minting (currency) and mining reforms in three stages. In 1325 he introduced, alongside silver coins, gold currency – **ducats** (bi-metallism). To improve the silver currency he introduced in 1329, on the model of the Czech *groš*, a Hungarian **groš** and eliminated the annual exchange of coinage. In order to replace the profits from this exchange, he imposed a new group (**portal**) tax already in 1323. Two new mints were established, in Kremnica and Smolník. These reforms also incorporated the reform of mining (1327). In 1328 the annual exchange of old coins for new was ended.

■ 1327
Because Charles Robert had not fulfilled his financial obligations to him, Albrecht the Austrian duke occupied Bratislava.
13 February – At a meeting in Trnava, Charles Robert concluded with the Czech king, John of Luxemburg, an alliance against the Habsburgs.
17 May – Charles Robert issued a decree regulating mining, according to which the owners of the land were not forced to exchange land upon which they found precious metals. However, they were to pay to the king duties (**urbura**) in the amount of 1/15 to 1/12 of the extracted metal. If a mine was leased to other persons, they were allowed to retain a third of the duties belonging to the king. Extracted material had to be turned over to the mint, for which the owners received monetary compensation.

■ 1328
21 September – After a war with Austria, Bratislava again reverted to Hungary.
8 November – Charles Robert bestowed the privileges of a city upon Kremnica.
– A court of inquisition was established in the Esztergom diocese.

■ 1330
17 April – Felicián Zach, a supporter of the late Matthew Csák, attempted to assassinate Charles Robert and his family at Visegrád. The queen and the successor to the throne, Louis, were slightly injured. The assassin was hanged, drawn and quartered and his family cruelly punished.

■ About 1330
Approximately 30 mining mills were in service in Kremnica and its environs.

■ 1335
August – The plenipotentiaries of the Hungarian, Czech and Polish kings met at Trenčín Castle. The Czech king was represented by Margrave Charles of Moravia, who later became the King and Emperor Charles IV.
October – A meeting of King Casimir the Great of Poland, King John Luxemburg of Czechia and King Charles Robert of Hungary took place at Visegrád. Margrave Charles also was present. The Czech king surrendered his claims to Poland and the Polish king gave up his claims to Silesia.

■ 1336
6 January – On the basis of the Visegrád agreement, Charles Robert bestowed privileges upon Czech and German merchants coming into Hungary along the so-called old Czech road. With this he attempted to circumvent the Vienna **warehousing right** that hindered commerce along the Danube.

■ 1339
July – Charles Robert concluded with Casimír, the Polish king, a treaty concerning mutual succession in the case of death without heirs.

■ **1342**
16 July – Charles Robert died.
21 July – Louis the Great (1342 – 1382) was crowned as the Hungarian king.
– The first written evidence for the existence of a school in the village of Diviaky nad Nitricou comes from this period. Another document about a village school in Tekovský Hrádok comes from 30 May 1378.

■ **1344**
The first written evidence about the existence of a **hammer mill** (*hámor*) in Štítnik. There is more evidence about hammer mills in Slovakia during the second half of the 14th century.

■ **1347 – 1349**
King Louis undertook a campaign to the kingdom of Naples in order to set on the throne his relative, Charles Durazzo. After departing with the main military force and leaving behind weakened Hungarian garrisons, his enemies again took over their lost positions.

■ **1348**
7 April – The Czech king Charles IV founded the first university north of the Alps in Prague, at which students from Slovakia also studied. They are mentioned for the first time after 1367.

■ **1350**
April to **October** – Louis undertook a second campaign to the kingdom of Naples. He was injured in a battle near Aversa on 26 July. Despite partial success, he was not able to secure his permanent influence in Naples. The Hungarian garrisons could not be maintained and the war concluded in 1352 with a peace mediated by Pope Clement VI.

■ **1351**
11 December – Louis issued a decree that confirmed the **Golden Bull** of Andrew II. In further provisions the **yeomanry** were formally made equal with the higher **nobility**. The nobility was not to sell or bestow their land upon the church or laymen. In case a noble family died out the land reverted to the king. The serfs were allowed to move freely, but only after payment of duties to the landlords. They paid the landlords a tax, the **ninth,** just like the landlords' towns. Cities with walls did not pay the ninth. Less significant **cloisters** (monasteries) and church institutions did not have the right to issue validated copies of charters.

■ **1364**
12 May – A university was established in Cracow. Hundreds of students from Slovakia studied there during the course of the 14th century and later.
5 October – King Louis fixed the payment of **tolls** (*mýto*) on the road from Košice, through Spiš, Liptov, Turiec, and Žilina, in the direction of Wroclaw. Along this road were transported metals extracted from the mining region of central Slovakia.

■ **1365**
12 March – A university was founded in Vienna. Like universities in Prague and Cracow, it had a great influence upon the intellectual culture of Slovakia.

■ **1367**
1 September – A university was founded in Pécs. It probably ceased to exist around 1390.

■ **1369**
27 February – On the order of King Louis, Žilina abandoned the law code of Těšín and accepted the Krupina law code. The towns and villages in northwestern Slovakia then formed a group that followed the principles of this **city law.**
7 May – King Louis bestowed a coat of arms upon the city of Košice. It is the oldest privilege granting an urban coat of arms in the whole of Europe.

■ **1370**
The so-called *Zipser Willkür*, or Spiš Law, codified the then existing legal customs derived from the *Saxon Mirror (Sachsenspiegel)*.
5 November – Casimir, king of Poland, died and, according to the agreement of

1339, Louis the Great was elected king of Poland.
17 November – Louis had himself crowned in Cracow.

■ **1370 – 1380**
The building of the royal castle in Zvolen took place on the Italian model of a square castle.

■ **1376**
The city council in Bratislava issued the first known statutes for the bakers, shoemakers and butchers of Bratislava. There still is no evidence in them for the existence of **guilds** for these crafts.

■ **1377**
Pastor Henrich from Veľké Tŕnie (today Vinosady near Modra) prepared an illuminated missal (liturgical book). It shows that important written documents were also produced outside of well-known copying centers (*scriptoria*).

■ **1378**
The first part of the Žilina City Book containing the German law was prepared. The provision that people who did not master German could give evidence at courts in their native language (Slovak) is evidence for the strong influence of Slovaks in this city.

■ **1381**
7 May – Louis the Great bestowed upon the Slovaks of Žilina privileges that allotted to them a number of places on the city council equal to those held by the Germans. The elected **magistrate** was to be alternately a Slovak and a German. This was already a tradition and the king confirmed it at the request of the townspeople.

■ **1382**
10 September – Louis the Great died in Trnava showing symptoms of leprosy.
17 September – Maria the daughter of Louis, was crowned (1382 – 1395). Co-regent was Elizabeth, the second wife of Louis. The ac-

tual ruler and advisor of the queen mother was the **palatine**, Nicholas Goriansky.

■ **1384**
May to June – The Polish nobility, according to previous negotiations, accepted Jadwiga, the younger daughter of Louis, as queen.
15 October – Jadwiga was crowned in Cracow.

■ **1385**
August – Sigismund of Luxemburg, the son of the emperor and Czech king, Charles IV, who was to have become, according to treaty, the husband of Maria, invaded western Slovakia with an army and occupied the counties of Bratislava and Nitra. In this way he wanted to achieve the realization of his claims.
3 September – Charles the Small, of the Neapolitan branch of the Anjous, landed in Dalmatia in order to enforce his claim to the Hungarian throne. Under pressure both queens agreed to the marriage of Sigismund and Maria in the autumn of 1385. At the end of the year Sigismund left Hungary in order to mobilize an army against Charles the Small.
31 December – Charles the Small, without respecting the position of the queens, had himself crowned king in Székesfehérvár.

■ **1386**
7 February – The conspirators, Blasius Forgách and the palatine Nicholas Goriansky, with the knowledge of Queen Elizabeth, seriously wounded Charles the Small. They imprisoned him in Buda and later in Visegrád, where he died of his wounds on 24 February. His assassination was the signal for the murder of the royal entourage and the Italian merchants living in Buda.
18 February – The Polish queen Jadwiga married the Lithuanian prince Vladislav Jagiello, who became king of Poland on 4 March. The Polish-Lithuanian Union had begun.
Spring – Sigismund, with his brother the Czech king Wenceslas IV, invaded Hungary and began to build fortifications near Gyor.
1 May – The queens negotiated with Sigis-

mund and Wenceslas IV. They recognized the pledge of the borderlands in western Slovakia to the margrave of Moravia and declared them to be debts of the Hungarian crown.

25 July – Supporters of the Neapolitan party ambushed the train of the queens in Sriema. The queens were captured and imprisoned in the fortress of Krupa and later in Novigrad in Dalmatia.

■ 1387

Beginning of the year – During the siege of Novigrad, Queen Elizabeth was garroted and her body flung over the walls in order to dissuade the attackers continuing the siege further. In the general confusion and uncertainty, the Hungarian nobility subscribed to the candidacy of Sigismund as king.

31 March – The coronation of Sigismund Luxemburg (1387 – 1347) took place. However, before this, he had to pledge that he would not elevate foreigners to ecclesiastical dignities, that he would have only Hungarian nobles in his council, and that he would respect the laws of the country.

■ 1388

The serfs in Jablonov revolted against the Spiš prior, Nicholas, who endeavored to deprive them of their privileged position.

■ 1389

15 June – In the battle at Kosovo polje, Turks defeated the Serbs, who lost their independence. The Turkish Empire thus became the immediate neighbor of Hungary.

■ 1390 – 1391

John Literát from Madočany falsified charters on the orders of the nobility of Liptov and Turiec for which he was burned. The king ordered a revision of the charters of these counties. Thus originated the Liptov and Turiec registers, containing a digest of the oldest charters of these counties.

■ 1390, 1394

14 February 1390 and 24 February 1394 – The cities of Košice and Cracow concluded agreements concerning mutual trade. These agreements improved their commercial relationships, delimitated spheres of influence, and eased mutual relations. They mutually respected the **warehousing right**.

■ 1395

17 May – Queen Maria died of injuries she had suffered when she fell from a horse.

■ 1396

19 March – The Czech and German king Wenceslas IV named Sigismund as his deputy (vicar) in the empire.

28 September – The Turkish sultan Bajazid defeated the army of Sigismund strengthened with knights from western Europe in a battle near Nicopolis. The undisciplined conduct of the French knights led to confusion and finally defeat. Sigismund saved himself by fleeing on a Venetian ship and at the end of the year he returned to Hungary through Dalmatia.

■ 1397

Beginning of the year – The Moravian margrave Prokop invaded northern Slovakia and took possession of Turiec, Liptov, and the castle of Likava. His troops dislodged domestic forces from this territory.

29 September to **October** – At a diet in Timisoara, King Sigismund issued a decree adding to the provisions of the **Golden Bull** of 1222 and the decree of Louis of 1351. It set the portal tax at three *groš* for each **portal**. Every 20 **farmsteads** had to equip one warrior for war. It ordered the return of royal land (even that which had been mortgaged). The provisions of the diet were directed against foreigners who were to be expelled from the country, and the Jews who were not to serve in offices of an economic character. These provisions did not extend to the royal favorite Stibor of Stiborice and several bishops.

■ Around 1400

In Trnava appeared some manifestations of the **Waldensian heresy,** which were subjected to investigation by the **inquisition**.

■ **1401**

28 April – Sigismund was imprisoned in the castle at Buda. He was blamed for the poor administration of the country and for preferring foreigners. He was taken to Visegrád and then to the castle of Siklós.

11 June – A partial diet in Topoľčany deposed Sigismund and offered the crown of Hungary to Vladislav Jagiello, who did not accept the offer.

Summer – Stibor of Stiborice and the Moravian margraves Prokop and Jošt took control of western Slovakia and conquered several castles and fortified cities that remained loyal to Sigismund. The military intervention and diplomatic activity of the Czech king Wenceslas IV, Sigismund's brother, contributed to the liberation of Sigismund in the autumn.

29 October – At a diet in Pápa, Sigismund, according to an agreement with the rebellious nobility, pledged not to seek revenge against the rebels for his imprisonment.

■ **1402**

22 January – For services which Trnava, Sopron, Levoča, Bardejov and especially Bratislava and Trnava had rendered in the war with the rebels, Sigismund bestowed upon them the **warehousing right**.

26 August – Ladislas of Naples, the son of Charles the Small, landed in Dalmatia in order to continue the war of the Neapolitan Anjous against Sigismund.

14 September – Sigismund concluded a treaty with the Austrian duke Albrecht, concerning mutual succession in case either died without heirs. This agreement became the basis for the further aspirations of Habsburgs to the Hungarian throne up to 1526.

21 September – At a diet in Bratislava the Hungarian estates confirmed the agreement of Sigismund with Albrecht.

■ **1403**

Beginning of the year – Sigismund remained in the Czech kingdom and thus enabled Ladislas of Naples to occupy Dalmatia and obtain followers among the Hungarian nobility. The army of Ladislas penetrated the central parts of Hungary.

July – Sigismund quickly returned to Hungary. Stibor of Stiborice defeated Ladislas of Naples near Gyor.

5 August – Ladislas of Naples had himself crowned king of Hungary at Zadar. He left the leadership of his military operation to his generals and did not leave Dalmatia.

9 August – In Bratislava, Sigismund issued a decree forbidding any payment in the Czech or Hungarian kingdoms to the papal curia in Rome and called for the rejection of Pope Boniface IX.

1 September – In Zadar the papal legate, Cardinal Acciaujoli issued a letter excommunicating Sigismund and his followers.

August to **September** – The army of Sigismund captured Buda, Esztergom and other cities that the rebels and the army of Ladislas of Naples had occupied.

6 October – At the diet in Buda, Sigismund bestowed pardons to those insurgents who had surrendered. All of the donations made during the time of disturbances were annulled and property was returned to its original owners if they had received amnesty.

■ **1404**

6 April – In Bratislava Sigismund issued the decree **placetum regium** (it pleases the king) that limited the rights of the papal curia in Hungary.

■ **1405**

13 March – Sigismund issued a decree for the country that outlined several provisions of the so-called minor decree (**Decretum minus**).

15 April – Sigismund issued the minor decree. Its goal was to create a single **estate** of the cities on royal land. However, the decree did not create a country-wide estate or status, legally or politically, for townspeople nor did it legalize their participation in the Hungarian diet even though the ruler, from time to time, invited them to it.

Mid-November – Sigismund married Barbara, the daughter of Herman Cillei, and thereby strengthened his family tie to the magnate league of the Goriansky and Cillei.

■ **1408**
12 December – Sigismund founded the Order of the Dragon. In addition to himself and his wife, twenty-two of the most prominent nobles of domestic and foreign origin were members. Among them the king acted as the „first among equals". The members of this order influenced the policy of the kingdom.

■ **1409**
Beginning of the year – Sigismund's army was victorious over the insurgent feudal land-owners in Bosnia and Dalmatia, where they had fought since in 1407. The loss of adherents who had joined Sigismund forced Ladislas of Naples to terminate his engagement in this area.
9 July – Ladislas of Naples sold to the Venetians the Dalmatian ports and fortresses that he held for 100,000 gold florins. Sigismund did not recognize this and still sought to exercise his claims to Dalmatia. Thus, instead of Ladislas, the Venetians became his enemies.
20 December – Sigismund concluded a treaty with the order of the German knights (**Teutonic Order**) that was directed against Poland.

■ **1410**
20 March – The Czech reformer Jerome of Prague delivered a sermon in Buda that aroused the anger of the Sigismund and his court. Jerome was imprisoned but he was able to escape.
6 – 18 April – At a meeting in Kežmarok with Grand Prince Vitold of Lithuania, Sigismund unsuccessfully sought to dissuade the Poles from war with the Teutonic Order. During the negotiations a great fire broke out in Kežmarok. King Vladislav of Poland, waiting in Nowy Sacz, did not participate in the negotiations.
15 July – The army of the Teutonic Order was defeated in a decisive battle between the crusaders and the Polish army near Grünwald. Hungary did not directly participate in the war.

September to **October** – The Poles repulsed smaller Hungarian forces that, under the leadership of Stibor from Stiborice, invaded the area of Stary and Nowy Sacz.

■ **1410 – 1413**
Ulrich Rauchenwarter, the former magistrate of Bratislava, instigated unrest against the city council.

■ **1411**
21 July – After repeated votes the electoral princes elected Sigismund as the German king in Frankfurt am Main. The first elections took place on 20 September and 1 October 1410 but the votes of the electoral princes were distributed to between Sigismund and Margrave Jošt of Moravia.
4 October – At the diet in Bratislava, Sigismund named Duke Albrecht of Austria as his heir and son-in-law. His two-year old daughter Elizabeth was declared the heir to the Hungarian throne if he died without male descendants.
11 November – The representatives of the kings of Poland and Hungary met in Šramovice on the Polish-Hungarian border where they agreed on a truce to 15 August 1412. In addition, they guaranteed free trade to merchants from both countries.
End of the year – A war between Venice and Hungary broke out, in which the military commander of Sigismund, Pipo Scholari, took several cities in Friaul and the border city of Tarvisio.
– The oldest evidence for the production of cannons in Slovakia, at Bardejov, comes from this year. Further evidence about the production of cannons comes from Bratislava (1414), Trnava (1428) and Prešov (1429).

■ **1412**
15 March – Sigismund concluded a peace with King Vladislav of Poland and Grand Prince Vitold of Lithuania in Stará Ľubovňa. Sigismund was interested in making peace with the Poles because he was threatened in the south by the Venetians.

19 April – The first consultation among the five cities of eastern Slovakia (Košice, Levoča, Prešov, Bardejov and Sabinov) about prosecuting debtors took place. This can be considered the basis for the future **league of five cities** (*Pentapolitana*).

Autumn – Sigismund personally took to the field with an army against Venice. More than six years would pass before he returned to Hungary (1419).

8 November – Sigismund mortgaged to Vladislav, the Polish king, 13 Spiš cities of the Saxon community and three towns and the castle of Stará Lubovňa for 37,000 *kôp* (piles) of Czech *groš*. The mortgage was redeemed only after the division of Poland in 1772.

■ **1413**

17 April – Sigismund concluded a truce with the Republic of Venice for a period of five years, which legitimized the territorial gains of both sides.

27 September – 25 December – Before King Sigismund the city of Bratislava accused the former magistrate Ulrich Rauchenwarter of embezzling 13,000 florins, misuse of his office, violating urban privileges, and stirring up discord before the election of a new magistrate. Rauchenwarter later died in the city prison of Bratislava.

9 December – According to an agreement with King Sigismund, Pope John XXIII summoned a council of the church to convene in Constance on 1 November of the following year.

■ **1414**

After leaving Italy, Sigismund devoted himself to the affairs of the German Empire.

1 November – The Council of Constance opened.

8 November – In the presence of his wife Barbara, Sigismund was crowned as German king in Aachen.

25 December – Sigismund arrived with his entourage in Constance.

■ **1415**

29 May – The Council of Constance de-

posed the anti-Pope John XXIII, who attempted to thwart the council by his flight (29 March).

4 July – The Roman Pope Gregory XII announced his abdication through his legates.

6 July – Master John Hus of the University of Prague was burned after the council declared his teachings heretical.

21 July – Sigismund left Constance for Perpignan to negotiate the abdication of the anti-Pope, Benedict XIII. The negotiation was not successful and the **schism** continued.

■ **1416**

Spring – Sigismund left for France where he attempted to mediate peace in the Hundred Years' War between the French and English.

Summer – Sigismund, with his entourage, crossed the English Channel.

15 August – By an agreement concluded in Canterbury, Sigismund transferred his support to the English.

■ **1417**

26 July – The council deposed the anti-Pope Benedict XIII in his absence.

11 November – The election of a new pope, Martin V, took place.

■ **1418**

22 April – The Council of Constance was adjourned although it had not fulfilled one of its main tasks, the elimination of schism in the church. Later popes did not recognize all of its decisions, especially those that were in conflict with the idea of the supremacy of the pope over the council.

Second half of the year – Sigismund remained in Germany where he resolved the affairs of the German Empire.

■ **1419**

6 February – Sigismund left Passau for Bratislava travelling through Vienna. During the first half of the year he resolved the internal problems that had accumulated in Hungary during his six-year absence. The war with Venetians continued. Already in April 1418, they had occupied the territory in northern Italy belonging to the patriarch of Aquilea, a supporter of Sigismund.

2 July – A consultation of the cities with the king took place in Buda.

16 August – The Czech king Wenceslas IV died of apoplexy after a revolt in Prague. Shortly before his death he appealed to Sigismund for assistance.

Autumn – In the southern part of the kingdom the Hungarian army attacked the Turks.

December – Sigismund concluded a peace with the Turks for five years in Oradea.

■ **1420**
17 March – In Wroclaw the papal legate declared a crusade against the Czechs.

14 July – The **Hussites** defeated the army of Sigismund at Vítkov hill near Prague.

28 July – Some of the Czech nobility crowned Sigismund as the Czech king.

1 November – The Hussites defeated the army of Sigismund at Vyšehrad in Prague.

■ **1421**
3 – 7 June – The diet of the Czech estates in Čáslav deposed Sigismund from the Czech throne.

28 September – Sigismund gave Duke Albrecht of Austria five cities in Moravia and Czechia as a guarantee for a loan and promised him all cities and castles that he could regain from the **Hussites**. Albrecht loaned him 60, 000 florins for conducting the war and was engaged to Elizabeth, Sigismund's daughter.

October 1421 – April 1422
Sigismund undertook a second campaign against the Hussites. After several defeats near Kolín, Kutná Hora and Nemecký Brod, the Hungarian army withdrew to Moravia where garrisons were left until 1426.

■ **1422**
13 December – Stibor of Stiborice issued the first document in Slovakia written in Czech. This was a debenture note containing Slovakisms.

■ **1423**
18 April – Sigismund decreed privileges for the Romany people in Spiš.

4 October – Sigismund gave Albrecht, in feudal tenure, the margravate of Moravia and appointed him heir to the Czech Kingdom after his death.

■ **1424**
22 May – The king bestowed upon his wife Barbara the mining cities of central Slovakia together with the royal castle in Zvolen.

■ **1427**
17 March – During a military campaign against the Turks, Sigismund issued a military code in Brasov in Transylvania that was intended to protect the population against pillaging by the army.

■ **1428**
January to **February** – The first campaign of the Hussites under the leadership of Prokop Holý invaded Slovakia near Skalica and penetrated Slovak territory up to Bratislava. They ravaged the region of the Small Carpathians and burned the suburbs of Bratislava.

End of May – The Turks defeated the army of Sigismund at the siege of the fortress of Golubac on the Danube. Serbia and Walachia had to submit to Turkey.

■ **1429**
28 March – 9 April – A meeting between Sigismund and a Hussite delegation took place at the castle in Bratislava. Prokop Holý and Peter Payne, a teacher at Charles University, represented the Hussites. Because of the uncompromising stance of both parties the negotiations were unsuccessful.

■ **End of the 1520s – 1530s**
The rebuilding of the castle of Bratislava as the second residence of Sigismund (the first was in Buda) took place.

■ **1430**
6 March – Sigismund bestowed upon Bratislava the right to mint coins as compensation for

the damages suffered in the war against the Hussites. This and other privileges were later extended.

23 – 28 April – Hussite troops led by the captain Velek Koudelník invaded Hungary. In battles with the Hungarian army at Trnava and Šintava the leader of the Hussites fell. After an indecisive result they successfully withdrew to Moravia.

July – Sigismund left Bratislava for the imperial diet and traveled through Vienna to Nuremberg.

■ 1431

3 March – Pope Martin V summoned a council of the church to meet in Basle.

18 March – A disputation between Hussite theologians and professors of the University of Cracow took place. The bishop of Cracow, Zbigniev Olésnicki, placed the city under an **interdict**.

End of March – The enraged Hussites attacked an area around Cracow and penetrated into northern Slovakia, pillaging the Carthusian monastery in Lechnica.

1 April – Part of this army, under the leadership of Dobeslav Puchala, pillaged and burned Levoča.

September – After a battle near Domažlice (14 August 1431), the Orphans, under the leadership of Ján Čapek from Sáně, and the Taborites, led by Prokop Holý, invaded northern Slovakia in two columns, pillaged Žilina, left a garrison in Lednica and traversed Turiec to reach Liptov.

27 September – Through cunning the Orphans and Taborites were able to capture Likava castle, where they also left a garrison.

October – The Hussites invaded the upper Nitra region, left troops in Topoľčany and took Nitra.

Around 19 October – Disagreeing on the division of looty, the Hussite army divided. The Taborites crossed the Váh River near Hlohovec, pulled down bridges behind them, and returned to Moravia. The Orphans continued to plunder southern Slovakia and, when they did not succeed in crossing the Váh near Hlohovec, they proceeded northward along the left bank.

Around 11 November – A Hungarian army defeated the Orphans near Ilava, where they had tried to cross the Váh. They lost the majority of their warriors and looty.

Fall – After the battle at Domažlice, in which he did not take part, Sigismund left Germany for Italy with a small military force comprised of Hungarian knights and soldiers from the Swiss Confederation. The goal of his journey was his coronation as emperor.

25 November – Sigismund was crowned king of Italy with the Lombard iron crown in Milan.

18 December – Sigismund concluded a treaty with the north Italian states against the Venetians.

■ 1432

Beginning of the year – Sigismund left Milan for Piacenza, Parma and Sienna.

24 June – Under the leadership of Blažek of Borotín, the Hussites took possession of Trnava by cunning and left a garrison there. Previously they had seized Skalica where they also left a detachment.

July 1432 to May 1433 – Owing to military weakness, Sigismund remained surrounded by enemies in Sienna. He requested reinforcements from Hungary. However, these were not sufficient to break through the encirclement.

27 November – The Hussite garrison from Trnava attempted to take Bratislava with the help of conspirators in the city, who were to have opened the city gates at the agreed upon signal. They were led by a Moravian knight, Peter Kuděj (Kutěj). The conspiracy was discovered and Kuděj died in prison.

November – The Hussite detachment in Lednica, with assistance of reinforcements from Moravia, captured Považská Bystrica, Rajec, Nemecké Pravno, and Prievidza.

■ 1433

20 January – From Sienna Sigismund sent suggestions to Hungary for the organization of its defense against the Hussites and the Turks.

4 January – 14 April – A delegation of Czech Hussites participated in the meetings of the Council of Basle. The result was the acceptance of the *compacta* (agreement) and the introduction of communion in both forms (bread and wine). At the end of April, the legates of the council together with the representatives of the Hussites left for Prague for further negotiations.

Mid-February – The detachment of Hussites in Trnava together with the garrison from Skalica again attempted to take Bratislava, but without success.

7 April – Pope Eugenius IV mediated peace between King Sigismund and the Venetians with the Florentines. Therefore, in his conflict with the Council of Basle, Sigismund took the side of the pope.

12 – 21 April – Under the leadership of John Pardus of Hrádok and Frederick of Strážnice, the Taborites invaded southern Spiš through southern Poland.

25 April – Hussite soldiers captured and looted Kežmarok.

April – The Hussites devastated Spišská Nová Ves, the monasteries in Spišský Štiavnik, and the stones of refuge (*lapis refugii*) near Levoča.

8 – 23 May – Wreaking havoc everywhere, the Hussites marched through Liptov, Turiec, and the Považie region to Kežmarok. There they looted the mint located outside the city's fortifications.

Around 11 June – The Hussites returned to Moravia.

31 May – After mutual negotiations, Pope Eugenius IV crowned Sigismund in Rome as Emperor of the Holy Roman Empire of the German Nation. After his coronation, Sigismund left for the Council of Basle.

August – Blažek from Borotín negotiated with the Hungarian estates in Buda but without result.

■ **1434**

March to **April** – Frederick from Strážnice attacked Spiš from Poland. A second invasion was undertaken from Žilina to Ružomberok. The expected reinforcement from the garrison in Topoľčany did not arrive, as they themselves were surrounded.

30 May – A battle took place at Lipany between the radical Taborites and the more moderate Hussites from Prague allied with the Czech **Calixtine** (Utraquist) nobles. The Taborites were defeated and their leader, Prokop Holý, died in the battle. After this battle, Hussite garrisons in Slovakia were no longer able to expect much help from Czechia.

June – The Hussite garrison in Trnava undertook a circuitous campaign through southern Slovakia. They burned Sv. Jur. They advanced from Bratislava, which was not taken, through the Žitný ostrov (Rye Island), to Nitra County as far as Šurany, and then turned to return to Trnava.

Second half of the year – The commanders of the Hussite garrisons returned a ransom for the occupied fortresses and cities.

8 October – Sigismund returned to Bratislava through Vienna.

■ **1435**

8 March – At a diet in Bratislava Sigismund issued the so-called major decree (*Decretum maius*) that reformed state and judicial administration. It also ordered an audit of the **tolls** in all counties at a general assembly of the nobility.

12 March – Sigismund issued a decree focused on defenses against the Hussites. It contained an order that a cavalryman had to be put in place for every 33 serfs and that the nobles without serfs had to fight in the county army under the leadership of the county administrator. The king pledged to secure at his own expense the defense of western Slovakia against the Hussites.

Before 12 May – The Hussite occupiers left Trnava.

■ **1436**

After 27 May – In Kežmarok Hungarian and Polish ambassadors negotiated about the return of the Spiš cities but without success.

5 July – The Czech estates accepted in Jihlava an agreement with Council of Basle, the so-called Basle *compacta*.

8 July – For its services in the battles against the Hussites, Sigismund bestowed a coat of arms upon Bratislava.

14 August – At a diet in Jihlava the Czech estates confirmed Sigismund as the Czech king. He departed for Prague with his entourage.

3 November – Sigismund confirmed the old privileges of the Jews in Hungary.

■ 1437

Sigismund sojourned in Czechia where he suppressed the remnant opposition of the radical Hussites (Ján Roháč z Dubé).

9 December – Sigismund died in Znojmo on his way to Hungary.

18 December – The diet in Bratislava accepted Albrecht Habsburg as king of Hungary on the basis of previous agreements and the last will and testament of Sigismund.

■ 1438

1 January – The coronation of Albrecht (1438 – 1439) took place.

18 March – Albrecht was elected king of Germany in Frankfurt am Main.

April – Albrecht left for Vienna and Czechia.

6 May – The Czech Catholic estates elected Albrecht as Czech king and crowned him on 29 June.

July – Polish forces struck Spiš and Šariš. The conflict in eastern Slovakia lasted until the beginning of 1439.

■ 1439

June – A Turkish army under the leadership of Sultan Murad II attacked the border region of Hungary.

August to **October** – Hungarian forces under the leadership of King Albrecht advanced against the Turks but, because of an outbreak of dysentery, they had to withdraw. No armed encounter with the Turks occurred.

27 October – During the withdrawal of the military expedition, Albrecht died in Neszmély near Komárno.

■ 1440

20 – 21 February – Awaiting the birth of her son, the widowed Queen Elizabeth secretly had the royal crown brought from Visegrád to Komárno (the courier was her chambermaid).

22 February – Elizabeth gave birth to a son, Ladislas (Posthumous). This changed the political situation in Hungary.

8 March – In Cracow, a delegation of the Hungarian estates offered the crown to Vladislav Jagiello.

15 May – Elizabeth had Ladislas Posthumous (1440 – 1457) crowned. After the coronation, in fear of enemies, she carried off her son and the royal crown to Vienna. The German king Frederick III was to be his guardian until he came of age.

17 July – In Székesfehérvár, the supporters of Vladislav III celebrated his coronation as king of Hungary. Both coronations were performed by the archbishop of Esztergom, Cardinal Dionysius of Seč.

Prior to 22 August – Elizabeth engaged the services of the Czech Catholic nobleman Ján Jiskra of Brandýs to defend the interests of Ladislas Posthumous in Hungary during his minority. After arriving in Slovakia, Jiskra was temporarily taken prisoner near Hronský Beňadik. Later he captured the castle in Zvolen and by military force gradually took control of the castles and the cities that the queen entrusted to his administration. In addition to Zvolen, these were the castles of Spiš, Šášov, Revište, Ľupča, Šariš, the mining cities of central Slovakia, as well as Košice, Prešov and Bardejov.

■ 1440 – 1445

A league of the five cities in eastern Slovakia (*Pentapolitana*) was established that consisted of Košice, Levoča, Prešov, Bardejov and Sabinov (**league of five cities**).

■ 1441

12 March – Jiskra's forces took Šariš Castle.

16 October – Jiskra took Kežmarok that supported Vladislav Jagiello of Poland. He occupied Podolínec and the castle of Richňava.

■ 1441 – 1459

Discrimination by the city council of Kremnica against a townsman of Slovak origin, Stanko Vilhelmovič is an indication of nationality conflicts in the cities. The rulers Ladislas V (1453) and Matthias Corvinus (1459) intervened on his behalf.

■ 1442
January to **February** – Vladislav III besieged Bratislava, which supported Queen Elizabeth.
13 December – In Gyor Elizabeth concluded a treaty with Vladislav. She recognized him as king of Hungary, but in return demanded the recognition of the right of her son, Ladislas Posthumous, to the Hungarian throne.
17 December – Elizabeth died unexpectedly in Gyor.

■ 1443
The struggles between the Jagiellonian and the pro-Habsburgs parties in Hungary continued. Jiskra postponed concluding a truce until he succeeded in taking Spiš castle in mid-August.
1 September – In Spišká Nová Ves, Jiskra concluded a one- year truce with Vladislav III, who was represented by Simon Rozgonyi.
Mid-June to the **end of the year** – John Hunyady and Vladislav were drawn into a war with the Turks. They captured Niš and Sofia and penetrated up to the Balkan foothills. The approach of winter forced them to withdraw.

■ 1444
Around 15 June – Vladislav gathered an army for a campaign against the Turks. In Szeged, the emissaries of the Turkish sultan conveyed a favorable peace offer to Hungary. The king concluded peace with the Turks for ten years.
4 August – At the insistence of the papal legate, Cardinal Giuliano Cesarini, the king broke the peace with the Turks and resumed the war.
10 November – In a battle near Varna in Bulgaria, the Hungarian army suffered a defeat at the hands of Sultan Murad II. King Vladislav (also called Varnenčík) and Cardinal Cesarini perished in the battle. John Hunyady was captured.

■ 1445
April to **May** – The Hungarian diet recognized the claim of Ladislas Posthumous to the throne of Hungary. During his minority the administration of the country was entrusted to seven captains who supervised separate territories. In Slovakia these were Ján Jiskra, Pongrác from Liptovský, Svätý Mikuláš, and Imrich Bubek. The diet further ordered that the German king Frederick hand over Ladislas Posthumous. At this diet the cities participated in the drawing up of the laws of the country for the first time.
– The first reports about the **Brethren** in Slovakia appear. This was a group of deserters from the army of Jiskra who built fortified camps. Already in 1445 Jiskra had agreed to their liquidation.

■ 1446
6 June – A diet of the **Hungarian estates** elected John Hunyady (1446 – 1453) as the regent of the country. However, the function of the captains was not abolished. Noteworthy is a reference that the emissaries of Bratislava did not understand the discussions held at the diet in Hungarian.
13 September – John Hunyady and Ján Jiskra concluded a truce for three years at Kremnica. Jiskra pledged to pay his mercenary soldiers regularly so that they would not pillage the country. He retained the administration of and income from the cities of Košice, Kremnica, Levoča, Prešov and Bardejov, as well as from the Spiš and Zvolen castles, together with the income from the **thirtieth.**
November to **December** – John Hunyady turned against Frederick III and occupied territory of Lower Austria.

■ 1447
25 March – The function of the seven captains was abolished by the Hungarian diet. All power was transferred to the regent, John Hunyady.
21 July – In Rimavská Sobota a truce confirming the agreement of 13 September 1446 was concluded between Jiskra on the one side and the supporters of John Hunyady, John Ko-

morovský, and Pongrác from Mikuláš, on the other.

■ 1448
16 – 18 October – John Hunyady was defeated by the Turks in a battle at Kosovo polje.

■ 1449
Pongrác of Mikuláš and the Komorovský brothers, in the service of John Hunyady, pillaged the lands of Spiš administered by Jiskra. Later they concluded a treaty with him.

4 May – Ján Jiskra concluded a peace with the cities of Košice, Levoča, Bardejov, Prešov, and Kežmarok, as well as with Pongrác of Mikuláš.

24 June – At the diet in Pest the Hungarian **estates** informed the papal curia of the spread of the Hussite heresy in Spiš and Šariš counties and about the reception of the sacrament in both species (bread and wine), for which they blamed Czech soldiers in Slovakia.

5 December – In Kremnica John Hunyady concluded a truce with Ján Jiskra that was to last until 25 June of the following year.

■ 1450
Prior to 28 March – John Hunyady and the Hungarian estates concluded a peace with Ján Jiskra in Mezökövesd that legitimized the existing situation.

22 October – John Hunyady concluded a peace with the German king Frederick III. Ladislas Posthumous was to remain in Vienna until he was eighteen years of age. In addition to Devín, Frederick retained several border fortresses and territories.

■ 1451
22 January – The oldest entry in Slovak in the **Žilina city book**.

7 September – Ján Jiskra achieved the greatest victory over John Hunyady and his allies in a battle near Lučenec.

■ 1452
February and March – The estates of Hungary met in Bratislava. Emissaries were sent to Vienna to demand that the Austrian estates hand over Ladislas Posthumous.

24 August – Jiskra concluded peace with Hunyady in Kremnica. His domain was reduced to Levoča, the Spiš castle, and the income from the **thirtieth** in Kežmarok and Stará Ľubovňa.

4 September – Emperor Frederick III handed over Ladislas Posthumous to Ulrich Cillei.

■ 1453
Beginning of the year – The diet in Bratislava confirmed John Hunyady in the offices of regent and captain general.

29 January – Ladislas V presented his coronation oath and the diet recognized him as king of Hungary. It regarded his coronation of 1440 as valid. Ladislas V again named John Hunyady as the captain general of the country.

6 February – The diet stripped Jiskra of all his lands and banished him from Hungary. After his departure, the movement of the **Brethren** began to gather strength.

29 May – Sultan Mehmed II took Constantinople and with this the Byzantine Empire became extinct.

October – Ladislas V left for Czechia and on 28 October was crowned as the Czech king in Prague.

■ 1454
King Ladislas V recalled Jiskra in order to suppress the Brethren. He returned to him the administration of the cities in Spiš and Šariš and the mining cities in central Slovakia.

November – Jiskra was victorious over the Brethren near Trebišov.

■ 1455
Jiskra attempted to seize Kežmarok, which was defended by his former captains Bartoš and Brcál.

■ 1456
4 – 22 July – Turkish forces led by Sultan Mehmed II besieged Belgrade, which was defended by a weak garrison under the leadership of Michael Szilágyi. The defenders were encouraged by the Franciscan friar John Capistrano.

22 July – John Hunyady arrived to help the besieged and was victorious over the superior Turkish forces, which numbered a hundred thousand troops.

11 August – John Hunyady died of the plague in Zemun.

October – Riots and revolts stirred up by the Brethren erupted among the serfs in the Zemplín region.

■ **1457**
14 March – Ladislas Hunyady, the oldest son of John Hunyady, was accused of betraying the king and the murder of Ulrich Cillei.

16 March – Ladislas Hunyady was executed after a short trial in Buda.

Fall – King Ladislas left for Czechia and took with him Matthias, the younger son of John Hunyady, as a prisoner.

23 November – Ladislas V died in Prague, where he was awaiting the arrival of the French princess who was to become his wife. Modern medical science, by examination of his remains, has refuted the suspicion that he was poisoned.

■ **1457 – 1458**
The thirtieth tax book of Bratislava documents the foreign trade of Hungary. Precious metals and cattle predominated among exports, while the main imports were textiles (up to 75 per cent) and the products of artisans. The export of wine from Bratislava likewise was extensive, but it is not recorded in writing, since the townspeople of Bratislava were exempt from paying the **thirtieth.**

■ **1458**
24 January – In Buda, the Hungarian nobility elected and proclaimed Matthias Hunyady, later called Corvinus, king of Hungary in his absence, since he had from the autumn of 1457 been interned as a hostage in Prague. The maternal uncle of Matthias, Michael Szilágyi, became regent.

14 February – Matthias arrived in Buda. He was ceremonially enthroned in the Church of the Blessed Virgin Mary since the crown of St Stephen had been taken to Vienna in **1440**

by Queen Elizabeth, the mother of Ladislas Posthumous.

Spring – Led by Sebastian from Rozhanovce, the royal army defeated detachments of the Brethren led by the captains Ján Talafúz and Peter Axamit in the battle of Sárospatak. Axamit fell in the battle, while Talafúz was able to escape to Šariš Castle.

August – Under pressure from Matthias, Michael Szilágyi resigned the office of regent. This was one of the first steps taken by King Matthias to strengthen the power of the ruler.

Summer – Matthias summoned the military mobilization (**insurekcia**) of the **nobility** for a campaign against the Turks, which was successful in minor engagements in Serbia in October. Subsequently an extraordinary military tax (*subsidium*), amounting to one florin for every chimney (that is house), was levied throughout Hungary.

■ **1459**
17 February – Opposition magnates elected the German king and emperor, Frederick II Habsburg as king of Hungary (as rival king to Matthias).

Spring – A struggle lasting several months between the armies of Matthias and Frederick III broke out on the Hungarian-Austrian borders.

■ **1460**
April – Emissaries of Matthias and Frederick III concluded a peace at Olomouc.

■ **1461**
10 January – Matthias called upon the upper Hungarian (or Slovak) cities to fight against Ján Jiskra and the Brethren.

1 May – Matthias Corvinus married Catherine, the daughter of the Czech king, George of Podiebrad.

■ **1462**
3 April – In the name of King Matthias, John Vitéz, archbishop of Esztergom, concluded an agreement with Frederick III in Graz according to which the emperor promised to return the crown of St Stephen for an indemnity of 80 thousand florins. But he reserved the

right to use the title king of Hungary and a claim to the Hungarian throne in the event that Matthias did not have any legitimate offspring (**16 June 1463**).

Spring – Matthias concluded a treaty with Ján Jiskra, according to which the king elevated him to the status of baron and accepted him, together with his soldiers, into royal service. As compensation for relinquishing several castles in Slovakia, Matthias paid Jiskra 25 thousand florins.

10 August – Matthias levied an extraordinary tax for the redemption of the crown of St. Stephen amounting to one florin for every **portal** (dwelling) in Hungary. At the same time he levied an extraordinary tax upon all the free royal cities (for example, Bardejov had to pay 2000 and Košice 5000 florins).

■ **1463**
19 July – The treaty and peace of **3 April 1462** between King Matthias and Emperor Frederick III was ceremonially confirmed in Wiener Neustadt.

September – Matthias led an army against the Turks. The expedition ended successfully with the capture of the castle and capital city of Bosnia, Jajce (25 December 1463).

■ **1464**
29 March – The coronation ceremony of Matthias with the crown of St Stephen took place in Székesfehérvár.

March – Matthias reformed the royal chancellery and judiciary.

27 May – Matthias issued a golden bull for Bratislava, in which he confirmed all privileges and rights granted by the preceding rulers.

■ **1465**
29 May – Pope Paul II entrusted to John Vitéz, archbishop of Esztergom, the establishment of a university in Bratislava according to the wishes of Matthias.

■ **1467**
30 January – In a battle near Veľké Kostoľany, Matthias decisively defeated the

Brethren when he captured their last camp. Ján Švehla, the Brethren's captain, and approximately 150 brethren were sentenced to death and hanged near Čachtice. Some of the defeated Brethren entered the service of Matthias and became the basis of the so-called **Black Army**.

March – Matthias implemented extensive monetary and tax reforms that enabled him to increase royal income substantially (according to estimates, around 800 thousand florins annually).

20 July – The university, the **Academia Istropolitana**, began to function in Bratislava. Along with the royal court, this, the only university in Hungary, disseminated **humanism**, **Renaissance** scholarship, and higher education in general.

18 August – A revolt of the estates erupted in Transylvania against Matthias, which he suppressed within a month. The leaders of the revolt were pardoned.

■ **1468**
31 March – As the executor of the papal anathema, King Matthias undertook a military expedition into the Czech Kingdom against his former father-in-law King George of Podiebrad, who was excommunicated (**excommunication**) and declared deposed from his throne by Pope Paul II. Gradually the troops of Matthias occupied much of the territory of Moravia.

■ **1469**
3 May – Matthias was elected Czech king by representatives of the Czech Catholic estates in Olomouc.

5 June – The diet of the Czech estates rejected the election of Matthias as the Czech king and, at the suggestion of King George of Podiebrad, recognized the succession of Vladislav Jagiello (who in 1471, after the death of King George, he was crowned and became the Czech king).

2 November – The Czech army defeated the army of King Matthias at the battle of Uherský Brod and unexpectedly invaded the Považie region.

■ **1471**

June – Led by Archbishop John Vitéz and the bishop of Pécs, John of Cazma (Johannes Pannonius), the Hungarian magnates hatched a conspiracy against King Matthias.

2 October – The Polish prince Casimir Jagiello, the son of the king of Poland, Casimir IV, to whom the conspirators had offered the crown, invaded Hungary with an army of 12,000 soldiers and briefly occupied a part of Slovakia, including Nitra, from whence he withdrew to Poland at the end of December.

19 December – Matthias reconciled with the leader of the conspiracy, John Vitéz, whom, however, he later imprisoned. Until his death (8 August 1472) Vitéz remained in royal disfavor, as did his nephew, the bishop and humanist John of Cazma (Johannes Pannonius).

■ **1472**

May – Matthias concluded a truce with the Polish king Casimir IV and his son, the Czech king Vladislav.

■ **1473**

A Slovakized translation of the Magdeburg law was copied into the **Žilina City Book** and was valid for Žilina and several other cities in central Slovakia **(1378)**.

5 June – Andrew Hess printed the *Hungarian Chronicle* in Buda, the oldest known Hungarian incunabula.

■ **1474**

August – Matthias, at the head of a military expedition, occupied a substantial part of Silesia where, until December, he fought against the armies of the Czech king Vladislav and the Polish king Casimir IV.

8 December – Matthias accepted the offer of Casimir IV and concluded a truce with him for a period of two and half years. This enabled him to concentrate on putting in order his relations with the Ottoman Empire on the southern border.

■ **1475**

24 April – John Thurzo (a native of Levoča), a citizen of Cracow and Levoča, contractually confirmed his pledge to King Matthias that the flooded mines in the mining cities of central Slovakia would be drained.

■ **1476**

15 February – During a campaign against the Turks, King Matthias captured the important fortress of Sabac in Serbia.

■ **1477**

12 June – Matthias declared war on Frederick III who, through his recognition of the Czech king Vladislav as a vassal of the empire, essentially denied the right of Matthias to the Czech crown. The Hungarian-Austrian war, during which Matthias gradually conquered all of Lower Austria, ended only in 1487.

■ **1478**

28 March – The ambassadors of King Matthias and the Czech king, Vladislav, concluded a truce in Brno by which the Hungarian-Czech war, which had lasted with interruptions for almost 10 years, was brought to an end.

30 October – In Buda and on **7 December** in Olomouc, the peace agreement concluded between Matthias and the Czech king Vladislav was proclaimed. Both rulers retained the Czech royal title; Vladislav ruled Czechia and the rule of Moravia, Silesia and Lusatia devolved upon Matthias. According to the agreement Vladislav was allowed to obtain the separated lands of the Czech crown for a sum of 400 000 florins but only after the death of Matthias.

■ **1479**

21 July – King Matthias and King Vladislav personally ratified the peace treaty at Olomouc.

21 October – Matthias bestowed upon his illegitimate son John Corvinus extensive lands in Transylvania and the titles count of Hunyady and duke of Liptov.

25 October – The prior of Spiš, Gašpar Bak, wrote several prayers in the „Slovak language" on the occasion of the anniversary of his ordination as priest. The Spiš prayers are a significant evidence for the development of the Slovak language in the Middle Ages.

■ **1480**
The Bratislava canon Ján Han de Wep issued a printed letter of indulgence to the townswoman Agnes of Bratislava, which is the oldest of known Slovak **incunabula**. Two other incunabula (issued in 1477 and 1478) are also possibly from Bratislava since they are typographically similar with the above-mentioned letter of indulgence.

■ **1481**
29 March – In light of the impoverishment of the mine operators, King Matthias allowed the city of Banská Štiavnica to establish a joint mining company.

■ **1485**
1 June – After a five-month siege, Matthias occupied Vienna, which became his new residence.
December – The Hungarian diet in Buda accepted several legal clauses that dealt with the competence of the **palatine**.

■ **1486**
21 and **26 May** – Matthias forbade with the threat of capital punishment, national conflicts between the German and the Slovak townspeople in Trnava in connection with the election of the magistrate and ordered that the election take place according to the old customs.
12 June – Matthias campaigned unsuccessfully for the throne of the Holy Roman Empire of the German Nation. The imperial diet in Frankfurt am Main elected as the Roman-German king, Maximilian Habsburg, the son of Emperor Frederick III.

■ **1487**
16 December – A truce was concluded in Sankt Pölten in Austria that ended the war between Matthias and Frederick III.
26 December – At a meeting of the seven mining cities in Košice, a mining law was written as the basis for the development of the league of the upper Hungarian mining cities (in Slovakia these were Gelnica, Smolník, Rožňava, Spišská Nová Ves, and Jasov).

■ **1488**
20 March – An illustrated *Hungarian Chronicle* authored by Master John Thuroczy (Ján z Turca) was printed in Brno. Shortly after (3 June) the chronicle was reprinted in Augsburg.

■ **1489**
23 June – The royal free cities took an oath to King Matthias that they would recognize and support his son John Corvinus as successor to the Hungarian throne. Eventually several **magnates**, the captains and castellans of the royal castles, as well as the **county administrators** took the same oath.

■ **1490**
6 April – King Matthias died in Vienna. In Hungary a struggle was unleashed among several contenders for the royal throne.
15 July – At the Rákos diet in Pest, Vladislav II Jagiello was elected king of Hungary. The Hungarian and Czech kingdoms thus were joined in a personal union. The illegitimate son of King Matthias, John Corvinus, became the Croatian-Slavonian *bán* (governor). Vladislav II immediately had to defend his claim to the Hungarian throne in a war against his own brother John Albrecht, whose armies penetrated up to Pest, as well as against the Roman-German king Maximilian I, whose armies took Vienna during the summer and, at the beginning of the autumn, occupied a large part of Transdanubia.

■ **1491**
20 February – Near Košice Vladislav II concluded a truce with John Albrecht, who gained part of Silesia and received Prešov and Sabinov in mortgage.
Fall – The army of the Polish prince John Albrecht again invaded Hungary, occupied Stropkov castle, and pillaged the counties of Šariš and Zemplín.

7 November – Vladislav II and Maximilian I concluded a peace treaty in Bratislava. It became the basis for an agreement between the Jagiellonian and the Habsburg dynasties that secured their mutual rights of succession.

24 December – In a battle near Prešov, Stephen Zápolya defeated John Albrecht, who definitively renounced his claim to the Hungarian throne.

■ 1492

February – The Hungarian diet accepted several laws strengthening the position of the **magnates** and **nobles** at the expense of royal power and, at the same time, hardening the obligations of the serf farmers and the cities and towns of the landlords. All until-then free cities not encircled by walls also were obliged to pay the **ninth**. The hereditary **county administrator** of Spiš, Stephen Zápolya, was elected as palatine.

September – The lower Hungarian chief captain, Paul Kinizsi, defeated and dispersed near the river Sava the legendary **Black Army** (established by King Matthias), which had laid waste the environs because they had not been paid for a long time.

■ 1494

19 April – Vladislav II, the Hungarian and Czech king, met the Polish king John Albrecht in Levoča, where they negotiated questions concerning their dynasties.

15 November – John Thurzo and his son George concluded in Bratislava a preliminary contract concerning the establishment of the Hungarian Trade Company (*Ungarischer Handel*) with the Fugger banking family of Augsburg.

26 December – The Hungarian royal treasurer, Sigmund Ernust, leased the mines of Banská Bystrica to John Thurzo and his son George for a period of 12 years.

■ 1495

16 March – The agreement establishing the **Thurzo-Fugger Company** called Hungarian Trade (and later Neusohl Copper Trade – *Neusohler Kupferhandel*) was concluded. It

gradually became the largest producer of copper in the world at its time. This prosperous company had warehouses and agencies throughout all of Europe and functioned as a private company until 1525, when it was seized by the royal administration for a brief period. The co-owner John Thurzo set up the first **foundry** to separate copper from silver in the region of Banská Bystrica.

April – After several years of armed conflict on the Hungarian-Ottoman borders, Vladislav II concluded a peace with Sultan Bajazid II to maintain the status quo for three years. The peace treaty was later extended several times so that up to 1512 the Hungarian kingdom and the Ottoman Empire were officially not in a state of war.

■ 1498

Mikuláš Bakalár-Štetina, born in Slovakia in the Považie region and a graduate of the University of Cracow, began to work as a book printer in Pilsen. All of the incunabula and post-incunabula prints he issued were in Czech with a small number of Slovakisms. Twenty-nine titles that he published during the period 1498 – 1514 have been preserved. Especially prominent among them was the *Writing about the New Lands and about the New World (Spis o nowych zemiech a o nowem swietie* – 1504), which belongs among the very first extensive reports of the overseas discoveries of Amerigo Vespucci.

■ 1499

1 November – 14 November - The diet of the Czech estates sat in Bratislava and accepted a resolution known by the name *Zůstanie prešpurské*, which became the basis for Vladislav's regulation of the Czech country, approved on 11 March 1500.

■ 1504

8 May – The Hungarian diet at Rákos field accepted several resolutions that favored the lesser nobility. Serfs were forbidden to move to another landlord without the approval of the sheriff or to hunt game or fowl.

12 October – John Corvinus, the Croatian ban

and the illegitimate son of King Matthias Corvinus, died.

■ **1508**
4 June – Vladislav II had his son Ladislas crowned king of Hungary at Székesfehérvár.

■ **1506**
20 March – Vladislav II and Maximilian I, the Roman – German king (and later emperor), secretly concluded a dynastic agreement about their relationship and a possible mutual succession to the throne despite the fact that the Hungarian estates had rejected the possible accession to the Hungarian throne of a foreign dynasty through the so-called Rákos decisions of 13 October 1505. Immediately after the disclosure of the Jagellonian-Habsburg dynastic agreement, the Hungarian nobility compelled Vladislav II to declare war on Maximilian I (7 May). The military conflict, during which the army of Maximilian occupied Bratislava, ended with the conclusion of a peace treaty on 19 July 1506.

■ **1514**
9 April – As papal legate, Thomas Bakócz, archbishop of Esztergom, published a papal bull in Buda calling for a crusade against the Turks.
Spring – An army of 40,000 crusaders, made up predominantly of peasants and led by the Transylvanian yeoman George Dózsa, turned against the nobility. The peasant **Dózsa insurrection** was cruelly suppressed by the nobility led by John Zápolya at the end of July.
18 October – The diet of the estates assembled in Buda. It accepted several laws directed against the peasants and serfs as punishment for the Dózsa insurrection. Among other things, free movement and the bearing of arms were forbidden to the serfs (**serfdom**). At the same time, the basic labor and tax obligations of the serfs to the authorities were established and their „eternal bondage to the soil" was decreed. The diet also received and approved the *Three-part book of the common law of the glorious Hungarian kingdom and affiliated countries* by Stephan Werboczy, known under its short title, the **Tripartitum.**

It opened the way to the so-called second **servitude** and was used in Hungarian judicial practice until the end of **feudalism.**

■ **1516**
13 March – After the death of Vladislav II, his ten-year old son Louis II Jagiello ascended the Hungarian throne.

■ **1517**
The **Tripartitum** of Werboczy was printed in Vienna and became one of the most frequently-issued Hungarian books during the feudal era.

■ **1521**
28 August – A Turkish army captured Belgrad, which was a crucial Hungarian fortress on the southern border. With this the anti-Turkish defensive perimeter fell apart.
1 September – King Louis II allowed the count of the chamber of the Kremnica mint, Alexius Thurzo, to strike new, devalued silver coins. But even this measure did not avert the deepening economic and resulting social crises in the Kingdom of Hungary.
– During the year, followers of the Lutheran reformation began to appear in several of the royal free and mining cities in Slovakia.

■ **1523**
April to **May** – The Hungarian diet accepted articles concerning punishing the followers of Luther with death by burning at the stake. A similar legal provision was also accepted at the diet of 1525. However, the regulation remained without practical effect.

■ **1525**
19 May – In Banská Bystrica and its environs a strike of the miners erupted that later grew into an armed insurrection of the miners.

■ **1526**
13 April – A court in Banská Bystrica, under the chairmanship of the Palatine Stephen Werboczy, condemned several leaders of the revolt of the miners to death and ordered the confiscation of their property.

3 August – New disturbances of armed miners occurred in Banská Bystrica. They set fire to part of the city and destroyed mining equipment.

29 August – The Hungarian army suffered a catastrophic defeat at the hands of the Turks in the battle near Mohács. King Louis II, the last Jagiello on the Hungarian throne, perished in the battle. This date marks the end of the Middle Ages in Slovak history and the beginning of the Early Modern Era.

The beginning of the Early Modern Era (1526 – 1711)

The disaster at Mohács at the end of August 1526 and the extinction of the royal Jagiello dynasty symbolically signified the end of the Middle Ages in Hungary. Gradually central Europe came to be the center of attention of the contemporary European public. For almost one and a half centuries, southern Slovakia was the border between two different civilizations, the Christian and the Islamic, with all the consequences brought by the proximity of two deadly enemies. The new era that pushed the Middle Ages into the past was characterized by considerable contradictions. The territory of today's Slovakia already was an organic component of Europe-wide power-politics. It became the arena of wars against the Turks, the defensive rampart of Christianity, and of regular revolts of the estates of the Hungarian nobility, which repeatedly reiterated the slogans of the freedom of religion and of the estates. In Slovakia, each movement on the European political stage was attended by concrete consequences in terms of tremendous human and material losses.

In Slovak history, the early modern era is characterized by several important factors. For four centuries, Hungary was part of the huge Habsburg Empire, which was essentially a conglomeration of countries at different levels of social, economic and cultural development. Only the person of the ruler united them. During the whole Early Modern Era the Habsburg dynasty attempted to establish for their confederated state at least partial internal unity. This obviously meant that the prerogatives of the privileged classes had to be delimited. Exploiting the foreign political situation, the Hungarian nobility worked against the efforts of the court of the ruler, for example, in the Fifteen and Thirty Years' Wars and other Europe-wide military conflicts. Under the cloak of religious freedom, the estates sought above all else to protect their own prerogatives and privileges.

However, in the Early Modern Era radical changes in the life of society took place. Under the influence of the new ideas of humanism, Reformation and Counter-Reformation, the medieval view of the world and man began to disintegrate. Modern ideas often penetrated Slovak environment unnoticed, frequently in a very distorted or even deformed form. Humanism and the Reformation entered the territory of Slovakia at almost the same time. They penetrated the fields of schooling and education most markedly, but also those of science, literature, and the fine arts. Every religious and intellectual stream very quickly understood the importance of education in the struggle against its opponents. This had a positive influence upon the development of schooling and changes in educational structure at all levels of society. Every city or larger town had a Latin school. University-like institutions also began to function. The Early Modern Era was marked by an unprecedented growth in the intelligentsia, the development of literary works and of centers of printing. European intellectual and artistic currents (Renaissance, Baroque) likewise elicited changes in aesthetic perceptions, which were reflected by changes in the cities and countryside.

The germ that became the national consciousness process began to develop during the Early Modern Era. Above all it expressed itself in the political struggles of the urban inhabitants, which, alongside the religious, took on a national hue. This process acquired a new dimension when the investigation of the beginnings of Christianity in Hungary discovered the first evidence concerning the Great Moravia mission of Cyril and Methodius. These initial insights gradually assumed a more integrated form for which the designation Baroque Slavicism has become common.

■ **1526**
10 November – In Székesfehérvár a part of the Hungarian feudal estates elected John Zápolya as king. The following day he was ceremonially crowned by the bishop of Nitra, Štefan Podmanický.
17 December – In Bratislava the Hungarian diet elected Ferdinand Habsburg as king of Hungary. The reigns of the two rival kings were characterized by a war that especially affected the population and territory of Slovakia and produced a complete economic decline until the death of John Zápolya in 1540.

■ **1528**
8 January – Ferdinand I established the **Hungarian Chamber** in Buda that administered the royal lands and state revenue.
27 January – Sultan Süleyman I recognized John Zápolya as king of Hungary and concluded an alliance with him.
8 March – In a battle at Seňa near Košice, the Habsburg mercenary army led by John Katzianer defeated the forces of John Zápolya, who fled to Poland. He returned to Hungary at the beginning of November.
30 June – Habsburg forces occupied Trenčín Castle, one of the most significant possessions of John Zápolya.
– A map of Hungary was printed at Bavarian Ingolstadt in 1523 that had been drafted by Lazarus (Roseti), the secretary of Archbishop Thomas Bakócz. The woodcut, the oldest preserved map of Hungary, is 55 x 78.5 cm and indicates topographically, in addition to mountains and rivers, around 1400 localities, 290 of which are situated on the territory of today's Slovakia.

■ **1529**
10 May – Süleyman I left Istanbul for Hungary with an army of 200,000. The Turkish army gradually occupied the central part of the Carpathian basin, namely Buda. At the end of summer it even invaded Austria from which it withdrew at the beginning of fall after unsuccessfully besieging Vienna.
Beginning of August – The representatives of the central offices of Hungary fled Buda and the Hungarian Chancellery of King Ferdinand was dissolved. Shortly thereafter, its functions were assumed by the Hungarian office of the Court Chancellery in Vienna.
18 August – John Zápolya did homage to the sultan on the field of Mohács, thus recognizing the supremacy of the Ottomans.
Summer – In fear of the advancing Ottoman army, the city council of Bratislava had three churches, a hospice and several houses torn down so that the Turks could not fortify them. Although an Ottoman army did not attack Bratislava, as it proceeded along the right bank of the Danube to Vienna, it looted Rusovce and Čunovo.
25 September – The Turks attacked Vienna and laid siege to the city. The garrison of King Ferdinand and the armed townspeople of Vienna resisted, however, so that the Turks turned and marched away on 16 October.
21 December – At the suggestion of Emperor Charles V (the brother of Ferdinand) Pope Clement VII excommunicated (**excommunication**) John Zápolya and his followers.

■ **1530**
September – With the consent of John Zápolya, numerous Turkish columns undertook the first direct invasion of the territory of southern and south-western Slovakia that was under the rule of Ferdinand and carried away into captivity many of the inhabitants. They pillaged the lower and central Váh River valley up to Piešťany and the Hron River valley up to Svätý (today Hronský) Beňadik. The

Turks devastated not only undefended villages but also several towns (Hlohovec, Vráble, Topoľčany, Zlaté Moravce).

24 November – The paper mill in Levoča, which was at that time the only one in Hungary burned down. It was set afire by the soldiers of the captain of the castle of Orava, Mikuláš Kostka (in the service of John Zápolya), who devastated Spiš county.

– Documentary evidence indicates that there was a regular (weekly) postal service between Vienna and Bratislava.

■ **1531**

2 July – Ferdinand I renewed the activity of the **Hungarian Chamber** with its seat in Bratislava. The maintenance and supplying of garrisons of the royal castles was within its competence.

Spring to **summer** – A military expedition of Sultan Süleyman, the goal of which was to conquer Vienna, ended at the Transdanubian fortress of Koszeg. From 10 to 28 August the garrison of the castle was able to fend off the superior forces of the Turks, so that the sultan discontinued his campaign. He contented himself with pillaging western Hungary, Carinthia and part of Croatia.

■ **1536**

19 November – A session of the Hungarian diet in Bratislava decided, by law article 49/1536, that Bratislava was to be the capital of the Kingdom of Hungary. It was the capital city until 1783, when the central offices moved back to Buda. It remained the coronation city until 1830 and the seat of the Hungarian diet until 1848.

4 December – The army of King John Zápolya was able to seize Košice by treachery. Many townspeople of German nationality were expelled from the city.

■ **1538**

24 February – The emissaries of Ferdinand I and John Zápolya concluded a secret peace treaty in Varadín. (Until then both kings had concluded 11 truces that, however, they broke one after the other). Each recognized the other as king of Hungary and each retained rule over the territory he controlled. Ferdinand ruled the western part of the country, almost all of Slovakia, Croatia and part of Transdanubia. Zápolyai ruled in Transylvania and in central and northeastern Hungary including Košice.

■ **1540**

17 (or 21) – July John Zápolya died.

13 September – A part of the Hungarian nobility at the Rákos diet declared the two-month old John Sigismund (the son of John Zápolya) king of Hungary, but he was never crowned. The sultan recognized his election. This became a pretext for the further escalation of tension between the Ottoman Empire and Ferdinand I who, in accordance with the peace of Varadín (of 24 February 1538), claimed the rule of all of Hungary.

■ **1541**

29 August – The Turks occupied the castle of Buda and, at the same time, the territory between the Danube and the Tisa, as well as the right bank of the Danube from Csákvár to Pécs. Thus Hungary was divided into three parts. Buda became the center of a new pashalik (*ejálet*) of the Ottoman Empire. For the occupied lands it gradually introduced a **Turkish administration**. Bratislava became the capital of the **Kingdom of Hungary**. Transylvania, by the will of the sultan devolved upon John Sigismund Zápolya, became an autonomous principality although it was dependent upon the Ottoman Empire.

■ **1543**

10 August – After a two-week siege, the Turks took and occupied Esztergom. Trnava became the seat of the **archbishop** and the chapter of Esztergom.

3 September – The Turks occupied the traditional coronation city of the Hungarian kings, Székesfehérvár.

23 November – The Hungarian diet met in Banská Bystrica. It accepted several legal articles concerning the defense of the kingdom against the Turks, including a law according to which every peasant and tenant owing a house had to pay, in addition to the existing rents in money and goods (*naturalia*), two florins as a *subsidium* (an extraordinary tax for the army). From all taxes collected, 80 per cent was used for defensive purposes in the various counties and the royal Hungarian Chamber took 20 percent.

■ **1546**

2 November – At a synod in Prešov the representatives of the Evangelical parishes from the 5 free cities of eastern Slovakia (Bardejov, Košice, Levoča, Prešov, and Sabinov) declared their allegiance to the Augsburg Confession, although they remained within the Catholic Church.

– Ferdinand I ordered that the administration of all of the mines of Hungary be assumed by the Lower Austrian Chamber in Vienna. The Copper Trade Company of Banská Bystrica became the property of the state treasury, since the Fuggers, to whom they had belonged until then, were no longer interested in leasing them.

■ **1547**

19 June – The Emperor Charles V Habsburg and Sultan Süleyman I concluded a peace at Edirne, Turkey. The peace related to all territories ruled by Ferdinand I and de facto confirmed the division of Hungary into three parts: the Pashalik or *ejálet* of Buda as an immediate part of the Ottoman Empire, the principality of Transylvania, which was a vassal state of the Turks, and the significantly-trimmed kingdom of Hungary (also called Royal Hungary), of which today's Slovakia comprised a significant part. This treaty, concluded for a period of five years, obliged Ferdinand I to deliver 30,000 ducats each year to the Turkish sultan as a „courteous gift".

■ **1548**

26 October – A session of the Hungarian diet began in Bratislava. It accepted several laws strengthening the Catholic Church that were, at the same time, directed against various heretical (Protestant) sects, especially the Anabaptists, who had fled persecution in the German lands. Traversing Czechia and Moravia, they created the first independent *haban* or Anabaptist settlements (courts) in western Slovakia around 1545.

■ **1549**

September – The rector of the school in Bardejov, Leonard Stöckel, compiled the first Evangelical confession for five cities of eastern Slovakia (Levoča, Košice, Sabinov, Prešov, and Bardejov), known as the *Confessio Pentapolitana*. This confession was conciliatory towards Catholicism but sharply focused against the Anabaptists and other radical sects.

■ **1551**

4 April – Ferdinand I decreed that, in view of the actual composition of the population, Slovaks, Germans and Magyars should have parity of representation on the city council of Trnava.

Fall – Ferdinand's military intervention in Transylvania became the pretext for another Turkish war, which during the following year directly afflicted southern Slovakia and, with minor pauses, lasted until 17 February 1568.

■ **1552**

9 July – The army of the Pasha of Buda, after a four-day siege, captured Dregel castle killing the entire 80-man garrison led by Captain George Szondy (Šucha). By the end of the month the Turks had occupied Šahy, Balassagyarmat, Szécsény, and Hollókö, thus disrupting the entire Ipeľ defensive line.

10 August – In a battle near Plášťovce the Turks defeated a Habsburg mercenary army alongside which fought conscripted units (**banderia**) from Slovak counties and cities. This was the first large battle against the Turks on the territory of Slovakia. It confirmed and consolidated Ottoman power in the Ipeľ valley.

■ **1554**

September – The Turks captured Fiľakovo

which became the seat of a newly established Turkish district (**sandjak**). It further was divided territorially into **náhijas**. From the *sandjak* of Fiľakovo the Turks undertook expeditions especially against the mining cities of central Slovakia but also into the territory of Spiš.

■ **1555**
According to the plan of the archbishop of Esztergom, Nicholas Oláh, the city and chapter schools in Trnava were merged. Among others, a future generation of Catholic clergy was trained here without charge in a three-year course study. Alongside instruction in rhetoric, dialectic, arithmetic, classical languages, theology, and singing, care was taken that the pupils mastered the national languages current in Hungary and that there was always at least one teacher (master) who spoke the Slovak language.

■ **1556**
In Trnava a guild of Slovak journeymen cobblers was established whose statute belongs among the oldest guild articles written in Slovak. The guild of Slovak potters in Trnava, which was established 1567, also had a statute in Slovak. In the sixteenth century the hatters in Banská Bystrica (1594), potters, drapers, tailors, smiths, and furriers in Žilina had articles in Slovak.
23 August – Charles V Habsburg abdicated the imperial throne in favor of his brother Ferdinand I, the king of Hungary and Czechia, who as the Roman-German king (elected on 5 January 1531) and later as the crowned emperor (14 March 1558) assumed the rule of the Holy Roman Empire of the German Nation. From the time of Ferdinand, with only a short hiatus (1742 – 1745), the Austrian branch of the Habsburgs, later the Habsburg-Lothringen dynasty, held the title of Holy Roman Emperor and ruled the Holy Roman Empire of the German Nation until its dissolution in 1806.
– Ferdinand I established a court war council in Vienna that was the highest administrative and coordinating military organ for all of the lands of the Habsburg Empire. It functioned until the dissolution of the monarchy (1918).

■ **1559**
On the model of the confession of the cities of eastern Slovakia (*Confessio Pentapolitana),* the seven mining cities of central Slovakia (Kremnica, Banská Štiavnica, Banská Bystrica, Nová Baňa, Pukanec, Banská Belá and Ľubietová) accepted a Lutheran confession of faith known as the *Confessio Heptapolitana* or *Montana*. The confession of the Fraternity of the Pastors of the 24 Spiš Cities (*Confessio Scepusiana*), accepted in 1569, had a similar, if slightly more radical, character vis-à-vis Catholic teachings. These confessions were an expression of the more moderate Evangelical (Lutheran) **Reformation,** which was in particular characterized externally by communion in both species (bread and wine), the introduction of German or Czech as a liturgical language, the simplification of worship services, as well as of the embellishment of churches, and permission for the marriage of the clergy.

■ **1560**
The humanist Martin Rakovský of Turiec (an official of the Hungarian chamber and later the vice county administrator of Turiec) issued a versified *Book about the estates* in Latin in Vienna. It was concerned with the various strata of the population and the causes of societal change. The culmination of the work of Rakovský is represented by the versified Latin work *Concerning secular authority* published in Leipzig in 1574.
– A Catholic synod in Trnava decided that every parish was to establish a school or, in the case of the poorer parishes, maintain a teacher in common who would teach writing, reading, singing and religion.

■ **1561**
Nicholas Oláh, the archbishop of Esztergom, for the very first time in Hungary invited the **Jesuit** order to Trnava to establish a Jesuit college there. After a promising be-

ginning and the gradual opening of five classes with approximately 100 pupils, the Jesuits had to leave the city (and Slovakia) in 1567 because of financial difficulties. The college was closed. At the same time, there were a total of 200 pupils in the other schools in Trnava.

■ **1562**
4 April – The Turks were victorious over an army of the chief captain of the mining cities, John Balassa in a battle near Sečany. His army also included bands (**banderia**) from the counties and contingents from the mining cities of central Slovakia.

■ **1563**
8 September – Maximilian I Habsburg was crowned king of Hungary in Bratislava. From 1563 to 1830 the coronations of 19 kings and queens of Hungary took place in Bratislava.
13 November – Ferdinand I approved laws accepted at the diet in Bratislava. The nobility living in the royal free cities were ordered to share the burdens and obligations of the cities equally with the townspeople. At the same time, they could buy houses and hold property in the city. This made possible the infiltration of the nobility into local government.
– A reorganization of the anti-Turkish defenses took place. On the territory of western and central Slovakia up to Muráň, a Cisdanubian chief captaincy of the mining cities was established with its headquarters in Nitra and later, depending upon the military situation, in Šurany (1568 – 1581), Levice (1581 – 1589), Nové Zámky (1589 – 1663) and, after their fall, in Komárno (1663 – 1686). In eastern Slovakia and along the Tisa up to Transylvania, an Upper Hungarian chief captaincy headquartered in Košice (up to 1686) was created. A smaller part of southwestern Slovakia belonged under the Transdanubian chief captaincy headquartered in Gyor.

■ **1564**
17 May – At a consultation in Banská Štiavnica, military regulations for the defense of the mining cities of central Slovakia were accepted. They became the basis for the effective defense of this region against the Turks.
26 July – After the death of the emperor and Hungarian king Ferdinand I, his son Maximilian I ascended the throne (as Emperor Maximilian II).

■ **1566**
1 May – An army led by Sultan Süleyman left Istanbul for a campaign in Hungary. During the expedition the Turks, after a siege of one month, captured the important fortress of Szigetvár, commanded by the Croatian magnate Nicholas Zrínyi, on 8 September. His heroic death was echoed in Slovak oral folk and romantic literature. In the summer, supported by the armies of John Sigismund Zápolya, the Ottomans invaded the Slovak borderlands, where their advance was halted by the army of the emperor led by Lazarus Schwendi.
10 May – Archbishop Nicholas Oláh established the seminary of St. Stephen in Trnava for the training of Catholic clergy.

■ **1567**
24 February – The Calvinists in Hungary definitively separated from the Lutherans and established their own church organization at a synod in Debrecen.
1 April – At the order of the ruler, the **Spiš Chamber,** with its headquarters in Košice, was formed from the Upper Hungarian (Spiš and Košice) subsidiary administrations of the **Hungarian Chamber**. It was the highest economic organ in Upper Hungary, i. e. in the counties of eastern Slovakia and the Tisa River valley.

■ **1568**
17 February – At Edirne, in Turkey, Maximilian I and Sultan Selim II concluded a peace that ended the first period of Turkish expansion into Hungary. Part of the agreed peace was the provision that Maximilian would pay the Ottoman Empire 30,000 florins annually for 8 years.

1571
New Songs on the Seven Penitential and other Psalms (*Písně nové na sedm žalmů kajících i jiné žalmy*) was published in Prague by the Slovak Ján Silván. It is an important representative of Protestant spiritual work based upon Slovak historical, popular and folk songs.

1573
16 February – The so-called New or **Maximilian Mining Code** came into effect. It took into account regulations from the existing mining codes of Banská Štiavnica and Kremnica.

1575
July – The Turks took the castles of Modrý Kameň and Divín after a hard struggle.

1576
12 October – After the death of Emperor Maximilian I, the Hungarian king, his son Rudolf I ascended the throne as Emperor Rudolf II. According to the accounts of the Court Military Council, 16,801 soldiers were registered in 48 Hungarian **castles** on unoccupied territory. At the same time, according to imperial estimates, more than 40, 000 Turkish soldiers occupied the 66 Ottoman castles in Hungary.

1580
October – After several years of construction, the modern fortress of Nové Zámky was officially turned over for use. In subsequent years its fortification continued.
31 December – Rudolf I forbade the building of a Protestant academy in Levoča.

1581
The printery of David Guttgesell in Bardejov published a translation by Severín Škultéty of the *Small Catechism* by Martin Luther, the oldest book printed in Slovak in Slovakia.

1582
24 February – Pope Gregory XIII (1572 – 1585) ordered a reform of the **Julian calendar:** 4 October was immediately followed by 15 October.

1586
19 May – Rudolf I granted the priory of Turiec in Kláštor pod Znievom to the Jesuits. Thus, after a nineteen-year absence, the Jesuit order settled again on Slovak territory in Hungary.

1588
28 January – With the agreement of the Hungarian diet (sitting in Bratislava since November), the ruler ordered the introduction of the **Gregorian calendar** in Hungary. Thus 21 October was to be followed immediately by 1 November. The implementation was not total, however. The old Julian calendar continued to be used in places even during the following century. The Orthodox Church continues to use it today.

1593
22 June – The Turkish army of the Bosnian pasha was defeated by Sisak in Croatia, at the beginning of another war with the Turks known as the „Long" or the Fifteen Years' War.

1594
In Bratislava, the printer Ján Walo issued the first handbill newspaper in Slovakia *Two Accurate Reports* (*Zwo Warhafftige Newezeitung*). It provided information about the defeat of the Turks in battles at Novohrad and Buda (1593) and about an unusual heavenly phenomenon (a comet) over Constantinople.

1599
Spring to **end of summer** – Turkish and Crimean Tatar forces pillaged the Slovak border region and even penetrated the hinterlands. They ravaged the Považie region up to Beckov, as well as the area around Nitra and Levice, Krupina, Zvolen and Banská Bystrica.
– The general of the Jesuit order, Claudius Aquaviva, ordered the implementation of a unified school order and the organization of Jesuit schools, the *Order of Studies of the Society of Jesus (Ratio studiorum Societatis Jesu)*. The order went into effect in Slovakia during the 17 century in connection with the process of re-Catholicization and the estab-

lishment of Jesuit schools. In the 16th century the **Jesuits** had colleges in Trnava (1561 – 1567), Kláštor pod Znievom (1586 – 1598) and in Šaľa (1598 – 1605).

In Slovakia at the end of the 16th century, at least 132 schools functioned. About sixteen of the city and eight of the noble schools were gymnasia (secondary schools).

■ 1603

The Slovak scholar and professor at the university of Prague, Laurence Benedict from Nedožery, wrote and published in Prague the first systematic grammar of Czech (*Grammatica bohemica*), in which he referred to the separate status of Slovak and exhorted the Slovaks not to neglect the cultivation of their native language.

■ 1604

6 January – Giacomo Barbiano di Belgiojoso, the imperial commander and chief captain of upper Hungary, forcibly seized St. Elizabeth's Church in Košice from the Protestants (Evangelicals) and turned it over to the Catholics. At the same time he ordered the banishment of all Protestant clergy from Košice. Similar re-Catholicization measures were inaugurated in the remaining royal free cities at the instigation of the imperial court and the Catholic hierarchy.

1 May – Rudolf I refused to confirm the religious freedom demanded by the Hungarian diet and, disregarding the diet, ordered the maintenance of the then existing anti-Reformation laws, which called forth considerable anger from the Protestant part of the nobility.

October – An attack by imperial soldiers on the castles and lands in Bihar county of Stephen Bocskai, a Transylvanian magnate, led to the eruption of the first anti-Habsburg uprising of the estates (**Bocskai's insurrection**). The Protestant segment of the nobility, in particular, joined the uprising, which was militarily supported by the Ottoman Empire.

16 October – Representatives of the five free cities of eastern Slovakia (*Pentapolitana*) decided to support the insurgents (**September 1549**). Several of the Slovak mining cities followed their example at the beginning of November.

■ 1605

Spring – The imperial army retreated from eastern Slovakia before the insurgents who advanced through central and western Slovakia, taking Trnava (5 May) and penetrating Transdanubia, Upper Austria and even Moravia and Silesia. The ravaging army of the insurgents, comprised especially of **hajduks**, was halted and forced to retreat by an offensive of the imperial army at the beginning of summer.

11 November – In Pest, Grand Vizier Lalla Mehmed handed over the royal crown to Bocskai, by which the sultan showed that he recognized him as king of Hungary. Bocskai accepted the crown only as a gift and refused coronation.

■ 1606

9 February – In Vienna the court of the ruler concluded a truce with the supporters of the Bocskai insurrection. The truce subsequently was confirmed by a treaty, the Peace of Vienna, signed on 23 June.

11 September – At the mouth of the Žitava River the plenipotentiaries of the Habsburgs and the Ottoman Empire signed a treaty that ended the so-called Fifteen Years' War (22 June 1593). The Peace of Žitava, concluded for 20 years, confirmed partial modifications of the mutual borders (only an insignificant part of southern Slovakia remained under Ottoman hegemony) and obliged the ruler of the Habsburg Empire to pay the sultan a one-time tribute of 200 thousand florins. Emperor and King Rudolf declined to recognize the peace, which his brother Archduke Matthias exploited, joining with the Hungarian and Austrian estates in an attempt to usurp the throne.

■ 1608

May – At the head of a confederate army of the Hungarian, Austrian and Moravian estates, Archduke Matthias took the field against his brother Rudolf, who was based in Prague.

25 June – Rudolf I (II) abdicated in favor of his brother Matthias the rule of Hungary and the Austrian patrimonial lands. Rudolf nonetheless retained the titles of Roman-German emperor and Czech king.

16 November – At a coronation diet in Bratislava Matthias was elected king of Hungary. At the same time, the estates exacted a guarantee of complete religious freedom, even for the serf population. King Matthias II also confirmed the laws strengthening the position of the magnates, for example, by renewing and filling the positions in the central offices or by naming the principle officers of the country (**palatine**, **chancellor**, treasurer or **tavernicus**), dividing the diet into two tables or chambers (the upper made up of the **magnates** and **prelates,** the lower made up of representatives of the county nobility, the **yeomanry**, the lower clergy and representatives of privileged cities). Law article 13 equalized the status of nationalities in the free cities.

■ **1609**

11 November – The diet convened in Bratislava and, among other things, approved the amending of previously published articles concerning parity in the representation of Germans, Slovaks and Hungarians in the organs of local governance (**nationality laws of 1608**). George Thurzo was elected palatine.

■ **1610**

23 January – At the instigation of the diet, the ruler approved a new delineation of the portal tax, according to which a **port** (*portal*), as the basic tax unit, was made up of 4 serf (peasant) houses or 12 houses of tenants (cotters) or agrarian workers.

28 – 30 March – Under the patronage of Palatine George Thurzo, the **Synod of Žilina** was held.

■ **1611**

Under the leadership of the archbishop of Esztergom, F. Forgách, a Catholic synod sat in Trnava. In the spirit of the canons and decrees of the Council of Trent (1545 – 1563) it accepted provisions that became the starting point for an effective re-Catholicization. One of these was the renewal of the invitation to the **Jesuits**, who set up new colleges in Humenné (1614), Trnava (1615) and later in other cities.

■ **1614**

22 January – A synod of Spiš and Šariš Evangelicals met in Spišské Podhradie. It accepted a resolution about the establishment of a superintendency of the five eastern Slovak cities and a Spiš-Šariš superintendency, by which the Evangelical Church of the Augsburg Confession established its own organizational structure in eastern Slovakia also.

■ **1615**

6 May – The emissaries of King Matthias II and of the Transylvanian prince Gabriel Bethlen agreed on an alliance in Trnava.

15 July – In Vienna, the representatives of Sultan Ahmed I and King Matthias II prolonged the Peace of Žitava (1606) for another 20 years.

■ **1616**

28 September – King Matthias II named the Jesuit rector of Turiec, Peter Pázmány, as the archbishop of Esztergom.

November – Troops of the Transylvanian prince, Gabriel Bethlen, attacked eastern Slovakia, thus beginning **Bethlen's insurrection**.

■ **1617**

Daniel Sculteti revived a printery in Levoča.

■ **1618**

27 February – Representatives of King Matthias II and Sultan Osman II again prolonged the peace of Žitava in Komárno.

26 June – A leader of the insurgent Czech estates, the physician Ján Jessenius, whose parents came from Turiec in Slovakia, was arrested in Bratislava.

1 July – The cousin of Matthias II was crowned in Bratislava as King Ferdinand II of Hungary.

■ **1619**
20 March – King Matthias II died in Vienna. His cousin Ferdinand II succeeded him.
26 May – King Ferdinand II called the diet to Bratislava, at which the Hungarian estates declined to intervene militarily against the Czech estates.
7 September – After occupying Košice, the *hajduk* army of Bethlen tortured to death the Jesuits Štefan Pongrác and Melchior Grodeczki, as well as a canon of Esztergom, Marek Križin, who refused to repudiate their faith. They entered into history as the **martyrs of Košice**.
21 September – The Transylvanian prince, Gabriel Bethlen, summoned the Protestant estates to Košice. They proclaimed him the administrator of the country.
14 October – After the soldiers of Gabriel Bethlen occupied Bratislava, the insurgents obtained the royal regalia and the crown from the palatine.
11 November – The Transylvanian prince, Gabriel Bethlen, summoned at Bratislava a diet that declared religious freedom for all of the population.

■ **1620**
15 January – Representatives of the Czech, Moravian, Silesian, Austrian, and Hungarian Protestant estates concluded a treaty of alliance.
25 August – The estates, meeting at a diet in Banská Bystrica, deposed the Habsburgs from the throne. They elected Gabriel Bethlen as king of Hungary but he did not accept coronation.
28 October – Three thousand cavalrymen led by the Hungarian chancellor, Simon Péchy, set out to provide military assistance to the Czech estates. However, they reached White Mountain (*Biela hora*) only on 8 November, after the battle.

■ **1621**
1 January – The Transylvanian prince Gabriel Bethlen summoned a diet in Trnava. The deputies indicated that they were in favor of reconciliation with the sovereign.

23 June – The scholar and physician Ján Jessenius was executed in Prague.
31 December – King Ferdinand II and Gabriel Bethlen concluded a peace in Mikulov.

■ **1622**
20 March – On the basis of the Peace of Mikulov, the Transylvanian prince, Gabriel Bethlen, returned the royal crown to Bratislava castle.

■ **1623**
15 August – Gabriel Bethlen's army of ten thousand left Alba Iulia for a second campaign against King Ferdinand II.
29 September – The archbishop of Esztergom, Peter Pázmány, founded a college in Vienna for the training of priests, the Pazmaneum.
17 October – Troops of the Transylvanian prince, Gabriel Bethlen, occupied Trnava.

■ **1624**
9 May – In Vienna, King Ferdinand II and the Transylvanian prince, Gabriel Bethlen signed a treaty based on the Peace of Mikulov.
20 August – Archbishop Peter Pázmány founded a boarding school in Trnava for the training of young nobles.

■ **1625**
25 February – In Istanbul, French, English, Dutch and Venetian emissaries requested Gabriel Bethlen to support them in their war against the Habsburgs.
28 May – In Novohrad, Ferdinand II and the Turkish sultan Murad IV prolonged the Žitava treaty (11 September 1606).
– The Brewer printery began functioning in Levoča. During the 17th century it published the majority of secular and religious baroque literature in Slovakia.

■ **1626**
25 August – The Transylvanian prince, Gabriel Bethlen, departed Alba Iulia with an army of twenty thousand for his third campaign against Ferdinand II.
11 September – The archbishop of Esztergom, Peter Pázmány, issued a letter of foundation

for the Jesuit residence and college in Bratislava.

20 December – King Ferdinand II and Gabriel Bethlen concluded a truce in Bratislava based on the Mikulov treaty.

■ **1627**
8 February – Gašpar Weindl completed the first successful attempt to use gunpowder as blasting powder in the Upper Biber Shaft (*Horná Biberštôlňa*) in Banská Štiavnica.
31 July – On the basis of a mandate of King Ferdinand II against the non-Catholic estates in the patrimonial lands (in Czechia 1628), emigrants began to arrive in western Slovakia.
13 September – In Szöny (Komárno county) plenipotentiaries of King Ferdinand II and Sultan Murad IV prolonged the peace for a further 25 years.

■ **1629**
6 March – In the German Empire, the King and Emperor Ferdinand II decreed that property secularized since 1552 be returned to the church.
29 May – With support from the palatine of Hungary, M. Eszterházy, the Italian architects Antonio and Pietro Spazzo began to erect the university church in Trnava in the baroque style (it was finished on 30 August 1637).

■ **1630**
2 February – King Ferdinand II convened the diet in Bratislava, which decided that nobility could be bestowed only on persons living in Hungary. The grant of land to Gabriel Bethlen was declared invalid.

■ **1631**
3 April – In Košice, the emissaries of King Ferdinand II and Prince George I Rákóczi agreed to recognize the election of the prince and that Rákóczi had to disarm the discontented **hajduks**.
17 August – At Gönc near Komárno an agreement was concluded concerning amnesty for the rebellious serfs in eastern Hungary who had revolted against the pillaging armies.

■ **1632**
14 February – The archbishop of Esztergom, Peter Pázmány, left for Rome with a commission from King Ferdinand to negotiate with Pope Urban VIII for assistance for the war against the Turks.
4 March – After two days of interrogation and torture, Peter Császár, the leader of the peasant uprising in eastern Slovakia, was executed.
November – An outbreak of the plague in Bratislava and Trnava claimed a large number of victims among the population.

■ **1633**
6 May – Emissaries of King Ferdinand II and the Transylvanian prince George I Rákóczi negotiated in Prešov about their mutual relations.

■ **1634**
30 November – King Ferdinand II called the diet to meet in Sopron. It accepted a prohibition on fraternizing with the Turks or of provoking them militarily, allowed the nobility to own houses in the royal free cities and prohibited serfs from appealing against the decision of a landlord's court.

■ **1635**
12 May – Archbishop Peter Pázmány founded in Trnava a university with theological and philosophical faculties. It became a center of education and the Counter- Reformation. Lectures at Trnava University began on 13 November.

■ **1636**
The most frequently published Evangelical hymnbook, the *Harp of the Saints* (**Cithara Sanctorum**), compiled by Juraj Tranovský, was first published in Levoča.

■ **1637**
21 September – King Ferdinand III, who ascended the throne after the death of his father Ferdinand II, convened the diet in Bratislava. It discussed the sending of a peace mission to the Porte. The landlords had to admit tax

collectors to their estates and to pay duties on goods that they exported for sale abroad.

– The rector of Trnava University, Martin Palkovič from Chtelnica, conferred the first 24 bachelor's degrees on graduates.

– The printery of Václav Vokál, a Czech exile, began to operate in Trenčín. It issued many publications in the Czech language.

■ **1638**

12 November – The Transylvanian prince George I Rákóczi began negotiations concerning an anti-Habsburg alliance with the emissary of the French King Louis XIII.

■ **1639**

January – George I Rákóczi empowered his emissaries in Istanbul to negotiate secretly with the emissaries of European powers concerning an anti-Habsburg alliance.

– A synod of the Hungarian bishops in Trnava decided to ask the king for assistance in order to obtain the remission of church contributions to the papal see in Rome.

■ **1640**

31 August – The Jesuits concluded their activities in Humenné and resettled in Uzhgorod.

■ **1642**

In Levoča the work of the Czech exile Jakob Jakobeus, *Tears, Sighs and Pleas of the Slovak Nation* (*Gentis Slavonicae lacrimae, suspiria et vota*), was published. It was the first defense of the nation.

– Members of the Piarist order arrived in Podolínec.

– The newly named archbishop of Esztergom, George Lippay, began to build a summer palace in Bratislava (finished 1666).

■ **1643**

26 April – In Stockholm, Kristina, queen of Sweden, confirmed a treaty of alliance between the French king Louis XIII and the Transylvanian prince George I Rákóczi.

■ **1644**

2 February – George I Rákóczi invaded east-

ern Slovakia (**Insurrection of George I Rákóczi**).

■ **1645**

18 July – Units of George I Rákóczi and the Swedish general Leonard Torstensson joined forces near Brno.

16 December – In Linz a peace treaty ended hostilities between King Ferdinand III and the Transylvanian prince, George I Rákóczi.

– The first friars of the Capuchin order came to Bratislava.

■ **1646**

24 August – King Ferdinand III called the diet to Bratislava, which confirmed religious freedom. The churches confiscated since 1608 had to be returned to the Evangelicals.

– The work of the Jesuit Melchior Inchofer from Koszeg, *Ecclesiastical Annals of the Kingdom of Hungary* (*Annales ecclesiastici regni Hungariae*) was published in Rome. It deals with the beginnings of Christianity in Great Moravia and in Hungary.

■ **1647**

16 June – Ferdinand IV, the son of Ferdinand III, was crowned king of Hungary. However, he did not reign but he died during the lifetime of his father (9 July 1654).

14 July – The town of Pezinok received from King Ferdinand III a charter of privileges and became a royal free city.

■ **1648**

7 September – In a battle below Calvary Hill in Banská Štiavnica, the domestic defenders fended off an attack by the Turks.

24 October – The Peace of Westphalia, which ended thirty years of continuous war among the European states, was signed in Münster.

– A university printery began to operate in Trnava. During the 17th century it was the most productive printery in Hungary.

■ **1649**

25 January – King Ferdinand III called the diet to meet in Bratislava, at which he promised to maintain the border castles and garrisons.

1650
25 February – In Istanbul the emissaries of King Ferdinand III and Sultan Mehmed IV prolonged the peace based on the Žitava treaty of 1606 for another 22 years.
– Members of the Merciful Brethren Order arrived in Spišské Podhradie.

1652
26 June – Václav Lobkovitz, the chairman of the Court Military Council, forbade garrisons of castles to provoke armed skirmishes with the Turks.
25 August – Four of the Eszterházy brothers fell in a battle with the Turks near Vozokany (Tekov). They were buried with pomp on 26 November in Trnava.

1655
27 June – Fifteen-year old Leopold I was elected king of Hungary by a diet in Bratislava.
– The first Jesuit novitiate in Hungary opened at Trenčín.
– The Catholic hymnal *Catholic Songs* (**Cantus catholici**), compiled by Benedikt Sölöši, was published in Levoča.

1656
In Kláštor pod Znievom, the **Jesuits** opened a paper-mill to meet the needs of the university printery.

1657
26 February – In Jasov, the bishop of Eger, Benedict Kisdi, established an endowment of forty thousand florins for the foundation of a Jesuit university in Košice (**7 August 1660**).
2 April – King Ferdinand III died in Vienna. Leopold I succeeded to the throne.

1658
2 June – An assembly of Catholic ecclesiastics in Trnava called for more energetic Counter-Reformation measures.

1659
21 July – King Leopold I called a diet in Bratislava to discuss taxes. The Kremnica ducat was to equal the quality of the Vienna ducat.

1660
May – The imperial general Louis de Souchés came to Bratislava in order to avert the threat of a Turkish attack.
7 August – King Leopold I confirmed the rights and privileges of **Košice University** with a golden bull.

1662
16 February – King Leopold I ordered the introduction of work in three shifts in the mines.
1 May – King Leopold I convened the diet in Bratislava. The Protestants withdrew because the king would not accept their demands.

1663
12 April – Grand Vizier Köprülü Mehmed, the pasha of Edirne, advanced into Hungary with an army of 120,000 soldiers. After arriving in Buda (15 June), he decided on the conquest of Nové Zámky. On 7 August the advanced guard of the Ottoman army unexpectedly defeated, near Parkán (Štúrovo), detachments of the garrison of Nové Zámky led by A. Forgách. On 16 August the grand vizier besieged Nové Zámky, which was defended by 3,500 men.
2 September – The Crimean Tatars, Walachians, Moldavians and a part of the Turks devastated a substantial part of western Slovakia, the middle Považie region and Moravia.
25 September – After a siege of 39 days, Nové Zámky capitulated. The garrison was allowed to go to Komárno. Nové Zámky became the seat of a new **ejálet**.

1664
16 May – General Louis de Souchés defeated the army of Pasha Küčük Mehmed near Žarnovica.
1 August – An imperial army led by Raimund Montecuccoli defeated the Turks near St. Gotthard and halted a Turkish drive towards Vienna.

10 August – In Vasvár Emperor Leopold I concluded peace with the Turks.

■ **1665**
24 September – Palatine Francis Wesselényi, together with Archbishop George Szelepcsényi and General Louis de Souchés, laid the foundations of a new fortress in Leopoldov on the Váh River.
– The printery of Ján Dadan began to operate in Žilina. It published books primarily in the Czech language.

■ **1666**
3 April – In Kláštor pod Znievom, the Magistrate Ján Kužel as well as the jurists Martin Kmeť and Matej Pohánka, who had refused to fulfill their obligations to the landlord, were executed on the order of the plenipotentiary of Palatine George Makaj.
5 April – In Štubnianske (Turčianske) Teplice, Peter Zrínyi began to organize with Francis Wesselényi a movement of the magnates against the Habsburgs (**Wesselényi Conspiracy**).
– The so-called New Fort in Komárno was constructed according to the plans of a military engineer of Scottish origin, Francis Wimes.
– In Žilina, Štefan Pilárik published his reflective epic poem *The Fate of Stephen Pilárik (Sors Pilarikiana),* in which he recorded his personal experience as a prisoner of the Turks, into whose hands he had fallen in 1663.

■ **1667**
2 January – The law faculty of **Trnava University** began to operate.
16 October – An Evangelical college opened in Prešov (**Prešov Collegium**).

■ **1668**
July – At a meeting in Turčianske Teplice the anti-Habsburg conspirators decided that, despite a lack of foreign support, they would begin an armed insurrection.

■ **1669**
14 April – King Leopold I convened an assembly of the upper Hungarian estates in Prešov which, after the Protestants presented their grievances, ended on 29 May without success.

■ **1670**
13 April – In Vienna, the leaders of the conspiracy, Peter Zrínyi and Francis Fangepan, betrayed their associates.
10 December – The imperial army occupied Orava Castle belonging to Stephen Thököly, a member of the conspiracy, who had died on 4 December. The garrison of the castle surrendered.

■ **1671**
3 January – An extraordinary court in Bratislava under the presidency of Ján Rotthal summoned more than 200 nobles and punished them with the confiscation of all or part of their property for their alleged participation in the conspiracy against the king. František Bóniš from Zemplín was the only one condemned to death.
30 April – In Vienna the leaders of the conspiracy, Peter Zrínyi, Francis Frangepan and Francis Nádasdy, were executed. On the intercession of the Jesuits, Francis I Rákóczi was freed on the payment of a fine of 400,000 florins.
16 September – An extraordinary court in Bratislava condemned and publicly executed the preacher of the Czech Brethren and visionary Mikuláš Drábik, for writing about the decline of the Habsburgs.

■ **1672**
5 September – The serfs in Turá Lúka attacked members of a commission who intended to take the Evangelical church by force.
20 October – A *Kuruc* unit under Gašpar Pika invaded Orava and, with the help of the local population, took Orava Castle.
25 November – The imperial general Johann Sporck ordered the execution, by impalement, of the leader of the uprising Gašpar Pika, as well as of 25 magistrates from Orava and Liptov counties for their part in the armed rebellion.

– Members of the Order of the Merciful Brethren arrived in Bratislava. The Poor Claires began the systematic instruction of girls.

■ 1673

27 February – The administration of the Kingdom of Hungary was entrusted to an eight-member council of regency (cabinet of the country) led by the grand master of the German Knights, John Gaspar Ampringen (until 1681). For a time a consistent **absolutism** was introduced into Hungary.

25 September – The archbishop of Esztergom, George Szelepcsényi, summoned 33 Protestant pastors before an extraordinary court (**Bratislava court**).

■ 1674

5 March – Seven hundred Protestant pastors and teachers were summoned to the court in Bratislava. Approximately 350 of them appeared.

■ 1675

March – The **Bratislava court** condemned the Protestant pastors who refused to convert to the Catholic faith and sold them as galley slaves to Naples.

■ 1676

The preachers Tobiáš Masník and Ján Simonides, who had been redeemed from the galleys in Naples by the German merchant George Wetzl, arrived in Halle.

■ 1678

Imrich Thököly led his army from its Transylvanian exile into eastern Slovakia (**Thököly insurrection**).

– Daniel Sinapius-Horčička published in Latin a collection of Slovak proverbs and adages, *Latin-Slovak New Market (Neoforum Latino-Slavonicum)* in Leszno.

■ 1679

5 February – King Leopold I concluded peace with the French king Louis XIV at Nijmegen. Imrich Thököly was left without French support.

■ 1680

Summer – The *kuruc* detachments of Thököly undertook an expedition into Moravia.

■ 1681

28 April – King Leopold I convened a diet in Sopron, which granted amnesty to the participants in the **Thököly insurrection**. It confirmed old privileges and proclaimed the freedom of religion.

■ 1682

16 September – In Fiľakovo Pasha Ibrahim crowned Imrich Thököly as „king of central Hungary" and turned over to him the royal regalia. For an annual tribute of 40,000 *thaler*, Sultan Mehmed IV guaranteed the defense of his kingdom.

■ 1683

18 March – An Ottoman army (120 – 180,000 men), led by Sultan Mehmed IV, left Edirne for Hungary. On 25 June it left Székesfehérvár for Vienna, which it reached and besieged on 14 July.

25 July – Bratislava surrendered without a fight to the forces of Imrich Thököly. Earlier the crown and the royal regalia had been taken from the castle to Austria.

7 August – Trnava was engulfed by an inferno in which 4, 000 people perished.

12 September – The allies defeated the army of the Turks at Vienna, which meant the beginning of the end of Turkish hegemony in central Europe.

12 October – The imperial army inflicted a crushing defeat on the Turks near Parkán (Štúrovo).

■ 1684

12 January – In Bratislava King Leopold I granted amnesty to those participants in the **Thököly insurrection** who laid down their arms and promised to be loyal to him. Representatives of 17 counties and 12 cities, as well as several magnates, came to Bratislava.

■ 1685

7 July – Allied anti-Turkish armies besieged

Nové Zámky. It fell to the hands of the Emperor after an attack on 19 August.

11 September – General Schultz occupied Prešov after a two-month siege.

■ **1686**
2 September – Buda, the center of the Ottoman Empire in Hungary, fell to the royal forces after a two-month siege. This was definitively the end of Turkish hegemony.

■ **1687**
5 March – With the permission of King Leopold I, General Anton Caraffa erected a tribunal with twelve members in Prešov that, from March to September 1687, executed 24 townspeople suspected of preparing a new uprising (**Prešov Slaughter**).

18 April – King Leopold I convened in Bratislava a diet that enacted an amnesty for the participants in the **Thököly insurrection** and dissolved the tribunal in Prešov. It accepted the Habsburgs in the male line as the hereditary sovereigns of Hungary and abrogated the 31st article of the **Golden Bull** of Andrew II from 1222, which anchored the right of the estates to resist the sovereign.

9 November – Leopold I had his nine-year old son crowned as King Joseph I of Hungary in Bratislava. He was the first king of Hungary to be attired in the national dress of a Hungarian nobleman at his coronation.

■ **1688**
24 January – František Klobušický, the deputy administrator of Zemplín, turned over Thököly's royal regalia to King Leopold.

■ **1689**
15 November – Archbishop Leopold Kollonich, the president of the Hungarian Chamber, developed a plan for the financial and administrative reorganization of Hungary, the *Work for Organizing the Kingdom of Hungary* (*Einrichtungswerk des Königreichs Ungarn*).

– The professor and poly-historian, Martin Szentiványi began to publish the three-volume encyclopedic work *Rare and Diverse Products of Miscellaneous Sciences* (*Curiosiora et selectiora variarum scientiarum miscellanea*) in Latin in Trnava.

■ **1691**
10 December – The Court Chamber forbade the recruitment of miners as soldiers. Recruited miners had to be discharged.

■ **1692**
P. Eszterházy had the first permanent walled theater in Hungary built in the seminary of St. Mary in Trnava.

■ **1693**
23 January – King Leopold I decreed that in Turiec, Zvolen, Hont and Tekov counties Jews could settle no closer than seven miles from the mining cities.

– During his service in the imperial army, the Italian engineer Count Luigi Ferdinando Marsigli carried out a complex survey of the Danubian basin (topography, hydrology of the Danube, archaeology, mining, zoology etc.), the results of which he published in the work *Danubius Pannonico – mysicus...* (Amsterdam 1726).

■ **1694**
During his studies in the Roman archives a Jesuit professor at Trnava University, Martin Cseles from Ružindol discovered documents concerning the beginnings of Christianity in Great Moravia (**Baroque Slavicism**).

■ **1696**
The work of Tobiáš Masník, *The Rules of Written Slovak, How it has to be Properly Written, Read and Printed* (*Zpráva Písma slovenského, jak se má dobře psáti, čísti a tisknouti*) was published in Levoča.

■ **1697**
11 September – The imperial commander Prince Eugene of Savoy inflicted a devastating defeat on the Turks near Zenta, in which 30,000 Turkish soldiers fell.

■ **1699**
26 January – The peace treaty of Karlovac

confirmed the results of the war with the Ottoman Empire.

16 February – King Leopold I confirmed the creation of an ecclesiastical union and bestowed upon the Greek Catholic clergy the same rights as the Roman Catholic clergy.

■ **1700**
1 November – Joseph Longueval, the French emissary in Vienna, revealed the contents of a letter of the county administrator (*župan*) of Šariš county, Francis II Rákóczi, addressed to the French king Louis XIV in the name of domestic conspirators. The letter was a request for support.

■ **1701**
18 April – Francis II Rákóczi was captured in Veľký Šariš and escorted to imprisonment in Wiener Neustadt. Captain Gottfried Lehman helped him to escape to Poland on 8 November. On 14 November King Leopold offered for the capture of Francis II Rákóczi a reward of 10,000 florins, if taken alive, or 6,000 florins, if dead.

■ **1702**
8 April – Through the mediation of influential Polish magnates, Francis II Rákóczi, in exile in Brzezany in Poland, established contact with the French king regarding the preparation of an anti-Habsburg insurrection.
– In Trnava the first topographical work of Samuel Timon, *Topography of Hungarian cities and towns (Celebriorum Hungariae urbium et oppidorum topographia)* was published in Latin.

■ **1703**
6 May – From exile in Poland, Francis II Rákóczi appealed to the population of Hungary to fight for freedom (**Insurrection of Francis II Rákóczi**). On 16 June he returned to his lands in Mukačevo, where Ruthenian serfs and the defeated *kuruc* soldiers led by Thomas Esze joined him.
28 August – Rákóczi issued an edict in Satu Mare that freed the serfs fighting under his banner from feudal dues. In September the *kuruc*

soldiers under the leadership of Ladislas Ocskay occupied southern and central Slovakia.
15 November – In a battle near Zvolen, *kuruc* soldiers led by Nicholas Bercsényi defeated the imperial army and took the mining cities.

■ **1704**
January – The political manifesto of Francis II Rákóczi to the population of the Christian countries was published in Trnava. He appealed to them to rise up against the Habsburgs.
27 – 28 May – The *kuruc* soldiers of Nicholas Bercsényi defeated a larger imperial army near Smolenice. The *kuruc* insurgents also took Košice on 31 October.

■ **1705**
3 January – A new copper coin of lower value, called the *libertáš*, went into circulation. It had catastrophic consequences for the economy of the country.
12 September – Francis II Rákóczi called a diet to meet in Sečany, which enacted freedom of religious confession.

■ **1706**
13 April – The Transylvanian prince Francis II Rákóczi and King Joseph I concluded a two-week truce in Trnava.
Spring – As a result of the poor economic situation, the Economic Council (*Consilium oeconomicum*), the chief economic organ of the insurgents, was compelled to issue price controls for foodstuffs and artisan products.

■ **1707**
1 January – Turiec County issued a circular letter that expressed dissatisfaction with the orders of the insurgents.
31 May – The meeting of the **Ónod diet** began. Representatives of Turiec County who criticized the policy of the insurgents were killed. The diet in Ónod deposed the Habsburgs from the Hungarian throne on 16 June.
3 October – The count of the chamber in Banská Štiavnica used gunfire to disperse

striking miners who were protesting the payment of wages in worthless copper coins.

■ **1708**
3 August – In a battle near Trenčín the imperial general, Sigbert Heister, defeated the insurgents who lost more than 3,000 men.
28 August – Ladislas Ocskay, the *kuruc* brigadier, went over to the side of the emperor with his whole brigade after being defeated in battle.

■ **1709**
14 July – King Joseph I decreed an amnesty for all of the insurgents who surrendered within four weeks except for Francis II Rákóczi and his deputy Nicholas Bercsényi.
Summer – Hungary was afflicted with an epidemic of the plague that lasted until 1714.
10 December – King Joseph I mandated thereturn of Catholic churches and schools that the Protestants had confiscated during the insurrection.

■ **1710**
22 January – The defeat of the *kuruc* army near Romhány broke the resistance of the insurgent army.
1 February – The *kuruc* general, Stephen Andrássy, opened the city gates of Levoča to the emperor's army.
24 September – In Nové Zámky, the garrison of the insurgents, who had held the fortress from 1704, capitulated to the emperor's forces.

■ **1711**
25 February – Francis II Rákóczi and N. Bercsényi left for Poland where they sought to obtain help from the Russian czar, Peter I.
17 April – King Joseph I died unexpectedly in Vienna and Charles III ascended the throne.
30 April – Peace between the insurgents and the king was concluded in Satu Mare. This ended the final rebellion of the estates, **the Insurrection of Francis II Rákóczi** (Peace of Satu Mare).

Era of Reforms (1711 – 1780)

The conclusion of the Peace of Satu Mare in 1711 was not only the end of the last armed insurrection of the Hungarian nobility, but also was a turning point in the development of Slovakia, Hungary and the whole of central Europe. The peace was concluded with a compromise. The ruling Habsburg family retained the Hungarian royal crown; the nobility preserved their prerogatives and privileges, especially their exemption from taxation. No longer was the territory of Slovakia exposed to devastating forays and it ceased to be the center of military operations of the Ottoman Empire or domestic armed conflicts. This did not mean, however, that martial events did not affect it. The population continued to pay taxes and to comprise the rank and file of huge regular armies that conducted destructive wars outside this territory. Changes in the nationality structure of the country also was a result of the pacific development in the 18th century. The lands in southern Hungary, freed from the Turks, promised the desired land and a new future to the population of the northern regions. A new wave of colonization to the depopulated regions of the lower lands began. Slovak immigrants also went there.

The 18th century is usually described as „the Century of the Enlightenment" or the „Age of Reason". The reason for this is the presupposition that the previous „dark" age of religious intolerance, of captive spirits, of a world of superstition, miracles, myths, magic and incomprehensible mysteries was replaced by a period of „enlightened" reason that provided rational explanations of unexplained secrets of nature and man. The ideas of the disseminators and popularizers of the Enlightenment proceeded from theories of natural law, according to which each person is by nature free and all people are equal. The royal court became the promoter of these ideas. A result of reform activity was that the economic and cultural levels of the empire improved. The state gradually took control of the economy, regulated relations between the landlords and the serfs, organized and administered schools, health care and other spheres of the life of society.

Foreign political failures compelled the ruler's court to implement several basic reforms in Hungary. The first, the land registry (*urbarial*) regulation, was connected with securing a regular and stable tax revenue. It injected order into the then uncontrolled legal relationship between the landlord and the serf. In essence, its goal was to secure the economic prosperity of the serfs/farmers, the main taxpayers of the state. The products of the guilds also were regulated. The first manufactures developed. During this period the first state school institutions were established and a reform of university studies took place. In Banská Štiavnica an academy began to function that was the predecessor of technical higher schools (universities). A medical faculty opened at the University of Trnava, which was, however, transferred to Buda in 1777. Under the title *Ratio educationis,* school reform radically changed the content, methods and goals of the educational-training process in accordance with the spirit of modern conceptions and views.

In the 18th century elements of the defense of the nation began to prevail in the ideology of the Slovak nationality. A typical example is the first political defense of the Slovak nation by the pastor of Dubnica, Ján Baltazár Magin. Alongside Hungarian patriotism, the Great Moravian tradition and the defense of Slovaks as a autochthonous population, there also developed a national defensive theory about the hospitable acceptance of the Magyars and a contractual theory concerning the development of the Hungarian state, scientifically modified by the poly-historian Matej Bel and by Adam František Kollár from Terchová. In its various mutations it essentially endured up to the mid- 19th century. A no less important manifestation of this period was the creation of a cultured western Slovak language at the university and educational center in Trnava. It became the basis for the first codification of a literary Slovak language by Anton Bernolák.

■ **1712**
3 April – King Charles III (VI) convened a diet in Bratislava, which prematurely terminated discussions on 2 August because of an epidemic of the plague. The diet proclaimed the leaders of the uprising to be traitors and declared invalid the laws accepted by the **Ónod diet** and the later diets of the insurgents in Sečany and Sáarospatak.

■ **1713**
18 March – The bandit captain, Juraj Jánošík from Terchová, was cruelly executed in Liptovský Sv. Mikuláš.
11 April – A peace treaty ending the War of the Spanish Succession was signed in Utrecht.
19 April – King Charles III (VI) proclaimed the **Pragmatic Sanction,** which regulated the succession of the Habsburg dynasty.
Summer – An epidemic of the plague claimed approximately 400 victims in Bratislava.

■ **1714**
6 March – King Charles III (VI) abjured claims to the Spanish throne by the peace treaty of Rastatt.
8 September – Charles III called the diet to Bratislava, which decided that new magistrates were not allowed to be elected in the free cities except in the presence of royal commissioners.
– More than 3,000 serfs left Šariš County. Fifteen villages were completely deserted.
– In Tekov County 3,160 serfs raised 8,481 head of draft cattle and worked 12,680 hectares of arable land and 3, 302 hectares of meadows.

■ **1715**
15 June – Law no. 101/1715 went into effect, forbiding serf emigration without the written consent of the landlord. The diet decided that the ruler had the right freely to decide the religious questions of the Protestants.

22 August – As a result of an epidemic of the plague which lasted until 3 January 1716, 222 people died in Trenčín and 114 left the city with symptoms of the disease.
– A countrywide census of the tax-paying population took place.
– As a consequence of crop failure and starvation 1,144 serf families fled Liptov County.
– In Slovakia about 8,000 artisan workshops operated. Nearly 40,000 people worked as craftsmen.

■ 1716
5 August – Prince Eugene of Savoy defeated 60,000 troops of Grand Vizier Ali near Petrovaradin.

■ 1717
17 August – The Turkish garrison of Belgrade surrendered to the Imperial army under Eugene of Savoy, after a month-long siege.
October – Urban Celder, a *kuruc* warrior who tried to organize a military uprising against the king in 1714, was executed in Košice.
– There were 56 pensioners in the „hospital" (poorhouse) of St. Ladislas in Bratislava.

■ 1718
21 July – King Charles III (VI) concluded peace with the Turks for 25 years in Požarevac.
– Thirty-four furnaces (**foundries**) and **hammer-mills** for working iron operated in Gemer.
– The first book of sermons in the Slovak language, *Of the bread of the first fruits (Panes primitiarum aneb chleby prvotín)* by Alexander Máčaj was published in Trnava.

■ 1720
A census of the tax-paying population of the whole country took place. About 65,000 people lived in the royal free and mining cities of Slovakia. There were 4, 500 Germans, 3,000 Slovaks and 1,500 Magyars in Bratislava. In Komárno there were 792 houses, in Bratislava 608 and in Banská Štiavnica 694.
– The first Slovak colonists began to settle in Csaba in the „lower lands", which had only 58 households.

■ 1721
15 March – A commission made up of 24 Catholics and Protestants began to function in Pest. Its task was to resolve religious questions.
March – The printery of Ján Pavol Royer in Bratislava began to issue the Latin newspaper, *Nova Posoniensia (New Pozsony)*. Matej Bel initiated its publication, but it ceased to exist in September 1722.
– For the *Althandel* shaft in Nová Baňa, the English engineer Isaac Potter installed the first Newcomen steam engine on the European continent for pumping water from mines.

■ 1722
20 June – Charles III (VI) summoned to Bratislava the diet that accepted the **Pragmatic Sanction**.
– Slovak colonists settled the city of Sarvas in the „lower lands" (**emigration**).
– In Banská Štiavnica an open revolt of the miners erupted against a radical reduction of wages.
– Count Nicholas Pálffy founded a **manufacture** (factory) in which five master drapers worked to produce cloth in Malacky.
– The professor of Hungarian law at the university in Trnava, Michael Bencsik, published the work *The Most Recent Noble Diet (Novissima diaetae nobilissima)*, which led Ján Baltazár Magin to write a political defense (**Magin's Apology**).

■ 1723
King Charles III (VI) implemented a reform of the judiciary. He organized four new district (territorial) courts, two of which were located in Trnava and Prešov.
– A law article directed the counties to regulate the pay of salaried workers and servants according to local conditions.
– The sculptor Dávid Ignác Zirn and the painters Ján Grinberg and Juraj Lipský from Trenčín worked on the reconstruction of the castle in Dubnica nad Váhom, which continued until 1730.

■ **1724**

20 January – Charles III (VI) delimited the competency of the **Vice-Regency Council** with its seat in Bratislava, which renewed its activities on 21 March.

■ **1725**

The Vice-Regency Council directed that those who intended to study in other countries must have individually authorized travel documents.

– Together with two partners, the merchant Teofil Gottlieb Sterz founded a cloth factory in Banská Bystrica that produced 1,120 bolts of cloth annually.

■ **1726**

8 February – The Vice-Regency Council in Bratislava assumed the administration of censorship. Until then it had been conducted by the chancellor of Trnava University. It ordered that printers were obliged to send 3 copies of each work for evaluation.

– According to an order of the Vice-Regency Council the renewal or election of the magistrate of the city of Trenčín had to take place on 31 December. Prior to this it had taken place, according to an old custom, on the feast of St. John the Evangelist (27 December).

■ **1728**

17 May – King Charles III (VI) convened the diet in Bratislava. However, he did not come to an agreement with the deputies on taxation and the registration of taxpayers. For the rest of his life, the king did not convene the diet again.

23 July – In Szeged, six men and six women charged with witchcraft were burned, another man was decapitated, and 28 persons were imprisoned.

– The first political defense of the Slovak nation, *Thorns...or Apology* (*Murices...sive Apologia*), by the pastor of Dubnica, Ján Baltazár Magin (**Magin's Apology**), was published in Púchov.

■ **1729**

6 July – The city council of Bratislava issued fire regulations containing 20 points.

– The Hungarian diet accepted a law against higher fees for the acceptance of new masters into the **guilds.**

■ **1730**

4 February – The Vice-Regency Council forbade the city council in Levoča to borrow money without royal approval.

– Since 1721, 6,471 children had been baptized, 2,165 marriages celebrated and 7,571 inhabitants buried in Bratislava.

– The Jesuits founded the Confraternity of the Holy Rosary in Žilina in order to intensify the spiritual life of the students.

■ **1731**

February – An extraordinary tribunal in Bratislava, under the leadership of John Pálffy, condemned the Evangelical superintendent Daniel Krman to life imprisonment for insulting the Catholic religion.

21 March – King Charles III (IV) issued an order concerning the regulation of non-Catholic religions, the so-called **Resolutio Carolina**.

■ **1732**

5 April – After the death of Palatine Nicholas Pálffy (20 February 1732), King Charles III (IV) named as viceroy his future son-in-law, Francis of Lothringen (Lorraine).

28 October – Imrich Eszterházy, the archbishop of Esztergom, dedicated in the Cathedral of St. Martin in Bratislava the chapel of St. John the Almoner, decorated by Rafael Donner.

– Šaštín became a place of pilgrimage.

■ **1733**

1 February – After the death of the Polish king August II of Saxony, the War of the Polish Succession began.

16 October – Charles III (VI) ordered the establishment of a thirtieth office (an office for the collection of duties), with its seat in Bratislava under the administration of the Court Chamber.

– Professor Samuel Timon published in Latin the work *Picture of Ancient Hungary (Imago antiquae Hungariae...)* in Košice.

■ 1734
20 October – On the basis of the **Resolutio Carolina** King Charles III permitted four superintendencies for the Evangelicals and Calvinists to be established.
– 341 pupils attended the Evangelical lyceum in Bratislava.

■ 1735
23 October – Charles III (VI) appointed Samuel Mikovíni as the imperial surveyor. He was entrusted with teaching mathematics at the mining school in Banská Štiavnica.
– The first part of the extensive work of Matej Bel, *Historical-Geographic Notes about New Hungary (Notitia Hungariae novae historico-geographica)* was published in Latin in Vienna.
– The sculptor Rafael Donner completed the ornamentation of the main altar of St. Martin's Cathedral in Bratislava.

■ 1736
12 February – The marriage of Maria Theresa to the Tuscan duke, Francis of Lothringen (Lorraine) took place in Vienna.
2 May – King Charles III (VI), allied with Russia, began an unsuccessful war against the Turks.
– The viceroy, Francis of Lothringen, founded a textile **manufacture** in Šaštín that produced cotton cloth and other cotton products.
– The pharmacist Hieronymus Petzelt published the first catalog of medicines used in Trnava.
– Anton Galli da Bibiena, an Italian painter and decorator, began to paint the dome of the Church of the Trinitarians in Bratislava (completed in 1740).
– The building of a Calvary began in Košice (completed in 1758).

■ 1737
– The work of Francis Kazy *History of the University of Trnava (Historia Universitas Tyrnaviensis)* was published in Trnava on the 100th anniversary of its foundation.

■ 1738
1 August – King Charles III (VI) issued a constitution for the Bratislava **guild** of the Slovak cobblers, which was intended only for Slovaks.
– A health commission was established under the Vice-Regency Council to organize public health service.
– In Banská Štiavnica, Jozef Karol Hell, a master mining engineer, constructed a reciprocating machine for pumping out water.

■ 1739
1 September – The emissaries of King Charles III (VI) and Sultan Mahmud I concluded a peace in Belgrade.
– An epidemic of the plague in Slovakia spread and lasted until 1742.

■ 1740
20 October – Charles III (VI) died in Vienna and, according to the **Pragmatic Sanction**, his daughter Maria Theresa assumed rule. During her reign many important reforms (**Theresian Reforms**) were implemented.
11 October – Jakub Surovec (born 1715), the leader of a band of bandits, was executed in Brezno. Popular tradition incorrectly associated him with Jánošík.
16 December – Frederick II, the Prussian king, invaded Silesia, which he claimed in return for recognizing Maria Theresa's right of succession.

■ 1741
26 January – John Pálffy, the chief justice, circulated an appeal to the counties that the nobles take the field to fight against the invading Prussians.
10 April – Frederick II, the king of Prussia, defeated the Austrian army at Mollowitz and occupied Silesia.
14 May – The sovereign, Maria Theresa, summoned the diet to Bratislava. It confirmed the prerogatives of the nobles and approved extraordinary military assistance for the defense against the Prussians.
25 June – Maria Theresa, the daughter of Charles III, was crowned in Bratislava as Queen of Hungary.
11 September – The Hungarian estates as-

sembled at a diet in Bratislava voluably demonstrated their willingness to defend the throne of the young queen and proclaimed their willingness to sacrifice their own blood and lives for her cause.

■ **1742**
12 February – Austrian and Hungarian soldiers occupied Munich, the seat of Charles Albert, the German emperor and the cousin-in-law of Maria Theresa.
11 June – The emissaries of Maria Theresa and the Prussian king Frederick II signed a peace treaty in Wroclaw by which Maria Theresa gave up Silesia.
– The painter Paul Troger began to paint the altar picture and ornamentation of the Church of the Elizabethan order in Bratislava (completed in 1743).

■ **1743**
12 May – The coronation of Maria Theresa as Queen of Bohemia (Czech queen) took place in Prague.

■ **1744**
August – Frederick II, the Prussian king, occupied Prague but he had to withdraw at the end of the year.
– In Banská Štiavnica the building of a Calvary began (completed in 1751). Devotion to the Way of the Cross (via dolorosa) began to spread at the same time.
– In this year the mines in Banská Štiavnica administered by the state produced 9,261 talents (hrivna) of silver and 2,429 talents of gold.

■ **1745**
22 April – Maximilian III, the Bavarian elector and Holy Roman Emperor, concluded peace with Maria Theresa in Füssen and recognized her succession as ruler of the Habsburg lands only.
4 October – Following the death of the Emperor Maximilian, Francis of Lothringen, the husband of Maria Theresa, was crowned as German (Holy Roman) emperor in Frankfurt am Main.

25 December – Maria Theresa and the Prussian king Frederick II concluded a peace in Dresden, which confirmed the loss of Silesia.
– Bratislava Pharmaceutical Schedule (Taxa pharmaceutica Posoniensis), the work of Ján Just Torkoš concerning the preparation of medicine, was published in Bratislava in Slovak, German, Latin and Hungarian.

■ **1746**
November – Maria Theresa founded the Theresian College (Collegium Teresianum) in Vienna, a school to educate young nobles.
– Emperor Francis I Lothringen founded a factory in Holíč for the production of faience (ceramics).
– In Tekov County 5,562 peasant farms cultivated 35,754 hectares of arable land and 7,755 meadows and bred 18, 563 head of draft cattle.
– Teaching at the mining school in Smolník began.
– Pavel Doležal published a textbook of Czech, A Slavic- Bohemian Grammar (Grammatica Slavico-Bohemica) in Bratislava.
– The work of the secondary-school teacher, Ján Purgina, A didactic poem concerning electrical force (De vi eletrica carmen didacticum), was published in Latin in Trnava.

■ **1747**
Queen Maria Theresa issued the ordinance, Constitutiones et rescripta, which substantially limited the control of mining by the mining cities.
– The first members of the Notre Dame Congregation arrived in Bratislava, where they established a school for girls (**religious orders**).
– Johann A. Segner, a Bratislava native and professor at the University of Jena, publicly demonstrated his invention, the so-called Segner wheel (a reciprocating water engine).

■ **1748**
18 October – A peace treaty was signed in Aachen, which concluded the War of the Austrian Succession.

– Maria Theresa renewed an older prohibition of publishing papal bulls without the approval of the monarch.

■ **1749**

Maria Theresa ordered the imprisonment of those Catholics who wished to convert to another religious faith.

– In this year the revenue flowing into the state treasury from the **thirtieth** reached 547,000 florins.

– The Vice-Regency Council informed Joseph Illésházy, administrator of Trenčín County, of the sovereign's decision to erect a protective dike along the Váh River near Trenčín.

– The engineer Jozef Karol Hell put a water-column pump into operation in Banská Štiavnica.

■ **1750**

– In Hungary the Jesuits, with an annual income of 350, 000 florins, had 884 members and administered 30 secondary schools (gymnasia), 18 boarding schools, six academies and the Universities of Košice and Trnava.

– Queen Maria Theresa regulated the amount of stole fees (payments for the performance of priestly services).

– The school of the Congregation of Notre Dame in Bratislava was attended by 73 pupils.

– In Soľná Baňa near Prešov 32,000 hundredweight of salt were extracted from four shafts.

– In Bratislava Ján Michal Landerer established the largest printing company in Hungary, which functioned without interruption until 1854.

– Count Joseph Illésházy had the mortuary chapel of his family in the parish church at Trenčín rebuilt (completed in 1752). The sculpted work on the altar was by Ľudovít Gode, a pupil of Rafael Donner. The reconstruction cost 3,514 florins.

■ **1751**

17 April – Queen Maria Theresa summoned a diet to Bratislava at which she requested an increase in taxes.

19 August – Maria Theresa issued a decree that imposed more severe penalties for apostasy (deserting the Catholic faith). Only Catholic bishops were allowed to approve mixed marriages of Catholics and Protestants. Catholics were not allowed to attend non-Catholic schools.

1 November – The ruler issued new military regulations (*Regulamentum militare*) concerning the disposition and maintenance of troops.

– The Slovak population of Banská Bystrica presented to the diet a complaint against the privileges of the German townspeople.

■ **1752**

26 October – Queen Maria Theresa ordered that a physician and a physician's assistant be maintained in each county.

■ **1753**

Maria Theresa reformed the program of study at **Trnava University**.

– In Banská Bystrica the master engineer Jozef Karol Hell constructed a pump driven by compressed air.

– The construction of a university observatory in Trnava began using the plans of the astronomer Maximilian Hell.

■ **1754**

11 January – In Rome, Pope Benedict XIV granted permission for Maria Theresa to reduce the number of church holidays. Apart from Sundays, only 16 holidays were retained.

22 January – Queen Maria Theresa published regulations concerning the control of the licensing of physicians.

■ **1755**

4 January – Maria Theresa published toll regulations that imposed a duty of 30 per cent on goods imported into Hungary.

19 August – The health commission, responsible to the Vice-Regency Council in Bratislava, published the *Plain Health Regulations (Planum regulationis in re sanitatis)* regulating fees paid to health workers.

26 August – The Royal Chamber accepted nine-point general regulations for local governments, which limited their existing prerogatives.

– Hugolín Gavlovič completed in Pruské the manuscript of the most famous baroque work, *The Shepherds School, A Storehouse of Morals* (*Valaská škola, mravúv stodola*).

■ 1756
29 August – Frederick II, the Prussian king, invaded and occupied Saxony, including the capital Dresden. This was the beginning of the Seven Years' War.

– Queen Maria Theresa forbade the imposition of the death sentence for sorcery by Hungarian courts.

– Maria Theresa directed that even people of other faiths pay the stole fees due to Catholic clergy.

– A black plague epidemic broke out in Slovakia and lasted until 1758.

– Andrej Jaslinský, a professor of philosophy, published the work *Foundations of Physics (Institutiones Physicae)* in Trnava.

■ 1757
18 June – The army of Maria Theresa under Count Daun defeated Frederick II, the Prussian king, near the Czech town of Kolín. By a daring attack on 16 October, 5,000 men of the Hussar divisions, led by Count Andrej Hadik, occupied Berlin.

– A smallpox epidemic spread in Slovakia and lasted, with brief pauses, until 1766.

■ 1758
14 August – By his first brief (*breve*), Pope Clement XIII bestowed on Maria Theresa the title of Apostolic Queen.

8 November – The queen ordered the county of Nitra to confiscate heretical books from the Anabaptist *Habans* in Sobotište (**26 October 1548**).

■ 1759
25 July – In Skalica, the **Jesuits** celebrated the 100th anniversary of their arrival in the city.

12 August – Austrian and Russian armies defeated the army of Frederick II, the Prussian king, near Kunersdorf.

– Queen Maria Theresa decreed that legal questions arising even from purely Protestant marriages fell within the competence of the Catholic bishops.

– The cornerstone of the Trinity Statue in Banská Štiavnica (completed in 1764), designed by the sculptor Dionýz Stanetti, was consecrated.

■ 1760
11 September – Maria Theresa established a personal Hungarian guard of 120 men under the leadership of Count Leopold Pálffy.

– Maria Theresa created an eight-member state council as her advisory organ regarding suggestions for reforms.

– In Trnava 147 Jesuits, 63 Franciscans, 50 Poor Claires and 50 Ursulines (**religious orders**) lived in four cloisters.

■ 1761
– The queen ordered the **guilds** to have their old guild privileges confirmed.

– The reconstruction of Bratislava Castle (completed in 1765) began under the direction of Francis Anton Hillebrandt.

■ 1762
22 March – The Hungarian Royal Court Chamber demanded that the Vice-Regency Council prepare a report about the state of the royal free and mining cities.

1 October – A consultation of officials at the emperor's court in Vienna decided to establish a „practical mining school" in Banská Štiavnica (**3 April 1770**).

– The city bank of Vienna issued the first paper money.

– Johann Lucas Kracker began to paint an altar picture and the internal ornamentation of the Premonstratensian church and monastery in Jasov (completed in 1764).

■ 1763
15 February – The emissaries of Queen Maria Theresa and King Frederick II of Prussia signed a peace treaty in Hubertsburg that

ended the Seven Years' War (begun 29 August 1756).

9 June – The department of mineralogy opened at the mining academy in Banská Štiavnica.

28 June – An earthquake affected Bratislava, Komárno and Buda.

21 July – Count F. Eszterházy founded a state orphanage in the castle in Tomášikovo for 75 boys and 25 girls.

14 September – In Senec, Queen Maria Theresa founded a school to train specialists in the area of the economy, the *Collegium oeconomicum* or Economic College. The Piarists ran the school.

– In Trenčianske Bohuslavice, Francis Anton Maulbertsch completed wall paintings in the castle of Count Anton Erdödy.

■ **1764**

3 April – Joseph II, the son of Maria Theresa, was crowned King of the Romans in Frankfurt am Main. He was elected Holy Roman Emperor in 1765.

Spring – The Latin work of Adam František Kollár, *On the Source and continuity of the use of legislative power in the Holy Apostolic Kingdom of Hungary (De originibus et usu perpetuo potestatis legislatoriae circa sacra apostolicum regum Ungariae)*, was published in Vienna. It elicited antagonism from the Hungarian nobility and the Pope.

17 June – Maria Theresa summoned the diet to Bratislava. In view of its unsuccessful discussions, she did not convene a diet again.

14 July – The printer Ján Michal Landerer began to issue a newspaper, *Pressburger News (Pressburger Zeitung)*, in Bratislava.

– The Kremnica mint provided the sovereign's court with 17,399 talents of silver and 378 talents of gold as well as providing 4,117 talents of silver to the coinage office in Vienna.

– The work of Jozef Bencúr concerning the absolute power of the ruler *Hungary Always Free (Ungaria semper libera)* was published in Vienna.

■ **1765**

18 February – At the order of Queen Maria Theresa, the executionerburned in the main square of Bratislava the anonymous work *Persecution of Reason (Vexatio ad intelectum)* directed against the absolutist efforts of the sovereign.

18 August – The Emperor Francis of Lothringen, the husband of Maria Theresa, died in Vienna. On 21 September the sovereign declared her son, Joseph II, who was elected Holy Roman Emperor, co-ruler.

15 November – The Royal Chamber established a standard mode of electing local governments. The townspeople with a right to vote cast balls into several urns marked with the names of the candidates.

■ **1766**

10 April – Maria Theresa forbade the importation of textiles, glassware and other products into Hungary.

– A group of merchants from Vienna and Bratislava founded a factory to make heavy cotton cloth in Bernolákovo.

– Pavol Adámi, a professor at Universities of Vienna and Cracow, published a Latin work *Hydrology of Trenčín County (Hydrographia comitatus Trenchiniensis)* in Vienna.

■ **1767**

23 January – Queen Maria Theresa regulated serf relationships (**Theresian urbár**) by patent.

18 May – Maria Theresa ordered the burning of books with subversive contents.

– Emperor Joseph II ordered that papal bulls were to be published in churches only with his permission.

– Wolfgang Kempelen founded a manufacture to produce heavy cotton cloth in Bratislava. Count Windischgrätz established a factory in Teplička nad Váhom for producing linen.

■ **1768**

28 April – Maximilian Hell, a native of Banská Štiavnica and the director of the imperial observatory in Vienna, together with his assistant Ján Šajnovič, from Trnava, left for a two-year scientific expedition to Norway.

– Queen Maria Theresa ordered that conviction for witchcraft be based only on irrefutable evidence.

■ **1769**

17 July – By a personal decree, Maria Theresa took **Trnava University** under her personal control. This meant it was controlled by the state.

17 November – The queen directed that Trnava University be expanded to include a medical faculty. The Vice-Regency Council promulgated the Queen's decision concerning the establishment of a medical faculty on 14 December.

– A freemason lodge, At the Virtuous Traveler (*Zum tugendhaften Reisenden*), was founded in Prešov.

– The work of Adam František Kollár in Latin *Concerning the Origin, Spread and Settlement of the Ruthenian Nationality in Hungary (Humilissimum pro memoria de ortu, progressu et in Hungaria incolatu gentis Ruthenicae)* was published in Vienna.

■ **1770**

3 April – The school of mining in Banská Štiavnica was renamed the Mining Academy by a decree of the Mining Chamber in Vienna.

17 September – The Vice-Regency Council in Bratislava directed the counties to carry out a census of the population.

4 October – The Vice-Regency Council issued health regulations (*Regulamentum sanitatis*).

1 November – Based on a patent of Maria Theresa, the Vice-Regency Council issued regulations to reorganize university studies (*Norma studiorum*).

7 November – Lectures began at the medical faculty of **Trnava University**.

– Approximately 20,000 Romany lived in Slovakia.

– There were more than 22,000 artisan workshops in Slovakia. More than 12,000 workers labored in the state mines in the mining region of central Slovakia.

■ **1771**

– In March a „revolt of the women" to defend the old rights of the city took place in Prievidza.

– In Bratislava a supplement to the *Pressburg News (Pressburger Zeitung)* entitled the *Pressburg Weekly (Pressburgische Wochenblatt)*, dealing with natural science and economic topics, began to be published. Its publication ceased in 1773.

– A university botanical garden was founded by the medical faculty in Trnava.

■ **1772**

1 June – The Vice-Regency Council in Bratislava published data from the census of the population, *Conscriptio animarum.*

5 August – As a consequence of the First Partition of Poland in Petersburg, Queen Maria Theresa obtained Galicia, with a population of three million, and the Spiš cities that had been mortgaged to Poland on 8 November 1412.

– In Smolník a new mint was established, in which predominantly copper coins were minted.

■ **1773**

21 September – Maria Theresa promulgated the papal brief of 21 July suppressing the **Jesuit** order.

23 September – The queen ordered landlords to surrender to the serfs the abandoned settlements they had seized during the past 30 years.

November – The Vice-Regency Council in Bratislava created a commission that was to prepare a reorganization of the school system.

– The work *Introduction to Mining (Einleitung zu der Bergbaukunst)* by Krištof Traugott Delius from Smolník was published in German in Vienna. It later was translated into several languages.

■ **1774**

19 August – Queen Maria Theresa bestowed the property of the dissolved Jesuit residence in Trnava upon the local university.

■ **1775**

1 May – Maria Theresa issued a toll patent which regulated exports and imports within the empire.

30 June – A so-called normal school training teachers for elementary schools opened in Bratislava.

12 October – Maria Theresa issued a regulation against vagabonds, according to which they were to be rehabilitated by starting to work; the sick and the elderly were to be placed in poorhouses.

– The painter Ján Baptista Bergl completed the decoration of the vaults in the church of the Paulist cloister in Horné Lefantovce.

■ **1776**

15 January – Maria Theresa issued a decree, on the basis of which three new bishoprics were established: Banská Bystrica, Spiš and Rožňava.

22 March – Maria Theresa forbade torture to obtain confessions.

5 August – School districts were formed to administer school matters, at the suggestion of Jozef Ürményi, the chairman of the education commission. In Slovakia they were headquartered in Bratislava, Banská Bystrica and Košice.

9 November – The newly erected Theater of the Estates, today the Slovak National Theater, opened in Bratislava.

30 November – A new Evangelical church on Konventná Street in Bratislava, the so-called Large Church, was consecrated.

■ **1777**

22 February – The musician Francis Riegler organized a concert in his home in Bratislava at which 30 musicians performed.

22 August – Maria Theresa issued the regula

tion entitled **Ratio educationis** concerningthe reorganization of the system of education in the monarchy.

24 August – The last lectures were given at **Trnava University,** ending almost 150 years of its existence. On 26 September Queen Maria Theresa directed that the university move to Buda.

November – A royal academy opened in Trnava with a law faculty and a philosophical faculty.

■ **1778**

13 March – A war between Prussia and the Habsburgs erupted over the Bavarian succession.

– The population in the royal free and mining cities of Slovakia consisted of 58,122 males, of which 36,770 were adults: 7,590 artisans and merchants, 6,072 journeymen, and 10,133 hired day-workers and servants. Females numbered 62,327, of which 14,006 were servants and hired day-workers. There were 1,225 orphans registered.

– The city schools in Slovakia were attended by 8,793 male and 2,238 female pupils.

■ **1779**

13 May – Emissaries of Maria Theresa and the Prussian king, Frederick II, signed a peace treaty in Těšín.

– Samuel Tešedík, an Evangelical pastor, founded the Agricultural-Industrial Institute in Sarvas. Young people from the villages were educated in practical subjects at this, the first specialized agricultural school in Hungary.

At the Threshold of the Modern Era (1780 – 1848)

A complicated process that transformed a society of estates into a civil society also took place in central Europe during the nineteenth century. Four sovereigns reigned during the first stage, 1780–1847. The brothers Joseph II and Leopold II were representatives of enlightenment ideas and reforms. During the reign of the former, enlightenment absolutism climaxed, removed class differentiation and prejudices, and laid the foundations for equality before the law. Joseph II attempted to transform the complex Habsburg federation into a unified state. German was introduced as the official language to replace Latin and, at the same time, the cultivation of the vernacular languages was supported. The elimination of privileges, together with a general modernization, also raised national consciousness. The nation was becoming so important a value that it began to be associated with political institutions, especially with the state (national state). Thus, in this period, another complicated process took place, traditionally called the national revival; it is now more precisely called the formation of modern nations. National movements of differing strength and unequal influence engaged in this process in central Europe. Even their programs and concepts of the nation and state were different. One advocated the principles of national equality, the second the assimilation of minority nationalities and the creation of a state consisting of a single nation. The second concept was represented by modern Magyar nationalism. Its rapid ascent was associated with the outrage of the Hungarian middle nobility at the radical reforms of Joseph II. During the resistance to Josephinism, traditional Hungarian nationalism began to be identified with Magyarism, Hungarian was advocated as the language of the homeland and the Magyars were considered as the only repository of civilization in Hungary. This was the foundation of the Magyarization that the Magyar reform movement regarded as part of a general modernization.

The first generation of Slovak national revivers advocated the enlightenment and Josephinian reforms, promoted the advancement of education, the resolution of language questions, and emphasized the antiquity of the Slovaks. They developed the Great Moravian and Cyril- Methodian tradition and founded learned societies and associations. However, they did not show that they were able to overcome the different concepts of the nation that were a result of various confessional traditions. The Catholic followers of Bernolák regarded the Slovaks as a distinct tribe (nation) and therefore codified a literary language (Bernolák's Slovak). Conversely, Evangelical intellectuals (George Ribay, Ján Hrdlička, Ondrej Plachý, Samuel Rožnay, and Bohuslav Tablic), faithful to their intellectual tradition, considered the Slovaks and the Czechs a single tribe and the language of the Protestant Czech Bible the Slovak literary language. This dualism complicated the development of Slovak national life and slowed the creation of national unity and Slovak politics. Much time and energy was required to overcome this.

The French revolution hampered rather than aided enlightenment reforms in central Europe. Its terror called forth a defensive reaction in the monarchy. Emperor Francis II forsook the path of reform and renewed a „proven" form of government. The „new" absolutism was definitively confirmed and established after the Congress of Vienna. Its leading representative was the most significant Austrian politician of the first half of the nineteenth century, Prince Clement Wenceslas Metternich. He obtained great power, especially during the reign of the incompetent Ferdinand V. In Hungary, however, even at this time, absolutism could not be completely implemented. The Habsburgs had to share power with the traditional organs of the estates, in which the Magyar noble opposition gradually obtained important positions. During the 1820s, a second generation of Slovak revivers were opposed to its conception of „one state – one nation" and the emerging policy of assimilation. In many political works (national defenses) they challenged the legitimacy of Magyarization and the superiority of the Magyars, while they defended the principles of federalism and the equality of nations. They found support in the idea of Slavic mutuality. The Slovak revivers, especially Ján Kollár and Pavol Jozef Šafárik, were among the leading creators of the idea of Slavic mutuality.

During the 1830s, the wave of revolutions in Europe, the revolt of peasants in eastern Slovakia that confirmed that serfdom was not sustainable, and the lack of industrial development and insufficient capital in Hungary had a significant impact upon the political thought of the younger generation. On the Magyar side the followers of Kossuth did not hide their radical opposition to the policies of Vienna or their support for radical Magyarization. On the Slovak side the followers of Štúr rejected the isolation of the older national revivers in their studies. They wanted to appeal to the public and to lay the foundations for independent Slovak politics. They urged the large-scale modernization of life and the advancement of the non- privileged classes, the common people. Due to patient, day-by-day work they overcame the interior weakness of the national movement and the absence of any important center. The strengthening of national life was part of this modernization. They overcame divisions in the movement by identifying with the idea of the national particularity of the Slovaks and by codifying a new literary language (Štúr's Slovak). They co-operated with the followers of Bernolák. With them, they organized the basis of a movement and created a Slovak political program. Many of their reform goals (with the exception of national rights) were achieved at the beginning of the revolution of 1848, which brought the long era of feudalism to a close.

■ **1780**
1 January – The very first newspaper in Hungarian, *Magyar hírmondó,* was issued in Bratislava.
29 November – Maria Theresa died. Her son, Joseph II, became the Hungarian and Czech king (King of Bohemia). However, he did not present himself for coronation and thus the Hungarian nobility in particular referred to him by the derisive nickname „Hat King". **Enlightenment absolutism** reached its height during his reign.
– Juraj Papánek published his work *History of the Slovak Nation – About the Kingdom and Kings of the Slovaks (Historia gentis Slavae – De regno regibusque Slavorum)* in Pécs. In it, he depicted Great Moravia as a Slovak state and produced a list of old Slovak kings, by which he sought to strengthen the claims of the Slovaks to an equal status in Hungary.

■ **1781**
13 October – Joseph II issued the **Edict (Patent) of Toleration.**

■ **1783**
1 July – The very first Slovak newspaper, the *Pressburg News (Prešpurské noviny)* began to be published in Bratislava. It promoted enlightenment ideas. Its editor, Štefan Leška, published it twice a week in Slovakicized Czech. It ceased publication around the middle of 1787.
9 December – Joseph II directed that the Vice-Regency Council be transferred from Bratislava to Buda and later took the Hungarian crown jewels to Vienna. Thus, the impor-

tance of Bratislava declined significantly and Buda was raised to the status of capital city of Hungary. However, the coronation of the sovereign continued to take place in Bratislava and the Hungarian diet met there until 1848.
– Jozef Ignác Bajza published the novel *The Adventures and Experience of the Youth, Rene (René mládenca príhodi a skúsenosti)* in which he unsuccessfully attempted to elevate the every-day language of the common people to the status of a literary language.

■ **1784**
11 May – Joseph II ordered the introduction of German to replace Latin as the official language in the central, county, and city organs of Hungary. This elicited strong opposition from the Hungarian **nobility** and the growth of Magyar nationalism.
14 May – The Royal Academy (1777) began to function in Bratislava after being transferred from Trnava.
1 June – One of the two Catholic general seminaries in Hungary, established by edict of the ruler, opened in Bratislava. It educated priests in the spirit of the enlightenment, taught them practical disciplines and a knowledge of the native language, so that they would be able to disseminate culture among the believers. The Catholic seminaries provided a strong impulse for the activities of **followers of Bernolák.**
– Juraj Sklenár published the work *The oldest location of Great Moravia and the first invasion of it by the Magyars (Vetustissimus Magnae Moraviae situs).* He placed Great Moravia

in the region of Morava in Serbia. In this way he wanted to demonstrate that the Slovaks had not surrendered to the old Magyars and thus the Slovaks were not a subjugated nation, but had a claim to equal rights in Hungary.

■ **1785**

18 March – The ruler dissolved local county government and divided Hungary into ten regions (districts), each headed by an appointed royal commissioner. The regions of Nitra, Banská Bystrica and Košice were located on the territory of Slovakia. By the nationalization of public administration and the ending of noble self-government, Joseph II wanted to restrict the power of the nobility, strengthen the centralization of the empire, and consolidate the **Josephinian reforms.**

May – O. Plachý began to publish in Banská Bystrica the *Old Newspaper of Literary Art (Staré noviny literního umění)*, in the language of the Protestant Czech Bible. He published articles that promoted enlightenment reforms, scientific discoveries and the principles of equality and tolerance. It ceased publication at the beginning of 1786.

22 August – Joseph II issued an edict on the **abolition of servitude.**

■ **1786**

1 January – A civil code was issued followed by a criminal code, about one year later, based upon the principle of the equality of all classes before the law. Capital punishment was restricted to periods of martial law only. Joseph II gradually separated the judicial from the political power.

September – The first international congress of mining and foundry specialists took place in Sklené Teplice. Its participants studied the amalgamation method of producing silver, which was demonstrated by Ignác Anton Born in the foundry newly established in the town. The very first international society for mining sciences was founded at the congress.

27 December – The king issued a decree concerning the cultivation of the native languages by which he increased interest in their ad-

vancement. This also encouraged a group of Slovak students at the general seminary in Bratislava to create a group of patriotic philologists that prepared a codification of the first literary language (Bernolák's Slovak). The members of this circle later formed the core of the **followers of Bernolák**.

■ **1787**

Anton Bernolák completed the work *Philological-critical dissertation concerning Slovak Letters (Dissertatio philologico-critica de litteris Slavorum)*. This Latin work codified the first literary Slovak language based on a cultivated western Slovak, which had developed largely due to the work of **Trnava University**.

■ **1788/1789**

Winter – The Hungarian nobility took a stand against the obligatory purchase of grain for the imperial army and the drafting of recruits into its ranks. The imperial power resorted to expropriation. This only increased the opposition of the nobility.

■ **1789**

10 February – The ruler issued a new tax code. Compulsory serf labor was replaced by a monetary payment and the tax obligations of the serfs, who kept 70 per cent of their income, were reduced. The state received 12.5 per cent and the landlords and communities 17.5 per cent. This, the most radical reform of Joseph II, was a daring step towards the abolition of serfdom.

■ **1790**

26 January – Because of the great opposition of the nobility, Joseph II on his deathbed revoked the **Josephinian reforms,** except for the Edict of Toleration and the abolition of servitude.

20 February – Joseph II died at the age of 50. His younger brother Leopold II, also an advocate of enlightenment reforms, ascended the throne.

1 April – The first theatrical performance in the new city theater in Košice took place in German. Košice was the sixth city in Hungary to have a permanent theater after Pest, Bratislava, Sopron, Buda and Sibiu. It could seat 1000 people. At the end of the 18th century the population of Košice was about 8,000 people.

10 June – After 26 years a diet of the Hungarian estates met in Buda and on 11 November relocated to Bratislava. It forced the sovereign to recognize Hungary as an „independent" kingdom with its own constitution. The diet reserved the right to negotiate modifications in the relations between serfs and the nobility and confirmed the privileges of the nobility. It accepted the first law giving preference to Hungarian (the establishment of departments of Hungarian at universities, academies and gymnasia, where Hungarian became a non-compulsory subject). This marked the beginning of **Magyarization**.

– Anton Bernolák published a grammar of the new Slovak literary language in Latin (*Grammatica Slavica*).

– Juraj Alojz Belnai published in Bratislava his *Demands of the non-noble population of Hungary (Reflexiones cunctorum Hungariae civium...),* a work addressed to the Hungarian diet. In it he demanded equality of persons, access of the educated non-nobles to high office, freedom of ownership, and popular representation for all classes.

■ **1791**
– Wolfgang Kempelen, a native of Bratislava, published the work *Mechanism of Human Language together with the Description of a Talking Machine (Mechanismus der menschlichen Sprache nebst der Beschreibung einer sprechenden Maschine)* in Vienna. One of his inventions was a machine that mimicked the human voice. The nature of this „talking machine" is still shrouded in mystery.

■ **1792**
1 March – Leopold II died. His son Francis II became Holy Roman emperor and king of Hungary and Czechia (Bohemia).
24 May – The king opened a session of the

diet in Buda. It accepted the second Magyarization law, which introduced Hungarian as a compulsory subject in all schools in Hungary. The broader knowledge of Hungarian would eventually make it the official language of the country.

First half – Followers of Bernolák founded the **Slovak Learned Society** in Trnava.

– Juraj Fándly issued the first volume of his most significant educational work, *The Diligent Domestic and Agricultural Steward (Piľní domajší a poľní hospodár).*

■ **1793**
9 September – An assembly of Gemer County protested against more severe censorship and demanded the freedom of the press.

– Juraj Fándly published, in Latin, *A Brief History of the Slovak Nation (Compendiata historia gentis Slavae)* in Trnava. Drawing upon the work of Juraj Papánek, he depicted Great Moravia as a state of Slovaks and Svätopluk as their king. He also responded to the first Magyarization laws by demanding the establishment of departments of Slovak at the higher schools and the Pest University.

■ **1794**
May – Ignác Martinovič founded two secret organizations in Pest that comprised the nucleus of the **Hungarian Jacobins**.

■ **1795**
20 May – Five participants in the Jacobin movement were beheaded in Buda, including Ignác Martinovič and Jozef Hajnóczy.
24 October – Austria, Russia and Prussia partitioned remnant Poland.

– A decree was issued concerning the censorship of all publications and the review of books from the time of Joseph II, and forbidding the works of French authors.

■ **1796**
6 November – The king ceremonially opened a session of the Hungarian diet in Bratislava. It approved military assistance (50,000 soldiers)

to the imperial government in Vienna for the war against France.

12 November – The Hungarian diet elected as **palatine** the younger brother of Francis II, the Archduke Joseph, who had been viceroy until then. He held this office until his death in 1847.

■ **1797**

Gregory Berzeviczy published in Levoča his first national economic work, *Commerce and Industry in Hungary (De commercio et industria Hungariae)*. In it he criticized the backward conditions in Hungary and argued for free enterprise and free trade.

■ **1798**

Martin Schwartner, a native of Kežmarok and an outstanding political scientist, published the *Statistics of the Kingdom of Hungary (Statistik des Königreichs Ungarn)* in Pest that made public important information about contemporary life in Hungary.

■ **1800**

The first factory for stoneware in Hungary was established in Kremnica. During the 1840s its products were considered the best in Hungary. About a year later the same kind of industry was established in Košice as a joint-stock company.

■ **1801**

31 August – Archduke Charles became the president of the Court Military Council (Hofkriegsrat). He immediately began to reform the less than efficient imperial army (he abolished life-long service, required more civil behavior by officers towards the private soldiers, a simpler way of achieving a general mobilization, and the like).

■ **1803**

12 December – The Department of Czechoslavonic Language and Literature began to function at the Evangelical lyceum in Bratislava and was headed, until 1850, by Professor Martin Palkovič. During the 1830s and 40s,

the nucleus of the Slovak national movement **(followers of Štúr)** formed within the department.

■ **1804**

11 August – Francis II proclaimed himself the hereditary emperor of Austria as Francis I.

– The diocese of Košice was established by separating it from the Bishopric of Eger. Its first bishop was Andrew Szabó, the former rector of the General Seminary in Bratislava.

■ **1805**

17 October – A session of the Hungarian diet began in Bratislava. It passed laws that enabled the counties and the courts to conduct business and correspond with the highest imperial and Hungarian offices in Hungarian. In Slovakia this was fully or partially respected only in Hont, Bratislava, Zemplín and Novohrad counties.

15 November – French units occupied Bratislava two days after entering Vienna and prior to the battle of Austerlitz (Slavkov) (2 December 1805).

26 December – The Peace of Bratislava, which confirmed the victory of Napoleon at Austerlitz, the Battle of the Three Emperors, was signed in the Primate's Palace. The Habsburg monarchy lost Tyrol, Venice, Dalmatia and Istria but obtained Salzburg. It had to recognize the hegemony of France in Italy and in southern and western Germany.

– A state arms manufacture, one of the largest in Hungary, was established in Liptovský Hrádok. Four years later Jozef Kraft established a similar munitions plant in Banská Bystrica.

■ **1806**

6 August – Francis II resigned the dignity of Emperor of the Holy Roman Empire of the German Nation. After one thousand years the Holy Roman Empire ceased to exist.

4 November – The king issued a new (second) *Education order (Ratio educationis)* for Catholic schools. It ordered that instruction in the primary schools take place in the native language. In higher schools instruction in practical subjects (natural sciences, geography, architecture, etc.) was expanded and Hungarian was to be taught as a compulsory subject. It also recommended the establishment of schools for girls.

– The two-headed eagle was officially adopted as the coat of arms of the Austrian Empire and black and gold as its colors. Joseph Haydn had composed its national anthem already in 1796. Red, white and green became the colors of Hungary.

– In Levoča Gregory Berzeviczy published anonymously his most significant work, *Concerning the Situation and Character of Small Farmers in Hungary (De conditione et indole rusticorum in Hungaria)*, copies of which were confiscated. In it he criticized the privileges of the nobility, suggested the abolition of compulsory serf labor, the taxation of the nobility and the attainment of the equality of people.

■ 1807

30 August – A department of forestry was established at the academy in Banská Štiavnica. Its first professor was Heinrich David Wilckens. On 6 October 1846 the school received a new constitution and name, the Royal Academy of Mining and Forestry.

– Fourteen mining and iron entrepreneurs from Gemer joined together to establish the Muráň Union. It owned several blast furnaces and iron ore mines and specialized in the production of pig iron. Until the 1850s official business was conducted in Slovak.

■ 1808

13 September – The Malohont Learned Society was established. Its members were primarily Evangelical clergy and yeomen. Its most prominent members were Matej Holko, Jr. and Ján Feješ. It advocated national tolerance, Hungarian patriotism and popularized new scientific discoveries. It published 25 volumes of an annual in Latin (*Sollenia)* and had a noteworthy library in Vyšný Skálnik. It was dissolved in 1855.

■ 1809

8 February – The royal court in Vienna decided to initiate a new war against Napoleon. Led by Archduke Charles, nearly 200,000 soldiers marched into Bavaria at the beginning of April where, however, they were defeated by Napoleon.

13 May – After a rapid advance, Napoleon occupied Vienna. Two days later he turned to the „Hungarian nation" and appealed for it to rise up against the Habsburgs and declare the independence of Hungary. The frightened nobility did not respond to the appeal.

14 July – French units occupied Bratislava after a siege and bombardment of several weeks. Napoleon decisively defeated the Archduke Charles at the battle of Wagram. In the summer they blew up Devín castle.

8 October – Prince Clement Wenceslas Metternich, until then the Austrian ambassador in France, became the minister of foreign affairs of the monarchy (until 1848) after the resignation of Count Johann Filip Stadion.

■ 1810

16 May – The **Learned Society of the Mining Region** was founded at the parsonage of Bohuslav Tablic in Kostolné Moravce. It was a counter-weight to the learned societies that advocated the spread of Hungarian and **Magyarization**. It published economic and geographic-historical works and was concerned with investigating the native country, ethnography and the natural sciences. It helped to establish the Department of the Czechoslavonic Language at the lyceum in Banská Štiavnica.

■ 1811

15 March – The bankruptcy of the state was proclaimed throughout the monarchy. It had been caused by the war against Napoleon. Paper money was devalued to one-fifth of its previous value.

2 September – The Hungarian diet met in Bratislava. It unsuccessfully demanded the complete **Magyarization** of education, opposed the financial policies of the court, the use of new paper money in Hungary, and the imposition upon Hungary of one-half of the state debt of the monarchy. The sovereign prorogued its session on 26 May 1812. The next diet was called only 13 years later. This concluded the period of cooperation of Vienna with the Hungarian estates.

– The mining and iron entrepreneurs in Gemer founded the Rimava Coalition. In 1831, Slovakia produced 78 per cent of the pig iron and 64 per cent of the cast-iron within Hungary.

■ 1812
14 March – Austria and France signed a treaty of alliance in Paris. The Austrian monarchy obligated itself to establish auxiliary units made up of 30,000 soldiers to assist in Napoleon's invasion of Russia.

3 July – Professor G. Palkovič began to publish the *Weekly or Imperial-Royal National News (Týdenník aneb císařské královské národní noviny)* in Bratislava. It was published until 1818.

10 August – The ruler issued a regulation directed against **Magyarization**. The counties and courts had to conduct business in the language spoken by the population. In subsequent years the attempts to Magyarize the public administration weakened.

■ 1813
28 – 31 January – The Austrian monarchy signed a truce with France. It sought to play the role of a mediator between France and its enemies. But, due to the intransigence of Napoleon, even Austria declared war on France.

■ 1814
22 May – Count John Hunyady organized the first horse derby in Hungary in Mojmírovce.

18 September – The **Congress of Vienna** began to discuss peace and a new order in Europe.

■ 1816
1 June – A new currency, devalued by 40 per cent, was placed into circulation in the Habsburg monarchy. At the same time the sover-eign ordered that an Austrian national bank be established.

– Francis I ordered the establishment of a new Greek-Catholic bishopric in Prešov.

– A metallurgical world congress, concerned with the smelting of gold-bearing ores, took place in Banská Štiavnica.

■ 1817
19 May – Count Juraj Sedlnitzky was named as the president of the supreme police and censorship office by Francis I. Until 1848 he set up such an ingenious police system with a net of secret agents that, in this period, the monarchy was a model police state.

■ 1818
July 1818 to **1820** – A wave of discontent and riots, with peasants demanding better social conditions and refusing to pay local taxes in cash, took place on the property of the Pálffys in the Malacky area. About 7,000 serfs armed themselves. Only the intervention of the army prevented the riots from turning into armed conflict.

■ 1819
12 June – Alexander Rudnay became the archbishop of Esztergom. He cooperated with followers of Bernolák and supported the publication of Slovak religious literature.

19 November – In Spišská Kapitula, the bishop of Spiš, Ján Ladislav Pyrker, established the first institute for teachers in Hungary. Its organizer was a follower of Bernolák, Juraj Páleš and the language of instruction was the Slovak language of Bernolák (Bernolák's Slovak).

▣ 1821
25 May – The sovereign named Prince Metternich as the House, Court and State Chancellor. After Francis II he was the second most influential person in the monarchy. The political system of this era is often referred to as **Metternichian absolutism**.

■ 1822
8 September – A church synod for all of

Hungary began in Bratislava. On the initiative of Cardinal Alexander Rudnay, it decided to translate the Bible into the languages of the nations of the Kingdom of Hungary. The translation into Bernolák's Slovak was prepared by Canon Juraj Palkovič. The first volume was published in 1829 in Esztergom, the second volume appeared in 1832.

– The counties in Hungary refused to pay taxes in non-debased silver currency and to equip 23,000 new soldiers. The emperor forbade communication between the counties and appointed commissioners for them. The intervention of the army, and the imprisonment and the dismissal of many county officials definitely suppressed the open opposition of the counties.

■ **1823**

– Samuel Mičko had a chemical bleaching plant built in Bardejov. In it domestically produced or manufactured linen received its final treatment. The bleachery was larger than facilities in other cities and annually treated 186,000 meters of cloth. At this time, up to 10, 000,000 meters of linen cloth with a value of 5 – 6 million florins were produced domestically or in manufactures in the northern region. Usually peddlers (mainly from Orava) and Orthodox merchants (Greeks, Serbs, Armenians) marketed the cloth.

■ **1824**

Ján Kollár published his *Daughter of the Slavs (Slávy dcera)* in Pest. Other, substantially expanded editions were issued in 1832, 1845 and 1852. This work particularly influenced the younger intellectuals of all Slavic nations by its new optimistic concept of nation, patriotism and **Slavic mutuality**.

– The Club of Slovak Students was established at the Evangelical lyceum in Kežmarok.

■ **1825**

15 September –The **Hungarian diet** began its session in Bratislava. It discussed agricultural reforms, the problem of small peasant farms and extending the use of Hungarian for official business. The deputies did not demonstrate any desire for change and did not pass any important laws. The diet concluded on 18 August 1827.

– In Buda, Canon Juraj Palkovič began to publish Bernolák's six-volume *A Slovak, Czech, Latin, German, Hungarian Dictionary (Slovár slovenskí, česko-laťinsko-ňemecko-uherskí)*. It contained 5,302 pages and glossed 31,000 words.

– A *Reader (Čítanka)* by Ján Kollár was published in Buda in which the author used a Slovakized Czech. About one year later, in his work in German, *A History of the Slavic Language and Literature according to all Dialects (Geschichte der slawischen Sprache und Literatur nach allen Mundarten)* Pavol Jozef Šafárik differentiated between the Czech and Slovak languages and characterized the Slovaks as a distinct nation. As a reaction to the negative attitude of the Czechs, Kollár began to adhere consistently to the Czech literary language and the idea of a Czechoslovak tribal unity.

– Bedřich Schnierch constructed the first suspended roof in the world in Banská Bystrica. This type of construction has been used a great deal, especially in the 20th century (e.g. the Olympic stadiums in Munich and Tokyo).

■ **1826**

30 April – At a conference in Pest, Ján Kollár agreed with Martin Hamuljak, Ján Herkeľ and Ján Koiš to establish the Slovak Readers' Club. It was the first common cultural organization of the followers of Bernolák and the adherents of the Czech literary language.

29 September – The king named Count Francis Anton Kolowrat-Liebstein as the interior minister. He had a decisive influence upon internal policy while his rival, Clement Wenceslas Metternich, controlled foreign policy.

– Ján Herkeľ published his *General Foundations of the Slavic Language (Elementa universalis linguae slavonicae)* in Buda. In it, alongside the rules of a „Slavic Esperanto", he also developed the idea of the literary unity of the Slavs.

■ **1828**
– The inventor Štefan Anián Jedlík, a native of Zemné near Nové Zámky, constructed and demonstrated to students in Gyor the very first motor which worked on the electro-magnetic principle (electro-motor).

■ **1829**
August – At the Evangelical lyceum in Bratislava the **Czechoslavonic Society** was established. It became the nucleus of the Slovak national movement during the mid-1830s.

■ **1830**
22 August – Gašpar Fejérpataky-Belopotocký founded a theater company in Liptovský Mikuláš, which presented the new play of Ján Chalupka, *Kocúrkovo* (Podunk, Hicksville). This presentation marks the beginnings of Slovak amateur theater.

11 September – The session of the Hungarian diet that accepted new Magyarization laws (correspondence in Hungarian between the Vice-Regency Council and judicial institutions, decisions of the courts in Hungarian, a knowledge of Hungarian as a condition for holding office) began in Bratislava. Due especially to Count Széchényi, a **Magyar reform movement** that advocated modernization reforms was established. The diet concluded on 20 December 1830 because of the spread of cholera.

28 September – Ferdinand V was crowned king of Hungary. This was the last coronation to be held in Bratislava.

29 November – Šariš County introduced the use of Hungarian in government offices and the judiciary. The complete or partial conduct of business in Hungarian was gradually introduced in other Slovak counties, the last of which were Spiš (1840) and Turiec (1841).

■ **1831**
29 May – Hungary renewed a military cordon on the border with Galicia because of the cholera epidemic. However, it was too late, for cholera spread quickly, especially in east-ern Slovakia, and penetrated the whole of Hungary.

19 July – The first mass expression of discontent occurred in Košice. The population suspected that officials had poisoned them intentionally, withheld anti-cholera medicine, and failed to implement preventive measures. The discontent grew into the **insurrection of the peasants of eastern Slovakia.**

4 November – The ruler dissolved the martial law courts (proclaimed on 14 August 1831). By then, 119 of the peasant rebels had been executed and more than 4,000 had been condemned to prison or to receive corporal punishment. Other accused received relatively lesser penalties from the regular courts.

■ **1832**
20 April – Professor Juraj Palkovič began to publish the journal *Tatranka*.

– The first textile factory in Hungary to introduce a steam driven machine was the clothing factory in Halič.

– The first sugar mill in Hungary was built in Veľké Úľany by the businessman Mikuláš Lačný. In 1850 there were 21 sugar mills in Slovakia and 63 in the Kingdom of Hungary.

19 December – Deliberations of the **Hungarian diet** began in Bratislava. It accepted another Magyarization law (Hungarian became the language of law, the official language for judicial proceedings), at least a partial liberation from feudal obligations (the right of serfs freely to dispose of their property and the produce of their farming), and, by imposing a tax on urbarial (communal) land, questioned the tax-exemptions of the nobility. At the so-called long diet, which concluded on 2 May 18?? the young, radical wing under the leadership of Louis Kossuth was able to gain the upper hand in the **Magyar reform movement.**

■ **1833**
5 January – On the initiative of J. B. Guoth, the Slavic Medical Society was founded by a group of Slovaks studying medicine in Pest.

– H. Klein, a friend of Ludwig van Beethoven, founded the Society for Church Music in Bratislava. In this way the rich musical life in Bratislava achieved an organized form.

January – Michal Kunič published his German work *Reflections concerning the Establishment of the Hungarian Language (Reflexionen über die Begründung der magyarischen Sprache)* in Zagreb. In it he refuted the arguments of the supporters of Magyarization. Even more pronounced in its opposition to them was the work of Samuel Hojč, *Do we have to become Magyars? (Sollen wir Magyaren werden?)*, also written in German.

– The owners of several ironworks in Štítnická dolina founded the joint-stock company Concordia.

■ **1834**
1 August – The **Club of the Devotees of Slovak Language and Literature** was founded in Buda.

– Ľudovít Matej Šuhajda, an Evangelical pastor in the lower lands (southern Hungary), published his *Legal, Historical and Linguistic Aspects of Magyarism in Hungary (Der Magyarismus in Ungarn, in rechtlicher, geschichtlicher und sprachlicher Hinsicht)* in Leipzig in German. In the spirit of the equality of nations, he suggested the transformation of Hungary into a federal state of several nations.

■ **1835**
16 April – Alexander Boleslavín Vrchovský suggested the reorganization of the **Czechoslavonic Society** to make it a center of the national movement.

12 December – After the death of Francis I (II), the reorganized Privy State Council met. Archduke Louis became its president; its members were the Archduke Francis Charles, Francis Anton Kolowrat-Liebstein, and Prince Clement Wenceslas Metternich. Because of the mental incompetence of the new ruler, Ferdinand I (V), it was the most important imperial organ.

■ **1836**
February – The almanac *Fruits (Plody)*, the first ideological and literary manifesto of the

younger generation of Slovaks (**followers of Štúr**) who joined the Czechoslavonic Society was published in Bratislava.

24 April – On a commemorative outing to Devín Castle a group of students at the Bratislava Evangelical lyceum pledged themselves to be faithful to liberty, to cultivate the life of the nation, and to take second names of Slavonic origin.

Spring – On the model of Bratislava, a Czechoslavonic Society was also founded by students at the Evangelical lyceum in Banská Štiavnica.

– Karol Kuzmány published the almanac *Hronka* in Banská Bystrica. It promoted the values and views of Romanticism.

■ **1837**
1 February – The district conference appointed Ľudovít Štúr as the deputy professor of the Department of Czechoslavonic Language and Literature at the Bratislava Evangelical lyceum.

5 April – Due to a decision of the Vice-Regency Council banning student societies in Hungary (20 September 1836), the **Czechoslavonic Society** halted its activities. Its members began to gather in the Institute of Czechoslavonic Language and Literature (Slavic Institute, Slovak Institute).

End of June – A group of radical young Slovaks founded the secret society **Mutuality** (*Vzájomnosť*).

June – In Pest, Ján Kollár published in German the treatise *Concerning Literary Mutuality between the Various Tribes and Dialects of the Slavic Nation (Über die literarische Wechselseitigkeit zwischen den verschiedenen Stämmen und Mundarten der slawischen Nation)*. It was the most consistent justification of the idea of **Slavic mutuality.**

– The first workshop in the world equipped with a machine for braiding steel cable, which replaced hemp ropes in the mines, was put into operation in Štiavnické Bane.

– Construction began on the first horse-drawn railroad in Hungary, from Bratislava to Trnava. On 27 September 1840 the tracks reached Sv. Jur and on 1 June 1846 Trnava.

– Pavol Jozef Šafárik published in Prague *Slavic Antiquities (Slovanské starožitnosti)*, a work important for its information about ancient Slavic history.

■ **1838**
September – Since Ľudovít Štúr left to study in Halle, Benjamín Pravoslav Červenák assumed the position of deputy professor in the Department of Czechoslavonic Language and Literature.

■ **1839**
5 June – The Hungarian diet began deliberations in Bratislava which ended on 13 May 1840. New laws were passed permitting redemption from serfdom with the approval of the feudal lord, the settlement of Jews in the royal cities, and introducing the use of Hungarian in all political and judicial proceedings and as a subject at all levels of education.

■ **1840**
First quarter – A group of Slovak patriots prepared a petition to the Hungarian diet to halt the intensifying Magyarization and to cancel Magyarization laws in order to free national life. The petition did not exclude the option of establishing an independent Slovak diet.
May – Jozef Maximilián Petzval, a native of Spiš and professor at the University of Vienna, calculated the parameters for a lens that reduced by many times the time needed to expose and complete a daguerreotype.
8 – 11 September – A general convention of the Evangelical Church of the Augsburg Confession (Lutheran) took place in Pest and approved the policy of open **Magyarization**. Count Karol Zay, elected as general inspector, articulated the idea of a uni-national Hungary and advocated the use of Hungarian in all areas of Evangelical life as well as union with the Calvinists (Union).
September – Students at the Evangelical lyceum in Levoča issued the almanac *Jitřenka*, which supported the endeavors of the students in Bratislava. It elicited a wave of anti-Slovak reaction in Magyar circles that called for intensifying **Magyarization**.

– The Krompachy-Hornád Iron-Works Company was founded.

■ **1841**
The first two volumes of *Poems (Básne)* by Ján Hollý were published in Buda at the expense of the Club of Devotees of Slovak Language and Literature.
– In Leipzig, the playwright Ján Chalupka anonymously published in German *The Writings of Count Carl Zay (Schreiben des Grafen Carl Zay)* that repudiated the Magyarization policy in the Evangelical Church.
– Using the pseudonym Thomas Világosváry, Ján Pavol Tomášek, a professor at the Levoča Evangelical lyceum published in Hungarian his work, *Language Peace in Hungary* in Zagreb.
– An amateur theater company, called the Nitra Slovak National Theater, was founded in Sobotište, fulfilling the ideas of the **followers of Štúr** concerning a theater for the common people.

■ **1842**
5 January – A savings bank began to operate in Bratislava as the first banking institution in Slovakia. During the first year, deposits reached 480,000 florins. For a long time the savings bank was among the largest in Hungary.
5 June – A Slovak deputation led by Pavol Jozefi delivered the **Slovak petition to the throne** to the president of the state conference in Vienna, the Archduke Louis. It also visited Prince Clement Wenceslas Metternich and Francis Anton Kolowrat-Liebstein.
15 – 16 June – At the general convention of the Evangelical Church in Pest, a sharp conflict erupted between the supporters of the petition to the throne and the pro-Magyar party. The latter characterized the former as betrayers of the native land and of Protestantism.
14 November – The palatine, the Archduke Joseph, received the Evangelical superintendent, Pavol Jozefi, and promised to fulfill the just demands contained in the appeal.
27 November – At a ceremonial session of the Hungarian Academy of Sciences, Stephen

Széchenyi spoke against the radical Magyarization of Louis Kossuth and called for respect for the rights of non-Magyars in Hungary. However, Széchenyi assumed that they would gradually and naturally be assimilated.
– Karol Kuzmány led the group that published the *Evangelical Hymnal (Zpěvník evanjelický)* in Pest.
– The first volume of the *Catholic Hymnal (Katolický spevník)* by Ján Hollý was published. The second volume was published in Vienna in 1846.
– Ján Čaplovič published the German pamphlet *Slavism and Pseudomagyarism (Slavismus und Pseudomagyarismus)* in Leipzig, which argued against the views of Karol Zay and explained that Magyarization was being advocated mainly by those who themselves had been Magyarized. The pamphlet was one of the numerous publications from the 1830s and 40s that called for the equality of nations in Hungary and their peaceful co-existence.

■ 1843

14 February – At a conference in Bratislava, Ľudovít Štúr, Ján Francisci, Samuel Vozár, Ján Kalinčiak, Ján Gáber-Lovinský and Samuel Štúr agreed on the need to codify a new literary language. It was to express the idea of the national particularity of the Slovaks to which the **followers of Štúr** adhered.
8 March – The Palatine Joseph challenged Karol Zay to take a stand for the renewal of national toleration in the Evangelical schools that Zay promised.
18 May – The palatine opened the session of the Hungarian diet in Bratislava, which lasted until 13 November 1844. The diet rejected modernizing social reforms but introduced a law that required the use of Hungarian in all areas of public administration and judicial proceedings.
11 – 16 July – Ľudovít Štúr, Jozef Miloslav Hurban and Michal Miloslav Hodža agreed in Hlboké on the basic rules for a new literary language (Štúr's Slovak) and decided to prepare a grammar for it based on that which had been developed primarily by Štúr in the works *The Slovak Language or the Necessity*

of Writing in this Language (Nárečja slovenskuo alebo potreba písaňja v tomto nárečí) and *The Study of Language and Slovak Literature (Náuka reči a literatúry slovenskej)*, both published in 1846.
31 December – The Bratislava convention of the Evangelical Church, after an extensive and lengthy investigation, dismissed Ľudovít Štúr from his position as deputy professor of the Department for Czechoslavonic Language and Literature. Štúr subsequently devoted himself only to scholarly, journalistic and political activity.
– The Czech Count Leopold Thun published in German *The Place of the Slovaks in Hungary (Die Stellung der Slowaken in Ungarn)*, in which he took issue with Francis Pulszky who had advocated the Magyarization and assimilation of the Slovaks.
– Ľudovít Štúr published in Leipzig in German *The Complaints and Laments of the Slavs in Hungary over the Illegal Encroachments of the Magyars (Die Beschwerden und Klagen der Slawen in Ungarn über die gesetzwidrigen Uebergriffe der Magyaren)*. This treatise analyzed Magyarization practices and emphasized that language is the most characteristic feature of each nation and a condition of its existence.

■ 1844

5 – 6 March – Twenty-two students withdrew from the Evangelical lyceum in Bratislava to protest against the dismissal of Ľudovít Štúr. The majority of them went to Levoča. Shortly thereafter a center of the young Slovak movement was established there. On this occasion Janko Vlastimil Matúška composed the text of the anthem *Lightening Flashes above the Tatras (Nad Tatrou sa blýska)*, which is now the national anthem of the Slovak Republic.
19 May – A Slovak delegation presented a new **Slovak Appeal to the Throne** to the Archduke Louis in Vienna.
June and **July** – Jozef Miloslav Hurban published the second edition of the almanac *Nitra* in Bratislava. It was the first publication in Štúr's Slovak. It presented and defended the idea of Slovak national particularity.

26 – 28 August – The constituting assembly of the first nation-wide cultural club **Tatrín** took place in Liptovský Mikuláš.

6 October – Louis Kossuth, Count Casimir Batthyányi and their colleagues founded a club in Bratislava to protect the Hungarian economy from cheaper imports from the western part of the monarchy. Its members were obliged to purchase only domestic products.

■ **1845**

9 February – On the initiative of Samuel Jurkovič, the Farmers' Club was founded as the first self-help credit cooperative on the European continent. Modern entrepreneurship also was gradually implemented in Slovakia.

1 August – The first copy of the **Slovak National News** *(Slovenské národné noviny)* was published in Bratislava.

6 August – At a meeting of the Tatrín Club in Liptovský Mikuláš, its participants were introduced to the lyrical poem by A. Sládkovič, *Marína*, the first important work of art written in Štúr's Slovak.

6 August – The constituting meeting of the Union of Slovak Youth took place. It was an association of student societies at the higher Evangelical schools. Ján Francisci, who worked at the lyceum in Levoča, became its president.

16 September – A group of young followers of Bernolák founded the Pohronský Association (Pohronský Spolok) in Banská Bystrica. It focused on cultural activities, education, the study of Slovak history, and language and literature. It contributed to a rapprochement with Evangelical intellectuals and to the strengthening of national unity.

– After long disputes, the German work of Ľ. Štúr, *The Nineteenth Century and Magyarism (Das neunzehnte Jahrhundert und der Magyarismus)*, in which he analyzed the basis of Magyarization, was published in Vienna.

■ **1846**

May – A volume of collected papers inspired by Kollár, *Arguments about the Need for a Single Literary Language for the Czechs, Moravians and Slovaks (Hlasové o potřebě jednoty spisovného jazyka pro Čechy, Moravany a Slováky)*, was published in Prague. In it the authors argued against the literary language of Štúr and the principle of the national particularity of the Slovaks.

12 – 16 June – Following the lead of students at the Catholic seminaries in Vienna and Trnava, seminarians in Pest declared their support for the new literary language. After the questionnaire project of Andrej Radlinský, Štúr agreed with such modifications of his language that would bring it closer to the Bernolák's version of literary Slovak.

9 – 17 August – The first industrial exposition on the territory of Slovakia took place in Košice and Prešov. The first such exhibition in Hungary had been held in Pest in 1842.

1 November – The first horse-drawn railroad in Hungary was put into service between Bratislava – Trnava – Sereď.

Fall – As a result of poor harvests and floods, famine spread through the northern counties of Slovakia and claimed thousands of victims. The result was a new wave of emigration to the lower lands (southern Hungary).

– Jozef Miloslav Hurban began to publish the journal *Slovak Views on science, arts and literature (Slovenskje pohladi na vedi, umeňja a literatúru)*, which helped to form views of Slovak history and culture.

■ **1847**

10 August – The fourth meeting of Tatrín Club took place at the parsonage of Jozef Urbanovský in Čachtice. At this meeting, a significant number of supporters of the Catholic Bernolák movement participated for the first time. This demonstrated the dynamic growth in the process of unifying the nation. The participants accepted Štúr's Slovak as the national literary language.

12 August – A central committee of the founders of **temperance clubs** was established, on the initiative of Štefan Závodník, at the parsonage of Juraj Holček in Veselé. It was to direct the activities of almost 500 temperance clubs in Slovakia.

Mid-September – At an audience with the new palatine Stephen, Ondrej Caban and Juraj Holček requested that he approve the by-laws of the Tatrín Club. The palatine received them with hostility.

11 November – The Palatine Stephen opened the last diet of the Hungarian estates held in Bratislava. It approved reforms advocated by the **Magyar reform movement.**

21 December – Ľudovít Štúr, the deputy for the city of Zvolen and the leading personality of the Slovak national movement, presented the Slovak political program to the diet in a speech which was also published in the **Slovak National News**. It demanded the abolition of serfdom, equality before the law and a guarantee of the basic national rights of the Slovaks.

26 December – A telegraph line between Vienna and Bratislava was put into service. In 1850 a telegraph line was installed from Bratislava through Štúrovo to Pest.

End of the year – Štefan Marko Daxner and Ján Francisci drafted a petition for the abolition of serfdom and for the conduct of official business in the county institutions in Slovak. They did not have time to present it to the diet because of the sudden outbreak of the 1848 revolution.

– The first firemen's corps in Slovakia was established in Prešov. Fire-fighting associations spread widely during the 1860s.

Between Vienna and Pest (1848 – 1867)

D ecisive struggles concerning the modernization of society in central Europe took place in the two decades between 1848 – 1867. They determined whether elements of harmony would be strengthened or contradictions multiplied. Especially during the eighteen revolutionary months of 1848 – 1849, the principles of societal organization changed radically. Centuries old serfdom and feudal differentiation into the privileged and unprivileged were eliminated and equality before the law was legislated. Absolutism disappeared. A constitutional system was introduced for the first time. The revolution opened the way for capitalism and a civil society. The nation became the new principle for organizing society. Life in the new milieu did not become more harmonious but rather more complicated. This was caused especially by conflicts between the yearnings of the representatives of the non-Magyars for national liberty, which had been subdued but which, after March 1848, rapidly rose to the surface, and the aims of the reform- oriented middle nobility, the leaders of the Magyar revolution. The latter preserved some of prerogatives of the estates, refused to recognize the rights of other nationalities of Hungary, and pursued a policy of Magyarization. The national movement did not call just for linguistic and cultural rights but also for autonomous status. These contradictions and the conflict between Kossuth and imperial Vienna concerning the competence of Hungary were manifested in a great civil war. On one side of the conflict was the Magyar revolution of Kossuth. On the other side were the non- Magyar nations and imperial Vienna, which promised to respect the equality of all nations and to transform the monarchy into a modern federal state (Austrian federalism).

For the first time, the Slovak question was at the center of political events. Even if it did not belong among the main problems of the revolution, „high politics" was seriously concerned with it. At least for a short time, the Slovak national movement created its first representative political organ, the Slovak National Council, led an armed struggle for national liberty and, for the first time, officially demanded the fulfillment of Slovak demands through constitutional law. It first struggled for the autonomy of Slovakia within the Kingdom of Hungary. From the fall of 1848 it sought secession from Hungary and an autonomous position within the monarchy. However, the Slovak representatives did not have strong support. Thus the attainment of their program depended especially upon imperial Vienna. In the monarchy, the traditional aristocratic forces, represented by the young Emperor Francis Joseph I, were victorious. They rejected liberal principles (the basic rights of citizens, representation, elections, federalism) and gave preference to proven values and the implementation of a consistent centralism which led to the renewal of absolutism. While neo-absolutism limited the gains of the revolution, it respected its chief aims and created the preconditions for the modernization of industry, transportation and education. The modest gains of the revolution in no way corresponded to the great energy expended by the Slovak representatives and Slovakia remained a part of the Kingdom of Hungary. However, during the 1850s Magyarization did not threaten Slovak national life.

Neo-absolutism merely „postponed" many problems. These reasserted themselves after its fall in 1860. The old conflicts and suppressed ambitions, especially the unresolved constitutional and national contradictions, emerged with a new urgency. The sovereign acknowledged the right to autonomy of the traditional historical units (the crown lands), not of the nationalities. The politically and economically very strong Hungarian constitutional opposition rejected this model. As in 1848 – 1849, it pursued a policy that would make Hungary into an independent country and its development as the Magyar national state. Its non-Magyar residents would have only modest language and cultural rights. This policy drove the non-Magyar politicians, including Slovaks, to intensified action. They rejected historic claims and demanded, on the basis of natural law (the ethnic principle), the guarantee of the equality of nationalities, the federalization of the monarchy as a whole, or of Hungary, and the recognition of autonomous constitutions for their lands. In the case of the politically weak Slovak national movement this was expressed especially by activities connected with the Memorandum of the Slovak Nation. Vienna responded to the radical demands of the Magyar constitutional opposition and the struggles of the non-Magyar movements by freezing constitutional conditions in Hungary. However, after defeat in the Austrian-Prussian war (the Seven Weeks War) in 1866, it was necessary to accept the Magyar constitutional concept. This was reflected in the constitutional arrangement between Austria and the Kingdom of Hungary (today characterized as the Austro-Hungarian Compromise). The Compromise concluded years of temporary arrangements and struggles for a constitutional transformation of the monarchy. The monarchy became a confederation of two states under the name Austria-Hungary. In Hungary the powerful position of the old aristocracy and the middle nobility was strengthened and the hegemony of the Magyars over other nations was definitively confirmed. The Compromise buried Slovak constitutional ambitions and opened the way to radical Magyarization.

■ **1848**

15 January – At a session of the diet, Ľudovít Štúr demanded the enactment of instruction in Slovak in lower schools and the use of the native language at divine worship services.

3 – 6 March – The Magyar reform movement, represented by Louis Kossuth, demanded in the diet the abolition of absolutism, equality before the law, and an independent Hungarian government.

6 March – At the diet, Štúr supported the demand for civil reforms and for the immediate abolition of serfdom.

13 March – Influenced by the French Revolution, an uprising in Vienna forced the resignation of the detested Prince Clement Wenceslas Metternich, eliminated **absolutism,** and opened the way to a **constitutional monarchy**.

15 March – A large assembly in Pest accepted the declaration that became a basis for the **March Laws** in the sphere of citizen rights and constitutional relations.

18 March – The Hungarian diet accepted the most important of the **March Laws**.

22 March – The miners in and around Banská Štiavnica demanded an improvement in their social conditions. The government pacified the movement only at the end of April.

23 March – Count Louis Batthyány presented the Hungarian government to the diet.

28 March – The **Liptov Demands** were accepted at a popular assembly in Liptovský Mikuláš.

27 – 30 March – The peasants in five villages of Hont County revolted under the leadership of the poet Janko Kráľ and the teacher Ján Rotarides. They demanded the complete abolition of serfdom, the right to use Slovak in offices and schools. After the revolt was suppressed, its leaders became some of the first prisoners of the new government.

31 March – In his article *The New World (Nový svet),* Ľudovít Štúr welcomed the revolutionary changes and expressed his hope that freedom would spread on the basis of national needs.

2 April – In Vienna, approximately two thousand people participated in the largest of a series of meetings of representatives of the Austrian Slavs. The most popular orator was Ľudovít Štúr.

11 April – The king signed new laws and closed the diet in Bratislava.

28 April – A popular assembly in Brezová pod Bradlom accepted the **Nitra Demands**.

5 May – As a reaction to peasant disturbances, anti- Jewish pogroms and the pace of the Slovak national movement, the Hungarian government and the palatine declared a state of martial law that restricted freedom of assembly and freedom of speech.

11 May – A small popular assembly at Ondrášová spa (part of Liptovský Mikuláš) proclaimed the **Demands of the Slovak Nation**.

12 May – Bertalan Szemere, the minister of the interior, ordered that a warrant be issued for the arrest of Ľudovít Štúr and then of Jozef Miloslav Hurban (on 22 May) and Michal Miloslav Hodža (on 1 June).

2 – 12 June – The **Slavic Congress** at which Jozef Miloslav Hurban presented the **Demands of the Slovaks and Ruthenians of Hungary** took place in Prague.

2 July – Jozef Miloslav Hurban spoke at the Croatian diet in Zagreb. Influenced by his fiery speech, the Croatian politicians promised to the Slovaks assistance in seeking a resolution of the Slovak question.

5 July – The **Hungarian diet** began discussions in Pest that were characterized by strong Magyar nationalism. It demanded that the competence of Hungarian government organs be broadened, the acceptance of laws concerning the formation of the Hungarian army (*honvéd*), and the issue of paper money (Kossuths). This led to growing tensions with Vienna.

20 August – The Bratislava-Vienna railway line was ceremonially put into service.

16 September – A **Slovak National Council** was established in Vienna.

18 – 28 September – The **September Uprising,** the first independent armed action of the Slovaks in modern history, took place.

19 September – In the name of the Slovak National Council, Ľudovít Štúr declared the independence of Slovakia from the Hungarian government (autonomy) at an assembly in Myjava.

28 September – A mob in Buda assassinated Francis Lamberg, the newly appointed royal commissioner and imperial military commander for Hungary.

3 October – The king dissolved the Hungarian diet, declared martial law in Hungary and named *Ban* Jozef Jelačič as the chief military commander. The Hungarian diet declared the manifesto to be illegal. Led by Louis Kossuth, a revolutionary Committee for the Defense of the Homeland assumed power. It fulfilled the role of the provisional government of Hungary until April 1849.

6 October – A revolt erupted in Vienna in defense of Kossuth's power and against strengthening the positions of the conservatives and the ambitions of the Slavs. The king took refuge in Olomouc and the majority of the diet in Kroměříž. Led by Alfred Windischgrätz and Jozef Jelačič, the imperial army suppressed the uprising only at the end of October.

26 October – Viliam Šulek, Karol Holuby and, later, four other participants in the September Uprising were hanged after being condemned by courts martial. Several hundred others were arrested.

2 December – Ferdinand V abdicated in Olomouc. The 18 year-old Francis Joseph I became emperor. A new imperial government, led by Felix Schwarzenberg had already assumed its duties on 21 November. These changes consolidated the situation, halted the revolutionary movements, strengthened the position of the older classes and led to a new structure for the empire (**Austro-Slavism**).

Beginning of December – At the suggestion of the new prime minister Prince Felix Schwarzenberg, Count John Majláth, a Magyar old conservative, prepared the first draft of a plan for the reorganization of Hungary. He suggested that it be divided immediately into seven national districts including a district for the „Carpathian Slavs". The shape of the Slovak autonomous administration was made more concrete in further drafts for the imperial government. Majláth's proposals helped to speed up the development of a new Slovak political program that was represented, in particular, by the **March Petition**.

4 December – Slovak volunteers in the imperial army began an offensive in the Kysuca region. They defeated the Kossuth guard on 9 December 1848 at Budatín near Žilina. However, they withdrew to Moravia (**Winter Campaign**) after the battle.

14 December – The imperial army invaded Hungary and, without encountering much resistance, occupied the country while the majority of Kossuth's insurgents withdrew to the region beyond the Tisa River. The Hungarian diet and government transferred to Debrecen.

■ **1849**

1 January – By a victory at the second battle of Budatín, the Slovak volunteers opened a way into the interior of Slovakia.

9 January – The minister of the interior, Count Francis Stadion, presented a plan for dividing Hungary into national administrative units to the government. Slovakia would be one of them.

13 January – After the arrival of the volunteers, a popular assembly took place in Martin. It recalled the pro-Kossuth county representation and elected a temporary Turiec administrative council (also called a national council). New offices and national councils were established also in Orava, Liptov and Zvolen counties and in several other cities in central and eastern Slovakia. They conducted business in Slovak and were staffed by pro-imperial middle nobles and Slovak patriotic bureaucrats.

29 January – Jozef Miloslav Hurban publicly submitted a new Slovak program for the first time at an assembly in Martin. It was based upon **Austro-Slavism** and demanded the separation of Slovakia from Hungary and an autonomous status for it within the monarchy.

5 February – A victory at Branisko over the Slovak volunteers and imperial units by the Magyar army of Gen. Arthur Görgey left open a way of retreat to Prešov and Košice.

7 March – The king dissolved the imperial diet and proclaimed the **Dictated Constitution**.

Mid-march – **Slovak government confidants** began to work in Vienna as advisors of the government.

20 March – A Slovak delegation led by Jozef Kozáček presented the **March Petition** to the king in Olomouc.

End of March – The Magyar army began a successful counter-offensive. By the beginning of May it had forced the imperial army from the territory of Hungary.

14 April – In Debrecen the Hungarian diet deposed the Habsburgs from the Hungarian throne, declared the complete independence of Hungary and named Kossuth as regent.

10 May – A new corps of Slovak volunteers (**Summer Campaign**) began to be formed in Skalica.

21 May – Francis Joseph I and Czar Nicholas I signed an agreement in Warsaw concerning Russian military assistance to suppress the Magyar revolution. Together with the imperial army, Russian units began an offensive at the beginning of June and occupied Košice on 24 June.

22 June – After condemnation by a court martial, the teacher J. Langsfeld was executed in Kremnica. He had fought in the ranks of the Slovak volunteers. After the withdrawal of the imperial army from Hungary, including the territory of Slovakia, during May and June 1849, he had ambushed units of the Hungarian army (*honvéd*) with a small armed guerilla group. After condemnation by Hungarian courts martial, about 33 Slovaks, who had taken a stand against the Magyar revolutionary powers, were executed during 1848-49.

24 June – The imperial commissioner of Hungary, Karl Geringer, named Ľudovít Štúr, Jozef Miloslav Hurban, Jozef Kozáček, Michal Miloslav Hodža and others as the Slovak popular confidants. They had to acquaint the Slovak public with Habsburg policies and the aims of the Slovak volunteers.

10 July – *Slovak News* (*Slovenské noviny*) edited by Daniel Lichard and Andrej Radlinský began to be published in Vienna.

28 July – The Hungarian diet in Szeged adopted nationality laws. Certain national (language) rights were granted to non-Magyars. This did not influence events because it came too late.

13 August – The Magyar army capitulated at Siria near Arad. Its commander, Arthur Görgey, surrendered his weapons into the hands of the Russians. The imperial high command in Hungary led by Július Haynau responded to this with a heavy-handed punishment of the insurgents.

10 September – The **Slovak government confidants** published a memorandum in which they demanded the separation of Slovakia from Hungary and the establishment of an individual Slovak crown country within the empire.

17 September – A meeting of leading politicians about the future of Hungary in Vienna. They decided to preserve Hungary and to separate from it Transylvania, Croatia, and the Voivodina, but not Slovakia.

6 October – The former Hungarian prime minister, Louis Batthyány, was executed in Pest. A total of about 120 military and political representatives of the Magyar revolution were executed.

7 October – A delegation of about 100 members presented a petition for the establishment of a Slovak crown country to the king in Vienna. With this the **Petition Movement** in the **autumn of 1849** ended.

21 November – The Slovak volunteer corps was ceremonially disbanded in Bratislava.

21 December – The interior minister, Alexander Bach, with the aid of Ján Kollár, declared the so-called old Slovak (Slovakized Czech) the official language in Slovakia.

■ 1850

20 April – Andrej Radlinský and Ján Palárik began to publish in Banská Štiavnica the weekly *Cyrill and Methodius* (*Cyrill a Method*) in old Slovak. It defended liberal ideas and the formation of a Slovak ecclesiastical province.

1 July – The government ordered that Slovak newspapers be published in the Czech language.

30 August – The king named Štefan Moyzes bishop of Banská Bystrica. He gathered around himself Catholic patriots. Together they intensified the national life and developed a system of Slovak schools (**Slovak gymnasia in the 19th century**). Shortly thereafter, Štefan Kolarčík became the bishop of Rožňava and Ladislav Zábojský was named the bishop of Spiš. Ján Scitovský, another native of Slovakia, became the primate of Hungary and, in 1853, a cardinal. However, he supported Magyarization in the Catholic Church.

13 September – Alexander Bach, the minister of the interior, introduced a temporary arrangement for the political administration of Hungary. The provisional government (**provisorium**) was incorporated into the uniform system of the absolutist monarchy.

1 October – The customs border between the Austrian part of the monarchy and Hungary was abolished. The Habsburg Empire was created a single customs region.

16 December – A railway line between Bratislava and Štúrovo was opened, which at the same time completed the rail connection between Vienna and Pest.

– The first postage stamp in the Habsburg monarchy was issued.

■ 1851

13 April – The emperor constituted his new personal and advisory organ, the Imperial Council, under the leadership of Baron Karl Kübeck. Its importance grew at the expense of the government.

20 August – By a cabinet letter, the king relieved the government of its constitutional responsibilities and dissolved it as a collective organ. It remained only his advisory organ. The ministers were only to be administrators of their respective departments.

31 December – With the issue of the **Sylvester Patents** the Emperor Francis Joseph I laid the legal foundations for a **neo-absolutism** traditionally called Bach's absolutism.

■ 1852

16 – 17 February – The miners in Banská Štiavnica revolted against poor social conditions.

5 April – Felix Schwarzenberg died. The king did not fill the post of prime minister. With his closest circle, he assumed the direct supervision of the state.

6 July – The Rimavská Coalition, the Muráň Union and the Society of Gemer Iron Producers merged into Rimava-Muráň Iron Company. Alongside state companies it was the largest industrial enterprise in Slovakia.

– Martin Hattala published *A Short Grammar (Krátka mluvnica)* in Bratislava. On the authority of a conference of leading intellectuals, he adapted some norms of Štúr's Slovak so that it was akin to Bernolák's Slovak.

– After the reforms of Hattala, this literary Slovak within a few years became the generally accepted form of the language.

– Ľudovít Stárek, an amateur historian, re-discovered the forgotten Roman inscription in Trenčín. It showed that a Roman unit had penetrated up to Trenčín in the year 179.

■ 1853

19 January – The definitive organization of the political administration of Hungary was established and, with this, the **provisional government** ended.

2 March – The emperor confirmed by an urbarial patent the abolition of serfdom and the right of peasants to ownership of the land listed in the urbarial registers. The patent resolved disputed questions of the use of forests and pastures, ordered the consolidation of land holdings and their delineation (the separation of the pastures of the peasants from those of the landlords) and established the amount of state reparations due to the landlords.

■ 1854

1 May – The emperor suspended martial law in Hungary.

11 May – A funerary monument by Vavrinec Dunajský dedicated to the poet Ján Hollý was unveiled in Dobrá Voda near Trenčín. Public collections for it had taken place since 1851. Leading Slovak activists, who participated in the unveiling, viewed the ceremonies as an expression of national solidarity.

■ 1855

18 August – The Habsburg monarchy signed a concordat with the Holy See. It abolished the **Placetum regium** and returned to the Catholic church some rights in education, the right to acquire property and to maintain its own administration, which were previously subordinated to the state or the king and thus broadened the church's influence upon public life (supervision of schools, participation in censorship).

– The Austrian gas company founded the first gasworks in Slovakia in Bratislava. Within ten years the city was illuminated by 209 lamps and, in winter, by an additional 167 lamps. Bratislava was one of the first cities in Hungary, along with Pest and Timisoara, to be illuminated by gas. Gas companies were established in Košice (1868), Banská Štiavnica (1880), Nitra (1890), Trnava (1900) and Komárno (1901).

■ 1856

12 January – Ľudovít Štúr died as a result of an injury while hunting. After 1849 he had published in Prague *About National Songs and Tales of the Slavic Nations (O národních*

písních a pověstech plemen slovanských
1853) and *Slavdom and the World of the Fu-*
ture (Das Slawenthum und Welt der Zukunft),
written in German (published in 1867 in Russia). In them he espoused **panslavism**.

■ **1859**
22 August – After defeats on the Italian battlefields of Magenta and Solferino, the emperor
dismissed Alexander Bach and other unpopular representatives of neo- absolutism. Bach
became the ambassador of the empire to the
Holy See.
1 September – The **Protestant Patent** was issued.

■ **1860**
5 March – The ruler convened the so-called
expanded Imperial Council. It gradually became the parliament of the Austrian part of
the monarchy.
20 October – The emperor issued the **Octo-**
ber Diploma by which he relinquished absolute power and determined the principles of
a future constitution.
– In the United States, Gejza Mihalóczi
formed the first military unit of emigrants of
Slovak and Czech origin and, from 1861,
other Slavs also. The Slovak Lincoln Rifle
Company fought in the Civil War on the side
of the Union. Mihalóczi fell in the war, having attained the rank of colonel. The first Slovak to become a general in the American
army was Eugen Kozlaj (1865).

■ **1861**
Second half of January – Štefan Marko Daxner issued the pamphlet *Voice from Slovakia*
(Hlas zo Slovenska), in which he precisely
analyzed the situation in the monarchy on
the basis of natural law and demanded a guarantee for the equality of nations in Hungary
and its new structure.
9 February – Jozef Miloslav Hurban presented
a memorandum to the ministry of the interior
in Vienna, in which he criticized the national
oppression of the Slovaks and, in the spirit of
Austro-Slavism, demanded the incorporation
of Slovakia as an autonomous unit with its

own government and diet into a confederated
empire.
26 February – The ruler issued the **February**
Constitution.
19 March – Ján Francisci started publishing in
Buda the *Pest-Buda News (Pešťbudínske ve-*
domosti), which became an organ of the Slovak national movement, especially of the
Old School (Stará škola).
29 April – After elections, a broadened imperial council (parliament) convened in Vienna.
6 – 7 June – The **Slovak national assembly**
that adopted the **Memorandum of the Slovak**
Nation took place in Martin.
22 August – The ruler dissolved the **Hungar-**
ian diet, which had been in session from the
beginning of April because it was dominated
by a radical anti-Vienna mood and had attempted to renew the state sovereignty of
1848. In Hungary the renewal of constitutional arrangements was halted for a time
and a **provisional government** was introduced.
12 December – A delegation led by Štefan
Moyzes presented the **Vienna Memorandum**
of the Slovaks to the sovereign. Francis
Joseph I sent it to Hungarian state organs,
which filed it away.

■ **1862**
27 July – The ruler ordered the Hungarian
viceroy to prepare a draft of a nationality
law. The commission was comprised largely
of old noble conservatives, who delayed work
and advocated the idea of a single Magyar
(Hungarian) nation in the law.
16 September – The first Evangelical secondary school (gymnasium) in Revúca was ceremonially opened (its director was Augustín
Horislav Škultéty).
– At the world exhibition in London, Dionýz
Štúr, an employee of the Imperial Geological
Office in Vienna, received a gold medal for
a set of geological maps on which the region
of Slovakia was also depicted.

■ **1863**
2 January – In a petition to the sovereign, 42
communities in Spiš protested against being

forced to use Hungarian and called for the use of Slovak in county offices.

17 February – The ruler directed that the points of the **Memorandum of the Slovak Nation** be taken into account in the preparation of the Nationality Law.

4 August – The **Matica slovenská** was ceremonially opened in Martin. For Š. Moyzes, who had been named by the ruler as his privy councilor on 3 August, the villages along the road from Žiar nad Hronom (Sv. Kríž) to Martin erected triumphal arches. The opening of the Matica was the culmination of the celebration of the millennium of the arrival of Cyril and Methodius in Great Moravia.

10 September – Francis Joseph I received a delegation led by Štefan Moyzes that thanked him for approving the opening of the Matica slovenská and for his gift of 1000 florins. The emperor's attitude at least partially subdued the anti-Matica attacks from the Magyar side. However, the delegation was not resolute in demanding a resolution of the Slovak question.

4 October – The Croatian National Theater was opened in Zagreb with *The Tinker (Drotár)*, a play by the Slovak playwright Ján Palárik.

5 October – Daniel Lichard began to publish the journal *Horizon (Obzor)* in Skalica, which had a positive influence upon the promotion of modern entrepreneurship and business education. It ceased publication in 1905.

■ **1864**
22 April – After the discovery of secret anti-Habsburg organizations in Hungary, the sovereign dismissed Anton Forgách from the office of court chancellor and appointed Herman Zichy who was sympathetic to the demands of the non-Magyar nationalities. However, he was forced to leave office on 26 June 1865, under pressure from the Magyar opposition and because of the unfavorable international situation.

In November – Ján Francisci was named as the chief county administrator (*hlavný župan*) of Liptov County. This elicited enthusiasm from some of the Slovak public and the hope

that the Slovak question would be satisfactorily resolved. Letters of thanks were sent to the sovereign and the court chancellor by 87 communities of Liptov. Ján Francisci was recalled on 10 September 1865 after the political situation changed.

2 December – Influenced by Herman Zichy, the ruler issued an order that the languages of the non-Magyar nationalities be respected in the conduct of official business.

– A state hospital was established in Bratislava. It became an important medical research institute and a center for the medical profession.

■ **1865**
27 July – The cabinet of the prime minister Anton Schmerling resigned in Vienna. It was replaced by the government of Richard Belcredi, which was more conciliatory towards the demands of the Magyar constitutional opposition.

20 September – The sovereign abrogated the **February Constitution**, dissolved the **provisional government** and renewed the constitutional order in Hungary.

14 December – The sovereign opened a new **Hungarian diet** in Pest-Buda. The adherents of **dualism** constituted the overwhelming majority in it.

– The Vienna entrepreneur Michael Thonet established the first factory for bent-wood furniture in Hungary in Veľké Uherce. It employed about 300 workers.

■ **1866**
17 June – The Austrian-Prussian war broke out and small- scale battles took place around Bratislava. After a decisive victory at Sadowa, Prussia gained the upper hand in German unification. The weakened position and international isolation of the Habsburg Empire was used by the Magyar opposition to speed up the attainment of a constitutional settlement with the Austrian side.

■ **1867**
28 January – The **Mutual Aid Society** was established in Revúca and became a model for financial institutions in rural Slovakia.

7 February – Richard Belcredi, the opponent of unilateral concessions to the Magyar constitutional opposition, resigned and Ferdinand Beust assumed the leadership of the imperial government. He expected that a quick agreement between Vienna and Pest would strengthen the political stability of the monarchy.

20 February – After negotiations for a settlement concluded, the ruler named the members of a newly established independent Hungarian government. Count Julius Andrássy became prime minister.

20 May – A meeting of the imperial council began in Vienna. It considered constitutional agreements with Hungary prepared by Ferdinand Beust, the imperial court, Francis Deák and Julius Andrássy.

May to June – A Slavic congress took place in Moscow. Andrej Radlinský, Janko Jesenský, and Pavol Mudroň comprised the Slovak delegation. Like the Czech representatives, they expressed their disagreement with the dualist arrangement of the empire.

8 June – Francis Joseph I agreed to be crowned king of Hungary in Buda. By this he symbolically confirmed the constitutional settlement.

28 July – The king signed a resolution of the Hungarian diet concerning the Austrian-Hungarian (Magyar) constitutional settlement.

21 December – The ruler approved a new constitution for the Cisleithan part of the empire. In this culminated the process of compromise and the monarchy became a federal state (**dualism**).

– The first steam boiler and the first steam engine in Slovakia were produced by the Kachelmann engineering factory in Vyhne.

– Officials approved the by-laws of a self-help cooperative credit society in Revúca, the first in Hungary. There were 70 such societies active in Slovakia by the end of the 1880s.

Modernization deformed by strong national oppression (1868 – 1918)

T he constitutional settlement of 1867 was a definite turning point in the development and character of the monarchy. It considered only the interests of the two strongest political groups, the Hungarian-Magyar and the Austrian-German. The anti-Vienna mood in Hungary was silenced for a time and the long-lasting struggle over constitutional power between Vienna and Budapest was sidetracked. The monarchy was outwardly stabilized. However, at the beginning of the 20th century, the traditional political tensions between the two main centers of power acquired new dimensions. Crises of dualism attended the monarchy up to its collapse in 1918.

After the Compromise, the economy and whole way of life was significantly modernized within the constitutional regime in Hungary. The conditions for this had been prepared during the preceding decades. Industrialization and the building up of the transportation system of the Hungarian state was especially supported by tax relief, legislation (the so-called industrial laws) and state orders. Gigantic building and industrial activity took place, especially in Budapest, where tens of thousands of Slovaks went to work. Alongside Budapest, Slovakia continued to retain its position as the most industrialized region of Hungary. The food-stuff (milling and distilling), paper, wood, textile and glass industries, as well as foundries, machine works and the mining of iron ore, particularly flourished. Before the war, a railway network was constructed and new branches of industry were established (chemical and electrical technology and the production of electric power).

The social structure of society also changed. From the old privileged classes and some of the successful individuals from the lower classes, especially Jews, sprang forth modern businessmen and the upper middle- classes. The number of small farmers declined and the number of workers increased. However, economic modernization in Hungary lagged behind the growth of the population and took place much more slowly than in Cisleitha. The concentration of capital and production was also much less and the growth of the cities was slower. Double-employment spread, especially in the mountain and foothill regions of Slovakia, typified by the so-called metal worker-farmer. People began to leave for work overseas, especially in the United States of America, primarily from those regions where the land had been sub-divided to a bizarre degree and agriculture had not been modernized, resulting in a relative overpopulation with its negative consequences (hunger, poverty, illnesses etc.). Emigration from Slovakia reached massive proportions, so that the Slovaks rank among those nations with the highest proportion of emigrants.

The same course of rapid change characterized the cultural sphere. New ideas, socialism and liberalism, penetrated the Slovak milieu, especially at the beginning of the century. Life was becoming secularized. However, the most characteristic phenomenon of social conditions was nationalism. Hungary resolutely persevered in building a Magyar national state. After 1867, Magyarization became an important element of the policy and ideology of the state. It reached massive proportions and penetrated all spheres of life, most significantly education, public administration, the army, the churches, and even business. It especially affected the urban, and the more propertied and/or educated classes. Its strength was bound to the political regime of Hungary which, unlike the Cisleithan region of the monarchy, did not become democratic. It retained many of the features of an aristocratic society of estates.

The policy of strong national oppression from the Magyar side elicited opposition and a defensive reaction from the non-Magyars and affected the growth of national contradictions in Hungary. The Compromise outflanked Slovak policy, especially its pro-Vienna center in Martin. Once again Slovakia felt left out of the decision-making process and was not able even to rely on the occasional understanding of Vienna. It reacted with critical journalism and electoral passivity to the aggressive Magyar nationalism and the enforcement of Hungarian patriotism. At the end of the century, Slovak policy underwent clear changes. It became differentiated (left, center, right) and realistic-pragmatic tendencies were strengthened. It even achieved some success (for instance, a few deputies in the diet). Despite persecution the circulation of Slovak newspapers increased, as did the very modest Slovak supply of capital.

A conspicuous deformation of Slovak political thought and culture took place during the last half-century of the Kingdom of Hungary. In this era, when in most other nations the ideas of their own strength and greatness prevailed, the Slovaks had their energy drained merely in the defense of their national existence. Sometimes they reacted to the omnipresent Magyarization by rejecting some of the new phenomena of civilization and by „withdrawing" to idyllic surroundings that strengthened the feeling of insignificance and isolationism and a „plebeian" mentality.

The First World War brought misfortune, tragedy and a large-scale decline in living conditions. However, it called forth a more favorable political constellation for which a substantial part of Slovak politicians had waited for a long time. Its representatives believed that the Slovaks would be emancipated from national oppression only through a great catastrophe and external assistance. Already at the beginning of the war, Slovaks and Czechs in the United States and Russia spontaneously accepted the idea of an independent Czecho-Slovakia. It had found a resonance in their thought as one alternative, even before the war. When, alongside the disappearance of Austria-Hungary in 1918, this idea also was adopted by the great powers of the victorious alliance, radical changes in the structures in central Europe and the status of Slovakia were decided. With the establishment of Czecho-Slovakia the writing of a new chapter in the history of the Slovaks began, which was to eliminate many of the deformations from the 19th century.

■ **1868**

2 January – Ján Nepomuk Bobula started to publish, in Pest, the *Slovak News (Slovenské noviny)* that became an organ of the **New School**.

31 January – Twenty-one communities of Spiš presented a petition demanding the equality of Slovaks and Magyars, that the borders of the counties be drawn according to nationality, and that Slovak be used in the administration and in secondary schools. It was presented to the diet by the Ruthenian deputy, Adolf Dobriansky, on 24 February. He delivered a similar petition from the Liptov region on 23 May.

9 February – A General Workers' Socialist Association was founded in Pest. In this international association, based on the principles of Lasalle, Slovaks were organized alongside Magyar and German workers. The program was published in three languages.

25 March – The **New School** established a Slovak National Democratic Association in Pest.

17 November – The ruler approved the Hungarian-Croatian constitutional settlement that confirmed the autonomous status of Croatia in Hungary (internal administration, religion, education, and judiciary).

6 December – The monarch signed the **Nationality Law** of the Hungarian diet and the union of Transylvania with Hungary.

■ **1869**

3 March – The Book Publishing Joint-Stock Company was founded in Martin, the first national printery with a publisher. Ján Francisci became its president.

29 March – The newly established workers' club, Forward (*Vorwärts*), organized the first public socialist assembly in Hungary in Bratislava.

22 July – The representatives of the **New School** presented a petition with 70,000 signatures to the minister of education, Joseph Eötvös, that demanded the establishment of Slovak secondary schools (5 Slovak and 6 partially Slovak secondary schools).

4 August – The assembly that founded Žive-na, a society of Slovak women, took place in Martin.

21 October – Jozef Miloslav Hurban was sentenced to six- months imprisonment and fined 400 florins for publishing the article *What Does History Teach Us? (Čomu nás učia dejiny?)*. It was one of the first politically colored judicial processes after the Compromise.

30 October – The Slovak Catholic secondary school in Kláštor pod Znievom began instruction. Previously, in 1867, an Evangelical lower secondary school had begun activity in Martin.

11 November – The publication company Minerva was founded in Budapest with a capital of 40,000 florins and its own printery. It closed by the end of 1872.

14 December – The St. Vojtech (Adalbert) Society, an institution for spreading religious culture and the publication of Slovak Catholic literature, was established in Trnava. It was initiated by Andrej Radlinský who became its honorary president. It published *Catholic News (Katolícke noviny)* and the journals *Vojtech* (Adalbert) and *St Adalbert Pilgrim (Pútnik svätovojtešský)*.

■ **1870**

13 March – The name of *Pest-Buda News* (*Pešťbudínske vedomosti*) was changed to the *National News* (*Národné noviny*) and began to be issued in Martin. It became the organ of the **Slovak National Party**. Svetozár Hurban Vajanský and Jozef Škultéty were the editors for the longest period.

1 August – A law about the organization of the counties was passed. The counties were administered by county committees and assemblies comprised half of elected and half of appointed representatives, called *virilisti* (the payers of the highest taxes). This system of representation maintained the privileges of the propertied and old families. The same principles also characterized the community law of 1871.

24 August – Jozef Kozáček was elected president of the Matica slovenská to replace Štefan Moyzes who had died.

■ **1871**
6 June – A conference in Martin established the organizational principles of the **Slovak National Party**.
7 November – The **Old School** (Viliam Paulíny-Tóth) and the **New School** (Ján Nepomuk Bobula) concluded an agreement that they would not publicly attack each other, would inform each other about their activities and act jointly on basic questions. The agreement was maintained until the election in June 1872, in which the Slovak National Party did not win any seats whereas the New School won three.
– The first factory for the production of matches in Slovakia was established in Bytča. Match factories were established soon after in Trnava, Nižný Komárnik and Banská Bystrica.

■ **1872**
27 February – The ruler signed a law of the Hungarian diet concerning small businesses which definitively dissolved the guilds and made it possible for small manufacturers to associate freely in small business associations. With 500 producers, the Association of Bagmakers in Myjava ranked among the largest in Slovakia.
18 March – The railway line Košice-Poprad-Žilina opened with connections to Bohumín (Košice-Bohumín line). Service began on the Vrútky-Zvolen-Pest line in August.
23 October – A conference of the representatives of the **New School** took place in Pest. So that it would be acceptable to the Hungarian government and comply with **dualism**, it accepted a moderate program (the establishment of two Slovak secondary schools, state support for the Matica slovenská, representation of Slovaks in the state administration) and changed its name to the Party of the Settlement.
– The by-laws of the Slovak Choral Society in Martin were officially approved. Associated with it was an actors' group that became the nucleus of the Slovak amateur theater.
– Baron Gregory Friesenhof founded the Agricultural Society of the Nitra Valley. It pro-

vided farmers with information about how to cultivate new crops and breed animals, as well as new agricultural techniques, and it organized expositions. Its headquarters were in Žabokreky nad Nitrou.

■ **1873**
8 April – The newspaper *Concord (Svornosť)* appeared in Banská Bystrica. In cooperation with the vice- administrator (*podžupan*) of Zvolen County, Béla Grünwald, it intensified Magyar nationalism and was disrespectful towards the Slovak national movement, whose institutions, especially the Matica slovenská, it considered pan- Slavist.
9 May – The Vienna stock-exchange collapsed, followed by the first great economic crisis in Austria-Hungary, which lasted until 1880. On the one hand, production declined by about 25 per cent, which lowered the living standards of the majority of society. On the other hand, the modernization of the economy, industrialization, and the concentration of capital speeded up. In Slovakia the foundry, textile, and agricultural industries were especially affected.
10 August – The Hungarian Carpathian Society, one of the first tourist organizations in the Kingdom of Hungary, was founded. It led to the start of organized tourism in the High Tatras, the construction of huts and paths, the protection of nature and the founding of a rescue service. Its headquarters were in Kežmarok.
– Dynamit-Nobel, a firm based in Vienna, established the largest factory in Austria-Hungary for producing chemicals and explosives in Bratislava.

■ **1874**
20 August – The Evangelical secondary school (gymnasium) in Revúca was closed on the orders of the government and of the minister of education, Augustín Trefort. This was followed by the closing of the Catholic gymnasium in Kláštor pod Znievom on 30 December and of the Evangelical gymnasium in Martin on 5 January 1875. The government pursued the course of a radical **Magyariza-**

tion. Until 1918 not a single Slovak secondary school existed in the Kingdom of Hungary.

26 November – The ruler signed a new law of the Hungarian diet concerning **voting rights**. It retained educational and property requirements so that the right to vote was held only by 5 – 7 per cent of the population.

■ **1875**
1 March – Deák's ruling Party of the Settlement and the opposition Party of the Left-Center merged to form the **Liberal Party.**
6 April – Koloman Tisza, the minister of the interior, dissolved the **Matica slovenská**. Thus Slovaks lost the last institutional manifestation of their national particularity. The government confiscated the property of the Matica and later transferred it to the Hungarian- Patriotic Slovak Educational Association (**1885**).

■ **1876**
3 April – The ruler approved a law about servants, which allowed them to be punished physically and degraded the status of servants and their families on large estates and in the houses of wealthy farmers.

■ **1877**
6 May – Viliam Paulíny-Tóth died. Pavol Mudroň became the president of the Slovak National Party and served to 1914.

■ **1878**
Beginning of July – Because of persecution, violence and machinations, the leadership of the Slovak National Party decided not to participate in the August elections for the Hungarian diet.

■ **1879**
1 March – Karol Hanzlíček began to publish in Bratislava *The Truth (Die Wahrheit)*, the first newspaper for workers in Slovakia.
22 May – The ruler signed an act of the Hungarian diet concerning the compulsory teaching of Hungarian in elementary schools and the obligation of teachers to master Hungarian.

■ **1880**
16 – 17 May – The founding congress of the General Workers Party of Hungary was held in Budapest and declared its adherence to social democratic principles. Karol Hanzlíček suggested its name. Delegates from Bratislava, Košice and Komárno participated in the congress.

■ **1881**
30 May – One of the three main laws about state support for industrial undertakings was passed. On the basis of these laws, businessmen could be freed from the payment of taxes for 15 years, receive rebates for transportation, obtain support for the purchase of new equipment, and offered free land and the like. These laws were a precondition for the modernization of industry (**industrialization**) and contributed to the growth of cities in Hungary.
– After nearly 30 years, *Slovak Views (Slovenské pohľady)* again began to be published in Martin. Aside from political questions, it was devoted mainly to Slovak culture and to strengthening the national identity of the Slovaks. Its spiritual leaders were primarily Svetozár Hurban Vajanský and Jozef Škultéty.
– By a merger of the Rimava-Muráň and the Salgótarján companies the Rimamuráň-Salgótarján Joint-Stock Iron Company, the largest mining-smelting concern in Hungary, was established.

■ **1882**
15 March – Slovak students founded the club Detvan in Prague. Its first president was Jaroslav Vlček. It organized educational and cultural programs, informed the Czech public about the life and status of Slovaks and promoted an interest in events in Slovakia. It cooperated with Czech Slovakophiles whose numbers grew at this time.

■ **1883**
20 November – The Upper Hungary Magyar Educational Society (FEMKE) was founded in Nitra and became active in 10 counties. Through its cultural activities, courses in Hun-

garian, newly-established libraries, and child care, they strengthened not only Hungarian patriotism and education but also tried, in particular, to denationalize (that is, assimilate) Slovak youth.

■ **1884**
1 June – The leaders of the Slovak National Party again confirmed its withdrawal to political passivity. By not participating in the elections, the Slovak National Party protested against the machinations and violence connected with them, as well as against the discriminatory electoral law.
15 June – The first city telephone network in Slovakia opened in Bratislava. The second was in Košice (1891).
21 December – An artists society was founded in Bratislava as the first association of visual artists in Slovakia.

■ **1885**
2 February – The constituting assembly of the Tatra Bank took place in Martin. Together with the Ružomberok Credit Society (1879), it was one of the two largest financial institutions with Slovak capital. By the turn of the century, many credit societies and cooperatives operated alongside 130 banks and savings banks in Slovakia. Slovak funds made up 14 per cent of their capital.
30 June – A seven-member delegation, made up of members of the last committee of the Matica slovenská, delivered a petition to the ruler, which requested that the prohibition of the Matica slovenská be cancelled and that it be permitted to renew its activities and that its property be returned. At the beginning of July, they delivered the petition to Koloman Tisza, the prime minister of Hungary, as well.
– The Hungarian-Patriotic Slovak Educational Association of the Kingdom of Hungary was founded in Budapest and received the property of the Matica slovenská. It was supported by the Hungarian government. Its presiding officers were the Bishop of Spiš, George Császka, Michal Zsilinszky, Béla Radvánszky and Béla Grünwald. It published the *Slovak News (Slovenské noviny)* and conducted edu-

cation and propaganda in the spirit of Magyar ideas about the state and the suppression of the national consciousness of the Slovaks.

■ **1886**
21 October – The first Slovak newspaper in the United States, the *American-Slovak News (Amerikánsko-slovenské noviny)*, was published in Pittsburgh. Janko Slovenský published it first in the Šariš dialect and later Peter Rovnianek published it in literary Slovak. It had a circulation of 30,000.

■ **1887**
3 August – In Martin, the Živena Society opened an exhibition of Slovak embroidery and pictures with Slovak themes of the Czech painter, Jaroslav Věšín. The exhibition manifested national particularity, the attractiveness of Slovak folk culture, and demonstrated an ability to organize a complex undertaking despite strong national oppression. It elicited a favorable international response.

■ **1887/1888**
As during the cholera epidemic of 1874, the authorities organized the transportation of poor orphans, half- orphans and children with parents from northern Slovak counties to the lower lands (southern Hungary) with the help of FEMKE (**20 November 1883**). A total of about 600 children were evacuated; around 300 of them returned home. Their suffering and the cynicism of officials produced a scandal at home and abroad.

■ **1889**
30 January – Archduke Rudolf, the heir apparent to the Habsburg throne, committed suicide in Mayerling. The circumstances still remain a mystery. The Archduke Francis Ferdinand, who favored the abolition of dualism and the federalization of the Empire, became the heir presumptive to the throne.

■ **1890**
16 February – Peter Rovnianek founded the National Slovak Society (*Národný slovenský spolok*) in Pittsburgh. He attempted to sur-

mount the isolation and the confessional distinctions of the Slovak immigrants as well as to support socially weak individuals and national life in Slovakia.

February – The cement works in Ladce was the first to produce Portland cement in Slovakia. It was among the most modern cement works in Hungary.

9 March – Koloman Tisza resigned as the prime minister of the Hungary after 15 years. His term was marked by the stability of the dualist system, rapid economic growth and a tactless national policy.

1 May – Mass demonstrations of workers took place in Hungary for the first time. An improvement of working and social conditions in Slovakia was demanded by workers in Bratislava, Košice, Bardejov and Liptovský Mikuláš, where soldiers intervened.

28 August – Karol Löw, an entrepreneur from Brno, opened a textile mill in Žilina. Together with the textile mill in Ružomberok (1895), it was one of the two largest factories of its type in Hungary.

7 – 8 December – The Social Democratic Party of Hungary was established in Budapest under the leadership of Paul Engelmann. Six delegates from Slovakia participated: four from Bratislava and two from Vrútky. Karol Hanzlíček was the co-author of the report to the congress.

– Tile stove workers in Bratislava founded the first trade union organization in Slovakia. Workers of a tile stove factory in Modra also applied for membership.

■ **1891**
28 January – 100 Slovak miners perished in a mine accident in Mount Pleasant, Pennsylvania.

9 April – An act concerning free Sundays for workers was passed. Another about obligatory sickness insurance in industry, transportation and commerce was passed in 1892.

28 April – The ruler approved legislation of the Hungarian diet concerning pre-school child-care institutions, which fostered the use of the Hungarian language.

15 May – A 150 member Slovak delegation led by Pavol Mudroň participated in the opening of a jubilee Czech exhibition in Prague. By this they demonstrated Slovak support for the Czechs.

– A small steam railway was put into service in Košice. It was the beginning of urban public transportation in Slovakia. In 1895, four kilometers of tram-tracks were opened in Bratislava.

■ **1892**
Repeated failures of potatoes, cabbage and grain crops led to much starvation, especially in mountainous northern Slovakia. The terrible social conditions forced masses of the poor to emigrate to the United States (**emigration**).

22 May – The first large assembly of workers (2,000) in Bratislava demonstrated for a general right of suffrage. Gradually this was also demanded by other political groups at mass meetings. It was attained, however, only with the establishment of Czecho-Slovakia in 1918.

23 – 24 July – A Romanian national conference in Sibiu proclaimed Romanian-Slovak solidarity. In January 1893 it was joined also by representatives of the Serbs from the Vojvodina. This signified the beginning of cooperation among the non-Magyar nations. The Slovaks were represented at the conference by Miloš Štefanovič, Samuel Daxner, Ján Botto and Gustáv Augustiny.

2 August – Monetary reform began in Austria-Hungary. Prior to 1900, the crown was gradually introduced as the unit of currency. The crown had half the value of the older **florin**.

8 September – Officials forbade the solemn unveiling of a monument to Jozef Miloslav Hurban in Hlboké. Svetozár Hurban Vajanský reacted to this by writing his article *Hyenism in Hungary (Hyenizmus v Uhorsku)*. For this he was sentenced to one year in prison.

17 November – The monarch named Alexander Wekerle to be the prime minister of Hungary. He was the first and last non-noble in this office. During 1894/95 he achieved the adoption of the so-called church political laws.

– Hungaria, the first factory in Slovakia for the production of artificial fertilizers and sulfuric acid, was founded in Žilina. It was a subsidiary of a factory in Budapest.

– In Krásny Brod, Medzilaborce, and later in Strážske (1894) and elsewhere, oil refineries were founded. Experimental drilling for crude oil was conducted in northern and eastern Slovakia and Galicia. The most significant refinery was Apollo in Bratislava (1895).

– The first public electric plant in Hungary was put into service in Gelnica. In 1893 city electric plants were established in Kežmarok and Plešivec and by 1900 they had been established also in Spišská Nová Ves, Bratislava, Ružomberok, Košice, Banská Bystrica, Prešov and Lučenec.

– After reconstruction and modernization, the paper-mill in Slavošovce was the largest in Hungary. The second largest was the paper-mill in Ružomberok (reconstructed in 1894); the third was in Harmanec.

■ 1894

7 May – The Evangelical Church accepted a new constitution at a synod in Budapest. The borders of its districts were drawn in such a way that its Slovak members did not have a majority in any of them.

9 December – The ruler signed the first three church- political laws of the Hungarian diet (obligatory civil marriages, the religion of children of mixed marriages, and the administration of registers by the state), which proclaimed the freedom of religious confession, increased the role of the state at the expense of the churches and fostered Magyarization.

■ 1895

14 January – King Francis Joseph I appointed the new government of Desiderius Bánffy. After a moderate beginning, it became famous for its unyielding assimilation policies and sharp interventions against the workers' movement and the representatives of non-Magyar nations, as well as for many political trials.

28 – 29 January – The Catholic Popular Party (Néppárt) was constituted. Ferdinand Zichy became its president. It declared its allegiance to a traditional, conservative orientation and the encyclicals of Pope Leo XIII, sought to weaken liberalism and the workers' movement, and demanded the abolition of the church- political laws and the strengthening of church influence in politics. Initially it pledged to respect the rights of the non-Magyars. Therefore it was supported by Slovak Catholics (František Skyčák, Andrej Hlinka) and even by the Slovak National Party. However, the promise was not kept.

15 May – A Czecho-Slavic ethnographic exhibition opened in Prague that was visited by 2 million people. An individual, abundant exposition presented Slovak folk art. The exhibition contributed to Czecho-Slovak cooperation and aroused the interest of the broader Czech public in the Slovaks.

10 August – A **congress of non-Magyar nationalities** took place in Budapest. After it concluded, the Bánffy government began to persecute severely the representatives of the national movements.

22 August – The **Slovak Museum Society** (*Muzeálna slovenská spoločnosť*) officially began its activity.

16 October – The ruler signed an act of the Hungarian diet that guaranteed freedom of confession for the Jews also.

– Isabella, the wife of Archduke Friedrich, founded the Isabella Society in Bratislava. It established embroidery workshops in several places in Slovakia, which employed up to 800 embroiderers. The society obtained a gold medal at the World's Fair in St. Louis. Its production, folk embroidery, was found even in the courts of several rulers.

■ 1896

6 – 16 April – At the first modern Olympic games in Athens, the Slovak Alojz Sokol (Szokolyi), in the uniform of Hungary, won third place in the 100 meter dash.

2 May – The monarch opened the first subway on the continent and the Millennial Exhibition in Budapest. This marked the culmination of the grandiose celebration of the millennium (the 1000th anniversary of the arrival of the Magyars in the Carpathian basin). It presented the civilizing ascent of Hungary, as well as the idea of a Magyar Hungary. Magyar nationalistic enthusiasm intensified during the celebration.

7 May – Slovakophiles and members of the Detvan Club founded the **Czechoslavonic Union** (*Československá jednota*) in Prague.

27 July – The ruler approved legislation concerning the redemption of contracted serfs and cotters (**želiari**). This concluded the half-century journey towards the elimination of **serfdom** in Hungary.

19 December – The first film presentation in Slovakia took place in the Schalkház Hotel in Košice. Until now it has been assumed that the first projection took place on 25 December in Bratislava (where the Hotel Carlton is now located).

– The Stollwerk firm opened in Bratislava one of the most significant factories for the production of chocolate and candies in Europe.

■ **1897**

January – The *People's News (Ľudové noviny)* began to appear in Martin. Anton Bielek and Andrej Hlinka, the editors, issued it outside the framework of Néppárt, as they did not agree with the policy of the Slovak National Party. The „hlasists" and Milan Hodža cooperated with them. Later they represented a newly developing current of Slovak Catholic thought.

1 May – The first Slovak social-democratic newspaper, *New Times (Nová doba),* began to appear in Budapest. Its publisher was the boilermaker František Tupý and the editor was the wood-carver Gustáv Švéni.

21 June – 18 July – In Budapest 15,000 brickyard workers, largely Slovak and Polish, engaged in a strike for higher wages, shorter working hours, an improvement in housing and the like. It was the largest strike of industrial workers in Hungary up to that time.

23 August – 16 September – A strike of 20,000 building trades workers, the majority of them Slovaks, took place in Budapest.

– The Society of Spiš Physicians obtained one

of the very first industrially produced X-ray machines thanks to Vojtech Alexander.

■ **1898**

15 February – A law went into effect that required a community to have only one official name. The law and political practice enforced the use of the Magyar name.

27 April – The Tranoscius Society was organized in Martin and focused on the publication and distribution of Slovak Evangelical religious literature. Its first president was Juraj Janoška.

29 June – Young liberal intellectuals began to issue the journal *Voice (Hlas)* in Skalica. Its publisher and editor was Pavol Blaho and later Vavro Šrobár. From the magazine the group received the name **hlasists.**

10 September – The Italian anarchist Luigi Luccheni assassinated the Austrian empress and Hungarian queen, Elizabeth Habsburg (Sissi), in Geneva.

■ **1900**

4 – 5 January – A court trial of 28 leading Slovak patriots took place in Banská Bystrica. They were accused of inciting disorder during the welcome of Ambro Pietor on his return from prison in Pest. The persecution of Slovak patriots and social democrats climaxed between 1898 and 1909. In 89 court trials about 500 individuals were sentenced to a total of 83 years in prison and were fined 40,000 crowns.

■ **1901**

11 April – After 17 years, influenced by a more tolerant policy of the government of Koloman Széll, the Slovak National Party decided to renew its electoral activity. Its electoral program demanded respect for the **Nationality Law**, the abolition of the church political laws, the enactment of the universal right to vote and the like. In the October elections, four Slovak representatives were elected to the diet, which had more than 400 deputies.

7 August – The reconstruction of the organization of Slovak National Party began. A new leadership was elected, which represented all currents of Slovak politics, except for the social democrats, and also included members from outside Martin. The ability of the party to operate was also strengthened by its network of district agents.

■ **1903**

4 July – Milan Hodža began to issue the *Slovak Weekly (Slovenský týždenník)* in Budapest. On 27 February 1910 it became the *Slovak Daily (Slovenský denník)*. It had the highest circulation of the Slovak newspapers in Hungary, was oriented especially towards the farmers, supported active practical politics, modern entrepreneurship and the cooperation of the Slovaks with the other nationalities in Hungary and with the Czechs (**18 February 1912**).

1 – 15 August – The first joint exhibition of Slovak painters (Tomáš Andraškovič, Jaroslav Augusta, Karol Lehotský, Gustáv Mallý, Emil Pacovský and Gustáv Obendorf) took place in Žilina. The Group of Slovak Painters in Hungary adhering to the ideas of the Slovak national movement was founded at it. Because of the opposition of the authorities, the exhibitions took place in Moravian towns. Jozef Hanula, Július Kern and the Czech Miloš Jiránek exhibited their works within the framework of the group.

1 August – The industrial exhibition of Upper Hungary opened in Žilina at which almost 350 small producers and several larger enterprises from five Slovak counties exhibited. It lasted until 15 September and was visited by about 60,000 people.

■ **1904**

19 – 24 April – A strike of railway workers took place that was suppressed by the government of Stephen Tisza. By this time the railway network in Hungary had by and large been built. In 1900, 72 per cent of the current railway track in Slovakia (2,600 km) was in service; by 1914 it was 90 per cent.

1 October – The *Slovak Workers News (Slovenské robotnícke noviny)*, the organ of the Slovak Social Democratic Party of Hungary, began to be published in Bratislava. It supported the principles of the Second International and, in addition to social issues, defended the national rights of the Slovaks.

■ **1905**

26 January – 4 February – For the first time since the Compromise, the **Liberal Party** did not win the elections. They were won by a coalition of parties that demanded the abolition of the Compromise or a new settlement that would give greater independence to Hungary.

18 February – Ten Romanian, Serbian and Slovak (Milan Hodža, František Skyčák) representatives formed a common club in the diet, the so-called Nationality Party of the diet. Its president was Theodor Mihali and its secretary was Milan Hodža. Together they sought to obtain the right of universal suffrage.

11 – 12 June – The **Slovak Social Democrat Party of Hungary** was founded in Bratislava.

18 June – The ruler appointed the **caretaker government** of Gejza Fejérvári. This angered the victorious coalition, which found itself in opposition.

13 August – A convention of friends of Slovakia took place in Hodonín. In addition to representatives of the Czechoslavic Union, several Czech deputies as well as Milan Hodža and Pavol Blaho participated.

September – Jozef Murgaš successfully performed the first public experiments in Wilkes-Barre, Pennsylvania USA, that contributed to the perfecting of wireless telegraphy. He received 11 patents from the American patent office for inventions that advanced the development of radio-telegraphy.

14 December – The founding of the **Slovak Peoples' Party** was proclaimed in Žilina. It was to be a party with a large membership and a counterweight to the Magyar parties and the passive Slovak National Party. In addition to Catholics (Andrej Hlinka, Ferdiš Juriga and František Skyčák) those representing other currents of thought (Milan Hodža, *Hlasists*) supported it. It demanded adherence to the Nationality Law and the enactment into law of the right of universal suffrage. It had established itself organizationally and intellectually (in the spirit of Catholicism) prior to the First World War.

– Filip Lenard, a native of Bratislava, received the Nobel Prize for physics for 1905. During the Nazi government in Germany he became a protagonist of a so- called pure German physics.

– In 1905, 50,000 people from Slovakia emigrated to the USA (the largest number for a single year prior to World War I). Extensive **emigration** was recorded also in subsequent years.

■ **1906**

19 February – After unsuccessful negotiations between the bureaucrat government and the opposition of coalition parties, the ruler dissolved the diet. Its building was occupied by soldiers. The government banned public assemblies.

17 March – Andrej Áchim founded the Independent Socialist Farmers Party of Hungary in Békéscsaba. It had strong support even among Slovak farmers in the lower lands. Milan Hodža, who sought to found a Slovak agrarian movement (**4 July 1903**), cooperated with it.

29 April – 8 May – Elections took place. They were marked by machinations and fraud that exceeded that of all previous elections. Seven Slovak representatives were elected to the diet, the largest number until then. Six of them declared allegiance to the people's party, one to the national party. As a consequence of its lack of success in the elections, the **Liberal Party** was dissolved.

26 November – 6 December – The trial of Slovak politicians who allegedly incited disorder during the pre-election campaign took place in Ružomberok. Andrej Hlinka was sentenced to two years and Vavro Šrobár to one year in prison while another 11 received lesser sentences. In Bratislava Ferdiš Juriga was sentenced to two years in prison.

– The Agricultural School in Košice changed its name to the Agricultural Academy. It fulfilled an important role in popularizing modern agriculture.

– The Transylvanian political scientist Aurel Popovici published the book, *The United States of Greater-Austria (Die vereinigten Staaten von Gross-Österreich)*. In it he rejected **dualism** and connected the preservation of the monarchy to its federalization (**Austro-Slavism**). The Federation would be made up of 15 autonomous states including Slovakia. The author also prepared a model constitution for the United States of Greater Austria. The views of Popovici approximated those shared by the so-called Belvedere group around the heir to the throne, Francis Ferdinand (**September 1908**).

– Karl Renner, the Austrian Social Democrat, published the work *The Foundations and Development Goals of the Austrian-Hungarian Monarchy (Grundlagen und Entwicklungsziele der Österreichisch-ungarischen Monarchie)*. In it he suggested the division of the empire into national units united by a weak central power. Cultural autonomy was to be secured for national groups living outside a compact national territory. The work was greatly appreciated by Slovak politicians.

■ **1907**

26 May – The most significant association of Slovak organizations in the United States, the Slovak League in America, was established at a large assembly in Cleveland, Ohio. Its presidium was made up of Štefan Furdek, Peter Rovnianek and Albert Mamatey.

2 June – The monarch signed the so-called Apponyi Laws (named for the minister of education, Albert Apponyi). They increased the responsibility of the state for the financial resources needed for education and teachers. However, they also advanced the complete **Magyarization** of primary schools. They forbade teachers to participate in national life, their pay was conditional upon the results of so-called patriotic training and required the use only of approved textbooks. Pupils were to have an active mastery of Hungarian after the fourth school year. The laws were complemented by a government regulation of 1909 that required the teaching of religion only in Hungarian.

10 October – A general strike for the right of universal suffrage took place in Hungary. Approximately 100,000 people demonstrated in front of the building of the Hungarian Diet in Budapest. The largest demonstration in Slovakia was in Bratislava (12,000 participants).

27 October – The **Černová tragedy** took place.

– In Prešov, the journal *Our Banner (Naša zastava)* began to be issued in the Šariš dialect with the support of the state authorities. By emphasizing the so-called *Slovjak* union, it sought to isolate the eastern Slovaks from the other Slovaks and to hasten the process of their Magyarization.

■ **1908**

May – In the so-called Kovačica process, 35 Evangelical believers were convicted of having protested the introduction of Hungarian divine services. Kovačica was a Slovak village in the Vojvodina.

August – The **Czechoslovak Union** organized a meeting of representatives of Czechs and Slovaks in Luhačovice, which subsequently became an annual event. The union founded branches in the Czech lands and obtained supporters in Slovakia who cooperated with it.

6 October – A directive was issued according to which Bosnia and Herzegovina were annexed to Austria-Hungary. This step was one of the modest results of the attempts of the monarchy to obtain a stronger position in the Balkans. But, at the same time, it led to a worsening of its relations with Russia and Serbia.

■ **1909**

August – A conference of young people supporting the aims of the **Hlasists** took place in Martin. It decided to establish the journal *Currents (Prúdy)*, which began publication in Budapest in November. It was edited by Bohdan Pavlů, Ivan Markovič and Vladimír Roy. This group also published the *Journal of Slovak Youth (Sborník slovenskej mládeže)*.

■ **1910**

1 – 10 June – The last election in Hungary took place. It was won by the National Party of Labor (60 per cent of the votes), established after the dissolution of the **Liberal Party** led by Stephen Tisza. Slovak nationalists and the populists campaigned together and won three seats as representatives.

– The cooperatives Lipa, in Martin, and Union for financing domestic industry in Skalica, were established using Slovak capital. Both produced in particular folk products and lace and competed with the Isabella society (**1895**). Their products met with great success at an exhibition in London organized by Robert William Seton-Watson in 1911 as well as at an exhibition in Vienna in 1913.

■ **1911**

28 June – A delegation of the Slovak National Party led by Pavol Mudroň delivered to Charles Khuen-Héderváry, the Hungarian prime minister, a memorandum that demanded adherence to the Nationality Law, the founding of Slovak primary schools, the renewal of the Matica slovenská and the return of its property. The government did not respond to the memorandum.

August – Leading personalities of the Slovak National Party (Pavol Mudroň, Matúš Dula), Milan Hodža, and the former *Hlasists* participated in a conference in Luhačovice (**August 1908**). In addition to cultural questions they considered cooperation in economic matters, especially strengthening the position of Czech capital in Slovakia.

September –Together with the Romanian, Juliu Maniu, Milan Hodža presented a secret memorandum to the heir to the throne, Francis Ferdinand. It outlined the federalization of the monarchy as a solution of the national question. Slovakia was to be an autonomous unit.

■ **1912**

18 February – Milan Hodža founded the Central Cooperative for Agriculture and Commerce in Budapest that helped to establish cooperatives of all kinds and defend their interests. It published the journal *Economic Horizon (Hospodársky obzor)*. Through the agrarian movement Hodža sought to raise the economic and social status of the farmers.

23 May – As part of the struggle for a universal right to vote and the improvement of social conditions, 100, 000 workers demonstrated in Budapest. The police and soldiers intervened against them. „Bloody Thursday" claimed 9 lives and 150 wounded. The largest assembly in Slovakia took place in Žilina.

6 – 7 August – The Slovak National Party transformed itself organizationally into the Central Club of the Slovak Nationality Party of the diet. The Central Club was comprised of 620 members of the party; additional members were active in the regions. In this way the leaders of the Slovak National Party sought to bring about closer cooperation among Slovak representatives and the Nationality Party of the diet.

■ **1913**

March – A delegation of the Slovak National Party led by Matúš Dula visited the heir to the throne, Francis Ferdinand. This indirectly confirmed the correctness of the political orientation of Milan Hodža towards the policy of the Belvedere group (**1906**) and the expected abolition of dualism and the federalization of the monarchy.

29 July – The **Slovak People's Party** was definitively established at a conference in Žilina. This ended the differentiation process in the Slovak national movement. Its leadership was comprised of Andrej Hlinka, Ferdiš Juriga, František Skyčák, Ignác Grebáč-Orlov and Florián Tománek. As a conservative party it sought to solve social problems in the spirit of papal encyclicals and according to Catholic social teachings.

– The largest amount of iron ore until that time was mined in Slovakia, 1,200 thousand tons, that is, 58 per cent of the total amount mined in Hungary. Among the numerous smelters and iron-works the largest were the iron-works in Podbrezová (the largest factory in Slovakia employing 3,000 people) and in Krompachy (1,900 employees).

■ **1914**

26 May – At a conference in Budapest the representatives of all Slovak political groups, with the exception of the Slovak People's Party, agreed to create the Slovak National Council as a representative organ for the whole nation.

3 June – Štefan Banič constructed a parachute and successfully tested it by jumping from a skyscraper in Washington. His idea was perfected by American military engineers so that the parachute began to be used by the United States Army.

28 June – The Serbian student Gavrilo Princip assassinated the heir to the Austrian throne, the Archduke Francis Ferdinand, and his wife in Sarajevo.

28 July – Leopold Berchtold, the Austrian-Hungarian Foreign minister, informed the Serbian government by telephone, of the declaration of war. This began the **First World War**.

6 August – The **Slovak National Party** declared its loyalty to the Habsburg dynasty and the monarchy. At the same time, during the war, it halted activities that would have led to persecution. Despite the pressure of Magyar politicians it did not even once express loyalty to the Hungarian government or renounce Czecho-Slovak cooperation.

10 September – The Slovak League in America issued a memorandum that demanded the right of Slovaks to self-determination by establishing their statehood. This statehood was not, however, more concretely defined (**26 May 1907**).

18 September – At an audience with the Russian Czar, the president of the Slovak club *Beseda* (Symposium) in Warsaw, Jozef Miloslav Országh, presented the idea of creating a joint state of Czechs and Slovaks with close ties to Russia. Representatives of the Czechs in Russia also approached the Czar with a similar idea.

23 November – After a massive offensive in Galicia, the Russian army occupied Humenné and, later, the greater part of northwestern Slovakia, from which it withdrew on 7 May 1915 under pressure from the Austrian army.

It was the only direct contact of Slovakia with the tactical front during the war.

■ 1915

11 March – The entry of the representatives of Slovakia into the Union of Czech Societies in Russia created the Union of Czecho-Slovak Societies in Russia. Its president was Bohumil Čermák and its vice-president Jozef Miloslav Országh. It organized the **Czecho-Slovak Legions**.

6 July – Tomáš Garrigue Masaryk, who had emigrated from Austria-Hungary in December 1914, began his public activity. In Geneva he expressed support for the policy of the Triple Entente, the division of the monarchy, and an independent Czecho-Slovak state. In May he had delivered to the British foreign secretary a memorandum about the need to create Czecho-Slovakia. He submitted a similar memorandum to the French government.

22 August – A bi-weekly newspaper, *Czechoslovak Independence (Československá samostatnost)* began to be published in Paris. It was edited by L. Sychrana and the Slovak Ivan Markovič. It became the organ of the Czechoslovak National Council in April 1916. As of 1 July 1917 its other press organ was *La Nation Tcheque.* It had been founded in the spring of 1915 by Tomáš Garrigue Masaryk and the French professor Ernst Denis.

15 September – The Hungarian government banned the *Slovak Daily (Slovenský denník).* Its editor, Anton Štefánek, left to work in Prague where he mediated contacts between Czech and Slovak politicians.

22 October – Representatives of Slovaks and Czechs in the United States concluded the **Cleveland Agreement**.

■ 1916

February – The Czech Foreign Committee in Paris was transformed into the **Czechoslovak National Council**.

21 November – After the death of Francis Joseph I, who had ruled longer than any other Hungarian monarch, his great-nephew Charles ascended the throne (Charles I (VII) as Austrian emperor, Charles IV as king of Hungary).

■ 1917

Transition from January to February – Three monarchs, the German emperor Wilhelm II, the Austrian emperor Charles I (VII), and the Bulgarian emperor Ferdinand I, met at Piešťany spa. During the meeting Wilhelm II received a telegram that the United States had terminated diplomatic relations with Germany and he issued a decree for an unrestricted submarine war. The meeting ended without results.

March – A subsidiary of the **Czechoslovak National Council** was created in Russia. Masaryk was able to obtain the permission of the provisional Russian government for the mass recruitment of Czech and Slovak prisoners of war for the **Czecho-Slovak Legions**.

1 May – For the first time during the war, the celebration of 1 May took place in Slovakia. It ended as a demonstration for peace and against hunger. It reflected the very bad economic situation, the shortages of goods, especially foodstuffs, and the social condition of the poor.

30 May – The Czech representatives in the imperial council presented a petition that had been signed by 222 Czech writers. It demanded that the Czech lands and Slovakia be joined into an autonomous unit within a federally organized monarchy. The Hungarian government delivered a sharp protest against this.

2 July – The **Czecho-Slovak Legions** in Russia took part in their first battle near Zborov (Ukraine); 3,500 legionnaires, of which 150 fell and 800 were wounded, helped the Russian army to victory.

17 August – The French government concluded an agreement with the **Czechoslovak National Council,** according to which the national council became the highest political authority of the Czecho-Slovak troops in France.

21 August – A group led by Hodža negotiated with some Czech politicians in Vienna about the inclusion of Slovakia into a future Czecho-Slovak state. The groups around Vavro Šrobár, Andrej Hlinka and Emanuel Lehocký were also informed of some of the negotiations.

■ 1918

6 January – Czech deputies to the imperial and country parliaments accepted the so-called Three Kings (Epiphany) Declaration in Prague. It demanded the establishment of a state unit by joining the Czech lands and Slovakia. The Austrian – German political public reacted to the declaration with a demand to create a German Czechia entity. The Magyar politicians attempted to persuade, unsuccessfully, the Slovak politicians to promise loyalty to an integrated Hungary.

8 January – President Woodrow Wilson presented to congress the 14 point program of the United States for the ending the war. The tenth point contained the federalization of Austria-Hungary with broad autonomous rights for its nations.

26 March – The Russian branch of the **Czechoslovak National Council** signed an agreement with the Soviet government about the transfer of the **Czecho-Slovak Legions** to Vladivostok. After a peace agreement between Germany and Soviet Russia was signed in Brest-Litovsk, the legions were transferred to the western front as part of the French army. Accidental conflicts with Magyar prisoners in Čeljabinsk and attempts of the Soviet power to disarm the legions led to clashes with them and later to the participation of the legions in the foreign intervention against Soviet Russia.

8 – 10 April – A congress of suppressed Austrian-Hungarian nations took place in Rome. There the representatives of foreign liberation movements of the Italians, Poles, Romanians, Czechs (Edvard Beneš), Slovaks (Milan Rastislav Štefánik and Štefan Osuský), and the Yugoslav nations declared their desire for political and economic independence.

30 April – The Hungarian government forbade the importation of Czech newspapers into Slovakia in order to stop the penetration of news about the liberation movement into the Czech lands.

1 May – A demonstration took place in Liptovský Mikuláš, which accepted the **Mikuláš Resolution**.

23 May – An insurrection of Slovak soldiers, afraid of being posted at the front, took place in Trenčín. They were supported by the population of the city.

24 May – A confidential consultation of the leadership of the **Slovak National Party** took place in Martin. Of the 24 participants at the meeting, Vavro Šrobár and Andrej Hlinka in particular declined to link the future of the Slovaks with Hungary and supported a political connection with the Czechs. Accepted by the meeting, this conclusion strengthened the arguments of the foreign resistance.

30 May – The **Pittsburgh Agreement** was signed.

2 – 8 June – The soldiers of the 71st infantry regiment mutinied in Kragujevac, Serbia. It was made up largely of Slovaks from Trenčín county. Forty-four of the mutineers were summarily executed.

13 June – The Czecho-Slovak National Committee was established or, better put, renewed. It gradually took power and passed the first laws of the new state. It also had a Slovak section. Its chairman was Karol Kramář.

20 – 29 June – A general strike took place in Hungary as a response to the shooting of striking workers in Pest (19 June). In Slovakia workers in Vrútky, Nové Zámky, Zvolen and Krompachy went on strike against the war and hunger.

29 June – The French government recognized the **Czechoslovak National Council** as the supreme organ of the Czechs and Slovaks and the basis for a future Czecho-Slovak government. On 9 August it was diplomatically recognized by Great Britain, on 3 September by the United States of America.

12 September – Representatives of the national party in Budapest agreed on the need to establish the **Slovak National Council** (1918) as the a representative organ of the Slovaks.

14 October – Edvard Beneš announced to the allied states the formation of a provisional Czecho-Slovak government in Paris (Tomáš

Garrigue Masaryk – president, Edvard Beneš – foreign minister, Milan Rastislav Štefánik, who was stationed in Siberia with the Czecho-Slovak legions – minister of defense).

16 October – The Emperor Charles issued a manifesto concerning the federalization of the Cisleithian lands. It precipitated protests from the Magyar politicians, who feared the possible federalization of Hungary, as well as from the politicians of nations that inclined towards the creation of independent states.

17 October - Tomáš Garrigue Masaryk delivered to the American government the **Washington Declaration** in the name of the provisional Czecho-Slovak government.

19 October – Ferdiš Juriga, the only Slovak deputy active in the Hungarian diet, presented the declaration that the Hungarian diet did not speak for the Slovaks, who had the right to decide freely on a constitutional basis, and that their single representative is the **Slovak National Council (1918)**.

24 October – Soldiers in Rimavská Sobota abandoned their barracks and the garrison dissolved. Likewise 500 soldiers in Tisovec went home. In this period the number of deserters increased. This „green cadre" took refuge in the mountain regions. Most of them (approximately 4,000) hid in the Small Car-pathians. After the founding of Czecho-Slovakia they disbanded or fought to force Hungarian units from Slovakia.

27 October – The new and last foreign minister of Austria-Hungary, Count Julius Andrássy, sent a note to the president of the United States. It declared the willingness of the monarchy to begin negotiations about a truce immediately. It was an expression of the abdication of power and a signal to the huge national liberation movements demanding the declaration of independent states.

28 October – Edvard Beneš negotiated in Geneva with a delegation of the Czecho-Slovak National Committee, led by its president, Karol Kramář. They agreed that Czecho-Slovakia would be a republic and Masaryk would be its president.

– A large demonstration in Prague approved the proclamation of an independent **Czecho-Slovakia**. That evening, the national committee that led the movement passed the first law concerning the foundation of Czecho-Slovakia. Vavro Šrobár signed it on behalf of the Slovaks.

30 October – The **Slovak National Council** was founded at an assembly in Martin. It declared its support for the new state by accepting the **Declaration of the Slovak Nation**.

Slovakia in Czecho-Slovakia between the wars (1918 – 1939)

In the inter-war period Slovakia was a part of the Czechoslovak Republic founded on 28 and 30 October 1918. This state was born due to changes among the powers caused by the First World War. It was incorporated into the system of international relations of post-war Europe as required by the victorious allied great powers, especially France.

Slovak politicians saw in the union with the Czechs a promising solution advantageous for both sides. The new state entity relieved the Slovaks of the pressure of Magyarization of the preceding decades, introduced a parliamentary democracy, raised the level of education of the population, stimulated the development of science and the arts, and made public events accessible to the citizens. However, it also brought new problems: Slovaks were not recognized as a distinct nation and the new state was built upon the principle of centralism. Emigration, a slowing down of economic development, the problem of the accessibility of significant positions for the new Slovak intelligentsia, corruption, political fragmentation and an unnatural progressiveness were phenomena that deeply influenced Slovak society. Slovak statehood did not exist. Only Czecho slovak statehood existed, and this the ruling circles understood as a more developed Czech statehood. In these conditions the Slovak nation was not able to take full advantage of the possibilities offered by the democratic political system. Among the political parties, only Hlinka's Slovak People's Party and the Slovak National Party consistently sought to advocate Slovak national rights. Through parliamentary means they pursued a policy advocating the distinctiveness of the Slovak nation and the idea of autonomy, the self-administration of Slovakia within the framework of the Czecho-Slovak state. This exclusively democratic program did not meet with the understanding of the official government structure that continued to adhere to an ethnic and state Czechoslovakism. In the 1920s the resolution of the Slovak problem was considered „premature". During the 1930s, after the victory of national socialism in Germany, it was „too late". Neighboring states understood the Czecho-Slovak state as a competing power without a tradition. A solution might be the revision of the borders. The state did not succeed in building up a firm base of support among its neighbors and was not able to count on their help in the case of an armed conflict with a gradually strengthening Germany. The policy of appeasement of France and Great Britain towards German ambitions in central Europe brought a fundamental change in the life of the Czecho-Slovak state and in the solution of the Slovak question. The Munich agreement of 29 September 1938 stripped from Czecho-Slovakia the border regions inhabited by a German minority. The rest of the state was left practically defenseless in the face of further German expansion. It is a sad fact of the time that, as a consequence of this significant weakening of the power of the Czechoslovak Republic, Slovak statehood was able to be implemented in the form of autonomy (6 October 1938). Germany did not have an interest in the further existence of the Czecho-Slovak state, even if it was transformed according to its own conception. It was interested in Czechia becoming a part of Germany. With this as a goal, Germany supported those Slovak politicians who sought to create an independent Slovak state. The history of this epoch, which lasted twenty years and five months, concluded with the emergence of the Slovak state on 14 March 1939.

■ 1918

31 October – The executive committee of the **Slovak National Council (1918)** held a meeting in Martin. It considered the proposal of the Czech lawyer Pantůček concerning the future position of Slovakia within a Czecho-Slovak state. The executive committee expressed the view that, after the completion of a transitional period lasting at most ten years, the constitutional relationships would be resolved on the basis of an agreement between the representatives of Czechia and Slovakia.

– The Emperor Charles named Michael Károlyi prime minister of Hungary by telephone and Károlyi took his oath by telephone.

1 November – Michael Károlyi requested the Emperor Charles to be released from his pledge of the previous day. The emperor complied but declined to relinquish the Hungarian throne.

3 November – In the name of the Austrian-Hungarian army, Field Marshall Hermann von Kövess signed an armistice with representatives of the Italian army in the Villa Giusti near Padua. A condition of the armistice was the reduction of the Austrian-Hungarian army to 20 divisions, a reduction of the artillery by half and the free movement of the allied armies within the territory of the former monarchy. The armistice went into effect on 4 November.

3 November – A group of demonstrators in Prague pulled down the statue of the Virgin Mary in Old Town Square. The movement against the Catholic Church found its expression on **8 January 1920** with the establishment of a new church named the Czechoslovak Church.

4 November – The national committee in Prague named the so-called provisional Slovak government with its headquarters in Skalica (Vavro Šrobár – Prime Minister, Ivan Dérer –

military and police, Anton Štefánek – education and Pavol Blaho – supply of foodstuffs and goods). At the same time as the government the first Czech soldiers entered Slovakia. After the departure of Šrobár, Štefánek and Dérer for Prague, only Pavol Blaho remained in Skalica. The activity of the government ceased with the creation of the Czecho-Slovak government in Prague on **14 November 1918**.

8 November – The **Slovak National Council** issued a call to the Slovak Nation for the founding of local Slovak national councils.

12 November – The Republic of German Austria was proclaimed in Vienna. The evening before, the Emperor Charles had abdicated as Emperor of Austria, but continued to be the king of Hungary (**13 November 1918**, **16 November 1918**).

– A conference of the American-Ruthenian National Council took place in Scranton, Pennsylvania (USA) at which 67 per cent of the delegates were in favor of the union of Sub-Carpathian Ruthenia with the Czecho-Slovak state on the condition of political autonomy. This decision was confirmed by a meeting of the Ruthenian national councils in Uzhgorod on 8 May 1919.

13 November – The commander-in-chief of the eastern army of the allies in the Balkans, Frandet d'Esperey, concluded a separate armistice with the government of Michael Károlyi in Belgrad, despite the armistice of 3 November 1918. The administration of Hungary, with the exception of Croatia, remained within the competence of Hungarian officials. This actually legalized the exercise of Magyar state power in Slovakia.

– The Czecho-Slovak National Committee proclaimed a provisional constitution, according to which the provisional national assembly was not elected but established by enlarging the national committee to 256 members. Elections in the Austrian part of the monarchy in 1911 were crucial. The number of Slovak representatives, selected by Vavro Šrobár and Matúš Dula, had been stipulated as 40 and in March 1919 this was raised to 54 later to 58. With this, the number of representatives in the Prague parliament was 270. However, according to the number of inhabitants, Slovakia had a claim to 69 representatives.

– A Magyar delegation led by the Hungarian primate, John Csernoch, visited the Emperor Charles in Eckartsau, Austria, and asked him to abdicate the Hungarian throne. Charles signed a proclamation as king of Hungary by which he abdicated the state power he had exercised until then.

14 November – The provisional national assembly met for the first time in Prague. Without a vote, the Czecho-Slovak state deposed the Habsburgs from the throne, declared itself a republic, and elected Tomáš Garrigue Masaryk president. An all-nation coalition government was established under Karol Kramář. The Slovaks were represented in it by the minister of war, Milan Rastislav Štefánik, and the minister of health, Vavro Šrobár, later plenipotentiary minister for the administration of Slovakia.

15 November – The Károlyi government, considering itself the government of the kingdom of Hungary, protested against the arrival of Czech soldiers in Slovakia and sent Magyar soldiers there.

16 November – At an assembly of un-elected delegates of the Magyar national councils, the Hungarian People's Republic was declared.

29 November – The chief of the joint military mission of the allies in Budapest, Lieutenant Colonel Ferdinand Vyx, protested the occupation of Slovakia by Czech soldiers to the Czecho-Slovak plenipotentiary representative in Budapest, Milan Hodža.

3 December – Lieutenant Colonel Ferdinand Vyx delivered the decision of the supreme allied military command to Michael Károlyi. According to it, as an allied state, Czecho-Slovakia had the right to occupy Slovak territory. The allied decision did not however, define line of demarcation (**6 December 1918, 24 December 1918**).

5 December – The high command of the Czecho-Slovak army in Slovakia issued an order confirming the command of the Guard of Slovak Liberty. The Guard of Slovak Liberty (*Garda Slovenskej Slobody*, later renamed the First Regiment of Slovak Liberty) was made up of Slovak volunteers and consisted of 168 officers and 3,200 private soldiers. Its headquarters were in Uherské Hradiště and later in Ružomberok. The Slovak volunteers originally were subordinated to the Slovak National Council (1918). The Guard of Slovak Liberty participated in the military occupation of eastern Slovakia, forcing out Polish and Magyar units. It was disbanded in March 1919.

6 December – Milan Hodža agreed with the Hungarian minister of defense, Albert Bartha, on a provisional line of demarcation unfavorable for Slovakia. The Rye Island, the cities of Bratislava and Košice, and a great part of southern Slovakia would belong to Hungary. His intention was to hinder the plebiscite for Slovakia being prepared by the Károlyi government and to achieve the quick departure of Magyar troops from Slovak territory.

7 December – Vavro Šrobár was commissioned as the minister of the Czecho-Slovak government to lead the plenipotentiary ministry for the administration of Slovakia. On 12 December he arrived in Žilina where he began to conduct business with 14 officials. The ministry was located in Žilina until **4 February 1919** when it was relocated to Bratislava.

10 December – The Prague parliament accepted a law that abolished noble titles and the rights and privileges based on them. Former nobles were forbidden to use their title with their names.

11 December – Viktor Dvortsák and his followers declared an independent Slovak People's Republic in Košice. The seat of the government was to have been Prešov. Dvortsák was a representative of the Hungarophile current. His state collapsed on 30 December 1918 with the arrival of the Czecho-Slovak army in Košice.

19 December – In Žilina the **Slovak People's Party** (SĽS) renewed its activities under the leadership of Andrej Hlinka. The renewal of the party was motivated by the need to de-

fend the rights of Slovak Catholics and the particularity of the Slovak nation.
– The Prague parliament enacted into law a working day of eight hours.

21 December – President Tomáš Garrigue Masaryk returned to Prague from the United States.

24 December – In the name of the allies, Lieutenant Colonel Ferdinand Vyx delivered a note to the Károlyi government of Hungary that established the demarcation line between Slovakia and Hungary. It followed the Danube river up to its juncture with the Ipeľ and then ran along the river Ipeľ up to Rimavská Sobota, which belonged to Slovakia, and then in a straight line to river Uh. The line then followed the river Uh up to the Uh pass. Károlyi accepted the note and on 29 January 1919 the Czecho-Slovak army completed the occupation of Slovakia (**4 June 1920**).

26 December – A congress of the Slovak Social Democratic Party took place in Liptovský Mikuláš. The delegates decided to establish a common party with the Czech social democrats. The merger of the two parties took place at the XII congress of the Czechoslovak social democrats in Prague on 27 – 30 December 1918.

■ **1919**

1 January – Minister Vavro Šrobár issued a regulation concerning the renewal of the Matica slovenská that called for its first general assembly to meet in Martin on 5 August 1919 (**4 August 1863**, **6 April 1875**).
– The Czecho-Slovak army occupied Bratislava.

8 January – Vavro Šrobár issued a regulation dissolving all local national councils on the territory of Slovakia. Their liquidation lasted until March. The **Slovak National Council (1918)** also became a victim of centralization and was dissolved on 31 January 1919.

18 January – A peace conference ceremonially opened in Paris. A Czecho-Slovak delegation participated in it. By this the other states collectively recognized the Czecho-Slovak state.

20 January – An agreement about the dispatch of a French military mission to Czecho-Slovakia was signed. The agreement subordinated the high-command of the Czecho- Slovak army to France. Another agreement was signed on 10 September 1919 about the operation of the mission. After 1 January 1926 the chief of the French military mission was to be an advisor to the ministry of national defense. It cost the Czecho-Slovak Republic 18 million crowns annually to maintain the French mission. The preference given to the French influence in the Czecho-Slovak military relations led to a worsening of relations between the Czecho-Slovak Republic and Italy.

30 January – After negotiations with representatives of the Evangelical Church of the Augsburg Confession (Lutherans), Vavro Šrobár issued a directive concerning temporary regulations for this church in Slovakia. It confirmed its right to self-administration (**17 February 1919, 18 January 1921, 22 October 1922**).

4 February – Minister Vavro Šrobár transferred his office from Žilina to Bratislava. The local Magyar socialists welcomed him with a general strike of the railway workers and the employees of the postal and telegraph service. After a short interruption, the strike continued on 12 February together with a mass demonstration of the Magyars, during which Czecho-Slovak soldiers, after being provoked, shot eight people.

17 February – Vavro Šrobár named a temporary 26 member general council for the administration of the Evangelical Church of the Augsburg Confession in Slovakia. Juraj Janoška became its clerical president (**18 January 1921, 22 October 1922**).

25 February – An enabling law and a regulation of the ministry of finance concerning the stamping of Austrian- Hungarian bank-notes made possible the introduction of a new Czecho-Slovak currency. The author of the successful currency reform of the new state was the minister of finance, Alois Rašín. He was assassinated by a leftist anarchist on 5 January 1923.

20 March – Lieutenant Colonel Ferdinand Vyx presented Michael Károlyi with a note about the creation of a neutral zone along the demarcation line. The zone was extend 50 kilometers into Magyar territory.

21 March – A republic of councils was declared in Hungary. The Social Democratic Party was merged into the Communist Party.

25 March – Influenced by events in Hungary, Minister Vavro Šrobár declared martial law in Slovakia.

16 April – The provisional National Assembly accepted a law about **land reform**. The law dealt with the confiscation of land holdings of more than 150 hectares of agricultural land or over 250 hectares of land in aggregate.

27 April – The Czecho-Slovak army began to occupy territory to the south of the line determined by the allied military command. Another goal was to occupy Sub-Carpathian Ruthenia. On 5 May it reached the Hungarian town of Miškolc. The action was coordinated with the Romanian army.

4 May – The plane carrying General Milan Rastislav Štefánik, the minister of war, on a flight from Italy crashed during a landing at the airport in Vajnory. Štefánik and the crew were killed. The crash was probably caused by a shot fired at the aircraft. After Štefánik's death the portfolio of minister of war remained unassigned. The cause of Štefánik's death still remains mysterious.

20 May – The Hungarian Red Army invaded Slovakia. It violated the line of demarcation and occupied Košice, Prešov, Bardejov, Banská Štiavnica, Nové Zámky, Zvolen and other towns. A terror against nationally conscious Slovaks was unleashed in the occupied lands. An attempt to link up with deserters from the army of Soviet Russia did not succeed.

13 June – The French premier Georges Clemenceau, the president of the peace conference, sent a note to the communist government in Budapest that demanded a cessation of the military operation and so determined the definitive border between Czecho-Slovakia and Hungary.

16 June – A popular assembly declared a Slovak republic of councils. Antonín Janoušek, a Czech worker, stood at the head of this state entity, which was completely dependent upon Budapest. Behind it was an attempt to influence the peace conference in Paris so that the integrity of Hungary would be renewed. With the departure of the Magyar army from Slovakia on 5 July 1919 the Slovak republic of councils collapsed.

24 June – A truce was concluded and the Magyar army was to leave Slovakia by 5 July. The Czecho-Slovak army had lost 3,694 troops, the Hungarian Red Army had lost 4,141 soldiers.

27 June – Parliament passed a law concerning the founding of a university in Bratislava to replace the Hungarian Elizabeth University, which had been dissolved. The university, was named after Jan Amos Comenius by a government regulation of 11 November 1919 and was to have three faculties: medical, legal and philosophical (**3 July 1940**).

28 June – The German delegation signed the peace treaty in Versailles, France. Germany recognized the independence of Czecho-Slovakia and withdrew from the region of Hlučín.

8 July – President Tomáš Garrigue Masaryk named a new government led by the social democrat Vlastimil Tusar. Slovaks were represented in it by the ministers Milan Hodža, Vavro Šrobár and Ivan Dérer, who were centralist politicians. The previous government of Karol Kramář had faced a crisis when the national democrats resigned from it in May 1919.

27 August – A delegation of the **Slovak People's Party** made up of Andrej Hlinka, František Jehlička and Štefan Mnoheľ secretly traveled through Poland to France in order to inform the peace conference in Paris about the unfavorable position of the Slovak nation in centralist Czecho-Slovakia. Andrej Hlinka returned to Slovakia on 4 October 1919. He was arrested and imprisoned for two months. František Jehlička remained abroad and promoted the idea of a federated Hungarian state.

10 September – The Austrian delegation signed the peace treaty in Saint-Germain-en-Laye, France. Austria recognized the independence of Czecho-Slovakia and its borders by this treaty.

16 September – The National Republican Party of Farmers with an agrarian program was organized in Bratislava. It sought to draw upon the tradition of the **Slovak National Party** when it merged with it to form an electoral bloc on 11 January 1920 in Turčiansky sv. Martin. Thus the Slovak National and Farmers' Party was established. After losing the elections, the Slovak National Party declared its independence again on 30 March 1921. In 1922 the National Republican Party merged with the Czech agrarians under the name the Republican Party of Agricultural Workers and Small Farmers (Agrarian Party).

23 November – The constituting assembly of the Magyar Compatriots Christian-Socialist Party took place in Košice. The party formulated a program of **autonomy** for Slovakia. It understood autonomy as the elimination of Czech influence in Slovakia and the inclination of Slovakia to Hungary (**6 June 1936**).

11 December – A nostrification (certification) law was adopted. Joint stock companies with enterprises in Czecho-Slovakia had to relocate their foreign headquarters and have them officially registered. A total of 231 companies, until then located in Austria and Hungary, were relocated and certified.

■ **1920**

8 January – Dissatisfied Roman Catholic clergy in Prague founded a new church, the Czechoslovak Church, and invited people to leave the Catholic Church. The immediate cause for founding the church was the intervention of the new archbishop of Prague, František Kordáč, in disbanding the reformist Unity of Catholic Clergy. In 1930 about 800,000 people declared their membership in the Czechoslovak Church. It did not find support in Slovakia.

17 February – The constituting assembly of the Magyar Compatriot Party of Small Farmers and Agricultural Workers took place in Komárno. In 1925 the party took the name Hungarian National Party. It gradually adopted the **autonomy of Slovakia** as its program but with the expectation that this would result in more rights for the Hungarian-speaking minority (**23 November 1919, 6 June 1936**).

29 February – The unelected provisional national assembly accepted the constitution of the first **Czechoslovak Republic**, a language law and other important laws. The constitution defined the Czechoslovak Republic as a democratic republic with a president elected by the parliament. The preamble began with the words, „We, the Czechoslovak nation", an expression of **Czechoslovakism**. The language law designated a fictive „Czechoslovak language" as the „official language of the state". National minorities had the right to use their language in offices and courts in the districts where they made up more than 20 per cent of the population.

1 March – The Slovak National Theater in Bratislava opened with the first performance of Smetana's opera „The Kiss" (Hubička).

18 March – The Slovak economist Kornel Stodola founded the Danube Fair in Bratislava. Its original name was the Oriental Fair.

22 March – The Spiš German Party was established in Kežmarok. The party had a regional character, closely cooperated with Magyar minority parties and was completely subordinate to their policy. In disappeared in 1938 by merging with the German Party in Slovakia (*Deutsche Partei in der Slowakei*), (**1929, 28 March 1935**).

18 April – Elections for representatives to the assembly according to the new electoral system took place. State-wide, the Social Democratic Party was victorious and received 25.7 per cent of the vote. In Slovakia it obtained 39.4 per cent of the vote. The Agrarian Party obtained 18.6 per cent of the vote, which put it in the second place in Slovakia, while in third place was the People's Party with 18.1 per cent of the votes.

25 May – President Tomáš Garrigue Masaryk named a new government led by Vlastimil Tusar. During the Tusar government a powerful political group was formed, the so-called **government five**.

27 May – Tomáš Garrigue Masaryk was elected as president for the second time by the National Assembly.

4 June – In the Grand Trianon Palace near Paris a peace treaty with Hungary was signed. Edvard Beneš and Štefan Osuský signed for the Czecho-Slovak state, while August Benárd and Alfréd Drasche-Lázár signed it for Hungary. The treaty definitively established the state borders of Hungary and obliged it to respect the rights of national minorities. For Hungary Trianon meant partial military and financial limitations. The treaty went into effect on 26 July 1921.

28 July – The supreme council of the Allies decided on the division of Těšín region between Poland and Czechoslovak Republic. Upper Orava and Spiš (25 villages with a population of 22,523 Slovaks) devolved to Poland. Edvard Beneš, the foreign minister, waived a plebiscite and yielded to the decision of the supreme council without consulting with parliament or the government.

9 August – The Czecho-Slovak government issued a decree concerning neutrality in the military conflict between Poland and Soviet Russia when the Red Army stood before Warsaw. The Těšín crisis and the attitude of the Czecho-Slovak government was the reason for a chilling in the relationships between the two states during the inter-war period.

14 August – A treaty was signed creating a defensive alliance between Czecho-Slovakia and the Kingdom of the Serbians, Croatians and Slovenians, which was directed against Magyar revisionism and a restoration of the Habsburgs. This treaty was supplemented by the Czechoslovak-Romanian treaty of alliance of **23 April 1921** (the Little Entente).

14 September – As a result of a crisis in the Social Democratic Party, in which a strong communist left-wing had formed, Prime Minister Vlastimil Tusar, submitted his resignation.

15 September – President Tomáš Garrigue Masaryk named a **caretaker government** led by Ján Černý. The ministers Martin Mičura and Vladimír Fajnor represented the Slovaks in it.

19 September – A congress of the left-wing of the Slovak Social Democratic Party convened in Martin. The right-wing withdrew on 7 November. A complete rupture of the social democrats in Slovakia occurred.

25 – 28 September – The left-wing of the Social Democratic Party arranged a state-wide congress. Its primary goal was to mobilize a majority of the working class for the revolution.

10 October – Soldiers, incited by propaganda, shot dead two farmers at an assembly of the **Slovak People's Party** in Námestovo.

22 October – A Slovak-American, Ignác Gessay, founded in Bratislava the Slovak League in Slovakia. This non- partisan association fostered Slovak national consciousness, culture, education and information. Its presiding officers were Method Matej Bella, Vojtech Brestenský and Anton Granatier. Within the Slovak League a school foundation (*školská matica*), led by Alois Kolísek and Ferdiš Juriga, functioned. Prior to 1938 it established 277 Slovak schools in linguistically mixed regions of Slovakia. The Slovak League merged with the **Matica slovenská** in 1948.

13 November – Pope Benedict XV informed a secret consistory (advisory body of cardinals) that three Slovak bishops had been named: Ján Vojtaššák for Spiš, Marián Blaha for Banská Bystrica and Karol Kmeťko for the Nitra diocese. Their solemn consecration took place on 21 February 1921 in Nitra, the cradle of Christianity in Slovakia (**3 March 1973, 19 May 1988, 17 March 1990**).

24 November – At the initiative of Milan Hodža, representatives of Slovak political parties founded a political committee that was to pursue the same goals on questions of political administration, land reform and the economy. However, it had only a short life-span. Slovak politicians were not united on the question of the legislative **autonomy of Slovakia**.

9 December – After intervention by the police, the Social Democratic Party recovered the People's House (*Lidový dům*) in Prague, which the left-wing faction of the party had seized. The executive committee of the left-wing faction of the Social Democratic Party called for a general strike.

10 December – As a result of the strike declared at several locations in the state, clashes of the police with workers occurred. Four workers were shot dead in Vráble.

■ **1921**

16 January – A congress of the left wing representatives of the Social Democratic Party from Slovakia and Sub-Carpathian Russia assembled in Ľubochňa. Its participants accepted 21 conditions for entry into the Communist International.

18 January – A synod of the Evangelical Church of the Augsburg Confession (Lutherans) assembled in Trenčianske Teplice. Juraj Janoška and Vladimír Fajnor were elected its presidents. The synod approved the constitution of the Evangelical Church of the Augsburg Confession on 10 May 1922. The Czecho-Slovak government approved it on 10 May 1922 (**30 January 1919, 22 October 1922**).

7 March – In Piešťany, representatives of 100 enterprises, until then organized in the Territorial Union Hungarian Industrialists, founded the Central Association of Slovak Industry, which became an important economic and political force. By the mid-1930s 700 companies were members.

23 April – The Czechoslovak Republic signed a treaty of alliance with Romania. The alliance of the Czechoslovak Republic, the Kingdom of the Serbians, Croatians and Slovenians, and Romania, called the Little Entente, was completed with the treaty between Romania and the Kingdom of the Serbians, Croatians and Slovenians of 17 June 1921. The specified obligations of the states of the Little Entente were limited to fighting against Hungarian revisionism and an attempt to return the Habsburgs to the throne (**14 August 1920, 23 October 1921**) .

3 May – The constituting general assembly of the Artists Forum of Slovakia (*Umelecká beseda Slovenská*) was held in Bratislava. The society had three sections: music, literature and the visual arts. It promoted and supported Slovak art. The senior member of the society was the architect Dušan Jurkovič. In 1939 it merged with the Society of Slovak Artists and the Association of Slovak Artists to form the Society of Slovak Artists. In 1946 it was re-established using the original name. Mikuláš Bakoš became its president. It was enlarged by a film and theater section. In 1950 it merged with the Slovak section of the Union of Czechoslovak Visual Artists. It was re-established in 1990.

14 – 16 May – The founding congress of the **Communist Party of Czechoslovakia** took place in Prague. The congress accepted 21 conditions for entry into the Communist International and requested the acceptance of the party into this international communist organ. The program of the Communist Party of Czechoslovakia was revolution, the dictatorship of the proletariat and the nationalization of the means of production.

26 September – President Tomáš Garrigue Masaryk named a new government with Edvard Beneš, a Czechoslovak national socialist, as prime minister. The Slovaks were represented in it by the ministers Martin Mičura, Vavro Šrobár and Ivan Dérer.

23 October – Czecho-Slovakia and the Kingdom of the Serbians, Croatians and Slovenians declared a partial mobilization in order to thwart an attempt by Emperor Charles to return to the Hungarian throne. This attempt was suppressed by the Hungarian army. Charles was exiled to the island of Madeira, where he died on 1 April 1922.

26 November – The deputies of the **Slovak National Party** withdrew from a joint parliamentary club with the Czechoslovak People's Party. Andrej Hlinka explained this step by citing fidelity to the program of the **autonomy of Slovakia**, which the Czech Peoples Party rejected, as well as the unfulfilled agreement concerning the establishment of three Slovak Catholic secondary schools.

– Juraj Siakeľ, of American Slovak origin, directed the first Slovak film, Jánošík, about the fate of the legendary robber Juraj Jánošík.

■ **1922**

22 January – Parliament passed a law establishing the Bratislava stock exchange. The ex-change began to operate on 26 June 1922. Its first president was Kornel Stodola, who had contributed greatly to its establishment.

25 January – With the assistance of the German Christian Social Party, the Slovak People's Party submitted to parliament the first official proposal for **autonomy of Slovakia** prepared by the lawyer Ľudovít Labaj.

3 August – The congress of the Slovak People's Party assembled in Žilina and accepted a memorandum reiterating the complaints and demands of the Slovak nation. It proposed the **autonomy of Slovakia** as a way out of the desolate economic, cultural and political situation. The document was sent to President Tomáš Garrigue Masaryk and, after its translation into foreign languages, was disseminated abroad (**21 June 1923**).

4 October – The Czechoslovak Republic consented to the Geneva protocol about economic assistance to Austria.

7 October – President Tomáš Garrigue Masaryk named a new government led by the agrarian Antonín Švehla. The ministers Jozef Kállay, Ivan Markovič and Milan Hodža represented the Slovaks in it.

22 October – The ceremonial consecration of the first two Slovak bishops of the Evangelical Church of the Augsburg Confession, Juraj Janoška and Samuel Zoch, took place in Liptovský Mikuláš (**30 January 1919, 17 February 1919, 18 January 1921**).

■ **1923**

6 March – The parliament adopted a law on the defense of the republic. The law confirmed the trend towards the centralization of the state. It contained paragraphs concerning sanctions for activities directed against state unity or its constitutional agents. Directed against the communists, it actually punished attempts to establish **autonomy of Slovakia.**

15 June – The constituting general assembly of the Society of Slovak Writers was held in Bratislava. Vavro Šrobár and Janko Jesenský alternated as presidents. After the establishment of the first Slovak Republic, Valentín Beniak became its president. In this period the membership of the society doubled. The journal *Elán* was the official publication of the society (**18 June 1945**).

21 June – The club of the deputies and senators of the Slovak People's Party empowered the vice-chairman of the party, Vojtech Tuka, to present the Žilina memorandum of **3 August 1922** to the council of ambassadors in Paris and the League of Nations in Geneva. Tuka fulfilled this assignment.

18 August – The conference of ambassadors decided to present to the Council of the League of Nations the dispute between Czecho-Slovakia and Poland over the Javorina region. The **Slovak People's Party** suggested the exchange of the Javorina for Slovak villages in Poland (**28 July 1920**). On 12 March 1924 the council approved a demarcation line defined by the International Arbitration Court in the Hague. Javorina remained a part of Slovakia.

30 September – County elections took place in Slovakia. They were won by the **Slovak People's Party,** which became the strongest Slovak political party.

6 October – The Czechoslovak state airline was established in Prague.

29 October – The first flight of the Czechoslovak airline, by an A 14 (Brandenburg), took place on the Prague-Bratislava route (**1 July 1930**).

■ **1924**

25 January – Czecho-Slovakia and France, represented by the foreign ministers Edvard Beneš and Raymond Poincar, signed a treaty of alliance and friendship in Paris. The parties pledged to take measures to secure their mutual interests if either were threatened. The treaty did not contain an obligation of mutual military assistance as was the case in a similar treaty between France and Poland in 1921.

2 October – At a session of the League of Nations in Geneva, the representatives of 44 states approved the Geneva protocol. Its text was prepared by the Czecho-Slovak foreign minister Edvard Beneš and the Greek politician N. Politis. It was a general guaranty pact. The signatories pledged not to resolve con-

flicts by war but by means of the arbitration court in the Hague or by a decision of the League of Nations. Great Britain stood out against the protocol and other states declined to ratify it. The only state that ratified the protocol was the Czechoslovak Republic.

■ **1925**

6 July – The papal **nuncio** and dean of the diplomatic corps, Francesco Marmaggi ostentatiously left Prague. The reason for this was the raising of a Hussite rather than the state flag over the Prague castle on the state holiday commemorating the burning of Jan Hus. Tense relations with the Vatican continued until the signing of the **modus vivendi** of 17 December 1927.

5 – 16 October – An international conference of foreign ministers took place in Locarno in Switzerland. Germany concluded with France, Belgium, Italy and Great Britain the so-called Rhineland Mutual Guaranty pact, which guaranteed the immutability of the Versailles border between Germany, France, and Belgium. Germany declined to conclude such a pact with the Czechoslovak Republic or Poland. Only less significant arbitration agreements were concluded with them. France concluded a guaranty treaty with the Czechoslovak Republic and Poland.

17 October – The broader executive committee of the **Slovak People's Party** decided to rename the party **Hlinka's Slovak People's Party** (HSPP). The reason for the change was to differentiate it from the Czechoslovak People's Party, which had decided to establish its own branch in Slovakia, led by Martin Mičura, before the parliamentary elections.

15 November – Parliamentary elections took place. State-wide the agrarians won with 13.66 per cent of the vote, while the second strongest party with 13.14 per cent of the votes was the Czechoslovak Communist Party. In Slovakia Hlinka's Slovak People's Party won with 34.3 per cent, second was the Agrarian Party with 17.4 per cent and third was the Communist Party of Czechoslovakia with 13.9 per cent of the votes.

9 December – President Tomáš Garrigue Masaryk named a new government. The agrarian Antonín Švehla became prime minister again. The ministers Jozef Kállay, Milan Hodža and Ivan Dérer represented the Slovaks.

18 December – The representative of the Communist Party of Czechoslovakia in parliament, Bohumil Šmeral, delivered a speech in which he outlined a change in the tactics of the party on the nationality question. According to it, each nation in the Czechoslovak Republic had the right to self-determination and even to secede. He characterized the results of the elections in Slovakia as a plebiscite that had repudiated „the bureaucratic Czech nationalist centralism of Prague". The new tactics, supported by various memoranda, were used up to 1928.

■ **1926**

18 March – President Tomáš Garrigue Masaryk named a **caretaker government** led by Ján Černý. This was because of a controversy between the agrarians and the social democrats in the governing coalition. The Slovaks were represented by Jozef Kállay and Juraj Slávik.

23 May – Andrej Hlinka, together with a seven member delegation, traveled to a eucharistic congress in Chicago. Separate delegations were made up of the Slovak **bishops**, representatives of the St. Vojtech (Adalbert) Society, and the Svorad student society in Bratislava. The delegates met with Slovak compatriots in the United States.

22 June – The **Agrarian Party** pushed through the introduction of fixed agrarian tariffs.

25 June – Parliament approved the so-called congruency law modifying the salaries of the clergy of the churches and religious societies. This measure was to meet the demands especially of the priests of the Catholic Church who, after the confiscation of church property, had insufficient financial support. The congruency adjustment was systematically paid only after 1930.

27 September – The Holy See named Pavol Gojdič as the apostolic administrator of the Greek Catholic diocese (the *Eparchy* of Prešov). Pope Pius XI named him a bishop on 22 February 1927.

2 October – Regular radio broadcasting began in Bratislava. The first test of broadcasting already had taken place in Košice in December 1925 (**15 June 1939, 28 April 1948, 24 May 1991**).

12 October – President Tomáš Garrigue Masaryk named a new government. Again the prime minister was Antonín Švehla. Neither representatives of the social democrats nor of the national socialists were included in the government. Jozef Kállay and Milan Hodža represented the Slovaks. For the first time German ministers became members of the government. They represented the German Christian socialists (Robert Mayr-Harting) and the German agrarians (Franz Spina).

2 December – The constituting assembly of the Šafárik Learned Society (which officially used the Czech version of its name, *Učená společnost Šafaříkova*) took place in Bratislava. Its goal was scientific research of Slovakia and Sub-Carpathian Ruthenia. The society held to the ideology of **Czechoslovakism**. Its first president was Professor Augustín Ráth and its secretary was Professor Albert Pražák. The society published the journal *Bratislava* and during its existence published 37 issues. In 1939, after the first **Slovak Republic** was created, the society was disbanded and its property put into the hands of the newly founded Slovak Learned Society.

■ **1927**

15 January – The opposition **Hlinka's Slovak People's Party** joined the government and obtained two ministerial portfolios. Jozef Tiso became the minister of health and physical education; Marek Gažík became the minister for the unification of laws and the organization of the administration (he was later replaced by Ľudovít Labaj). The government was comprised of a broad coalition of agrarians, populists, national democrats and tradesmen. **Hlinka's Slovak People's Party** withdrew its ministers from the government on 5 October 1929 because of the political trial of Vojtech Tuka.

22 April – Pope Pius XI, by the bull *Celebre apud Slovaccham Gentem,* declared the Virgin Mary of the Seven Sorrows to be the patroness of Slovakia. With this the Vatican emphasized the particularity of the Slovak nation and the territory it occupied.

27 May – Parliament elected Tomáš Garrigue Masaryk president for the third time.

24 June – Lord Rothermere, the English press magnate, published an article, „The Place of Hungary under the Sun", in his newspaper, *The Daily Mail*. Together with the Hungarian government he began a propaganda campaign for a revision of the Treaty of Trianon, which had been concluded on **4 June 1920**. The wave of protests in Slovakia against Hungarian revisionism increased.

14 July – Parliament passed a law concerning changes in political administration. According to this law a so-called **regional system** was established for the whole territory of the Czechoslovak Republic. Slovakia, which until then had been divided into counties without a central administrative organ, obtained a regional administration with limited competencies. The new law went into effect in Slovakia on 1 July 1928.

■ **1928**

1 January – Vojtech Tuka published a philosophical discussion of the state, „The Tenth Year of the Martin Declaration", in the daily newspaper *The Slovak (Slovák)* . It presumed the existence of a secret clause of the Martin Declaration (**30 October 1918**). According to Tuka, „a juridical vacuum" (*vacuum juris*) would arise after 30 October 1928 and the Slovaks had the right to decide their own future. The article was the impulse for initiating the political trial of Vojtech Tuka (**5 October 1929**).

20 January – The Czecho-Slovak government approved the text of the **modus vivendi** with the Vatican. The agreement meant a normalization of relations between the states.

27 August – Representatives of the Czechoslovak Republic together with those of other states signed the so-called Kellogg-Briand Pact in Paris. The pact outlawed war as a political means. It was binding only on its signatories and did not contain any sanctions for the violation of its conditions. Therefore it was without practical effect.

23 September – On the summit of Bradlo near the town of Brezová, the statue of General Milan Rastislav Štefánik, the magnificent work of the Slovak architect Dušan Jurkovič, was ceremonially dedicated.

■ **1929**

1 February – President Tomáš Garrigue Masaryk named a new government led by the agrarian František Udržal. The ministers Milan Hodža, Jozef Tiso and Marek Gažík represented the Slovaks.

18 – 23 February – The fifth congress of the Communist Party of Czechoslovakia took place in Prague. A radical wing led by Klement Gottwald was able to push through its program. It carried out an internal purge of the party under the guise of bolshevizing.

5 October – The regional court in Bratislava sentenced Vojtech Tuka, professor of law and deputy of **Hlinka's Slovak People's Party**, and his companions (Alexander Mach and Anton Sznacký). Accused of high treason and espionage for Hungary, in a political trial and despite a lack of evidence, Tuka was condemned to 15 years in prison (he spent eight and a half years in prison). Mach and Sznacký were released.

8 October – The ministers of **Hlinka's Slovak People's Party**, Jozef Tiso and Ľudovít Labaj, submitted their resignations, to protest the result of the trial of Vojtech Tuka. Other reasons were conflicts within the leadership of Hlinka's Slovak People's Party and the dissatisfaction of its voters with the results achieved for Slovakia by the participation of its representatives in the government.

27 October – Elections to parliament took place. The agrarians were victorious statewide with 15 per cent of the votes. In Slovakia **Hlinka's Slovak People's Party** won with 28.26 per cent of the votes, the agrarians were second with 19.53 per cent and the communists were third with 10.66 per cent.

17 November – The Czechoslovak Republic changed its currency to the gold standard.

The crown was to contain 44.58 mg of pure gold.

7 December – President Tomáš Garrigue Masaryk named a new government again led by the agrarian František Udržal. The Czechoslovakist ministers Juraj Slávik and Ivan Dérer represented the Slovaks.

– Shortly before the parliamentary elections a Carpathian German Party (*Karpathendeutsche Partei*) was established. The party had an activist program and sought to free the Germans of Slovakia from Magyar influence. On 10 October 1938 it was renamed the German Party (*Deutsche Partei*) (**28 March 1935**).

■ **1930**

8 May – **Hlinka's Slovak People's Party** presented a second proposal for the **autonomy of Slovakia** in parliament. Its author was the lawyer Karol Mederly.

1 July – The first international airline route of the Czechoslovak Republic was established between the cities of Prague and Bratislava and Zagreb in Croatia (**29 October 1923**).

■ **1931**

19 January – Under the presidency of Kornel Stodola, a National Economics Institute for Slovakia and Sub-Carpathian Russia (NÁRUS) was established. NÁRUS brought together the younger and middle generations of Slovak national economists (Imrich Karvaš, Peter Zaťko, Vojtech Brestenský, Ján Štetina and others). It prepared projects for the **industrialization** of Slovakia and sent several memoranda to the government requesting support for the realization of their goals.

25 May – Gendarmes fired upon demonstrators in Košúty in southern Slovakia. Three persons lost their lives. The demonstration had been organized by the **Communist Party of Czechoslovakia**. A manifesto of protest was signed by 34 Czech and Slovak writers and journalists.

December – Industrial production, which had been maintained at 80 per cent of the level in 1929, began to decline rapidly as a result of the economic depression.

■ **1932**

16 February – Representatives of the Czechoslovak Republic, Romania and Yugoslavia signed the organizational treaty of the **Little Entente (14 August 1920)**.

12 May – The general assembly of the **Matica slovenská** met in Martin. The assembly rejected the candidacy of the old committee and elected a new committee without Czechs and Czechoslovakists. At the same time, it approved a revision of the *Rules of Slovak Orthography* (*Pravidlá slovenského pravopisu*) by the Czech linguist, Václav Vážný, who had tried to bring the Slovak and Czech languages closer; 128 Slovak writers, translators and journalists had protested against the rules of Vážný.

25 – 26 June – About 370 representatives of the younger Slovak intelligentsia met in Trenčianske Teplice in order to find a common solution to the Slovak question, irrespective of differences in their political orientation. They accepted a manifesto that rejected centralism. The younger Slovak generation declared its support for autonomy. They differed only on the degree of autonomy, which ranged from federalism to regionalism. The congress demanded a just social order and criticized immorality and corruption in politics.

16 October – On the 90th anniversary of the speech of Ľudovít Štúr in the **Hungarian diet**, the leading personalities of **Hlinka's Slovak People's Party** and the **Slovak National Party** met in Zvolen. They were united by a common interest, the **autonomy of Slovakia**, as was shown by the creation of an autonomist bloc. The presidents of both parties, Andrej Hlinka and Martin Rázus, emphasized that national unity stood above religious confession in politics.

29 October – President Tomáš Garrigue Masaryk named a new government led by the agrarian Jan Malypetr. Milan Hodža and Ivan Dérer represented the Slovaks in it.

12 – 16 November – A wave of opposition to foreclosures led to shootings by gendarmes that took the lives of three people in the village of Polomka (16 November). Three people also were shot during foreclosures in

Čierny Balog (7 June 1933). The stricter attitude of financial authorities in Slovakia in comparison to those in Czechia during the economic crisis is demonstrated by the fact that the expenses of foreclosures, interest for delayed payments and penalties in 1934 yielded 6,150, 000 crowns in Slovakia and only 4,800,000 crowns in Czechia.

28 – 29 December – A working congress of the Slovak autonomists took place in Trenčín. The congress appealed for the cultivation of national unity and concord and condemned class and confessional discord. It was here that Andrej Hlinka uttered his well-known slogan „We will not renounce the uniqueness of the Slovak nation even at the price of the Republic".

– Karol Plicka's documentary film, *Along the Mountains, Through the Valleys (Po horách, po dolách)* received the gold medal at the international exhibition of photographic arts in Florence. His later film, *The Earth Sings (Zem spieva)*, the first Slovak sound film, received a prize at the Bienniale in Venice in 1934.

■ **1933**
28 February – Labor offices recorded the highest number of unemployed. In the whole of the Czechoslovak Republic 919,083 were unemployed, of whom 110,171 were from Slovakia. At the end of February 1936 there were 860,393 unemployed in the Czechoslovak Republic, of whom 141,340 were in Slovakia. While unemployment throughout the whole state declined by about 6 per cent after 1933, in Slovakia it grew about 28 per cent. In 1937 an economic revival led to a decline in unemployment also in Slovakia.

24 May – Tomáš Garrigue Masaryk was elected president for the fourth time.

12 – 15 August – A celebration of the 1,000[th] anniversary of the consecration of the first Christian church in Slovakia (under Pribina) took place in Nitra. The celebration was organized by the government. Participants in the celebration forced the appearances of Andrej Hlinka and Martin Rázus, who had been left out of the official program. Tens of autonomists lost their jobs after a demonstration and

several were imprisoned. For a time, the publications of **Hlinka's Slovak People's Party** were not permitted to be published.

■ **1934**
19 February – The government of the Czechoslovak Republic resolved that it would not deny the right to asylum to former members of the Austrian Social Democratic Party and its para-military organization, the *Schutzbund*. Centers of Austrian immigration were Prague and Brno; there were refugee camps in Volary, Žatec, Znojmo, Nýrsko and Hodonín, and in Slovakia in the cities of Bratislava and Trnava. About 1,300 people emigrated from Austria to Czecho-Slovakia in 1934. The majority of them decided to go to the Soviet Union.

9 June – The Czechoslovak Republic initiated full diplomatic relations with the Soviet Union.

10 June – The Czecho-Slovak football (soccer) team lost to Italy in the finals of the world championship in Rome and received the silver medal (**20 June 1976**).

■ **1935**
28 March – An electoral agreement concerning a common approach in the coming parliamentary election was concluded between the Sudeten German Home Front (*Sudetendeutscher Heimatfront*) and the Carpathian German Party (**22 March 1920, 1929**).

16 May – Czecho-Slovakia and the Soviet Union signed a treaty of alliance. Its second article laid down that military assistance would be provided only if the victim of an attack was offered assistance by France.

19 May – A parliamentary election took place. The opposition Sudeten German party won with 15.18 per cent of the votes in the whole of Czecho-Slovakia. In Slovakia the autonomist bloc grouped around **Hlinka's Slovak People's Party** obtained 30.12 per cent of the vote, the agrarians were second with 17.64 per cent, and a bloc made up of the Hungarian National and the Christian Socialist parties was third.

4 June – President Tomáš Garrigue Masaryk named a new government led by the agrarian

Jan Malypetr. The ministers Ivan Dérer and Milan Hodža represented the Slovaks.

5 November – When Malypetr was elected the chairman of the assembly of deputies, President Tomáš Garrigue Masaryk named a new government led by the agrarian Milan Hodža. He was the first Slovak to serve as the prime minister. The Hodža government lasted until 22 September 1938.

14 December – The seriously ill 85 year-old President Tomáš Garrigue Masaryk resigned. The month before he had recommended Edvard Beneš as his successor.

18 December – The parliament elected the foreign minister Edvard Beneš as president.

20 December – Prime Minister Milan Hodža took over the leadership of the foreign ministry. He held this office until 29 February 1936 and sought to implement, without great success, his plan for cooperation among the Danubian states.

■ **1936**
30 May – 1 June – The first congress of Slovak writers met in Trenčianske Teplice. A joint resolution, signed by 51 writers, expressed fidelity to „the struggle for freedom and the great ideals of mankind" and resolved „that our literary work was in harmony with the desires of the people for social liberty and justice".

6 June – The unifying congress of the Magyar Christian Social Party and the Magyar National Party took place in Nové Zámky (**23 November 1919, February 1920**).

19 – 20 September – A congress of **Hlinka's Slovak People's Party** took place in Piešťany. It approved a resolution of the radical wing of the party (Karol Sidor, Alexander Mach, Anton Vašek and Ján Ďurčanský) that called for a decisive struggle for the **autonomy of Slovakia** and declared unity with the anticommunist front of nations, motivated by Christian principles.

December – From 1919 to 1936, 202,038 persons emigrated from Slovakia, of whom 67,436 settled in other European states while 134,794 went overseas. With 1,174 emigrants for each 100,000 Slovaks, Slovakia ranked first among European nations in 1924.

■ **1937**
25 June – After a long struggle, parliament passed a law founding the Slovak Technical University in Košice. After the **Vienna Arbitration** it had to move and from 1939 it was permanently located in Bratislava.

26 June – A law for a provisional adjustment in the position of the governor of Sub-Carpathian Ruthenia was passed. It was the first concrete step towards putting into practice the autonomy of the Sub-Carpathian Ruthenians guaranteed by the constitution and the international treaty of Saint-Germain-en-Lay (**10 September 1919**).

14 September – The former president of the Czechoslovak Republic, Tomáš Garrigue Masaryk, died at the age of 87.

– Slovak painters achieved extraordinary success at the world's fair in Paris. Ľudovít Fulla was awarded the grand prix and a silver medal, while Martin Benka and Mikuláš Galanda were awarded silver medals.

■ **1938**
11 – 13 March – Germany annexed Austria (*Anschluss*). Austria ceased to exist as a sovereign state and became a part of the German Reich. The border of the Czechoslovak Republic with Germany was lengthened, so that Slovakia became an immediate neighbor of Germany.

28 March – Adolf Hitler, the German chancellor and President (from 1934), conferred in Berlin with representatives of the Sudeten German Party, Konrad Henlein and Karl Hermann Frank. He asked them to put forward unacceptable demands in their negotiations with the Czecho-Slovak government about a solution for the German minority question.

21 May – The Czecho-Slovak government decreed a partial mobilization. The reason was the inadequately-confirmed movement of German soldiers along the borders with Czecho-Slovakia.

30 May – Adolf Hitler responded to the partial mobilization of Czecho-Slovakia by issuing detailed instructions for the military liquidation of the Czechoslovak Republic.

5 June – The daily newspaper *Slovák* published a new proposal of **Hlinka's Slovak People's Party** concerning **autonomy of Slovakia**. Its authors were Ferdinand Ďurčanský, Martin Sokol and Aladár Kočiš.

5 June – A demonstration for the **autonomy of Slovakia** took place in Bratislava. President Peter Pavol Hletko of the Slovak League in America showed the assembly the original **Pittsburgh Agreement** of 30 May 1918. Here Andrej Hlinka made his last public appearance.

6 June – The agrarians arranged a demonstration in Bratislava, at which Milan Hodža declared support for the legal equality of the Czechs and the Slovaks according to the slogan „I'm a lord, you're a lord" (*ja pán – ty pán*). He considered legislative autonomy to be detrimental for Slovakia and that a solution might be decentralization on the basis of a nationality statute.

2 August – The first unit of the **Hlinka Guard** was founded in Trnava.

16 August – Andrej Hlinka died. His funeral became a day of reconciliation for Slovak politicians.

19 September – The ambassadors of Great Britain and France in Prague delivered a note to the Czecho-Slovak government, the so-called Anglo-French plan. The plan suggested a withdrawal from the border territories where the population was more than 50 per cent German. If it was rejected, France would decline to offer guarantees to the Czechoslovak Republic (**5 – 16 October 1925**).

21 September – The Czecho-Slovak government changed its initial attitude favoring the rejection of the Anglo-French plan and accepted it under diplomatic pressure.

22 September – The government led by Milan Hodža resigned. It was replaced by a **caretaker government** led by General Jan Syrový. Vladimír Fajnor represented the Slovaks in it. Two days later, two additional Slovak ministers, Matúš Černák and Imrich Karvaš became members of the government (**3 October 1938**).

23 September – At the instigation of Great Britain and France, the Czecho-Slovak government decreed a general mobilization as a reaction to Hitler's rejection of the Anglo-French plan in negotiations with Neville Chamberlain in Godesberg.

29 – 30 September – A conference of the four great powers took place in Munich: Germany (Adolf Hitler), Italy (Benito Mussolini), France (Edouard Daladier) and Great Britain (Neville Chamberlain). The representatives of the great powers accepted the **Munich Agreement** about the withdrawal of Czecho-Slovakia from border territories populated by the German national minority.

30 September – The Czecho-Slovak government accepted the decision of the Munich conference. The position of the government was confirmed by a committee of the coalition majority in the parliament.

3 October – The Slovak minister in the Prague government, Matúš Černák, presented an ultimatum to the government: if Slovakia did not receive autonomy within 24 hours, he would resign from the government. He did so, which caused the fall of the Syrový **caretaker government**.

4 October – a new Syrový **caretaker government** was created. Vladimír Fajnor and Imrich Karvaš represented the Slovaks in it.

5 October – President Edvard Beneš resigned and flew to Great Britain on 22 October.

6 October – The executive committee of **Hlinka's Slovak People's Party** met in Žilina to decide the **autonomy of Slovakia**. The presidium of the Hlinka's Slovak People's approved the **Žilina Manifesto,** in which they declared Slovak autonomy. In view of the serious situation, representatives of other Slovak political parties came to Žilina. After joint negotiations, they united on the autonomy of Slovakia and accepted the **Žilina Agreement**. – Jozef Tiso was named plenipotentiary minister for the administration of Slovakia.

7 October – The first government of autonomous Slovakia was established: Jozef Tiso – prime minister and minister of the interior, Pavol Teplanský – minister of finance, public works and agriculture, Ferdinand Ďurčanský – minister of justice, social welfare and health, Matúš Černák – minister of education and Ján Lichner – minister of transport.

9 October – Negotiations began in Komárno between Czecho-Slovakia and Hungary concerning a withdrawal from the southern territory of Slovakia, which was inhabited by a Magyar national minority. The negotiations resulted from the **Munich Agreement**. The Hungarian party disrupted them on 13 October with a note from Budapest demanding that the great powers resolve the dispute (**2 November 1938**).

9 October – The ministry of the interior of autonomous Slovakia suspended the activity of the **Communist Party of Czechoslovakia** and the organizations in Slovakia affiliated with it. In Czechia the activity of the Communist Party of Czechoslovakia was suspended on 20 October 1938. The Czecho-Slovak government dissolved it on 27 December 1938.

10 October – Under the leadership of Franz Karmasin, the Carpathian German Party was renamed the German Party (*Deutsche Partei*). It was the only political party of the Slovak-Germans and functioned until 1945.

– The government of autonomous Slovakia established a state secretariat for German national minority matters in Slovakia (*Staatssekretariat für die Angelegenheiten der deutschen Volksgruppe in der Slowakei*), headed by Franz Karmasin. The state secretariat functioned within the Slovak government and its task was to foster the interests of the German minority.

– The German army occupied a small part of Slovak territory opposite Bratislava on the right bank of the Danube, together with the village of Petržalka. Petržalka was visited by Adolf Hitler on 25 October 1938.

11 October – The first autonomous government of Sub-Carpathian Ruthenia led by Andrej Bródy was named.

21 October – Adolf Hitler issued a military directive concerning the liquidation of „remnant" Czecho-Slovakia by the occupation of Czechia and Moravia and the secession of Slovakia. According to another directive from 7 December 1938, this was to be a pacific action carried out by peaceful armed forces.

2 November – Representatives of Germany (Joachim von Ribbentrop) and Italy (Galeazzo Ciano) accepted an arbitration decision in Vienna. The **Vienna Arbitration** decided that Slovakia had to give part of its southern territory to Hungary. It was a success for Hungarian revisionism.

8 November – The Slovak branches of the Czechoslovak People's Party, the Czechoslovak National Socialist Party, the **Agrarian Party**, the National Democratic Party, the Tradesmen Party, and the National Community of Fascists issued a common declaration to the Slovak public, according to which Hlinka's Slovak People's Party became the actual and only representative of the will of the Slovak nation. The new name of the party was Hlinka's Slovak People's Party – Party of Slovak National Unity. After a vote of its executive committee, the **Slovak National Party** united with this party on 15 December 1938.

21 November – Devín, a memorable historic place for the Slovaks at the confluence of the Danube and Morava rivers, was annexed to Germany.

22 November – Parliament accepted a law concerning the **autonomy of Slovakia**.

30 November – The former president of the supreme administrative court, Emil Hácha, was elected president of the Czecho-Slovak state.

1 December – President Emil Hácha named a new government. The agrarian Rudolf Beran became prime minister. Karol Sidor became the deputy prime minister. The ministers of the autonomous Slovak government were, at the same time, members of the central council of ministers. Slovak attachés were assigned to departments of the common ministries of defense, foreign affairs and finance.

17 December – The Prague parliament approved the so-called empowerment law. The central government was authorized to change the constitution and constitutional laws and to assume the exceptional power to govern by decree. The representatives of **Hlinka's Slovak People's Party** were able to push through a proposal that this law would be voted on only after the election of the president and the naming of a government. This was because they feared a reduction in the **autonomy of Slovakia**. Slovak consent to the law was also conditional upon the naming of Slovak government delegates to the ministries for the whole state.

18 December – Elections for the autonomous Assembly of the Slovak Region took place in Slovakia. The single slate of candidates of Hlinka's Slovak People's Party – Party of Slovak National Unity obtained 97.5 per cent of the votes. Of 100 candidates, 63 were elected to the assembly.

23 December – The Prague government issued a regulation concerning political parties. New political parties could be established only with the consent of the central government. The government had te authority to dissolve a political party if it endangered public order. The regulation legitimized the authoritarian system built up after the **Munich Agreement**.

– After an agreement with the Slovak autonomous government, the Prague government directed the transfer of 9,000 Czech state employees from Slovakia to Czechia, while Slovak state employees had to return to Slovakia. After the establishment of the first **Slovak Republic** in 1939, Czechs who had come to Slovakia during the inter-war period had to leave the country. The evacuation of Czech employees from Slovakia was halted in 1940. Of 120,000 Czechs who had originally settled in Slovakia, about 30,000 remained in Slovakia.

■ **1939**

18 January – The Assembly of the Slovak Region was ceremonially opened in Bratislava and elected Martin Sokol as its president.

12 February – Elections for an autonomous assembly of Sub-Carpathian Ruthenia took place. Thirty-two delegates were elected.

– At the initiative of General Alois Eliáš, a secret meeting of the Czech members of the central government, except for Rudolf Beran, František Chvalkovský and Jan Syrový, took place in Unhošť near Nouzov (Czechia). The participants agreed to military action against the autonomous Slovak government, which

was accused of separatism (**9 – 10 March 1939**).

28 February – In Berlin, ministers of the Slovak autonomous government negotiated economic assistance for Slovakia with the authorized agent for the German four-year plan, Hermann Göring. Göring promised assistance on the condition that Slovakia declare independence.

6 March – The presidium of the Slovak autonomous government and the assembly agreed that they were in favor of gradually establishing an independent Slovak state but were against declaring it quickly.

7 March – The German governor in Austria, Arthur von Seyss-Inquart, traveled to Bratislava. In negotiations he urged Karol Sidor, the deputy prime minister of the central government and Jozef Tiso, the prime minister of the Slovak government, to declare independence immediately.

9 – 10 March – President Emil Hácha dismissed from office all the ministers of the Slovak government with the exception of Pavol Teplanský. Slovakia was occupied by strong units of the Czech army; 253 Slovaks, advocates of making Slovakia independent rapidly, among them Vojtech Tuka, Alexander Mach, and Matúš Černák, were sent to prison in Moravia. The president immediately named a new Slovak government led by Jozef Sivák on 10 March.

11 March – President Emil Hácha named a new Slovak government led by Karol Sidor.

12 March – Karol Sidor met in Bratislava with a German delegation (Arthur von Seyss-Inquart, Wilhelm Keppler and Joseph Bürckel), which presented to him a draft of a telegram addressed to Adolf Hitler with the text for the declaration of the independence of Slovakia and a list of names for the government of the new state. Karol Sidor refused this initiative.

13 March – Jozef Tiso received an official invitation to Berlin from Adolf Hitler. A meeting of the presidium of **Hlinka's Slovak People's Party** and the Slovak government decided that he should go. Jozef Tiso flew to Berlin from Vienna with the deputies Štefan Danihel and Ferdinand Ďurčanský. Jozef Tiso negotiated with Joachim von Ribbentrop and Adolf Hitler. Hitler informed him that he wished to resolve the „Czech question" by occupying Czechia. He offered German guarantees if the independence of Slovakia was declared; otherwise he would leave Slovakia to its fate (to Hungarian aspirations). Tiso refused the text of the declaration of independence of the Slovak state that was given to him. He contacted Karol Sidor and Emil Hácha by telegraph and suggested that the Slovak assembly be convened. Emil Hácha complied and called for the Slovak assembly to meet on 14 March.

The First Slovak State (1939 – 1945)

The following six years centered on the existence of the first Slovak republic as the natural expression of Slovak national sovereignty. Its establishment meant the realization of the basic right of the Slovak nation to self-determination. The Slovak state was born in unfavorable conditions when the influence of Nazi Germany dominated the whole of central Europe and southern Slovakia was annexed by Hungary. Germany had urged the establishment of the Slovak state, so that it could achieve the collapse of the Czecho-Slovak state from within. This did not mean, however, that the idea of the Slovak state was foreign to Slovakia or imposed from outside.

The Slovak Republic appeared as an internationally recognized state, which was established a six months before the eruption of the Second World War. The sovereignty of the state was restricted by relations with Germany, by the treaty of 1939 concerning protective relations and by the result of the Salzburg negotiations (1940). Despite these limitations, some of the Slovak governmental figures sought a way to weaken German influence. Slovakia began to be built as an authoritarian state aiming at a corporate order. In its concrete form this was expressed in the suppression of parliamentarianism, in the creation of united labor and youth organizations, in the emphases upon the national unit and in the persecution of persons with other political ideas, especially from the political left. The constant German influence and the interference of Germany prevented the Slovak state from developing according to its own conception. The corporate system was not put into practice. The struggle among pro-German radicals and a group of more moderate individuals, which was manifested externally in the competition between the Hlinka Guard and Hlinka's Slovak People's Party, created internal tensions and provided Germany more space to maneuver. The moderate groups finally forced the radicals into a more defensive position. The educational level of the population during the first Slovak Republic, Slovak art and culture, industry and social welfare continued to rise. The noteworthy growth of the economy can be ascribed to the independence of the state and to a boom in several branches of production directly dependent on the war.

The Second World War bound Slovakia more firmly to Germany. Notwithstanding the war and the participation of the Slovak army on the eastern front, in comparison with the surrounding countries life was peaceful in Slovakia. For political crimes punishments were moderate and the regular courts of the Slovak Republic convicted 2,809 persons of them (extraordinary courts did not exist until 1945). Not a single death sentence for political crimes was carried out.

A special chapter is the Slovak relationship to the Jewish population in this period. It begun with economic limitations and passed through several stages. Finally, the variant of the policy of the radical pro-German group and Germany itself was implemented. Jews were expelled from the economic life of the country and their isolation was followed by their deportation to concentration camps.

After 1943, the British-American-Soviet coalition was definitively against the existence of an independent Slovak state and pushed for the renewal of the Czecho-Slovak state. This position was respected also by the domestic underground movement, which created the Slovak National Council in 1944 and prepared for an armed uprising. The uprising erupted prematurely and therefore was not able to attain its goal. In essence it was an armed opposition to a German occupation of Slovakia. The Slovak Republic ceased to exist in 1945 with the arrival of Soviet troops, and Slovakia again became a part of Czecho-Slovakia. The significance of this short period in the history of the Slovaks is that the Slovak nation demonstrated that it was able to build its own state in extraordinarily unfavorable circumstances. Despite its incontestably negative aspects, the first Slovak Republic represents an important experience that raised national and state consciousness.

■ 1939

14 March – The Slovak assembly convened in Bratislava. The assembly first accepted the resignation of the government of Karol Sidor. Jozef Tiso acquainted the deputies with the negotiations in Berlin. After his presentation the 57 deputies present voted by acclamation (by standing up in their places) on the question: „Do you agree with the declaration of an independent Slovak state?" Shortly after noon, all of the deputies present voted in the affirmative. The adoption of a law concerning an independent Slovak state followed. Following this, the presidium of the Slovak assembly named the first government of the Slovak state. Jozef Tiso became its prime minister.

– After the situation in Slovakia was clarified, Adolf Hitler approved the request of František Chvalkovský, the Czecho-Slovak foreign minister, that negotiations between Hitler and Hácha take place in Berlin. Emil Hácha departed for Berlin.

15 March – President Emil Hácha negotiated with Adolf Hitler in Berlin. Hitler made known his decision to annex Czechia to the German Empire. At the same time, he cautioned Hácha that the German army would cross the Czech borders at 6:00 (i.e. within four hours). Hácha signed a declaration that placed the fate of the Czech nation and of the country in the hands of the leader of German Reich, Adolf Hitler.

16 March – In Prague Emil Hácha signed Hitler's decree concerning the Protectorate of Czechia and Moravia.

23 March – The German foreign minister, Joachim von Ribbentrop signed a treaty in Berlin establishing a protective relationship between the German Reich and the Slovak state, which was to be valid for 25 years. Germany bound itself to defend the political independence and the territorial integrity of Slovakia. Germany set up a so-called defensive zone in western Slovakia demarcated by the ridges of the Small and White Carpathians and the Javorníky Mountains. Slovakia obligated itself to organize its own armed forces, foreign policy, and economy in close harmony with Germany. Slovak members of the government had already signed the agreement on 18 March 1939 (Vojtech Tuka and Ferdinand Ďurčanský) and 19 March 1939 (Jozef Tiso).

– The Hungarian army invaded eastern Slovakia from the occupied territory of Sub-Carpathian Ruthenia. Its advance was halted by volunteers from the **Hlinka Guard** and members of the Slovak army which was just being formed. A military truce was signed on 25 March followed by an agreement concerning new borders on 4 April. Slovakia lost 386 km^2 to Hungary with a population of 41,000, of which only 309 were Magyars.

24 March – A government regulation for the preventive custody of enemies of the Slovak state was issued. The regulation empowered the minister of the interior to arrest persons who „have aroused or who are arousing serious apprehensions that would be obstacles in building the Slovak state". For this purpose an interment camp was established in Ilava. From March 1939 until March 1945 about 3,100 persons were interned here (some of them convicted criminals), of which several hundred persons were interned in Ilava in 1944 – 45 by German occupation forces. In the prisons of regional courts, 3,595 persons (of which 2,857 were Slovaks) were imprisoned for political crimes between March 1939 and April 1945.

4 April – The government issued a regulation concerning the Slovak National Bank. The bank was to be responsible for the stability of the currency, the regulation of the general system of payments and the granting of credits for the national economy.

– The government issued a currency regulation setting the value of the Slovak crown as equal to that of 31.21 milligrams of pure gold.

15 June – The Slovak Broadcasting Company Ltd. was founded (**2 October 1926, 28 April 1948**).

21 July – The Slovak assembly accepted a constitution and a new name, the first **Slovak Republic**. The constitution was based upon liberal-democratic elements (the separation of state powers) and Christian elements (the papal encyclicals *Rerum novarum* of 1890 and *Quadragesimo anno* of 1931). It reflected the influence especially of the constitutions of the authoritarian political systems in Portugal and Austria. The constitution legally established the exceptional position of Hlinka's Slovak People's Party in the state.

25 July – The Slovak assembly accepted a law concerning the internal public administration. Slovakia was internally divided into six counties (*župy*) each with a capital city: Bratislava (Bratislava), Nitra (Nitra), Trenčín (Trenčín), Tatra (Ružomberok), Šariš-Zemplín (Prešov), and Pohronská (Banská Bystrica).

1 September – Units of the **Hlinka Guard** and the Slovak army participated in a German military operation against Poland. Slovakia thus participated in the first military campaign of the **Second World War**. It was a violation of the previous agreement according to which Slovakia would be passive. The Slovak army recorded 18 dead, 46 wounded, and 11 missing. Slovak units withdrew to Slovakia by 15 September 1939. Slovakia retained the territory of 25 Slovak villages that had devolved to Poland on 28 July 1920. On 22 December 1939 the Slovak assembly adopted a law concerning the incorporation of this territory into the **Slovak Republic**.

30 September – 1 October – A congress of **Hlinka's Slovak People's Party** took place in Trenčín that elected Jozef Tiso as its president. The moderate wing led by Jozef Tiso obtained predominance in the narrower presidium of the party.

26 October – The Slovak assembly unanimously elected Jozef Tiso president of the Slovak Republic. Vojtech Tuka became the prime minister.

7 November – The Slovak film joint-stock company Nástup was established. On the basis of a government decree of 18 January 1940 it obtained a monopoly over producing, importing, exporting and distributing 35 mm films (**23 June 1945**).

22 November – Milan Hodža, in exile in Paris, established the **Slovak National Council (1939)** in opposition to the Czechoslovak National Committee of Edvard Beneš.

■ **1940**

26 January – The Slovak government accepted a resolution concerning the creation of the Slovak museum in Bratislava. The new museum was established by the merger of independent museum societies: the Slovak National Museum Society, the Agricultural Museum and the Forestry Museum.

22 February – The Slovak assembly passed a **land reform** law. As implemented, only a part of the land was distributed, namely the land bought or confiscated from Jewish owners. The other land remained the property of the state.

8 May – The government issued a regulation about support for the construction of factories and employee housing. Tax-reductions of up to 50 per cent were introduced (**19 November 1940**).

21 May – After several months of conflict between the radical and the more moderate group, Jozef Tiso accepted the resignation of Alexander Mach as the main commander of the **Hlinka Guard**.

3 July – The Slovak assembly passed a law about the Slovak University, which consisted of Catholic and Evangelical theological faculties, legal, medical, philosophical, and the newly established natural science faculties (**27 June 1919**).

27 – 28 July – A Slovak delegation made up of Jozef Tiso, Alexander Mach and Vojtech Tuka conferred in Salzburg with Joachim von Ribbentrop and Adolf Hitler. At the **Salzburg Negotiations**, Germany substantially intervened in the internal politics of Slovakia so as to limit its sovereignty (the departure from political life of Ferdinand Ďurčanský, the foreign and interior minister, and the installation of Alexander Mach as the minister of the interior).

3 September – On the initiative of Vojtech Tuka the Slovak assembly accepted a law which authorized the government to do everything necessary to exclude Jews from economic and social life (**9 September 1941**). The exclusion of Jews from political life and the restriction of their influence in economic areas had been initiated by previous laws.

4 October – The government of the first Slovak Republic issued a regulation concerning the Commercial College in Bratislava, which was founded by the chambers of commerce and industry. In 1952 the school was renamed the University of Economics.

19 November – The Slovak assembly passed a law about support for building up industry. It thus created the legal basis for the industrialization of Slovakia. The law replaced the Hungarian law from 1907 concerning support for industrial enterprises, which had been valid but not applied in the first Czecho-Slovak Republic.

24 November – In Berlin, the Slovak prime minister and foreign minister, Vojtech Tuka, together with the German foreign minister, Joachim von Ribbentrop and representatives of Japan and Italy, signed a protocol about Slovakia's entry into in the Triple Alliance. Hungary and Romania had previously joined the Pact (**12 December 1941**).

26 November – The Slovak assembly passed a law concerning the protection of the Slovak Republic. It dealt with all acts directed against the existence of the state, its constitutional agents and its legal order.

■ **1941**

1 May – The Slovak National Library was established at the Matica slovenská in Martin.
– The government introduced allowances for the children of workers. To pay for the allowances a separate fund for family allowances was created. This system of family allowances was taken over in 1945 by the renewed Czecho-Slovak state.

22 June – The German ambassador Hans Elard Ludin informed Vojtech Tuka, the prime minister, of the declaration of a state of war between Germany and the Soviet Union. To the question of how Slovakia would conduct itself, Vojtech Tuka, without consulting with other constitutional representatives, expressed a willingness to enter the war on the side of Germany.

23 June – The Slovak army joined Germany in the military attack on the Soviet Union. Two Slovak divisions were put on the eastern front. The President and government systematically reduced their numbers (**Second World War**).

24 June – President Jozef Tiso rejected Tuka's suggestion of the text of a declaration about the voluntary entry of Slovakia into the war. A new text was drafted by Tiso in which, alongside an expression of solidarity with Germany, it was asserted that part of the Slovak army had already crossed the borders of Slovakia.

18 July – The British and Soviet governments definitively recognized the Czecho-Slovak government in London. The prime minister was Jan Šrámek, but actual power and the competence to make decisions belonged to Edvard Beneš, who was considered president in exile.

9 September – The Slovak government issued a regulation concerning the legal status of Jews, known as the **Jewish Code**. The Slovak Catholic and Evangelical bishops protested against the regulation with a special memorandum of 7 October 1941.

25 November – In Berlin Vojtech Tuka, the Slovak prime minister, signed the accession agreement of Slovakia to the pact against the Comintern.

12 December – Vojtech Tuka, the Slovak prime minister, sent a telegram to Adolf Hitler in Berlin in which he asserted that Slovakia would maintain its treaty obligations arising from its membership in the Triple Alliance and declare war upon Great Britain and the United States. He had not consulted with anyone about this step (**24 November 1940**).

■ **1942**

25 March – The deportations of Jews from Slovakia to German concentration camps began. The directive for deportations was issued by Vojtech Tuka, the prime minister, after agreeing with Germany without the knowledge of the president, parliament and the other members of the government. Slovakia was the first independent state that deported the greater part of its Jews. At the same time, it was the first state which suspended deportations in October 1942 after reports about the extermination of the Jews. (To the end of 1942 approximately 58,000 Jews had been deported). The deportations were resumed in October 1944 after the arrival of the German army in Slovakia. The total number of Jews deported was approximately 70,000, of which about 67,000 perished in German concentration camps.

2 July – The Slovak assembly passed a law about the Slovak Academy of Sciences and the Arts. The task of this, the highest scientific institution, with its seat in Bratislava, was to develop and organize Slovak scientific research (**22 February 1946, 26 June 1953**).

22 October – The Slovak assembly passed a law concerning **Hlinka's Slovak People's Party**. Under the law Jozef Tiso recieved the title of „leader". The law about Hlinka's Slovak People's Party strengthened the position of Jozef Tiso vis-à-vis the radicals (Alexander Mach, Vojtech Tuka).

■ **1943**

12 December – Edvard Beneš signed an agreement in Moscow, valid for 20 years, concerning friendship, mutual assistance and post-war cooperation between **Czecho-Slovakia** and the Soviet Union. The agreement guaranteed the renewal of the Czecho-Slovak state and was the first to legalize Soviet policy in central Europe and create the pre-conditions for making the renewed Czecho-Slovakia a Soviet satellite.

25 December – After four months of negotiations, the opposition political groups in Slovakia, the communists, former agrarians and nationalists, concluded the **Christmas Agreement** concerning the creation of a joint organ of resistance, the **Slovak National Council** (1944) that would, at an appropriate moment, assume political power in Slovakia.

■ **1944**

10 April – The Soviet military command decided to expand the 1st Czecho-Slovak Independent Brigade in the Soviet Union into the 1st Czecho-Slovak Army division (16,000 soldiers).

14 March – An exhibition of contemporary Slovak literature opened in Bratislava. In the five years of the existence of the Slovak Republic, 3,927 books were published, of which 3,286 were original Slovak works and 447 were educational and scientific literature. The remainder were translations.

11 May – Pope Pius XII named Karol Kmeťko, the **bishop** of Nitra, a titular **archbishop** (*ad personam*).

11 August – Alexander Mach, the minister of the interior, declared martial law within the territory of the Slovak Republic, to take effect on 12 August. It was directed against the partisan movement.

21 – 31 August – Partisan counter-intelligence executed about 100 persons in Sklabiňa.

27 August – The partisans assassinated František Slameň, a deputy in the Slovak Assembly, and three other persons in Brezno. Slovak soldiers and partisans occupied Ružomberok and liquidated a small unit of the SS. The murder of Germans in Ružomberok began.

28 August – In the courtyard of the barracks in Martin, a squad of Slovak soldiers shot 32 German officers, soldiers and physicians, led by Lieutenant Colonel W. P. Otto. This group had returned from Romania. Influenced by this and further partisan actions, the German ambassador, Hans Elard Ludin, presented President Tiso with an ultimatum that demanded the intervention of German military forces. Jozef Tiso, who until then had resisted such a solution, consented.

29 August – The first German units entered Slovak territory. Ferdinand Čatloš, the minister of national defense, urged the population in a radio broadcast to offer assistance to the German army. The commander of the underground military command in Banská Bystrica, Lieutenant Colonel Ján Golian, gave the password that was the agreed signal for an armed insurrection against the German army. (**Insurrection of 1944 – Slovak National Uprising**).

31 August – The high command of the German Army Group of the Northern Ukraine ordered the army division Heinrich to disarm two Slovak divisions under General Augustín Malár, located in eastern Slovakia. The disarmament took place on the same day without resistance. This made it impossible for the Slovak divisions to take part in the uprising.

1 September – The insurgent Slovak National Council issued a declaration in Banská Bystrica that it alone had the right to speak in the name of the Slovak nation. At the same time it declared the renewal of the Czecho-Slovak state.

5 September – In Bratislava President Jozef Tiso named a new government led by Štefan Tiso.

8 September – The 1st Ukrainian front of the Soviet army together with the 1st Czecho-Slovak army corps began a common eastern Carpathian operation to penetrate the well-constructed German defenses in the Carpathians in order to reach Slovakia.

17 September – The congress at which the Communist Party of Slovakia and the Slovak Social Democrats merged took place in Banská Bystrica. Only a few individuals expressed disapproval of the merger with the communists. The parties merged under the name Communist Party of Slovakia.

19 September – The first railway train with German evacuees was dispatched from eastern Slovakia to Germany. On 27 October Berlin ordered a general evacuation of Slovak-Germans. About 100,000 (80 per cent) members of the German speaking minority left Slovakia before April 1945.

6 October – Members of the 1st Czecho-Slovak army corps fighting in the Soviet army entered Slovak territory with Soviet soldiers in the area of the Dukla Pass.

27 October – After a two month battle the German army occupied Banská Bystrica, the center of the **Insurrection of 1944**. In the battle 4,000 insurgents fell and 15,000 were captured. A large portion of the prisoners were transported to German concentration camps. The Slovak government and president was able to have some of these returned to Slovakia from the end of November 1944.

The Gradual Sovietization of Slovakia (1945 – 1968)

In 1945 the war ended and the Czecho-Slovak state was restored. Negotiations that took place during the war (1943 – 1945), when it still did not exist, decided its political dependency upon the Soviet Union. A policy of compliance towards the Soviet Union and the domestic communists who, after 1945, became a government party, limited the sovereignty of this state. The political system of the National Front was an artificial coalition of the communist and other parties, which enabled the communists to control and direct them. National committees (analogous to soviets) were characteristic of the new so-called „people's democracy". Thousands of people left Slovakia to go abroad, among them many leading personalities of its cultural life, before the new pro-soviet system was introduced at the end of the war. This was the first Slovak political emigration that reached massive proportions.

Czechs and Slovaks entered into the new state entity with very different wartime experiences. While the Czech nation had lost its statehood throughout the war and had the Protectorate forced upon them, the Slovak nation had obtained its statehood. The terror unleashed by the Nazis in the Protectorate of Czechia and Moravia cannot be compared with the relative peace and stability which reigned in the first Slovak republic. The events of the war directly affected Slovakia twice, in the form of the uprising of 1944 and the arrival of the tactical front in 1944/45. It had not been fought with such intensity in Czechia, and the Soviet security service (NKVD) did not carry off to Soviet work camps as many people from Czechia as from Slovakia.

The return to conditions existing before 1938 was not possible, although the views of some politicians concerning the Slovak question had not changed at all. The Slovak nation clearly expressed its will in the elections of 1946 when it supported the Democratic Party. In Czechia the communists were victorious. The electoral victory of the democrats was a mere gesture because the communists together with other Czech parties completely repressed the authority of Slovak organs in the state. This made it impossible for the results of the election to be reflected in practice. State security was already controlled by the communists. It staged an „anti-state conspiracy" in the fall of 1947 that led to extensive arrests and purges in offices. The way was open to the definitive seizure of power by the communists. The lack of unity among non-communist parties in Czechia, which assented to or flirted with Marxist ideology brought disastrous results not only in the election of 1946 but also during the government crisis in February 1948. The government crisis, which could have mobilized the democratic forces in the state, presented the communists with the opportunity to finally seize power in the state. Although other political views were tolerated to a limited degree until 1948, after the communist state coup massive persecutions took place, most intensively during the first half of the 1950s. The new regime also persecuted the churches, especially the largest, the Roman Catholic Church. State and party functions were combined and everywhere consistent cadre politics was implemented. The importance of the secret police grew. The Czecho-Slovak state was a part of the so-called eastern bloc and its military and economic structures. Slovakia was affected by the communist program of collectivization and industrialization. Both processes were implemented without consideration of the real needs of Slovakia. Basic industries and the processing of raw materials and partially finished goods were concentrated in Slovakia; gigantic foundry, chemical and armaments factories were built. Slovakia was not able to develop in accordance with its cultural and spiritual traditions and its economic possibilities. Its traditional cultural institutions were completely paralyzed, the Slovak national organs were not able to make independent decisions and existed more on paper than in reality.

The communist regime had two faces. To the world it showed its maturity and advantages, internally it was based on lawlessness and the violation of basic human and national rights and liberties. It persecuted every expression of opposition. Despite this, groups and individuals opposed it. In distinction from the surrounding states of the eastern bloc, however, opposition to the system did not grow into mass dissatisfaction and open confrontation. The renewal and democratization process in the Communist Party and in society that began in the spring of 1968 brought great hope. The process of renewal had its limits determined by the reformed communist leadership, but it was able to address the whole of society, which saw in it the opportunity for a gradual implementation of fundamental rights and liberties. Its fruit was the renewal of Slovak statehood in the form of the Slovak Socialist Republic within a federal Czecho-Slovak state. The intervention of the armies of five Warsaw pact countries during the night of 20 – 21 August 1968 suffocated the promising process of renewal.

■ 1945

3 January – Six of the leading figures of the uprising of 29 August 1944 were condemned to death in absentia by an extraordinary court established at the supreme court in Bratislava under German pressure. Additionally an extraordinary military court condemned seven persons to death in absentia.

14 January – A congress of the younger Slovak generation supporting **Hlinka's Slovak People's Party** met in Piešťany. Its participants issued the manifesto „For the Life of the Nation, for the Maintenance of the State", in which they expressed their support for the further existence of the Slovak state.

27 February – A decree of the presidium of the **Slovak National Council** ordered the confiscation of the land of „Germans, Magyars, and traitors of the nation". It was the basis for other **land reform**.

22 – 29 March – The **Moscow negotiations (1945)** between representatives of Czech political parties, Edvard Beneš and the Slovak National Council took place. They agreed on the creation of the National Front, associating all political parties, and on who was to comprise the government of post-war Czecho-Slovakia. The key portfolios were to be held by the Communist Party of Czechoslovakia. The **Košice government program** suggested by the communists was accepted at the negotiations. The **Slovak National Council (1945)** was recognized as the supreme organ of legislative and executive power in Slovakia.

4 April – Soviet soldiers drove German units from Bratislava. The liberation of Slovakia by the Soviet army, the 1st Czecho-Slovak army corps, and the Romanian army was completed on 1 May. The Soviet security organ, the NKVD, deported about 10,000 citizens from Slovakia for forced labor in the Soviet Union. The Slovak government and President Jozef Tiso fled into exile in Kremsmünster in Austria. About 10,000 Slovaks emigrated from Slovakia.

– The Czecho-Slovak government, led by the social democrat Zdeněk Fierlinger, took the oath of office before President Edvard Beneš in Košice.

5 April – The Czecho-Slovak government accepted the **Košice government program**.

8 May – The Slovak government of Štefan Tiso concluded an agreement with the representatives of the commander of the American 3rd Army, W. A. Collier. It subordinated itself and its policies to the commanding general of the 20th corps of the American 3rd Army and were under his protection. This was the last legal act of the government of the first Slovak Republic. However, the agreement was not respected and members of the Slovak government were turned over to the Czecho-Slovak state.

9 May – The Soviet army entered Prague, the capital city of the renewed Czecho-Slovak state.

10 May – The government of Zdeněk Fierlinger arrived in Prague.

15 May – The **Slovak National Council** issued a regulation concerning retributive courts (**retribution**).

2 June – The Czecho-Slovak government and the presidium of the **Slovak National Council** concluded the so-called first Prague Agreement concerning the delimitation of the competency of state-wide and Slovak organs. The agreement defined only state-wide matters. The board of commissioners, until then responsible only to the **Slovak National Council**, assumed responsibility for executing the decrees of the president of the republic and the laws of parliament.

18 June – The commission of the interior dissolved the Society of Slovak Writers on the pretext of collaboration. A new society with the same name, and with Ladislav Novomeský as president, began to function on 29 November 1945 (**4 – 6 March 1949**).

21 June – President Edvard Beneš issued a decree concerning the confiscation and distribution of land owned by Germans, Magyars, traitors and collaborators.

23 June – The Slovak Film Society (Slofis) was founded.

29 June – The Czechoslovak Republic signed a treaty in Moscow with the Soviet Union about Sub-Carpathian Ruthenia. The treaty annexed Sub-Carpathian Ruthenia to the Ukrainian Soviet Socialist Republic and it thus made it a part of the Soviet Union.

17 July – 2 August – A conference of the United States of America, the Soviet Union and Great Britain in Potsdam near Berlin recognized the need for the transfer of the German national minorities from the Czechoslovak Republic, Poland and Hungary. Until this time a so-called „wild transfer" had been carried out.

2 August – President Edvard Beneš issued a decree concerning the state citizenship of the resident Germans and Magyars. Both national groups lost their state citizenship and the rights of citizens in the republic. Some of the three million strong German minority were expelled from Czechia even before the acceptance of legal regulations concerning the transfer. By the end of October 1946, 32,450 Germans, who had not left during the evacuation (**19 September 1944**), had been transferred from Slovakia.

19 October – President Edvard Beneš issued a decree concerning currency reform. The decree introduced the Czecho-Slovak crown as the unit of currency throughout the whole state. The exchange with the currency used until then, the Czech Protectorate crown and the Slovak crown, took place on a 1:1 ratio. This exchange rate did not conform to reality. For black market goods the exchange rate in force was 1:10 in favor of the Slovak crown. The 1:1 ratio was to assuage Czech public opinion. Slovakia obtained a promise that it would be compensated with the release of blocked deposits and investments.

24 October – President Edvard Beneš signed a decree for the **nationalization** of banks, mining and smelting companies, private insurance companies and food-stuff industries. Nationalized were 3,000 factories with 61.2 per cent of all industrial employees. It was a serious encroachment upon private ownership and property relationships.

23 November – The Czecho-Slovak minister of foreign trade, Hubert Ripka signed a secret agreement in Prague with the plenipotentiary of the Soviet government, I. Bakulin, concerning the mining of uranium ore in the Czecho-

slovak Republic. The Czechoslovak Republic was entitled to retain only the ore and concentrates necessary for its economic and scientific needs. The remaining ore had to be exported to the Soviet Union. The agreement was to be valid for 20 years.

– Units of the Soviet Red Army left the Czechoslovak Republic at the end of the year, but the Soviets left behind a network of their agents. The Soviet army remained on the territory of the surrounding states (except for the American zone of occupation in Germany).

■ **1946**

22 February – A law of the **Slovak National Council** again re-constituted the Slovak Academy of Sciences and the Arts as the supreme Slovak scientific institution (**26 June 1953**).

27 February – A Czecho-Slovak – Hungarian agreement was concluded in Budapest for the exchange of population (the Slovak minority in Hungary for the Hungarian minority in Slovakia) and regarding the property of those being resettled. From Hungary 71,787 persons came to Slovakia; from Czecho-Slovakia 89,660 persons went to Hungary. On the basis of a decree about general work obligations, 44,129 Magyars were transferred to Czechia and 362,679 persons were re-Slovakicized (accepted Slovak nationality).

30 March – In the cottage of the Farmer's Bank in Harmónia near Modra, the leadership of the **Democratic Party** concluded an agreement with the Catholic wing of the party, which had originally wanted to establish their own political party. The Catholic wing abandoned this idea and agreed on a common approach with the leadership of the Democratic Party. The agreement is known in history as the **April Agreement.**

11 April – Representatives of the government and the **Slovak National Council** accepted the so-called second Prague Agreement concerning the delimitation of the competence of state-wide and Slovak organs. The government obtained the right to intervene in personnel matters in all departments in Slovakia.

26 May – The election to the Constitutional National Assembly took place. In Slovakia the **Democratic Party** was victorious with 62 per cent of the votes, the **Communist Party of Slovakia** obtained 30.4 per cent of the votes. In Czechia the Communist Party of Czechoslovakia was victorious with 40.17 per cent. Throughout the whole state the communists won the elections with 37.94 per cent of the votes.

19 June – Parliament elected Edvard Beneš as the president of the Czechoslovak Republic. The government of Zdeněk Fierlinger submitted its resignation.

27 June – Representatives of the National Front of Czechs and Slovaks signed the so-called Third Prague Agreement in Prague. The Slovak commissioners felt themselves to be in a subordinate position towards the ministries and the board of commissioners towards the government. The ministers obtained the right to exercise their authority through their own ministries.

2 July – President Edvard Beneš named a government led by the communist Klement Gottwald.

13 August – The communist Gustáv Husák became the chairman of the board of commissioners despite the fact that the parliamentary election of **26 May 1946** had been won by the **Democratic Party**.

■ **1947**

1 January – The two-year plan legislated by the Prague parliament began to be implemented. This was a plan to renew and reconstruct the economy destroyed by the war. The two-year plan was initiated by the **Communist Party of Czechoslovakia**. **Nationalization** and the two-year plan were the first step towards regulating the economy through directed plans and subsequent five-year plans.

15 April – After a political trial, the **retribution** national court in Bratislava passed judgement on Jozef Tiso, the president of the first Slovak Republic. When the majority in the government voted against granting clemency, the sentence, execution by hanging, was carried out on 18 April.

7 July – The Czecho-Slovak government unanimously resolved to send a delegation to

Paris for a conference of those countries that had an interest in participating in the Marshall Plan (a plan of economic assistance for the European countries). The delegation's participation was cancelled three days later as a result of direct pressure from Joseph Visarionovich Stalin.

14 September – The commission for the interior issued a report about the „uncovering of an anti-state conspiracy" in Slovakia. In collusion with Slovak emigrants, illegal groups allegedly wished to renew the Slovak state and were prepared to assassinate Edvard Beneš. The „conspiracy" was organized by the state security controlled by the communists and its goal was to compromise the Democratic Party (general secretaries and deputies Ján Kempný and Miloš Bugár, and the deputy prime minister Ján Ursíny). The security service arrested 707 people in connection with the „conspiracy". The autumn political crisis began as planned by the Communist Party of Czechoslovakia and the Communist Party of Slovakia and created the immediate preconditions for the realization of the **communist state coup**.

31 October – Led by Gustáv Husák, six members of the board of commissioners presented their resignations. In a letter to Klement Gottwald, Husák falsely claimed that two commissioners from the **Democratic Party** also had submitted their resignations.

19 November – The presidium of the Slovak National Council named a new board of commissioners. From the original nine departments in this 15 member organ, the Democratic Party lost three departments, one to the Party of Freedom and the other to the Social Democratic Party in Slovakia, while the third seat went to an appointed specialist.

■ **1948**

13 February – The Czecho-Slovak government voted on a resolution that Václav Nosek, the communist minister of the interior, cancel an order of the regional security commander transferring eight non-communist district commanders from Prague.

20 February – In view of the failure to fulfill

the resolution of the government of 13 February, the ministers from the Czechoslovak Party of the National Socialists, the Czechoslovak People's Party, and the Democratic Party resigned from the government. Resignations were submitted by 12 of 26 ministers, i.e. a minority.

21 February – Gustáv Husák, the chairman of the board of commissioners, recalled the commissioners of the Democratic Party against the law, but with the justification that the resignation of the ministers of the Democratic Party also meant resignation from the board of commissioners.

– Action committees began to be established after an appeal from Klement Gottwald. Their goal was to remove „reactionary and subversive elements" from public life. The action committees dismissed 28,000 state and public employees throughout the state. Seven thousand students (24 per cent) were expelled from universities.

25 February – President Edvard Beneš accepted the resignations of the ministers from 20 February. At the same time he confirmed the decree naming a new government as it had been presented to him by the prime minister, Klement Gottwald. After the Communist State Coup, a political dictatorship was installed. It began a massive wave of emigration. In the years 1948 – 1950, 23, 354 citizens emigrated from the Czechoslovak Republic.

23 March – The **Slovak National Council** issued a regulation concerning **labor camps**. People were not assigned to them by the decision of a court but by the decision of a three member committee of the commission of the interior. The question of **labor camps** in Czechia was regulated by the law on forced labor camps of 25 October 1948, which also had a state-wide impact. Throughout the Czechoslovak Republic more than 80,000 persons served sentences in the forced labor camps.

28 April – Slovak Radio Broadcasting was merged with Czech Radio Broadcasting to form Czechoslovak Radio Broadcasting (**2 October 1926, 15 June 1939, 24 May 1991**).

29 April – The state court in Bratislava com-

pleted proceedings against one group of the „anti-state conspiracy in Slovakia". On the basis of fabricated charges, Ján Ursíny, the former deputy prime minister, received a sentence of 7 years in prison, his press attaché Otto Obuch 30 years, Ladislav Čulen 18 years and Jozef Fickuliak 10 years (**14 September 1947**).

9 May – The Constitutional National Assembly accepted a new constitution of the **Czechoslovak Republic**. It declared the „victory of the working class" in February 1948 and established the new form of the state, a people's democracy, with an asymmetrical constitutional arrangement (Czech organs did not exist, Slovak organs only had limited autonomy). It permitted private enterprises with up to 50 employees and the ownership of up to 50 hectares of land. This principle was violated as the liquidation of urban small production and **collectivization** began in 1949.

15 May – After a fabricated political trial, the state court in Bratislava sentenced the general secretaries of the **Democratic Party** and deputies Ján Kempný and Miloš Bugár to six years, Ľudovít Obtulovič to eight years, Jozef Staško to six years, Peter Maxoň to seven years, and Ferdinand Jurčovič to seven years in prison.

30 May – Parliamentary elections took place. The voters could vote only for a single list of candidates compiled by communists or deposit blank ballots in the ballot box. Through a propaganda campaign and by the manipulation of the election results, the single list of candidates in Slovakia received 84.91 per cent of the votes; 13.98 per cent of the voters turned in blank ballots. In Czechia the single list of candidates received 87.12 per cent of the votes and 9.32 per cent turned in blank ballots. Throughout the state the single list of candidates received 89.2 per cent of the votes. The results of the election were intentionally falsified.

2 June – President Beneš signed a letter of resignation, in consequence of his refusal to sign the new **constitution**.

14 June – The national assembly elected Klement Gottwald president of the Czechoslovak Republic.

15 June – President Klement Gottwald named a new government led by Antonín Zápotocký.

29 June – The **Slovak National Council** approved a law concerning the Slovak National Gallery.

29 July – 14 August – The XIV Olympic Games took place in London. The Slovak boxer Július Torma won the gold medal in the category up to 67 kg. Torma was considered one of the boxers with the best technique in the world.

15 – 16 August – A conference of Czech and Slovak Roman Catholic **bishops** took place in Nitra. It accepted a memorandum claiming that the new regime had begun to intensify attacks against the church, especially against the bishops. The government's response was to prohibit most of the Catholic periodicals (in September 1948).

3 September – The former President of the Czechoslovak Republic, Edvard Beneš, died.

29 September – The Comunist Party of Czechoslovakia and the Communist Party of Slovakia merged into an organizationally unified party. Its chairman was Klement Gottwald; the general secretary was Rudolf Slánský. The Communist Party of Slovakia became a merely regional organization of the Communist Party of Czechoslovakia.

16 October – The national assembly accepted law No. 231 about the defense of the people's democratic **Czechoslovak Republic**. It was an expression of the struggle of the communist regime against „reactionary forces". Between 1948 and 1954, 45,000 citizens of Czecho-Slovakia were condemned under this law and its supplement, law no. 86 of 1950.

27 October – The national assembly approved the first five-year economic plan for the years 1949 – 1953. The plan concentrated on the heavy machine and metal industries. It was based upon Soviet experience. The main tasks were the **industrialization** of Slovakia and the gradual **collectivization** of agriculture.

21 December – The Prague parliament accepted a law concerning the regional organization of the state. Nineteen regions (*kraj*), were created on the territory of the state, 13 in Czechia and 6 in Slovakia. In Slovakia the regions were: Bratislava, Nitra, Banská Bystrica, Žilina, Košice, and Prešov. A regional national committee and a regional organization of the **Communist Party of Czechoslovakia** was created in the capital of each region (**9 April 1960**).

– The Slovak graphic artist Vincent Hložník received an honorable mention for his work in Forte dei Marni in Italy. He obtained further awards in Venice and Leipzig in 1958 and in Varna in 1981.

■ 1949

5 – 8 January – The Council for Mutual Economic Assistance (COMECON) was established in Moscow. The Czechoslovak Republic was one of the six founding members.

17 February – Alexej Čepička, the minister of justice, presented an ultimatum at a meeting with the Roman Catholic **bishops**. He demanded a clear declaration of loyalty to the government from the church, the revocation of the suspensions of the clergy cooperating with the regime, and the suspension of clergy condemned for alleged anti-state activity.

22 – 23 February – The national assembly accepted a law concerning Unified Farmers' Cooperatives. It created the preconditions for the „socialization" of the country-side that accompanied the **collectivization** of the land.

4 – 6 March – The founding congress of the Union of Czechoslovak Writers took place in Prague. With this the independent Society of Slovak Writers was degraded to the Slovak section of the new state-wide organization (**6 April 1954**).

22 March – A conference of the Czech and Slovak Roman Catholic **bishops** in Dolný Smokovec discussed the ultimatum of Alexej Čepička of **17 February**. Listening devices were discovered in the meeting rooms. With this, negotiations between the church and the state ended.

25 April – The presidium of the **Central Committee of the Communist Party of Czechoslovakia** approved a directive about the further struggle against the Roman Catholic Church: forbidding Catholic societies, halting the church press, establishing church bureaux led by a church secretary at the regional and district national committees, the organizing and support of a „renewal movement of Catholics" loyal to the political regime, the development of a national church independent of the Vatican.

25 – 29 May – The 9th congress of the **Communist Party of Czechoslovakia** took place in Prague. The congress accepted „a general line for the building of socialism". The party emphasized the intensification of the class struggle, especially in the countryside, and stressed the need for a resolute dissemination of Marxist-Leninist ideology in every area of life and the need for socialist **industrialization** and **collectivization**.

15 June – At a secret meeting in Prague, the Czech and Slovak Catholic **bishops** approved a pastoral letter to the faithful. It condemned attacks against the church, the efforts of the state to bring the church under its control and to make of it an obedient tool of its policy, for example, through the schismatic **Catholic action**. The bishops maintained that, particularly in Slovakia, monastic houses had been emptied by force and the priests taken away in trucks.

14 October – The Prague parliament unanimously approved the so-called church laws, which created a state office for church matters in Prague, whose director was Alexej Čepička, and a Slovak office for church matters in Bratislava, directed by Gustáv Husák and, from 1950, by Ladislav Holdoš. These laws and later government regulations subordinated all churches to state supervision and made them completely dependent upon the state. State approval was necessary for pastoral work.

27 October – The Slovak Philharmonic began its activities. The orchestra had been established in 1948 by a law of the **Slovak National Council**.

■ **1950**
31 March – 4 April – A show trial of representatives of religious orders took place in Prague. Of the ten accused, nine Czechs and one Slovak, the Redemptorist Ján Mastiliak, received the most severe sentence, life imprisonment. This was the beginning of a well-prepared attack against monastics accused of espionage and anti-state activity.

13 – 14 April – During the night members of security and police units began a state-wide action „K" to occupy the monasteries and intern monks and other religious. In Slovakia 56 monasteries, in which 850 monastics lived, and parish offices were occupied. By the end of May, 1, 002 monastics were interned in Slovakia.

28 April – The action „P" climaxed when, with the help of state organs, Greek Catholics were forced to become Orthodox believers. In Prešov the Ukrainian National Council organized an assembly of „restoration commissions." This non-representative organ approved a manifesto concerning the conversion of Greek Catholic believers to the Orthodox faith. The government took note of this decision on 27 May. Although there did not exist any legal basis for the decision to dissolve the Greek Catholic Church, Greek Catholic believers were outlawed (**13 June 1968**).

18 May – The parliament in Prague adopted a law concerning universities. The new law adopted an organization and system of studies on the Soviet model. Thorough purges and the establishment of cadres among the students and the teachers at universities began. „Bourgeois nationalism and bourgeois ideology" became the greatest enemy at Slovak universities.

20 May – A ministry of national security was organized. The first minister was Ladislav Kopřiva. He was followed by Karol Bacílek. The new ministry made possible the widening of illegal incursions against the citizens and the state security obtained practically unlimited power. Under the supervision of Soviet advisors the state security began to produce fabricated accusations. From October 1948 to

January 1953 the state court condemned 233 persons to death. Of these, 178 were executed. From 1951 to 1953 hundreds of Soviet advisors were active in 600 functions in the Czechoslovak Republic (not including experts for the mining of uranium).

24 – 27 May – The 9th congress of the **Communist Party of Slovakia** was held. It focused on the **industrialization** of Slovakia and the uncovering of those propagating so-called Slovak bourgeois nationalism in the party.

12 July – The national assembly approved a new criminal code and criminal procedure. The national committees obtained broader criminal jurisdiction. They used this especially against the small farmers (**collectivization**).

16 July – The supreme court sentenced a group of defendants accused of participating in the activities of the **White Legion,** an anti-communist organization. For Anton Tunega, Albert Púčik and Eduard Tesár the punishment of life imprisonment was changed to the death penalty. The execution of these three young opponents of the communist regime took place in Bratislava on 20 February 1951.

29 – 31 August – The police and security organs carried out the action „R", the occupation of female cloisters and the internment of nuns. From 137 cloisters and houses of religious orders in Slovakia 1,962 nuns were interned.

1 September – The minister of national defense ordered the establishment of the first four centers of Auxiliary Technical Battalions (*Pomocné technické prápory* – PTP) in Czechia. They were intended for „politically unreliable and asocial persons" (clerics, monastics, so-called kulaks, former entrepreneurs, and some of the intelligentsia). Up to 1954, 60,000 people served in the battalions. Of these 22,000 were „politically unreliable". About 5,500 individuals from Slovakia were included in this category.

19 – 21 October – The trial of the partisan commander Viliam Žingor, who was suspected of wanting to become a Slovak Tito, was held in Bratislava. State security fabricated a „dangerous armed group" led by Žin-

gor, whose members did not know or had seen one another only once. Žingor was condemned to death and executed. Another 142 persons were condemned in connection with the Žingor process. All but three of the important Slovak partisan commanders became victims of the communist system that they had helped to create.

■ **1951**

10 – 15 January – A show trial of the Roman Catholic **bishops** Ján Vojtaššák and Michal Buzalka and the Greek Catholic bishop Pavol Gojdič took place in Bratislava. Buzalka and Gojdič were condemned to life imprisonment and died in prison. The 74 year-old Vojtaššák was condemned to 24 years in prison.

21 – 24 February – The Central Committee of the Communist Party of Czechoslovakia considered so-called Slovak bourgeois nationalism. Štefan Bašťovanský made a presentation on this problem. Vladimír Clementis, Gustáv Husák and Ladislav Novomeský were consequently expelled from the Communist Party (**24 – 27 May 1950, 21 – 24 April 1954**).

25 June – The communist leadership approved the action „77,000 office workers to production". A total of 77,500 office workers in Czechia and 5,800 in Slovakia had to go into manufacturing. The criterion for unreliability in Slovakia was membership and activity in **Hlinka's Slovak People's Party**, the **Hlinka Guard**, Hlinka Youth, or the **Democratic Party**. Eventually 51,215 office workers were transferred to production (66 per cent of the planned number).

■ **1952**

1 February – The commission for the interior prepared several variants of action „B", the removal of „bourgeois and unreliable elements of the state" from the cities to the villages. Action „B" affected a high proportion of the Slovak intelligentsia. For example, 678 families had to leave Bratislava and 136 families left Martin. Action „B" ended in September 1953.

20 – 27 November – A show trial took place of „the leadership of the anti-state conspiracy center", led by the former general secretary of the **Communist Party of Czechoslovakia**, Rudolf Slánský, before the senate of the state court in Prague. Eleven of the accused were condemned to death and executed, among them the former minister of foreign affairs, Vladimír Clementis, and three were sentenced to life imprisonment (one of whom was the former deputy minister of foreign trade, Eugen Löbl).

■ **1953**
14 March – President Klement Gottwald died. Antonín Zápotocký was elected president by the national assembly on 21 March.
30 May – The national assembly passed a currency reform law. The reform was initiated by Soviet advisors. It fixed the exchange rate at 5:1 for 300 Kčs per person in cash and for up to 5,000 Kčs in deposits in saving accounts. Salaries, wages, and cash were calculated according to the same formula. Remaining cash and deposits in banks were exchanged at a ratio of 50:1. The reform affected especially the workers and farmers, whose proportion of the savings was 79.65 per cent. Protests against the reform erupted in strikes at 129 factories. Security forces arrested 472 persons. The ration system was cancelled contemporaneously with the currency reform.
26 June – The **Slovak National Council** approved a law concerning the Slovak Academy of Sciences that reshaped it according to the Soviet model (**2 July 1942**, **22 February 1946**).
3 July – On the basis of a previous decision of the commission for information and propaganda, the commission for the interior issued an order for the dissolution of the **Matica slovenská**. Only the Slovak National Library remained from the Matica. The commission for the interior cancelled this order on 4 April 1954. The Matica activities remained paralyzed (**27 April 1954**, **27 June 1968**).
5 July – The first annual folklore festival took place in the typical Slovak village of Východná at the foot of the High Tatra Mountains. From a regional event it gradually became an international festival.
4 – 5 September – The Central Committee of

the Communist Party of Czechoslovakia decided to abolish the office of chairman of the party and to introduce the office of the first secretary of the party. Antonín Novotný was the first to be elected to this office. The meeting also conceded that mistakes had been made in the **collectivization** of agriculture. But, despite its declared voluntary nature, collectivization continued to be advanced by force.

■ **1954**
6 April – A conference of the Union of Czechoslovak Writers in Prague accepted new by-laws that transformed the Slovak section of this organization into the Union of Slovak Writers (**22 April 1963**).
21 – 24 April – A trial of a group of so-called Slovak bourgeois nationalists from the ranks of former Slovak communists took place in Bratislava. On fabricated charges Gustáv Husák was condemned to life imprisonment, Ivan Horváth to 22 years, Daniel Okáli to 18 years, Ladislav Holdoš to 13 years, and Ladislav Novomeský to 10 years in prison (**21- 24 February 1951**).
27 April – **The Slovak National Council** passed a law concerning the **Matica slovenská**. The law changed the societal character of the Matica and transformed it into a scientific institution with library, bibliographical, archival and publication activities.

■ **1955**
11 – 14 May – A conference took place in Warsaw of European socialist states (Albania, Bulgaria, Czecho- Slovakia, Hungary, the German Democratic Republic, Poland, Romania and the Soviet Union) concerning peace and security in Europe. The conference participants signed a treaty of friendship, cooperation and mutual assistance, and a resolution about creating a joint command for the armed forces of all the Warsaw Pact states.

■ **1956**
3 November – After test television transmissions in Bratislava (1953) and in Košice

(1956), regular television transmissions began from the Bratislava television studio.

19 – 20 April – The Central Committee of the Communist Party of Czechoslovakia discussed the conclusions of the 20th congress of the Communist Party of the Soviet Union (the criticism of the personality cult and its removal from public life, the theses concerning peaceful co-existence of different political systems and various paths to socialism). The central committee did not in fact take any steps to remedy the terror of the previous period.

22 – 29 April – At their second congress, Czech and Slovak writers came forward as the conscience of the nation. They called for the leading party and government organs to learn from the consequences of the injustice previously committed on a mass scale (**22 April 1963**).

■ 1957

13 November – Antonín Zápotocký , the president of the Czechoslovak Republic, died. Antonín Novotný was elected as its new president on 19 November.

■ 1958

2 – 3 April – The Central Committee of the Communist Party of Czechoslovakia discussed a report of Antonín Novotný and delineated the direction towards the completion of the building of socialism.

16 – 18 May – The congress of the **Communist Party of Slovakia** took place in Bratislava. The participants spoke about the role of Slovakia in the „final stage in building the material-technical basis of socialism". They also discussed the struggle against former supporters of Hlinka's Slovak People's Party (Ľudaks). Antonín Novotný and leading figures of the Central Committee of the Communist Party of Czechoslovakia were behind this campaign, which led to new political show trials and the screening of party workers.

12 August – A government regulation was issued concerning the establishment of the Pavol Jozef Šafárik University in Košice. It was to consist of a philosophical faculty located in Prešov and a medical faculty located in Košice.

11 – 13 December – A meeting of the Council for Mutual Economic Assistance in Prague accepted a resolution about building the pipeline *Družba* to deliver oil to the **Czechoslovak Republic**, Poland, Hungary and the German Democratic Republic. With this, the Slovnaft company in Bratislava grew in importance. An inter-governmental agreement about the pipeline was signed in Moscow on 11 December 1959.

– The Slovak photographer Martin Martinček received the gold medal at the international exhibition „How Children of the World Play" in Neuchatel in Switzerland. He received further awards in 1960 in Budapest and in 1965 in Saõ Paulo and Leipzig.

■ 1960

9 April – The Prague parliament passed a law concerning the territorial division of the state. Ten regions (7 in Czechia and 3 in Slovakia) were created on its territory. In Slovakia these were the Western Slovak Region (Bratislava), the Central Slovak Region (Banská Bystrica), and the Eastern Slovak Region (Košice). The law was a step towards a more centralized administration (**21 December 1948**).

5 – 7 July – A state-wide conference of the **Communist Party of Czechoslovakia** asserted that socialism had been victorious in Czecho-Slovakia. The conference discussed a draft of a new **constitution**.

11 July – The national assembly approved the new **constitution** that confirmed the victory of socialism in the country and prepared for the transition to communism. The name of the state, the Czechoslovak Republic was changed to the Czechoslovak Socialist Republic. According to article four, the leading force in society and the state was the Communist Party of Czechoslovakia. The constitution radically limited the authority of the **Slovak National Council** by abolishing its executive organ, the board of commissioners.

■ 1961

26 – 27 January – A state-wide conference

about the Eastern Slovak Ironworks character-ized the building of this integrated metallurgi-cal factory as one of the most important goals of the third five-year plan.

■ **1962**

17 June – The Czecho-Slovak football (soc-cer) team lost to Brazil in the finals of the world championships in Santiago de Chile. It received the silver medal (**20 June 1976**).

■ **1963**

3 – 4 April – The Central Committee of the Communist Party of Czechoslovakia ac-cepted a report concerning the violation of party principles and socialist legality during the period 1949 – 1954. This began a process that rehabilitated the communists purged during this period. Karol Bacílek was re-moved from the office of the first secretary of the Central Committee of the Communist Party of Slovakia and Bruno Köhler from the office of secretary of the Central Committee of the Communist Party of Czechoslovakia, while Alexej Čepička and Ladislav Kopřiva were expelled from the party. The rehabilita-tion process and compensation for the injus-tice of the previous years of the communist regime had only a symbolic character and was understood as an internal matter of the Communist Party.

22 April – A conference of the Union of Slovak Writers met in Bratislava. Several Slo-vak writers including, in particular, Ladislav Novomeský, criticized the power of the gov-erning clique of Antonín Novotný and de-manded truthful and objective interpreta-tions of the most recent history of Slovak literature.

13 May – Pope John XXIII consecrated the corner-stone of the building of the Slovak In-stitute of Saints Cyril and Methodius in Rome. The Institute focused on publishing religious literature in Slovak and on spiritual care for Slovaks abroad. The clerics Anton Botek, Šte-fan Náhalka and Dominik Hrušovský ren-dered great service in its development.

20 September – President Antonín Novotný dismissed Viliam Široký from his function as prime minister and named Jozef Lenárt as the new prime minister. Before the results of the investigation of the so-called Kolder commis-sion, which was researching the political show trials of the 1950s, were to have been made public, Antonín Novotný had to sacri-fice, in his own interests, the compromised Široký.

27 November – The treaty of friendship, mu-tual assistance, and post-war co-operation be-tween the Czechoslovak Socialist Republic and the Union of Soviet Socialist Republics (**12 December 1943**) was extended for an-other twenty years.

18 – 19 December – The Central Committee of the Communist Party of Czechoslovakia discussed the problem of so-called Slovak bourgeois nationalism. There were inconsis-tencies between the rehabilitation of purged communists and ascertaining responsibility for the show trials.

– The Slovak director Peter Solan received a prize at the San Francisco film festival for his film *The Boxer and Death (Boxer a smrť*).

■ **1964**

The Slovak painter and graphic artist Albín Brunovský received a prize at the Biennial of Graphic Art in Lugano. He received other prizes in 1967 (Paris, Ljubljana), 1976 (Ber-lin), 1977 (Seattle), 1980 (Krakow, Frechen), 1982 (Leipzig), 1985 (Varna) and in 1988 (Pescara).

3 December – An agreement about the build-ing of a gas pipeline from the Soviet Union to the Czechoslovak Socialist Republic was signed in Moscow.

■ **1965**

11 March – The Czecho-Slovak team de-feated the Canadian team (8:0) at the world championship for ice hockey in Tampere, Fin-land. For Canada, it was their greatest defeat in the history of the world championship. The Czecho-Slovak team won the silver me-dal. The Slovak goal-tender, Vladimír Dzuril-la, was named the best goalie of the cham-pionship. Another Slovak player, Jozef Golonka, also received recognition.

1966

12 – 14 May – The congress of the Communist Party of Slovakia in Bratislava elected Alexander Dubček as the first secretary of its Central Committee.

3 June – An American astronaut of Slovak descent, Eugene A. Černan, made his first flight into space as the co-pilot of the Gemini space capsule. He completed another flight in 1969 to photograph the surface of the moon. In 1972, as commander of the space capsule Apollo 17, he walked on the moon.

5 – 7 December – At a conference of Slovak linguists in Smolenice a specific theory of language culture and the Slovak literary language was elaborated and accepted. The conclusions of the conference were formulated as „Theses concerning Slovak". The theses emphasized the representational, as opposed to the communicative, function of the language. Slovak was characterized as the national language of the Slovaks that had to fulfill the role of a state language (**8 May 1968**).

– The motion picture, **A Shop on Main Street** (Obchod na Korze) was honored with an Oscar Academy Award. In it J. Króner, a Slovak actor, played a leading role.

1967

27 – 29 June – The 4th congress of the Union of Czechoslovak Writers met in Prague. A group of writers openly called attention to the growing crisis in society and the bureaucratic character of the policies of Antonín Novotný. Novotný had the publication of the press organ of the union, *Literary news (Literární noviny),* halted and expelled several writers from the **Communist Party of Czechoslovakia.**

7 September – An international jury awarded the prizes for the first competitive exhibition of illustrations of literature for children and young people, the Bratislava Illustrations Biennial (BIB). During the first year 278 artists from 25 countries participated with 3,236 illustrations. Since 1967 the Biennial has regularly taken place every other year.

30 – 31 October – Alexander Dubček spoke in the plenary session of the Central Commit-

tee of the Communist Party of Czechoslovakia and suggested a new concept for the work of the party. He demanded a democratization of relationships in the party and the preparation of a new program for the party. He criticized its conservatism and sectarianism. Antonín Novotný accused Dubček of Slovak nationalism.

– The documentary film *The Enchanted Valley (Zakliata dolina),* directed by Štefan Kamenický and filmed by O. Šághy, received the Silver Plaque of St. Mark at the 1967 international festival of documentary films in Venice.

1968

3 – 5 January – A plenary session of the Central Committee of the Communist Party of Czechoslovakia agreed that the office of president of the state and the function of the first secretary of the Central Committee were not to be held by the same person. Antonín Novotný was dismissed as the first secretary of the central committee. He was replaced by Alexander Dubček, the first Slovak in the highest office of the party.

14 – 15 March – The **Slovak National Council (1945)** met in Bratislava. It approved a proposal to strengthen the jurisdiction of Slovak national organs. A special commission drafted the document „The Position of the Slovak National Council towards the current period in the development of society", which introduced the demand for a federal arrangement of the Czecho-Slovak state.

15 March – The **Matica slovenská** issued a demand that Antonín Novotný resign from the office of president. On 19 March the universities in Bratislava joined in this demand. The reason for the dissatisfaction of the Matica with Novotný lay in his anti-Slovak orientation and his undignified behavior during his visit to its seat in Martin in September 1967.

21 March – President Antonín Novotný informed the presidium of the Central Committee of the Communist Party of Czechoslovakia that he was resigning his office. The next day he informed the national assembly of his decision.

23 March – The leading representatives of the communist parties of the Soviet Union, Czecho-Slovakia, Poland, Hungary, Bulgaria, and the German Democratic Republic met in Dresden. The participants sharply criticized the delegation of the Communist Party of Czechoslovakia led by Alexander Dubček and alleged that in the Czechoslovak Socialist Republic the work of people was dishonored, the security service and army were berated, and the Czechoslovak Communist Party spoke about democracy as if there had not been any until now.

30 March – General Ludvík Svoboda was elected president of the Czechoslovak Socialist Republic by the national assembly.

1 – 5 April – The Central Committee of the Communist Party of Czechoslovakia accepted a program document which admitted that previously democratic rights and liberties had been suppressed, laws violated, and power misused, that Communists and non-communists were affected. It stated that the leading role of the Communist Party should be to guarantee the rights and liberties of the citizens. The document further emphasized the partnership role of the members of the National Front and demanded a reduction of the influence of state security (ŠtB). A federal arrangement of the state and the implementation of economic reforms through greater independence for enterprises were designated as priorities.

7 April – A preparatory assembly of the Slovak Organization for the Defense of Human and National Rights (SONOP) met in Bratislava. It was the first organization with this focus in the Czechoslovak Socialist Republic. Its founder was Emil Vidra. In particular, the organization brought together former political prisoners. SONOP was renewed on 5 October 1990. Club 231 was founded in Prague on 31 March 1968 and was an association political prisoners sentenced according to law no. 231 (**16 October 1948**).

8 April – President Ludvík Svoboda named a new government led by Oldřich Černík.

17 April – A group of Evangelical pastors led by Pavol Valášek, which sought the internal renewal of the Evangelical Church of the Augsburg Confession, was formed in Čertovica. It later created a preparatory committee for the Association of Evangelical Clergy.

13 – 14 May – In Moravian Velehrad 2,500 clergy and laymen participated in the state-wide constituting assembly of Work of Conciliar Renewal. It was led by Bishop František Tomášek of Prague. The bishop of Trnava, Ambróz Lazík, became the president of the Slovak committee of the organization. Other important figures of the group in Slovakia were the secretly ordained **bishops** Ján Chryzostom Korec and Peter Dubovský. The organization's goals were to implement the decisions of the Second Vatican Council in the lives of believers and to enforce religious rights and liberty in the Czechoslovak Socialist Republic.

29 May – 1 June – The Central Committee of the Communist Party of Czechoslovakia considered the current political situation. Alexander Dubček maintained that they had obtained the trust of the citizens in the policies of the Communist Party. At the same time he mentioned that intensifying anti-communist tendencies were eliciting a conservative reaction from some functionaries of the party. According to Dubček, the dissemination of unreliable reports about the danger of a military intervention of the states of the Warsaw Pact were damaging the current political course of the Communist Party of Czechoslovakia. The party's central committee decided to call an extraordinary congress for 9 September 1968 (**22 August 1968**).

13 June – The government accepted a resolution about renewing the activities of the Greek Catholic Church. However, the resolution did not sufficiently redress the injustices that the Greek Catholics had endured during the previous three decades (**28 April 1950**).

24 – 26 June – The national assembly passed a constitutional law concerning a federal arrangement for the Czechoslovak Socialist Republic. It also accepted a law about the judicial rehabilitation of those unjustly condemned, the number of which was estimated to be about 105,000 (**8 July 1970**).

27 June – The **Slovak National Council** approved a law about the **Matica slovenská**. Alongside of its existing scientific activities concentrated in six departments, the Matica again became an association with the right to establish local branches (**27 December 1973**).

27 June – Radio, television and several newspapers made public the appeal „2000 Words". Its author was the Czech journalist Ladislav Vaculík. The appeal demanded a speeding up of the democratization process, the inclusion of communists in this process, and the founding of citizen committees and commissions. The leadership of the Communist Party of the Soviet Union viewed the „2000 Words" as a direct appeal to counter-revolution.

15 July – A joint meeting of the highest representatives of the communist parties of the Soviet Union, Poland, Bulgaria, the German Democratic Republic and Hungary was held in Warsaw. In a letter addressed to the Central Committee of the Communist Party of Czechoslovakia, they expressed their fear of a counter-revolutionary withdrawal of the Czecho-Slovakia from the socialist bloc. The states of the Warsaw Pact regarded the fate of socialism as a common matter. The Central Committee of the Communist Party of Czechoslovakia unanimously rejected the Warsaw letter.

29 July – 1 August – A confidential meeting between the delegation of the politbureau of the Communist Party of the Soviet Union led by Leodnid Iljich Brezhnev and the delegation of the presidium of the Central Committee of the Communist Party of Czechoslovakia led by Alexander Dubček took place in Čierna nad Tisou. The Soviet side demanded that the leadership of the Communist Party of Czechoslovakia be changed, that censorship of the media be reintroduced, and that the K 231 and KAN organizations be banned. The Czechoslovak Communist Party expressed its willingness to halt the spread of „anti-socialist tendencies" with democratic methods. The delegations agreed that a meeting of the representatives of the six communist parties would take place in Bratislava on **3 August 1968**.

3 August – A joint consultation of the leading representatives of the communist parties of the Czechoslovak Socialist Republic, the Soviet Union, Poland, Hungary, Bulgaria and the German Democratic Republic took place in Bratislava. The text of the joint communiqué contained the formula that the defense, support and strengthening of the achievements of socialism are „the common international obligation of all socialist countries". This formulation later served as a justification for the military intervention in Czecho-Slovakia (**21 August 1968**).

18 August – Alois Indra, the secretary of the Communist Party of Czechoslovakia and an opponent of the process of renewal in Czecho-Slovakia, secretly flew to Moscow. In a meeting with Leodnid Iljich Brezhnev he discussed the political steps to be taken after the arrival of intervening armies in Czecho-Slovakia. After the intervention a „revolutionary government and tribunal" led by Alois Indra was to be created and approve the military action retroactively.

Years of Dashed Hopes and Normalization (1968 – 1989)

The arrival of the intervention troops of the Warsaw Pact in August 1968 meant the forcible end to the process of social renewal in society. The subsequent policy of normalization substantially acceded to the demands of the Soviet Union and removed all democratic residues of the spring of 1968. The persecution of activists of the renewal process was joined to an extensive purge of the Communist Party and by the screening of party personnel. Censorship was reintroduced and the involvement of citizens in public matters was made impossible. A mass emigration to western democratic countries followed. The power of conservative communists in offices was strengthened and, supported by their patrons in Moscow, they used their power to intervene against anything that could be characterized as dissent. The attention of the citizens was intentionally directed away from public affairs. Citizens reacted with a flight to privacy and by withdrawing into the environment of the family. Success was achieved through a policy of social corruption that compensated for the loss of liberty with material advantages. The economic successes emphasized at congresses of the Communist Party were the result of extensive growth based upon state subsidies, the lack of a competitive environment, and a plundering of domestic natural and raw material resources. Despite the threat of persecution, the number of people who did not passively observe the normalization regime and who initiated activities directed towards the revival of human, national, and citizen rights grew. Dissidents, working individually and in groups, distributed *samizdat* (self-published) literature to the people and created secret discussion and education centers. Opposition to the existing political regime in Slovakia was represented in particular by Christian activists from the Roman Catholic Church who sought to achieve religious, national and citizen rights and liberties.

The federalization of the state, a fruit of the process of renewal, paradoxically was introduced only during the period of normalization. However, empowered by the normalization policy, the existing communist system hindered the functioning of the federation in practice. Therefore, the Czecho-Slovak problem remained open and unresolved. A certain political relaxation in the country occurred during the mid-1980s. The activities of opponents of the communist regime and the dissatisfaction of the citizens increased. The changes that took place in the Soviet Union after Michail Sergejevich Gorbachov became the head of the party leadership were an important factor. The first great public demonstration for religious and citizen liberty took place in Bratislava in March 1988. Police units dispersed it by force. The demonstration of Bratislava university students on 16 November and the Prague university students on 17 November 1989 led to an open confrontation of forces that developed into a political opposition.

■ **1968**

20 – 21 August – The presidium of the Central Committee of the Communist Party of Czechoslovakia met in Prague. Its conservative faction (Alois Indra, Drahomír Kolder, Vasil Biľak, Emil Rigo and Miloš Jakeš), partially informed about the approaching military intervention, proposed a declaration, a document condemning the process of renewal in the country and inclining towards the critique contained in the Warsaw letter (**15 July 1968**). During the discussion, at about 23:30, the prime minister, Oldřich Černík, reported the military invasion of the Czechoslovak Socialist Republic by five states of the Warsaw Pact. Zdeněk Mlynář, a member of the presidium, suggested the text of a resolution condemning the invasion. Seven of its members voted for the resolution, 4 voted against it.

– Shortly before midnight of 20 – 21 August, the military invasion by the five states of the Warsaw Pact (the Soviet Union, German De-

mocratic Republic, Poland, Hungary and Bulgaria) began. It was the largest military operation in Europe since the end of the Second World War. Participating in it were 27 divisions (500, 000 to 600,000 men), 800 aircraft, 6,000 tanks, 2,000 artillery and special rocket units. The expected and planned „request for assistance" [invitation letter] was not publicized by Czecho-Slovak radio or the Czecho-Slovak Press Agency.

21 August – In the name of the non-existent workers- farmers government of Alois Indra, organs of the KGB, the Soviet secret police, in cooperation with agents of State Security (ŠtB), arrested Alexander Dubček, Josef Smrkovský, František Kriegel, Josef Špaček, Čestmír Císař, and other leading state and party representatives of the renewal process during the early morning hours and deported them to the Soviet Union.

– The mass media of the five states of the Warsaw Pact participating in the invasion,

published the text of an invitation letter by which anonymous representatives of the **Communist Party of Czechoslovakia** turned to the Soviet Union and the „fraternal socialist states" with a request for help against counter-revolution and an alleged threat of civil war.
– President Ludvík Svoboda declined to name a new „revolutionary government" led by Alois Indra as suggested by Soviet officials. With this, the plan to legalize the occupation failed.

22 August – Because the invading armies still had not cut the cable network of the Central Committee of the Communist Party of Czechoslovakia, an extraordinary congress of the party took place at Vysočany in Prague. Of a total number of 1,543 invited delegates, 1,219 participated. The lower participation of delegates from Slovakia was the result of communication difficulties caused by the intervention. The congress declared that „socialist Czechoslovakia would never accept either the administration of military occupation or the authority of domestic collaborators". It recognized only the legally elected representatives of the state and the Communist Party of Czechoslovakia. The congress elected the new leadership of the party and confirmed Alexander Dubček in his position.

23 – 26 August – The **Moscow negotiations** took place between the Czecho-Slovak delegation led by President Ludvík Svoboda and the leadership of the Soviet Communist Party. Ludvík Svoboda again declined the Soviet offer. However the Soviets imposed upon the delegation the so-called Moscow protocol that guaranteed the presence of Soviet troops in Czecho-Slovakia as long as the „threat to socialism" had not passed. The presidium of the **Central Committee of the Communist Party** was obliged to declare the extraordinary Vysočany congress of the **Communist Party of Czechoslovakia** (**22 August 1968**) invalid and to promise extensive purges.

26 – 28 August – An extraordinary congress of the **Communist Party of Slovakia** took place in Bratislava. On the first day of the congress the delegates accepted a resolution that condemned the occupation by five states of the

Warsaw Pact and expressed support for the extraordinary Vysočany congress of the **Communist Party of Czechoslovakia**. On 27 August Gustáv Husák returned from Moscow and attended the congress. He made known to those present the results of the **Moscow negotiations** and obtained the revocation of the original resolution of the congress. He openly declared his own support for the renewal process of 1968 and the program of Dubček. Gustáv Husák became the first secretary of the Central Committee of the Communist Party of Slovakia instead of Vasil Biľak.

31 August – A plenary session of the Central Committee of the Communist Party of Czechoslovakia met in Prague. It approved the Moscow protocol (**23 – 26 August 1968**) as a condition for a gradual **normalization**. Gustáv Husák and Ludvík Svoboda were co-opted as members of the central committee and elected to the presidium of this party organ.

28 September – According to the Czecho-Slovak police, during the invasion of Czecho-Slovakia, the occupation army of the five Warsaw Pact states killed 94 persons (53 were shot, 38 were killed by military vehicles, and 3 persons died in other ways), seriously injured 335 persons and slightly injured 500 individuals.

16 October – After discussions in Moscow, in which Alexander Dubček, Gustáv Husák and Oldřich Černík participated, an agreement was signed in Prague for the temporary presence of Soviet troops on the territory of the Czecho-Slovak state. The agreement was approved by the Czecho-Slovak government and accepted by the national assembly on 18 October (228 voted for it, 10 abstained, and 4 voted against it).

27 October – The national assembly accepted a constitutional law concerning the Czecho-Slovak federation. It was ceremonially signed at the restored castle in Bratislava on 30 October 1968. The law came into force on 1 January 1969. The state became a compound entity, a **federation** of two national republics, the Slovak and the Czech. State organs for the federation and the republics were created (**20 December 1970**).

1 December – Since 21 August 1968, 6,384 individuals had emigrated from Slovakia. From December 1968 to October 1969 an additional 4,223 persons emigrated.

13 December – A meeting of Slovak writers took place in Bratislava. They expressed clear support for the process of renewal in society. The dogmatic Marxist writers resigned from their offices in the presidium of the Union of Slovak Writers (**11 June 1969**).

■ 1969

1 January – The Slovak Socialist Republic was established in accordance with the law concerning the Czecho-Slovak **federation**.

30 March – At the world championship in ice hockey, the Czecho-Slovak team won the bronze medal. Their double victory over the team of the Soviet Union (21 March and 28 March) was considered a great success. It was the occasion for mass demonstrations against the occupation forces in Czecho-Slovakia and against the start of **normalization** (**11 March 1965, 20 April 1972**).

17 April – The Central Committee of the Communist Party of Czechoslovakia met and elected a new presidium for the committee. Alexander Dubček was replaced by Gustáv Husák as its first secretary.

21 May – The Slovak soccer (football) club Slovan Bratislava defeated the Spanish team FC Barcelona 3 to 2 in the Cup Champions' Cup final in Basel. It thus became the first soccer team from the former eastern bloc to win this cup.

11 June – The founding congress of the Union of Slovak Writers as an independent organization took place in Bratislava. Andrej Plávka was elected its chairman (**31 May 1972**).

25 – 29 September – In Prague the **Central Committee of the Communist Party of Czechoslovakia** discussed the current political situation. Gustáv Husák presented a report that raised doubts about the ideas of Dubček and the entire political development since January 1968. The mandates of the delegates at the extraordinary congress of the Communist Party of Czechoslovakia (**22 August 1968**) were abolished, several of the preced-

ing resolutions of the party were annulled and 80 members of the reform wing of the central committee were expelled from the party.

– The film director Dušan Hanák was awarded a prize at the Biennial of Young Art in Paris for the documentary film *Mass (Omša)*. His later work, *Pictures from the Old World (Obrazy starého sveta)* received recognition at film festivals in Lyon, Leipzig, Montreal and Los Angeles.

■ 1970

9 January – The government of the Slovak Socialist Republic accepted a resolution concerning the question of the churches in Slovakia. It contained directives to dampen religious activity, forbade the importation of religious literature from abroad, limited the teaching of religion and renewed the institution of atheism.

28 – 30 January – The **Central Committee of the Communist Party of Czechoslovakia** took up the question of party personnel (cadres). It approved a letter of the central committee addressed to all basic organizations about „the exchange of party membership cards". The result of the screening and purge was the expulsion of 67,000 and the cancellation of 259,000 party memberships; 147,000 members of the party voluntarily relinquished their membership.

5 – 6 February – The **Central Committee of the Communist Party of Slovakia** discussed questions of personnel, the economy, and the „exchange of party membership cards". With the support of Gustáv Husák, Jozef Lenárt, who was inextricably connected with the conservative Brezhnev group in the Communist Party of Czechoslovakia, was elected the first secretary of the **Communist Party of Slovakia**.

19 – 21 June – The preparatory general assembly of the Slovak World Congress, linking many Slovak associations and organizations abroad, was held in the American Hotel in New York City. The congress declared itself in favor of the process of European integration, in which Slovaks would freely and immediately participate. The Slovak World Congress rejected the continuity of the first **Slovak Republic** (1939 – 1945) and revived the demand for Slovak statehood by appealing to the right of self-determination and ideas of sovereignty and democracy. The definitive form of the Slovak World Congress was achieved at its founding general assembly in Toronto 17 – 20 June 1971. The industrial entrepreneur Štefan B. Roman became the president of the Slovak World Congress.

6 May – The highest representatives of the Union of Soviet Socialist Republics, Leodnid Iljich Brezhnev and Alexej Nikolajevich Kosygin, and the Czechoslovak Socialist Republic, Gustáv Husák and Lubomír Štrougal, signed a treaty of friendship, co-operation, and mutual assistance between Czecho-Slovakia and Soviet Union at Prague castle. It was to be valid for 20 years.

8 July – The federal assembly accepted amendments to the law of judicial rehabilitation which had halted the process of judicial rehabilitation from 1968 (**24 – 26 June 1968**).

5 November – The Czechoslovak Socialist Republic and the Union of Soviet Socialist Republics signed a commercial agreement in Moscow valid for the period 1971 – 1975.

10 – 11 December – At a meeting of the **Central Committee of the Communist Party of Czechoslovakia**, an evaluation of the results of the purges in the party was made (**28 – 30 January 1970**). The ultra-left group in the central committee pushed through the document, „Learning from the crisis development in the party and society after the 13th congress of the **Communist Party of Czechoslovakia**". The document was full of demagogic and false assertions that a counter-revolution was being prepared in the Czechoslovak Socialist Republic and that therefore the „international assistance" of the five Warsaw Pact states on 21 August 1968 was needed.

20 December – After a previous decision of the **Central Committee of the Communist Party of Czechoslovakia,** the federal assembly adopted constitutional law no. 125, which in-itiated a series of legal changes and amendments to the constitutional law concerning the federation of **27 October 1968**. Under the guise of „strengthening the socialist state", the industrial branches of fuel, energy, transport, communications, and machine production were transferred to the competency of the central government in Prague. The office of state secretary in the federal central organs was abolished and the number of central organs of the **federation** was increased. The receipts and expenditures of the federal budget were increased at the expense of the republics.

■ **1971**

13 – 15 May – A congress of the Communist Party of Slovakia took place in Bratislava. It stressed the success of **normalization** and asserted that in the years 1965 – 1970 the national income grew by 61 per cent. Jozef Lenárt was confirmed as the first secretary of the **Central Committee of the Communist Party of Slovakia**.

25 – 29 May – The 14th congress of the **Communist Party of Czechoslovakia** took place in Prague. It confirmed the policy of **normalization** and focused future efforts on a growth in productivity and the national income. The congress dogmatically emphasized the leading role of the **Communist Party of Czechoslovakia** in society. A two-year candidacy period was introduced to make more strict the selection of future party members. Gustáv Husák was confirmed as general secretary of the party.

7 October – The federal assembly approved a law concerning the five-year plan.

■ **1972**

3 – 13 February – The XI Winter Olympic Games took place in the Japanese city of Sapporo at which the Slovak figure skater Ondrej Nepela won a gold medal.

20 April – The Czecho-Slovak team beat the team of the Soviet Union in the finals of the ice hockey world championship in Prague and thus won the gold medal. It was the second time Czecho-Slovakia had won the ice-hockey world championship. The first was in Stockholm in 1949. In the 1970s the Slovak Stanislav Mikita, a native of Sokolče near Liptovský Mikuláš and a star of the Chicago Black Hawks of the National Hockey League, ranked among the best hockey players in the world (**30 March 1969, 25 April 1976**).

31 May – The second congress of the Union of Slovak Writers took place in Bratislava. It was held in the spirit of **normalization**. The main presentations were delivered by Andrej Plávka and a representative of the **Central Committee of the Communist Party of Slovakia**, the ideologue Ľudovít Pezlár. The congress criticized the process of renewal of 1968, approved new by-laws and introduced a „program of engaged socialist literature, a program of **socialist realism,** and the renewal of the principles of Marxism-Leninism in literary criticism".

13 – 14 December – The federal assembly adopted as a law the previous resolution of the **Central Committee of the Communist Party of Czechoslovakia** and the government of the Czechoslovak Socialist Republic about increasing assistance to families with more children and young married couples (an increase in family subsidies and the introduction of loans for young married couples).

■ **1973**

3 March – The consecration of three Roman Catholic bishops, Július Gábriš (Trnava), Ján Pásztor (Nitra), and Jozef Feranec (Banská Bystrica), took place in Nitra. Thirteen bishoprics remained without bishops in the Czechoslovak Socialist Republic (**13 November 1920, 17 March 1990**).

22 March – The federal assembly re-elected Ludvík Svoboda president.

9 May – Czecho-Slovak television began regular color transmissions.

3 – 4 July – The **Central Committee of the Communist Party of Czechoslovakia** took up the question of the socialist training of the younger generation. Alongside an improvement in the quality of teaching at secondary schools and universities, increased attention had to be devoted to influencing the youth in the spirit of Marxist-Leninist ideology and atheism.

11 December – Willy Brandt, the social democratic chancellor of the Federal Republic of Germany, and Walter Scheel, the German minister of foreign affairs together with the prime minister of the Czechoslovak Socialist Republic, Lubomír Štrougal, and the minister of foreign affairs, Bohuslav Chňoupek, signed in Prague a treaty of mutual relations between both countries. The treaty partners did not find a suitable formula to nullify the Munich Agreement. The German side essentially legalized the communist system as a partner for cooperation.

27 December – The normalization law of the **Slovak National Council** dissolved the membership base of the Matica slovenská (**27 June 1968**).

– The Slovak photographer Karol Kállay was recognized by UNESCO for the year's most beautiful book. He obtained this prize also in 1974 and 1975. In 1992 the German periodical *Geo* declared him the photographer of the year.

– The Slovak director Juraj Jakubisko received a prize at the festival in Budapest for his film *Construction of the Century (Stavba storočia)*. He was awarded a prize in 1975 in Varna for the film *Omnia* and in 1978 in Oberhausen for the film *Drummer of the Red Cross (Bubeník Červeného kríža)*.

■ **1975**

28 – 29 May – The federal assembly approved a supplement to the law of federation (**27 October 1968**). If the president was unable to carry out the functions of his office for more than year, the federal assembly could elect a new president. At the suggestion of the central committees of the Communist Party of Czechoslovakia and of the National Front of the Czechoslovak Socialist Republic, the federal assembly elected Gustáv Husák president (29 May).

3 – 4 June – The 1st state-wide congress of Catholic clergy in the pro-regime organization *Pacem in terris* took place in Brno. Antonín Veselý was elected its chairman. By its decree *Quidam episcopi* of 8 March 1982, the Vatican Congregation for the Clergy forbade clergy to be members of this organization.

7 – 8 July – The **Slovak National Council** elected as its new chairman Viliam Šalgovič, the former minister of the interior who was closely connected with the Soviet KGB.

■ **1976**

25 – 27 March – A congress of the **Communist Party of Slovakia** took place in Bratislava. It evaluated the preceding five year period as „one of the most successful periods in the building of a socialist Slovakia." The Slovak Socialist Republic's proportion of the total industrial production of the state was 26.6 per cent and of gross agricultural production 32.7 per cent. Jozef Lenárt was again elected as the first secretary of the Central Committee of the Communist Party of Slovakia**.**

12 – 16 April – The 15th congress of the **Communist Party of Czechoslovakia** took place in the Palace of Congresses in Prague. It was asserted that the economic potential of the state had grown by about one third and confirmed a preference for the chemical industry and machine production while programs in the areas of electronics and electro-technology where throttled. Statistical manipulation artificially increased the standard of living, since the national income and wages having actually stagnated. This was brought about by a policy of economic growth at any price (a disproportionate growth in investment costs and the high energy consumption of the machine industry).

25 April – At the European and world ice hockey championship in Katowice, Poland, the Czecho-Slovak team won the gold medal when it tied with the team from the Soviet Union in the final game. On the Czecho-Slovak team Slovakia was represented by several hockey players, including the brothers Peter and Marián Šťastný (**11 March 1965, 30 March 1969, 20 April 1972**).

20 June – The Czecho-Slovak soccer team, under the leadership of the Slovak trainer Jozef Vengloš, beat the team of the Federal Republic of Germany at the European championship in Yugoslavia and won the European title. Eight Slovaks were part of the Czecho-Slovak team (**10 June 1934**).

22 June – The federal assembly approved the law concerning the sixth five-year plan.

17 July – 1 August – The XXI Olympic Games took place in Montreal. The Slovak cyclist Anton Tkáč won the gold medal for the 1000 m sprint. He was the world champion in this event in 1974 and 1978.

11 November – The president of the Czechoslovak Socialist Republic, Gustáv Husák, named a new federal government with Lubomír Štrougal as prime minister.

■ **1977**

1 January – A group of opposition intellectuals sent a letter to the highest state and party figures, in which they expressed appreciation that the government of the Czechoslovak Socialist Republic had signed international pacts on human rights and demanded that they also apply these rights in practice. The free opposition association was called Charter 77, after the name of its first document. The ruling circles reacted with propaganda, a slander campaign and the arrest, trial and imprisonment of the chartists. According to an incomplete list, since its presentation in 1997 to 1989, the declaration Charter 77 was signed by at least 1,886 persons from throughout Czecho-Slovakia (**24 April 1978, dissidents**).

16 September – The prime ministers of the Czechoslovak Socialist Republic and Hungary, Lubomír Štrougal and George Lázár, signed in Budapest an inter-state agreement concerning the Gabčíkovo-Nagymaros system of dams and power plants on the Danube. The annual production of electrical energy of 3,900 gW (three quarters produced in Gabčíkovo and one quarter in Nagymaros) was to be distributed between the two states in the ratio of one as to one (**13 May 1989, 2 May 1994, 5 September 1997**).

30 December – By the constitution *Praescrip-*

tionum Sacrosancti Pope Paul VI separated the territory of the Trnava administrative area from the province of the Archbishop of Esztergom and determined the borders of the dioceses in Slovakia. By the apostolic constitution *Qui divino* the pope established a separate Slovak ecclesiastical province. Thus, from the ecclesiastical perspective Slovakia became independent.

■ 1978

24 April – Seventeen **dissidents** who had signed Charter 77 established the independent organization The Committee for the Protection against the Unjustly Prosecuted (VONS). Its goal was to make known to public at home and abroad cases of criminal prosecution, imprisonment and political persecution of individuals by the communist state apparatus (**1 January 1977**).

21 June – The federal assembly approved a law concerning the system of primary and secondary schools, which introduced compulsory school attendance for ten years.

17 December – The nuclear power plant in Jaslovské Bohunice near Trnava, the first in the Czechoslovak Socialist Republic, began trial operations.

■ 1979

12 February – A meeting of Czechoslovak counter-intelligence with the participation of the minister of the interior, Jaromír Obzina, took place in Prague. The meeting asserted that while in Czecho-Slovakia there were 3,090 Roman Catholic clerics, „our agency is represented in the circle of the Catholic clergy by about 11.5 per cent of the members; among non-Catholic clergy by about 10.4 per cent". The meeting decided to establish a new network of agents to function in the illegal church structures (Action Dampen), to support loyal clergy from *Pacem in terris* in the case of conflict between church and state, and to infiltrate intelligence agents into the Vatican.

1 April – Summer time (daylight savings time) was introduced into the Czechoslovak Socialist Republic.

■ 1980

22 May – Gustáv Husák, the general secretary of the **Central Committee of the Communist Party** was re-elected president of the Czechoslovak Socialist Republic.

8 November – The newly-built highway Prague – Brno – Bratislava (317 km) was ceremonially put into service.

■ 1981

20 – 23 March – The 16th congress of the **Communist Party of Slovakia** was held in Bratislava. Industrial production in the Slovak Socialist Republic had increased by 33 per cent since 1975; in agriculture by 10 per cent. Slovakia's share of the production of the entire state increased to 29.4 per cent and its share in the creation of the national income of the **federation** was 29.2 per cent. Jozef Lenárt was again elected First Secretary of the **Central Committee of the Communist Party of Slovakia**.

6 – 10 April – The 16th congress of the **Communist Party of Czechoslovakia** took place in the newly-built Palace of Culture in Prague. Not even the manipulation of statistics could hide falling production, the high level of incomplete constructions, slow growth or rather the stagnation of the national income. Everything showed the lack of elasticity of the centrally-directed planned economy. The state artificially supported the growth of foreign trade with other socialist states. The congress maintained that the volume of foreign trade with these countries increased by 65 per cent (84 per cent was with the Soviet Union). Gustáv Husák was re-elected general secretary of the **Communist Party of Czechoslovakia**.

■ 1982

8 February – Following on a decision of the Tripartite Commission (United States of America, Great Britain and France) and the treaty between the Czechoslovak Socialist Republic and the United States of America of 5 July 1974, 18.4 tons of monetary gold, which had been confiscated by Germany during the war and stored in the United States after it, was returned to the Czecho-Slovak state.

10 November – Leonid Iljich Brezhnev, the general secretary of the Communist Party of the Soviet Union responsible for the invasion of the Czechoslovak Socialist Republic on **20 – 21 August 1968** by five Warsaw Pact states, died.

■ **1983**
24 November – At a meeting of the **Central Committee of the Communist Party of Czechoslovakia** Gustáv Husák announced that, in the interests of increasing the defensive potential „of socialist society", the government of the Czechoslovak Socialist Republic had concluded an agreement with the council of ministers of the Soviet Union for initiating preparatory work to develop missile complexes on the territory of Czecho-Slovakia for operational-tactical purposes. By rearming with modern nuclear weapons the Soviet Union and its allies reacted to the firmer policy of the President of the United States, Ronald Reagan, towards the states of the Warsaw Pact.

■ **1985**
11 March – The Communist Party of the Soviet Union elected Michail Sergejevich Gorbachov, a politician with a reform program, to be its general secretary.

■ **1987**
7 June – The Marian year declared by **Pope** John Paul II began. It lasted until 15 August 1988. It brought about a revitalization of Catholicism in Slovakia, especially in the form of numerous pilgrimages (Levoča, Šaštín, Staré Hory and Marianka).
9 April – Michail Sergejevich Gorbachov officially visited Czecho-Slovakia. On 11 April he arrived in Slovakia and visited Bratislava. The people greeted him in the hope of impending political changes. Despite expectations, Gorbachov did not comment upon the events of 1968.
28 September – Pope John Paul II expressed to **Cardinal** František Tomášek his dissatisfac-

tion with the suppression of the Catholic Church in Czecho-Slovakia and called for determination and firmness. The words of the Holy Father found an echo among the Moravian Catholics, who prepared a petition with 13 points. The petition, supported by Cardinal Tomášek, demanded that vacant bishoprics be filled, the separation of church from the state, and the free publication and dissemination of religious literature and the like. By the end of April 1988 this petition had been signed by 500,000 citizens of the Czechoslovak Socialist Republic, of which two-thirds were from Slovakia.

17 December – At a meeting of the **Central Committee of the Communist Party of Czechoslovakia,** the general secretary, Gustáv Husák, requested to be released from the highest party office. The resignation of Gustáv Husák was the result of a growing ambition for power on the part of Ladislav Adamec, Miloš Jakeš and Vasil Biľak, which they had clearly expressed since the spring of 1987. The new general secretary of the **Communist Party of Czechoslovakia,** Miloš Jakeš, was unable to overcome the conservatism of the period of normalization.

– State security prepared a state-wide project, „Wedge" (*Klin*), approved by its chief, Major General Alojz Lorenc. The goal of the project was to defuse the forming political opposition by accentuating differences between ex-communists and non-communists and by systematically discrediting several public figures (for example, Ján Čarnogurský) and initiatives (Bratislava Aloud, environmentalists, the underground Church movement) in the media. The project was implemented until November 1989.

■ **1988**
25 March – After an official request by the Catholic activist František Mikloško, a silent 30 minute demonstration took place on Hviezdoslav Square in Bratislava demanding the naming of Catholic **bishops**, complete religious freedom, and the rights of citizens. The city and state organs did not permit the action. Nevertheless, 10,000 citizens partici-

pated in the „candlelight demonstration". The police intervened against the peaceful assembly with batons, water cannon and sprinkler trucks. The intervention was followed from the Carlton hotel by the prime minister of the Slovak Socialist Republic, Peter Colotka, the minister of the interior, Štefan Lazar, and of culture, Miroslav Válek, as well as by the prominent communists Viliam Šalgovič and Gejza Šlapka. The police arrested about 100 participants in the demonstration.

19 May – Pope John Paul II named Monsignor Ján Sokol a **bishop** and the administrator of the archdiocese of Trnava. He was consecrated on 12 June 1988.

■ **1989**

13 May – Without consultation with the government of the Czechoslovak Socialist Republic, the Hungarian side halted construction work on the dam at Nagymaros. This violated the inter-state treaty of **16 September 1977** (on 25 May 1992 it was annulled by Hungary). The construction work on the Slovak side of the Danube continued and, on 24 October 1992, the Danube was dammed (**2 May 1994, 5 September 1997**).

26 July – **Pope** John Paul II named **Bishop** Ján Sokol to be the archbishop and metropolitan of the Slovak ecclesiastical province (**30 December 1977**).

9 September – František Tondra was consecrated as the **bishop** of Spiš.

The First Steps in Democracy – An Independent State

The year 1989 brought an open confrontation between the opposition and the political forces of the communist regime, which could no longer rely upon the assistance of the Soviet Union. The representatives of the old state and party leadership consented to a compromise solution. They agreed to call democratic elections and share power with the opposition. The opposition convincingly won the election of 1990 and thus assumed responsibility for further developments. The former opposition inherited the problems of the past, the most burning of which was the future direction of the country and the reform plans connected to this. Nationality and social problems came to the foreground. Leading Czech and Slovak political figures attempted to solve them. But they differed on specific conceptions. The Czech model emphasizing centrally led reforms and processes of transformation, regardless of their impact and the economic peculiarities of Slovakia, elicited mistrust from the Slovaks. This, alongside the new regime's assertion of authority and the transformation of the federation from the „functional" to „actual", strengthened concerns about the interests and needs of Slovakia. Despite many discussions, it was not possible to find a solution satisfactory to both sides, and, on 1 January 1993, two independent states were established. The creation of the Slovak Republic occurred peacefully by a division of the federation after the federal parliament passed the relevant legislation. The establishment of the second independent Slovak Republic confirmed the ability of the Slovak nation to administer its own state in a manner corresponding to the character and interests of the Slovak nation in the spirit of its best traditions. The years between 1993 and 1995 were characterized by the difficult work of creating structures suitable for an independent state. The young state had to solve complicated economic, social and cultural problems. Its important geopolitical location made its situation even more difficult. Sharp domestic political controversies needlessly drained vital energy. The Slovak Republic now exists as an independent democratic state and has the will and sufficient motivation to be an equal partner with the other European and world nations.

16 November – Slovak university students demonstrated in Bratislava for academic liberty and democracy.

17 November – On International Students' Day Czech students demonstrated in Prague. The police brutally intervened against the demonstrators and several were wounded. The students went on strike and demanded an investigation of the inappropriate police intervention.

19 November – An opposition political initiative, Public against Violence (*Verejnosť proti násiliu* – VPN) was founded in Bratislava on the premises of a city organization, the Union of Slovak Visual Artists. VPN rejected the violence that had occurred in Prague **17 November 1989** and demanded the purging of Stalinists and their methods from public life. An opposition movement with the name Citizens Forum (*Občianske fórum* – OF) was created in Czechia. A wave of demonstrations against the communist system and in support of the opposition began in cities and towns throughout Czecho-Slovakia. The demonstrations continued until December 1989.

24 November – Miloš Jakeš resigned as the general secretary of the **Central Committee of the Communist Party of Czechoslovakia** and was replaced by Karel Urbánek.

25 November – VPN (Public against Violence) formulated its first program declaration. It demanded the transformation of the **Slovak National Council** into an actual parliament of the Slovak nation, the introduction of the freedom of the press and of conscience, entreprenuership, the rights of assembly and association, the abolition of the leading role of the **Communist Party of Czechoslovakia**, the elimination of ideology from schools and culture, the separation of the church from the state, the equality of all forms of ownership and a functional, consistently democratic, **federation** of Czechs and Slovaks.

27 November – A symbolic two-hour strike took place at the instigation of Public against Violence, Citizens Forum and the organizations of university students. The strike demonstrated the dissatisfaction of the opposition with changes in the leadership of the **Communist Party of Czechoslovakia**. It demanded the abolition of the leading role of the Communist Party of Czechoslovakia, free elections, the formation of an independent commission to investigate the events of **17 November 1989** and space for the opposition in the media.

29 November – The federal assembly resolved to remove article 4 of the Czechoslovak Constitution of 1960 pertaining to the leading role of the Communist Party in the state and society (**11 July 1960**). The law was adopted by a still un-reconstructed parliament, made up of communists, and signed by President Gustáv Husák and Prime Minister Ladislav Adamec.

5 December – The minister of the interior decided to get rid of the barbed wire and barricades, symbols of the „iron curtain", on the border with the Republic of Austria. Barriers were also removed along the border with the Federal Republic of Germany.

7 December – President Gustáv Husák accepted the resignation of the federal government led by Ladislav Adamec. It was the last government established by the **Communist Party of Czechoslovakia** according to its own principles. The formation of a new government was entrusted to Marián Čalfa.

8 December – The presidium of the **Slovak National Council** dismissed the prime minister of the Slovak Socialist Republic, Pavol Hrivnák, and entrusted the formation of a new government to Milan Čič.

10 December – Gustáv Husák named a government of „national reconciliation" led by Marián Čalfa. At the same time, the president announced his resignation in a letter to the federal assembly.

28 December – The federal assembly in Prague elected Alexander Dubček as its chairman.

29 December – The federal assembly unanimously, by acclamation (323 votes), elected as president of the Czechoslovak Socialist Republic Václav Havel, the representative of the opposition, playwright and journalist.

1990

23 January – The federal assembly adopted a law by which the government guaranteed the Communist Party of Czechoslovakia legal protection and made possible its transformation.

6 February – Pope John Paul II named Monsignor Ján Chryzostom Korec to be the **bishop** of Nitra diocese. His enthronement took place in Nitra on 25 March 1990 (**29 June 1991**).

12 February – The assembly of the Christian Democratic Movement took place in Nitra.

1 March – The **Slovak National Council** passed a constitutional law concerning the name, state symbol, state flag, state seal, and state anthem of the **Slovak Republic**. The name „Slovak Socialist Republic" was changed to the „Slovak Republic". The state symbol chosed was the historic double-armed cross. The Czech Republic accepted a law concerning its state symbols on 23 March 1990.

17 March – Alojz Tkáč was consecrated as the **bishop** of Košice. One day later Eduard Kojnok was consecrated as the bishop of Rožnava and on 19 March Rudolf Baláž was consecrated as the bishop of Banská Bystrica. The prefect of the Congregation for the Evangelization of Nations, **Cardinal** Jozef Tomko, consecrated all three bishops (with Ján Chryzostom Korec who had been secretly consecrated as bishop in 1951 as co-consecrator). With this all of the bishoprics were filled (**13 November 1920, 3 March 1973**).

29 March – A constitutional law about changing the name of the state from the „Czechoslovak Socialist Republic" to the „Czecho-Slovak Federal Republic" was proposed in the federal parliament. The proposal initiated discussion about the constitutional arrangement of the state.

20 April – The federal assembly accepted the new constitutional law concerning the name of the state. The name „Czecho-Slovak Federal Republic" was changed to the „Czech and Slovak Federal Republic."

21 April – Pope John Paul II officially visited Czecho-Slovakia. After celebrating masses in Prague and Velehrad, he was welcomed to Slovakia on 22 April. At the airport in Vajnory near Bratislava he celebrated mass. He pointed out the heroism of the persecuted church in the past and called for a life without fear under new conditions (**30 June – 3 July 1995**).

8 – 9 June – The first democratic elections took place in the Czech and Slovak Federal Republic. In the Slovak Republic, the Public Against Violence (VPN) movement was victorious with 29.34 per cent, second was the Christian Democratic Movement (KDH) with 19.20 per cent, third was the Slovak National Party (SNS) with 13.94 per cent, and fourth was the **Communist Party of Slovakia** with 13.34 per cent of the votes. The Hungarian Coalition received 8.66 per cent of the votes. In Czechia the Citizens' Forum (OF) was victorious with 49.5 per cent of the votes (**5 – 6 June 1992**).

22 June – Representatives of social and political organizations in Komjatice (district of Nové Zámky) formulated an appeal that the **Slovak National Council** legislate that the Slovak language was the „single state and official language in Slovakia without exception". By the end of October 1990 more than 230,000 citizens had signed the appeal (**5 October 1990**).

26 June – At the first session of the **Slovak National Council** the deputies elected a new presidium and František Mikloško as its chairman.

27 June – The presidium of the **Slovak National Council** named a new government for the Slovak Republic led by Vladimír Mečiar (VPN). The new government was a coalition of the Public against Violence (VPN) and the Christian Democratic Movement (KDH).

5 July – After the first free election, the federal assembly re-elected Václav Havel as president of the Czech and Slovak Federal Republic (234 delegates voted for and 50 voted against him).

9 August – Czecho-Slovak negotiations about a new division of powers between the **federation** and the republics concluded in Trenčianske Teplice.

25 October – The **Slovak National Council**

approved a language law that declared Slovak to be the official language, although the use of Czech was permitted in official contacts. In districts where the Hungarian minority made up at least 20 per cent of the population, it was possible to use Hungarian in official correspondence. Because Slovak was not accepted as the state language and the 20 per cent threshold appeared low, demonstrations occurred in Bratislava. From 25 October to 19 November several citizens declared hunger strikes to force changes in the language law. During October mass demonstrations took place in favor of the draft of a language law that had been prepared by the **Matica slovenská**.

24 November – Pavol Uhorskai was installed as the general **bishop** of the Evangelical Church of the Augsburg Confession (Lutheran) in Bratislava.

12 December – The delegates of the federal assembly approved a jurisdictional law. In the Czech and Slovak Federal Republic sovereignty was retained by the central federal state. The laws of **federation** were to override to the laws of the individual republics. The jurisdictional law preserved a unitary federation. At the same time discussions took place (up to 1992) about the character of new constitutions for the individual republics and the federation.

■ **1991**
1 January – In the Czech and Slovak Federal Republic price controls for most commodities were revoked (according to the law about prices, no. 526/1990) and a negative turnover tax from food-stuffs was removed. Foreign trade was partially liberalized and internal convertibility of currency was introduced.
– The manner of re-distributing financial resources from the federal budget to the budgets of the republics in force to this date was abolished. After the founding of an independent Slovak Republic, the budget deficit of the Slovak Republic from 1991 became a part of its state debt (**1 January 1993**).
22 February – The federal assembly approved a law concerning non-judicial rehabilitation

that was intended to remedy the wrongs caused by the communist regime from 1948 to 1990. It made possible the restitution of the property of the victims.

11 March – A nation-wide assembly arranged by the **Matica slovenská** in support of a declaration of sovereignty by Slovakia took place in Bratislava.

27 March – The last Soviet tank left the territory of the Czech and Slovak Federal Republic. Before the withdrawal of Soviet troops, which was supervised by a special parliamentary commission created on 20 September 1990, there were 73,500 soldiers, 16,001 military families with 39,931 family members on the territory of the Czecho-Slovakia.

23 April – The presidium of the **Slovak National Council** removed Vladimír Mečiar (VPN) from the office of prime minister of the Slovak Republic and reconstructed the government. Ján Čarnogurský, the chairman of the Christian Democratic Movement (KDH), was named prime minister.

1 May – A schism in the Public against Violence (VPN) took place after an internal controversy between the groups of Fedor Gál and Vladimír Mečiar. Vladimír Mečiar was elected head of the political gremium of the organizational committee of the Movement for a Democratic Slovakia (HZDS), which seceded from the VPN. Ján Budaj and Milan Kňažko, leaders of the November mass demonstrations, joined the HZDS.

22 May – The deputies of the Czech National Council met behind closed doors to discuss the eventual dissolution of the Czech and Slovak Federal Republic.

24 May – The **Slovak National Council** approved privatization laws. On 1 October 1991 registration for coupon booklets began. In the coupon privatization, regulated by law no. 92/1991, each citizen of the Czech and Slovak Federal Republic was able to obtain „his share" of state property. The first wave of coupon privatization lasted from May 1992 to December 1992. Throughout Czecho-Slovakia the property of 1,491 joint- stock companies (in the Slovak Republic 503, in the Czech Republic 988), with a total book value of 299 billion crowns (in the Slovak Republic 87 billion and in the Czech Republic 212 billion), was offered. This large privatization was preceded by a small privatization that focused on smaller enterprises.

– The **Slovak National Council** adopted a law that established Slovak Radio (**2 October 1926, 15 June 1939, 28 April 1948**).

29 June – Pope John Paul II named 23 new cardinals, among them the **bishop** of Nitra, Ján Chryzostom Korec.

16 November – The prime minister of the Czech and Slovak Federal Republic, Marián Čalfa, signed in Brussels an agreement on the association of Czecho-Slovakia with the European Community. A unilateral declaration that the Czech Republic and the Slovak Republic shared in its implementation was appended to this agreement.

18 November – Gustáv Husák, the former president of the Czechoslovak Socialist Republic and general secretary of the Central Committee of the Communist Party of Czechoslovakia, died in Bratislava.

December – Industrial production in the Slovak Republic fell about 24.7 per cent in comparison to 1990, building production about 33.6 per cent and agricultural production was reduced by about 23.9 per cent. Unemployment approached 12 per cent. Extensive economic changes adversely affected the structure of Slovak industry, which had been especially hard hit by the conversion from military production and the collapse of the eastern market (COMECON officially ceased at a meeting in Budapest on 28 June 1991).

■ **1992**
3 – 8 February – A meeting took place at Milovy (near Žďár nad Sázavou, in the Czech Republic) of a joint expert commission of the Czech National Council, the Slovak National Council, and the governments of the Slovak Republic, the Czech Republic, and the Czech and Slovak Federal Republic concerning a proposed treaty on constitutional arrangements. The Czechs originally refused to enter into a treaty and would allow only an agreement. Finally they acceded to a treaty, with-

out legal liability, between the Slovak and the Czech national councils, and not between the Slovak and the Czech Republics as the Slovak side had suggested. The result of the negotiations in Milovy was the draft of a treaty with a preamble which stated that the treaty was concluded between „the people of the Slovak Republic and the people of the Czech Republic". This was a fundamental retreat from the position which the Slovak side, especially the Christian Democratic Movement, had espoused.

10 February – The president of the government of the Czech and Slovak Federal Republic, Marián Čalfa, publicly stated that „the final solution of the form of Slovak statehood would be taken up only by the victors in the approaching elections". As the highest representative of the government, he thus devalued the principle of a treaty solution between the Czech Republic and the Slovak Republic even before negotiations took place in the Slovak and the Czech national councils about the proposed treaty.

12 February – The presidium of the **Slovak National Council** discussed the proposed treaty from **8 February 1992**. Ten members (3 from the Civic Democratic Union – Public Against Violence, 2 from the Christian Democratic Movement, 1 from the Democratic Party, 1 from the Co-existence and 2 from the Hungarian parties) voted for the proposal, and 10 members (4 from the Christian Democratic Movement, 2 from the Movement for a Democratic Slovakia, 1 from the Slovak National Party, 1 from the Party of the Democratic Left, 1 from the Civic Democratic Union – Public Against Violence) voted against it. Thus the treaty was not approved and could not be introduced at a plenary session of the Slovak National Council.

5 March – The presidium of the Czech National Council adopted a resolution that „there is nothing to discuss". The discussions between the Czech National Council and the Slovak National Council were officially suspended on 11 March 1992.

7 March – The draft treaty from Milovy (**3 – 8 February 1992**) led to a schism in the coalition Christian Democratic Movement, which split into the Christian Democratic Movement led by Ján Čarnogurský and the Slovak Christian Democratic Movement (later Christian Social Union) led by Ján Klepáč.

28 March – Alexander Dubček was elected the chairman of the Social Democratic Party of Slovakia in Bratislava.

7 May – By a vote of 73 for and 57 against, the **Slovak National Council** rejected a declaration of the sovereignty of the Slovak Republic,which was supported by the deputies of the Slovak National Party, the Movement for a Democratic Slovakia, and the Slovak Christian Democratic Movement. For acceptance a three-fifths majority (90 votes) was necessary.

5 – 6 June – Premature parliamentary elections took place in the Czech and Slovak Federal Republic. In the Slovak Republic the Movement for a Democratic Slovakia was victorious with 37.26 per cent of the votes, the Party of the Democratic Left (mainly the transformed Communist Party of Slovakia) came in second with 14.70 per cent, the Christian Democratic Movement received 8.88 per cent. The fourth strongest party was the Slovak National Party with 7.42 per cent of the votes, while the Hungarian Coalition also received 7.42 per cent of the votes. In the Czech Republic the coalition of the Civic Democratic Party and the Christian Democratic Party was victorious with 29.8 per cent of the votes.

8 June – Representatives of the victorious parties, the Slovak Movement for a Democratic Slovakia and the Czech Civic Democratic Party met in Brno. Diametrically different ideas were put forward: the idea of a „functional federation" was supported by the Civic Democratic Party; that of a confederation with international recognition for the Slovak Republic was supported by the Movement for a Democratic Slovakia.

17 June – The Civic Democratic Party (Václav Klaus) and the Movement for a Democratic Slovakia (Vladimír Mečiar) negotiated about the composition of the federal government in Prague. Václav Klaus declared that he was in-

terested in the office of the prime minister of the Czech Republic (which he obtained on 2 July 1992) and would not accept any other office in the federal government. Both sides agreed that each republic would have its own budget and that the distribution of funds from the federal state budget would be halted.

19 – 20 June – Negotiations between the Movement for a Democratic Slovakia and the Civic Democratic Party took place in Bratislava. They agreed to reduce the number of ministries in the federal government and to parity in the number of ministries they filled. Moreover, the federal government was to understand its mandate as temporary.

23 June – At a constituting meeting of the **Slovak National Council** in Bratislava the deputies elected as its chairman, Ivan Gašparovič, the former prosecutor general of the Czech and Slovak Federal Republic.

24 June – The presidium of the **Slovak National Council** accepted the resignation of the government of Ján Čarnogurský and named a new government of the Slovak Republic led by Vladimír Mečiar.

25 June – At the constituting meeting of the federal assembly in Prague the deputies elected Michal Kováč of the Movement for a Democratic Slovakia as their last chairman.

2 July – In Prague castle President Václav Havel named the new (and last) federal government with Ján Stráský as prime minister. The government had only 10 members (4 Civic Democratic Party, 4 Movement for a Democratic Slovakia, 1 Christian Democratic Union Czechoslovak People's Party, and 1 independent proposed by the Movement for a Democratic Slovakia). The departing government of Marián Čalfa had submitted its resignation on 26 June 1992.

3 July – The election of the president of the Czech and Slovak Federal Republic took place in the federal assembly. The sole candidate, Václav Havel, failed to obtain the majority of votes necessary in either of the two rounds.

13 – 19 July – The Fifth World Festival of Slovak Youth was held for the very first time on Slovak soil in Martin.

17 July – The **Slovak National Council** approved the *Declaration of the Sovereignty of the Slovak Republic.* Voting for the acceptance of the declaration were the deputies of the Movement for a Democratic Slovakia, Slovak National Party, and the Party of the Democratic Left (113 for, 10 abstained and 24, mostly from the Christian Democratic Movement and the Hungarian parties, voted against). President Václav Havel reacted to the adoption of the declaration by resigning his office (20 July 1992). The functions of the president devolved upon the federal government.

22 – 23 July – A conference of representatives of the Movement for a Democratic Slovakia and the Civic Democratic Party took place in Bratislava. At its conclusion they announced that they would attempt to follow a legal process for the dissolution of the **federation** into two independent states.

26 August – The prime ministers of the Slovak and the Czech republics, Vladimír Mečiar and Václav Klaus met in Brno. They agreed on a date for the dissolution of the **federation**, namely 1 January 1993. The precise wording of the agreement between the prime ministers was not published.

1 September – The **Slovak National Council** accepted the Constitution of the Slovak Republic. Voting for acceptance of the constitution were 114 deputies of the Movement for a Democratic Slovakia, the Slovak National Party and the Party of the Democratic Left. Sixteen deputies from the Christian Democratic Movement and the Hungarian coalition voted against it and 4 abstained. The preamble to the constitution notes the struggle of the Slovaks for national existence and their own statehood, the Cyril-Methodian spiritual heritage and the historical legacy of Great Moravia. The constitution is based upon the principle of the natural right of the Slovak nation to self-determination. According to the first article of the constitution, the Slovak Republic is a sovereign, democratic, and legal state.

– On the highway Prague-Brno-Bratislava, not far from Humpolec, a BMW 535 carrying the former chairman of the federal assembly Alexander Dubček crashed under still insufficiently explained circumstances. Alexander Dubček suffered serious injuries of which he died on 7 November 1992 in Na Homolke hospital in Prague.

1 October – After refusing a draft law about the manner of dissolving the **federation**, the federal assembly adopted the proposal of the Czech social democratic deputy Miloš Zeman, concerning the creation of a commission to prepare legislation for the transformation of the Czech and Slovak Federal Republic into the Czecho-Slovak Union. This proposal was supported also by the Movement for a Democratic Slovakia, because of the failure of the Czech Civic Democratic Party to keep its side of their agreement.

6 October – Further negotiations were conducted between the prime ministers of the Czech (Václav Klaus) and Slovak (Vladimír Mečiar) republics in Jihlava. Both sides again confirmed that they would respect the agreed procedure for the dissolution of the Czech and Slovak Federal Republic.

29 October – The prime ministers of the Czech and Slovak republics, Václav Klaus and Vladimír Mečiar, signed an agreement for tariff union between the Czech and the Slovak republics and fifteen additional bi-lateral agreements.

13 November – The federal assembly approved a law for the division of federal property between the Czech and the Slovak republics using a 2:1 ratio.

25 November – The federal assembly accepted a constitutional law for the dissolution of the Czech and Slovak Federal Republic. On 31 December the Czecho-Slovak state ceased to exist.

■ **1993**

1 January – The independent Slovak Republic came into being. The deputies of the National Council of the Slovak Republic and the government of the independent Slovak Republic met together in a solemn session. The deputies took an oath of loyalty to the Constitution of the Slovak Republic and accepted a declaration that stated: „On 1 January 1993 the Slovak Republic became an independent and democratic state. As a sovereign, independent, and legal state the Slovak Republic is one of the two successor states of the Czech and Slovak Federal Republic. The National Council of the Slovak Republic confirms its will and readiness to become a regular member of the United Nations Organization ....and equally declares its interest in membership in the Council of Europe and the status as a contracting partner of the European agreement on the defense of human rights and fundamental liberties. ...The National Council of the Slovak Republic solemnly declares that the Slovak Republic is continuing in the democratic tradition and the humanistic legacy of our forefathers and is prepared to initiate and maintain diplomatic relations with all democratic states of the world". Already in the first hours of its existence the independent Slovak Republic was diplomatically recognized by 62 countries of the world.

– The Slovak Republic became a full member of the International Monetary Fund and the Organization for Security and Cooperation in Europe (OSCE).

12 January – The French foreign minister, Roland Dumas, arrived for an official visit to the Slovak Republic. It was the first visit of a representative of a foreign government to the independent Slovak Republic.

16 January – The Slovak Republic became a member of the World Bank.

19 January – At a session of the General Assembly of the United Nations in New York, the Slovak Republic was accepted as the 180th member state. The Slovak state flag was ceremonially raised in front of the United Nations building.

22 January – The Slovak Republic was accepted as a special observer at the Council of Europe.

2 February – The National Council of the Slovak Republic adopted a law concerning the separation of the currencies of the Czech and Slovak republics.

8 February – A new currency, the Slovak crown (Sk), began to be used in Slovakia.

9 February – The Slovak Republic became a member of UNESCO.

15 February – In a secret ballot, 106 of the deputies of the National Council of the Slovak Republic voted for the candidate of the Movement for a Democratic Slovakia, Michal Kováč, to become president of the Slovak Republic.

8 March – President Michal Kováč named Milan Čič as the president of the constitutional court of the Slovak Republic.

2 April – In Bratislava an options and futures exchange, the first in central or eastern Europe, began to function.

12 April – At the 89th session of the Inter-parliamentary Union in New Delhi in India, the Slovak Republic became a member of the organization.

23 June – The Slovak Republic signed an agreement of association with the European Community in Brussels.

30 June – The Slovak Republic became the 31st member of the Council of Europe.

10 July – The National Bank of the Slovak Republic devalued the Slovak crown by 10 per cent.

8 August – The remains of the writer Jozef Cíger Hronský, which had been brought from Argentina to Slovakia (3 July 1993), were buried in the National Cemetery in Martin in the presence of President Michal Kováč and Prime Minister Vladimír Mečiar.

9 August – The trade balance of the Slovak Republic concluded with a surplus of 2.9 billion Sk.

17 August – The government of the Slovak Republic accepted an agreement of association with the European Community. The agreement was signed in the Kirchberg European Center in Luxemburg on 4 October 1993. The European parliament ratified it on 27 October 1993 and the National Council of the Slovak Republic ratified it on 15 October 1993.

29 September – The National Council of the Slovak Republic adopted a law for mitigating some of the property injustices inflicted upon churches and religious societies during the communist regime.

September – During the first nine months of its existence the Slovak Republic had been recognized by 122 states of the world. Diplomatic relations with Slovakia were maintained by 106 states. The Slovak Republic opened embassies and consular offices in 53 states of the world.

20 November – In Bratislava, police arrested three forgers of plates for one-thousand crown bank notes. They also found 91,000 plates and printing equipment in their possession.

22 December – The National Council of the Slovak Republic adopted a law on the state budget allowing a deficit of 14 billion Sk.

■ 1994

9 March – At a session of the National Council of the Slovak Republic, President Michal Kováč presented a report on the state of the Slovak Republic. On 11 March 1994 the national council passed a vote of no confidence in Prime Minister Vladimír Mečiar. Eighty-two opposition deputies participated in the secret ballot. The deputies of the Movement for a Democratic Slovakia and the Slovak National Party abstained. The dismissal of Vladimír Mečiar was the result of a long-standing crisis among the leading politicians of the HZDS, the first signs of which were evident already in March and November 1993.

12 March – The republican presidium of the Movement for a Democratic Society decided that the movement would go into opposition.

14 March – President Michal Kováč entrusted Jozef Moravčík with the formation of a new government. The new government was named on 15 March.

17 March – The National Council of the Slovak Republic unanimously agreed on the dates **30 September – 1 October 1994** as the period for premature parliamentary elections.

2 May – Hungary and the Slovak Republic submitted their dispute over the dam building project of Gabčíkovo-Nagymaros to the International Court of Justice at the Hague (**5 September 1997**).

June – The Slovak Republic was the first country of the Visegrád four to sign an international agreement with Russia regulating conditions for travel without visas.

30 September – 1 October – Premature parliamentary elections took place in Slovakia, in which 18 political parties participated. The coalition of the Movement for a Democratic Slovakia and the Farmers Party of Slovakia was victorious with 34.96 per cent of the votes. The coalition of the left, grouped under the name Common Choice (Party of the Democratic Left, the Social Democratic Party of Slovakia, Party of the Greens in Slovakia, and the Farmers' Movement) received 10.41 per cent, the Hungarian Coalition 10.18 per cent, the Christian Democratic Movement 10.08, the Democratic Union 8.57, the Alliance of the Workers of Slovakia 7.34, and the Slovak National Party 5.40 per cent of the votes. 75.65 per cent of the voters participated in the elections.

November – Envoys of the German Federal Republic and France delivered *demarches* of the European Union, in which they expressed their alarm at certain development in political life after the parliamentary elections as well as the hope that Slovakia would continue on the path of democratic reforms (**16. November 1995**).

December – The index of consumer prices in 1994 had increased by 174 per cent in comparison to 1989. The cost of living had risen 161.1 per cent in the same period. The average monthly income had risen to 6,285 Sk, which was a growth of 103.4 per cent over 1989. The purchasing power of the population, however, represented only 75 per cent of their purchasing power in 1989. The consumption of foodstuffs had declined by 23 percent.

■ 1995

1 February – Representatives of 21 states from the 33 member countries of the Council of Europe signed in Strasbourg the framework agreement on the protection of national minorities. The Slovak Republic was among the signatories. The agreement forbids discrimination against minorities and obligates the state to protect them. A point of dispute remained the definition of national minorities. The National Council of the Slovak Republic ratified the agreement on 21 June 1995.

19 March – In the Martignon Palace, the Paris residence of the French premier, the prime ministers of the Slovak Republic and Hungary, Vladimír Mečiar and Gyula Horn, signed a basic treaty for good neighborly relationships and friendly cooperation between the two countries. Since its ratification the treaty has been open to various interpretations.

31 March – Pope John Paul II issued a bull elevating the bishopric of Košice to the status of an **archbishopric**. An independent ecclesiastical province of Košice was established with Rožňava and Spiš as its sufragan bishoprics (**30 December 1977**).

27 June – Prime Minister Vladimír Mečiar, after the conclusion of a summit meeting of the states of the European Union in Cannes, presented the French Foreign Minister with the official request of the Slovak Republic for entry into the European Union. According to the appended memorandum, 7,600 companies with foreign participation operated in the Slovak Republic and the private sector produced 61.2 per cent of the gross domestic product. The banking sector was made up of 30 banks (in 1991 there were only two state banks in the Slovak Republic) and its basic capital had reached 24.6 billion Sk (820 million US $).

30 June – 3 July – Pope John Paul II arrived for an official visit to the Slovak Republic. On 1 July in Košice he declared as saints the three blessed **martyrs of Košice**. He visited Bratislava, Nitra, Košice, Prešov, Šaštín and the High Tatras.

Summer – The number of unemployed in the Slovak Republic reached 339,000 (13.3 per cent).

31 August – Michal Kováč Jr., the son of the president of the Slovak Republic, for whom an arrest warrant had been issued in the Federal Republic of Germany, was kidnapped on the road from Svätý Jur to Bratislava.

15 November – The National Council of the Slovak Republic adopted a law on the state language. According to the law, the Slovak language was intended to unite all citizens of the Slovak Republic. The law left intact the rights of the national minorities. Its adoption was approved by 108 deputies, while 17 deputies (Hungarian Coalition) voted against it, 17 deputies (Christian Democratic Movement) abstained and 8 deputies were not present. The legislation was signed into law by the president of the Slovak Republic, Michal Kováč.

16 November – After the *demarches* of the European Union and the United States of America which pointed out several undemocratic measures, the European Parliament adopted a resolution addressed to the Slovak government. The resolution, initiated by the liberal and socialistic factions of the European parliament, repudiated the exclusion of deputies from the Democratic Union from the National Council of the Slovak Republic (on the basis of questionable signatures on the petitions which had made it possible for the party to take part in the campaign) and criticized the attempts to force the president to resign, the dismissal of three investigators into the case of the kidnapping of the president's son, Michal Kováč Jr., and attacks upon opposition journalists who wrote about the case. The European parliament called upon the government to adhere to democratic principles (**December 1996, 15 July 1997**).

December – The Czech government of Václav Klaus approved an agreement between the Czech Republic and the Slovak Republic concerning the definitive delineation of the state borders. From its original length of 285 km the border was shortened to 251 km (**4 January 1996**).

■ **1996**

4 January – The interior ministers of the Slovak and the Czech republics, Ľudovít Hudek and Jan Ruml, signed an agreement in Židlochovice about the borders between the two states (**December 1995, 25 July 1997**).

22 – 23 January – The Slovak prime minister, Vladimír Mečiar, and the Ukrainian prime minister, Leonid Kučma, conferred about the relations of Slovakia and Ukraine at Štrbské

Pleso in the High Tatras. The prime ministers of Slovakia and Ukraine signed eight documents concerning mutual co-operation on 5 – 6 March 1997 in Uzhgorod.

29 – 30 January – A delegation of Slovak government and business figures led by Vladimír Mečiar visited the Yugoslav Federal Republic. They signed four inter-governmental agreements.

31 January – The Slovak parliament adopted a banking law that introduced mortgage banking.

9 February – The commissioner of the European Union, Hans van den Broek, ceremonially opened the office of the delegation of the commission of the European Union in Bratislava.

11 – 12 February – A Slovak government delegation visited Croatia.

29 February – 2 March – The Russian Foreign minister, J. Primakov made an official visit to Slovakia.

27 March – The National Council of the Slovak Republic adopted a law on the immorality and illegality of the communist system. After the law was passed, a commemorative plaque was installed in the entry hall of parliament with the words: „The participants in the anti-communist struggle deserve our thanks for the fall of the communist regime and the restoration of democracy in Slovakia. For this we thank them".

12 April – The cornerstone was laid for the first highway tunnel in Slovakia, under Branisko Mt.

16 April – In the presence of Vladimír Mečiar and the ambassadors of Czechia, France, Germany and Russia, the director general of the Slovak Electric Company Karol Česnek signed basic suppliers' contracts with 11 domestic and foreign firms for completing the first two blocks of the nuclear power plant in Mochovce.

29 – 30 April – The general secretary of NATO, Javier Solana, took part in a conference in Bratislava.

2 May – As the presiding country of CEFTA (Central European Free Trade Association), Slovakia organized in Bratislava a meeting of the ministers of culture from Czechia, Bulgaria, Estonia, Lithuania, Latvia, Hungary, Poland, Slovenia, Croatia, Yugoslavia, Romania and Ukraine.

6 May – President Michal Kováč signed a letter of ratification of the Slovak-Hungarian treaty (**19 March 1995**).

11 May – The Slovak prime minister, Vladimír Mečiar, met with W. Cimoszewicz, the Polish prime minister, in Starý Smokovec.

17 – 20 May – Alexij II, the Patriarch of Moscow and of all the Russia visited Slovakia.

23 May – Vladimír Masár, the governor of the National Bank of Slovakia, signed an agreement in Moscow concerning a Russian loan in the amount of 80 million dollars in order to complete the building of the nuclear power plant in Mochovce.

21 June – The National Council of the Slovak Republic accepted changes in the number of members in its special control organ to supervise the activity of the Slovak Information Service. An opposition deputy also became a member of this organ. Additional opposition deputies to control the Slovak Information Service and military intelligence were added on 19 November 1997.

26 June – The Slovak prime minister, Vladimír Mečiar, visited Strasbourg and confirmed, before the parliamentary assembly of the Council of Europe, Slovakia's interest in joining NATO.

3 July – The National Council of the Slovak Republic adopted a law about a new territorial and administrative arrangement for the Slovak Republic. It created eight regions (*kraj*): Bratislava, Trnava, Trenčín, Nitra, Žilina, Banská Bystrica, Prešov and Košice. On the territory of Slovakia 79 districts (*okres*) were created (**25 July 1939, 21 December 1948, 9 April 1960**).

6 July – Hillary Clinton, the wife of the American president, and the American ambassador to the United Nations, Madeleine Albright, made a short visit to Slovakia. They met with President Michal Kováč and Prime Minister Vladimír Mečiar.

19 July – The minister of foreign affairs of the Slovak Republic, Juraj Schenk, delivered a completed questionnaire for the European Union to Georgios Zavvos, the ambassador of the European Union to the Slovak Republic.

19 July – 4 August – The XXVI Summer Olympic Games took place in Atlanta (USA). A contingent of 71 athletes went to the Olympics as the first representatives of an independent Slovakia. Slovakia won three medals: a gold medal was won by Michal Martikán (water slalom), a silver medal by Slavomír Kňazovický (canoeing) and a bronze by Jozef Gönci (shooting). Among the participating states the Slovak Republic was placed 43rd, that is in the first third. (Athletes from 197 countries participated).

27 August – President Michal Kováč solemnly installed three new ministers in crucial posts, namely the ministries of the interior, of foreign affairs, and of the economy. It was a positive signal that Slovakia wished to conduct a more active and transparent foreign and domestic policy.

13 – 14 September – A summit of the prime ministers of the member countries of the Central European Free Trade Association met in Jasná.

19 September – The deputies of the National Council of the Slovak Republic deliberated concerning the report of the supreme control office about the illegal export of grain in 1995 and the first quarter of 1996 from Slovakia.

9 – 10 October – The President of India, Shankar Dajal Sharma, paid a visit to the Slovak Republic.

20 – 22 October – Leni Fischer, the chairman of the Parliamentary Assembly of the Council of Europe, visited Slovakia.

4 November – A tri-lateral meeting of the prime ministers of Slovakia, Austria, and Hungary took place in Piešťany (**15 December 1997**).

8 – 9 November – Prime Minister Vladimír Mečiar and Pavol Hamžík, the minister of foreign affairs, participated in the summit of the prime ministers of the states of the Central European Initiative.

4 December – The deputies of the National Council of the Slovak Republic from the gov-

erning coalition parties voted to take away the parliamentary mandate of Deputy František Gaulieder of the Movement for a Democratic Slovakia.

23 December – Jean-Luc Dehaene, the prime minister of Belgium, visited the Slovak Republic.

December – The European parliament adopted a resolution that called on the Slovak parliament to reconsider its decision to deprive František Gaulieder, the former deputy of the Movement of a Democratic Slovakia, of his seat. This request was repeated in October 1997.

– In 1996 there were, according to the data of the ministry of health, 1,594 drug dependent citizens. The number of undiscovered and undocumented drug addicts is, according to experts, 10 to 12 times higher (40 per cent are in the category 14 – 19 years of age).

– Foreign investment in the Slovak Republic in 1996 amounted to $186 per capita in American dollars (in Hungary it was $1,518, in Slovenia $1,057, in Czechia $659 and in Poland $311.) The foreign trade deficit reached 64,537 billion Slovak crowns.

31 December – The Slovak Republic maintained diplomatic relations with 121 states. In Bratislava 30 countries and the Sovereign Order of the Knights of Malta maintain diplomatic offices. The remainder of those active in the Slovak Republic are based abroad (especially in Vienna and Prague). Throughout the world, Slovakia is represented by 59 embassies and permanent missions at the United Nations, the European Union, the Organization for Security and Cooperation in Europe and the Council of Europe.

■ **1997**

9 January – The opposition political parties (Christian Democratic Movement, Democratic Union, Democratic Party) together with the parties of the opposition Hungarian coalition (Hungarian Christian Democratic Movement, Coexistence, Hungarian Civic Party) began a petition campaign for a referendum on the direct election of the president of the Republic by the citizens of Slovakia.

14 February – The National Council of the Slovak Republic adopted a law about Slovaks living abroad.

– 86 deputies of the National Council of the Slovak Republic accepted the proposal of the Movement for a Democratic Slovakia to conduct a referendum with three questions: 1. Are you in favor of Slovakia's entry into NATO? 2. Are you for placing nuclear weapons on the territory of Slovakia? 3. Are you for locating foreign military bases on the territory of Slovakia? (**13 March 1997, 18 March 1997**).

5 – 6 March – Ivan Gašparovič, the chairman of the National Council of the Slovak Republic, participated in a meeting in Brussels of the speakers of the parliaments of the associated countries. He consulted with the speaker of the European parliament, José María Gil-Robles, about the integration of the Slovak Republic into the European Union.

12 March – The deputies of the National Council of the Slovak Republic rejected a proposed law concerning the direct election of the president. The deputies decided to exempt the General Credit Bank and the Investment and Development Bank from privatization.

13 March – President Michal Kováč declared a referendum to take place on 23 – 24 May 1997. The referendum questions included those from the National Council of the Slovak Republic from **14 February 1997** and a question about the direct election of the President: Do you agree that the president of the Slovak Republic should be directly elected by the citizens of the Slovak Republic according to the enclosed proposal for a constitutional law? (**17 April 1997**).

18 March – The deputies of the National Council of the Slovak Republic accepted a resolution recommending that the citizens affirmatively answer the question about the entry of the country into NATO.

22 – 27 March – Prime Minister Vladimír Mečiar visited Japan. He consulted with the Emperor Akihito and the prime minister, Rjutaro Hashimoto.

2 – 4 April – Accompanied by 4 ministers, Vladimír Mečiar visited Turkey, where he signed several agreements about mutual cooperation.

14 April – The governor of the National Bank of Slovakia requested the governor of the Czech National Bank to expedite the return of Slovak gold.

17 April – Members of the Central Commission for Referenda of the Slovak Republic, in which the opposition held a majority, decided that citizens would receive only one ballot paper with four questions in the referendum being prepared (**13 March 1997**).

14 May – The National Council of the Slovak Republic adopted a law on the revitalization of enterprises.

– The 26th regional conference of Interpol took place in Piešťany with the participation of representatives from 42 countries of Europe.

21 May – The constitutional court held that the constitution did not forbid changing the constitution by referendum, but that it was a mistake to connect a proposed draft for a constitutional law with the question concerning the direct election of the president. The minister of the interior, Gustáv Krajči, ordered that ballots be printed with three questions only, that is, without the question about the direct election of the president (**13 March 1997**).

23 – 24 May – The referendum took place in Slovakia. The refusal of some of the district electoral commissions to accept ballots without the question about the direct election of the president made it impossible for some of the citizens to express their views. The required percentage of participation in the referendum was not reached. Only 9.5 per cent of qualified voters cast their votes. The referendum was declared invalid.

26 May – Pavol Hamžík, the minister of foreign affairs, submitted his resignation. On 11 June he was replaced by Zdenka Kramplová.

3 – 6 June – Public transport drivers in Bratislava, the capital city of the Slovak Republic, went on strike.

3 July – The representatives of the opposition parties, Christian Democratic Movement, Democratic Union, Democratic Party, Slovak

Democratic Socialist Party and the Party of the Greens of Slovakia, signed an agreement in Bratislava about creating an election coalition, which was named the Slovak Democratic Coalition on 11 July (**2 December 1997**).

8 – 9 July – At the Madrid summit of NATO, the Czech Republic, Poland and Hungary were invited to begin negotiations concerning membership in NATO. Slovakia was not considered for the first stage of the expansion of the alliance.

15 July – The European Commission in Strasbourg approved the evaluation of the candidacy of ten European countries for European Union membership. It recommended that in the first wave of expansion, discussions about admission to the EU take place with only six countries (Hungary, Poland, Czechia, Estonia, Slovenia and Cyprus). Five states (Slovakia, Bulgaria, Lithuania, Latvia and Romania) would have to wait longer for membership although each of them had concluded an agreement of association, which made possible individual preparation for admission. According to the evaluation, Slovakia failed to meet the political criteria required for entry into the EU. The evaluation noted the tensions between the government and the president, the attitude of the government during the time of the referendum, the absence of opposition parties in the parliamentary control of the Slovak Information Service, the failure to investigate the kidnapping of Michal Kováč Jr. and the death of Robert Remiáš connected with this case, as well as attacks upon opposition journalists. It recommended improvements in dealing with the Hungarian minority and the adoption of a law on the use of the languages of national minorities. The Slovak government delegation explained its objections to the evaluation in September 1997 in Brussels. The Vice Chairman of the European Commission, Leon Brittan, did not accept its arguments (**16 November 1995, 12 December 1998**).

17 July – The World Year of the Slovaks, prepared by the **Matica slovenská,** began in Martin.

25 July – The Slovak and the Czech republics exchanged the settlements of U Sabotů and Sidonie. The treaty between the two states concerning common borders went into effect (**December 1995, 4 January 1996**).

20 – 21 August – The Polish president, Aleksander Kwasniewski, visited Slovakia.

25 September – The international court in the Hague delivered its judgment in the controversy between the Slovak Republic and Hungary over the building of the Gabčíkovo-Nagymaros dams. The court recognized as justified the steps taken by the Slovak Republic after the unilateral abrogation of the international treaty by Hungary (**16 September 1977**). The court did not recommend the abandonment of already completed construction. Commissions from both states were to resolve other questions within six months (**13 May 1989, 2 May 1994**).

10 October – Deputies of the National Council of the Slovak Republic adopted a declaration concerning the integration of the Slovak Republic into the European Union. One hundred and thirty-one deputies voted for the resolution, and no one voted against it.

10 – 11 October – A working meeting of the Slovak prime minister, Vladimír Mečiar, with the Czech prime minister, Václav Klaus, took place in Piešťany. The prime ministers agreed on three inter-state agreements and the re-activation of the commission to resolve the division of federal property.

17 October – President Michal Kováč and Prime Minister Vladimír Mečiar signed a joint declaration in Bratislava about the expansion of the European Union. They expressed a desire to renew the trust of the member states of the European Union in the Slovak Republic as regards the fulfillment of the political criteria. Its goal was to obtain for the Slovak Republic a supplemental invitation to the negotiations on integration. Although both pledged mutually to abstain from attacks on one another, tensions between them grew.

2 December – Five chairmen of the opposition parties of the Slovak Democratic Coalition and three representatives of the opposition parties of the Hungarian coalition signed a declaration of cooperation. The Hungarian parties received places in the shadow government (**3 July 1977**).

12 December – President Michal Kováč used his constitutional right and ordered a halt to criminal prosecutions of all persons in the Technopol case including that of his own son (**31 August 1995**).

12 – 13 December – At a summit of the heads of state and the governments of the associated countries, it was definitely decided that Slovakia would not be included among the first six countries with which intensive bilateral discussions would begin in April 1998. However, the Slovak Republic was included as one of the 11 states that would participate in the ceremonial opening of the discussion process in March 1998.

15 December – A trilateral meeting of the prime ministers of Austria, Slovakia and Hungary took place in Vienna (**4 November 1996**).

■ **1998**

23 – 24 January – The presidents of 11 European states (eight from the countries of the former eastern bloc), met in Levoča. They discussed the topic *A Civil Society – The Hope of a United Europe.*

29 January – The first round of the presidential election took place in the national council. Neither this nor any of the four other rounds were successful (**2 March 1998**).

13 February – Prime Minister Vladimír Mečiar ceremonially opened the super-highway section between Vienna Road in Bratislava and the border of the Slovak Republic with Hungary. The project connected Slovakia with Austria, while at the same time connecting with the north-south highway leading through Hungary. The highways sections Horná Streda – Ladce (45 km) and Hybe – Važec (10 km) in central Slovakia were opened on 10 and 14 September 1998.

2 March – The term of office of President Michal Kováč ended. The president met with members of the government and turned over to them the part of his jurisdiction delimited by the constitution.

3 March – The government cancelled the decision of Michal Kováč concerning the declaration of a referendum on 19 March 1998. Prime Minister Vladimír Mečiar declared an amnesty for criminal acts committed in connection with the abduction of the president's son Michal Kováč Jr. and the preparation of the referendum (**13 March 1997**).

25 March – The opposition Slovak Democratic Coalition organized a demonstration in Bratislava. It began a petition campaign for the direct election of the president and for a just electoral law. By the middle of May 1998 it had collected 400,000 signatures.

5 April – The founding congress of the Party of Civil Understanding was held in Bratislava. Rudolf Schuster was elected as its president.

23 April – Nine Slovak Catholic bishops sent a letter to the Slovak government and the National Council of the Slovak Republic, expressing their concern about the situation in Slovakia. They noted the polarization of society, the artificial evocation of national hatred, the lack of interest in solving the problem of organized crime, the creation of a wealthy class with uncontrollable power, attempts to manipulate the elections through the prepared electoral law, and the international isolation of Slovakia. They demanded that it hold democratic elections, make possible the election of a president, and provide objective information through Slovak television.

20 May – Deputies of the National Council of the Slovak Republic adopted an amended electoral law. According to it, each political party that was part of a pre-electoral coalition had to obtain more than five per cent of the vote in order to obtain a place in parliament. The law aroused the antipathy of the opposition.

8 June – The start-up of the reactor of the first block of the atomic energy electric plant in Mochovce began at a minimal controlled level. The first turbine-generator of the atomic energy electric plant was put on line on 4 July 1998.

21 June – A congress at which Hungarian parties (Hungarian Christian Democratic Movement, the Hungarian Civic Party and Co-existence) merged took place in Dunajská Streda. It created the Party of the Hungarian Coalition.

27 June – Delegates of the Christian Social Union (formerly the Slovak Christian Democratic Movement) and the Slovak Green Alternative decided on merging their parties with the Slovak National Party at an extraordinary congress.

June – Unemployment in Slovakia reached 13.8 per cent (374,735 persons).

4 July – The founding congress of the Slovak Democratic Coalition took place in Trnava. Representatives of five opposition parties (Christian Democratic Movement, the Democratic Union, the Democratic Party, the Social Democratic Party of Slovakia and the Slovak Green Party) formally created a single party (**20 May 1998**).

14 July – The National Council of the Slovak Republic adopted a constitutional law that assigned some of the president's jurisdiction to the prime minister and some to the chairman of the parliament during periods when the presidency is vacant.

20 July – Flooding in eastern Slovakia claimed more than 50 victims and caused 3.3 billion Sk in damages.

13 August – A petition against the privatization of Slovak strategic enterprises was signed by 620,281 citizens (**25 – 26 September**).

24 September – On the occasion of the 53rd general assembly of the United Nations in New York, Zdenka Kramplová, the minister of foreign affairs, presented a statue of Saints Cyril and Method as a gift of the Slovak Republic to the UN. The sculptor was Andrej Rudavský.

25 – 26 September – Parliamentary elections took place. Participating in them were 84,24 per cent of the voters. The Movement for a Democratic Slovakia, with 27 per cent of the votes, won a slim victory. The Slovak Democratic Coalition obtained 26.33 per cent, the Party of the Democratic Left 14.66 per cent, the Hungarian Coalition Party 9.12 per cent and the Party of Civil Understanding 8.01 per cent.

– In the referendum on the privatization of strategic enterprises, 44.25 per cent of the voters participated. Because the number of those participating did not reach the required 50 per cent of the voters, the referendum was invalid.

28 October – Representatives of four political parties, The Slovak Democratic Coalition, the Party of the Democratic Left, the Hungarian Coalition Party and the Party of Civil Understanding, signed an agreement in Bratislava to create a coalition government. With this, the future government would be able to obtain the support of 93 out of 150 deputies and thus have enough votes to change the constitution. A twelve-member coalition council was established by the agreement.

29 October – Jozef Migaš, the chairman of the Party of the Democratic Left, was elected by the deputies as the chairman of the National Council of the Slovak Republic.

30 October – The chairman of the National Council of the Slovak Republic, Jozef Migaš (as acting head of state), named a new government led by Prime Minister Mikuláš Dzurinda (Slovak Democratic Coalition). The distribution of portfolios in the new government was: Slovak Democratic Coalition 9, Party of the Democratic Left 6, Hungarian Coalition Party 3, and the Party of Civil Understanding 2.

5 – 6 November – At the head of a government delegation, Prime Minister Mikuláš Dzurinda visited Brussels. He met with Jacques Santer, the chairman of the European Commission, and with José María Gil-Robles, chairman of the European Parliament, and the general secretary of NATO, Javier Solana. Mikuláš Dzurinda appealed for the rapid inclusion of Slovakia in the European Union and NATO. Before the end of the year the prime minister visited Austria and Poland, where he met with the prime ministers and the Polish president, Aleksander Kwasniewski.

12 December – At its summit in Vienna, the Council of Europe decided that the earliest evaluation of Slovakia and other candidate countries for entry into the European Union would be prepared by the European Commission in the fall and presented at the Helsinki summit of the European Union in December 1999 (**15 July 1997**).

19 December – Local community elections took place in the Slovak Republic.

■ **1999**

11 January – Ján Ducký, the former minister for the economy (HZDS) and the Director of the Slovak Gas Company, was murdered in Bratislava. It was the first murder of an important politician since 1989.

20 January – A rocket was launched from the Bajkonur cosmodrome in Kazakstan with Ivan Bella, the first Slovak astronaut on board. Slovakia became the 21st country in the world to have its own astronaut. After a successful flight, I. Bella returned to earth on February 28 1999.

24 March – The government of Slovakia acceded its consent to the request of NATO to use Slovak airspace for operations against Yugoslavia. On April 6, the government approved also the overflight of military aircraft of the Alliance and, on April 23, acceded to the passage of military equipment and members of the armed forces of NATO through the territory of Slovakia.

1 May – the ceremonial breakthrough of the first Slovak highway tunnel under Branisko took place.

29 May – For the first time in history, the citizens of the Slovak Republic decided the presidency by direct election. Rudolf Schuster (1990 – 1992 ambassador to Canada, since 1994 the mayor of Košice) was elected in the second round of the presidential election. Schuster obtained 1,727, 481 votes (57.18 %). His oponent, V. Mečiar, obtained 1,293,642 votes (42.82 %). In the election 75.45 % of the registered voters cast their ballots.

June 1999 – During the first half of 1999 60 % of Slovak exports went to states of the EU and 30 % to states of the Višegrad Four.

15 July – Kofi Annan, the General Secretary of the UN, visited Bratislava.

8 November – The Prime Minister Mikuláš Dzurinda became the first representative of Slovakia in the seven years of its existence to be received in the White House by the President of the USA, William Jefferson Clinton. W. J. Clinton promised to support the efforts of Slovakia to become a member of NATO.

The Ministry of the Interior registered a new political party named Smer, led by Robert Fico, formerly a member of the SDĽ.

24 November – In Bratislava, the Prime Ministers of the Slovak and the Czech republics, Mikuláš Dzurinda and Miloš Zeman, signed an intergovernmental protocol concerning the distribution of the remaining part of the gold reserve from the former State Bank of Czecho-slovakia. With the exchange of stock by the General Credit Bank and the Commercial Bank, the return of Slovak gold (4.124 t) was cleared. On November 22, 1999 the government of M. Zeman decided that, for a symbolic payment of 1 Czech crown, it would buy the so-called Slovak debt in the amount of 25.8 billion Czech crowns from the Czech National Bank.

10 – 11 December – The tenth summit of the EU took place at Helsinki in which M. Dzurinda, the Prime Minister of the Slovak Republic took part. The summit decided to begin negotiations about the entry into the EU of Slovakia, Latvia, Lithuania, Malta, Bulgaria and Romania. It set 31 December 2002 as the date for the ratification of a new agreement about the EU, so that the EU would be prepared to accept new members.

■ **2000**

15 February – The Slovak Republic officially began negotiations for entry into the EU.

18 March – The assembly of the opposition party, HZDS, decided on the transformation of the citizens' movement into a populist party. V. Mečiar remained its chairman.

11 May – The Prime Minister of the Slovak Republic, M. Dzurinda, received the general secretary of NATO, George Robertson, in Bratislava.

17 May – The National Council of the Slovak Republic approved a law about the free access to information that was to go into effect on 1 January 2001.

14 June – The President of the Slovak Republic, R. Schuster, was hospitalized in Bratislava. When his medical condition deteriorated rapidly, he was transferred on June 28 to Innsbruck. He resumed his office on November 20, 2000.

28 July – The council of the Organization for Economic Cooperation and Development (OECD) decided to accept the Slovak Republic into the club of the economically most advanced countries in the world.

23 October – The German Prime Minister, Gerhard Schroeder, visited Slovakia at the invitation of M. Dzurinda.

23 October – At its convention, the Christian Democratic Movement (KDH) elected Pavol Hrušovský as its chairman.

1 November – Prince Charles of Great Britain visited the Slovak Republic at the invitation of President R. Schuster.

11 November – A referendum on early elections took place in the Slovak Republic. 818,480 citizens (20.03 % of the total number of voters) participated In it. Because participation did not exceed 50 %, the referendum was not valid.

14 November – Negotiations between representatives of the EU and the Slovak Republic took place in Brussels.

18 November – In Bratislava delegates to the constituting congress of the SDKÚ (Slovak Democratic and Christian Union) elected M. Dzurinda as the chairman of the new party. The SDKÚ was formed from parts of the SDK (Slovak Democratic Coalition). The original party, SDK, continued to function.

24 November – At the Vatican the Prime Minister of the Slovak Republic, M. Dzurinda and the Papal Secretary of State, Cardinal Angelo Sodano, signed a basic concordat between the Slovak Republic and the Vatican.

ABOLITION OF SERVITUDE – one of the most important economic and social reforms of Joseph II (**Josephinian reforms**)*. It was proclaimed for Hungary on **22 August 1785** by Joseph II. It eliminated the status legalized by the *Tripartitum* of Werbőczy at the beginning of the 16th century. The landlords had perpetrated many injustices against the serfs, who had lost almost all their personal freedom and were bound to the soil. The landlords often did not respect even the **Theresian urbár** and arbitrarily increased the serfs' obligations and took their land. The patent abolishing servitude was based upon Enlightenment principles of natural law. It sought to end the unbridled suppression, lack of legal rights, dissatisfaction and backwardness of the serf farmers. It recognized the human dignity, strengthened the civic consciousness and restored the personal freedom of the serfs. They were able to move, while the landlord was not permitted to bind them to the soil, to expel them or settle them in other areas. They could freely establish families, work in various jobs, send children to school, and dispose of their property. They remained bound only economically, through the leasing of land, to their superiors. Their obligations were defined by the *urbár* or other contracts. This reform weakened feudal relations but did not resolve the ownership of the land and preserved the obligations of the serfs. On **10 February 1789** Joseph II proclaimed a tax reform that limited the obligations of the serfs to the payment of money dues and infringed upon the foundations of **serfdom**. However, after his premature death, it was not put into effect. /DŠ/

ABSOLUTISM – a form of monarchic government. It is characterized by the unlimited executive and legislative power of the sovereign, allegedly derived from the will of God. After the feudal era, it culminated in the nationalization of public administration, the centralization of power and the abolition of the principles of the **monarchy of the estates.** It began to be implemented in the 15th century (reign of Matthias Corvinus), and in the **Habsburg monarchy** from the 16th century. The ruler asserted his power through numerous state offices, the police, the army and the church. Formally all offices were advisory organs of the ruler. To replace the autonomous administration of the estates by hereditary lords, the ruler established state offices to which he appointed educated officials. He limited, sometime even abolished, the rights of the nobility and historic entities. In contrast to the Austrian and Czech lands, in Hungary the Habsburgs were not able to permanently establish absolutism due to the strong opposition of the estates, which resorted to armed insurrections. Except for the brief periods (for example, the 1760s) of **enlightenment absolutism** or **neo-absolutism**, Hungary preserved the marks of statehood and significant independence from the dynasty; the nobility kept their privileges and the country its autonomous organs. In Hungary the Habsburgs had more or less to respect the rights of the domestic estates and to share power with their organs (**Hungarian diet, counties**). Due to this, the Hungarian nobility built up a strong self-awareness, patriotic feeling and a sense of independence. Hungary preserved the attributes of statehood even during **Metternichian absolutism**. In the **revolution of 1848-49** the empire was transformed into a **constitutional monarchy** for a short time. /DŠ/

ACADEMIA ISTROPOLITANA – more properly the Istropolitanian University, the first university on the territory of Slovakia. King Matthias Corvinus requested its establishment and Pope Paul II issued the chartering bull on **19 May 1465**. The university began to function on **20 July 1467**. The University of Bologna served as its model. Its organizer and chancellor was John Vitéz of Sredna, the Archbishop of Esztergom and a learned humanist; its vi-

---

* Bold type indicates particular headword.

ce-chancellor was George Schomberg, the dean of the Bratislava chapter. Because the archives have not been preserved, little is known about its internal organization, the number of students, or details of its activities. It is presumed that faculties of arts (philosophy) and of theology functioned, but the existence of law and medical faculties is debatable. Humanist scholars were associated with the university: the mathematician Johann Müller-Regiomontanus, the astronomer Martin Bylica of Olkusz, and the theologian and lawyer Giovanni Gattus from Italy. Vavrinec Koch of Krompachy also worked at the University of Vienna. A conflict between King Matthias and Archbishop Vitéz, who joined a conspiracy against the king, led to the imprisonment of Vitéz and the dismissal of several teachers from the university. Some went to the royal court in Buda, a center of Hungarian **humanism**. There are no primary sources concerning the dissolution of the Istropolitana. When King Matthias transferred his seat to Vienna in 1485, he probably lost interest in supporting it. As early as 1492, weapons were stored in its building and a written record notes that the Istropolitana had long disappeared. /JB/

ADAMITES – religious sect in, but not limited to, the Hussite movement. In the first phase of the dissemination of Hussitism, free thought views from Picardy also penetrated Czechia. Therefore, their disseminators (the most radical part of the Hussite movement) were also called Picards. They repudiated the sacrament of the altar, called for a return to nature, the cult of nakedness, and sexual promiscuity. At the beginning of 1421, under the leadership of the priest Martin Húska, also called Loquis, the community sought refuge in the countryside near the Lužnice and Nežárka rivers, where they established their own commune due to controversies with the people of Prague and the city of Tábor. After Martin Húska was burned, they were led by another priest, Peter Kániš. When their eccentricity increased and threatened surrounding villages, Jan Žižka put to death the Adamites in his own army, intervened against them mi-

litarily and, after destroying their settlements, burned all those who remained, including Peter Kániš, in April 1421. /JB/

AGRARIAN PARTY – a political party on the right oriented towards the small farmers. Milan Hodža, Pavol Blaho and Vavro Šrobár contributed to the formation of the agrarian movement in Slovakia at the transition from the 19th to the 20th centuries. They maintained close contacts with the Republican Party of the Czech Countryside founded in 1899. After the establishment of the Czechoslovak Republic in 1918, the National Republican Farmers' Party was founded with aid of Vavro Šrobár and Milan Hodža on **16 September 1919** in Bratislava. Before the parliamentary elections on 11 January 1920 it attempted to utilize the tradition of the **Slovak National Party** and merged with this party to establish the Slovak National and Farmers' Party. After losing the elections, it withdrew from the unified party on 30 March 1921. One of its disagreements with the Slovak National Party was over the question of the **autonomy of Slovakia**. At a congress in Prague, 28 – 29 June 1922, the Slovak agrarians merged with the Czech agrarians to form the Republican Party of the Agricultural and Small Farm People. The party had a centralist character, accepted the position of **Czechoslovakism**, sought to resolve the Slovak question through regionalism (for example, by increasing the authority of the organs of executive power in Slovakia, and the modernization of agricultural and industry through state subsidies). It was a member of all of the coalition governments of the first and second Czechoslovak Republic and of the **government five**. According to the election results, it was the strongest party in Czechia and throughout the country as a whole and the second strongest in Slovakia. Its chairman was Antonín Švehla and Milan Hodža the deputy chairman. It was supported in Slovakia by the Union of Slovak Farmers, the League of Agricultural Co-operatives, and the League of Farmer Mutual Relief Funds and interest organizations. It used the first **land reform** to strengthen its position. On **6 October 1938** the Slovak agrarians signed the **Žilina**

agreement and took a position in favor of the autonomy of Slovakia. Later a crisis emerged in the party over its future direction. After negotiations with the **Hlinka's Slovak People's Party**, the two parties merged on **8 November 1938**. Former agrarians (Ján Ursíny, Jozef Lettrich) made up the decisive element of the civic underground opposition (**Christmas Agreement**) in the first Slovak Republic. The participants in the **Moscow negotiations** (1945) agreed to prohibit the Agrarian Party in the renewed Czechoslovak Republic. The Slovak agrarians continued their activities in the **Democratic Party**. /RL/

ALLOD (Latin **Allodium**) – originally inheritance; inherited land in contrast to land purchased or acquired in other ways. It appeared for the first time among the ancient Germani. In Hungary, from the 14th century, this term designated land in the possession of the landlord (allodial land) in distinction to land in the hands of serfs (rustical land). From the 16th century the proportion of allodial land increased and it was also called dominical land. The landlords erected manors (farmsteads) on this land, which the serfs were forced to work (**serfdom**). /JB/

ANNALS – historical written sources that record events in a chronological sequence without providing detailed descriptions or seeking to establish connections between them. They belong among the oldest sort of historical literature. Most were the work of anonymous authors (annalists). They recorded events either on separate pages or in already existing formats, Easter charts, calendars and the like. The most important events (the deaths of popes, sovereigns, and church dignitaries, and wars, as well as unusual events, natural catastrophes and the like) were noted in them. Annals had already developed in antiquity and the oldest medieval annals from the 8th century followed their tradition. The Frankish annals that recorded the years 741 – 829 are the most significant. Also important are the Fulda annals that recorded events to 901. Both are important sources for the oldest history of the Slovaks. The oldest annals in Hungary are the Bratislava annals from the mid **11th century**, recording events to 1276 in the so-called Pray Codex. Other annals, especially from the German regions (Altaic, Bertinian, Hildesheim, Regensburg, Salzburg etc.), also existed. In the 13th and 14th century annals declined and were replaced by **chronicles** as a higher form of historical written source. /JB/

APPRENTICES see **Guilds**

APRIL AGREEMENT – an agreement between the leadership of the Democratic Party and some Catholic politicians. The new political representation that came to power in Slovakia in 1945 after the arrival of Soviet troops did not fulfill the expectations of a great part of the citizens. Under the pretext of removing the influence of the Catholic church on leading offices of the state, it nationalized church schools, limited the Catholic press, and dissolved religious societies. Many clerics were brought before people's courts (**retribution**). With the dissolution of Hlinka's Slovak People's Party, Catholic believers also lost a political representation reflecting their national and religious orientation. While the Communist Party of Slovakia supported the idea of establishing a new party for Slovak Catholics, the overwhelmingly Evangelical leadership of the Democratic Party sought their integration. Already in 1945 several Catholic representatives in the Prague parliament (Ján Kempný, Miloš Bugár, Andrej Cvinček) had been accepted into the Democratic Party. Because discussions concerning an independent party for Catholics encountered obstacles in the National Front and parliamentary elections were approaching, the majority of Catholic activists decided in favor of an agreement with the Democratic Party, approved on **30 March 1946**. The agreement required the replacement of religiously intolerant persons in politics, stated that the views of the Democratic Party on the question of education and schools were identical with those of the Catholic Church, established a narrower presidium of the Democratic Party and created two new positions as general secretaries for Ján Kempný and Miloš Bugár. The ratio between Catholics and Evangelicals was to be 2:1 in the candidate lists and 7:3 in party organs, financial, economic and interest organizations. The executive committee of the Democratic Party informed the public about the signed agreement on 5 April 1946, hence the name "April Agreement". Under pressure from the communists the presidium of the Democratic Party distanced itself from the agreement on 9 November 1947. /RL/

ARCHBISHOPS – in the Catholic Church, the high ecclesiastical dignitaries presiding over ecclesiastical provinces, which have to include at least two bishoprics. They exist in the Roman Catholic, eastern Orthodox and Anglican churches. Archbishops have the right to call church synods within their provinces, i.e. on the territory subordinated to them. They conduct visitations, have judicial authority in church matters and other ecclesiastical rights. In addition to metropolitan archbishops, the pope also bestows the dignity of titular archbishop upon important bishops, papal nuncios, and the like. With the penetration of Frankish missionaries, the Salzburg archbishopric and the Passau bishopric claimed ecclesiastical authority in the territory of the later **Great Moravian Empire**. At the transition of the 9th to the 10th centuries the territory of Slovakia belonged to the Moravian ecclesiastical province, at the end of the 10th century to the province of the Mainz archbishopric, and from the beginning of the 11th century to the province of the Esztergom archbishopric (**1000**). In 1135 the archbishopric of Kalocsa and in 1804 the archbishopric of Eger were established in Hungary. The bulk of the territory of Slovakia belonged to the province of Esztergom. After the establishment of the Eger archbishopric, the Slovak bishoprics of Spiš, Košice and Rožňava, and some parishes in Slovakia in the bishopric of Satu Mare, as well as the Greek Catholic bishoprics of Prešov and Mukačevo, were subordinated to it. The authority of the bishopric of Mukačevo also extended into eastern Slovakia. The archbishop of Esztergom was the Hungarian primate with the right to crown the king and to fill the office of chancellor. After 1918, as a result of constitutional changes,

links with the archbishoprics of Esztergom and Eger were loosened. Apostolic administration was established in Trnava in 1922, and in 1937 in Košice and Rožňava. The reorganization of ecclesiastical administration was effected on **30 December 1977** with the establishment of an archbishopric in Trnava and the elevation of the bishopric of Košice to an archbishopric (**31 March 1995**). /JB/

ARCHDEACONRY – a territorial administrative unit of the Catholic Church. From the 4th century archdeacons assisted **bishops** in caring for church property, in the exercise of judicial authority, and in the care of the poor. In the 9th – 10th centuries their authority was extended to the administration of part of the territory of bishoprics. The Bratislava and Nitra archdeaconries (from the 11th century) are the oldest in Slovakia. A network of archdeaconries was created in the 12th century. The Šaštín, Komárno, Hont and, in later centuries, the Novohrad, Turňa, Abov-Novohrad, Uh, Hradno, and other archdeaconries were established. Archdeaconries were subdivided into vice archdeaconries, from which were created rural deaneries headed by a rural dean. Theoretically, ten parishes were subordinated to the rural dean. /JB/

ART NOUVEAU (art of the new style, also in central Europe the Secession or Vienna Secession style) – an artistic movement at the end of the 19th and the beginning of the 20th centuries. It found expression in all areas of culture but especially in architecture, the applied arts, furniture, glassware and every-day fashion. It sought a return to nature and its popular motifs were animals, flowers, trees, ornaments and the human face. It was characterized by oval shapes, curves, mosaic embellishments and the use of diverse materials. The art nouveau movement originated in Germany (Munich) and Austria-Hungary (Vienna). The Viennese Gustav Klimt and the Czech Alfons Mucha were among the most famous art nouveau painters. Art nouveau influenced the early works of Gustáv Mallý, Martin Benka, Alojz Rigele and Anton Jasusch. In architecture it was grandly implemented in the building of new sections in the larger cities (Vienna, Prague, Budapest and Bratislava). Especially noteworthy in Slovakia are the buildings by the chief representatives of the so-called Hungarian art nouveau, Edmund Lechner and Dušan Jurkovič. Jurkovič, who was inspired by folk, especially wooden, architecture, also designed the Štefánik monument on Bradlo Hill as well as military cemeteries in Poland and the Ukraine. /DŠ/

AUSTRIA-HUNGARY (Austro-Hungarian Monarchy / Empire) – a federal state unit in central Europe. It developed from the **Habsburg Monarchy** after the Austrian-Hungarian (Magyar) Compromise of 1867 and was based upon **dualism**. It was the official name of the entity from 14 November 1867 and had an area of 622,000 km^2 (without Bosnia and Hercegovina). It was comprised of two state units, Cisleitha (Austria and the Czech lands, Dalmatia, the Littoral, Bukovina and Galicia) and Transleitha (Hungary). They were symbolically separated by the Leitha River. In Cisleitha the political system was more democratic, life was in general more cultivated, power and the laws took into account, at least partially, the national needs of the "small" nations and, after 1907, there was general suffrage. In the Kingdom of **Hungary** the old noble class obtained almost unlimited power. It was represented in particular by the governments of the **Liberal Party**. These governments ignored the **nationality law**. The discriminatory **right to vote in Hungary** made it easier for them to implement a radical **Magyarization**. The Kingdom of Hungary was transformed into a country of national oppression, intolerance and mistrust. In the **First World War**, Austria-Hungary, fighting on the side of Germany, was defeated. With the military defeat the monarchy also ceased to exist. Its territory passed to **Czecho-Slovakia**, Austria, and Hungary and in part also Yugoslavia, Romania, Poland and Italy. /DŠ/

AUSTRO-SLAVISM (also Austro-federalism) – the political program of some representatives of the Slavic nations in the **Habsburg Monarchy**. It was formed in the 1840s and appeared as an integrated concept in the spring of 1848 when it was advocated in particular by Czech liberals (Karol Havlíček-Borovský, František Palacký). It rejected Kollár's **Slavic mutuality,** his idea of a pan-Slavic nation and vision of **pan-Slavism,** as unrealistic and harmful. It considered the Habsburg Monarchy to be the most appropriate state entity for small, central European Slavic nations. Austro-Slavism was seen as providing protection from German and Magyar hegemony, Russian expansion and a guarantee of Slavic liberty. It demanded the transformation of the monarchy into a federal and constitutional state based on natural rights and national equality. Autonomous units were to have their own parliaments and executive powers, and in them official business was to be conducted in the national languages. Austro-Slavism dominated the **Slavic Congress**. In the fall of 1848 the new imperial government in Vienna and the imperial diet in Kroměříž declared their support for its principles. It was also adopted by Slovak politicians who demanded the separation of Slovakia from the Kingdom of Hungary and the establishment of an autonomous Slovakia within the framework of the monarchy (as a district, crown land, or grand principality). They expressed their demands especially in the **March Petition** and in the **Petition Movement in the fall of 1849**. However, the Habsburg politicians introduced **neo-absolutism** instead of federalization in the empire. A disappointed Ľudovít Štúr and some members of his group supported pan-Slavism. With the renewal of a **constitutional monarchy** in 1860, Austro-Slavism again became a relevant issue and was demanded in particular by those in the circle of Jozef Miloslav Hurban (**9 February 1861**). However, Magyar politicians rejected this possibility and Vienna deferred to them. Austro-Slavism revived again just before the **First World War.** It was advocated by Francis Ferdinand, the heir to the throne, and his co-workers (e.g. Milan Hodža), who wanted to eliminate **dualism** and federalize the monarchy. It became irrelevant after 1918. /DŠ/

AUTONOMY OF SLOVAKIA (from the Greek *autonomos* – having its own laws) – in the broadest sense of the word, self-government, distinctness, or independence. In politics and law it means the self-administration of territorial or cultural units within the framework of a larger administrative unit. The struggle for the autonomy of Slovakia on a national and territorial basis is closely connected with the formation of the modern Slovak nation in the 19th century. Slovak politicians publicly expressed it for the first time in the **Demands of the Slovak Nation** in 1848. A further key document, the **Memorandum of the Slovak Nation** of 1861, demanded the autonomy of Slovakia within the context of the Kingdom of Hungary. Autonomy was a continuing demand of the majority of Slovak politicians up to the **First World War**, when an important change took place in the Slovak political program. In October 1915 representatives of American Slovaks and Czechs signed the **Cleveland Agreement** that proposed joining the Czech and Slovak nations in a federal union of states with a fully autonomous Slovakia. The **Pittsburgh Agreement** of **31 May 1918** confirmed the autonomy of Slovakia within the framework of Czecho-Slovakia. A delegation of the Slovak League in the United States brought photo-copies of it to Slovakia in April 1919. In Czecho-Slovakia the question of Slovakia was regarded as an internal problem of the state. Instead of autonomy, a centralist model of the state and the ideology of **Czechoslovakism** was implemented. The Pittsburgh Agreement, whose binding force was disavowed by Tomáš Garrigue Masaryk, became the basic starting point for the efforts of Slovak autonomists associated with **Hlinka's Slovak People's Party** and the **Slovak National Party**. Both parties sought to achieve autonomy through constitutional means (**25 January 1922, 8 May 1930, 19 August 1938**). Other important political parties were branches of Czech centralist parties and did not consistently assert the distinctness of the Slovak nation. The many years of struggle for the autonomy of Slovakia ended after the **Munich Agreement** with the signing of the **Žilina Agreement** and the publication of the **Žilina Manifesto** on **6 October 1938**. A constitutional law concerning the autonomy of Slovakia was adopted by the Prague parliament on **22 November 1938**. A struggle over jurisdiction, mistrust between the autonomous and the central government and, in particular, the dominant influence of Germany in central Europe, led to the dissolution of the Czechoslovak Republic and to the creation of the first **Slovak Republic** on **14 March 1939**. /RL/

AVARS – a nomadic tribal alliance led by the Turko-Tatars. Some historians associate them with the Juan Juan rulers of Mongolia in the 4th and 5th centuries, others with the Hephtalites, the so-called White Huns. Some suppose the participation of both elements in their ethnic composition. The Avars appeared for the first time in the northern foothills of the Caucasus in 558. They came into contact with the Byzantine Empire, which used them in struggles with other tribes to the north of the Black Sea. In 561 they moved around the arch of the Carpathians and undertook unsuccessful raids into central Germany. After returning to the southern Ukrainian steppes, they subdued the Antia who lived there. As allies of the Pannonian Longobards, they destroyed the empire of the Gepids along the Tisa (Tisza) River and in Transylvania in 568. After an agreement with the Longobards, they took control of Pannonia in the same year. The Longobards departed for northern Italy. The Avar Empire extended from the Vienna area of the Danube basin to the Don. It became a threat to the Byzantine Empire, which had to pay an annual tribute as early as 570. Under the rule of the *kagan* Bajan, the Avars conquered Sirmium (Sriem – Mitrovica) in 562. In 601 the Byzantine military commander Priscus undertook a successful campaign against the Avars in the Tisza region. An uprising of the Slavs living north of the Danube, under the leadership of the Frankish merchant Samo, in 623 – 624 and an unsuccessful siege of Constantinople in 626 broke Avar power. Changes in the Danubian basin and the Balkans occurred in the 7th century in connection with the migration of other tribes to this territory. Bulgarian tribes under the leadership of Asperuch (Isperikh) migrated to the Balkans in 678 – 680 and other tribes came with them. The empire of the Khazars developed north of the Black Sea and the Byzantine Empire stopped paying the Avars annual tribute. The eclipse of Avar domination was brought about by the expeditions of the Frankish ruler Charlemagne and his son Pipin who, in **796**, destroyed the seat of the Avar *kagan* in the Danubian basin. As a nomadic league, the Avars lived from looting and from the exploitation of the subjugated population whom they considered slaves. They built large fortifications for themselves-stockades surrounded by earthen escarpments. The last mention of the Avars dates from **822**. /JB/

BACH'S ABSOLUTISM see **Neo-absolutism**

BANDERIUM – in general a battle flag (standard, colors), but also a ceremonial mounted detachment or escort (armed band or entourage). In the Hungarian military system during feudalism, an armed unit fighting under the banner of the one who organized, armed and led them. Although the creation of the banderial military arrangement is usually ascribed to Charles Robert, long before, during the reign of the Árpáds, soldiers had fought under the personal banner or standard of the **king**, castle captains (*špáni*), county administrators (*župani*), or **magnates**. At the transition from the 13th to the 14th centuries, during a period of feudal warfare and the decline of royal power, the *banderia* of the nobles, specifically made up of their retainers or courtiers (*dvorníci*), servants and serfs, were very numerous (for example, the army of Matthew Csák of Trenčín had up to 5,000 warriors). In the 14th and 15th centuries the establishment of the banderial system was completed under several legal arrangements. The Hungarian military power was made up of the following types of *banderia*: royal (those of the king and queen), of standard-bearing lords, or regional **barons** and, depending on wealth, of other magnates and **prelates**, and of counties led by the *župan* or county administrator, in which, in the case of a conscription (*insurekcia*, insurrection), all nobles who were obliged to provide military service were enlisted, together with *portal* soldiers drawn predominantly from serfs of the pertinent county (*stolica*). As a rule, contingents raised by chartered cities, subordinated to the *banderia* of the counties. While the strength and composition of individual types of *banderia*, the number and types of troops differed, cavalry predominated. The most heavily armed served in the royal *banderium,* the core of which was made up of the king's own escort, body guards, court knights and mercenary soldiers. The majority of the *banderia* of the lords numbered between 50 and 400 men (however, under the banner of John Hunyady, 10,000 men often served). Light cavalry and infantry predominated in the *banderia* of the counties; but they were often inadequately equipped and armed. The banderial arrangement, together with institutionalized conscription (*insurekcia*), was the essence of Hungarian military power up to the end of the Middle Ages. An exception was the period of the reign of Matthias Corvinus who, for financial compensation, relieved the magnates of the responsibility to establish *banderia* because he preferred to maintain a predominantly mercenary army (the **black army**). After the battle at Mohács in 1526, under the Habsburgs, the banderial arrangement gradually lost its significance because mercenary soldiers and, from 1649, regular armies came to form the core of the armed forces. *Banderia* were abolished in Hungary in 1848. /VS/

BARON – a member of the upper nobility (**magnate**), in the medieval system of feudal tenure (**fief**-holding) originally a member of the entourage of the ruler or a vassal immediately subordinate to the king. In the Kingdom of Hungary from the 13th century until the end of the Middle Ages, only the highest provincial dignitaries and officials (in other words, provincial barons by virtue of office) were designated as barons in the narrow sense of the word. According to the *Tripartitum* of Werbőczy, these were: the **palatine**, the **chief justice**, the *vojvoda* or duke of Trans-

ylvania, the Croatian-Dalmatian and the Sla-
vonian *bán*, the treasurer (*taverník*), the chief
steward, the chief butler, the chief cup-bearer,
the chief groom, the Mačva and Severin *bán*,
and the administrator (*župan*) of Bratislava
and of Temes, as well as the prior of Vranje
(Aureanum). In the broader sense of the word,
the title baron also belonged to the wealthiest
and most influential provincial landlords and
to all former provincial dignitaries. From the
end of the 15th century baronies became hereditary titles. The barons were members of
the royal council and had the right (and from
the 15th century the obligation) to maintain
private armies and to fight under their own
standards, in other words, to have their own
banderia. In the hierarchy of nobility adopted
by law no. 1/1608, they constituted the lowest degree of the magnate estate below the
dukes (*knieža, vojvoda*) and **counts** (*gróf*) but
above the lower nobility (**yeoman**, *zeman*).
The barons had the right to sit at the upper table (later in the upper chamber) of the **Hungarian diet** (assembly). /VS/

BAROQUE – artistic style. It originated in Italy
in the 16th century. It spread into central Europe during the 17th century and climaxed
during the pacific 18th century. It was influenced by the climate of religious conflicts,
penetrated all areas of culture and characterized a way of life. In contrast to the Renaissance, it sought values in the supra-terrestrial or
ideal world and was characterized by pomp,
grandiose decoration, emotional intensity
and unrestrained fantasy. A specific form of
the baroque style was the playfully ornamental rococo. The beginning of the baroque style
in Slovakia is connected with the founding of
Trnava University. It was manifested in the
architecture of numerous churches, grand
cloisters, residences of the nobility in the villages and palaces in the cities. The most famous central European baroque architects
from Vienna designed buildings in Slovakia,
namely Francis Anton Hillebrandt in Bratislava, Johann Fischer of Erlach in Banská
Štiavnica and Francis Anton Pilgram in Jasov.
The outstanding sculptor J. Rafael Donner
spent his most creative years in Bratislava;

the portrait painter Ján Kupecký of Pezinok,
on the other hand, worked abroad. The most
beautiful fresco paintings in churches were likewise created by Austrian artists (Francis Anton Maulbertsch, Johann Lucas Kracker, Paul
Troger). The baroque style even influenced
popular culture, building and applied arts (for
example the work of the gold-smith Ján Szi-
lassy). Literature was characterized by an ornamental style and rich metaphors. The ephemeral nature of life was depicted in tragedies,
satires and sermons. The majority of scholars
wrote in Latin (Matej Bel); religious works (Juraj Tranovský, Benedikt Sölöši), books on travel and memoirs (Štefan Pilárik, Daniel Krman
Jr.) and humorous and ethical poetry (Hugolín
Gavlovič) were published in the native language. **Baroque Slavicism** was cultivated.
Courtly and noble theater, Latin school plays,
opera, ballet and hymns enjoyed popularity
(Juraj Bajan, Edmund Pascha). /DŠ/

BAROQUE SLAVICISM – the views of the Slovak
intellectuals on the Slavic or Slovak nation
during the baroque era of the 17th and 18th
centuries. Among its elements was the antiquity of the "Slavic nation" and the autochthonous existence of the Slovaks in Hungary that was claimed in the famous baroque
forgery, the so-called privilege of Alexander
the Great. The name *Slovak – Slav* was most
frequently derived from the word *slava*
(glory), sometimes from *slovo* (word) and
even from the word *člověk* (human being). Vigorously rejected was its derivation from the
word *sclavus* (slave). It stressed the diffusion
of the *Slavic nation* from the Adriatic to the
Baltic seas and eastward to the borders of
China. Baroque scholars also called attention
to the beauty and comprehensibility of the
Slavic language as one of the three liturgical
languages. They referred to the privilege of
Pope Nicholas I and the golden bull of Emperor Charles IV. All the qualities of the *Slavic
nation* were ascribed to the Slovaks. The most
significant representatives of baroque Slavicism were Jakob Jakobeus, Martin Szentiványi, Matej Bel, Samuel Timon and Ján Baltazár Magin. /VČ/

BASILICA – a Christian church of the most significant character. It developed from ancient buildings that served administrative, judicial or market purposes. (The original meaning of *basiliké stoá* was the royal hall). It had a longitudinal floor-plan with columned halls and lateral naves. The entry, a portal which projected from the floor-plan of the structure, was at the narrow end. The opposite end of a basilica was closed by a semi-circular floor-plan (*nike*). This type of building was adopted also by the first Christian churches that had three to five naves. The middle nave was broader and higher than the side naves and at the eastern end was closed by a semi-circular apse. Transverse naves, transepts placed between the lateral naves and the apse, began to be built during the early Christian era, while the space between the transverse nave and the termination of the building was lengthened. From this developed the presbytery (or choir, a space reserved for the clergy) typical of the **Gothic** style. The first basilicas were established in Slovakia during the era of the **Great Moravian Empire** (at Bratislava castle). The basilicas in Hronský Beňadik, Diakovce and Banská Štiavnica were built by the Benedictines in the **Romanesque** style, while later basilicas were built in the Gothic and Renaissance styles. This type of building was ignored during the baroque era. In terms of ecclesiastical (canon) law, a church received the status of basilica from the pope. In Slovakia the national shrine in Šaštín (1964), the pilgrimage church in Levoča (1984) and in Ľutina (1988) were declared basilicas. /JB/

BENEDICTINES – the oldest Catholic **religious order**. It was founded by Benedict of Nursia (480 to 543) who built the first monastery on the hill of Monte Cassino in southern Italy in 529. The Benedictines became a model for other **religious orders**. As missionaries they contributed to the Christianizing of Europe. From the mid 8th century as well as during the era of the **Great Moravian Empire,** Frankish Benedictines worked on the territory of the Danubian Slavs. The oldest Benedictine monastery of St Hippolytus on Zobor Mountain near Nitra was probably established at this time. It was renewed in the 11th century

after the establishment of the Hungarian state. The hermits St Svorad and St Benedict (**1032, 1034**) worked there. Other cloisters were in Hronský Beňadik (**1075**), Bzovík (**1135**), Krásna nad Hornádom (1143), Skalka near Trenčín (1224), in Ludanice (1242), Nové Mesto nad Váhom (1263) and elsewhere. During the **Reformation** several **cloisters** were closed; some were renewed later. During the 19th and 20th centuries the Benedictines devoted themselves to teaching in schools and had secondary schools in Trnava, Bratislava and Komárno. The Cistercian (1098) and the Premonstratensian (1121) orders were offshoots of the Benedictine order. /JB/

BERNOLÁK'S GROUP – a Catholic stream of the national revival movement named for its chief representative Anton Bernolák. It was active from the 1780s to the mid 19th century. Both clerical and secular intellectuals belonged to it (Juraj Fándly, Jozef Ignác Bajza, Ján Hollý, Juraj Palkovič, Martin Hamuljak, Alexander Rudnay, Andrej Radlinský and others). Centers of the Bernolák group were Bratislava (**1 June 1784**) and Trnava, later Pest and Esztergom, as well as towns with Catholic higher schools. The members of the group were united by the use of the literary Slovak language of Bernolák (**27 December 1786, 1 May 1787**), the concept of Slovak national particularity and the idea of the equality of nations. During the enlightenment the first generation supported the **Josephinian reforms**, criticized the privileges of the nobility and sought to ease the situation of the serfs and the poorer classes through education. They provided them with new knowledge about nature and society, and taught more modern ways of working the soil, of cultivating new varieties of plants and of breeding new types of animals. At the same time they promoted the consciousness of a Slovak national particularity, drawing upon the Great Moravian and Cyrilic-Methodian tradition. Organizational support for this generation was provided by the **Slovak Learned Society**. After its activity waned, the Bernolák group was revived in the 1820s. In the era of intensified national struggles they became supporters of **Slavic**

mutuality, translated the Bible (**8 September 1822**) into Bernolák's Slovak and published the Dictionary or *Slowár* (*1825*) by Bernolák. Ján Hollý wrote epic poetry and Martin Hamuljak founded the **Society of the Devotees of Slovak Language and Literature**. The views of the younger (third) generation of the Bernolák group resembled those of **Štúr's group,** as they accepted the concept of popular language as well as the new literary language of Štúr. This helped to overcome differences in the understanding of the nation based upon confessional allegiance. The unity of the Slovak national movement was confirmed within the **Tatrín** association. /DŠ/

BETHLEN'S INSURRECTION – a revolt of the nobility that began with the invasion of Hungary in **November 1616** by an army of the Transylvanian prince Gabriel Bethlen. It was joined by Hungarian Protestant magnates (George Rákoczi, Imrich Thurzo, George Széchy) in the hope of toppling the Habsburgs from the Hungarian throne. In the summer of 1619 Bethlen exploited the weak position in which Ferdinand II found himself after the revolt of the Czech estates. After he occupied Košice, Bethlen's adherents declared him the regent of the Kingdom of Hungary and the protector of the non-Catholic population. Because Bethlen's insurgents met only weak opposition, they traversed the whole of Slovakia and took Bratislava in October. The palatine turned over the Hungarian royal crown to Bethlen at Bratislava castle. After joining with the armies of the Czech and Moravian estates in November 1619 he set out against Vienna. An attack by the emperor's ally George Drugeth in eastern Slovakia forced Bethlen to forsake his allies. At the **diet** in Bratislava in January 1620 the nobility no longer wanted to continue the war against the emperor and only wished to have confirmed both the privileges of the estates and the distribution of the property taken from the Catholic Church. Therefore Bethlen concluded a truce with the emperor. Fighting between the insurgents and the imperial army was renewed when Bethlen, with consent of the sultan, allowed himself to be elected as king of Hungary at the diet in Banská Bystrica in August 1620. Because of the weak assistance provided by the Ottoman Turks and the loss of his noble followers, Bethlen was forced to sign a peace with the emperor. He returned the royal crown on **20 March 1622**. However, Bethlen was not satisfied with the conditions of the peace. Together with Protestant participants in the Thirty Years' War and with the direct assistance of the Ottomans, he undertook further raids into Slovakia in 1623 and 1626. He signed treaties with King Ferdinand II in Vienna in 1624 and in Bratislava in 1626. Bethlen surrendered the royal title and territory he had occupied. He became an imperial prince and received seven eastern Hungarian counties in usufruct for life. However, he gradually lost the duchies of Opolie and Ratibor and was deprived of payments for the maintenance of the border fortresses. /MK/

BIEDERMEIER – artistic style and fashion in the first half of the 19th century. It repudiated the severity of classicism. It was enriched especially by elements of pathos and heroism from **romanticism**. It spread primarily in the **Habsburg Monarchy** and the German states. The name was derived from two popular Viennese theatrical figures, Bieder and Meier, who, during the era of the Napoleonic wars, propagated the ideal of life in a quiet, modest family environment. Its adherents were predominantly the bourgeoisie, but it was also popular among the aristocracy and at the Habsburg court. It was a specific reaction to the sufferings caused by the Napoleonic wars, strong censorship and the police regime of the first half of the 19th century. It was characterized by the commonplace, carefree festive mood and the enjoyment of trifling things. In dwellings appeared simple, light and functional furniture, wall-paper and small ornaments – embroidery, porcelain cups, toys, trifles, glass, wooden and metal statuettes, and little angels. Biedermeier was eloquently reflected in music. In the city and the county palaces were heard the lesser works of Ludwig van Beethoven and Franz Schubert; new dances gained popularity on the promenades and, in popular entertainment, the polkas and waltzes of Strauss. Houses with carefully cultivated gardens and garden houses appeared on the outskirts of the cities. In the visual arts peaceful still-lifes, charming miniature landscapes and portraits prevailed. The Biedermeier style influenced the culture of the general public of the city and the countryside and the taste of central Europeans as a whole. /DŠ/

BISHOPS – ecclesiastical dignitaries in early Christian societies who cared for the spiritual teaching and economic administration of the dioceses entrusted to them. The name comes from the Greek (*episkopos* – overseer). From the beginning of the 2nd century they began to replace presbyters (elders) in church communities. The bishops of Rome, Constantinople, Antioch and Alexandria held the most significant positions during antiquity. In the Middle Ages the bishopric (diocese) became the basic element of ecclesiastical administration. Bishops had the right to ordain priests as well as administrative and judicial authority in ecclesiastical matters. They supervised theological teaching, conducted regular visitations of parishes entrusted to them and submitted reports to the papal curia about the state of the diocese. The insignia of bishops include a ring, crozier (an ornamented curved staff as a symbol of the pastoral function), pectoral cross and bishop's miter. Titular bishops do not preside over functioning dioceses. Because of the collegial nature of the office, consecrating bishops act on behalf of all the bishops in the act of consecration. The oldest bishopric on the territory of Slovakia was the Nitra diocese. After the fall of the **Great Moravian Empire** it probably disappeared. From the beginning of the 11th century Slovakia was part of the archbishopric of Esztergom (**archbishops**), from which, before **1086**, the Nitra bishopric was separated. Part of eastern Slovakia belonged to the bishopric of Eger. By separation from the archbishopric of Esztergom were established the bishoprics of Spiš, Rožňava and Banská Bystrica on **15 January 1776**. In 1771 the Greek Catholic bishopric of Mukachevo was established; from 1776 its seat was in Uzhgorod. A part of the territory of eastern Slovakia (Zemplín) was also under its authority. In 1776 the territory of the diocese of Nitra in the Nitra River valley was enlarged to include northwestern Slovakia (Trenčín county). In **1804** the bishopric of Eger became an archbishopric and a new bishopric in Košice was established. In addition to the new bishopric of Košice, the older bishoprics of Spiš and Rožňava became sufragan bishoprics of the archbishopric of Eger. In 1816 the bishopric of Prešov was separated from the Greek Catholic bishopric of Mukachevo. Both belonged to the province of the Esztergom archdiocese. After 1918 the Slovak bishoprics ceased to be part of the ecclesiastical provinces of Esztergom and Eger, which were limited to Hungary. Therefore, an apostolic administration (i.e. one directly subordinate to Rome) was created in Trnava in 1922 for the territory formerly belonging to the archbishopric of Esztergom. In 1937 such administrations were established in Košice and Rožňava. The organization of the Roman Catholic Church was modified only on **30 December 1977** by the establishment of an archbishopric in Trnava, to whose province the bishoprics of Nitra, Spiš, Košice, Banská Bystrica and Rožňava were assigned. The bishopric of Košice was elevated on **31 March 1995** to an archbishopric with a province encompassing the Košice, Spiš and Rožňava dioceses. The seat of the Greek Catholic bishop is in Prešov. Bishops in the Evangelical (Lutheran) church developed from the office of superintendents. From the last quarter of the 16th century the congregations of the Evangelical Church were associated into larger units called *contubernia* led by elders (seniors). In 1735 the *contubernia* were renamed seniorates. A higher organizational component was the superintendency associating several seniorates. They were headed by elected superintendents. The **Žilina synod of 1610** created an organizational structure for the Evangelical Church with three superintendencies. Later synods modified the number of superintendencies as well as their borders. In 1735 the superintendencies were renamed districts. Since 1919 the Evangelical Church of the Augsburg Confession of the Lutheran Church in Slovakia had two districts, an eastern and a western, each headed by a bishop. During the first Slovak Republic the independent German Evangelical Church of the Augsburg Confession seceded. In 1945 the original ecclesiastical organization was renewed. The seats of the superintendencies, districts and bishoprics are not permanent but change according to where the pastor elected as bishop lives, since he remains the pastor of his parish. /JB/

BLACK ARMY (Black Regiment) – the core of the standing mercenary army of King Matthias Corvinus. The name developed only after the death of Matthias Corvinus and its origins still have not been satisfactorily explained. It is often but inaccurately used to identify the whole mercenary army. Matthias began to form it from the first years of his rule, especially after he concluded an agreement with Ján Jiskra (**Spring 1462**) and when he accepted into his pay some of the former **brethren** after the battle near Veľké Kostoľany (**30 January 1467**). The standing army of Matthias, the most formidable and numerous units of which were armored cavalry and infantry of predominantly non-Hungarian origin, belonged among the most battle-worthy armies in Europe at that time. Thanks to it Matthias was on the whole successful in resisting Ottoman pressure in the Balkans and in conducting an expansionist policy in central Europe. He seized Moravia, Silesia, and Lusatia, as well as the Austrian lands. Gradual growth from an original 6 – 8,000 to nearly 15 – 20,000 mercenary soldiers (with a monthly pay of 3 to 5 **florins** per man) was made possible only by systematically increasing the tax obligations of the serfs and an almost annual collection of the extraordinary military tax (*subsidium*) in the amount of 1 florin from each settlement (*portal*). After the death of Matthias Corvinus the core of the mercenary army went into the service of Vladislav II. However, he proved unable to pay them. Thus the Black Army largely looted and devastated their own territory up to **September 1492**, when the main body was defeated in a battle near the Sava river

by the supreme captain of Lower Austria, Paul Kinizsi, leading noble *banderia* and a *portal* conscript army (insurrection, *insurekcia*). The edict of Vladislav II of 3 January 1493 dissolving the Black Army was a mere formality. /VS/

BOCSKAI'S INSURRECTION – the first insurrection of the estates. When the Transylvanian prince Sigismund Báthory surrendered his office and yielded the territory to the Emperor Rudolph II, the Habsburgs became responsible for defending Transylvania from the Ottomans. However, the Transylvanian nobility concluded a secret alliance with the Ottomans and acknowledged their vassalage. The struggle to become master of Transylvania was influenced by the war of the Habsburgs with the Ottomans and the rivalry between the Catholic and Protestant nobility over their economic and political positions in Hungary. In 1604 opponents of the Habsburgs won over Duke Stephen Bocskai to their idea of an insurrection. When the court discovered the preparations for an armed rebellion, it empowered the imperial general Giacomo Barbiano di Belgiojoso to confiscate the property of Bocskai in Bihar county (1604). Bocskai began an open struggle against the court in Vienna. With the *hajduks*, Ottomans, and his own units, he defeated Belgiojoso and advanced towards Košice. The eastern Slovak nobility and cities originally joined him, because they feared that their property would be confiscated and plundered. The warring parties reached stalemate on the battlefield and so negotiations began in 1605. After naming new noble commanders, the insurgents occupied even the central Slovak mining cities and western Slovakia except for Bratislava during the course of 1605. They undertook marauding raids into Moravia and Austria. Important figures of the insurrection, Stephen Illésházy and Valentine Drugeth, rendered great service in the new negotiations that concluded with the signing of the Peace of Vienna on 23 June 1606. Bocskai obtained the rule of Transylvania and the life-long use of Bihar, Bereg and Ugocsa counties. The privileged classes maintained all their prerogatives and religious freedom but not at the expense of the Catholic religion. All insurgents were amnestied. **Bethlen's insurrection** fought for similar aims. /MK/

BOGOMILS – a heretical sect in Bulgaria and the Balkans. It was based upon the teachings of the priest Bogomil, which derivaded from strict observance of New Testament practice. Their views were disseminated from the mid 10th century and penetrated other countries of the Balkans and the Byzantine Empire. They also influenced heretical movements in western Europe (**Waldensians** and Albigensians). The Bogomils reacted against the official church, church ceremonies, and the veneration of the saints and their relics. They condemned the killing of people and animals and therefore were vegetarians. They organized themselves into communities and regions led by elders. They also influenced Bulgarian literature, although the majority of their works were later destroyed. /JB/

BRATISLAVA COURT – an ecclesiastical court that condemned Protestant pastors. The **Counter-Reformation** reached one of its climactic moments on **25 September 1673** when an extra-ordinary court was convened in Bratislava by Archbishop George Szelepcsényi Pohronec to try 33 Protestant clergy from Turiec, Zvolen and Liptov counties. They were accused of affronts to the Catholic religion and the royal majesty and of being connected the Francis Wesselényi **conspiracy**. Led by Superintendent Joachim Kalinka, all of the indicted went into exile. On **5 March 1674** an additional 350 clergy (out of 700 summoned) came before the court. After longer or shorter imprisonment in Leopoldov or Komárno, nearly three-quarters of them converted to the Catholic faith. Pastors who refused to do so were taken to Naples and sold to serve as Spanish gallery slaves (**1675**). They were freed only after the intervention of the Protestant states. Daniel Sinapius-Horčička, Štefan Pilárik, Juraj Láni, Tobiáš Masník, Ján Simonides and others emigrated. Pressured by protests throughout Europe, the Emperor Leopold I nullified the validity of the Bratislava court in 1676. /VČ/

BRETHREN – military units of former Hussite warriors. After the defeat of the **Hussites** the Brethren associated themselves under the leadership of their former commanders (for example, Friedrich from Ostrog and Peter Šafranec) and penetrated Slovak territory. In **August 1440** Queen Elizabeth engaged the Czech nobleman Jan Jiskra of Brandýs for her service. He was to defend the interests and claims to the throne of her minor son, Ladislas V (Posthumous). Jiskra's army was made up of mercenaries, including many former Hussite warriors. Because they were not regularly paid, they attached themselves to Brethren groups operating in Slovakia. The first references to the Brethren date from 1445 when Jiskra consented to their liquidation. In 1447 the Brethren pillaged cloisters near Lechnica, Letanovce, in Jasov and Nové Mesto nad Váhom, waylaid commercial caravans, and robbed townspeople and serfs. In a period of feudal anarchy, it was not possible to move against them effectively, especially when the warring parties made use of their help. The Brethren occupied the fortresses they captured or established new fortresses or fortified camps. Before 1452 they had field camps at Zelená Hora near Hrabušice and in Haligovce in Spiš, in Chmeľov in Šariš and at the fortresses of Muráň and Plaveč. Later they built camps near Medzilaborce, Sabinov, on the summit of Hrádok in Šariš, on the summit of Tábor nad Krnčou, in Teplice in Spiš, in the area of the abandoned castle of Vyšehrad in Turiec and in Gajary. They captured the fortresses of Košeca and Sárospatak and, around 1461, were entrenched in Peter near Hlohovec and in Veľké Kostoľany. Until the end of the 1450s they had between 15-20,000 armed men and controlled 36 camps and fortified castles. In the camps of the Brethren the Taborite tradition was maintained, the spoils collectively divided, and commanders elected on the basis of bravery. They spread Hussite ideas in their milieu. However, they generally did not gain sympathy even among the serfs, because they lived by fighting and marauding which only worsened the situation of the domestic population. The Brethren movement spread after **1453** when Jiskra was stripped of his office and property and had to leave Hungary. King Ladislas V (Posthumous) recalled him in **1454** in order to fight against the Brethren. Among them were even some of his former commanders (Jan Talafúz, Bartoš from Hartvíkovice, Mikuláš Brcál) as well as nobles of Polish origin, Mikuláš and Peter Komorovský. After Matthias Corvinus ascended the throne, the war against the brethren intensified, especially when Peter Axamit, the commander of the Brethren, fell in battle near Sárospatak in the **spring of 1458**. The nobles Komorovský left the Brethren. King Matthias Corvinus liquidated the last remnants of the Brethren on **30 January 1467** with the capture of the field camp near Veľké Kostoľany. He hanged the commanders led by Captain Ján Švehla and offered service in his **Black Army** to the rest. /JB/

BROTHERHOODS (FRATERNITIES) – associations of priests or laymen in the Middle Ages. The most significant association of priests was the Brotherhood of the Pastors of the 24 Spiš Cities, the beginnings of which go back to 1248. It contributed significantly to strengthening the faith, spreading education and supporting students studying abroad. Its library contained many codices. During the Reformation the members of the Brotherhood of the Pastors converted to **Protestantism** and contributed to the spread of the new doctrine. It disappeared in 1674. Brotherhoods of laymen developed as religious-social organizations for mutual assistance, usually with the name *Corpus Christi* Brotherhood. The oldest known fraternity of this type was established in Bratislava in 1349 and later in Levoča, Kremnica, Hodruša, Banská Bystrica, Banská Štiavnica and elsewhere. In the mining cities the miners joined these brotherhoods and received from its treasury social support or, at the death of a member of the brotherhood, support for their families. The brotherhoods maintained chapels and altars in churches. In the 16th century the brotherhood in Bratislava had a rich library with the works of ancient authors. There also existed brotherhoods dedicated to the Virgin Mary and other saints.

In some cities religious brotherhoods of laymen became the nucleus of **guilds**. /JB/

CALIXTINES see **Hussites**

CANTUS CATHOLICI – the first Slovak Catholic hymnal. It was issued in Levoča in 1655 with the sub-title *Latin and Slovak Catholic Songs (Písne katholické latinské i slovenské)*. It contained 62 Latin hymns and more than 40 Slovak hymns. However hymns of Czech origin (180) predominated. It had many features in common with Tranovský's hymnbook, the **Cithara sanctorum** (which included about 100 hymns). Hymns of a doctrinal and liturgical character predominated in the hymnbook. The Slovak folk environment was manifest especially in songs with Christmas themes, carols and lullabies. Baroque elements were intentionally mixed with popular elements. The *Cantus catholici* did not appear often. Its second edition was published only in 1700 in Trnava. The author of the hymnal, Benedikt Sölöši, was a member of the **Jesuits** and a missionary in several cities in Slovakia. In the Latin introduction to the collection of hymns, he became one of the first authors to emphasize the Cyrilic-Methodian tradition and the glorious past of the Slovak nation. This was the earliest reference in Slovak literature to the Great Moravian era, which later, at the transition from the 17th and 18th centuries, became an integral part of the Slovak cultural milieu. /VČ/

CARDINAL (from the Latin *cardinalis* – hinge) – after the pope, the highest dignitaries of the Catholic Church. Originally this was the dignity of the priests of the most important churches in Rome and of the sufragan bishops of the Roman province; later clergy outside of Rome who made up the advisory council of the **bishop** of Rome were also named cardinals. The pope named the cardinals and their chief right was to elect a new pope. Originally they were few in number but in the 15th century the college of cardinals numbered around 24. During the western schism, the college of cardinals sought to encroach upon the power of the popes and at elections presented them with so-called electoral capitulation or conditions to which they had to adhere. The popes opposed this. Today the college of cardinals has 143 members named by the pope. Only those who have not yet reached 80 years of age now have the right to elect the pope. The cardinals working in Rome usually serve as the heads of various church offices (congregations) or work as papal emissaries (legates, ambassadors and nuncios in various states). Cardinals outside of Rome usually head a province or diocese. Among Hungarian cardinals, Alexander Rudnay was significant in Slovak history. Two Slovaks currently are cardinals, Ján Chryzostom Korec and Jozef Tomko. The symbols of the dignity of a cardinal are the red hat (now abolished), scarlet robes with a cappa magna (great cape), and (if also a bishop) a pectoral cross, ring and miter. /JB/

CARETAKER GOVERNMENT – an element of the constitutional system of the first Czechoslovak Republic. The constitution from **29 February 1920** defined the competence and mutual relations of the government, president and parliament. The president had relatively broad authority in his relationship to the government. He named and dismissed the prime minister and ministers. During a government crisis, when the government lost the ability to properly perform its duties, the president had the right to name the members of a caretaker government, which had to be composed of experts and not of parliamentary deputies and representatives of political parties. Named for a short time, its task was to pacify the political situation and to contribute to the normal functioning of executive power in the state. The first caretaker government in interwar **Czecho-Slovakia** was the government of Ján Černý (**15 September 1929** – 26 September 1921), and others functioned in 1926 (Ján Černý) and 1938 (General Jan Syrový – twice). /RL/

CASTELLAN – administrator of a castle (fortress) and the domain belonging to it. From the 13th century he was, at the same time, the commander of the castle garrison and thus the highest representative of the castle estate after the owner of the **castle,** who was the **king** or another landlord. Subordinate to him in the economic sphere was the *provisor* (accountant), who maintained the business accounts and other officials or sub-officials working directly among the serfs. With the waning of medieval castles, the position of the castellan weakened. When the castle lost its defensive function, he ceased to be the commander of the castle garrison and remained only the administrator of the buildings and sometimes also the forests of the landlord up until the decline of the feudal estates. /VS/

CASTLE (from the Latin *castellum* – castle, fortification) – a fortified center of state and regional administration, the seat of the feudal landlord. Some medieval castles developed by rebuilding original Slavic and old Slovak fortresses or developed in their immediate vicinity (Bratislava, Nitra, Devín). The oldest castles were the seats of **counts** and centers of county administration (**castle county**), later of **counties** (*stolice*), whereby some counties received the name of these older castles (for example, Bratislava, Nitra, Trenčín, Spiš, Gemer, Zemplín, Novohrad and Zvolen). After the Tatar (Tartar) invasion in 1241 the building of castles spread, especially those of the nobility, for which, however, royal permission was necessary. The castles of the nobility became centers of the estates and seats of the landlords. They had a fortified habitable tower (*donjon*) and larger castles had several habitable palaces and a castle chapel. In the lower parts were farm buildings, storehouses, and housing for the garrison and servants. Large castles often had several parts (upper, middle and lower castle) divided into zones by the walls, gates and towers. From the 16th century, when the use of firearms spread and the techniques of siege warfare were perfected, the nobility abandoned their old castles with their difficult approaches and moved into the central community of their estates, where they built manor-houses or new castles (palaces). Older castles fulfilled defensive functions and therefore had corner towers and embrasures (loopholes) etc., as well as a typical square floor-plan with enclosed inner courtyards, sometimes with arcades. Later castles were constructed with new elements of the **Renaissance** building art. However, some castles were reconstructed in this manner as early as in the 14th century (Zvolen castle). They lost their defensive function after the uprisings of the estates in the 17th century when Leopold I had several of them demolished as centers of noble resistance. Many castles were abandoned in the 18th and 19th centuries and, after the departure of the owners for palaces, only ruins remained. In the 19th century some of the nobles, out of nostalgia for older times, built castles on the ruins of old fortresses that were copies of medieval castles or were built according to individual designs. The terminological diversity of the concept of castle that has its equivalents in Latin (*arx, castrum*) and German (*Burg* – fortress, *Schloß* – castle or palace) also found its way into Slovak. The terms fortress (*hrad*) and castle (*zámok*) are equivalents and signify a fortified building on an elevation or on a plain (water castle). Castle (*kaštieľ*) denotes the inhabited noble seat with a park located in the center or at the edge of a village or urban settlement. /JB/

CASTLE COUNTY – a territorial administrative unit in early feudal Hungary also called a royal county. Its core was a royal **castle** that administered the territory belonging to it. Such castles were, for example, those in Bratislava, Nitra, Starý Tekov, Trenčín, Hont, Novohrad, Zvolen, Gemer, Spiš, Šariš and Zemplín. It is probable that many of them had this function in the era of Great Moravia also. From the 11th to the 13th centuries the Hungarian **king** used the castle counties to control the patrimonial state as his own private property. The main administrator of each castle county was a castle count (špán, župan) named by the king. Other officials helped him to fulfill this role, i.e. a count of the court responsible for the judiciary and a **castellan**

who organized the life in and around the castle. The royal soldiers operating in the castle county were subordinated to the castle commander. His subordinates were the centurion (sergeant), the corporal, the herald, and various collectors of payments and taxes. The royal judges, *biloti*, had a special position in the castle counties. The castle counties were transformed into **counties** (*stolica* – seat) at the end of the 13th and the beginning of the 14th century. /VS/

CATHOLIC ACTION – a movement of the laity in the Catholic Church. Pope Pius XI laid its foundation by the encyclical *Ubi arcano Dei* of 23 December 1922. The encyclical stressed the importance of the laity in the church and emphasized their activity in society. The Communist Party of Czechoslovakia misused the expression Catholic Action after the **Communist state coup**. The goal of the communist organized Catholic Action was to create, under the guise of an agreement of the state with the church, a mass movement of priests and believers independent of the Vatican and the bishops. The founding congress of Catholic Action took place in Prague on 10 June 1949. In it participated 253 persons, of whom 68 were "patriotic priests". They accepted the document *Declaration of Catholic Action* and elected a sixty member central committee led by F. Pujman, the director of the National Theater in Prague. The Slovak deputy and teacher Vojtech Török was elected the general secretary. The Slovak and Czech bishops reacted on **15 June 1949** with an illegal pastoral letter (a legal pastoral letter was not possible because of censorship). Priests were offered material advantages for signing the Declaration of the Catholic Action. By mid-July about 1,500 priests had signed the declaration. On 20 June the Vatican condemned Catholic Action in the Czechoslovak Socialist Republic and excommunicated every priest and layperson who had voluntarily consented to it. The priests began to retract their signatures. For reading the illegal pastoral letter and as a preventive measure, 107 priests were imprisoned. Slovak Catholics defended their priests. Proof of their indignation were the 59 demonstrations from May to July 1949. For participating in the disturbances 467 persons were condemned. The commotion around the Catholic Action culminated in the publication of a Vatican decree concerning the excommunication of members of the Communist Party on 14 July 1949. Catholic Action concluded without success. The leadership of the Communist Party of Czechoslovakia set out to fully isolate the bishops and prepared two church laws, adopted on **14 October 1949.** They placed the church fully under state control and made it economically dependent upon the state. The Czechoslovak Socialist Republic broke off diplomatic relations with the Vatican in March 1950. On **13 – 14 April 1950** male orders were dissolved by force, on **29 – 31 August 1950** the female orders, and on **28 April 1950** the Greek Catholic Church. The open campaign against the church culminated in a trial of three Slovak bishops, Ján Vojtaššák, Michal Buzalka and Pavol Gojdič (**10 – 15 January 1951**). /RL/

CELIBACY – the obligation of clergy and monastics in the Catholic and Orthodox churches to remain single and not to marry. Originally this requirement was applicable only for the higher clergy. Celibacy was implemented from the 5th century but not consistently and therefore it was discussed at several church councils (2nd Lateran Council, 1139 and the Council of Trent 1545 – 1563). Despite the efforts of the church hierarchy in Hungary, it generally became established only in the 13th century, when in 1279 the synod of Buda adopted provisions against married priests. During the **Reformation** attempts to abolish celibacy emerged also in the Catholic Church. But the Council of Trent rejected them. In 1742 Pope Benedict XIV allowed married Greek Catholic clergy as in the Orthodox church. At the 2nd Vatican council, 1962 – 1965, attempts again were made to abolish celibacy for Roman Catholic priests but were unsuccessful. /JB/

CHANCELLOR – the head of the chancellery of a secular or ecclesiastical dignitary. The title of chancellor appeared in Hungary in the first half of the 12th century. It was obtained by the administrator (*špán*) or head of the royal chapel, who prepared written documents. The prior of Székesfehérvár was the first to perform the function of chancellor. The chancellor's importance grew with an increase in the productivity of the royal chancellery. He also devoted himself to state matters and a vice-chancellor assumed the real leadership of the chancellery. The chancellor was one of the most influential members of the **royal council**. From the 14th century, after the division of the royal chancellery into a greater and a lesser chancellery, he became the titular head of the greater chancellery and received the title of the chief chancellor. At the same time he became a regular judge of the royal court. After 1526 the Hungarian chancellery declined and its functions were taken over by the Habsburg court chancellery in Vienna. From the 14th century the title chief chancellor devolved upon the archbishop of Esztergom who used it until the 19th century. /VS/

CHAPTER – permanent body of canons at important churches. The association (*collegium*) of the chapter is headed by a dean, provost, or prior. A cathedral chapter existed at the seat of the bishop. The oldest chapter in Slovakia was that of Nitra (probably already in the 11th century). At the transition from the 11th to the 12th century the Bratislava chapter was established and at the beginning of the 13th century the Spiš chapter. After the bishopric of Nitra was restored at the end of the 11th century, the Nitra chapter became a cathedral chapter. In **1543** Trnava became the seat of the cathedral chapter of Esztergom when the chapter and the archbishop fled Esztergom and the Turkish danger. After its transfer to Esztergom in 1820 a vicar of the archbishopric of Esztergom remained in Trnava. With the establishment of new bishoprics and archbishoprics the existing cathedral chapters changed their seats. Only in Bratislava did the cathedral chapter endure from the Middle Ages to the present. Before the 19th century, trials by ordeal were held before the oldest chapters in Nitra and Bratislava, and some chapter-houses were also **credible places** with the right to issue charters. Schools to train future clerics were established at chapter-houses. The oldest evidence for this comes from Nitra and dates back to 1111. A chapter was comprised of 12 to 24 canons. It was led by a dean, prior, or grand prior. In the cathedral chapters the deputy of the bishop, the vicar general, was a member. Other canons had precisely defined functions. The lector was responsible for worship services, the cantor (precentor) for liturgical singing, and the treasurer for the property of the chapter. The canons of the cathedral chapter assisted the bishop in the administration of the diocese. The priors or deans sometimes performed the function of archdeacons (**archdeaconry**). In addition to regular canons, chapters also had honorary members (honorary canons) who might be clerics outside the chapter. /JB/

CHIEF JUSTICE – judge of the country, a high official of the country in the Kingdom of Hungary. As the highest judge he represented the **king**. This office developed from the older institution of judge of the royal court, who was originally the **palatine**. In the 13th century, the chief justice himself constituted the so-called king's presence, which meant he presided over the royal law-court on behalf of the king. He was a member of the **royal council** and, together with the chamberlain, presided over the knights' court of honor. From the end of the 13th century he summoned the court into session at fixed terms designated by octaves (eighth days) after the appropriate ecclesiastical holiday. The octave courts decided all civil and criminal matters, including the confiscation of property or capital punishment. In accord with the strengthening of the **estates monarchy**, his authority was transferred to a collective organ, the royal court of appeals (*tabula*) over which he himself presided. The office of chief justice disappeared in the middle of the 19th century. /VS/

CHRISTMAS AGREEMENT – the constituting document of the underground movement. The underground Slovak National Council was established in September 1943. Its task was to consolidate opposition forces and, at a suitable moment, to assume power, join Slova-

kia to the **Czechoslovak Republic** and to join to the British-American-Soviet coalition. The so-called civic bloc and the communists had differing views of future cooperation. However, the communists had the advantage since, at the end of 1943, it was more or less clear that the Soviet army would occupy central Europe. According to communist representatives, the future Czechoslovak Republic had to be a federal state with a hyphen in its official name. The representatives of the civic bloc disagreed with this. Thus the agreement declared only the general principle of "equal with equal". The communists favored the separation of church and state, the civic bloc was against it. The immediate impulse for the Christmas agreement was the signing of the Czecho-Slovak – Soviet treaty of friendship, mutual assistance and post-war cooperation on **12 December 1943**. With this Edvard Beneš manifested his pro-Soviet orientation, which also had consequences for the non-communist resistance. The Christmas agreement declared the establishment of the **Slovak National Council (1944)**. It contained a decision to base the foreign policy of the future Czechoslovak Republic upon the Soviet Union as the protector of the freedom of small nations. It also declared cooperation with the United States and Great Britain. The internal organization of the Czechoslovak Republic was to be democratic, all fascist, racist, and totalitarian tendencies were to be extirpated and the freedom of religious confession guaranteed. But, at the same time, the influence of the church was to be excluded from setting state policy. These general formulations were a portent of the future political persecution of some of the citizens and interference in the affairs of the church. The Christmas agreement was signed in Bratislava on **25 December 1943** and was later sent secretly to Edvard Beneš in London. It was the starting point for the **Uprising of 1944 – the Slovak National Uprising**. /RL/

CHRONICLES (from the Greek *chronika*) – literary works describing events in a temporal sequence. They are written narrative historical sources. In contrast to **annals,** they not only ordered events in a chronological sequence, but also tried to explain them and to establish a connection between them. In a literary form they described historical events and provided facts about the life of society and data about natural phenomena, catastrophes, descriptions of the country and the like. Alongside the interpretation of historical events they contain moral lessons and examples worth following. *Gesta* had a character similar to chronicles. The oldest chronicles were produced at royal courts, in ecclesiastical and noble milieus and, from the 15th century, also in cities. Sometimes the chronological principle was intentionally violated by the author, who provided an interpretation of the facts or attracted the attention of the reader to gradations in the text. Therefore, chronicles stand at the periphery of historical and literary sources and it is not always possible to consider them reliable. The chroniclers intentionally took over whole passages from older chronicles or adapted them to fit their purposes. Their own contribution was the description of more recent events or the presentation of events that they had personally experienced. In the Middle Ages so-called world chronicles were popular. They described events from the creation of the world up until the period of the writing of the chronicle. In addition, real historical facts were often intertwined with fables, legends and unverified statements contained in older chronicles. The oldest information concerning the empire of Samo is contained in the Fredegar chronicle from the 7th century. Information about the Great Moravian empire to 906 is provided by the chronicle of the Abbot Reginon and its continuations. For the beginning of the 11th century the chronicle of Ditmar (Thietmar), the bishop of Merseburg, is important. Events of the 11th and the beginning of the 12th century are described in the Czech Kosmas chronicle (to 1125) and partially in the Galla Chronicle from the beginning of the 12th century. Hungarian chronicles deal most extensively with the arrival of the old Magyars into the Danubian basin. The oldest *Gesta* of the Hungarians (*Gesta Uhrov*), from the second half of

the 11th century, are not preserved. The Anonymous Chronicle, also called the *Gesta Uhrov*, appeared at the transition from the 12th to the 13th centuries. The chronicle of Šimon of Kéza that continues the *Gesta Uhrov* is from the second half of the 13th century. Hungarian chronicles from the 14th century include the chronicle of Master John of Šarišské Sokolovce, whose material was taken from the Buda and Dubnica chronicles. The *Viennese Illustrated Chronicle* written by Mark of Kalt, dating from the era of Louis the Great, is valuable for its graphic art. The *Viennese Illustrated Chronicle* also contains the oldest, most complete copy of the *Gesta Uhrov*. The chronicle of John of Turiec comes from the 1480s. The chronicle of Spišská Sobota describes events to 1457. A new element in the writing of chronicles was the work of the Italian humanist historians Peter Ransanus, who incorporated an overview of Hungarian history into the *Annals of All Times* (1488 – 1490), and Antonio Bonfini, who wrote a 28 volume Hungarian history (completed between 1491 – 1496), which had more of a literary than a historical value. Rich regional data are contained in the later chronicles of the citizens of Levoča, Konrad Sperfogl (first third of the 16th century) and Gašpar Hain (17th century). In late feudal era popular chronicles were prepared in villages. The writing of chronicles, certainly with other goals and perspectives, continues until the present. In addition to chronicles of various associations and organizations, community chronicles were written, which survive today with various modifications, and were regulated by law as early as 1920. /JB/

CITHARA SANCTORUM (*Harp of the Saints*) – one of the first printed Slovak Evangelical (Lutheran) hymnbooks. It was published in Levoča in 1636 with the sub-title *Old and New Spiritual Songs (Písne duchovní staré i nové)*. It was compiled by the religious exile Juraj Tranovský. After arriving in Slovakia from Czechia in 1629 he worked as the preacher at Budatín and in the service of the Illésházy family at Orava Castle and finally in Liptovský Mikuláš, where he died. He was a creative writer and the author of secular and religious works. The *Cithara sanctorum* contained religious songs from the domestic Slovak milieu, Czech songs, and hymns translated from German and Latin. The language used was a cultivated Czech. Slovak elements penetrated its later editions. The hymnbook served as a source of national consciousness. It was issued in more than 150 editions, supplemented by new hymns, especially of Slovak origin. Daniel Sinapius-Horčička compiled the edition published in 1648. The hymns carried the stamp of baroque religious poetry: lamentations about the difficult fate and the persecution of the Protestants, together with critiques of society connected with the contemporary vision of the end of the world. Social motives also were present. /VČ/

CITY LEAGUES – alliances, associations of cities for the protection of their interests. Most frequently they were geographically contiguous and consisted of cities with the same or similar economic and political interests, especially those which belonged to the same legal system. The oldest city league was the association of the 24 Spiš cities, the beginnings of which are documented by common privileges from 1271. Originally the number of localities sharing this legal system was greater but it stabilized at 24 cities at the end of the 14th century. The first conference of the mining cities of central Slovakia took place in 1388. Although these six cities obtained common privileges in 1405, they cannot be regarded as a league. They became a league only during the course of the 15th century. In 1453 Banská Belá joined them and their number was stabilized at seven: Banská Štiavnica, Banská Bystrica, Kremnica, Pukanec, Nová Baňa , Ľubietová and Banská Belá. In 1412 a conference of the five eastern Slovak cities (Košice, Levoča, Prešov, Bardejov, Sabinov) took place in Košice. A league of these cities was formed (*Pentapolitana*) only in the period 1440 – 1445. To a community of political, military and economic interests was added in the 16th century a common religious position, as the Protestants in the eastern Slovak cities accepted a joint confession of faith, the *Confes-*

sio Pentapolitana, in **September 1549**. Similarly the seven mining cities of central Slovakia accepted the *Confessio Heptapolitana* in 1559. The league of the seven mining cities of eastern Slovakia led by Gelnica was established in **1487** (Gelnica, Smolník, Telkibánya, Rudabánya – both in Hungary, Rožňava, Jasov and Spišská Nová Ves). Common sessions and conferences had taken place already in 1421, although in another grouping (Švedlár and Mníšek were present, while Rožňava, Jasov and Spišská Nová Ves were absent). /JB/

CITY RIGHTS – a collection of legal regulations by which individual cities governed themselves. The most wide-spread legal system was that of the Magdeburg law that was accepted by Székesfehérvár in 1327. This law was adopted by Trnava (1238), Krupina (before 1241), Nitra (1248), the Spiš cities led by Levoča (1271) and Podolínec (1292), which obtained it from Cracow. Žilina, which had been regulated by the Těšín law, adopted the Krupina law in 1369. The Krupina and Žilina law spread to the cities and towns especially in northern Slovakia and it was adopted even by communities with hereditary **magistrates** (*richtár, šoltýs*). The second great legal system was represented by the southern German Nuremberg law, which was first adopted in Hungary by Buda (1244). From there it was adopted by Banská Bystrica (1255), Komárno (1265), Bratislava (1291), Košice (new privileges of 1347), Bardejov (1370), Prešov (1374), Prievidza (1382) and other cities. Due especially to its law, Košice became a place of appeal for the other cities and towns of eastern Slovakia. The law of the mining cities, represented by the Banská Štiavnica law (from the 13th century) based on the Magdeburg law, was used by the six, and from the 15th century, the seven mining cities of central Slovakia. The Gelnica mining law (1276) was used by the six mining cities of eastern Slovakia and seven communities in Spiš. The law of the mining cities was also influenced by the Jihlava law that was adopted by the mining cities at the beginning of the 15th century. This arrangement of legal systems was completed in the 14th century, as the ruler discouraged the bringing of appeals in foreign cities (for example, Tešín for Žilina or Cracow for Podolínec). The law of some cities were combinations of two legal systems (Magdeburg and Nuremberg). From this it is clear that younger (daughter) cities did not always fully adopt the city law of the older (mother) cities. Decisive were city **privileges** by which the ruler regulated in detail the rights and obligations of the cities. The mother cities became places of appeal in judicial and administrative matters for the cities of their legal system. Among the basic city rights belonged the free election of the magistrate and the city priest, exemption from the authority of the royal county administrator (*župan*) and later the county organs, exemption from paying **tolls** (*mýto*) either in the whole territory of the country or in a specific circle and the market right. Among the obligations to the king were the turning over of taxes (*cenzus*), the hosting of the king in case of a visit to the city (*descenzus*), New Year's gifts and, in earlier periods, the responsibility of equipping a certain number of armed men for the royal army. In charters of privilege the mining cities received the right to look for ore deposits on their designated territory, to mine them, as well as the right to fell wood for mining needs and the like. A special right was the **mile right**. Towns and villages with a hereditary magistrate (*richtár*) were allowed to elect only the city council but some cities later acquired rights to the election of the magistrate by buying the hereditary magistracy. Other cities also had the **right of the sword** (to impose capital punishment) and important border towns had the **warehousing right**. As a special category of rights city rights were abolished in 1848. Many customs and rights, including of city ownership of property and the management and internal administration of the cities, survived into the following era. /JB/

CLASSICISM – an artistic movement based on the art of antiquity. It developed at the end of the 17th century in France and in the second half of the 18th century spread throughout all of Europe. It repudiated the **baroque** and adhered to the antique and in part to the **Renaissance**. The intellectual movement corresponding to classicism was the **enlightenment**. It was characterized by rational severity, simplicity and regularity and its ideal was the harmony of truth, beauty and the good. Classicism was expressed especially in architecture, literature, music and painting. In Slovakia it temporally coincided with the first phase of the Slovak national revival (1780 – 1820). The most interesting example of classical architecture is the Primate's Palace in Bratislava. In this period many urban dwellings (houses with upper corridors on interior courtyards), hospitals, office buildings and *redoutas* (casinos or ballrooms) were erected. The distinctive Austrian portrait sculptors Franz Xavier Messerschmidt and Vavrinec Dunajský and portrait and landscape painters Joseph Czauczik, Ján Rombauer and Jozef Božetech Klemens were significant. Popular concerts in the city and country palaces presented the works of Joseph Haydn, Ludwig van Beethoven, Wolfgang Amadeus Mozart and Johann Nepomuk Hummel. Some of these composers also gave concerts in Bratislava or worked for a time in Slovakia. Local artists composed and gave concerts in other regions of Slovakia. Literature was oriented towards educational prose (Jozef Ignác Bajza, Juraj Fándly), and artistic values were established especially by the poetry of Ján Hollý and Ján Kollár. German companies in particular performed in newly opened city theaters and comedies enjoyed popularity (Ján Chalupka). The heroism that was a part of the works of younger intellectuals and artists opened the way to **romanticism**. /DŠ/

CLEVELAND AGREEMENT – the first agreement about the co-operation of American Slovaks and Czechs during the First World War. It co-ordinated the goals of the Czecho-Slovak resistance against Austria-Hungary abroad, the struggle for national liberation and views concerning the internal arrangement of a common state for the Czechs and Slovaks. It was signed in Cleveland on 22 and 23 October 1915 by representatives of the Slovak League in America (Albert Mamatey, Samuel Daxner) and the Czech National Association as the supreme organizations of both nations in the new homeland. The text was suggested by the Czech National Association. Its primary goal was the attainment of independence for the Czech lands and Slovakia and a federal structure for the new state with complete national autonomy for the Czech and Slovak nations (assembly, political, financial, cultural administration, Slovak as the state language). The new state was to have a democratic character including general suffrage. The Cleveland Agreement was the result of the co-operation of Slovak and Czech organizations. The agreement made it easier for the Czech foreign committee, which was transformed in February 1916 into the **Czechoslovak National Council**, to publish the first declaration for the struggle against Austria-Hungary and for an independent Czecho-Slovak state on 14 November 1915. The **Pittsburgh Agreement** corrected aspects of this agreement that would have been detrimental to the authority of Slovakia. /DŠ/

CLOISTER (from the Latin *claustrum* – enclosure) – residence of a community of monastics of the Catholic Church, the Orthodox Church and the ancient eastern Christian churches (Armenian, Ethiopian, Coptic, Syrian and Melchite). Buddhism and Islam also had the institution of cloisters. Christian cloisters had origins in the hermitages of early Christian Egypt and Asia Minor. They developed by the gradual concentration of eremites (hermits) into communities that eventually built fortified structures which included worship, housing, service and farm buildings. The inhabited part, the so-called *clausura,* was closed to outsiders and especially members of the opposite sex. The first cloistered communities developed in the 4th century in the Byzantine Empire. In the west cloisters developed in the 4th to 5th centuries, especially in southern Italy. In both cases they were guided by the rule of Basil the Great, hence the name Basilians. They laid the foundations for Catholic cloisters. Cloisters were centers of learning. The oldest were built in remote places and were fortified like castles. The developing

mendicant **religious orders** built cloisters in cities, usually at the city limits where they were incorporated into the defensive system of the city. The majority of cloisters disappeared during the **Reformation**. In the era of the **Counter-Reformation** some of them were renewed or their buildings were obtained by new orders of the church. Joseph II abolished a significant number of the cloisters. Their buildings were transformed into state buildings or barracks, or served school and charitable purposes. On **13 – 14 April** and **29 – 31 August 1950** cloisters were abolished in the Czechoslovak Socialist Republic, the monastics were interned, and many valuable cultural and artistic artifacts were destroyed or stolen. /JB/

CODICES – manuscript books of a non-official character. The name comes from the Latin *caudex* – plate, which also signified joined wooden waxed tables. Early in the Middle Ages codices shaped like the books of today developed alongside scrolls, rolls of paper wound around two cylinders. They were pieces of papyrus or parchment bound together. Parchment was employed as a writing material up to the 14th century, when much cheaper paper began to be used. However, illustrated codices, used primarily for liturgical purposes, continued to be prepared from parchment. They were richly decorated with initials (ornamental initial letters of sections and chapters) and miniatures (illustrations in codices). The borders of the pages, the spaces between the columns, and the free spaces of the codices were embellished with ornamental figures or plant motifs that had only a decorative function and were not illustrations of the text. For illustrations in codices gold and occasionally silver ink was used and the background color was often purple. The book painting of codices was influenced by existing artistic styles (Romanesque, Gothic, Renaissance), but, on the other hand, book painting influenced wall and panel painting. Codices can be divided into liturgical, scholarly (from various areas of learning) and non-scholarly or entertainment (contemporary fiction) codices. The aforementioned codices of representational character, with rich pictorial decorations, comprised a distinct group. Centers for the production of codices were the **cloisters** where writing sections, *scriptoria,* existed. They specialized in copying liturgical codices to meet liturgical needs. Further centers for such production were universities, at which codices with scholarly content (philosophy and theology, especially) were primarily produced. It was not unusual for those concerned with the copying or creating of new codices to be prominent scholars, for example, city notaries, scribes, or priests outside the *scriptoria.* After the invention of printing, the preparation of manuscript books disappeared during the course of the 16th and 17th centuries and from the mid 15th century codices began to be replaced by printed books (*incunabula*). /JB/

COLLECTIVIZATION – the forced consolidation of land. In Slovakia it took place in several stages between 1949 and 1989. The goal of this process was the liquidation of the class of propertied, middle-sized farmers, by creating unified cooperative farms (JRD) a new type of "cooperative farmer", as well as the recruitment of workers for industry by their movement from villages to the cities. The Communist Party of Czechoslovakia used the minister of agriculture (Július Ďuriš) to obtain the land and politically exploit the farmers under the guise of land reform. As early as November 1948 the plenary session of the Central Committee of the Communist Party of Czechoslovakia approved the policy of "the socialist transformation of agriculture". The law on unified cooperative farms was subsequently passed (**22 February 1949**), and the basic political line adopted at the 9th congress of the Communist Party of Czechoslovakia (25 – 29 May 1949) called for the intensification of the class struggle in the villages. The national committees and the organs of power especially persecuted the "village plutocracy", the so-called *kulaks* (in Czechia those who owned 20 hectares, in Slovakia those who held 15 hectares of land and later even less), and under various pretences assigned farmers to **labor camps**, imprisoned, or reset-

tled them, together with their families. The failure to fulfill often unrealistic state delivery quotas or the refusal to join a unified cooperative farm were likewise reasons for punishment. A total of nearly 500,000 farmers in Slovakia were imprisoned or fined. Pressure on them moderated in 1955 but did not stop. In 1960 the "socialist sector" in Slovakia cultivated 67.5 percent of the soil. Existing cooperatives were combined and thus even larger agricultural enterprises were created. /RL/

COLONIZATION – the founding of settlements, the settlement of empty or sparsely inhabited territory. It can be internal or external. Internal colonization, realized especially by the yeomanry and thus referred to as a yeoman colonization, completed the settlement of the territory of Slovakia from the 12th to the 14th centuries. The rulers carved out land from the territory of the old Slovak villages and gave it to their loyal supporters, especially in Turiec, Liptov and the upper part of Trenčín county. External colonization took place when the ruler summoned colonists from abroad. These were especially miners, craftsmen and merchants, who were to support the domestic mining enterprises, production and trade. The first wave of colonists came from German lands at the middle of the 12th century and brought their own legal tradition, the so-called **German law**. This phase lasted until the 15th century. The term used for it, German colonization, is not completely accurate, because, under this law, which was more favorable than the domestic customary law, not only Germans were resettled but also members of other nations and even the domestic population, the Slovaks. In addition to the colonists who settled in the cities, there was also a village colonization under the emphyteutic or German law. The representative of the colonists was an hereditary **magistrate** (*richtár, šoltýs, fojt, advokát*), whose responsibility was to recruit the population and to establish a settlement with them. For this the new village was freed from taxes for several years or even decades. Sometimes this form of colonization is called "šoltýs colonization". The šoltýs (*lokator* – leasor) was usually a German, but the colonists themselves were Slovaks or Poles, Ruthenians or even Magyars. From the 14th to the 17th century colonization under the **Walachian Law** took place. This is imprecisely called the Walachian colonization, since in fact not only Walachians (from Romania) but also Ruthenians, Ukrainians, Poles, Slovaks and even German elements participated in it. The originally nomadic Walachians later permanently settled in the mountainous and foothill regions of northern Slovakia and along the upper Hron River. The final wave of colonization was based on the so-called "mountain farmer law", which settled the remnant of the unsettled territory in the mountainous and less fertile regions. It intensified especially in the 16th and 17th centuries when the Turkish wars, internal disturbances and insurgencies of the estates led to a deterioration in the position of the general population. They expected that by cultivating and fertilizing fallow fields they would obtain a more favorable position with the landlords. /JB/

COMMUNE see Občina

COMMUNIST PARTY OF CZECHOSLOVAKIA – a party of the radical left. It adhered to the teachings of Karl Marx, Friedrich Engels, Joseph Visarionovich Stalin and Vladimír Iljich Lenin. It pursued the ideology of class struggle, the introduction of a dictatorship of the proletariat, the creation of a classless communist society and advocated the elimination of private property and a materialistic world view. Its goal was a socialist revolution and the seizure of power in the state. A pre-condition for the establishment of communist parties in Europe was the victory of the Bolshevik revolution in Russia in 1917. The Communist Party of Czechoslovakia was formed by the crystallization of a radical current within the Social Democratic Party. In Slovakia it was established in Ľubochňa on **16 January 1921**. At the founding congress in Prague on 14 – 16 May 1921 it merged with the Czech left. On the order of the Communist International in Moscow, a congress in Prague (31 October – 4 November 1921) merged the "nationality sections" (Czechoslovak, Ger-

man, Hungarian, Polish and Jewish) into a single state-wide party under the name Communist Party of Czechoslovakia. During the inter-war period it was in opposition. It was the only political party in Czechoslovak Republic that, from the beginning, was controlled from abroad, from Moscow. It declared that social questions were to take priority over nationality and cultural issues. In the 1920s, on the orders of the Comintern, it proclaimed the right of nations to self-determination even to the point of secession. In elections in Slovakia it obtained 10 – 14 per cent of the votes. Support came from the workers and the small farmers, especially the non-propertied agricultural workers of Magyar nationality. In an attempt to intensify conflicts, bring about open confrontations and transform them into open revolution, it resorted to extra-parliamentary forms of pressure (strikes, demonstrations riots and marches). These actions often ended in bloodshed. Therefore its members and followers often were condemned under the law for the defense of the republic of **3 March 1923**. A more moderate policy was pursued in the years 1935 – 1938 in accordance with the international tactics of Moscow. The Slovak autonomous government was unwilling to work with parties adhering to Marxist ideology. The Communist Party of Czechoslovakia was suspended on **9 October 1938,** and dissolved by the Czechoslovak government (27 December 1938) and the Slovak autonomous government as well (23 January 1939). The party went underground. Led by Klement Gottwald, its leadership emigrated to Moscow, where it worked until 1945. In accordance with the decision of the Communist International in May 1939 the Communist Party of Slovakia was created as an independent party after the establishment of the first **Slovak Republic**. However, it did not become an independent section of Comintern. Members of its four underground committees were arrested by the Slovak security organs; the fifth committee (including Gustáv Husák, Karol Šmidke, Ladislav Novomeský), together with former leaders of the **Agrarian Party,** signed the **Christmas Agree-**

ment on **25 December 1943**, created the illegal **Slovak National Council (1944)** and took part in the preparations for and the carrying out the armed **Uprising of 1944**. After the renewal of the Czechoslovak Republic, the Communist Party of Slovakia initially tried to create a Czecho-Slovak **federation**. However, after the conference in Žilina on 11 – 12 August 1945, its policy was completely subordinated to that of Communist Party of Czechoslovakia. It participated in limiting the authority of the Slovak national organs and in preparing for the **Communist state coup**. After the coup, the Communist Party of Czechoslovakia – Communist Party of Slovakia became the single decisive political force in the state. (Its leading role in society was anchored in the constitution of **11 July 1960** and was maintained until **29 November 1989**). On 27 – 29 September 1948 the Communist Party of Slovakia lost its organizational autonomy and became a territorial organization of the Communist Party of Czechoslovakia. All important decisions of the Communist Party of Slovakia had to be approved in advance by the Central Committee of the Communist Party of Czechoslovakia. The regime of the communists carried out mass persecutions of citizens from all social groups, the church (**Catholic Action**), members of banned parties and even communists (for example **21 – 24 April 1954**), and forcibly implemented **collectivization** and **industrialization**. Communist power was maintained only with the help of the Soviet Union, by corruption and by creating an atmosphere of fear and violence. Especially after the occupation by the armies of the Warsaw Pact in 1968, its policies were rejected not just by **dissidents** but also by the majority of the people. /RL/

COMMUNIST STATE COUP – the seizure of complete power in the state by the Communist Party of Czechoslovakia. The Communist Party of Czechoslovakia obtained a decisive position in the political life of the **Czechoslovak Republic** as early as the **Moscow negotiations** in **1943** and **1945**, and contributed to the acceptance of the **Košice government program** and the introduction of a National Front system. From 1945 the Czechoslovak Socialist Republic belonged to the Soviet sphere of influence. As the ruling party, the Communist Party of Czechoslovakia's goal was to obtain absolute power. Its position in the Czech part of the state was strengthened by the elections of **26 May 1946**. In the fall of 1947 the foreign communist parties criticized the leadership of the Communist Party of Czechoslovakia for inclining to parliamentarianism. The worsening relationships between the eastern and western blocs speeded up the complete seizure of power by the communists. Non-communist parties in the Czechoslovak Socialist Republic were not able to counteract their aggressive tactics. In the period of political crisis, some of them agreed to halt the growing power of the Communist Party of Czechoslovakia (**13 February 1948**). However, their interests were very different and coordination among them was inadequate. The ministers of the Czechoslovak Party of National Socialists, the Czechoslovak People's Party and the Democratic Party agreed to hand in their resignations on 16 February. They failed to consult with the social democrats on this step and relied on the support of President Edvard Beneš. Their decision was motivated by the approaching congress of factory councils (22 February 1948), which was being prepared by the communist-dominated trade unions and was to declare a further **nationalization**. The resignations were intended to forestall the declaration of a government crisis, which the communists could use to obtain concessions at the formation of a new government and to speed up the calling of parliamentary elections. Expecting a crisis, the deputy of the Soviet minister of foreign affairs, Valerian Alexandrovich Zorin, flew to the Czechoslovak Socialist Republic and expressed Stalin's concerns about developments in the country. In case the peaceful seizure of power failed, the Soviet Army was to intervene. Klement Gottwald assured Zorin that the Communist Party of Czechoslovakia had the situation under control. On 20 February twelve ministers of three non-communist parties submitted their resignations (from the Democratic Party Štefan Kočvara, Ivan Pietor, Mikuláš Franek and Ján Lichner). This was a minority since fourteen ministers remained in office. The leadership of the Communist Party of Czechoslovakia decided to use the government crisis for a state coup using the pretext of a "reactionary conspiracy". Its practical realization was entrusted to the reserve units of police and the National Security Force and the People's Militia. The congress of the factory councils in Prague on 22 February (8,000 delegates), which declared a general strike for 24 February, was used as an extra-parliamentary form of pressure. During the crisis, the non-communist parties failed to use the parliament to dismiss the communist premier, Klement Gottwald. President Edvard Beneš accepted the resignation of the minority parties of the government on **25 February 1948** and confirmed the list of the new members of the government of the "revived" National Front that Gottwald presented to him. His decision was awaited by a communist demonstration of 250,000 people in Prague and thousands of demonstrators in other cities. In Slovakia the chairman of the board of commissioners Gustáv Husák resolved the crisis. After consulting with Klement Gottwald on 21 February, he illegally dismissed the commissioners from the Democratic Party. The period of the communist dictatorship followed. /RL/

CONCLAVE – closed space for the election of the pope, in a broader sense the assembly of cardinals at this election. Originally the **pope** was elected by the people and clergy of Rome. However, various external forces including the Italian (Roman) nobility and German emperors interfered with this. Therefore, in 1059, Pope Nicholas II transferred the right to elect the pope to the cardinals. In an attempt to completely exclude external influences, Pope Gregory X set out the conditions for the election of the pope at the 2nd Council of Lyon in 1274. The cardinals were to meet within ten days after the death of a pope. They had to be completely isolated from the world during the election. In order that the election would not be prolonged, after three days of

discussions they would have only one meal per day and, after a further five days, only bread and water. A two-thirds majority of the votes of the cardinals present was necessary to elect a pope. Later popes mitigated some of the provisions of this law. /JB/

CONGRESS OF NON-MAGYAR NATIONALITIES (nationalities congress) – demonstrative assembly of representatives of the Slovaks, Serbs and Romanians. It was the largest joint action of suppressed nationalities in the Kingdom of **Hungary**. It took place after several years of preparation on **10 August 1895** in Budapest. More than 600 delegates, 200 of them Slovaks, participated in it. One of the three chairmen was Pavol Mudroň. The goal of the congress was to promulgate a common program against national oppression and the non-democratic regime. The program contained 22 points, which asserted the integrity of Hungary but rejected the idea of a greater Hungary that had entailed **Magyarization**. It demanded the abolition of the **nationalities law** and the enactment of laws recognizing the equality of nations, the conduct of official business in the counties and communities in the mother tongue, educational and church autonomy for each nation, the liberalization of the policy of the regime (for instance, universal suffrage, the founding of primary schools and adherence to fundamental civic liberties), a revision of the church policy laws and the naming of a minister of the Hungarian government for each nationality. The congress elected a 12 member nationalities committee (for the Slovaks: Pavol Mudroň, Miloš Štefanovič, Samuel Daxner, Ján Vanovič) that was to coordinate cooperation, assert itself against oppression, call a new congress and inform both the domestic and foreign public about the nationalities question in the Kingdom of Hungary. The congress had considerable international repercussions. The Bánffy government reacted to it with the increased persecution of non-Magyar politicians. This was another reason why its grand aims were not fulfilled. /DŠ/

CONGRESS OF VIENNA – political negotiations concerning new arrangements for security and peace in Europe after the Napoleonic Wars. It began on **18 September 1814** and concluded on 9 June 1815 with the acceptance of a concluding document of 121 points. Representatives of more than 200 states and mini-states participated in it and it was presided over by the Austrian minister of foreign affairs, Clement Wenceslas Metternich. During the congress the number of the inhabitants of Vienna increased by about 100,000 people; 700 politicians and experts participated in the discussions. The congress decided that policy in Europe would be based upon conservative principles, which had been suppressed by the French revolution and Napoleonic power. It renewed the principle of legitimacy, which stressed the authority of monarchical power and dynasties and the principle of intervention that made possible external intervention in the case of the spread of revolutionary, liberal or national ideas and movements. It strengthened the shaken self-confidence of the absolutist regimes and the position of old ruling classes. The victorious powers abolished the territorial changes effected by the Napoleonic wars. Austria surrendered Belgium to the Netherlands and obtained territory in northern Italy, Galicia and Dalmatia. Security order and equilibrium in Europe were to be secured by the concerted action of the great powers, that is, their cooperation. The resolutions of the congress were most consistently fulfilled in Russia and the **Habsburg Monarchy,** where **Metternichian absolutism** reigned. After three peaceful decades, suppressed antagonisms erupted in the **revolution of 1848/1849**. Many resolutions of the congress became permanently valid in diplomacy (rules of protocol for example) and others (for example, the concert of powers, the prevention of conflict through negotiations) created the basis for political equilibrium in Europe up to the end of the 19th century, when the great powers divided into two hostile blocs. /DŠ/

CONSPIRACY OF FRANCIS WESSELÉNYI – one of the attempts of the Hungarian nobility to overthrow the Habsburgs. After the **Insurrection of George I. Rákoczi**, the Turks and the Habsburgs sought to preserve the agreed peace. However, it was often violated in the countryside. The imperial commanders of the border fortresses undertook predatory raids in Turkish territory or, in the service of the nobles and counties, sought to collect taxes there. On the other hand, the Turkish *begs* on the borders increased the taxes and payments for the serfs in the villages subject to them. The nobles began to accuse the emperor of a lack of interest in Hungary since he did not want to intervene against the Turks. They also were dissatisfied with the unfavorable Peace of Vasvár concluded on **10 August 1664**. Disputes over economic and religious questions were added to this. In April 1666, **Palatine** Francis Wesselényi began to recruit a noble opposition to the Habsburgs. Among those who joined it were important personalities of Hungary, the Croatian ban, Peter Zrínyi, the archibishop of Esztergom, George Lippay (died in 1666), the **chief justice** Francis Nádasdy, Francis Frankopán and other important **magnates**. They sought help from France and later were willing to yield Hungary as a vassal state to the Ottoman Empire. After collecting sufficient information about the preparation of the insurrection, the court in Vienna intervened firmly against them in 1669. Many nobles were investigated, arrested and brought before a court. The main leaders of the conspiracy were executed on **30 April 1671**. Others were condemned to the complete or partial loss of their lands. A vice-regal council assumed the government in Hungary on **27 February 1673.** The counties had to maintain imperial armies through an apportionment system (precisely regulated contributions of foodstuffs and feed), while the taxes of the subjects and pressure on the Protestants also increased. /MK/

CONSTITUTIONAL MONARCHY – a form of monarchy. It began to develop in the 17th century in England (from the Restoration of Charles II in 1660) and spread especially during the 19th century. It was a compromise between radical enlightenment views that regarded the people as the source of power and adherence to old **absolutism** or an **estates**

monarchy. Its basis was the division of power between the sovereign, government, and the "representatives of the people", the parliament, i.e. an equilibrium of power between the crown and the parliament. It was characterized by the equality of people before the law, a written constitution and popular representation. Until the **revolution of 1848/1849** the **Habsburg Monarchy** was a traditional absolutist state. Then **Metternichian absolutism** collapsed and the foundations of constitutional relationships were established. The sovereign shared power with the imperial government and assembly and, in Hungary, with the Hungarian government and diet. The constitutional monarchy did not develop further since **neo-absolutism** followed the defeat of the revolution. It began to be restored with the **October Diploma** of 1860, a restoration which was completed after the Austrian-Hungarian (Magyar) Compromise. The power of Francis Joseph I, during whose reign the government changed 42 times, was limited by the constitution, the Austrian assembly and Hungarian diet, and governments dominated by Austrian German conservatives and liberals and the Magyar great landowners. However, in the era of **dualism**, the ruler was not merely a symbolic figure in a parliamentary monarchy but also had a large share of the power. After the enactment into law of general suffrage in the Cisleitha part of the monarchy in 1907 the constitutional monarchy began to be influenced by popular elements. The monopoly of power in Hungary was held by the old propertied classes until the dissolution of Austria-Hungary. In the 20th century constitutional monarchy in European kingdoms has been replaced by parliamentary government. /DŠ/

COTTERS (ŽELIARI) (Latin *inquilini* – tenant, lodger) – members of the poorest strata of the subject population. They had various local names – *hoštáci, hofieri, domkári, chalupníci*. The cotters (tenants) occupied only a house and agricultural land with an area less than one eighth of a serf **farmstead**. They paid **feudal rent** to the landlords according to the area of land occupied. The *Theresian urbár* of 1772 required 18 days of work on foot (without draft animals) per year. The cotters without a house were called *podželiari* (sub-tenants) and usually lived as sub-tenants of the **peasants**. Their obligations to the landlord were specifically defined. They provided various services and, for example, worked as craftsmen, shepherds, couriers, fishermen and the like. In the 17th century the landlords began to demand compulsory work (*robota*) from the sub-tenants. The country-wide *urbár* (1772) required from them 12 days of labor on foot per year. Although the **March laws** of 1848 abolished feudal obligations and relationships, the cotters remained in a dependent relationship towards the former landlords because they lived on their property and, for the use of a house or lesser agricultural land, paid rent in money or in the form of work (*robota*). In the second half of the 19th century the share-croppers and day laborers were created from this social class. They became the free reserve in the labor force that was used for developing industry. /JB/

COUNCIL – assembly of the highest dignitaries of the Catholic Church (namely, diocesan bishops and other ordinaries) concerned with the most important questions of faith, dogma and current ecclesiastical-political matters. The first general (ecumenical) councils (325 – 787) laid the basis of the dogmatic unity of the eastern and western church. After the so-called eastern (great) **schism** in 1054 councils were held only in the western, Roman Catholic Church. By the removal of the three competing popes, the Council of Constance succeeded in surmounting the greatest crisis of the western church in the 15th century. At the same time, the Council of Constance and the subsequent council in Basle declared the supremacy of the council over the papacy (conciliarism), which the **pope** never recognized. The Catholic Church considers a general or ecumenical council to be one over which the pope himself presides. Some of the negotiations of the councils in Constance and Basle did not have this character. The doctrine of papal primacy and the infallibility of the pope in maters of faith and morals were declared by the First Vatican Council in 1870. The last ecumenical council, the Second Vatican Council (11 October 1962 – 8 November 1965) began a new stage in the history of the Roman Catholic Church. In addition to internal ecclesiastical questions (for instance, the introduction of liturgy in national languages), it took a positive stance towards non-Catholics and other Christian religions (ecumenism) and defined the role of Catholicism and Catholics in the modern era. /JB/

COUNT (*gróf,* earl) – a member of the higher nobility (**magnate**). During the reign of Charlemagne in the Frankish Empire, this title denoted the official at the head of a territorial-administrative province called a *gau*, from which, as a rule, counties later developed. In early feudal Hungary the position of count corresponded to that of a castle or county administrator, which in Latin was signified by the title *comes* (*špán* or *župan*). From the 15th century the title of count in Hungary began to be linked with the hereditary administration of some seats (*stolice,* counties) or propertied domains (for instance, the Hunyady as hereditary counts of Bystrica in Transylvania or the Zapolyas as hereditary counts of Spiš). From 1526, under the rule of the Habsburgs, the title of count was bestowed in the German-imperial manner, that is, without a grant of new estates to already existing lands. From **1608** counts constituted the middle grade of the magnate estate. In hierarchical rank, they stood below the **dukes** (knieža) and above the **barons**. Status as a count was expressed in heraldry by a nine-pointed crown in the jewel of the family coat-of-arms. /VS/

COUNTER-REFORMATION – an ecclesiastical-political movement in the 16th – 18th centuries. It focused on halting the spread of the **Reformation** and renewing the Catholic Church and was organized by the papal curia and the church hierarchy in cooperation with rulers of the Catholic faith. It began to be implemented especially after the Tridentine Council (1545 – 1563) and gradually succeeded in eliminating **Protestantism** in the Italian and Iberian peninsulas, in the greater part of France, Poland, and to a preponderant degree

in the kingdoms of Bohemia and of Hungary. It achieved partial success even in Germany, Switzerland and Holland. The beginning of the Counter-Reformation in Hungary was connected with the name of Nicholas Oláh, the archbishop of Esztergom. At the middle of the 16th century he called the **Jesuits** to Hungary. They contributed decisively to the success of the Counter-Reformation struggle. Also significant were the activities of Archbishop Peter Pázmány who, on 6 May 1635, founded a university in Trnava and personally reconverted to Catholicism members of important magnate and noble families. Royal and state organs joined in the Counter-Reformation conflict. In the struggle against religious opponents they also used force (**re-Catholization**). Frequently the unresolved religious question was the cause or pretext for the insurrections of the estates of the Hungarian **nobility**. In the 18th century force ceased to be utilized against the Protestants, although their persecution retained legal force. The **Toleration Patent** of Joseph II brought the Counter-Reformation in Hungary to an end. /VČ/

COUNTY (STOLICA) – basic territorial-administrative unit during feudalism in Hungary. Territorially the counties (*stolica,* seat) were a continuation of the **castle counties** and developed at the end of the 13th and beginning of the 14th centuries as the self-governing organization of the **nobility** in a given territory. In the 14th and 15th centuries, the noble community assumed responsibility for the whole public administration of political, economic and cultural life in the counties. There were about 70 counties in Hungary during the Middle Ages and after the final expulsion of the Turks. All or the major parts of the following counties were located on the territory of today's Slovakia: Abov, Bratislava, Gemer-Malohont, Hont, Komárno, Liptov, Nitra, Novohrad, Orava, Esztergom, Spiš, Šariš, Tekov, Trenčín, Turiec, Turňa, Uh, Zemplín and Zvolen. The link between the counties and the ruler and central state power was the administrator (*župan*, count), later the chief administrator. His deputy and later the highest elected officer of county self-government was the vice-administrator (*podžupan*, viscount). Usually four assistants (*slúžni*) worked with him. Together they made up the county tribunal (*sedria*). The main organ of self-administration of the county was the general congregation or the assembly of all nobles. The counties were a fundamental element of the political system of the estates in Hungary. They represented the main pillar of the middle and lower nobility (**yeomen**) in their struggles against the centralizing efforts of the Habsburg court (**absolutism**) as well as against the interests of the **magnates**. Up to the reign of Maria Theresa they regulated the relations of serfs, so that they were also an instrument for their suppression. The counties lost their estates or noble character in the **revolution of 1848/1849,** when they were replaced by the *župy* (counties or districts). Some institutions, modified functions or officers of the counties survived until 1918. /VS/

CREDIBLE PLACES (Latin *loca credibilia)* – were individually designated **chapters** (Bratislava, Nitra and Spiš) and **cloisters** (the Premonstratensian in Jasov, Leles, Šahy and Kláštor pod Znievom, the **Benedictines** on Zobor near Nitra and Hronský sv. Beňadik), which had the right to issue, copy and confirm charters at the request of the parties to them. They also housed the charters and thus served as a kind of public archives. They had authentic seals at their disposal. In addition, they also performed functions connected with the inspection of property deeds by the representatives of the state administration (*homo regius*), issued certificates for this, and transcribed the evidence of witnesses who came before them in some legal matters. They performed the function of public notaries. This was peculiar to Hungary. The existence of credible or trustworthy places was already attested in the renewal of the **Golden Bull** of Andrew II in 1231. Not all of the credible places mentioned continued to function. In the 14th century this activity of the cloisters had so expanded that, by a law of 1351, King Louis the Great forbade the smaller cloisters from issuing charters in public law matters. During this period the number of credible places stabilized. For the territory of Slovakia this function was performed also by the chapters of Esztergom, Buda and Székesfehérvár, as well as those close to southern Slovakia (Györ, Vác, Eger). In 1874 a law concerning royal public notaries ended the activity of the credible places. /JB/

CUBISM (from the French *cube* – cube) – designation for an artistic movement. It developed in France at the very beginning of the 20th century and spread throughout Europe. Cubism is based on the idea of the creative and constructive autonomy of a picture. As an artistic movement it was expressed both in painting and sculpture. It was in vogue in parallel with **functionalism** in architecture and used regular geometric forms. Heterogeneous and polymorphous depictions of reality were reduced to basic stereo-metrical values. The "discovery" of prehistoric art inspired it. Among the founders of cubism were the painters Georges Braque and Pablo Picasso as well as the sculptors Alexander Archipenko and Raymond Duchamp-Villon. Cubism influenced especially the works of Slovak painters such as Ľudovít Fulla, Mikuláš Galanda, Ján Mudroch, Sergei Charchoun, Ján Želibský, Ernest Zmeták and Milan Laluha. /RL/

CURIAL VILLAGE – a village in which nobles lived and had their own curia (from the Latin *curia*, court). During the 13th and 14th centuries a multitude of **yeomen** and their properties emerged as a result of the bestowal of noble privileges and the subdividing of large royal estates, especially around royal castles. Formally they had the same rights as the other nobles but, because of their weak economic position, they did not take part in the **diet**. Curial villages had neither a magistrate (*richtár*) nor self-administration. In addition to the nobility (curialists), **tenant farmers** (*želiari*) subtenant farmers and, exceptionally, a few serfs subordinated to the curialists also lived in the curial villages. Since the curialists did not have serfs, they had to pay land and, occasionally, military taxes. Therefore they were also called taxed nobles (*nobiles taxati*). Most of the curial villages were located in Turiec and in Liptov. Curial villages and the special status of curialists were abolished in 1848 with the adoption of the **March laws**. /JB/

CYRILIC see **Glagolitic**

CZECHOSLAVIC SOCIETY (also the Czechoslovak Society) – a national defense society in Prague, founded on 7 May 1896, for the support of culture in the remote regions of Czechia and Slovakia. From 1908 it was focused solely on assistance for Slovakia. In 1913 it had 22 local branches in Czechia with 3,477 members, of which approximately 150 were Slovaks. Its chairmen were František Pastrnek, Jozef Otto, Ján Rychlík, František Táborský and Joseph Rothnágl, and its membership included other leading Czech Slovakophiles. The society sent books to Slovakia, established libraries, financially assisted Slovak students and advised Slovak apprentices and agricultural workers in the Czech lands. It supported the investment of Czech capital in Slovakia, the publication of Slovak newspapers, organized discussions in Prague about Slovakia, published the *Slovak Reader (Slovenská čítanka)* and from 1907 to 1911 the magazine *Our Slovakia (Naše Slovensko)*. From **August 1908** it organized regular conferences between leading Czech and Slovak personalities in Luhačovice. The most important took place in **August 1911**. One of the topics of the conferences was the possible political union of Czechs and Slovaks, which appeared to be a realistic option during the First World War. The Slovak side welcomed the revival of Czecho-Slovak mutuality. However, the society understood it in the spirit of a Czechoslovak national union (**Czechoslovakism**), which was repudiated by the majority of Slovak politicians. Therefore, they adopted a reserved attitude towards its activity. The **hlasists** (Vavro Šrobár, Pavol Blaho, Anton Štefánek) had the closest contacts with the society. /DŠ/

CZECHOSLAVONIC SOCIETY (also Czechoslovak Society) – a self-education society of students at the Evangelical lyceum in Bratislava. Samo Chalupka, Karol Štúr, Daniel Lichard and Samuel Godra founded it in 1829. A professor of the lyceum was the nominal president but it was really led by a vice-president from the ranks of the students. Like German and Magyar societies, it originally educated its members, future clergymen and teachers, in the native language. In 1834 – 1835 the character of the society was changed, especially by Alexander Boleslavín Vrchovský, who maintained contact with secret Polish and Czech student societies. He so shaped it that it became the nucleus of the Slovak national movement, adopted a spirit of free thought and modern patriotism and urged social reforms and the development of Slovak national culture (**romanticism**). Its activity climaxed in 1835 – 1837 during the vice-presidency of Ľudovít Štúr. The number of members grew to 120. They were interested in political events and the position of the suppressed classes and the Slovaks. They obtained trustworthy local knowledge through contacts with patriots in the country and Slovak students and by travel throughout Slovakia. They were inspired by the idea of **Slavic mutuality**, organized excursions to historically significant sites, especially to Devín (**24 April 1836**), issued the almanac *Fruits (Plody)* in **February 1836**, improved libraries and at meetings presented their own poetry and scientific treatises. After the prohibition of student societies in Hungary, it disbanded on **5 April 1837**. Due to the efforts of Ľudovít Štúr, its activities were transferred to the Department of Czechoslavonic language and literature with the name Slovak (Slavic) Institute. Its heritage was preserved by the **Štúr group** and, shortly thereafter the radical students created the society Mutuality (*Vzájomnosť*). /DŠ/

CZECHO-SLOVAK LEGIONS – military units in the First World War (this name took hold only after it had ended). They were created with the assent of the states of the Entente by the **Czechoslovak National Council** (especially Milan Rastislav Štefánik), to which they were subordinated. They were its chief power base in the pursuit of state independence for the Czechs and the Slovaks and in its quest for diplomatic recognition by the states of the Entente. They fought alongside their armies against **Austria-Hungary** and Germany. They are referred to as the legions in France, Italy and Russia according to the places they were established and operated. In France they began to be formed in 1914 from the *Nazdar* Battalion, which was part of the Foreign Legion. There they developed into an autonomous army only on the basis of an agreement between the French government and the Czechoslovak National Council (17 August 1917). They had more than 9,000 men, of which 1,590 were Slovaks. There they were comprised mainly of prisoners of war from various fronts but also of 2,285 volunteers from the United States, of which 1,063 were Slovaks. They fought in northern France. The Czecho-Slovak Legions in Italy began to be formed after Italy joined the side of the allies. They were established on the basis of an agreement between the National Council and the Italian government (4 October 1917). They had 19,225 men, of which 1,203 were Slovaks. In battles with the Austrian-Hungarian army in northern Italy (for example, at the Piave river) they also fought against Slovak soldiers. The most numerous were the members of the Czecho-Slovak Legions in Russia where, after 1914, the nucleus was comprised especially of Czechs and of local (later also of captured) Slovaks. They grew more rapidly after the February revolution of 1917 and numbered about 60,000 soldiers, of which more than 3,000 were Slovaks. They first went into battle in the successful attack near Zborov (**2 July 1917**). According to the agreement of **26 March 1918,** they had to traverse Siberia to reach Vladivostok and from there to go to the western front in France. After attempts by the Soviet army to disarm them, especially after the so-called **Chelabinsk** confrontation in May 1918, they turned against the Soviet leaders and participated in the war against them, which lasted to the summer of 1920 when they left Russia. /DŠ/

CZECHOSLOVAK NATIONAL COUNCIL (also the National Council of Czechoslovakia) – the central organ of the Czechoslovak foreign re-

sistance during the First World War. It was formed in February 1916 from the Czech foreign committee. Its chairman was Professor Tomáš Garrigue Masaryk, the deputy chairman was the Slovak Milan Rastislav Štefánik and Edvard Beneš was secretary. Its headquarters were in Paris and it had branches in Russia, the United States of America and Italy. It issued the periodicals *The Czech Nation (La Nation Tchécque)* and *Czechoslovak Independence (Československá samostatnosť),* (**22 August 1915**). Its program was the liquidation of **Austria-Hungary** and the creation of an independent state for the Czechs and Slovaks. The public and the politicians in the countries of the Entente had been drawn into sympathy with this program earlier through publicity. It gradually initiated contacts with influential politicians, in France primarily due to Milan Rastislav Štefánik, in the United States with the help of Slovak and Czech compatriots. With their consent the council began to organize its own armed units, the **Czecho-Slovak legions**. Gradually it also obtained support for its program from the organizations of Slovaks and Czechs in the United States (**Pittsburgh Agreement**), Russia and other allied countries. It established secret contacts with Czech politicians at home and, through them, also with Slovak politicians. Its program was accepted also by the powers of the Entente in the spring of 1918, which officially recognized it as the representative of the Czechs and Slovaks (**29 June 1918**). On **14 October 1918** it declared itself to be the provisional Czecho-Slovak government and issued the **Washington Declaration**. During October it was recognized by France, Great Britain, Italy and Serbia. In public and diplomatic circles the National Council acted in the name of the "Czechoslovak nation". This formulation made it easier to justify itself, in influential circles which were poorly informed about central Europe, as the basis for a new national state. However, after the creation of Czecho-Slovakia, **Czechoslovakism** lost its actual justification and caused many misunderstandings. /DŠ/

CZECHO-SLOVAKIA – the state unit created on

28 and 30 October 1918, that disappeared on 14 March 1939, was renewed in **May 1945,** and again disappeared on **31 December 1992**. The idea of a Czecho-Slovak state was a continuation of federalist plans from the mid 19th century for the re-construction of the Austrian-Hungarian Monarchy. The **First World War** and the subsequent new power structures of Europe created a concrete opportunity to establish a Czecho-Slovak state. The first Czechoslovak Republic (to 6 October 1938) had an area of 140,446 km², within which Slovakia had an area of 49,021 km². It was established by joining together culturally and economically different lands, Czechia, Slovakia and Sub-Carpathian Ruthenia. National minorities (Germans, Magyars, Poles, Ruthenians, Ukrainians, Jews) made up more than 30 per cent of the population. In the constitution of **29 February 1920** the Czechoslovak Republic declared itself a parliamentary democracy with a separation of state powers into three branches – legislative, executive and judicial. It was based on the principles of equality and the protection of life, property and personal liberty. It guaranteed the right of assembly and the freedom of the press, conscience and confession, and stood for the protection of national minorities. However, the constitution was based on identifying the Czechs and Slovaks as the same nation (**Czechoslovakism**) and did not respect the existence of the Slovak nation. The executive power stifled the movement for the **autonomy of Slovakia**. Real power in the state was divided among the ruling political parties that made up the **government five**. A change occurred after the acceptance of the **Munich Agreement** and the declaration of the autonomy of Slovakia in 1938. From **6 October 1938** until **14 March 1939** the state was denoted as the second Czechoslovak Republic. It differed from the first through the introduction of an authoritative form of government and the autonomy of Slovakia. In the years 1918 to 1920 the name of the state was the Czecho-Slovak Republic or Czechoslovakia, with or without a hyphen. From 1920 to 1938 the name was used without a hyphen and in 1938 –

1939 with a hyphen. The second Czechoslovak Republic ceased to exist on **14 and 15 March 1939** as a result of the creation of the first **Slovak Republic** and the Protectorate of Bohemia and Moravia. Some of the Czech and Slovak emigrants who created the Czecho-Slovak National Committee in 1939 worked for the renewal of the Czechoslovak Republic. This committee was changed in 1940 into the provisional government with its headquarters in London. **Czechoslovakism** was a typical characteristic of this government, which was definitively recognized by the governments of the Soviet Union and Great Britain in 1941 and later by other victorious great powers. The leadership of the **Communist Party of Czechoslovakia** with its headquarters in Moscow had the main voice in setting the direction of the future state. On its initiative, the **Moscow negotiations,** where the **Košice government program** was accepted, took place in 1945. Sub-Carpathian Ruthenia withdrew from the renewed Czechoslovak Republic (with an area of 127,896 km², of which Slovakia covered 49,014 km²) and became a part of the Soviet Union. The Czechoslovak Republic fell within the sphere of power of the Soviet Union and proclaimed its support for a so-called people's democracy, which was to form the transition to socialism. It was once again established as an asymmetrical centralist state, within which there existed Slovak national organs with minimal authority and central organs in Prague with decisive power. After the expulsion of the German minority and the exchange of populations with Hungary, national minorities made up only five per cent of the population. A milestone in the development of the Czechoslovak Republic was the **Communist state coup** of **25 February 1948**. The new system declared its support for a people's democracy and became an ally of the Soviet Union. The period 1948 – 1955 was characterized by injustice on a massive scale and by **collectivization** and **industrialization**. According to the new constitution of 1960 the Czechoslovak Republic became a socialist state, the Czechoslovak Socialist Republic. The Stalinist regime maintained its continuity up until 1968 when a democratizing process took place in the Czechoslovak Communist Party and in society. This short period concluded with the intervention of the armies of Warsaw Pact states on **20 – 21 August 1968**. An important result of the renewal process was the transformation of the state into a **federation** of two national states. A period of **normalization** followed. This brought an improvement in the standard of living but also the return of a centralist state, a neo-Stalinist regime, and the indifference of the citizens to public matters. The activity of **dissidents,** who advocated citizen, religious and national rights and freedoms, intensified. The dissatisfaction with a communist regime, which could no longer depend upon Soviet support, led to open demonstrations by the citizens after **17 November 1989.** The result was that the leaders of **Communist Party of Czechoslovakia** agreed with the opposition and called the first democratic parliamentary election. The new legislative organ accepted a new name for the state, the Czech and Slovak Federal Republic. The Czech and Slovak representations were unable to reach agreement on the constitutional arrangement of the common state. Thus two independent states, the Slovak Republic and the Czech Republic, were established on **1 January 1993**. /RL/

CZECHOSLOVAKISM – the ideological and political current that was based upon the conviction that the Czechs and Slovaks made up one nation. Its principles were already formed at the end of the 18th century by the Czech and some of the Slovak, especially Evangelical, national revivers. It received its definitive form at the end of the 19th century. It denied the existence of a separate Slovak nation. It declared that the Slovaks had to give up their own national existence and, originally, also their literary language. This stance was justified by reference to the culturally and economically more developed Czech environment and to the traditional use of Biblical Czech as a liturgical language by the Slovak Evangelicals. At the transition from the 19th to the 20th centuries, it was espoused by the **hla-**

sists. After 1918 it was the official political and state ideology anchored in the constitution of 1920. It existed in an ethnic and political form that was in practice generally fused, especially in the Czech environment. In the census of 1921 only a Czechoslovak nationality was officially indicated. Czechoslovakism was advocated by President Tomáš Garrigue Masaryk and later by his successor, Edvard Beneš. Its most significant political adherents in Slovakia were Vavro Šrobár and Ivan Dérer. In the inter-war period **Hlinka's Slovak People's Party**, the **Slovak National Party** and, at least nominally for a certain time, the **Communist Party of Czechoslovakia** were openly opposed to Czechoslovakism. In its various forms and remnants it continued even after 1945. It was manifested in the attitude of part of the government machine towards the existence of Slovak organs, in the struggle against Slovak bourgeois nationalism, and in interference with the Matica slovenská (**3 July 1953**). The creation of a **federation** confirmed it was not sustainable. A free discussion of this question was launched only after 1989. In the 1991 census, only 3,464 people in Czechia and 59 persons in the Slovak Republic declared themselves to be of "Czechoslovak nationality". /RL/

ČERNOVÁ TRAGEDY (Černová Massacre) – the brutal intervention against Catholics in Černová near Ružomberok. The immediate cause was a dispute between the faithful in the village and the bishop of Spiš, Alexander Párvy, over the dedication of a new church in Černová. The citizens of Černová insisted that it should be dedicated by Andrej Hlinka, a native of the village, who had performed great service in the building of the church. However, at this time his ecclesiastical superior, Bishop Alexander Párvy, had suspended him from his priestly functions because he had campaigned for Vavro Šrobár in the elections of 1906. Against the will of the citizens, Párvy ordered that the pastor of Likavka dedicate the church on 27 October 1907. The villagers of Černová sought to obstruct the entry of the delegation coaches and gendarmes into the village. The Ružomberok police commander gave the order to fire. The gendarmes killed 15 persons; 10 were seriously injured and 60 slightly wounded. The courts imprisoned 38 Catholics. The event ranks among the greatest atrocities in Hungary in the era of **dualism** and aroused considerable hostility from the European public. It was condemned by world-famous personalities such as the French Slavicist Ernst Denis, the English journalist Robert William Seton-Watson (Scotus Viator), and the Nobel Prize laureates Björnstjerne Björnson and Lev Nicholajevich Tolstoy. The American public was informed of the atrocity especially by Slovaks living there. In the **Hungarian diet** the deputy Milan Hodža demanded an explanation from the government. Andrej Hlinka, on a lecture tour of Moravian and Czech cities, aroused great interest in the question of Slovakia in Prague and Vienna. The tragedy made the world aware of the national suppression of the Slovaks and of the fact that the regime in Hungary only had a veneer of democracy. /DŠ/

DEANERY see **Archdeaconry**

DECLARATION OF THE SLOVAK NATION – a document proclaiming the union of Slovakia with Czechia in **Czecho-Slovakia**. With the permission of the Hungarian government, a committee of the Slovak National Party gathered in Martin on **30 October 1918**. The specific goal of the morning meeting in the Tatrabank building was to accept a proclamation of the Slovak nation. It was based on a draft by the Lutheran pastor of Modra, Samuel Zoch. The final wording of the declaration was influenced by a message from a delegation of the National Committee in Prague, which resulted from a meeting with the Czecho-Slovak foreign resistance in Geneva (**28 October 1918**). The Czech politicians recommended the publication of a general declaration concerning a common state and stressed that the self-administration of Slovakia not be emphasized; this would be resolved later. In the afternoon of 30 October 1918 the official session of the committee of the Slovak National Party took place. It decided to found a **Slovak National Council (1918 – 1919)** and, in its name, accepted the Declaration of the Slovak Nation. According to the Declaration, only the Slovak National Council (thus not the Hungarian government) was authorized to speak and act in the name of the Slovak nation. Under the pressure of an unclear situation and in an attempt to emphasize a Czecho-Slovak orientation, the first point of the declaration stated that "the Slovak nation, linguistically, culturally and historically, is a part of one Czecho-Slovak Nation" (here, alongside the idea of a Czechoslovak nation, is also found the concept of a Slovak nation). The second point of the Declaration demanded "the unlimited right to self-determination on the basis of complete independence" for the Czechoslovak nation. With this the representatives of the Slovaks claimed membership in the emerging Czecho-Slovakia. The third and final point was a demand for the "immediate conclusion of peace on universal, Christian principles". The original Declaration has not been preserved. Immediately after its approval, Milan Hodža omitted the part demanding separate representation for the Slovaks at the peace conference and inserted a reference to the Andrássy note of **27 October 1918**. The Declaration was a cause of political controversy in the inter-war period. The so-called secret clause that has often been mentioned was in reality the minutes of a meeting of the committee of the Slovak National Council from **31 October 1918**. /RL/

DECRETUM MINUS (minor or lesser Decree) – issued by King Sigismund for the defense of the cities on **15 April 1405**. It dealt with the royal free cities and cities belonging to the royal domains. Its goal was to create a single estate (**estates**) of the cities. The decree introduced a single standard of measurement on the model of the Buda system of measures and guaranteed domestic merchants freedom of movement throughout the kingdom. Only domestic townspeople could engage in the retail sale of broadcloth. The formation of associations with foreign merchants with the intention of circumventing the provisions of the decree was forbidden. It also extended to townspeople the right to be tried by their own magistrate and the like. The king later modified some of the provisions, for instance, the free movement of domestic merchants without regard to the **warehousing right** of Buda. By this he wanted to punish the people of Buda for revolting against him in 1401 and 1403. However, the decree did not create a legal and political territorial estate from the townspeople nor did it legalize their participation in the **Hungarian diet**. This was attained only later. /JB/

DEMANDS OF THE SLOVAK NATION – the most integrated Slovak program during the "Spring of Nations". At the end of April 1848 it was clear that the grand idea of Ľudovít Štúr, public assemblies in the regions and the acceptance of a petition at a whole-nation assembly, would not be fulfilled. At the instigation of Štefan Marko Daxner and Ján Francisci, about 30 members of **Štúr's group** met in Liptovský Mikuláš on 10 May 1848 and accepted a lengthy document. Its demands included the intensification of the **March laws,** which could limit the influence of the aristocracy, accelerate the emancipation of the lower strata and suppressed nations, fulfill civic and national equality, and bring about a democratic regime in the Kingdom of Hungary. It demanded the abolition of the clauses which limited the freedom of the press, assembly and association and, what was an unusually radical demand in Hungary, the introduction of universal suffrage for males. They considered the abolition of the remnants of feudal privileges and dependencies (that is, the abolition of the forced serf labor of non-

urbarial farmers, and the allotment to the farmers of the land that the nobility had taken from them) as an additional necessary step towards modernization. They repudiated the idea of a single-nation Kingdom of Hungary and Magyar national supremacy and oppression. They proclaimed the right of each nation to its own independent life and the value of their fraternal coexistence. They demanded the reconstruction of the Kingdom of Hungary as a federal state. Slovak autonomy was to be represented in a national diet, symbols (colors, flag), and a national guard. Slovak was to be used in offices and schools, including the university and polytechnical schools. The demands were proclaimed at a poorly attended assembly on 11 May. Before their organizers could send them to the ruler, government and diet, the Hungarian regime declared this legal petition to be unconstitutional and pan-Slavic. A warrant was issued for the arrest of Štúr, Hurban and Hodža, and several of those involved were imprisoned. The weak Slovak movement found itself outlawed. Its nucleus continued its activity at the **Slavic Congress** in Prague. /DŠ/

DEMANDS OF THE SLOVAKS AND RUTHENIANS OF HUNGARY – Slovak program document for the **Slavic Congress** in Prague in 1848. Several suggestions for the future position of Slovakia were presented at the congress (a unit within the framework of the monarchy, a union with the Czech lands and the like). The position of the Slovak delegation was set forth officially in the Demands of the Slovaks and Ruthenians of Hungary. They were presented by Jozef Miloslav Hurban and were to become part of the final document of the congress. Unlike the **Demands of the Slovak Nation,** they did not mention social questions or a democratization of the regime but practically coincided with them on the constitutional and national questions. They demanded the recognition of the Slovaks as a nation, the federalization of Hungary, a Slovak diet, Slovak schools of all levels and the repudiation of national superiority. In contrast to the Mikuláš **Demands of the Slovak Nation**, they presented a more detailed definition of the autonomous position of Slovakia when they demanded the establishment of a Slovak-Ruthenian standing committee. This executive was to be subordinated to a national diet and not to the Hungarian government. Equal rights were demanded also for the Ruthenians of Hungary who did not have representatives at the congress. /DŠ/

DEMOCRATIC PARTY – a political party of the center. After the declaration of the uprising on **29 August 1944**, a so-called democratic club was formed by the non-communist resistance activists in Banská Bystrica at the beginning of September 1944. It was not yet a classic political party with an organized structure and membership base. Its leaders during the insurgency were Vavro Šrobár, honorary chairman, Ján Ursíny, chairman, and Jozef Lettrich, vice chairman. From the beginning, the leadership of the Democratic Party was in the hands of activists of the Evangelical faith from the former **Agrarian Party**. The Democratic Party and the Communist Party of Slovakia created the pattern of two parties that influenced post-war developments. Ján Ursíny was chairman briefly in 1945 and his successor, until February 1948, was Jozef Lettrich. The Democratic Party stood for Christian values and social justice and was oriented towards farmers. The dissolution of Hlinka's Slovak People's Party by the decision of the **Moscow Negotiations** of 1945 excluded the majority of Slovak Catholics from politics. This led to a conflict between the Communist Party of Slovakia and the Democratic Party, which attempted to gain Catholics for their ranks. Catholic activists in and outside of the Democratic Party concluded the **April Agreement** with the leadership of the Democratic Party on 30 March 1946. As a result, the Democratic Party achieved a resounding victory in the parliamentary elections of **26 May 1946** (62 per cent of the votes). However, it was not able to implement its electoral success in practice. It was hindered by the three Prague Agreements (**2 June 1945, 11 April 1946, 27 June 1946**) that restricted the authority of the Slovak legislative and executive organs. The communists attacked the De-

mocratic Party and accused it of anti-state activities (**14 September 1947**). In the fall political crisis (**19 November 1947**), the Democratic Party lost three commissioners. After the **Communist state coup** in February 1948, some of its leaders emigrated (Jozef Lettrich, Martin Kvetko), others became victims of political trials (Ján Ursíny, Ján Kempný, Miloš Bugár). The Party of Slovak Renewal, which existed until 1989, was created from the remnant of the Democratic Party and was under the control of the Communist Party of Slovakia. /RL/

DENÁR – a silver or, from 1760, a copper coin. In the Middle Ages the *denár* was the basis of the monetary system until the reforms of Charles Robert in the 14th century. The first *denars* in Hungary were minted under Stephen I (11th century) on the pattern of coins of the German Empire. Half *denárs*, *obols* (*heller*), were also minted. As a result of the annual exchange of coins the content of silver in the *denárs* was reduced. The Austrian or so-called Friesian *denárs,* minted in Friesach in Carinthia, also spread in Hungary at the end of the 12th century. From the 1260s the Viennese *denárs* (*pfennig,* pennies) circulated in Hungary and were used alongside domestic coins. In 1430, during the reign of Sigismund, quarter *denárs* (*kvartingy*), exchangeable at the rate of 1000 *kvartings* or 250 *denars* for one *florin,* began to be minted in Bratislava. By the end of Sigismund's reign the value of the quarter *denar* was so reduced in relation to the florin that 6,000 quarter *denárs* equaled one *florin.* By a reform of 1468 Matthias Corvinus sought to maintain the value of the *denár.* It remained a small coin until the beginning of the 17th century. A rapid decline in the value of small coins in this period led to the introduction of higher denominations. The minting of *denárs* ended after 1780, although they continued to be used until the introduction of the so-called Austrian currency in 1857. /JB/

DICTATED CONSTITUTION – a constitution issued by the supreme executive power without the approval of a representative organ (parliament, diet). This characterization is most frequently connected with the constitution of

March 1849. King Francis Joseph I dated it 4 March and it was published on **7 March 1849**, when the imperial diet was dissolved in Kroměříž in Moravia. The diet was to consider its own constitution on 15 March but, encouraged by successes against the Magyar army, the government and imperial court sought to avoid this. They considered liberal freedoms, the federalization of the monarchy and the decentralization of power as weaknesses and the road to new instability. Moreover, the imperial diet had no right to decide the future of the Kingdom of Hungary. The dictated constitution was conceived, in particular, by the minister of the interior, Francis Stadion (therefore it is also called the Stadion constitution). It respected new liberties such as the equality of nations and of people before the law, citizen rights and the abolition of serfdom. It was the first constitution valid for the whole monarchy. It was the culmination of traditional efforts to create a single Habsburg state. It declared a common Austrian citizenship, customs and commercial region, legal code and judicial system. It abolished the constitutions of the crown countries, granted them only limited provincial authority, and especially limited the independent position of the Kingdom of Hungary. Slovakia was not separated from Hungary but its secession in the future was conceded. It formally preserved a constitutional monarchy, allowed community self-administration, regional diets and a two-chamber imperial diet. However, it substantially increased the authority of the sovereign. It granted him executive power (through the ministers) and also expanded his legislative power. The modernization of the state through centralization underestimated the strength of historical particularity and national and liberal principles. Ultimately, the Habsburg government did not implement the constitution; it followed the path towards a **provisional government** in Hungary. It was abolished by the **Sylvester Patent**. /DŠ/

DIET see **Hungarian Diet**

DISSIDENTS (from the Latin *dissidere* – to differ, to have a different opinion) – people or groups that consciously defend norms of behavior, conduct and thought other than those officially recognized and implemented, primarily by the state. Dissent can be characterized as political, religious, artistic, intellectual and the like. In the narrow sense of the word the term dissident is used to designate those fostering resistance during the period of Communist totalitarianism. They issued self-published (*samizdat*) magazines, journals, monographs and declarations. During the 1970s and 1980s there appeared 20 Christian and 5 political-literary *samizdat* journals in Slovakia. The association of citizens, Charter 77, comprised largely of former communists, did not find a great response in Slovakia (**1 January 1977**). The core of dissent in Slovakia was a Christian movement to which was added, from the 1980s, environmental activist groups, artists, scientists, and former members of the Communist Party of Czechoslovakia affected by **normalization**. Among the significant representatives of the church and religious dissent in Slovakia during the years 1948 to 1989 were Viktor Trstenský, Ladislav Hanus, Ján Chryzostom Korec, Ján Krajňák, Silvester Krčméry, Vladimír Jukl, Ján Čarnogurský, Ivan Polanský, Martin Lauko, J. Vojtko, František Mikloško, Ladislav Stromček, Peter Murdza, Anton Semeš, Anton Srholec, Vladimír Ďurikovič, Peter Rúčka and Jozef Oprala. The representatives of civic dissent active in this period included, in particular, Miroslav Kusý, Dominik Tatarka, Hana Ponická, Jozef Jablonický, Milan Šimečka, Ján Langoš, Oleg Pastier, Ivan Hofmann, Ján Budaj, Vladimír Havrila and Ivan Kadlečík. The dissidents played an important role in the fall of the communist system (**17 November 1989**, **White Legion**). /RL/

DOMINICANS – an order of friars founded by the Spanish priest St Dominic in 1215 and confirmed by Pope Honorius III about one year later. It was active in the urban milieu. In 1232 it was entrusted with the **inquisition** against heretics. The Dominicans worked in the theological faculties of the medieval universities, most famously at Paris. The Dominicans settled in Hungary in 1221 and from 1275 had a cloister with a hospital and an alms-house for the elderly in Banská Štiavnica in Slovakia. They founded the most important cloister in Košice in 1303, which ceased to exist during the Reformation but was restored in 1680. Other cloisters were in Gelnica (1288), Trnava (1303), Veľký Šariš, Kremnica, Komárno and Trenčín. The Dominican nuns had houses in Humenné and Trebišov. They renewed their activities after 1989 when they re-established a cloister in Košice and founded houses in Žilina, Bratislava and a novitiate in Dunajská Lužná. /JB/

DONATION see **Privileges**

DÓZSA INSURRECTION – the largest anti-feudal insurrection in medieval Hungary named for its leader, George Dózsa. It was also known as the Farmers' or Peasants' War. It developed from an unsuccessful crusade that had been preached by Archbishop Thomas Bakócz of Esztergom in Buda on 9 April 1514. A papal bull promised the participants extensive indulgences. Its opponents and those attempting to frustrate the crusade were threatened with **excommunication**. The Hungarian **nobility** underestimated the Turkish danger and did not exhibit any desire to provide the material means necessary for or to participate personally in a war against the Ottoman Empire. The ranks of a crusader army that assembled near Buda in May 1514 were joined by masses of farmers, the urban poor, craftsmen, students and even minor **yeomen** and the lower clergy. A Transylvanian yeoman, George Dózsa Székely, became the commander of the approximately 40,000 man army of diverse nationalities. The order to dispatch an insufficiently armed crusade to the south of the country and the prohibition of further recruitment aroused strong resistance. It was accompanied by the conviction that the crusaders were being betrayed by the nobles. The crusaders did not obey the order and arrayed themselves against the feudal landlords. Franciscan preachers played an important role in propagating the uprising. A moderate wing of the insurgents demanded the secularization of ecclesiastical property while the radicals devastated noble courts, castles, and cloisters. After the army withdrew from Cegléd, where Dózsa issued a manifesto, additional followers joined the rebels. Although the uprising did not affect Slovakia directly, it found a broad response in Zemplín, Hont and Trenčín **counties** and in the mining cities of central Slovakia. At the beginning of July of 1514 the insurgent army controlled the Hungarian plain and part of Transylvania. Dissension within the leadership and betrayal by townspeople weakened the uprising. Well-armed noble forces led by the **Palatine** Sigismund Báthory and the strong *banderium* of John Zápolya defeated the main force of the insurgents on 15 July 1514 in the battle of Timisoara. The insurrection was quickly and violently suppressed throughout the whole country and its leaders were cruelly punished. Dózsa was burned and several tens of thousands of the rebels were hanged or slaughtered. The result of the uprising was the enslavement of the serfs and their attachment to the soil "for eternity" as legislated by the **Hungarian diet** (18 October 1514) and codified in the **Tripartitum** of Werböczy. /VS/

DUALISM – the form of the constitutional arrangement of the Habsburg Monarchy. The dualistic arrangement of the **Habsburg Monarchy** had a long-term effect, as the Habsburgs did not succeed in implementing **absolutism** in the Kingdom of Hungary. The **March laws** from the period of the **revolution of 1848/1849** legalized dualism for the first time. After the defeat of the Hungarian revolution, **neo-absolutism** incorporated the Kingdom of Hungary into a unitary empire but, in 1867, the Habsburg politicians were forced to consent to an Austrian-Hungarian (Magyar) constitutional settlement. It was a compromise of several approaches: one pole was represented by the radical attempts of some Magyar politicians to achieve the full independence of the Kingdom of Hungary; the opposite pole was the centralism of the Austrian-German politicians. From the Magyar side it was prepared in particular by Ferenc Deák and Julius Andrássy, who used as a starting point the constitutional position of the Kingdom of Hungary in 1848. For the Hungarian side dualism was based especially on law number twelve of **28 July 1867**, for the Austrian side the constitution of **21 December 1867**. The monarchy, which began to be known as **Austria-Hungary,** was transformed into a federation with two equal states, Cisleitha and Transleitha. Each had its separate legislative, administrative and executive power, its own organs (government and parliament), and broad autonomous authority. They were connected by a common sovereign, the ministries of defense, foreign affairs and finance and some imperial-royal institutions. Common matters were resolved by the so-called delegations, to which the imperial council and the **Hungarian diet** sent 60 representatives each. The Kingdom of Hungary met 30 per cent of the state expenditures of the monarchy. Every ten years the economic balance was renewed and elicited great tension and political crises. The dualistic arrangement did not respect the desires of the non-Magyars and the non-Germans for national freedom. There ensued a half-century of the severest suppression of the nations, and the **Nationality Law** formally guaranteed to them only modest rights in the Kingdom of Hungary. Dualism enabled the old circle of large-scale land-owners, represented especially by the **Liberal Party**, to maintain their monopoly of property and position of power up to 1918. After a period of stabilization, dualism found itself in a deep crisis at the end of the 19th century. However, Hungarian political forces did not liberalize the regime, refused to legislate general suffrage, did not consider the desires of the non-Magyars, but rather obdurately implemented the idea of a greater Hungary and **Magyarization.** /DŠ/

DUCATS see **Gold Pieces**

DUKE (knieža) – originally the chief of a tribal formation, then the ruler of a duchy and later the highest grade of nobility, a **magnate**. Samo (**623 – 658**) is considered the first duke in the history of the Slovaks. Several dukes ruled the Nitra duchy but only the last, Pribina, is known by name. He was expelled from Nitra in **833** by Mojmír I who annexed the duchy to the **Great Moravian Empire**. In Hungarian history, the Árpáds held the title of duke until the time of Duke Stephen (Vajk), who became the first Hungarian **king** in **1000**. As the Middle Ages proceeded, the title of duke was relatively rare in Hungary. It was held mostly by younger members of the sovereign's family if they were granted territory, in the form of a so-called appanage duchy (**Nitra appanage Duchy**), since a permanent duchy did not exist in Hungary. Unique was the title of duke of Liptov (*dux liptoviensis*), which John Corvinus, the illegitimate son of Matthias I, used from **1479**. In the later feudal period, only a few Hungarian magnate families or their off-shoots (for example, the Erdödy, Esterházy, Grassalkovich, Kohári and Pálffy) obtained the title of duke. From 1715 the title belonged permanently to the primate of Hungary, the archbishop of Esztergom. The sovereign dukes of the Habsburg family ruling the Austrian lands (and from 1526 also the Kingdom of Hungary) began regularly to use the title of Archduke of Austria in 1453. It belonged also other (non-sovereign) members of the Habsburg (later the Habsburg-Lothringen) dynasty, according to the **Pragmatic Sanction** (1713), and was used up to the dissolution of Austria-Hungary. The title duke was practically identical with the term *vojvoda* and, for a time, was practically identical with the term prince. /VS/

DVORNÍCI (courtiers, servants) – a population category in early feudal Hungary, the origins of which reach back to the era of Great Moravia. They lived in villages which had to offer services to the courts of the **magnates** or the sovereign. Their responsibilities were a specific form of **feudal rent**. They included craftsmen, smiths, carpenters, bakers and millers, as well as agricultural workers who specialized in several activities (vine growers, brewers) or those who offered services to the authorities (shepherds, hunters, fishermen, falconers, teamsters, singers, musicians, jesters and the like). The servant organization of the *dvorníci* declined with the developments of cities and the separation of the trades from agriculture in the 13th century. /JB/

EASTERN SLOVAK PEASANT UPRISING (also Peasant Insurrection, Cholera Uprising) – the most radical social uprising of peasants in the Kingdom of Hungary in the 19th century. It erupted in connection with the cholera epidemic that, despite the precautions of the state, spread from Galicia and Russia. Unpopular precautions were adopted, such as prohibiting work in fields, travel prohibitions, mass graves and the coating of wells with lime. In Hungary, cholera took 200,000 victims, especially peasants exhausted by hunger and undermined by poor hygiene. It was the most vulnerable classes of the poor who, in particular, perceived the precautions of the officials as intentional poisoning of the people, so that rumors of poisoning led to mass hysteria, hostility towards the authorities, the propertied and doctors. The first mass disturbance occurred on **19 July 1831** in Košice. At the end of July, after the eruption of revolts in Žipov near Trebišov, the uprising took on a mass character. Its center was Zemplín county, but it also affected Spiš and, to a lesser degree, Gemer, Šariš, Abov and other counties. Altogether about 150 communities and 45,000 subject peasants and even small yeoman and miners revolted. The insurgents were badly organized and they did not possess a unified leadership or even a clear program and goal. Local leaders dominated them (mayor Michal Pavúk from Žipov, the yeoman Peter Tašnády from Malé Raškovce). The elemental character of the uprising enabled many serfs to avenge by force long-term suppression even upon the innocent. They drove out landlords, bureaucrats, merchants and clerics, 24 of whom were killed and their property destroyed. The rebels wanted to distribute the land among themselves, so they burned old documents containing the charters of privileges of the landlords and the obligations of the serfs. During August and September the imperial army put down the uprising and the officials cruelly took their revenge upon its participants. On **4 November 1831** the ruler forbade further executions. The uprising convinced many of the anachronism of **serfdom** and strengthened the position of those who wished to remove it. /DŠ/

EJÁLET – an independent territorial-administrative unit with the status of a vice-regal province in the Ottoman Empire. It also was called *vilájet, pashalik* and *beglerbeglik*. It was headed by the sultan's governor (*beglerbeg* or pasha) who was directly subordinate to the Porte (the sultan's court). The *beglerbeg* was the supreme commander of the provincial army and, at the same time, the administrator of the *ejálet*, personally responsible for its management. Named by the sultan, he administered his province only for one year. Only exceptionally was the commission lengthened (in 145 years only about 75 men held the office of the pasha of Buda). The pasha decided who would be named to the office of *sandjakbeg* and to the other offices. As the deputy of the Ottoman sultan, he had the right to negotiate with enemies. He took into account the opinions of his advisory organ, the *díván*, when he issued more important decisions. The highest Turkish dignitaries in the *ejálet* were permanent members of the *díván*. These were the *defterdar*, who stood at the head of the financial and tax administration; the *kádí*, the judge in Sharia or Islamic law; the commander of the *janissaries* and the main officers of the Turkish provincial army. The first and most significant *ejálet* in Hungary was the Buda *ejálet* (**1541 – 1686**). The Buda *beglerbeg* transmitted the sultan's commands to other pashas and *ejálets* that developed in Hungary during the Turkish occupation. These were the Timisoara (1552), Eger (1596), Varadine (1660) and Nové Zámky (**1663**) *ejálets*. The Nové Zámky *ejálet* disappeared in **1685,** when the imperial army captured Nové Zámky and almost the whole territory of Slovakia was freed from Turkish rule. An *ejálet* was comprised of several *sandjaks*. /VS/

EMIGRATION – a temporary or permanent departure from a country. Emigration was one of the typical demographic and social phenomena of the modern history of the Slovaks. It had predominantly social, but in some periods also a religious, national and political character. It acquired a mass character for the first time at the beginning of the 18th century after the expulsion of the Turks from the Kingdom of Hungary. Up to the mid 19th century, thousands of farming families from the mountain regions of Slovakia, especially Evangelicals, settled the depopulated or sparsely inhabited fertile regions of the "lower lands" (southern Hungary). At the end of the century about 500,000 of them lived there. Despite the fact that they were most exposed to **Magyarization**, they contributed significantly to the formation of modern Slovak culture. Today their descendants live in Hungary, Yugoslavia (Vojvodina), Romania and Croatia. The Slovaks endured the largest wave of emigration at the end of the 19th and the beginning of the 20th century. The large number of Slovaks who emigrated placed them in the ranks of those nations that experienced the highest percentage of emigrants as a proportion of their total population. They went to large cities for work in factories, transportation, the building trades and commerce. More than 100,000 Slovaks lived in Budapest and 50,000 in Vienna. Some returned home, others were assimilated. The greatest Slovak emigration was to the United States in 1880 – 1914, which numbered more than 500,000 Slovak emigrants. In 1905 alone they numbered 52,000. Most of them settled on the east coast (especially in Pennsylvania, Ohio and New Jersey) or the mid-west (Illinois), where they worked in mines and factories as day laborers. The city with the greatest number of Slovaks was Pittsburgh. There were 277 Slovak societies operating in the United States in 1932. On **26 May 1907** the Slovak League was established and 230 Slovak newspapers and magazines were published up to 1939. American Slovaks contributed to the founding of Czecho-Slovakia (**Cleveland Agreement**). In the inter-war period emigration to the USA declined (due in particular to limiting quotas on the American side). Therefore, about 220,000 Slovak workers left for work in Canada, France, Belgium and Argentina. In the third wave, from 1945 to 1989, about 100,000 Slovaks, especially the educated, left Czecho-Slovakia. The majority of them were motivated by political rather than social reasons, especially by their opposition to the Communist regime, fear of persecution and the like (**4 April 1945**, **25 February 1948**, **1 December 1968**). About 350,000 Slovaks live in the Czech Republic, especially in Prague, around Ostrava and along the borders, where they hoped to obtain better working and social conditions. Many of the emigrants lost contact with their old country and renewed them only after 1989. At present, approximately 2.5 million Slovaks or their descendants live abroad. /DŠ/

EMPEROR (CAESAR) – the title of a ruler of the highest degree. Originally it was derived from the Roman name Gaius Julius Caesar and was a title of the Roman emperors who, beginning with Augustus, began to use the name Caesar in order to indicate their kinship (or successorship) to Caesar the Dictator. The highest powers of the state were concentrated in the hands of the Caesars, the emperors. Through the Roman emperors this title became a synonym for absolute power with claims to world-wide rule. After the fall of the Roman Empire, the imperial dignity in Europe was renewed by the Frankish family of the Carolingians, who ruled a state made up of remnants of the main parts of the former western Roman Empire. Charlemagne was crowned emperor by the pope in 800. The renewed imperial title of the western Roman Empire was considered the highest symbol of secular power in the whole western Catholic Christian world. The imperial title passed from the Frankish Carolingians to the German rulers. With the German king Otto I (936 – 973) the history of the Holy Roman Empire of the German Nation began to unfold. Almost all the Hungarian sovereigns of the Habsburg dynasty held the imperial title from the 16th century until **6 August 1806** when Francis II renounced it. From 1804 the Habsburgs used the title of Hereditary Austrian

Emperor. Hungary was never a part of the Holy Roman Empire of the German Nation and therefore the **king** of Hungary was never a vassal of the emperor. Despite this, they sought the imperial title. Among the successful was Sigismund of Luxemburg; among the unsuccessful Matthias Corvinus and Vladislav II Jagiello. /VS/

EMPHYTEUTIC LAW see **German law**

ENLIGHTENED ABSOLUTISM – a political system in the 18th century. The tradition of the older **absolutism** became linked with the idea of the **Enlightenment**. The sovereign used his supreme and unrestricted power to implement enlightenment reforms, the principle of human equality and dignity, and the modernization of society. He removed or weakened obsolete differences between the estates. The authority of the **nobility,** the historical units and their organs were subordinated to the central power, the position of the serfs was alleviated and education supported. The ruler established state organs with reform-minded and educated bureaucrats and a new legal code and thus created the basis for forming a civil society. In the **Habsburg Monarchy** it began during the reign of Maria Theresa (1740 – 1780) and culminated during the reign of Joseph II (1780 – 1790). Both tried to transform the monarchy into a modern united state. Maria Theresa accepted only some enlightenment ideas and a great part in the **Theresian reforms** was played by the enlightened circle around her (her husband Francis of Lothringen, her son Joseph II, the court councillors Gerhard van Swieten, Johann Ignaz Felbiger, Adam František Kollár and others). Joseph II personally initiated and defended the radical **Josephinian reforms**. Maria Theresa eliminated the sovereignty of the Austrian and Czech estates. Joseph II did the same for **Hungary**. They transferred some rights of the church to the state, laid the foundations of a state school system and obligatory school attendance, reformed secondary schools and universities, established technical schools and introduced unified weights and measures. They supported **manufactures** and practical education (the cultivation of new crops, hygiene and the eradication of superstition). Through the **Theresian** *urbár* (land registers), Maria Theresa tried to restrict the arbitrariness of the landlords, while Joseph II directly disapproved of **serfdom.** He viewed the population as citizens of the state and the ruler as only its first servant. /VŠ/

ENLIGHTENMENT – a philosophical current and intellectual movement in the 17th and 18th centuries emphasizing human reason and the freedom of man. At the same time, the term signifies a whole cultural-historical epoch directed against feudalism and the remnants of medieval thought. Attention was focused on reason based upon sensory experience and science to resolve conflicts and problems. It rejected anything that was against or beyond reason, that is, the secret and miraculous. Through the Enlightenment's dissemination of the ideas of the good, justice and scientific knowledge, its adherents sought to change society politically and ethically and thus remove its inadequacies. In art it inspired **classicism**. The underlying presuppositions for Enlightenment views first appeared in the Netherlands and England, but it flourished especially in France. The Enlightenment entered Slovakia during the first half of the 18th century and reached its apogee in 1780 – 1820. It influenced some professors at **Trnava University** (Andrej Jaslinský, Anton Revický, Ján Krstiteľ Horvát). Another circle of enlightened philosophers were members of the **Slovak Learned Society**, the Institute of Czecho-Slovak Language and Literature, the Malohont Learned Society, and the Learned Society of the Mining Region. As clergymen (Catholic and Protestant), they accepted idealism in philosophy, while in the social area they criticized the existing feudal social order and attempted to improve the situation of the peasants. They used the possibilities offered by the state. They were supporters of **enlightenment absolutism** and were in favor of the **Josephinian reforms**. They raised enlightenment ideas to the level of rational popular education and a struggle against social and religious backwardness. This education was focused on the struggle against superstition, progress in agriculture and the improvement of people's health. /MK/

ESTATES – under feudalism the social strata or groups internally linked by certain legal rights and having an exclusive or privileged position in society. Non-privileged groups or classes (for instance, freemen or subject farmers, serfs) were not granted the character of an estate. The number and authority of the estates differed in the individual countries of Europe. However, they had basic characteristics in common: participation in the legislative (**Hungarian diet**), executive and administrative offices and the judicial powers of the state (**estates monarchy**). The process of creating estates was not fluid or straightforward in Hungary. It began in the 13th century, when the **Golden Bull** of Andrew II in 1222 recognized the rights of the estates and culminated during the second half of the 15th century with the establishment of an estates society that continued up to the end of **feudalism**. The clergy, represented by the **prelates** or ecclesiastical dignitaries, constituted the first estate. The second estate was made up of the secular **nobility,** whose legal position was anchored, in particular, in the decree of King Louis I from **1351** that recognized the principle of the equality of all nobles. However, the long-standing differentiation of the nobility into higher and lower was formally incorporated into law in **1608**. With this the nobles were divided into two estates: the **magnates,** or higher nobility, and the **yeomen**, or the middle and lower nobility. The royal free cities made up the fourth estate that was established only during the reign of King Sigismund, when its representatives began to be invited to diets of the country. However, they had only one collective vote in the diet. The division of Hungarian feudal society into estates was formally abolished by the **March laws** of 1848. /VS/

ESTATES MONARCHY – a form of monarchy. In the oldest European kingdoms the sovereign ruled alone. However, he gradually bestowed part of his nominal lands upon loyal warriors. The ambitious new nobility struggled with the ruler to maintain their **prerogatives**, including their participation in the administration of the kingdom and the establishment of its organs. If they achieved success, weak kings often became pawns in their hands. The government of the aristocracy was frequently accompanied by anarchy, violence and an increased oppression of the peasants. An estates monarchy was created in Hungary in the 13th century, in particular after the promulgation of the **Golden Bull**, when its organs of self-administration, the **Hungarian diet** and noble **counties**, began to take shape. During the 14th and 15th centuries periods of strong rulers (the Anjous and Hunyadys), who suppressed the power interests of the nobility, alternated with periods when the country was divided up by the most wealthy families, who fought among themselves for power (at the transition from the 13th to the 14th, and from the 15th to the 16th centuries, the first half of the 15th century). Often the royal power impotently watched this struggle. In the 16th century, after the annexation of Hungary to the **Habsburg Monarchy**, Habsburg **absolutism** sought to suppress the estates monarchy in Hungary. /DŠ/

EXCOMMUNICATION – in general expulsion, the most severe ecclesiastical punishment signifying exclusion from the (Catholic) Church. It was in force already during the early Christian era. From the 12th century a distinction was made between the lesser excommunication, which meant exclusion from participation in the sacraments and ineligibility to fill church offices, and the greater excommunication which meant the complete exclusion from the church. Initially, even any kind of social contact with the excommunicated person was forbidden. From the time of Pope Gregory IX (1227 – 1241) a specific type of greater excommunication was the ceremonial declaration of the anathema. The affected person was excluded from participation in church ceremonies and the sacraments and no-one was allowed to communicate with him. The anathema had the character of a so-called restorative punishment, a ban that could be rescinded after a time. However, it could be rescinded only by the prelate who had imposed it or his superior. In the Middle Ages the right of excommunication belonged to the **popes**, synods, papal legates, prelates in ordinary (diocesan bishops), and, in the case of unoccupied bishoprics, chapters or priors, if this right was delegated to them. Although excommunication was an ecclesiastical punishment, in the Middle Ages and the beginning of the early modern era the excommunicated did not, as a rule, avoid secular punishment (for example, in the Holy Roman Empire of the German Nation excommunication usually was accompanied by the so-called imperial ban, *Acht und Bann*). Excommunication was applied to an increased degree in large-scale ecclesiastical disputes (the so-called great eastern **schism** of 1054, the great western schism of 1378 to 1417, and in the era of the Reformation). The most famous example of excommunication in older Slovak history was that of Matthew Csák, who was excommunicated by Cardinal Gentilis. At the same time, in 1311, an **interdict** was imposed on all of Matthew's estates. /VS/

FARMSTEAD (Latin *sessia*, settlement) – a tax unit and the basic unit of agricultural land. To the 16th century it was equal to the *porta* (**portal**). Its area was not precisely defined and it varied from 12 to 40 *jutros* (that is from 5 to 17 hectares) of arable land. The size of farmsteads was dependent upon the fertility of the soil and differed from region to region. Originally it represented one peasant farm; later it was divided into halves, quarters and smaller parts. A house, farm buildings (stall, barn), garden, arable soil, meadows and sometimes also a vineyard belonged to such a farmstead. **Peasants** could hold up to one-eighth of the farmstead; while **cotters** had tenure of less than one eighth. The urbarial provisions of Maria Theresa in 1767 introduced unified provisions for the size of farmsteads

as tax units. These regulations were completed with the promulgation of the **Theresian urbár** (1772). /JB/

FEBRUARY CONSTITUTION – a patent of 26 February 1861 issued by the sovereign Francis Joseph I. It is also called the Schmerling constitution (after the minister Anton Schmerling). It was a collection of basic laws supplemented by 46 appendices and was valid for the whole of the monarchy, including the Kingdom of Hungary. In contrast to the **October Diploma**, it reinforced the unity of the empire and its central power while limiting autonomous legislative and executive power. All of the 15 crown lands were to be representated in the imperial **Diet** (the so-called extended imperial council) and 123 of the 343 deputies were to come from the Kingdom of Hungary. In addition to imperial and territorial assemblies there also functioned a so-called narrower imperial council. Its authority did not extend to Hungary or Venice. In this way, federation established an inequality between the greater autonomy of Hungary (and Venice) and the lesser authority of the other crown lands. This created space for **dualism** in the future. Influential Magyar politicians were not satisfied with this constitution. They demanded the restoration of Hungary's independence and that its government be responsible to the **Hungarian diet** on the model of the **March laws**. When Hungarian deputies refused to take their seats in the extended imperial council in May 1861, the ruler dismissed the diet and appointed a **provisional government** (*provisorium*) for the country. The February constitution did not mention at all the rights of the so-called non-historic nations. This weakened their position and, especially in Hungary, created the possibility of radical oppression. A power struggle erupted between the Magyar politicians of Hungary and the Austrian German politicians after the constitution was issued. This further weakened the dualistic arrangement of the monarchy. /DŠ/

FEDERATION (from the Latin *foederatio* – alliance) – the connection of two or more states on the basis of common interests and a constitution. The exercise of state power is divided among central organs and the organs of the member states. A bond of states looser than a federation is called a confederation. The form of a federation and confederation and the jurisdiction of their organs are influenced by the concrete, specific conditions in which nations live. In central Europe a program of federation was outlined for the first time by the **Hungarian Jacobins** and the supporters of **Austro-Slavism**. The first program of a Czecho-Slovak Federation was the **Cleveland Agreement** of 1915. However, the federation was established by the division of the unitary Czechoslovak Socialist Republic into national states, the Czech Socialist Republic and the Slovak Socialist Republic, and was based upon the constitutional law signed in Bratislava on **30 October 1968** and effective from **1 January 1969**. The federal organs of the federation located in Prague were the government, the federal assembly (divided into a Chamber of the People with 200 deputies, elected from the territory of the whole federation, and a Chamber of Nations with 150 deputies of which 75 were elected in the Slovak Socialist Republic and 75 in the Czech Socialist Republic), the president and the constitutional court. In the Czech Republic the republican organs were the government and the Czech National Council and, in the Slovak Socialist Republic, the government and the **Slovak National Council (1945)**. During the era of **normalization** the federation lost its original significance. The law of the federation was changed and supplemented each year to the detriment of the republics and in favor of the Prague central administration. The federal organs gradually acquired responsibility for fuel, energy, transport, communications and industry. The number of central organs of the federation increased and in each the office of state secretary was abolished. At the expense of the republics, the income and expenditures of the federal budget were increased in 1971. Neither issuing banks in the republics nor a central bank were created and the old constitution of 1960 remained in force. A fundamental change occurred only in 1989. Politi-

cians and the public began to discuss the fate of the federation. Tendencies either to preserve "the strong center" and to create a federal state on the territorial principle or to create two independent states prevailed in the Czech Republic. The original importance of the sovereign republics and their free alliance was stressed in the Slovak Republic. Its fate was decided by the parliamentary elections of 5 – 6 May 1992. The forces that agreed on the creation of two independent states were victorious in both parts of the federation. The federal assembly approved a law for the dissolution of the federation on **25 November 1992**. The independent Slovak Republic and Czech Republic were established in a legal and pacific way on **1 January 1993**. The new Slovak Republic is the second independent state in modern Slovak history (**14 March 1939**). /RL/

FEUDAL RENT – an essential mark of **feudalism**. It was the obligation of the serfs settled on the land of the feudal landowner to turn over part of their production (natural rent, *naturalia*) or a money payment (monetary rent) or to work for a certain number of days on the landowner's own estate (labor, *robota*). The oldest form was natural rent. This was paid primarily in grain, wine and fattened domestic animals. Gradually it was stabilized at a tenth of the yield for the church, the **tenth** (tithe), and a further tenth from the remaining yield for the landlord, the **ninth**. Initially the *robota* or rent paid in labor was not high. With the expansion of the farming of the allodial land by the nobles, the *robota* responsibilities of serfs began to increase from the 16th century and reached three to four days per week with draft animals or six days without draft animals, for each farmstead. The productivity of this forced labor was low. Money rent, when the serfs paid their obligations to the landlord in money, was the most economically mature form of feudal rent. However, it presupposed a developed market economy and sufficient currency. It was practised especially in the medieval cities and the settlements established under the **German law**. /JB/

FEUDALISM – a social-economic system based on the feudal ownership of land that belongs to the sovereign, secular and ecclesiastical landlords, cities and the free population (**fief**, **estates**). The serfs, who worked the soil, found themselves dependent upon their lords (**serfdom**). Feudal property was divided into land in immediate tenure, the domain (*allodium*), and land that was cultivated by the serfs and for which they paid **feudal rent**, the *rustical*. Feudalism developed in the economically most mature countries that emerged from the western Roman Empire (in Italy, France, Spain, Germany, England) during the 5th – 6th centuries. In the Byzantine Empire, feudal relations transformed the existing political-economic system in the 6th to the 8th centuries. In central, northern and eastern Europe it began to prevail only in the 10th and 11th centuries. The **Nitra duchy** and the **Great Moravian Empire** in Slovakia were proto-feudal states, in which feudal relations began to be established and were then violently interrupted by the extinction of these entities. Historians distinguish between early feudalism (5th – 11th centuries), mature (high) feudalism (12th – 15th) and late feudalism (16th to the mid 17th century). However, this division is schematic and applies only to some western European countries. While feudalism gradually disappeared in western Europe during revolutions in the Netherlands (1566 – 1579), England (1642 – 1649) and France (1789 – 1795), in the Habsburg Empire the last remnants of feudalism were eliminated only by the **revolution of 1848/1849**. /JB/

FIEF (*Feudum*) – land which is leased in return for some kind of service. This concept was introduced into Slovak in form of the word léno (from the German Lehen, i.e. loan). The dependent relation of the vassal to the feudal lord is known as the feudal system and was developed in western and central Europe by combining Roman law with Celtic and German-Slavic ideas of group relations. It attained its classical form in the Frankish Empire in the 8th – 9th centuries. However, the beginnings of these relationships may already be noted at the end of the Roman Empire

when personally free farmers, "colonists", made a specific payment for rented land. A particular responsibility of the vassal was military service for the lord. The feudal lord was obliged to protect his own vassals. This relationship of loyalty between the landlord and vassal was concluded by a symbolic ritual. The kneeling vassal placed his joined hands into the open hands of his *seigneur*. Originally the *seigneur* bestowed land upon a vassal only temporarily, later for life (*beneficium*), and from the 9th century it became hereditary (*léno*, fief). The heirs also inherited the obligations and responsibilities to the lord. The vassal was required to perform state, judicial and public services in addition to military service. In Hungary, the system of vassalage took hold during the reign of the Árpáds when, in addition to the ruler, royal dignitaries (*župani* or counts) could bestow fiefs. The whole feudal system (**feudalism**) was gradually built upon this relationship. The highest lord was the **king** or the **emperor** who bestowed land and property upon the **nobility**, that is, his own vassals. Thus a social pyramid of relationships developed in which a vassal at the lowest level was not subordinate directly to the sovereign but to his own feudal lord. This was expressed in the well known catchword, "the vassal of my vassal is not my vassal". The serfs stood at the lowest level of the feudal system and received only the use of the land. They did not have a right to inherit it and were not its legal owners. The feudal landlord could confiscate it or expel them from it. For the use of the soil they had to turn over **feudal rent**, that is, products, money and labor for the benefit of the landlord. /JB/

FIRST WORLD WAR – until 1939 the largest military conflict in history. The immediate cause was the assassination of the Habsburg heir to the throne, Francis Ferdinand, on **28 June 1914**. It began with the declaration of war by **Austria-Hungary** on Serbia on 28 July 1914. The central powers led by Germany and Austria-Hungary fought against the powers of the Entente (France, Great Britain, Russia and from 1917, the United States of America). The army of Austria-Hungary mobilized 9 million men that included 400,000 – 450,000 Slovaks. Of these 70,000 fell and more than 60,000 were wounded. They fought in Ukraine, Russia, Serbia, Italy, Belgium and Romania. The front affected Slovakia only peripherally (**23 November 1914**), however the war bequeathed to it great consequences. After war was declared, basic civic rights were limited in Hungary, which was governed with the help of extraordinary measures. Under the guise of patriotism, Magyar chauvinism was strengthened; 600 Slovaks condemned for political acts were imprisoned by October 1914. Slovak politicians reacted to the situation by halting their activity (**6 August 1914**). The state subordinated the economy to the needs of the war and assumed the direction of important enterprises. This did not prevent, however, the growth of inflation, the creation of a black market and an insufficiency of foodstuffs and consumer goods. A rapid decline in the living standard and starvation called forth hunger marches, strikes and May 1 demonstrations of workers and of the poor. They demanded general suffrage, the end of the war and a just peace. The morale of the army also declined. During the course of 1918 more than 800,000 soldiers deserted, especially those who returned from captivity in Russia. In numerous garrisons soldiers mutinied against deployment to the front. The horrors of war led to the strengthening of opposition to national oppression. Some Czech politicians emigrated. They initiated contacts with Slovaks and Czechs in the United States, as well as with leading politicians of the Allied States. A common foreign resistance movement of Czechs and Slovaks was formed in 1915, led by the **Czechoslovak National Council.** Its program was the dissolution of Austria-Hungary and the creation of Czecho-Slovakia (**Cleveland Agreement**). **Czecho-Slovak legions** were formed from thousands of Czech and Slovak prisoners of war in Russia, France and Italy. About 25,400 Slovak volunteers fought in the American army. After negotiations for a separate peace with Austria-Hungary collapsed in the spring of 1918, even the allied governments supported the creation of Czecho-Slovakia. From 1917 there was public support for the Czecho-Slovak State in Czechia; from May 1918 also in Slovakia (**Mikuláš Resolution**). By the summer preparations were being made in the Czech lands to found the new state and on **13 July 1918** the Czechoslovak National Committee was established. In Slovakia efforts to establish a **Slovak National Council (1918 – 1919)** were strengthened. Shortly after the declaration of **Czecho-Slovakia (28 October 1918, 30 October 1918**), the armistice of 11 November 1918 ended the war, which was definitively concluded by the peace treaties of Versailles. /DŠ/

FLORINS see **Gold Pieces**

FOJT see **Magistrate**

FOUNDRY – an installation for the processing of metallic ores by smelting and refining by fire. Evidence of primitive furnaces in which copper ore was smelted comes from as early as the Old Bronze Age, evidence for the smelting of iron ores from the Hallstatt period. Foundry furnaces were used also during the period of Great Moravia (Pobedím). With the development of deep mining in the 13th century, foundries were established in the environs of the mines, sometimes in conjunction with **hammer mills**. Although the German colonist miners perfected the old furnaces, the principle of their construction remained the same. From the mid 16th century a new type of furnace began to be built, the so-called blow-pipe, into which air was forced with the help of bellows. Thus higher temperatures could be reached for smelting ore. In addition to the primary smelting of ore in furnaces, the separation and refining of the raw metal (through re-heating) at higher temperatures took place, which produced metals of a higher quality or separated out other metals (for example, copper from silver through a so-called decanting process). At the end of the 17th century the first blast furnaces appeared in 1680 in Dobšiná and in 1692 in Ľubietová. The 18th and 19th centuries saw further technical improvements and the introduction of new techniques for the processing of metallic ores in blast furnaces. The term foundry also signifies glass-works. The first written reports of them come from the 14th century (Sklené, Sklené Teplice). In later centuries the evidence about them increases. In the 19th century, when there were several tens of glass-works in Slovakia, the term forge ceased to be used for them. Glass foundries were located at places where quartz, limestone and sufficient beech wood were found, since these were used in the smelting of glass. In the Middle Ages guilds of builders and stone-cutters built foundries at the construction sites of large buildings (cathedrals, castles and the like). /JB/

FRANCISCANS – a religious order founded in 1209 by St Francis of Assisi. It had three components: the male order (founded in 1209), the female Order of Poor Claires (founded in 1212) and the tertiary or lay order (founded in 1221). The pope confirmed the order in 1223. Franciscans settled primarily in cities, where they were active especially among the poorest and belong among the so-called mendicant orders. They devoted themselves to preaching and teaching in schools and universities. They later also had their own universities. Because of internal discord, Pope Leo X divided the order into two orders in 1517: the more strict Minorites or Observantines and the more moderate Conventuals. In 1528 the Capuchin order separated from the other Franciscans, first as an offshoot and then, from 1619, as an independent order. The final reform of the Franciscans was realized by Pope Leo XIII in 1897. The Franciscans came to Hungary in 1228 and settled in important medieval cities. Before the Tatar invasion they were settled in Bratislava, Trnava and Nitra, before 1263 in Slovenská Ľupča, at the beginning of the 14th century in Levoča, Trenčín, Spišská Nová Ves and Čachtice, before 1397 in Vranov and around 1400 in Košice. After the Hussite wars during the second half of the 15th century they founded new **cloisters** especially in the regions influenced by the ideology of the Hussite movement (Skalica 1467, Hlohovec 1465), but also in other cities (Okoličné prior to 1476, Solivar before 1482, Fiľakovo before 1484). The more strict Franci-

scans, the Observantines, were active especially in southern Hungary against the **Bogomils** and the Patarines. During the 15th and 16th centuries they had their own independent province, the Salvatorian, while the Conventuals established the Marian province. At the beginning of the 17th century the number of cloisters declined as a result of the **Reformation**. During the period of **re-Catholicization** the Franciscans settled again in Levoča, Nové Zámky, Pruské, Nižný Šebeš, Okoličné, Kremnica, Komárno, Trnava, Malacky, Žilina, Trstená etc. Up to the 20th century they were among the most wide-spread **religious orders** in Slovakia. After 1989 cloisters were re-established in Bratislava, Trnava, Trstená, Nové Zámky, Hlohovec, Fiľakovo and in Prešov. /JB/

FREEMEN – a category of the free population that obtained its position for monetary contributions, services offered to the landlord, or by redemption from the obligations of serfdom. The children born from the marriage of a serf with a yeomen also became freemen. Freemen were usually more propertied than **peasants** but sometimes they were without property. This title was occasionally used to designate serfs temporarily freed from some of the obligations of serfdom or serfs with the freedom to move. A special group of free farmers were the *taxalists* settled on the dominical land of the landlord (*allod*) cultivated by the landlord under his own supervision. To rent this land they paid in money. Also personally free were those who leased the **royal rights**, taverners, millers, butchers and the like. They paid an agreed rent to the landlord. By the decree of Joseph II of **2 August 1785** concerning the abolition of **servitude**, all inhabitants of the Kingdom of Hungary became freemen. /JB/

FUNCTIONALISM – an architectural style, the beginnings of which date back to the 1890s. It reached its definitive form in the 1920s. The first propagators of functionalism were the Belgian architects. Anatole de Baudot was the first to use reinforced concrete in the building of the church of St John in Montmartre in Paris (1894). Reinforced concrete enabled the roofing of large spaces and changed the classic understanding of vaulting. The history of architecture began to write a new chapter. Functionalism renounced, for the sake of utility, the ornamentation and the facades previously used. It rejected the **art nouveau** movement, eclecticism and **cubism**. It was guided by the principle that form follows function. It emphasized the function of the individual parts of a building and the building as a whole. Because of its idea of the unity and integrity of a composition it obtained the name "the school of discipline". Functionalism created simple compositions from basic elements – squares, cones, spheres, cylinders and pyramids – united by light. It caught on in modern society with urbanization and the building of housing blocks, administrative buildings, ecclesiastical buildings, stadiums and the like. Dušan Jurkovič, Klement Šilinger, Alois Balán, Juraj Grossmann, Juraj Tvarožek, Bedrich Weinwurm and Michal Scheer were among the best Slovak functional architects. /RL/

GERMAN COLONIZATION see **Colonization**

GERMAN LAW – a compilation of legal norms adopted from German lands. It was also called the emphyteutic law. It began to spread into Slovakia from Silesia, Little Poland and Moravia during the **colonization** of the 13th century. It first spread to the Spiš, Šariš and Zemplín regions and reached the villages from the cities. Its was brought predominantly by immigrants from German lands and therefore was called the German Law. The law enabled the population to trade freely in immovable property (buy, sell, mortgage and the like). The representatives of the villages were recruiters (*locatori*) who brought colonists in to settle a designated territory under an agreement with a landlord. The newly built village was freed from paying taxes du-

ring the first years or even decades of its existence. The recruiter held the office of hereditary **magistrate** (*richtár*), also called *šoltýs*, *fojt* or *advocatus*. He had the right to maintain a mill, tavern, brewery, forge, slaughter-house and the like without paying taxes. The *šoltýs* had the right to 1 – 2 free "hides" (*lány*), that is the portions of land into which the whole village was divided. The office and property connected with the hereditary magistracy could be purchased or sold. **Feudal rent** was paid in money. From the 15th century landlords attempted to impose upon the population of these villages an obligation to provide compulsory labor (*robota*). Many villages founded under the German Law were in the upper part of the county of Trenčín, where the colonization activity was initiated by the townspeople of Žilina, at the beginning of the 14th century. These villages appealed to the Žilina law (**Žilina City Book**). Also under the German Law were the villages in the counties of Upper Nitra, Orava and Turiec, part of Liptov and from the 13th century, Spiš, from where it spread into Šariš and upper Zemplín, as well as into Gemer and part of the counties of Malohont and Zvolen. Remnants of the emphyteutic law were preserved up to the *urbarial* regulations of Maria Theresa (**Theresian urbár**). /JB/

GESTA (from the Latin *res gestae* – things done, deeds) – deeds, actions, events, occurrences recorded in a literary manner. They could deal with the history of a nation, state, tribe, a certain group of people or important individuals. They originated in ancient Rome, where some authors selected short moral lessons from extensive historical works. Epic poems celebrating heroic deeds (for example the *Song of Roland*) were also classified among the *gesta* in the Middle Ages. The term *gesta* also referred to some **chronicles**, for example, *The Deeds of the Ancient Hungarians (Gesta Hungarorum vetera)*, which appeared in the 11th century. They have not been preserved as a whole but parts of them were taken over into later chronicles. /JB/

GLAGOLITIC (hlaholic) – the oldest Slavic alphabet. It was compiled by Constantine (Cyril), even before his arrival in Great Moravia, on the basis of the minuscule letters of the Greek alphabet supplemented by other letters not known in Greek, probably from the Hebrew and Samaritan alphabets. After the expulsion of the pupils of Methodius from the **Great Moravian Empire**, glagolitic writing was maintained until the 11th century at the school in Ochrida (Bulgaria) and later on the Dalmatian islands. Its name was drawn from the word "glagol" or "hlahol" (word). The shapes of the glagolitic letters are made up from three Christian symbols – the cross, the equilateral triangle and the circle. The oldest documents written in glagolitic are the Kiev letters (in a copy from the 10th century), which are connected with the history of Great Moravia. A younger form of Slavic writing is the Cyrillic that developed in the Bulgarian region at the end of the 9th and the beginning of the 10th century. Its model were the letters of the Greek majuscule (uncial) alphabet. /JB/

GOLD PIECES (florins, ducats) – gold coins. King Charles Robert introduced them into Hungary in 1325 on the model of the Florentine ducat, hence the name florin. A florin weighed 3.558 g and the content of pure gold was very high (3.520 g). This value was maintained for several centuries and therefore the coins also became very popular abroad. Hungarian florins were first minted in Buda and from 1330 also in Kremnica. The nominal value of a florin served also in the computation of the relationship of small coins. During the reigns of the Anjous one florin was exchanged for 84 to 96 *denárs*, later 100 – 200 *denárs* and, during the reign of Sigismund, 250 *denárs or* more. While the value of *denárs* in relation to florins decreased during internal disturbances in the country, florins retained a stable rate of exchange. In the period 1458 – 1521, during the reign of Matthias Corvinus and his successors, one florin was exchanged for 100 *denárs*; later the *denárs* again declined in value. The Rheinish gold piece that was minted in the German lands was also in circulation in Hungary from the 16th century. It had a lower gold content and thus was valued at less than a Hungarian florin. The Rhei-

nish gold piece was equal to 60 *kreutzer* or about 100 to 120 *denars*. The exchange rate of florins varied when they were exchanged for other coins of lesser value. For example, in the 16th century in eastern Slovakia a florin was exchanged for 33 Polish *groschen* or 99 *denars*, a Rhenish gold piece for only 80 *denars*. From 1620 three types of florins existed in Hungary: the rural florin (*florenus rusticus*) with a value of 33 half *turaks* – 49.5 *kreutzer;* the short florin (*florenus brevis*) with a value of 50 *kreutzer;* and the drawn florin (*florenus tractus*) with a value of 3 Marian groschen or 52 *kreutzer* (*grajciarov*). In addition, the Rheinish (German) gold piece continued to be used in the country. These coins were in use until 1857, when a gold piece with a value of 100 *kreutzer* was introduced. From the introduction of the crown as currency in 1892 until the disappearance of Austria-Hungary (1918), the term *gulden* (gold piece) was used for the new monetary unit and one *gulden* was equal to two crowns. Gold coins were minted only in higher values (100, 20 and 10 crowns). The gold content and its value no longer corresponded to the original Hungarian florin. /JB/

GOLDEN BULL – charter or document with a golden seal (*bulla*). The seal was either completely of gold or of wax covered with gold foil. Golden bulls were issued by rulers for significant legal acts or when the person petitioning for the charter paid an appropriate fee for its issue. The best known is the Golden Bull of Andrew II from **1222** that confirmed the collective privileges of the Hungarian **nobility**. It was issued because of the dissatisfaction of the minor nobility or *servienti,* who were burdened by the frequent and costly military campaigns of the **king**. According to the Golden Bull, the royal *servienti* were directly subordinate to the king. They were to be judged only by the king at regular court sessions in Székesfehérvár, and not by the county administrator (*župan*). The lands of a noble without male heirs could be inherited by daughters or immediate relatives. Otherwise, they reverted to the ruler. The nobility were obliged to fight for the defense of the country (conscription, **insurrection**), but only for three months in foreign campaigns; the king had to cover the cost of longer campaigns (by paying for military service). The bull delimited the king's authority to make arbitrary grants of extensive lands to the nobility and forbade entrusting lands and offices to foreigners, especially to Jews and **Ismailites**. If the king did not adhere to these provisions, the nobility had the right to resist (*ius resistendi*). The provisions of the bull were confirmed, with minor modifications, in **1231**, **1233** and **1267**, and were incorporated into the decrees of later rulers (for example, Louis of Anjou, **1351**) and Werböczy's *Tripartitum*. The original Golden Bull of Andrew II has not been preserved. The oldest version is from 1318. Golden bulls were issued also on other occasions. For example, the charter of privileges for Trnava of **1238** issued by Béla IV and the confirmation of the privileges of Bratislava of **1464** by Matthias Corvinus both had a golden bull affixed. /JB/

GOTHIC – artistic and cultural style prevailing from the mid 12th century to the end of the 15th century and in central Europe to the beginning of the 16th century. The name comes from the era of the Renaissance, which regarded medieval art as barbaric and named it after the Goths, a Germanic tribe. The oldest Gothic monument is the cloister church of Saint Denis designed by Abbot Suger (1140 – 1143). From France the Gothic style spread throughout the whole of Europe and reached Slovakia in the mid 13th century after the Tatar invasion. Its most significant expression in architecture was in the construction of cathedrals. Its typical characteristics are the divided arch, vaults resting on ribs, thin columns, high, divided windows filled with colored glass, round windows (rosettes), and thin turrets (finials). Gothic architecture is dematerialized, with an open space optically directed toward the vertical. Sculpted decorations, also present on the exterior, used small reliefs, figures from mythology, animal or plant motifs and drapery. In painting the Gothic style was expressed especially in the 14th century in wall paintings, in altars with rich decoration and panel pictures (so-called winged altars spread especially in the 15th century) and in book painting (miniatures). It also was adopted by the artisan crafts, such as metal-casting, especially in the production of bells and baptismal fonts, gold-smithing and jewelers (monstrances), furniture making and the like. Only literature and theater did not significantly differ from that of the previous Romanesque era. In Slovakia the Gothic style first affected the eastern Slovak cities, especially Spiš and the mining cities. In Slovakia the **Romanesque style** continued to exist in parallel with the earliest phase of the Gothic and so developed a transitional Romanesque-Gothic style (1230 – 1280). The Premonstratensian and Cistercian orders especially contributed to the building activity. From the 14th century grand multi-nave churches were built or older ones were rebuilt in the cities. After 1305 the Minorite church in Levoča was built, at the beginning of the 14th century the parish church in Trnava and the church of the Poor Claires in Bratislava, from mid-century the cloister church in Hronský Beňadik, in the third quarter of the century the parish church in Levoča and the chapel of St John in the Franciscan church in Bratislava. The most significant monuments of Gothic architecture are the cathedral of St Elizabeth in Košice, whose construction began after the fire in 1385, and the cathedral of St Martin in Bratislava, both completed only in the 15th century, as well as other parish and cloister churches in Banská Štiavnica, Kremnica, Bardejov and other cities. Unlike the churches in the towns, the older village churches were not reconstructed. The expressive elements of countryside Gothic are chapels with family tombs (for example, the chapel of the Zápolya family in Spišský Štvrtok). Gothic architecture was also expressed in the building of castles, especially their residential parts (Zvolen castle was built in the period from 1370 to 1382), homes of townspeople and city-halls. During the second quarter of the 15th century an extensive reconstruction of the castle in Bratislava was carried out on the model of an Italian castle with a square floor-plan. In the late Gothic era, from the second half of the 15th century, more natural and realistic elements were reflected in artistic works and presaged the appearance of the **Renaissance**. The most significant representative of late Gothic sculpture is Master Paul of Levoča (1460 – 1542), who made the Levoča altar. /JB/

GOVERNMENT FIVE – an extra-constitutional operational political institution in the interwar Czechoslovak Republic. It was established during the first government of the social democrat Vlastimil Tusar in 1919 and 1920 and was comprised of the chairmen of the ruling coalition parties (**Agrarian Party**, the Czechoslovak National Socialist Party, the Czechoslovak National Democratic Party, the Czechoslovak Social Democratic Party and the Czechoslovak People's Party). The most important political and economic questions were discussed and decided within the closed group of the ruling five before parliament (national assembly) made its decision. As an unaccountable center of power, it reduced the significance of parliament, which was dependent upon its decisions. The empowerment law of June 1933 underscored the dependence of parliament upon the executive power and further exacerbated this development. /RL/

GRAJCIAR (*kreutzer*) – originally an Austrian, later a Hungarian small silver coin. In the Alpine countries it was minted from 1250 and had the value of four Viennese pennies (*Pfennige*). It came into circulation in the Kingdom of Hungary, where it originally had a value of 1.33 Hungarian *denárs*. It became an official monetary unit of Hungary only in 1538, when its value was equal to a *groš*. After the inflation around 1620 it had the value of two Hungarian *denárs,* as documents from eastern Slovakia and the central Slovak mining towns testify. Elsewhere in Slovakia it had approximately the value of 1.6 Hungarian *denárs.* Three *kreutzers* were equal to one Hungarian *groš* or 5 to 6 Hungarian *denárs.* After 1760 they were struck from copper. The introduction of Austrian currency in 1857 set the value of the *kreutzer* at a hundreth of a *florin.* After the introduction of the crown as a cur-

rency unit (1892), the name *grajciar* was used to designate the two *heller* coin. /JB/

GREAT MORAVIA see **Great Moravian Empire**

GREAT MORAVIAN EMPIRE – the oldest state of Moravians and Slovaks in the second third of the 9th and the beginning of the 10th century. The concept *Morábia megalé* was introduced into historiography by the Byzantine Emperor Constantine Porphyrogenetos in the work *Concerning the Administration of the Empire (De administrando imperio)* in the mid 10th century. Some historians interpret this as being Further Moravia (from the viewpoint of a Byzantine observer), in contrast to Near Moravia, which stretched along the Sava river in today's Croatia. The Great Moravian Empire originated after the forcible annexation of Pribina's principality of Nitra to the Moravia of Mojmír in **833** and especially after the accession of Svätopluk, who in **871** seized power in the struggle against Frankish aggression. Under Svätopluk (871 – 894) today's Lusatia and Silesia, southern Poland (Vistula region), Transtisa controlled by the Bulgarians, the duchy of Pribina or Koceľ and, in 890 – 894, Czechia were connected to its territory. To speak of the Great Moravian Empire as the first common state of Czechs and Slovaks is an overstatement since the Czech tribes in it were a subjugated ethnic group, living at the edge of the Great Moravian Empire. Indeed, they withdrew in 895, at the first opportunity (after the death of Svätopluk), and subordinated themselves to the Eastern Frankish Empire. The greatest historic significance of the Great Moravian Empire relates to the spread of Christianity in the native language, including the use of the liturgical Old Slavonic language. Its recognition was a unique phenomenon in the history of the church. Constantine and Methodius, who came to Great Moravia in **863**, created the very first Slavic letters based upon the Greek alphabet (**Glagolitic**). This made possible the development of culture and education. Although Frankish missionaries had previously spread Christianity among the Slovaks and Moravians, it was the mission of Constantine (Cyril) and Methodius that established it on a firm basis. They obtained from the papal curia authorization to conduct a further mission in this region and to build an ecclesiastical organization in Svätopluk's Empire. This promising development was later interrupted by the fate of Great Moravia and its dissolution. The development of Great Moravia halted for a time the pressure of the Eastern Frankish Empire on the middle Danubian basin. In **907** a three-day battle between the Bavarians and Magyars took place not far from Bratislava. It is assumed that the Great Moravian Empire had declined as a military and political power shortly before. As a result of this battle, the Slovaks lost their independence for more than a thousand years. As is documented in written sources, the most significant Great Moravian center was Nitra. Documents also refer to Mikulčice (city of Moravia), Devín (considered in the sources to be the strongest of Rastislav's fortresses), Staré Město near Uherské Hradiště (probably the seat of Methodius) and Bratislava. In Great Moravia dozens of fortified castles existed and served as centers of political, military and cultic power. It is indisputable that at several locations there is a continuity between later settlements and Great Moravian sites. /JB/

GREGORIAN CALENDAR (also Christian calendar) – the calendar presently used. The Christian church officially adopted the **Julian Calendar** at the council of Nicea in 325. At the same time it fixed the date for the celebration of Easter, the most important ecclesiastical holiday, as the first Sunday after the full moon following the spring equinox (21 March). Therefore Easter is a holiday that moves within a range of 35 days (22 March to 25 April). The Christian church enriched the calendar not only with movable festivals (for example, the Baptism of Jesus, Ash Wednesday, the Ascension, first Sunday in Advent) but also with many holidays falling on specific dates (especially the feasts of the saints of the Catholic Church). Differences from the original Julian calendar included the introduction of a seven day week (from the 4th century) and the counting of years after Christ (AD – Anno Domini, the Year of the Lord), which began

to be used from 525. Since the calendar was not concordant with the actual geophysical year, by a bull of **24 February 1582** Pope Gregory XIII ordered its reform. The numbering of the days was moved forward 10 days, so that Thursday, 4 October 1582 was followed by Friday, 15 October. This corrected calendar, known as the Gregorian calendar, is used today. Hungary, and thus Slovakia, accepted it in the fall of 1587 (when 21 October was followed by 1 November). The Gregorian calendar has only 97 leap years for every 400 years and not 100 leap years, as does the Julian calendar, and thus has a deviation of only 1.22 days for every 4,000 years. /VS/

GRÓF see **Count**

GROŠ (from the German *Grosch*) – a silver coin current from the 12th century and introduced from western Europe and Venetia. The Czech or the Prague *groš* that was first minted during the reign of Wenceslas II (1300) circulated in Slovakia from the beginning of the 14th century. In 1329 Charles Robert introduced the Hungarian *groš* minted in Kremnica on the model of the Czech *groš*. The Czech *groš* contained 3.59 grams of pure silver, the Hungarian *groš* 3.19 grams. One *florin* was equal to 17 *groš*, one *groš* to six *denárs*. The value of the silver in the *groš* gradually decreased and the Czech *groš* with a higher silver content was more popular. In 1370 – 1468 the minting of *groš* was halted in Hungary and renewed only by Matthias Corvinus. The new *groš*, the so-called coin with the Madonna (that is, with the image of the Virgin Mary), was valued at five Hungarian *denárs*, so that 20 *groš* equaled one *florin*. In the 16th century large *groš*, with a value of eight *denárs*, and small *groš*, with a value of 4 *denárs*, were struck. The *groš* was in circulation until the use of the so-called Austrian currency was halted in 1857. /JB/

GUESTS – (Latin – *hospites*) – the free inhabitants of foreign and domestic origin who, on the basis of **privileges** and under city, especially **German Law**, obtained a privileged position in the cities in Slovakia. Until the end of the 13th century these were predominantly Germanic colonists but included the Flemish,

Walloons and Italians (**colonization**). Poles, Czechs, Ruthenians, Walachians etc. arrived later. Since, from a legal perspective, the guests merged with the resident domestic population, the term is not used in later sources. A distinction is made only between full-fledged citizens and the remaining population of a city. /JB/

GUILDS – organizations of craftsmen or other producers or tradesmen during **feudalism**. They developed in western European cities during the 11th and 12th centuries. In Slovakia they appeared at the beginning of the 14th century, although the first written documentation comes only from the second half of the 14th century. They developed from **brotherhoods** that had a religious-social character. The development of guilds was not everywhere conditioned by the existence of brotherhoods since brotherhoods and guilds continued to exist in parallel. The articles (statutes) of the Košice furriers nominally dating from **1307** perhaps originated earlier. None of the first statutes for the bakers, cobblers and butchers issued by the city council in Bratislava in **1376** mention guilds. From the beginning of the 15th century guild articles were enacted which defined the manner and organization of production, the sale of products, the obligations and rights of guild members (including spiritual-religious duties), the election of guild organs and the like. The guild articles were issued by city councils, landlords and rulers. Guilds compiled them themselves or sometimes adapted them from other guilds and presented them for confirmation to the authorities. Where there were few craftsmen in one profession, they usually created guilds of related trades (for example, smiths, swordmakers, cutlerers, armorers and the like). The guilds were first established in the most significant cities. From the 16th century they spread to the towns of landlords in the countryside. In the 18th century, when the development of guilds culminated, there were more than 1,000 guilds in 160 cities and towns in Slovakia. The guilds were headed by the masters who were full-fledged members of the guilds. Journeymen worked with masters as a salaried workforce. The lowest category was the apprentices. Journeymen had to complete practical training with several masters both at home and abroad. In some guilds the right to become a master was limited to owners of real property in the city and required the production of a master work (masterpiece) and a suitable payment to the guild, as well as the provision of a banquet for the members of the guild. In an attempt to limit competition, the guilds restricted not only the number of products and the manner of sale but also the number or masters, journeymen and apprentices in the guild. Even the journeymen associated in their own guilds were limited by the masters and the authorities, so that social conflicts did not occur. The guilds had started to retard the development of production by the 18th century, but continued to exist alongside **manufactures**. They were dissolved by the law of **27 February 1872**. In addition to guilds of craftsmen or artisans, there also existed guilds of merchants. In Slovakia these were not as widespread, for the merchants formed the leading group of the population in the cities and did not need such organizations to defend their interests. /JB/

HABSBURG MONARCHY – the complex confederation of states with a common ruler from the Habsburg family. It was multi-national and was the greatest power in central Europe, even though its internal organization and territorial extent changed. It had various names until 1804, after which it was officially called the Austrian Empire. It was established in 1526 by joining together the Kingdom of Hungary, the Czech kingdom and the Austrian lands, in order to protect numerous nations from the Turkish threat. The Habsburgs cooperated with the **pope** and the Catholic Church and did not join the side of the **Reformation**. They gradually attempted to introduce **absolutism**, to limit the privileges of the nobility and to weaken the independence of historic lands and their organs in favor of the central power. They generally succeeded in implementing reforms in the Czech and Austrian lands where the Thirty Years' War strengthened their position. They were much less successful in the Kingdom of Hungary where, through the insurrections of the estates, the **nobility** hindered absolutism and **re-Catholicization** during the 17th century. After the Turkish wars and the **Peace of Satu Mare** (1711), the territorially restored Kingdom of Hungary defended its autonomous position. The War of the Spanish Succession strengthened the Habsburgs. They tried to modernize the monarchy and transform it into a unified state, in particular during the period of **enlightenment absolutism**. Their lack of success led to the repudiation of radical reforms and, after the **Congress of Vienna**, **Metternichian absolutism** became a pillar of the old order on the continent. However, it was toppled by the **revolution of 1848/1849.** The ruler promised to reorganize the empire upon the principle of **Austro-Slavism.** But, after the defeat of the Hungarian army, he installed **neo-absolutism** instead. National and constitutional strife intensified again during the 1860s. The weakened imperial power chose a seemingly simple solution and, in the Austrian-Hungarian (Magyar) constitutional compromise, the monarchy yielded to the path of **dualism**. Although it was temporarily stabilized under the new name **Austria-Hungary**, in the long term its decline was hastened. /DŠ/

HAJDUKS – a specific population group in the Kingdom of Hungary that formed at the end of the Middle Ages. Originally they were displaced groups of farmers that fled before the Turks or lost their homes in the wars. By the end of the Middle Ages some of them were living as cattle drovers (their name is derived from the Latin word *haidones* and the Hungarian word *hajtu*). Later they were engaged for service in border castles and in the armies of the Transylvanian princes. During the insurrections of the estates of the Hungarian nobles (**Bocskai's, Bethlen's Insurrection, kuruci**)

they made up the core of the insurgent armies. They also fought in the ranks of the regular Habsburg army as separate Hungarian infantry units during the 17th and 18th centuries. The Hajduks were concentrated especially in the county of Sabolc, where they occupied around six towns and had their own administration headed by a count (after 1871 by a captain), under privileges granted by Stephen Bocskai and confirmed by Rudolf II and Maria Theresa. In 1876 they were incorporated into the new county of Hajda. Like the population settled under the Walachian Law, the Hajduks were not a distinct ethnic group, but a specific occupational and legally defined social class, whose main function was military service. Therefore, the name Hajduk was also used to designate the constables and servants of the landlords and the counties. /VS/

HAMMER MILL (*hámor*, forge) – a facility for processing iron or copper. Its basic components were a forge for heating metal, bellows and a hammer driven by a water-wheel. Usually one to three hammers were employed. Hammer mills appeared in western Europe at the end of the 12th and the beginning of the 13th century. The earliest reference to a hammer mill in Slovakia comes from Štítnik in 1344. In 1357 there was probably a hammer mill on the outskirts of Nálepkovo (Vondrišel), and there is further evidence of hammer mills from the years 1376 (Jasov), 1383 (Dobšiná) and 1399 (Jelšava). In the following centuries they spread into all of the mining areas. Evidence for this is preserved in topographical names. In 1841 there were more than 200 hammer mills in Slovakia. Foundry-men were already associated in **guilds** in the 16th century. In the 19th century hammer mills were replaced by more modern methods of processing metals. Some remained in service until the 20th century and today are exhibits in open-air museums. /JB/

HERETICS – false believers, apostates from the faith. In the 11th and 12th centuries the term *kacír* originally signified a neo-Manichean sect, the so-called Cathari, the pure (from the

Greek – *katharoi*). The sect developed in southern France and northern Italy. The term *kacír* (heretic) was later used for all who criticized the core teaching of the church or secretly created religious sects. In Slovakia traces of the heretics can be observed in the manner of burial in the 11th and 12th centuries. In the 14th century the **Waldensians** spread into Hungary and Slovakia. At the beginning of the 15th century Hussite ideas (even if in small measure) penetrated Slovakia (Lukáš of Nové Mesto, Jurík of Topoľčany). In the 1440s – 1460s the **Brethren** were active in Slovakia and, like the **Hussites**, were considered heretics by the Catholic Church. After the spread of the **Reformation** in the 16th century, the Catholic Church considered all Protestants to be heretics. The Protestants, on the other hand, regarded the Anabaptists as heretics and persecuted them as did the Catholic Church, which had created the institution of the **inquisition**. The term heretic comes from the Greek *hairesis* – a philosophical opinion. /JB/

HLASISTS – a group of young liberals without clear-cut views or a firm organization. It was formed by Slovak students in Prague associated in the Detvan Club (**15 March 1882**) and in Vienna and Budapest at the beginning of the 1890s. They were especially inspired by the views of Professor Tomáš Garrigue Masaryk. The name was taken from the journal *Voice (Hlas)* that they published from **29 June 1898**. Its leading personalities were Vavro Šrobár, Pavol Blaho, Fedor Houdek and also, to a lesser extent, Milan Hodža. The Hlasists condemned national suppression and considered it the cause for the backwardness of the Kingdom of Hungary. They criticized the conservative program, passive policy and Russophilia of the core of the **Slovak National Party** in Martin. They did not view slogans as the best way of defending against **Magyarization** and promoting the civilizing advance of Slovakia but rather favored a politics that concentrated upon the everyday life of all classes, especially those constituting the backbone of Slovak society (propertied farmers and small entrepreneurs). They developed the "Štúrian"

approach of patient day-by-day work focused on arousing Slovak political consciousness and raising the level of social, cultural and economic life generally. They demanded the democratic reform of state administration and government, a general right of suffrage, free education, progressive taxation and the establishment of Slovak secondary schools and a university. They were supporters of Czecho-Slovak national unity, defended the utility of cooperation with the Czechs and worked with the **Czechoslavic Society**. Initially they cooperated with the Catholic Ľudáks but, as is demonstrated by the **Mikuláš Resolution**, more regularly with the social democrats. The Hlasist group did not obtain broad support and it disappeared in the first decade of the 20th century as a result of internal conflicts. A younger liberal generation, the Prúdists (named for the journal *Prúdy-Currents)*, declared their support for its views. The Hlasists and Prúdists were active in the founding of Czecho-Slovakia. However, their continued adherence to the position of **Czechoslovakism** made the resolution of the question of Slovakia more difficult. /DŠ/

HLINKA GUARD – an armed organization active in the years 1938 – 1945. The name "guard" referred to the historically well-known organization of Slovak volunteers in 1848/1849 and in the coup of 1918. Its attributive "Hlinka" acknowledged the influence of Andrej Hlinka, who did not, however, play any role in its creation. The idea of establishing a defensive guard emerged in connection with the preparation of the autonomist demonstration of **5 June 1938**. The first Hlinka Guard group was established in Trnava on **2 August 1938**. The guard was created without a mandate from the leadership of Hlinka's Slovak People's Party, as a spontaneous expression of the dissatisfaction of some of the younger generation with existing political parties. After the declaration of the **autonomy of Slovakia** on **6 October 1938** the number of its members rapidly increased. The reason for this was the political crisis, the passivity of the army and the gendarmes after the **Munich agreement,** and the determination to defend

Slovak autonomy, especially against Magyar revisionism. Karol Sidor, who held a protective hand over the guard, defended its existence to the conservative wing of Hlinka's Slovak People's Party (Jozef Tiso, Jozef Buday, J. Sivák). In mid-October 1938 the Hlinka Guard came under the command of the army and became a paramilitary organization by a decree of the autonomous government of 28 October 1938. Prior to 1939 it was not armed. The position of the guard changed after the Slovak Republic was established on **14 March 1939**. An order of **21 December 1939** declared it to be a semi-military organization with a voluntary membership. The status of the Hlinka Guard was defined only by the law of 5 July 1940. As the highest representative of the defensive power of the state, Jozef Tiso became its supreme commander. Actual power over the Hlinka Guard was held by its chief commander (1938 – 1939 Karol Sidor, 1939 – 1940 Alexander Mach, 1940 František Galan, 1940 – 1944 Alexander Mach, 1944 – 1945 Otomar Kubala). Lower sections of its command structure consisted of county, district and local commands. The Hlinka Guard also organized cultural events. Bureaucrats and teachers joined it, often under pressure. After the **Salzburg Negotiations** in July 1940 it was completely in the hands of Slovak pro-German radicals. It had combat and security roles, provided guard service in **labor camps** and participated in organizing the deportation of the Jewish population (**25 March 1942**). Reserve units of the Hlinka Guard were created on 21 September 1944 by an order of the supreme command of the Hlinka Guard. It also established units of volunteers to go into the field. Their task was to maintain order and fight against the insurgents. From October to November 1944 the Hlinka Guard, police, gendarmes, Hlinka Youth, and the Slovak labor service were subordinated to the ministry of national defense. This made possible the assignment of citizens to any one of these organizations on the basis of an induction order. Some of the reserve units of the guard fought with German armed units against the partisans in the **insurrection**

of 1944. It assisted in the executions in Nemecká and Kremnička. The history of the Hlinka Guard ended with the arrival of the Soviet army and the subsequent **retribution**. /RL/

HLINKA'S SLOVAK PEOPLE'S PARTY – a right-wing party with a national and Catholic orientation. The political awakening of the Slovak Catholics took place in 1894 within the framework of the Hungarian People's Party of Ferdinand Zichy. Their public activity was elicited by the need to react to contemporary needs in the spirit of the 1891 encyclical of Pope Leo XIII, *Rerum novarum*. Several Slovak Catholic and Evangelical figures campaigned as candidates for the diet in 1896, 1901 and 1905 on the program of the Hungarian People's Party (national rights, social program, church laws). Dissatisfaction with the failure of the Hungarian People's Party to fulfill its promises led to the founding of an independent Slovak People's Party on **14 December 1905** that nonetheless formally remained a part of the Slovak National Party. Confessional discord led to the founding of an independent Slovak People's Party in Žilina on **29 July 1913**. Andrej Hlinka became its chairman. It suspended its activity during the **First World War**. In 1918 its representatives actively took part in the formation of the **Slovak National Council (1918 – 1919)** and the acceptance of the **Declaration of the Slovak Nation**. The Slovak People's Party renewed its activity in Žilina on 19 December 1918 and was renamed Hlinka's Slovak People's Party on **17 October 1925**. After the **Czechoslovak Republic** was founded, government politics were dominated by **Czechoslovakism**, liberalism and by anti-Slovak and anti-Catholic tendencies under the guise of struggling against Magyarism and for progress. The Slovak Catholics' share in political power was minimal. Small farmers, in particular, comprised the voter base of Hlinka's Slovak People's Party. It advocated the **autonomy of Slovakia** as anchored in the **Pittsburgh Agreement** and defended the idea of the particularity of the Slovak nation. It was the strongest political party in Slovakia (28 – 34 per cent) after the county elections in 1923. Since the centralist government circles refused to meet its demands, it worked in opposition and became a part of the government coalition only on **15 January 1927**. It supported the acceptance of the **regional system** and the **modus vivendi**. After the trial of Vojtech Tuka on **5 October 1929** it again went into opposition, in which it continued until **6 October 1938**. It cooperated in particular with the Slovak National Party (**16 October 1932**) and achieved a dominant position with the establishment of an autonomous Slovakia. It considered the fragmentation of political groups as a superfluous, disintegrating force and therefore urged the unification of Slovak parties into a single party (**8 November 1938**) on a voluntary basis and, if necessary, by political pressure. The new party received the name Hlinka's Slovak People's Party – the Party of Slovak National Unity. It was the only Slovak party established upon national and authoritarian principles. The leadership of Hlinka's Slovak People's Party was in the hands of a moderate group led by Jozef Tiso (**1 October 1939**). Hlinka's Slovak People's Party was a counter-weight to the **Hlinka Guard** and the influence of German and Magyar minorities. The strengthening of the authority of the party led to the acceptance of the leader principle on 22 October 1942. The activity of the Hlinka's Slovak People's Party was forbidden on the territory of the insurgents by the Slovak National Council on **1 September 1944**. In March 1945 the **Moscow Negotiations** definitively decided to ban it. /RL/

HUMANISM – an intellectual movement connected with the **Renaissance** of art and culture. Its goal was to re-awaken man and develop the human personality in the spirit of the ideals of antiquity. It began in Italy in the 14th century. Humanists gathered, critically studied, expounded, published and translated manuscripts of Greek and Roman authors and sought to imitate these creations in their own work. Literary humanism was limited to schools and learned circles. Initially they used only Latin, which they tried to cleanse of medieval vulgarisms in order to restore its classical form. The humanists also began to write in the national languages. Although they used ancient models, they also respected the impulses of their times as expressed in the development of philosophy and free thought. For example, in his work *In Praise of Folly*, Erasmus of Rotterdam (1467 – 1536) proclaimed the need for an internal renewal of the church. The statesman, philosopher and political thinker Thomas More (1478 – 1535) wrote his vision of the ideal state in *Utopia.* In *The Prince,* the politician and political theoretician Niccolo Machiavelli (1469 – 1527) depicted a Renaissance personality who was relentless in the pursuit of his interests. Humanist ideas began to penetrate the Kingdom of Hungary during the reign of Matthias Corvinus. A library of valuable manuscripts was established at the royal court. After 1526 the Reformation contributed to the spread of humanism (Leonard Coxe, Ján Henckel, Valentín Eck). It also influenced Catholic theologians and intellectuals (for example, Archbishop Nicholas Oláh, John Sambucus, Zachariáš Rohožník-Mošovský). Libraries were built and schools were established, even in the countryside. The spread of the new ideas was helped by the invention of printing with movable type (Johann Gutenberg, mid 15th century). Printing presses began to be established in Hungary and Slovakia only during the second half of the 16th century. The first university in Slovakia, the **Academia Istropolitana,** functioned in Bratislava (1467). The first learned society (Sodalitas litteraria Danubiana), whose guiding spirit was Conrad Celtis, was established in Buda in 1490 and was later transferred to Vienna (1497). Its members included the Bratislava pastor Ursínus Velius and Štefan Monetarius from Kremnica. /JB/

HUNGARIAN CHAMBER – the highest financial and economic administrative office of the Hungarian monarchy in the modern era. It was established in Buda by King Ferdinand I in 1528 on the model of the chamber system tried and tested in the so-called Habsburg patrimonial (hereditary) countries. It was subordinated to the court chamber in Vienna. It was dissolved in 1529 because of the threatening danger of the Turks and was renewed in Bratislava on **2 July 1531**. Its Slovakian branch was the **Spiš chamber**. It administered finances, the taxes approved by the **diet**, the royal (crown) and chamber property, the salt and mining prerogatives and revenue from the royal cities. From the beginning of the 17th century it was almost exclusively concerned with the documentation, administration or control of the income and property of the king and the state (*erár*). In contrast with other contemporary institutions of the estates, it was the first institution of a modern (bureaucratic) type in the Kingdom of Hungary. This collective organ was initially composed of five, later of even more councilors, over whom the chamber prefect presided. The ruler named the prefect and councilors to office for life. The chamber met daily, except for Sunday and holidays. The office of the Hungarian chamber, in which professionally skilled administrators worked – recorders, clerks and accountants – was made up of three divisions: chancellery, treasury and accounting office. During the reign of the Emperor Joseph II (1780 – 1790) the chamber was replaced by the royal property (*erár*) office of the **vice-regency council**. Following the death of Joseph, the Hungarian chamber again renewed its activity and functioned up to 1848 when its functions passed to the ministries of the newly established government in the Kingdom of Hungary. /VS/

HUNGARIAN DIET (also county diet) – the highest assembly of the privileged **estates** and the supreme organ of legislative power in the Kingdom of Hungary. It developed from the institution of court days on the one hand and, on the other, from the gradual assumption of some of the functions of the Hungarian **royal council,** which had been established by the first Hungarian kings as an advisory organ in judicial and legislative matters. From the 12th century, as a result of their weakened patrimonial authority and according to actual needs, the kings convened general congregations or country-wide assemblies of the **nobility,** which were the direct predecessors of the diet. According to the **Golden Bull** of 1222, the diet was to be regularly convened each year in Székesfehérvár on the feast-day of Saint Stephen. The nobility had the right to participate personally and to present their proposals and grievances to it, but they were an unequal party in the proceedings, since they could only advise the king on his decisions. During the reign of the last Árpád, Andrew III, legislative competence was added to the activity of these assemblies (called a *parlamentum generale* or *publicum*). The assembly of the country's nobility that took place in September 1298 in Buda is considered the first diet in the proper sense of the word. It accepted several proposals that strengthened royal power and limited the arbitrariness of the **magnates** in the interests of the lower nobility. During the reigns of the Anjous, who ruled in an absolutist manner, diets were not summoned, except in 1351, when Louis I was forced to request approval from the nobility to collect an extraordinary tax. The regular activity of the country's assemblies was renewed only by Sigismund of Luxemburg. In the 15th century the diet became the supreme self-governing organ of the **estates monarchy**. The representatives of the royal free cities also began to participate more regularly in its discussions but had only one collective vote. The authority of the diet grew with the acceptance of the convention that only acts jointly approved by king and diet had the force of law. The scope of the activity of the diet significantly expanded until the end of the Middle Ages. It approved the levy of new taxes, elected the new king, the **palatine** and other high officers and judges of the country, controlled the administration of state finances and regulated the obligations of the subject population (**1514, servitude**). In old Slovak the name *rákoš* was used for the diet, after the name of the place at which the diet most frequently met at the end of the Middle Ages, Rákos field near Pest. The diet carefully protected its acquired authority even after the annexation of the Kingdom of Hungary to the **Habsburg Monarchy**. As a result of the occupation of a part of Hungary by the Turks, Bratislava became the seat of the diet until

1848. Only exceptionally would the diet find it necessary to meet elsewhere, for example in Banská Bystrica (1542 – 1543) or Trnava (1545 – 1547). During the period of the introduction of **absolutism** the diet was further subordinated to the ruler. But it also fulfilled the task of representing the Hungarian nobility and Hungarian statehood vis-à-vis the Habsburgs. The failure to respect the rights and **privileges** of the Hungarian estates and religious freedom, which the Habsburgs frequently violated, culminated in several insurrections of the estates in the 17th century. The rebellious Hungarian nobility assembled at special insurgent diets: Banská Bystrica (1621), Sopron (1681), Sečany (1705) and **Ónod** (1707). An important encroachment upon the internal organization of the diet was its division into two tables (*tabula)* or chambers in 1608. The upper table was established for the **prelates** and secular magnates. Its president, as well as that of the entire diet, was the palatine. The remaining nobles and feudal landowners belonged to the lower table. It was representative and in its discussions two delegates from each **county** (*stolica)*, as well as the representatives of the royal free cities and chapters, took part. Priories and abbeys were represented by one delegate each. The president of the lower table was the representative of the king (*personál)*. After the defeat of the **revolution of 1848/ 1849** the Kingdom of Hungary lost its constitutional freedom. By the **October Diploma** of 20 October 1860 a special provincial diet was established but it was dissolved in August 1861 to protest the **February Constitution**. After the Austrian-Hungarian Compromise a Hungarian diet of two chambers was restored. The upper chamber was composed of hereditary members. It was made up of Hungarian magnates (**dukes**, **counts** and **barons**) and the highest dignitaries of the Catholic Church (**archbishops, bishops**). Bourgeois political relations were considered only in the reform of the upper chamber in 1885, which resulted in its reduction from 750 to 360 members. The new part of this chamber was made up of 50 members who were named

for life by the ruler on the recommendation of the Hungarian prime minister. The lower chamber was representative and its members were elected deputies. The electoral reform of **26 November 1847,** which was motivated by power politics and national perspectives, made the requirements for election even more strict. This is shown by the fact that the proportion of those who had a right to vote was reduced from 6.7 per cent to 5.9 per cent of the total population of the Kingdom of Hungary. The legislative activity of the Hungarian diet from the end of the 18th century up to the dissolution of **Austria-Hungary** was based upon the state ideology of a single political nation (*natio hungarica*) and was the legal basis for the process of systematic **Magyarization**. Under dualism all non-Magyar nations and nationalities had negligible representation in parliament (less than 10 per cent), which resulted from purposeful electoral manipulation as well as from the significantly restricted **right to vote in Hungary**. The final act of the Slovak representatives in the diet was the intervention of Ferdiš Juriga. In the name of the **Slovak National Council,** he delivered a speech on **19 October 1918** on the self-determination of the Slovaks and all nations in Hungary. The diet of the Kingdom of Hungary ceased to function in October 1918 after the disintegration of the monarchy. /VS/

HUNGARIAN ESTATES see **Estates**

HUNGARIAN JACOBINS – a group of radical intellectuals. It was formed in the first half of 1794 under the influence of the French revolution and because of the abolition of **enlightenment absolutism** and the introduction of a conservative policy in the **Habsburg Monarchy**. There were two clandestine organizations of Jacobins in Hungary: the Society of Reformers and the Society of Freedom and Equality, numbering 200 – 300 people of noble and middle-class origin. The program of the Jacobins was developed by their leader, the former abbé and professor, Ignác Martinovič. It rejected all types of privilege, the monarchy and even the Habsburgs. The population of the Kingdom of Hungary would fight for independence in an insurrection. An independent Hungary would proclaim itself a republic, accept a constitution that would abolish the privileges of the nobility and the church and guarantee the equality of all the people before the law and the separation of powers. The Jacobins respected the principle of the equality of nations and, for the first time in modern history, suggested the territorial-political separation of Slovakia. The Kingdom of Hungary was to be a federal state made up of four national provinces, one of which would be Slovakia (*provincia Slavonica*). The central power would be concerned primarily with security and foreign policy and the autonomous entities would have wide jurisdiction, their own constitution, diet, executive power and a native official language. The authorities uncovered the radical plans of the Jacobins and many of them were arrested in the middle of 1794. Five were executed on **20 May 1795** and others were imprisoned. The movement was centered in Buda and Pest and had strong support especially among the Slovaks. Among the 49 indicted, there were more than 20 Slovaks or people connected with Slovakia (origin, schools, relatives and the like), among them the ideologist of the movement, Jozef Hajnóczy, and the translator of the Marseillaise, Francis Abaffy. /DŠ/

HUNGARY (Hungarian Monarchy, Kingdom of Hungary) – multi-national state in central Europe. Named after the old Hungarians (Magyars), its area was 320,000 km² in the second half of the 19th century. One of the states that took over impulses from the **Great Moravian Empire**, it was formed in the second half of the 10th century. Its first king was Stephen I. It was an independent state until 1526 and was ruled by the dynasties of the Árpáds, Anjous, Luxemburgs, Hunyadys and Jagiellons. From the 16th century it was ruled by the Habsburgs. The **Nitra Appanage Duchy** initially occupied part of Slovakia. From the beginning of the 12th century up to 1918 Slovakia formed an integral part of Hungary. The kings lost nominally unlimited power by making grants of property and, from the 13th century, Hungary was transformed into an **estates monarchy** with great power in the hands of the

Hungarian diet and the **counties**. After the Tatar invasion, stone fortresses, fortified cities and Gothic churches were built throughout Hungary. In the 14th century it became one of the most significant states of Europe. In the following century, the higher **nobility** used disputed successions to the throne and political crises to strengthen their power, solidify feudalism and legally establish **servitude**. With the Turkish invasion, it lost its independence in 1526 and became part of the **Habsburg Monarchy**. After Transylvania became independent and the southern and central parts were occupied by the Turks, the Habsburg Kingdom of Hungary was reduced to the territory of Slovakia, the western part of Hungary and Croatia. Bratislava became its capital. In addition to the wars with the Turks, the country was also destabilized by uprisings of the estates and struggles between the **Reformation** and **re-Catholicization**. After the Turks were expelled, the Habsburgs resolutely attempted to introduce **absolutism** in Hungary, which its nobility resisted. **Enlightenment absolutism** implemented the most energetic centralization and modernization. Although **Metternichian absolutism** respected the independence of Hungary, it came into conflict with the **Magyar reform movement.** This culminated in the **revolution of 1848/1849**. After a period of **neo-absolutism** and **provisional government,** the monarchy was transformed in 1867 on the basis of **dualism** into **Austria-Hungary**. In the Kingdom of Hungary a radical **Magyarization** ensued that contributed to its dissolution at the conclusion of the **First World War** in 1918. /DŠ/

HUSSARS – a type of light cavalry. Its name is directly connected with the word courier (*korzár*, from the Latin *cursor* – fast messenger), which was transformed into *gusar, husar* among Slavs in the Balkans in the 14th century and originally designated a robber on horseback. The development of the Hussars as a type of mounted troops is connected with the struggle of the Kingdom of Hungary against the expansionist Ottoman Empire. From the 15th century the Hussars in the service of the Hungarian **kings** were an effective counterpart to the Turkish cavalry, *sipahis*. In contrast to the heavy cavalry of the medieval knights and the cuirassiers of the modern era, the Hussars were not initially a distinctive cavalry force. Their extraordinary mobility was made possible by their light arms (sabers and lances, later replaced by short carbines and a brace of pistols). Originally their assignments were confined primarily to scouting, securing, or pursuing, but, with the development of fire-arms, their importance and participation in direct offensive operations gradually grew. They were distinguished by a characteristic uniform of Hungarian cut, notably a dolman and a short jacket with rich braid. The first two regular Hussar divisions incorporated into the Habsburg army in 1689 were raised in Slovakia. In the **Habsburg Monarchy** the Hussars were raised exclusively in Hungary but at the end of the 17th and the beginning of the 18th century Hussar divisions were established also in other European armies. It disappeared as a type of military unit after the First World War. /VS/

HUSSITES – adherents of a religious reform movement in Czechia (flourished 1415 – 1434). The sermons, public lectures and tracts of the religious reformer Jan Hus (ca. 1372 – 1415), who was influenced by the English reformer John Wycliffe (1320/30 – 1384), led his followers to form distinct communities before 1415. They introduced communion in both kinds, bread and wine from the chalice, for which they were called Calixtines. The chalice became a symbol of the Hussites. Despite the burning of Jan Hus in Constance, his teachings spread further in Czechia. Hussitism assumed a militant revolutionary form only in August 1419 when a radical wing threw councilors from the windows of the new town hall in Prague and began to plunder churches and cloisters in Prague. In the fall of 1419 and at the beginning of 1420 thousands of Hussites organized pilgrimages to the hills and built the city of Tábor that became the center of the Taborite radical wing. The warriors of Jan Žižka in eastern Czechia, the radical Orebites, were called "Orphans" after his death (1424). The center of the mo-

derate Hussites, the Calixtines, was Prague and the University of Prague. The Czech nobility generally supported the moderate wing and only the minor yeomanry joined the Taborites or the "Orphans", where they functioned as commanders. In **1420 – 1431** King Sigismund and the German estates undertook several crusades against the Hussites. The Hussites responded with raids into neighboring countries – Germany, Austria, Poland and Slovakia (**1428**, **1430**, **1431**, **1432**, **1433**, **1434**). The defeat of the last crusader campaign near Domažlice in 1431 led to negotiations between the representatives of the Hussites and the Council of Basle (1432 – 1433). The result of the negotiations was the so-called Basle compacts (*compacta*) by which the Catholic Church, under certain conditions, would allow the Hussites to take communion in both kinds. The Taborites rejected the compacts, which could be implemented only after the battle near Lipany in 1434, when the moderate Calixtines defeated the Taborites. The final acceptance of the compacts and the recognition of Sigismund as the Czech king took place only at the diet of Jihlava on **14 August 1436**. The Calixtines were accepted back into the Catholic Church. In 1462 Pius II abrogated the compacts and, with this, the Calixtine Hussites, again considered themselves outside the Catholic Church. /JB/

IMPRESSIONISM (from French *l' impression* – impression) – an artistic movement. It originated in France in the 1870s and significantly influenced painting, music and literature up to the 1920s. It was a negative reaction to realism. The painters Claude Monet, Camille Pissarro, P. Auguste Renoir, Paul Cézanne, Edgar Degas, Édouard Manet and Alfred Sisley were its founders. Slovak impressionistic painters included Ladislav Medňanský, Elemér Halász-Hradil, Ľudovít Čordák, Konštantín Kövári and, in their early works, Martin Benka, Gustáv Mallý and Maximilián Schurmann. Impressionists turned away from the immutable "tangible world" and attempted to capture the volatile, the ephemeral and the intangible. They discovered the secret of day-light and had a predilection for painting the sea, sylvan landscapes, the country-side and parks. They used the play of rays of sunlight, the contrast of light and shadows on forms and replaced traditional linear perspectives, outline drawing and local tones with the perspective of light that decomposed shapes. Impressionistic artists did not interpret the impression evoked by the subject but followed changes in the environment that permeated, decomposed and dissolved the subject. In literature impressionism sought to capture reality as a lyrical mosaic of colored shadings, the vibrating reflections of things and phenomena connected with the psychological states of a perceiving subject. It was characterized by spontaneous sensual intimations, the interaction of tone and significance. In literature it was represented by naturalism and symbolism (Anatole France, André Gide, Rainer Maria Rilke). In Slovak literature symbolism was accompanied by the so-called moderns (Ivan Krasko, Vladimír Roy, Ivan Gall), post-1918 neo-symbolism (Ján Smrek, Maša Haľamová) and lyrical expressionism and naturism (Ľudo Ondrejov, Margita Figuli). In music it was expressed in the works of Claude Debussy and Maurice Ravel and it influenced the Slovak composers Alexander Moyzes, Eugen Suchoň and Ján Cikker. /RL/

INCUNABULA – the oldest printed books. They appeared in the mid 15th century when Johann Gutenberg invented book printing. The graphic arrangement and letters were similar to medieval manuscripts, **codices,** because the first Gutenberg letters were modeled after the Gothic calligraphic minuscule. The model for later incunabula was the humanistic minuscule, the *antiqua*. The oldest woodcuts in incunabula are also imitations of drawn initials and miniatures, but certainly they are not as elegant because multi-color printing only developed later. Books published until 1500 are considered incunabula. Others are so-called old prints. About 1,500 items of incunabula are found in Slovakia. The majority are of foreign origin because permanent presses were established in Slovakia only during the second half of the 16th century. However, occasional presses were found there. The oldest known item printed in Slovakia is an indulgence letter from **1480** printed by an itinerant printer on the initiative of the Bratislava canon J. Han. /JB/

INDULGENCES – the bestowal of absolution from the consequence (*poena*) of sin by the remission of time in Purgatory, on the presupposition that the penitent has made confession and sacrificed a certain sum of money for ecclesiastical purposes. Connected with this were letters of indulgences or confessional letters that offered to their holders remission of time in Purgatory on the condition of confession. In 1300 **Pope** Boniface VIII introduced a new jubilee indulgence. A year marking the end of a century could be declared a year of grace. During the course of the 14th and the second half of the 15th century, because of the brevity of human life, the popes introduced a shorter interval between the jubilee years, of 50, 33 (the length of Christ's life) and then of 25 years. The penitents were to make a pilgrimage to Rome, but later it was sufficient if they sacrificed a sum equal to the costs of such a journey. Indulgences were given by preachers who misused their office and the bestowal of indulgences was degraded to the collection of money for a letter of indulgence without penance and purification from sins. This trade in indulgences was criticized even by representatives of the church who, however, did not have sufficient courage to end it since it was a source of income. Indulgences spread during the period of the western **schism**, which called forth revolutionary attitudes and, indirectly, also the development of the Hussite movement and the later activities of Martin Luther (1517). /JB/

INDUSTRIALIZATION (from Latin *industria* – industriousness, diligence, assiduity) – the establishment of industrial mass-production. The basis of modern industrialization in Slovakia was set from the mid 19th century; industrialization itself took place only after the Austrian-Hungarian (Magyar) settlement of 1867. On **30 May 1881**, and in 1890 and 1907, the Hungarian diet accepted important industrialization laws. Based on them, the state provided substantial financial support for the development of industry. Slovakia received about one third of this support and investment was directed towards the textile and food industries (distilleries) in particular. In 1900 there were 485 industrial enterprises in Slovakia with more than 20 employees and by 1910 their number had grown to 600. Their industries produced 17.1 per cent of the industrial production in Hungary. In Slovakia were located 53.7 per cent of the Hungarian paper industries, 33.7 of the textile, 27.4 of the leather-working and 26.9 per cent of the iron industries. Industrialization was connected with the building of roads and railways. With the founding of the Czechoslovak Republic, the process of incorporating Slovak industry into the new state market and competitive environment ensued. The government policy was intentionally unfavorable and included the limiting of state supplements, tariff policies, higher taxes on returns and the liquidation of factories. In comparison with Czech industry it developed more slowly and during the period of prosperity at the end of the 1920s, exceeded the pre-war level only insignificantly. During the great economic crisis (1929 – 1935) it stagnated completely. The pre-crisis level was surpassed again only in 1937 due to the boom in military production. The founding of the first **Slovak Republic** in 1939 brought a new impulse for the industrialization of Slovakia. The goal of the national economy was to maintain or increase economic independence and, at the same time, to integrate the Slovak economy into the world economy. German economic expansion and the war made the situation difficult. However, the existence of the independent state and its economy as well as the war-time boom hastened industrialization and its accompanying phenomena (the building of communications,

electrification). The number of workers in industry grew by 50 per cent in comparison with the pre-war period. After the conclusion of the **Second World War** a renewal of industrial enterprises began. One of the goals of the two-year plan of **1 January 1947** was to industrialize Slovakia by relocating there factories from Czechia, especially from regions from which Germans were expelled. In 1948 Slovak industry produced 13.2 percent of the total production of Czecho-Slovakia. An interruption in industrialization and a change in its character followed the 9th congress of the Communist Party of Czechoslovakia on 25 – 29 May 1949. The goal of this strong-arm Communist policy was to set up heavy industry in Slovakia and increase the size of the "working class" within the context of the five-year plan. In the 1950s large factories flourished (for example: ZŤS Martin, ZŤS Košice, Ferro-Alloy Factory Istebné, the aluminum plant in Žiar nad Hronom, Slovnaft Bratislava and the nickel forge in Sereď). New workers were obtained by forced **collectivization**. Energy demanding industries focused on the processing of raw materials and semi-finished goods which hindered self-sufficiency. This rapid and disproportionate industrialization brought long-term ecological and urban problems along with social improvements. /RL/

INQUISITION – (from the Latin *inquirere*) – an institution for searching out and judging **heretics**. From the beginning, the bishops of the Catholic Church took responsibility for the purity of church teachings in matters of both faith and liturgy and at church **councils** they addressed various deviations from the teaching and practice of the official church. Various sects developed outside the structure of the church, which used state power to pursue them. The inquisition reached its greatest extent in Spain where Pope Sixtus IV approved the Spanish inquisition in 1478 at the request of King Ferdinand of Aragon and Queen Isabella of Castile. It was specifically exempted from the supervision of the Roman (or Holy) Inquisition. It began its activity in 1480 in Seville. After the assassination of the inquisitor, Peter Arbues, in Aragon in 1492, all the Jews that did not accept baptism were expelled from Spain. This expulsion was also extended to the Muslims and the Moors. Some of these only formally accepted Catholic baptism and secretly retained their original faith (the so-called Moriscos). Estimates of the number of victims of the inquisition differ. It is possible that there were about 30,000 victims. The Spanish Inquisition was abolished by the revolution of 1820. The inquisition was not applied extensively in Slovakia. In **1328** an inquisition was ordered in the diocese of Esztergom. At the beginning of the 15th century a community of **Waldensians** was uncovered in Trnava. During the Hussite campaigns in Slovakia in 1428 to 1434 several nobles with their serfs joined the Hussites. However, this was not a mass phenomenon. Strict laws were issued against heretics – the Lutherans, who were to be punished with death and the confiscation of their property – only during the reign of Louis II (1523). With the spread of the **Reformation** in the Kingdom of Hungary, the conditions necessary to introduce an inquisition of the Spanish type did not exist and the penal laws against the Lutherans were largely ignored. /JB/

INSURRECTION (insurekcia) – in general an uprising; in Hungary during **feudalism** it was a system of armed readiness that, as a rule, required the **nobility** (or other social classes) to enlist (to rise with arms) and defend the country. The **king** proclaimed an insurrection. During an interregnum it was proclaimed by the **palatine** or regent. Depending on the degree of the threat to the kingdom, it could be for the whole country (a general insurrection) or regional (a particular insurrection). Its origins go back to the earliest period of the Hungarian state when permanent military service was performed only by soldiers of the royal entourage, recruited knights, or mercenaries from abroad, the royal servants (*servientes,* individuals immediately subordinate to the king) and garrisons of the fortresses of the *jobbagi* in the counties (**castle counties**). However, after an insurrection was declared, others were also obliged to perform military service if needed. This included the majority of the

privileged classes of the population, the future nobility, Jazyges, Cumans, the Spiš Saxons, and cities to the extent designated. Defensive obligations were, for a long time, basically regulated by the **Golden Bull** of Andrew II (1222). According to the bull, the insurrection obligation did not extend to campaigns in other countries. The institutions of the insurrection and the *banderium* were the major components of the Hungarian military up to the end of the Middle Ages. According to well-established custom, the personal insurrection obligation pertained only to members of the nobility. It was their only real social obligation and was considered a so-called blood tax. However, depending upon the size of their estates, all feudal landlords had to provide a certain number of soldiers at their own expense, usually taken from the ranks of their serfs. The decision to declare an insurrection and the number of soldiers needed was generally approved by the **Hungarian diet**. Since, as a rule, the basis for their determination was a farmstead (**portal** – *porta*), the name that was used for this type of armed force was the portal army. It comprised part of the county *banderia*. The possibility of calling an insurrection remained in force even after the establishment of a permanent army. For example, it was declared in 1741 (the War of the Austrian Succession) and, for the last time, in June 1809, when an insurrection army led by the palatine suffered a catastrophic defeat in the battle against the French army at Győr (**15 June 1809**). It was legally abolished in 1868 with the introduction of a general obligation of military service. /VS/

INSURRECTION OF FRANCIS II RÁKOCZI – the last and largest insurrection of the estates. When the court in Vienna sent a large portion of the imperial army to battlefields in Italy and France, those dissatisfied with the reign of the Habsburgs took advantage of the situation. It was initiated by the Calvinist population in the Transtisa region who wished to defeat the Habsburgs as a bastion of Catholicism in Europe. Their delegation sought out Francis II Rákoczi who was living in exile in Poland. In the meantime, an insurrection had already erupted. Rákoczi, a Catholic magnate, accepted the offer of the non-noble Calvinists. The insurrection recorded successes only after it was joined by leading imperial military commanders from Hungary. The insurgents occupied all of Slovakia. Peace negotiations took place in 1704 and again in October 1705 but without result. The poor economic situation created dissatisfaction throughout the whole of Hungary and in 1707 many counties decided to desert Rákoczi (**Ónod diet**). The military situation of the insurgents also worsened. After the defeat near Trenčín on **3 August 1708** no significant military success was achieved and the number of insurgent soldiers diminished sharply. Not even the serfs were willing to join the army even though they had been promised personal freedom and freedom from their obligations to the landlords. In **1710** Count John Pálffy, the imperial commander, tried to negotiate a peace, but Rákoczi was not willing to make greater concessions and sought other allies abroad. Until then, France had provided him with significant financial and military assistance. In other countries the insurrection was generally considered to be an internal matter of the **Habsburg Monarchy**. After the fall of Košice in April 1711 the **Peace of Satu Mare** was concluded (30 April 1711) and the insurgents laid down their arms. All received a general amnesty, including those who returned from exile within a year. Rákoczi, however, spent the remainder of his life in Turkey. /MK/

INSURRECTION OF GEORGE I RÁKOCZI – insurrection of the estates. After the death of Gabriel Bethlen, George Rákoczi became the prince of Transylvania. He maintained contacts with the Swedish king Gustavus Adolphus, who was a foe of the Habsburgs. Even after the king's death he continued the alliance with the Swedes and, from 1638, he was also allied with the French and waiting for an opportunity to attack Hungary. This occurred in 1643 when a Swedish army invaded Moravia. However, as a vassal of the Ottomans, Rákoczi had to wait for the consent of the sultan. This arrived only in 1644, after the Swedes had already withdrawn from Moravia. Rákoc-

zi attacked eastern Slovakia where, like Bethlen before him (**Bethlen's Insurrection),** he declared himself the protector of the non-Catholics. The cities opened their gates to him. He also occupied the mining cities of central Slovakia with Ottoman assistance. During the course of summer 1664 the imperial army regained the whole of Slovakia except for Košice, Prešov and Levoča, where Rákoczi had strong garrisons. The imperial army, weakened by hunger and the plague, had to withdraw before a new Rákoczi army. The emperor Ferdinand III assembled new forces and achieved several successes that his commanders were not able, however, to exploit. The Transylvanian nobility urged the conclusion of a peace treaty. The emperor was also forced to enter into negotiations by discord in the army. Rákoczi made large territorial demands but the imperial side was not willing to accept the religious demands of the Protestants. A compromise agreement was concluded in February 1645. When the Swedes again invaded Moravia, Rákoczi renewed the struggle. The sultan, threatened with the loss of Transylvania, forced Rákoczi to renew peace negotiations. A peace treaty was signed in Linz on **24 August 1645**. Rákoczi received the castle and estate of Tokay and the lifelong tenure of seven eastern Hungarian counties. The Protestants obtained religious freedom, even for the serfs, and the return of confiscated churches to them was promised. The power and economic conflict between the Hungarian nobility and the Habsburgs continued (**Wesselényi Conspiracy**). /MK/

INTERDICT – in general a prohibition; a kind of ecclesiastical punishment. In church law it was the most severe penalty after excommunication. Its origins date back to the 10th century. The interdict prohibited participation in ecclesiastical acts or the conducting of liturgical services. It was used to punish both clerical and secular individuals. The degree of prohibition depended upon the type of interdict and could be temporarily or permanently valid. The **pope**, **archbishops**, **bishops** and appropriate religious superiors had and have the right to pronounce an interdict as do others to whom the pope entrusts this function. They also decide whether to repeal it. The interdict could be personal, whereby the sacraments or participation in ceremonies were forbidden to the affected person, and, in the case of the clergy, could also prohibit participation in ecclesiastical life with the suspension of the right to vote for or obtain a dignity or function, or to receive a benefice. The interdict even could mean the complete prohibition of offering or receiving the sacraments or Christian burial. Another type was the local interdict that prohibited the performance of ceremonies in the defined territory. The local interdict was used especially as a tool to exert political pressure on secular authorities in the Middle Ages (for example the interdict of 1208 of Pope Innocent III against England and its king, John (Lackland); the interdict against Hungary of 1232 of Archbishop Robert of Esztergom; the interdict of 1412 of Pope John XXIII against Prague). The interdict is still used today. For example, in the modern history of Slovakia, it was used in 1906 by the bishop of Spiš, Alexander Párvy, against Andrej Hlinka. However, Pope Pius X revoked this as unjustified in 1909. /VS/

ISMAILITES – originally a Moslem Shiite sect. From the 11th to 14th centuries they were Bulgarian Muslims (Mussulman), groups of which lived in the southern parts of Hungary. In addition to agriculture and service in the royal army, they took up commerce, money-changing and the minting of coins, and leased the king's **royal rights**, such as the sale of salt, the collection of the **thirtieth** and the like. At the beginning of the 13th century, they were, apart from the Jews, the most significant commercial and financial group in Hungary. In the **Golden Bull** of 1222 King Andrew II, pressured by the nobility, forbade leasing to them the right to trade in salt and the collection of the thirtieth. However, later Ismailites were in the service of the rulers. For example, during the reign of Louis I, they minted coins bearing the head of a Turk and were sub-lessees of the royal chambers. In Hungary they were also called Saracens, the name originally used throughout Europe for Moslems

from the east. After the crusades this name was used also for the Turks. /JB/

JANISSARIES – members of an elite infantry force of the Ottoman army. The janissary corps developed around 1360 and was made up of approximately 1000 soldiers. The Ottomans selected children or youths from among captives, especially Balkan Slavs, Greeks and Albanians, who were converted to Islam and trained for military service with strict discipline and a barracks regime. The long-standing practice of obtaining young boys for the janissary corps was confirmed and regulated by a law of 1482 (abolished in 1685) on the taking of Christian children from the lands under Ottoman rule as a so-called blood tax (*devširme*). The janissary corps eventually grew so large that, during the second half of the 17th century, it had 50,000 members. It was disbanded by Sultan Mahmud II (1862). Janissaries legally were slaves of the sultan and were subject exclusively to his authority and that of their own military officers. Like the *sipahis* and the *martals,* they also served in the garrisons of Turkish fortresses in the occupied parts of Hungary and the borderlands. For instance, in 1669 of a total of more than 1,500 janissaries in the Kingdom of Hungary almost 1,000 served in Nové Zámky. The term janissary has the connotation of a renegade or traitor. /VS/

JESUITS – ecclesiastical **religious order** founded in 1534 by the nobleman and former soldier Ignatius of Loyola (1492 – 1556). He gave the order a firm constitution in 1539 and introduced military discipline based upon an unquestioning fulfillment of the commands of the superior of the order. The constitution of the order was confirmed by Pope Paul III in 1540. The Jesuits became the mobile shock troops of the Catholic **Counter-Reformation** in the 16th and 17th centuries. They also engaged in missionary activity in overseas lands (Asia and South America). They created their own independent state (1609 – 1767) on the territory of what is today Paraguay. They devoted themselves especially to the teaching of young people in order to counter the influence of secular education. Therefore they founded universities and secondary schools. The instruction in schools was directed by unified principles, the so-called *ratio studiorum* (**1599**). In 1773 Pope Clement XIV supressed the Jesuit order. In 1814 after the Napoleonic wars, it was restored by Pius VII. The Jesuits came to Hungary at the invitation of Archbishop Nicholas Oláh in 1561 and settled in Trnava. In the **re-Catholicization** of Slovakia they met with the resistance of the Protestant population and, after several years, had to leave Hungary. They returned in 1586 and obtained the monastery of Zniev. During **Bocskai's Insurrection** they again had to leave Hungary. They finally obtained a foothold in Trnava in 1615 and spread to several towns. From the 16th to the 18th centuries they had their residences in Banská Štiavnica, Banská Bystrica (1650), Bratislava (1626), Humenné (1614), Kláštor pod Znievom, Komárno, Košice (1631), Levoča (1673), Pezinok (a secondary school), Piargy, Prešov, Rožňava (1659), Ružomberok, Skalica (1660), Spišské Podhradie (1646), Šaľa, Štiavnik (after the Cistercians, 1696) and in Trenčín and Žilina (1685). Trnava was a Jesuit center during the late period of feudalism. They established several schools in Slovakia. From their founding, **Trnava University** (founded in 1635) and **Košice University** (1657) were under their influence. After the revival of the order, at the beginning of the 19th century, they settled in Bratislava and Trnava and later in Košice and Ružomberok. Since 1989 they have been active in Bratislava, Košice, Prešov, Trnava and Piešťany. /JB/

JEWISH CODE – government regulations on the legal position of Jews. After the establishment of the first **Slovak Republic** on **14 March 1939,** a solution to the so-called Jewish question was sought that would resolve the economic, political and cultural position of the Jewish population. In Slovakia, where the assimilation of Jews was less than, for example, in Hungary and Czechia, Jews were generally understood as an alien element. This was the result of old historical prejudices and experience, long-standing beliefs and a lack of mutual acceptance and acquaintance. The government of Jozef Tiso attempted to use the so-called 4 per cent key (the proportion of the Jewish inhabitants to the rest of the population). In 1940 there lived in Slovakia 88,951 Jews. The first government regulation that limited the civic rights of the Jews was issued on 18 April 1939. It defined the concept "Jew" in religious and not racial terms and restricted their participation in several professions. Until September 1939 a total of 47 government regulations restricting the position of the Jews were issued. However, the majority of them allowed exceptions. Gradually the property of the Jews was encroached upon, for example, by the land reform of **29 February 1940**, and the first Aryanization law of 15 April 1940. These laws certainly struck insensitively at the economic base of the Jews but did not fully exclude them from the economic life of the country. From March 1939 to the end of 1941 6,194 Slovak Jews left Slovakia. The **Salzburg Negotiations** of **28 July 1940** brought a basic change in their position. At the suggestion of Adolf Eichmann, Dieter Wisliczeny came to Bratislava as an advisor on Jewish questions to the Slovak government with the goal of stripping the Jews of their property and deporting them. The new prime minister, Vojtech Tuka, and the minister of the interior, Alexander Mach, demanded the rapid resolution of the so-called Jewish question. On **3 September 1940** the parliament empowered the government to carry out all measures for Aryanization, including the transfer of property into the hands of non-Jews that would completely strip the Jews of their property. An inventory of Jewish property was carried out, according to which 54,667 persons owned property worth 4,322,239,000 crowns and the debt on this property represented 1,134,582,000 crowns. The Jewish code was issued as a law on

9 September 1941 on the model of the so-called Nuremberg race laws. Hans Globke, the author of extensive commentaries on the Nuremberg laws, supervised the text of the code, which consisted of 270 paragraphs. The concept "Jew" was defined racially: a person who had at least three Jewish grandparents was a Jew. Those of mixed race were considered non-Jews. The conclusion of marriages between Jews and non-Jews was forbidden. Jews had to wear a designated label. Their personal freedom was radically limited. President Jozef Tiso succeeded in inserting paragraph 255 into the Jewish code, according to which he could make full or partial exemptions from the application of these regulations. Work began on establishing **labor camps** for Jews. A secret conference of German politicians in Wannsee on 20 January 1942 decided on the "final solution of the Jewish question", the extermination of the Jews. When Germany demanded that the number of workers in Germany from Slovakia be increased, the Slovak ministry of the interior offered at the negotiations to replace the demanded work force with 20,000 Jew from Slovakia. Germany systematically effected the solution of the so-called Jewish question by deporting them. In an agreement made without the knowledge of the government and the president, Vojtech Tuka pledged to deport the Jews. The deportations from Slovakia began on **25 March 1942**. For each Jew deported the Slovak government agreed to pay Germany 500 marks. /RL/

JOBBAGI – during feudalism in Hungary a category of people with privileges or a favored position but of whom some later became serfs. From the 11th to the 13th century, those termed *jobbagi* were free and internally differentiated by their privileges into classes, from leading dignitaries to common members of the army. Individual groups of *jobbagi* were differentiated by their social and legal status, the extent of property ownership, and often by the degree of subordination. The royal *Jobbagi* of the Sainted King represented a distinct and the most significant group. Their position and property derived from the time of King Stephen I or his immediate successors. Even the highest royal dignitaries (that is, **magnates**), for whom the name **baron** gradually came into use from the first third of the 13th century, were termed royal *jobbagi* in the **Golden Bull** of 1222. Much more numerous were castle *jobbagi*, who performed military and sentinel service in exchange for leases or grants of property and who sometimes also held lower administrative postions in the **castle counties**. In the 13th century, along with the royal retainers (*servientes*), some of the castle *jobbagi* and their sons became the nucleus of a new group of Hungarian nobles, the yeomen. From the end of the 13th century until 1848 the term *jobbagi* designated a class of **serfs** that included the inferior part of the original castle *jobbagi*. /VS/

JOSEPHINIAN REFORMS – far-reaching regulations, decrees and patents of Joseph II. With them **enlightenment absolutism** climaxed in the Habsburg Empire. They modernized and developed the monarchy as a unitary state into which Hungary was incorporated. The autonomy of the estates was replaced by a state administration with reliable bureaucrats. By organizing 10 districts directly subject to the ruler (**18 March 1785**), conducting a census of the population, numbering houses, and surveying the land, Joseph II prepared to introduce general taxation in Hungary. He forbade the importation of luxury products and limited the expenditures of the Habsburg court within the framework of a strict financial policy. A new criminal and civil code guaranteed equal rights and responsibilities for the citizens, abolished capital punishment, forbade work by children less than eight years old and reduced discrimination against the Jews. To replace Latin, German was declared the official language of the empire and, at the same time, the cultivation of domestic languages was supported. Joseph II limited the influence of the pope in the monarchy and subordinated the church to state power. He abolished the diocesan seminaries and established two general seminaries that were to train priests in the spirit of the enlightenment (**1 June 1784**). The origins of the **Bernolák**

group are connected with the Bratislava seminary. Joseph II abolished those **religious orders** that were not focused on providing health services or the training of youth (a total of 739 cloisters). From their property he established a fund to finance new parishes, schools and hospices for aged clergy. The radical Josephinian reforms were timely reactions to the problems of the era. However, the sovereign implemented them in an insensitive manner and enforced them through the police. The Hungarian nobles in particular openly boycotted the changes. With the exception of the **Toleration Patent** and the **abolition of servitude,** Joseph was forced to retract them on his deathbed. Some of the reforms were achieved with changes only in 1848. This failure predetermined the distorted path of central Europe towards a civil society. /DŠ/

JOURNEYMEN (tovariši) see **Guilds**

JULIAN (or Roman) CALENDAR – a calendar that began to be used in ancient Rome. The Roman calendar originally had 304 days and ten months. Even after the addition of two further months in the 7th century BC, the Roman lunar year, lasting only 355 days, did not correspond to the solar year. In Rome the year originally began on 1 March; from the 2nd century BC its beginning was moved to 1 January, when the Roman consuls assumed office. Each year was named after the consuls in office. The counting of years from the foundation of the city of Rome (*Ab urbe condita*), believed to have taken place in 753 BC, began to be used only from the time of Caesar Augustus. The names of the Roman months were drawn from the names of gods, festivals and ceremonies, but also numerals (the last four) and these are preserved today in the majority of European languages. Each month had three base days by which the remainder were determined: *Kalends* (the 1st day of the month, which corresponded to the new moon), *Nones* (the 5th or 7th day) and the *Ides* (the 13th or 15th day during the full moon). In view of the imprecision and disorder in the Roman calendar, which no longer corresponded to the actual (astronomic) year, Gaius Ju-

lius Caesar in 46 BC implemented a fundamental reform of the calendar. On the proposal of the astronomer and mathematician Sosigenes, 46 BC was extended by 90 days. The year's length was fixed at 365 days, with every fourth year as a leap (adjusting) year of 366 days. This calendar was named the Julian calendar and was later accepted by Christianity and used in Europe, including Hungary, during the Middle Ages until it was replaced by the **Gregorian calendar**. /VS/

KING – title of a sovereign, the highest monarchic dignity after the emperor. The institution of king was known in ancient times, although the ancient *basileus* in the Greek city-states or *rex* in ancient Rome did not have unrestricted power. During the era of the migration of nations the first so-called barbaric kingdoms were established on the former territory of the western Roman Empire. Kingdoms existed in England and Scotland in the early Middle Ages and others were later established on the Iberian peninsula (Castile and Aragon, later unified into the Kingdom of Spain), as well as in Denmark, Sweden and Norway. After the fall of the Frankish Empire the royal title was assumed by the monarchs in France and Germany. In the Middle Ages the pope initially claimed the right to name kings as well as the Holy Roman **emperors**, who customarily also held the title of German king. Even Svätopluk is called king (*rex*) in one document (charter). The Hungarian sovereign Stephen I received the title king in **1000** and in 1025 Boleslav I the Brave became the Polish king. The German emperor Henry IV bestowed the kingly dignity on the Czech prince Vratislav II (1085). In the early feudal Kingdom of Hungary royal power was the source of land tenure. The king of Hungary was the chief and final authority in all state matters. His sovereignty was enforced in all matters relating to the kingdom. During the feudal fragmentation and the **monarchy of the estates**, the original legislative function of the king was assumed by the Hungarian diet. Various **royal rights** belonged to the king. Royal power was strengthened again in the era of **absolutism**. Family inheritance and election were used to determine succession to the throne, which was originally based on seniority (the successor was the oldest male member of the family) and later on the principle of primogeniture (the first born son or, exceptionally, daughter). The Mojmír dynasty ruled Great Moravia while Hungary was ruled by the Árpáds, Anjous, Luxemburgs, Matthias Corvinus, the Jagiellons, John Zápolya and the Habsburgs. /VS/

KOŠICE GOVERNMENT PROGRAM – the program of the Czecho-Slovak government of Zdeněk Fierlinger accepted during the **Moscow Negotiations** in March 1945. Its draft was prepared by the Communists and the non-Communist elements of the resistance (Edvard Beneš, the representatives of the People's, Social Democratic, National Socialist and Democratic Parties) accepted it without criticism as a basis for negotiations. The program prohibited the **Agrarian Party**, **Hlinka's Slovak People's Party**, the Entrepreneurs' Party and the National Democratic Party. Discussions about the displacement of the Germans and the Magyars lasted five minutes, the same time as the discussions concerning **retribution**. The sixth chapter of the program recognized the Slovak nation and the **Slovak National Council (1945)** as holding legislative and executive power in Slovakia. The government bound itself to implement **nationalization**, **land reform**, a "cleansing" of public life, the nationalizing of schools and, in foreign policy, to pursue closer cooperation with other Slavic states, especially with the Soviet Union. The prospective members of the government signed the government program in Moscow on 29 March 1945. On the insistence of the Communists, the government in exile in London was not to be allowed to enter the territory of the revived Czechoslovak Republic as a functioning government. Therefore,

the whole government of Prime Minister Ján Šrámek submitted its resignation on a train still on Soviet territory. The new government, after taking its oath of office in Košice on **5 April 1945**, ceremonially proclaimed the government program that entered history as the Košice Government Program. /RL/

KOŠICE MARTYRS – victims of religious intolerance. On **7 September 1619** participants in the **Bethlen Insurrection** tortured to death in Košice three Catholic priests, Marek Križin, Štefan Pongrác and Melchior Grodeczki. Originally they urged them to convert to Calvinism and take an oath of loyalty to Bethlen. When they refused, they were tortured and beheaded during the night of 6 – 7 September. Their bodies later were transported to Trnava and buried. Even the Calvinist population recoiled in horror at the murder of harmless priests. Pope Pius X declared them blessed on **15 January 1905** in Rome. In 1995 a church was built in their honor in Košice. During the second visit to Slovakia of Pope John Paul II, he declared the three Košice martyrs to be saints, and their solemn canonization took place in July 1995. Their feast day is 7 September, the anniversary of their death. /VČ/

KOŠICE UNIVERSITY – a Jesuit university. The only universities in Hungary in the 17th century were in Trnava (**Trnava University**) and Košice. The bishop of Eger, Benedikt Kisdi, established a university (*studium generale*) in Košice on **26 February 1657**. The Emperor Leopold I approved this educational institution with a golden bull on **7 August 1660,** only after it had secured material resources. Philosophical and theological faculties opened in 1658. The first bachelor's and doctoral degrees were granted in 1661. The first rector was Martin Palkovič and he was succeeded by Michal Gribóci. A residence was established at the university that housed 400 to 500 students. Dissertations, scholarly works, textbooks and even calendars were published at the university press. Several famous professors worked at the university, among them George Berzeviczy, Samuel Timon and František B. Kéri. After the suppression of the **Jesuit** order

(1773), the university was taken over by the state. In 1777 it was transformed into a royal academy, a branch of the university in Buda, with the right to grant degrees to its students. /VČ/

KRUPINA LAW see **City law**, **Žilina Book**

KURUCI – participants in the struggles of the estates against the Habsburgs in the last third of the 17th century and the first decade of the 18th century. They participated especially in the rebellion led by Gašpar Pika (1672), the **Thököly Insurrection** and the **Insurrection of Francis II Rákoczi.** The core of the *kuruc* army was made up of serfs, including many Slovaks. After the Peace of Satu Mare (concluded in 1711), which ended the final insurrection of the Hungarian estates, also called the *Kuruc War*, the majority of the leaders of the rebellion emigrated while some of the *kuruc soldiers* lived as brigands. /VS/

LABANCI – members of the Habsburg imperial army in the second half of the 17th century and the beginning of the 18th century. The name was used during the era of the insurrections of the estates of Imrich Thököly during 1678 – 1687 and the **Insurrection of Francis II Rákoczi** (1703 – 1711), that is, in the struggle against the *kuruci*. So far it has not been possible to explain the etymology of the word *labanec* or *labanc*, which had a pejorative character. It was also generally used to designate supporters of the Habsburgs. /VS/

LABOR CAMPS (1941 – 1945) – centers for Jews and persons avoiding work. They began to be established in Slovakia in the fall of 1941. They were intended for the Jewish population, which lost civil rights and property under the Jewish code. The deportations of Jews from Slovakia to German concentration camps on the territory of Poland after **25 March 1942** led to the rapid completion of labor camps that could protect them against the threatened

deportation. Persons marked for deportation were temporarily placed in assembly camps. Labor camps for Jews were legally based on the decree of the ministry of the interior of 1 April 1942, derived from the law on the general labor obligation. Three work camps that had the character of state enterprises were established in Slovakia. The camp in Sereď (1,700 persons) specialized in cabinet-making and belonged among the most modern and productive enterprises in Slovakia. The camp in Nováky (1,300 persons) specialized in the production of ready-to-wear clothing and the camp in Vyhne (400 persons) focused on construction work. The camps were guarded by units of the **Hlinka Guard**. Along with the strict camp regime, they had their own self-administration and social and cultural establishments (hospitals, nurseries, schools, libraries, theaters). In addition to labor camps for Jews, there existed also Jewish labor centers, which housed smaller groups scattered throughout Slovakia (about 700 persons). The labor camps for Jews disappeared when the Uprising of August 1944 broke out. An assembly camp under German command was established at the location of the labor camp in Sereď, from which Jews were deported to extermination camps. Several labor centers for persons avoiding work also existed in Slovakia. /RL/

LABOR CAMPS (1945 – 1954) – were established after the restoration of Czecho-Slovakia in 1945 for Germans and Magyars destined for transfer to Germany and Hungary, for Slovaks accused of collaboration or condemned by people's courts, and for those who were placed into camps without a trial (on the basis of the decisions of a three-member committee of the commission for the interior). The camps were organized by district national committees. In the summer of 1945 there were 26,296 persons assembled in 63 camps, mostly Slovak Germans. They were often located at the sites of the earlier **labor camps (1941 – 1945)** – Svätý Jur, Ústie na Orave, Krupina, Nováky and Ilava. Initially there was no medical care in them and the spread of infectious diseases resulted in high mortality. Labor camps existed also after the communist coup in 1948. According to a regulation of the Slovak National Council of March 1948, "idlers", "subversives" and, later, opponents of collectivization were frequently sent there for political reasons without trial. At the end of 1948 there were 1,268 persons in the camps. In Slovakia they were established on the basis of a regulation of the Slovak National Council of 23 March 1945, while in Czechia and throughout the whole state their existence was regulated by law no. 247 of October 1948 concerning camps of forced labor. The last labor camp in Slovakia, at Ruskov near Košice, was closed in 1953. Persons from Slovakia were often placed in camps in Czechia, especially in Jáchymov, where there was a large camp near the uranium mines. Even after the dissolution of the labor camps, prisoners were used as a cheap work force. During the years 1948 to 1954 about 100,000 persons served sentences in them. In the assembly camps for monastics (**13 – 14 April 1950**) and in the prisons of Leopoldov and Ilava there were also labor obligations. /RL/

LÁN (hide, field) – the area of a farmstead in villages founded under the **German Law**, varying in different regions from 30 to 60 acres (*jutro*). Under the **Tripartitium** legal code it was 34 royal acres, about 15 hectares. This measurement was used until the introduction of the metric system in 1874. In the period of late feudalism this term also designated lesser areas measuring about 193 square cords (*siaha* = 1.8 meters). /JB/

LAND REFORM – the intervention of the state in the ownership and use of the soil. In Slovakia three land reforms were implemented. The first was linked with the establishment of **Czecho-Slovakia**. The National Committee in Prague had already issued a law in 1918 that forbade the purchase and sale of large estates. It was followed by the adoption of a confiscation law (**16 April 1919**) containing the main principles for the seizure and distribution of large land holdings. All property over 150 hectares of arable land and 250 hectares in total was subject to land reform, with possible exceptions directed both upwards and downwards. The land reform was implemented by the State Land Office. It extended to 1,407,162 hectares of land (29 per cent of all the land in Slovakia), 686,000 hectares of which were distributed. The land reform strengthened the position of the mid-sized farmers at the expense of the Magyar large estate holders. Colonization, a new phenomenon, was introduced especially in the plains of southern Slovakia. Along with Slovak colonists, Czech colonists also received land (2,000 farmsteads with an area of 25,000 hectares). This strengthened the position of the **Agrarian Party** that controlled the mechanism of land distribution. The expectations of the farmers were only partially satisfied. In Slovakia a third of them had to lease land in 1929. A second land reform took place during the first **Slovak Republic**. Under the law on land reform, the State Land Office obtained land by purchase or confiscation. The greater part of it was land owned by the Jews. The state distributed or sold 45,379 hectares to 22,538 persons. The third land reform took place in three stages from 1945 to 1948. It involved land confiscated from the original German and Magyar owners, as well as from Slovaks accused of collaboration with the Germans. Confiscated were 567,933 hectares of land. In 1947 the government undertook a revision of the land reform that had taken place during the first Czechoslovak Republic and confiscated church land (155,000 hectares). This violated the *modus vivendi* with the Vatican. After the **Communist state coup** in 1948, the new power nationalized all parcels of land over 50 hectares. It soon halted the distribution of land and began to use the arguments of their former political opponents about the harm of fragmentation and the need to create larger agricultural units. In February 1949 a law was adopted concerning united farm cooperatives and **collectivization** began to take place. /RL/

LEGENDS (from the Latin *ad legendum* – that which is to be read) – lives (biographies) of the saints written in the Middle Ages. They were based upon original stories about martyrs and saints. In addition to biographies and descriptions of the miracles ascribed to the saints, legends also recorded important historical events and everyday life. From 1643 the Jesuits in Antwerp issued the *Acta sanctorum* (*Deeds of the Saints*), in which legends were chronologically ordered according to individual days of the year. The most important legends from the period of Great Moravia are about the lives of Constantine and Methodius. They had developed already in the 9th century and were written in Old Slavonic. The legend about the Slovak eremites Svorad and Benedict, which was written by Maurus, the bishop of Pécs, comes from **1064**. Two legends (a greater and a lesser) of the life of the first Hungarian king, St Stephen, date from the end of the 11th century and the beginning of the 12th century. From this period also comes the Hartwig legend about King Stephen. In the 12th century the legend about Imrich and Gerhard, the bishop and martyr of Csanád, appears, while a legend about King Ladislas I was created at the end of the 12th or the beginning of the 13th century. Some legends were later reworked (for example, the final version of the legend of St Gerhard in the 14th century). /JB/

LIBERAL PARTY (also the Free Thought Party, in Hungarian, the *Szabadelvü Párt*) – the most influential political party in Hungary in the period of **dualism**. It was founded on **1 March 1875** and its president was K. Tisza. Up to 1905 the single governing party in Hungary, it supported dualism in the Kingdom of Hungary. It continued the tradition of the **Magyar Reform Movement** and was overwhelmingly victorious in elections, obtaining more than two-thirds of the votes cast. Its voter-base was the old large landowner class, the middle nobility, the new industrial magnates, bureaucrats and, from the end of the 19th century, also the middle class. It was representative of the political system in Hungary, which was not democratized and bore responsibility for the low political culture in the country and the policy of **Magyarization**. It supported the rapprochement of Austria-Hungary with Germany. While it was in power the Slovaks en-dured the greatest national suppression in the history of Hungary and its representatives and adherents contributed to the dissolution of the **Slovak gymnasia** and the **Matica slovenská**, supported cultural societies carrying out Magyarization and were responsible for the fact that for a long time not a single Slovak cultural institution could function in the country. The party supported modernization and industrialization, the building of railways, and the reform of the currency. For a long time it resisted the opposition, especially the Magyar nationalists, who demanded a revision or the abolition of the compromise. It lost hegemony in the **diet** only in 1905 and 1906. S. Tisza disbanded it and founded it anew as the National Party of Labor. It had a strong position among voters in Slovakia, where it obtained 70 – 80 per cent of the votes due especially to the limited **right to vote in Hungary**. /DŠ/

LIPTOV DEMANDS (the precise title is Demands of the Slovak Nation in the county of Liptov) – the first integrated Slovak political program that emerged during the **revolution of 1848/1849**. After it erupted, the national rights which L. Štúr had sought in the last **diet** of the estates were not sufficient. He himself invited his followers to organize public assemblies in the regions. The Liptov demands were the first result of this initiative. They were compiled on 27 March 1848 by a group of patriots at the parsonage of Michal Miloslav Hodža in Liptovský Mikuláš. This document welcomed constitutional liberties but was more progressive than the **March laws**. They defined the liberty of the people as a harmony of citizen and national equality and considered the declaration of national rights as the precondition for involving the lower classes in public life. They demanded the legal recognition of the particularity of the Slovak nation, its proportional representation in the Hungarian diet, the use of the Slovak language for instruction in the elementary schools and in the county offices, as well as for the publication of laws and official regulations. The demands recognized Magyar as the diplomatic language of the Kingdom of Hungary and sought only modest language rights. They were accepted with enthusiasm on 23 March 1848 in a county-wide, popular assembly of several thousand individuals in Liptovský Mikuláš. Those who initiated the action withdrew the petition under pressure from the council of the county, comprised exclusively of nobles, after the arrival of military units. The officials paid no further attention to it. It later inspired the **Nitra Demands**. /DŠ/

LITTLE ENTENTE – a military political alliance of the Czechoslovak Republic, Yugoslavia and Romania directed against Magyar revisionism and the restoration of the Habsburg dynasty. As early as the peace conference in Paris these states took a unified position, thanks to the Slovak diplomat Štefan Osuský. They responded to Hungarian demands to preserve the territorial integrity of Hungary with a joint memorandum on 25 February 1920. The Hungarian press derisively called this step "the Little Entente" (in imitation of the entente of the great powers of Europe). On **14 August 1920** an agreement between the Czechoslovak Republic and the Kingdom of the Serbians, Croatians and Slovenians (from 1929 Yugoslavia) was signed concerning mutual assistance in case of an unprovoked attack from the Magyar side. A secret military convention stipulated that, in case of an attack by one of the signatories upon Hungary, the other would preserve a friendly neutrality. A further step towards the establishment of the Little Entente was the Czechoslovak-Romanian treaty of alliance of **23 April 1921**. The triple pact culminated on **17 June 1921** with the Romanian-Yugoslavian agreement. The Little Entente was created in accord with French interests in central Europe. It secured the status quo established by the existing peace treaties. Despite the efforts of the Czechoslovak Republic, Austria and Poland declined membership in the Little Entente. The organizational pact of the Little Entente was signed on **16 February 1932**. At the suggestion of Edvard Beneš it was reorganized on the model of the League of Nations (council, secretariat). The Little Entente was to be transformed into an association of sovereign states that would out-

wardly constitute a single great power. It was decided to coordinate foreign policy through a permanent council of the Little Entente and to change the bi-lateral agreements to tri-lateral ones. In a further phase it was to achieve a unification of the armed forces and a deeper economic cooperation through an economic council of the Little Entente. After the prime minister M. Stojadinovič took office in 1935 Yugoslavia began to deviate from the Little Entente. This tendency was supported by Germany and Italy. In June 1936 Edvard Beneš unsuccessfully tried to create a pact of the Little Alliance directed against any kind of enemy and not just against Hungary. After the dismissal of the Romanian minister of foreign affairs, N. Titulescu, the Little Entente lost firm support also in Romania. Because of its limited validity, the Czechoslovak Republic could not depend on it in the crisis of 1938. After a revision of the borders in favor of Hungary in 1938 – 1941 a rapprochement between the first Slovak Republic, Romania and Croatia occurred. In this Hungary saw a revival of the Little Entente (**Vienna Arbitration**). /RL/

M

MAGDEBURG LAW see **City law, Žilina city book**

MAGIN'S APOLOGY – the oldest known defense of the Slovak nation. It was published in **1728** in Púchov in the printery of Daniel Chrastina at the expense of the county of Trenčín. It was written by the Catholic pastor of Dubnica, Ján Baltazár Magin, who had been entrusted with the task by the nobility of Trenčín county. It was a response to the views of Michael Bencsik, a professor of Hungarian law at **Trnava University**, who, in his work of **1722** on the occasion of a session of the country's diet in Bratislava, called the nobility and the whole population of Trenčín County "the remnants of Svätopluk who sold his country to the Magyars, and thus the Slovak people, into eternal serfdom". Ján Baltazár Magin worked with several lawyers to compile the Latin work *Barbs spread for the author of the writing of the most recent Diet or Defense of the glorious Trenčín county (Murices Nobilissimae et novissimae diaetae Posoniensis sive Apologia.).* Magin had a very precise idea about the territory inhabited by the Slovaks and distinguished them from the surrounding nations. He demonstrated the autochthony and antiquity of the whole "Slavic" nation in Hungary, was proud of Svätopluk and attempted to show that the Slovaks were members of the same political nation (in the Kingdom of Hungary) as the Magyars, the Hungarian nation (*natio hungarica*). Therefore both nationalities had the same rights and obligations. /MK/

MAGISTRATE (mayor, *richtár*) – representative of a city or town government or self-administration. The Slovak term comes from the German *Richter* and the Latin equivalent is *iudex.* This also shows the magistrate's dual function as a representative of the local government and judge. Earlier, to the end of the 13th century, the term *villicus* also designated the town mayor, but this term later referred only to the representative of the community administration of a village. Cities which obtained **privileges** from the ruler and utilized some sort of **city law** as a rule had magistrates (*richtár*) elected for a period of one year. The ruler confirmed the magistrate in office. The magistrate stood at the head of the city council comprised of council members (jurors, scribes, councilors), six to twelve and sometimes even more in number. From the 14th century there were broader councils of electors (*electa civitas*), which in the greater cities numbered from several dozen up to more than one hundred townsmen. These had specific authority, for example, at the election of the magistrate, in deciding economic questions in the city and the like. The separation of the judicial from the administrative function brought into being alongside the magistrate, who retained only a judicial function, an elected mayor (*mešťanosta, Bürgermeister*). In the cities and villages under the **German Law**

the office of hereditary magistrate existed. As a rule these were the founders of new communities (*lokátor*, from the Latin *locator* - leaseholder) and were responsible to the landlord in carrying out their office. They were called *šoltýs, fojt* or *advokát* (from the German *Schultheiss, Vogt* or *Advokat*). Village bailiffs (*villicus, vesník*), although elected by the village community, were responsible to the landlord for the performance of their function. In addition to the administration of the village and the holding of lower judicial proceedings, they, together with the constables (*drábi*) of the landlord, had to look after the regular collection of serf dues, **tenths** and **ninths,** as well as of state taxes. As a result of the harmonization of the legal types of medieval villages from the 16th century, the office and name of magistrate (*richtár*) were brought into agreement, and the function of baliff (*vesník*) was added to it. Data from the later period of feudalism provide information about the election of village magistrates. Serfs chose the magistrates from three candidates suggested by the landlord. After 1848 the function of magistrate was transformed into the office of mayor (*mešťanosta*) in most of the towns. In the villages magistrates were retained but lost their judicial authority. In vineyard communities, vineyard magistrates (*peregovia*) were elected. /JB/

MAGNATES – the most influential social class and later an estate in feudal Hungary. They were the first to hold the rights of nobles. They came mainly from the families of the Magyar warrior clans and partly from native Slavic and other families who gained admittance to the royal circle because of their military service. Most received large grants of landed property from the **king**. From the 13th century the terms **baron** and magnate were used synonymously for the powerful nobles. Nobles who filled the highest offices or dignities of the country or were members of the **royal council**, were considered barons in the narrow (legal) sense. However, in the broad sense of the word, the most politically influential and wealthy members of the higher nobility were also regarded as barons. Hereditary baronies came into use from the 16th century. Although the magnates were legally constituted as an estate only in 1608, during the whole preceding period their rights, privileges and influence far exceeded the rights and power of the other (middle and lower) **nobility**. The law of **1608** cited the noble titles (normally hereditary) of the magnates in the following order: **duke**, **count**, **baron**. The magnates and **prelates** constituted the upper table of the **Hungarian diet** and, after the **March laws** (1848) abolished the estates, its upper house. The use of noble titles was abolished by one of the first laws accepted after the establishment of the **Czechoslovak Republic**. /VS/

MAGYAR REFORM MOVEMENT (also Magyar liberal opposition, liberal middle nobility and the like) – the main political current in the Kingdom of Hungary in the 1840s. Its leading elements were the middle nobility and it had support especially in the counties and the Hungarian diet. It uniquely joined the reform ideas of liberalism with the traditional values of the estates. It began to be formed in the Hungarian diet in 1830 through the work of Count Stephen Széchenyi and in the 1830s it attempted to pursue a peaceful path of modernizing reforms through agreements with Vienna. It assumed a radical form during the second half of the 1830s after a younger generation (Louis Kossuth) entered politics. In 1845 several pro-reform opposition groups began to unite and established an opposition party in 1847. The movement demanded the abolition of **absolutism** and **serfdom**, the introduction of general taxation, equality before the law, the abolition of inalienable land (that which was not able to be sold) and of the **guilds**, the founding of banks and factories and the building of railways. It created a society for the protection of Hungarian industry in Bratislava. Economic and social modernization were conditioned by the growing independence of Hungary from the Habsburgs and its transformation into a Magyar national state. This led to **Magyarization,** which was implemented by force, especially during the era of Kossuth. It was directed in particular against

the Evangelical Slovaks, who sought to defend themselves with the **Slovak Petition to the Throne**, the activity of **Štúr's group** and the like. The constitutional ambitions of the movement resulted in conflicts with Vienna and with the non-Magyar national movements because of their national intolerance and assimilation policies. Only after the eruption of the **revolution of 1848/1849** was it able to achieve its aims through the acceptance of the **March laws**. The **Liberal Party** adhered in particular to the legacy of the Magyar reform movement. /DŠ/

MAGYARIZATION – attempts to make Magyars of the non-Magyar population of the Kingdom of Hungary. Although it contained elements of natural assimilation (spontaneity, voluntary acceptance), it was dominated by the resolute use of force. This form of national suppression accompanied the transformation of the Kingdom of Hungary from a state of estates into a modern state. The traditional **Hungarian nation** (*natio hungarica*) thus was given a Magyar form. Its main representatives were the middle **nobility**. Later the powerful Magyar ruling classes wanted to transform the Kingdom of Hungary into a Magyar national state even though the Magyars made up only 35 – 40 per cent of the population. They claimed that all of the population comprised a single Hungarian (Magyar) nation. They gave preference to the rights of the Magyars and to the Magyar language at the expense of the remaining six nations. The linguistic variegation was to be resolved by pursuing a policy of making Magyar the official language that resulted in the first Magyarization laws (**10 June 1790, 24 May 1792**). In the **Magyar reform movement** in the 1830s, Stephen Széchenyi advocated a moderate form of Magyarization. He viewed it as a natural and long-term process whose success could not be guaranteed by force, but by the dissemination and attraction of Magyar culture. During the transition from the 1830s to 1840s, the Magyar opposition movement was controlled by the young Kossuth generation, for whom a speeded up (radical) Magyarization was viewed as an expression of progress. It was directed against the Slovaks in particular and more especially against the Evangelicals, who defended themselves with the **Slovak Petition to the Throne.** The Magyars pushed through the **March laws** that opened the way to an unbridled forced Magyarization. Resistance to Magyarization flowed into civil war during the **revolution of 1848/1849**. It was dampened by **neo-absolutism** but, in the 1860s, it was once again appropriated by the Hungarian politicians. After **dualism** was attained in 1867 the official ideology of the state became the fictive unity of the Hungarian (Magyar) nation and Hungary as the national state of the Magyars. During the last half-century of the Kingdom of Hungary radical Magyarization reached massive proportions and was pursued by the ruling parties (**Liberal Party**) as well as by opposition political forces, often in an openly chauvinistic form. Seldom were heard critical voices from the Magyar side (Louis Mocsáry, Joseph Eötvös, Hungarian People's Party, Oskár Jászi, Social Democrats, Michael Károlyi). A weak protection of the non-Magyars was to be offered by the **Nationalities Law.** However, it was not respected. For Slovaks this was the most unjust period in the history of Hungary. Slovak politics remained on the periphery of events, its representatives were exposed to persecution and some chose **emigration** overseas. State power eliminated the modest support for national life and culture (**Matica slovenská**) and education (**Slovak gymnasia**), supporting instead Magyarizing cultural societies (**20 November 1883, 1885**). The number of Slovak primary schools fell from about 2,000 at the beginning of the 1870s to 377 in 1912. Slovak society was deformed socially (by an absence of propertied and educated classes), culturally (by the absence of cultural institutions) and psychologically (by inadequate self-consciousness, a feeling of insignificance). Nearly 2.5 million non-Magyars including about 500,000 Slovaks were completely or partially Magyarized in Hungary. /DŠ/

MANUFACTURE – an enterprise based upon the principle of a division of labor and manual production. It represented the transition between the traditional **guilds** and mechanized factories. Manufactures developed in England in the 16th century. In Slovakia the first manufacture was founded in Hubice by Archbishop George Szelepcsényi in the 1660s. However, the era of manufactures in Slovakia dates from 1725, after which the Habsburg court, especially during the period of **enlightened absolutism,** supported their development. They were founded by the dynasty, the nobility and the church, especially in the fields of textile production (68 per cent), ceramics, distilling and machine construction. The textile manufacture in Šaštín, owned by the wealthiest entrepreneur in the monarchy, Francis of Lothringin, the husband of Maria Theresa and Holy Roman emperor, was among the largest in central Europe. It employed 900 people. In contrast to the western part of the monarchy, manufactures were much fewer in Hungary also because the imperial court did not find sufficient resources in the country for investment, that is, it was not able to tax the Hungarian nobility, nor did the nobility develop an entrepreneurial sense. Therefore, only rarely were manufactures in Slovakia – there were about 270 in the 1840s – transformed into mechanized factories. They rarely became the starting point for modern **industrialization**. Among the exceptions was the manufacture in Halič that, in **1832**, became the first textile mill in which a steam engine worked. /DŠ/

MARCH LAWS – a collection of 31 laws of the **Hungarian diet** from March **1848**. They concluded the long era of **feudalism** and the period of **Metternichian absolutism** and opened the way to a civil society. Their leading advocates were the **Magyar reform movement** and the majority of the laws were supported also by **Štúr's group**. They went into effect on **11 April 1848** and abolished the compulsory labor (*robota*), the church **tenth**, the **ninth** of the landlords and other obligations of the serfs of *urbarial* property, introduced general taxation, abolished the inalienability of land, **the vice-regency council** and the Hungarian court chancellery as a symbol of **absolutism**. The Kingdom of Hungary greatly strengthened its independence from Vienna and set up its first independent government that was subordinate to the Hungarian Diet. Its prime minister was Louis Batthyányi and the minister of finance was Louis Kossuth. The laws significantly restricted the authority of the king and the imperial government. The imperial organs in Hungary were allowed to decide matters of war, finance and foreign affairs. The lack of a clear definition of the spheres of competence between Pest and Vienna led to a military conflict during the winter of 1848. The laws guaranteed human liberty and citizen rights (the freedoms of speech, the press, association and assembly) and allowed the citizens to bear arms (national guard). They proclaimed the equality of the people before the law and a system of popular representation. Because of the high property and educational requirements, the **right to vote in Hungary** was held by only six per cent of the population. The laws did not deal with the question of nationalities. Hungarian was declared the official language of Hungary and the path to a radical **Magyarization** was opened. This led to major conflicts between the Hungarian power and the non-Magyar movements in the **revolution of 1848/1849**. The first time the Slovak politicians adopted a complex approach in order to remove the superficiality and the national irritant of the March laws was in the **Demands of the Slovak Nation**. /DŠ/

MARCH PETITION – a program document of the Slovak national movement. It was prepared in February and March 1849 by patriots grouped around Ľudovít Štúr and Jozef Miloslav Hurban. It was based upon the principles of **Austro-Slavism** and the equality of nations, to which the imperial government also adhered. The original text of the petition demanded the establishment of a Slovak crown land to be called the Slovak Grand Duchy. The unexpected proclamation of the **dictated constitution** forced the authors to abandon this demand. In the name of the Slovak nation a delegation of about 30 members presented a revised petition to the new sovereign, Francis Joseph I, on **20 March 1849** in Olomouc and later also to the government in Vienna.

The delegation was led by the Catholic priest Jozef Kozáček, known for his activities at the imperial court. The petition demanded the recall of bureaucrats compromised by Magyarization, the separation of Slovakia from Hungary and its formation into an independent entity, a Slovak duchy, which was to be directly subordinate to Vienna and equal to the other Austrian lands. It was to have its own diet, executive offices and public administration. This program was pursued by leading Slovak politicians during all of 1849, the **petition movement of the fall of 1849** and also by the **Slovak government confidants**. However, the Vienna government delayed the federalization of the monarchy and openly rejected it in the fall of 1849. /DŠ/

MARKETS (Fairs) – places designated for the sale and purchase of goods. From the 11th century they took place regularly at crossroads, at important castles and near centers of state or ecclesiastical administration. The first written reports about markets come from the end of the 11th century when King Vladislav I (1077 – 1095) ordered that trade could take place only at markets. Originally they were held in market settlements and later in the medieval cities. The conduct of business at a market was regulated by customary rights and later a market was permitted on the basis of a royal privilege. The market right and the collection of income from it belonged among the so-called lesser **royal rights** that the king conferred upon townspeople. There were two types of markets, annual fairs (jarmoky from the German Jahrmarkt) and weekly or daily markets. Annual markets usually took place on the feast day (hody) of the patron saint of the church. Weekly markets originally took place on Sunday, but were shifted to other days of the week due to the opposition of the church. The oldest market places were near churches. This is the source of the name for Sunday in Hungarian (vasárnap) and the German word die Messe (used for both a fair and the mass). The terms of the annual and weekly markets were determined so as not to impinge upon the terms of neighboring markets. Several important cities had the right to hold several annual markets during the year. From the 14th century the ruler bestowed the right to conduct annual markets on several days before and after appropriate holidays. The maximum duration of a market was two weeks before and two after the appropriate holiday, thus four weeks (*kvindéna*). In order to increase the attractiveness of the market, the rulers bestowed upon traders and merchants the right to travel to and from the market without paying **tolls** and sometimes even exempted them from the **thirtieth**. From the 17th century an increase in market privileges often served only to confirme and enlarge the original market rights. Small towns and important villages also obtained the market right. Annual markets in important cities (Bratislava, Trnava, Levoča, Košice etc.) became meeting places of traders from distant regions and countries and so were, at the same time, centers of long-distance trade and local markets. The development of transportation in the 18th and 19th centuries reduced the importance of markets, as wholesalers established regular commercial connections with partners without the mediating function of markets. This trend continued in the 20th century. Markets became, rather, an attraction (Radvaň fair) or an opportunity for various merchants and retailers as in contemporary bazaars. /JB/

MARTALS – members of irregular and auxiliary units of the Ottoman army. Like the **janissaries**, they were recruited especially from among the Balkan Orthodox Christians, who performed services in the Turkish border fortresses and on Ottoman shipping on the Danube for pay or for a reduction of tax obligations. They were mainly active mainly during the 16th and 17th centuries when, after the fall of Buda (1541) and the Turkish conquest of part of Hungary, they are found on the Slovak frontier, where they made up a significant proportion of the garrisons of Turkish border fortresses and provided support to the **Turkish administration**. They were found in Esztergom and also in Štúrovo, Drégel and Divín. As groups of marauding and pillaging irregulars, they penetrated deep into the hinterland of the enemy, evoking panic and fear in the local population. /VS/

MARTIN DECLARATION see the **Declaration of the Slovak Nation**

MASTERS see **Guilds**

MATICA SLOVENSKÁ (1863 – 1875) – a nation-wide cultural society. Its establishment was considered in the 1820s and a concrete proposal was made by the **Slovak National Assembly** in Martin. After the sovereign approved its statutes (21 August 1862), it was founded on **4 August 1863** in Martin where it also had its seat. It was a continuation of the activities of the **Tatrín** club. Its first chairman was Štefan Moyzes. After his death, he was succeeded by Jozef Kozáček. The vice-chairman was Karol Kuzmány and later Viliam Paulíny-Tóth. It was the only nation-wide Slovak cultural institution with approved statutes. In the absence of political organs, it represented not only a center of the national life of the Slovaks, but also was a symbol of their national particularity that was especially important during the period of forced **Magyarization**. Although it was not allowed to establish local branches, it carried out a variety of activities. In 1873 it had 1,300 members many of them collective or institutional (communities, libraries, schools, societies). It was supported exclusively by gifts. Financial support was obtained by *grajciar (kreutzer)* collections to which about 10,000 individuals contributed; the Emperor Francis Joseph I gave it 1000 florins. It laid the foundations for Slovak museums, and for archival and library activity. Within the Matica, several sections were established that fostered, in particular, the development of ethnographic scholarly research. It published educational and scientific monographs, calendars and the first Slovak scholarly journal, the *Chronicles of the Matica slovenská* (*Letopis Matice slovenskej*) and instigated the activity of amateur theater and choral ensembles. During the period the Matica functioned, the cultural life in Slovakia was significantly enlivened, as was the sense of national cohesiveness and pride. Its activity was disliked by Hungarian political forces and they disparaged it for its pan-Slavism.

On **6 April 1875** it was closed down without an objective justification. Up until the founding of the **Slovak Museum Society**, no nation-wide cultural institution functioned in Slovakia. Several attempts to renew the Matica slovenská were rejected by the authorities and it was revived only on 1 January 1919. /DŠ/

MAXIMILIAN'S MINING CODE – legal regulations for the royal free mining cities issued by Emperor Maximilian I. Previously the Štiavnica and Kremnica mining law had regulated mining in the mining cities of central Slovakia. In 1548 King Ferdinand I took over these cities from his sister Mary. He entrusted the preparation of a new uniform mining code for all the mining cities to the Lower Austrian mining chamber. He wanted to limit their old **privileges** and to give preference to **royal rights** in mining at the expense of the liberties of the population of the mining towns. In this way he sought greater control over the production of the mines and an increase in the royal income, especially from the production of precious metals and copper. The new mining code was based upon codes in effect in Austria and Czechia. It was presented to the mining cities for study in 1550. The cities refused to accept it, since it would have abolished all of the city prerogatives and liberties. After negotiations that lasted from 1550 to 1571 and when Ferdinand I and Maximilian I insisted on its acceptance, they issued a compromise mining code in which the version presented to them was supplemented by a modified and modernized version of the Štiavnica and Kremnica mining codes. The mining cities accepted the code in 1570 and in 1571 it appeared in print. It is also known by the name New Mining Code. /MK/

MEMORANDUM ASSEMBLY see **Slovak national assembly**

MEMORANDUM OF THE SLOVAK NATION – a program document of the Slovak national movement. It was accepted by the **Slovak national assembly** in Martin. The draft was prepared mainly by Štefan Marko Daxner. It was linked to the constitutional efforts of the **revolution of 1848/1849**, but respected the Octo-ber **Diploma** and the **February Constitution.** It appealed to the principles of natural law and national equality before the law. It recognized the territorial integrity of the Kingdom of Hungary and the diplomatic character of the Hungarian language, but rejected the elevation of the Magyars above other nations in the country. It demanded the abolition of the laws that discriminated against the non-Magyar languages and nations, the legal recognition of the distinct existence of the Slovak nation and, within the Kingdom of Hungary, the separation of its territory under the name Upper Hungarian Slovak Province. This autonomous region was to be made up of the counties (*župy*) with a Slovak population and the Slovak language was to be used in the offices, courts and schools. The memorandum further demanded the establishment of a Slovak legal academy, a chair of Slovak language and literature at the University of Pest, state support for Slovak cultural societies and the proportionate representation of Slovaks in the **Hungarian diet**. Against a background of anti-memorandum campaigns instigated by the authorities, who accused the Slovaks of destroying the unity of Hungary and of promoting pan-Slavism, the elected delegation presented the memorandum to Koloman Tisza, the chairman of the diet, on 26 June 1861. The delegation lacked representatives from the so-called Slovak nobility. Before the diet was able to consider the memorandum, the ruler dissolved it on **22 August 1861**. The memorandum only outlined the Slovak demands. They were more concretely presented in the **Vienna Slovak Memorandum**. Up until 1918 they remained the basis of the policy of the **Slovak National Party**. /DŠ/

METTERNICHIAN ABSOLUTISM – the political system in the **Habsburg Monarchy** during the first half of the 19th century. Imprecisely named after the most significant politician, Prince Clement Wenceslas Metternich, in contemporary literature it is characterized as a cabinet absolutism. It rejected **enlightenment absolutism** and adhered to the tradition of the older **absolutism** and to the principles of the **Congress of Vienna**. Its creators were, in particular, the Emperor Francis I and the Chancellor Metternich. Francis himself decided every detail. Later, during the reign of the incapable Ferdinand V, power was concentrated in the hands of the highest state bureaucrats (Metternich, Kolowrat). It was characterized by a strict centralism, a ponderous bureaucratic system directed from above, loyal but not independent officials, censorship and a secret police. The net of agents and informers functioned reliably and thus, in this period, the monarchy became a model police state. The regime was accompanied by fear and distrust, although the 1820s to 1840s was characterized by a peace and quiet which was expressed in the *biedermeier* culture. From the 1830s Metternich's efforts to keep everything stable led to an ossification of the system and an inability to resolve new problems. Although it supported economic modernization (the building of factories, railways, banks and the like), it repudiated new ideological currents and did not understand the nationality question. National contradictions in the monarchy were stifled, not resolved, and the regime yielded to the Magyarization plans of the **Magyar reform movement**. It offered only weak protection to the threatened nations (**Slovak Petition to the Throne**). Absolutism was not fully implemented in the Kingdom of Hungary and Vienna shared power there with the Hungarian nobility and its organs of self-administration. Although it ended with the **revolution of 1848/1849** it inspired **neoabsolutism**. /DŠ/

MIKULÁŠ RESOLUTION – a political document from the First World War. It was prepared by Vavro Šrobár, in cooperation with the **Slovak Social Democratic Party of Hungary,** presented on 1 May 1918 to the assembly in Liptovský Mikuláš organized by the local social democrats. About three thousand workers applauded it enthusiastically. The resolution demanded peace, universal suffrage by secret ballot, better social conditions for workers (an eight-hour working day and the like); it declared opposition to the reign of one class and one nation over others and support for the freedom of the press and expression, free access to periodicals from Cisleitha, especially in Czech. It demanded respect for the right of nations to self-determination and the right of the Slovaks to manage their own affairs independently and to be joined politically with the Czechs. The resolution was based on the idea that the Slovaks were the Hungarian branch of the Czechoslovak nation. It developed in a period when the desire for the creation of an independent Czecho-Slovakia strengthened in Czechia and even the states of the Entente inclined towards this program. It was the first public expression of the Slovaks in Slovakia for a new constitutional alternative. It strengthened the self-consciousness and arguments of the foreign resistance, especially the **Czechoslovak National Council**, which was able to cite the will of the Slovaks in Hungary to create a common state with the Czechs. On **24 May 1918** the **Slovak National Party** also declared itself in favour of a Czechoslovak state. /DŠ/

MILE RIGHT – the right of cities to cut wood, quarry stone and the like within a radius of one or two miles. (In the Middle Ages one Hungarian mile was equal to 8,350 meters). This law forbade craftsmen to settle or conduct business or trade within this radius. This had a negative economic impact since a market could not be held there. The goal was to limit competition and to strengthen the position of the cities with the mile right. It was effective in the mining cities (Gelnica and the other mining cities of eastern Slovakia under the Gelnica law, as well as the mining cities of central Slovakia) and in other cities, especially in Žilina, where it was a remnant of the Těšín law (**city rights**). /JB/

MINERS' INSURRECTION (1525 – 1526) – the largest social movement and armed uprising of miners in Slovakia during the feudal era. The prelude was a dispute between the miners of Banská Bystrica and the city council between 1517 and 1519 concerning the administration of the financial resources of the *Corpus Christi* Brotherhood, a social support organization in which the miners had achieved a controlling interest. The payment of wages in debased (copper) coins and the consequent rising inflation impoverished the poor of the city and the mine workers dependent on wages and on the city market controlled by the city council. In the struggle against the city council and various owners of mining enterprises, the miners had the support, for a while, of the **Thurzo-Fugger Company**, which attempted to dominate the whole central Slovak mining region at the expense of the remaining mine operators. A strike and the first uprising of the miners in May 1525 ended with an agreement (19 May 1525), according to which the mine operators were obliged to pay wages in undebased silver coins. When this promise was not kept, the miners demonstrated publicly in June. The situation came to a head when, under pressure from the diet, the royal chamber expropriated the Thurzo-Fugger Company. However, it was unable to assure its further operation. Thus hundreds of miners and small craftsmen lost the source of their livelihood. The disorder spread also to the Banská Štiavnica mining area. In September 1525 an association of miners was created with its center in Špania Dolina, which also sought the release of reformation preachers from prison. In February 1526 another uprising broke out in Banská Bystrica. Armed miners occupied the buildings of the chamber and were in possession of practically the whole city for more than 10 days. But when soldiers arrived, the miners retreated to the hills. The investigation of the insurrection was entrusted to the Palatine Stephen Werbőczy, author of the *Tripartitum* and the county administrator of Novohrad, Gašpar of Raška. It was also considered a heretical uprising due to the involvement of popular reformation preachers. In April 1526 severe sentences were imposed upon the miners of Banská Bystrica and Hodruša. The treasury of the *Corpus Christi* Brotherhood was fined 1,070 gold florins by Werbőczy. Repressive measures and unresolved social demands led to the radicalization of the miners and another armed rebellion on **3 August 1526**. They invaded the town, looted and burned several houses belonging to citizens and demolished mining installations. They retreated from the

city just ahead of the arrival of an army of superior force, which had been organized by the nobility and the cities of Zvolen, Krupina and Banská Štiavnica. The leaders of the insurrection fled into the mountains and to Moravia. However, several were captured and executed in September 1526. The prosecution and execution of those condemned for participating in the insurrection continued during the following years. /VS/

MINING ACADEMY – the first higher school (university level) for mining in the world. The development of mining and the metal industry and the need for educated specialists was the impetus for the establishment of mining schools in Banská Štiavnica and Smolník during the first half of the 18th century. At the apex of specialized education stood the mining academy in Banská Štiavnica, founded during 1762 – 1764. Its first chair and department (chemistry and metallurgy) were established in 1763, the second department (mathematics, mechanics and hydraulics) was set up in 1765 and on **3 April 1770** a department for the study of mining theory was established. The school then officially received the name Mining Academy (Bergakademie). Mikuláš Jozef Jacquin was the first professor in the first department and among other specialists who later lectured there were Kristof Traugott Delius, Anton Scopoli, Mikuláš Poda and Ján Selecký. Lectures in forestry were also a part of the course in mining theory. The courses were free. Applicants for study were supposed to be at least 18 years old, to have graduated from a secondary school, and to have had at least one year (from 1797, two) of practical experience. In addition to theoretical lectures, the students were trained in laboratories and through practice in the mines, preparation plants and smelters. After three years of instruction the students completed an obligatory one-year internship (*practicum*) that concluded with an examination and a thesis. The school soon acquired a worldwide reputation. In 1808 an independent forestry institute was established that merged with the academy, which was re-named the

Mining and Forestry Academy. In April 1919 it moved to Sopron in Hungary. /MK/

MODUS VIVENDI (Latin – manner of living together) – a type of agreement of the Vatican with other states that regulates mutual relationships. A higher form is a concordat. A *modus vivendi* with Czechoslovak Republic was difficult to achieve. From the founding of the state, anti-church elements had considerable influence in the Czech lands. The Vatican recognized the Czechoslovak Republic and named a diplomatic representative in 1920. But relations remained tense. On **6 July 1926** the Holy See recalled its diplomatic representative, F. Marmaggi, from Prague. The reason was the character of the commemoration of Jan Hus. After this event both parties began to work on normalizing relations. The Czechoslovak government approved the text of a *modus vivendi* on **20 January 1928** and the Holy See ratified it on 2 February 1928. The government of the Czechoslovak Republic renounced in favor of the **pope** the right of nominating new bishops, on the conditions that future **bishops** and **archbishops** must be citizens of Czecho-Slovakia and that the papal curia inform it of their names in advance. In this way political objections would be avoided. No territory of the Czechoslovak Republic, not even Slovakia, could be subordinated to an ecclesiastical administration based on the territory of another state and the borders of the dioceses had to be confined within the borders of the state. The Vatican agreed with this, but with the condition that the compulsory state administration of church property be abolished. The text of the *modus vivendi* was not presented for approval to parliament, nor was it published as part of the legal code. Both sides sought to implement it gradually. On 2 September 1937 Pope Pius XI issued the bull *Ad ecclesiastici regiminis incrementum* that announced that an independent ecclesiastical province was to be established in Slovakia. This intention was thwarted by the revision of the border on **2 November 1938**. By the confiscation of church property (laws of 11 July 1947 and 21 March 1948) the Czechoslovak Republic violated the *modus vivendi* and the Vatican did not feel bound by it. As part of the anti-church policy of the Communist government of the Czechoslovak Republic, the last diplomatic representative of the Vatican, Ottavio de Liva, was expelled on 16 March 1950 and about four days later diplomatic relations with the Holy See were broken. After 1989 the relations between the state and the church were normalized (see also **30 December 1977**). /RL/

MONASTIC (and other religious) ORDERS – associations of monastics (monks) living together according to a common rule in special communities, **cloisters**, or monastic houses. Monastics take a vow of obedience to their superiors (including the **pope**), as well as vows of chastity and personal poverty, together with a vow of stability (a promise to stay in the same abbey). Some orders have male and female branches (second order). Some also have a third order (*tertiaries*) composed of laypersons. The members of male orders may be clerics or laymen, but non-monastic orders, like the Jesuits, Piarists and Dominicans, must have a majority of priests. Candidates for membership in an order take vows after they complete a preparatory period, the novitiate. The pope approves the establishment of orders; diocesan **bishops** may approve congregations, in the first instance. The superiors of male abbeys are abbots; of female, abbesses. Newer (non-monastic) orders and lay congregations have a broad palette of titles for superiors (prior, rector, guardian, superior etc.). In the 11th century so-called monastic canons who lived in communities developed as **chapters** (for instance, the Augustinians and Premonstratensians). The oldest order in Slovakia was the **Benedictine**. The Cistercian order was established on the model of the Benedictines. It was founded by Robert of Molesme in 1098 in the Benedictine abbey of Citeaux and was reformed in 1113. The Cistercians cultivated unsettled regions and constructed churches and cloisters characterized by a special style. In Slovakia they established communities in Bardejov (1247) and Spišský Štiavnik (1223), where Polish influences were apparent. Originally they were also present in Bzovík, but were replaced there by the Premonstratensians. A female branch of the Cistercians (founded in 1125) had a cloister in Bratislava from 1235 until the last quarter of the 13th century. The Poor Claires replaced them there in 1297. The Premonstratensians, founded in 1120 by St Norbert at Prémontré in France and confirmed by the pope in 1126, were also established on the model of the Benedictines. In Slovakia they established priories in Bzovík (1135), Leles (around 1181), Jasov (end of the 12th century), Šahy (1238), Kláštor pod Znievom (1251), and Nižná Myšľa near Košice (around 1288). Among the older orders of friars (who were not monks and did not take a vow of stability), the Augustinians had cloisters in Veľký Šariš (1270), Sv. Jur (1279), Nové Mesto nad Váhom (1310), Spišské Podhradie (1327 and a hospital 1400), Hrabkov (1334) and Bardejov (1380). The Carthusians, founded in 1084 by St Bruno of Cologne on the Rhine, came to Slovakia in 1299 and built a cloister at the "Rock of Refuge" (*Lapis refugii*) near Letanovce. They founded Červený Kláštor (The Red Cloister, **1319**) in Lechnica on the Dunajec River. The Carmelites (an order of friars) settled in Prešov around 1288. An off-shoot of the Augustinians was the Guardians of the Holy Sepulcher who settled in Chmeľov in Šariš (1212) and from there went to Lendak and Huncovce (1232) and perhaps to Richňava in Spiš County. The Antonites had a cloister and hospital at the end of the 13th century in Dravce and a hospital in Bratislava at the end of the 12th century. The Benedictines, Premonstratensians, Cistercians, Carthusians, Augustinians and several others belong among the contemplative orders. In addition to performing the liturgical offices, they were concerned with the copying of **codices**, teaching and the cultivation of virgin land. They introduced new agricultural methods on their lands, and built churches (building foundries) and the like. During the 13th century the new orders of so-called friars were established, such as the **Franciscans** and **Dominicans.** Their goal was to work among the population of the cities. The female order of the

Franciscans were the Poor Claires, founded by St Claire in 1212. In Slovakia they had cloisters in Bratislava from the end of the 13th century, in Trnava (1239) and Kežmarok. When the Capuchins separated from the Franciscans in 1525 (approved by the pope in 1528), they also provided the initiative for the establishment of a female offshoot of the order, the Capuchines, founded in 1538 in Naples. A canon of Esztergom, Eusebius, founded in 1225 the Hungarian order of the Paulines. Through the intercession of Cardinal Gentilis (1308) they obtained the right to follow the rule of St Augustine from Pope Clement V. They spread during the reign of Louis I and established cloisters in Lefantovce (1369), Marianka (1377), Beckov (1430), Trebišov (1504) and Trnava (1650). In the 14th and 15th centuries other cloisters of older orders (Benedictines and Franciscans) also were established. During the **Reformation** the majority of the cloisters ceased to exist and were renewed only during **re-Catholicization**. At that time new orders also arrived in Slovakia. For example the Paulines (Barnabites), founded by St Francis of Paula in Calabria (1435), founded a cloister in Šamorín (1690). In the 17th century the Trinitarians (an order founded in 1198) came to Slovakia and had cloisters in Bratislava Trnava and Ilava. The **Jesuits**, who were among the leaders of the Catholic **Counter-Reformation**, settled in Slovakia during the time of the Reformation. The Piarists (founded in 1621) were dedicated to teaching and had cloisters in Podolínec (1642), Prievidza (1666), Nitra (1701), Trenčín (1776), Banská Štiavnica (1774) and elsewhere. In the post-Reformation era cloisters were established by the Capuchins in Pezinok (1674), Bratislava (1676) and Holíč (1750) and by the Merciful Brothers in Spišské Podhradie, Bratislava and Skalica. Female orders also spread, for example, the Ursulines in Bratislava (1676), Košice (1698), Trnava (1724) and Modra (1907). The Elizabethan (1738) and the Notre Dame (1747) orders settled in Bratislava. The majority of the mendicant and contemplative houses were abolished by Joseph II in 1782 and 1787. Some of them were revived after his death. During the 19th century modern orders were established that did not build cloisters of the classic type. They adapted themselves to the demands of the times and were devoted to working with youth, for example, the Salesians (founded in 1859). They began to build houses in Slovakia only in the 1920s. The orders played an important role in the spread of culture and education, especially in the more remote past, when clerics were almost the only people who were able to read and write. A special category were the knightly orders established during the era of the crusades. The first of these was the Order of the Hospital of St. John, the Hospitallers (founded in 1099 in Jerusalem) who, after they resettled on Malta in 1530, were known as the Knights of Malta. In 1798 they were forced to leave Malta by Napoleon and from 1834 the order had its seat in Rome. It maintains diplomatic relations with more than 50 states. The Knights Templar were established in 1118 near the temple of Solomon in Jerusalem. Pressured by the French king, Philip IV the Fair, Pope Clement V dissolved the order in 1312. The Hospitallers obtained their property in Hungary. The order of the German knights (Teutonic Order) was established in Acre (Palestine) in 1191. After the withdrawal of the crusaders from Palestine, Marienburg in Prussia became the seat of the order. In 1236 the German knights united with the order of the Knights of the Sword. The order was reformed in 1929 and still exists today. /JB/

MOSCOW NEGOTIATIONS 1943 – political negotiations about the relationship between the Czechoslovak Republic and the Soviet Union during the Second World War and after its conclusion. After the definitive recognition of the Czechoslovak government in exile in London on **18 July 1941** Edvard Beneš looked for a way to cooperate more closely with the Soviet Union, since he anticipated the rapid conclusion of the war and the arrival of the Soviet army in central Europe. In March 1942 he presented the Soviets with the main principles of a future treaty. Edvard Beneš obtained the support of Franklin Delano Roose-

velt, the president of the United States of America, for the pro-Soviet policy. Great Britain was against the preparation of a treaty because it had agreed with the Soviet Union that neither of them would conclude treaties concerning borders and post-war matters with other countries during the war. It agreed to a treaty only at a conference in Moscow of the ministers of foreign affairs of the Soviet Union, United States and Great Britain in October 1943. The Czechoslovak Republic and the Soviet Union signed a treaty of friendship, mutual assistance and post-war cooperation on **12 December 1943**. They obligated themselves to mutual military assistance in the case of a German attack, recognized the principle of the non-interference in internal affairs and agreed not to conclude an alliance directed against the other treaty party. At the last moment, the Soviet government suggested a change in the period of validity from 5 to 20 years and the clause about its subsequent approval by the Czechoslovak parliament was omitted. Through the treaty, the still non-existent Czecho-Slovak state secured the support of a great power whose army would occupy its territory at the price of a voluntary sovietization and limitation of sovereignty. In Moscow Edvard Beneš negotiated also with the minister of foreign affairs, Viacheslav Michailovich Molotov and with Joseph Visarionovich Stalin and promised to coordinate foreign policy with the Soviet Union. He demanded the punishment of the Sudeten-Germans in Czechia and the Slovaks accused of collaboration with Germany. The economic memorandum he presented to Molotov specified that, in the post-war commerce of the Czechoslovak Republic, the Soviet Union would participate to a significant degree and called for the accommodation of the Czechoslovak production plan to the Soviet state plan, suggested the building of new communications in the east and the adaptation of military industries to meet the needs of the Soviet army. Beneš negotiated also with the leadership of the **Communist Party of Czechoslovakia** in Moscow (Klement Gottwald, Rudolf Slánský, Václav Kopecký and Josef

Šverma). He did not succeed in persuading them to let Communists join the government in exile, nor did they accept his suggestion that they create a single socialist party from the Communist Party of Czechoslovakia, national socialists and social democrats. He agreed to the Communist Party of Czechoslovakia obtaining key ministries in the new state as well as to the creation of national committees and the promulgation of legal norms for the punishment of "traitors and collaborators" (**retribution**).

MOSCOW NEGOTIATIONS 1945 – negotiations about settling internal political relationships in the new Czecho-Slovak state. The impulse for their initiation was provided by the leadership of the **Communist Party of Czechoslovakia** in Moscow and the Czechoslovak ambassador in the Soviet Union, Zdeněk Fierlinger. The Communist Party of Czechoslovakia was represented by five representatives, the national socialists by four, the social democrats by four and the "ľudáks" (Czechoslovak People's Party) by two. The delegation of the **Slovak National Council (1945)** comprised Vavro Šrobár, Ján Ursíny, Gustáv Husák, Jozef Styk, Jozef Soltész, Ladislav Novomeský and Mikuláš Ferjenčík. Edvard Beneš took part in the negotiations about the Slovak question and a delegation of the parties from London arrived in Moscow on 17 March. The negotiations took place **22 – 29 March 1945**. They revealed the Czech non-Communist parties' lack of preparation and their compliance with the Communist Party of Czechoslovakia. The result was an agreement about the personnel of the new government and a government program. The delegation of the Slovak National Council demanded that the new government proclaim the equality of the Slovak nation with the Czech nation, recognize the Slovak National Council as the Slovak government and parliament and secure the exclusive competence of Slovak executive organs in the departments of the interior, education, procurement, health, industry, agriculture, public works, social security and justice. Independent Slovak units subordinate to a common leadership were to be established in the army. Slovakia was to become an independent economic, tariff and currency entity temporarily. The delegates of the Slovak National Council were invited to the official negotiations on the third day (24 March). The Slovak National Council did not find any acceptance for their federal project among the Czech non-Communist parties and gained only partial support from the Czech Communists. The compromise achieved respected only a part of their demands. The Czech politicians, including Edvard Beneš, recognized the particularity of the Slovak nation, the principle of "equals with equals", and the Slovak National Council as the holder of legislative and executive power in Slovakia, but its final competence was to be settled only after the war. The Communist Party of Czechoslovakia succeeded in having the Communist Party of Slovakia recognized as an independent party. In the provisional National Assembly the Communists secured about twice as many seats as the other parties (the parliamentary faction of the Czech Communist Party had 51 and the Slovak Communist Party had 47 deputies) and obtained a third of the most important ministries in the central government. The Moscow negotiations concluded with the ceremonial signing of the **Košice government program**. /RL/

MOSCOW NEGOTIATIONS 1968 – political negotiations in Moscow. They contributed to the legalization of the intervention of the Warsaw pact armies in Czecho-Slovakia and reversed the renewal process of 1968. The situation after the arrival of the invading armies on **20 – 21 August 1968,** marked by the arrest and abduction of several of the leading representatives of the renewal process led by Alexander Dubček, was full of uncertainty and the threat of bloodshed. President Ludvík Svoboda officially requested a meeting with the Soviet leadership in Moscow. On **23 August 1968** the deputy chairman of the government, Gustáv Husák, the minister of national defense, Martin Dzúr, the minister of justice, Bohuslav Kučera and, at the specific wish of Moscow, Vasil Biľak, Alois Indra and Jan Piller flew with Svoboda to Moscow. On 25 August the Czechoslovak delegation was expanded to 18 members. After his arrival in Moscow, Ludvík Svoboda immediately met with Leonid Iljich Brezhnev and Alexej Nikolajevich Kosygin and obtained the release of the imprisoned leaders of the renewal process and their participation in the negotiations. He also obtained official Soviet recognition for the government of Oldřich Černík and the parliament led by Josef Smrkovský. This concession from the Soviet side was balanced by the condition that the Vysočany congress of the **Communist Party of Czechoslovakia** would not be recognized. The Czechoslovak delegation did not have a unified approach, because it was divided into supporters and opponents of reform. The burden of negotiating rested upon Ludvík Svoboda, Gustáv Husák, Alexander Dubček, Oldřich Černík and Josef Smrkovský. On 26 August the Czechoslovak delegation signed the Moscow protocol. It declared invalid the Vysočany congress of the Communist Party of Czechoslovakia of **22 August 1968**, promised to withdraw the Czechoslovak question from discussion by the Security Council of the United Nations, agreed to the presence of Soviet troops on the territory of Czecho-Slovakia until the completion of **normalization**, promised that the "Soviet model of socialism" would be strengthened and the government purged, and agreed that the border with the German Federal Republic was insufficiently defended. However, the action program (**1 – 5 April 1968**), which was the spirit of the renewal process, formally remained in force. After the return of the Czechoslovak delegation (27 August 1968) a short transitional period ensued. The end to illusions was brought about by the negotiations of Alexander Dubček, Oldřich Černík and Gustáv Husák in Moscow on 4 October 1968. A new agreement went beyond the framework of the Moscow protocols and greater authority was offered to the conservative forces in the party and state. As at the previous negotiations, Gustáv Husák and Oldřich Černík pursued a compliant policy towards the Soviets in the name of realism. Oldřich Černík was soon again in Moscow and negotiated a Czecho-Slovak-Soviet treaty concerning the temporary presence of Soviet troops on the territory of Czecho-Slovakia. Oldřich Černík and Alexej Nikolajevich Kosygin signed the treaty in Prague, on 16 October 1968. It did not limit the length of the stay of the army or the number of troops. It legalized the invasion and the right of Moscow to maintain an indefinite number of soldiers on the territory of Czecho-Slovakia. /RL/

MUNICH AGREEMENT – an agreement among the great powers concerning the German annexation of the territory of the Czechoslovak state occupied predominantly by a German minority. Its acceptance resulted from the negotiations of the Czechoslovak government with representatives of the German national minority and international negotiations between the German leader, Adolf Hitler, and the British prime minister, Neville Chamberlain, in Berchtesgaden and Bad Godesberg in Germany. In the negotiations Germany clearly declared itself for the annexation to its own territory of the part of the Czech state occupied by the German minority. On **21 September 1938,** pressured by the allies, the Czechoslovak government accepted the Anglo-French plan for a withdrawal from territory in which the population was more than 50 per cent German. If Czechoslovakia declined, this would be branded the cause for the threatening military conflict. After the unsuccessful negotiations of Hitler with Chamberlain in Bad Godesberg, Great Britain and France did not raise any objections to the mobilization that was declared by the Czechoslovak government on **23 September 1938**. The complicated crisis was resolved only at the conference in Munich on **29 – 30 September 1938**. Representatives of Germany, Great Britain, France and Italy accepted an agreement that established the conditions and manner of surrendering the Sudeten-German lands to Germany. It was to take place in four stages from 1 to 10 October 1938. The Czechoslovak government had to voluntarily release the Germans from their army and police and to provide for the release of political prisoners of German nationality. According to an appendix, the territorial demands of Poland and Hungary (**Vienna arbitration**) had to be settled within three months. The agreement was signed by Adolf Hitler, Benito Mussolini, Neville Chamberlain and Edouard Daladier. The representative of the Czechoslovak government was not invited to the negotiations. Through the Munich agreement the first Czechoslovak Republic lost 28,643 km^2 of Czech territory inhabited by 2,800,000 Germans and more than 800,000 Czechs. Czecho-Slovakia lost the capacity for an effective defense against a possible attack and important industrial regions and communications. The Munich agreement opened the door to the further political and economic penetration of central Europe by the Germans. The Czechoslovak government approved the Munich agreement on **30 September 1938**. During the course of the war the Czechoslovak government in exile in London obtained the annulment of the Munich agreement by France, Great Britain and Italy. /RL/

MUTUALITY (*Vzájomnosť*) – a secret society of students at the lyceum in Bratislava. It was founded in June 1837 at the suggestion of Alexander Boleslavín Vrchovský by fifteen of the radically inclined members of the forbidden **Czechoslavic Society** (for example, Jozef Miloslav Hurban, Michal Miloslav Hodža, Samo Chalupka, Ctibor Zoch and Augustín Horislav Škultéty). Its chairman was Benjamín Pravoslav Červenák. It was established on the model of Polish radical societies, maintained contacts with students of other Slavic nations, declared itself in favor of civic equality, national liberty and **Slavic mutuality**. It viewed the future of the Slovaks as being linked to a federation of free Slavic nations. It condemned feudalism and serfdom. It urged the education of the common people and considered the cooperation of Catholics and Evangelicals as an important condition for the creation of national solidarity. Its members gathered information about life in the regions, especially the position of the serf farmers, by travelling and by corresponding with patriots in the countryside. They collected it in a manuscript journal, *Mutuality letters (Vzájomnostné listy)*.

Several suggestions emerged for the founding of economic and cultural societies and journals within Mutuality. It ceased to exist in the summer of 1840 after the intervention of the police against secret associations. Its members made up the nucleus of **Štúr's group** who preferred legal public activity to radicalism. /DŠ/

NÁHIJE – the lowest territorial administrative unit of **Turkish administration**. It was headed by a commissioned officer of the Turkish army called a *subashi* or *cheribashi*. Fully established *náhije* were rare in the border *sandjaks*. Their formation or dissolution depended upon Turkish territorial conquests or losses. *Náhije* on the territory of Slovakia – either completely or partially – were: in 1578 – 1579, within the Fiľakovo *sandjak*, Fiľakovo, Rimavská Sobota, Veľký Blh, Plešivec, Rimavská Seč, Divín, Muráň and Štítnik *náhije*; 1631 – 1632, within the Esztergom *sandjak*, Esztergom, Tekovské Lužany, Vráble, Bátovce and Nové Zámky *náhije*; in 1664, within the Nové Zámky *ejalet*, Nové Zámky, Tekov, Komárno, Hont, Nitra, Žabokreky and Šaľa *náhije*. Some *náhije* (for example, Rimavská Seč) were only formally organized. This meant that although a register of the taxes (*defter*) due from villages belonging to the respective *náhije* was created, these *náhije* did not have their own administrative organs. /VS/

NATIO HUNGARICA (Hungarian Nation) – Hungarian nation (nation of estates). In Hungary during **feudalism** this term expressed membership in the classes with prerogatives and privileges irrespective of ethnic origin. In the modern era, together with the idea of the crown of St Stephen, it shaped the feudal estates ideology of the Hungarian **nobility** as the ruling class in the country. It was the basis for the constitutional ideology of Hungarianism or the consciousness of a Hungarian state citizenship and a Hungarian patriotism that were accepted even by the Slovak nobility. In the era of the formation of modern nations, a clear change in the existing attitude towards the "Hungarian nation" set in when, at the beginning of the 18th century, several noble ideologists of Magyar origin, in the spirit of the so-called conquest theory, began to deny to the Slovak nobility the right to declare themselves members of the *natio hungarica* (1722). A defense of the rights of the Slovaks was the core of **Magin's *Apology*** of **1728** as well as of other apologetic works (for example, by Samuel Timon, Juraj Papánek and Juraj Sklenár). From the end of the 18th century up to the mid 19th century the Magyar nobility not only identified itself with the *natio hungarica*, but also declared that they were its only representatives. The ideology of the "Hungarian nation" thus became a tool for **Magyarization** and the transformation of the multi-national Kingdom of Hungary into a Magyar state. /VS/

NATIONALITY LAW (1868) – a norm regulating the position of the non-Magyar nations in Hungary. The Hungarian diet accepted it on 6 December 1868 and it was a part of the intricate Austrian-Hungarian (Magyar) constitutional compromise and the creation of **dualism**. Under the guise of protecting the integrity of Hungary, it anchored the principle of a single Magyar (Hungarian) political nation, in which each citizen, irrespective of his language or nationality, was to be a full-fledged member. The non-Magyars, with the exception of the Croatians, were not recognized as specific nations. In the context of a fictitious single nation, it granted them nationality status and individual rights in education and culture. Magyar was declared the official language of the state in all spheres of public life. The native languages could be used in county organs, if it was requested by a fifth of its members, in the offices of communities, in the courts and in the churches. Communities and churches could establish primary, secondary and higher schools, for which they could select the language of instruction. At state schools the language of instruction was to be determined by the ministry of education. Nationalities might freely establish economic and cultural societies. The law violated the principle of the equality of nationalities, granted privileges to the Magyars that were detrimental to the other inhabitants of the country and legalized a radical **Magyarization**. In addition, during the subsequent decades, it was not respected in practice, which further intensified national suppression in the Kingdom of Hungary. Slovak political forces generally repudiated it and demanded adherence to it or its abolition depending upon the circumstances. /DŠ/

NATIONALITY LAW ARTICLE OF 1608 – legal norm guaranteeing a parity of representation of nationalities in local governments. It was adopted by the **Hungarian diet** in Bratislava in 1608 and revised in 1609. It enabled the Hungarian **nobility** to expand their power at the expense of the royal free cities. Its members were able to settle in the royal free cities and to buy houses there, but they did not have to pay city taxes. In the organs of city government, Germans, Slovak, and Magyars were to have parity of representation. Although this law meant a victory of the nobility, especially of Magyar origin, it also strengthened the self-consciousness of the Slovak townspeople who previously had struggled against the German patricians. The sharpest conflict occurred in Krupina where, after 1610, a German, a Magyar and a Slovak alternated as magistrate and each of the individual nationalities had three representatives on the city council. In 1614 a revolt of the Slovak population erupted during the election of a new city pastor, which became the pretext for their cruel punishment. Their leader, Daniel Caban, was murdered, the remainder of the insurgents were beheaded and many of the Slovak townspeople were banished. Nationality struggles between Slovaks and Germans in Banská Bystrica did not follow such a bloody course, but complaints about the violation of the nationality law article in the 17th and 18th centuries often could be resolved only by the sovereign. /VS/

NATIONALIZATION – the transfer of private ownership into state ownership. The president of the Czechoslovak Republic, Edvard Beneš, issued the first decree concerning the nationalization of foreign trade companies and the film industry on 11 August 1945. His four nationalization decrees followed on **24 October 1945**. Their goal was to transfer the most important industrial enterprises from private ownership to that of the state. Decree number 100 nationalized mines, several of the large energy enterprises, iron-works, steel-works, rolling-mills, foundries, smelting works with more than 400 employees, metal-processors, electro-technical enterprises and factories for precision mechanics and optics with more than 500 employees, arms factories, building enterprises with more than 150 employees and textile enterprises with more than 400 employees. Decree no. 101 nationalized the majority of sugar mills, distilleries, breweries and mills, decree no. 102 the banks and decree no. 103 private insurance companies. The decrees were adopted by parliament on 28 October 1945. In aggregate 61.9 per cent of industry was nationalized, in Slovakia 59.4 per cent. From 1950, 28 October was celebrated as the day of nationalization, in order that the other important event linked to this date, the declaration of the Czechoslovak Republic, would be forgotten. The nationalization initiated by the social democrats significantly transformed the structure of the economy. It created the conditions for the transition to a planned directive economy. The Czechoslovak Republic was the first European state that implemented nationalization to such an extent after the war. The **Communist state coup, on 25 February 1948,** led to the nationalization of all enterprises with over 50 employees. From 1949 even private tradesmen and small business were affected in the name of socialization. In agriculture, **collectivization** was a form of nationalization. /RL/

NEO-ABSOLUTISM – the political regime in the **Habsburg Monarchy** during the 1850s. It is also called Bachian absolutism after Alexander Bach, the minister of the interior. The path to neo-absolutism was already indicated by the **dictated constitution** and was legalized by the **Sylvester Patents**. It did not mean a return to the inflexibility of **Metternichian absolutism**. Rather, it joined traditional notions of **absolutism** with a willingness to modernize all areas of life. On the one hand, it confirmed the abolition of serfdom, the equality of people before the law, the modernization of the judiciary, a tax code, schools, especially middle schools, supported the building of railways and mass production factories. On the other hand, it negated many of the achievements of the revolution. It abolished the constitutional form of the government and laws were issued by the ruler in the form of decrees. Local autonomous government was replaced by a system of offices controlled from above. Loyal, mostly talented bureaucrats, especially Austrian Germans and Czechs, were appointed to these offices. Basic human rights, such as freedom of assembly, speech and association, were again replaced by censorship, police surveillance and a many-branched network of its agents. Neo-absolutism granted to the crown lands only a symbolic authority and the monarchy was steadily built up as a single state controlled from a single center. At the apex of the complex hierarchy stood the sovereign Francis Joseph I. The army enjoyed great respect and the concordat of **18 August 1855** strengthened the position of the Catholic Church. German became the official language of the monarchy, although in legal proceedings it was possible to use the national languages. After the **revolution of 1848/1849** the central power treated Hungary as a conquered country. A **provisional government** was introduced, Hungary's autonomous rights were abolished and it was incorporated into the unified empire. After the state of emergency ended, Archduke Albrecht, the viceroy, governed Hungary. Absolutism suppressed the claims of the national movements and expressions of national identity, although it also offered protection from **Magyarization**. More Slovaks obtained positions in state offices, **Slovak gymnasia** were established and the **Pro-**

testant **Patent** was issued. The unpopular regime found itself in a crisis in 1859, which the ruler resolved by dismissing the highest bureaucrats and by issuing the **October Diploma.** This led to the renewal of a **constitutional monarchy**. /DŠ/

NEW SCHOOL (Nová škola) – a political current of the Slovak national movement in the 1860s and 1870s. Its views were opposed to those of the **Old School** and it began to emerge in the **Slovak National Assembly** and was definitively established in 1868 when it accepted the name New School. On **23 October 1872** it was renamed the Slovak Party of Equalization. Its center was in Budapest, where it had the publishing house Minerva and published the *Slovak News (Slovenské noviny)*. Among its representatives and adherents were clerics, entrepreneurs, nobles, students and workers living in Budapest. It was led by Ján Nepomuk Bobula, Jozef Zarzetsky, Ján Palárik, Ján Mallý-Dusarov and Jozef Viktorin. Its program was not well-defined and its political orientation was not firm. In trying to achieve success it conducted itself in an opportunistic manner. It devoted attention to social questions and the workers, supported the efforts of the Magyar political left to democratize political life but, at the same time, cooperated with the conservative nobility who expressed sympathy for some of its efforts. It sought to obtain the so-called Slovak nobility for its Slovak policy. It considered the **Memorandum of the Slovak Nation** and especially the demand for Slovak autonomy as untimely if not unrealistic. It criticized the **Old School** for too little activity and its orientation towards Vienna and Czarist Russia. It believed in an agreement with the Magyar politicians (deputies, ministers) and therefore did not demand a constitutional settlement for the Slovak question. It defended the integrity of the Kingdom of Hungary, its independence from Vienna and respected **dualism** and the privileged position of the Hungarian language. However, it demanded that **Magyarization** cease and that the culture of the Slovaks be allowed to develop, as well as the use of the Slovak language in offices, the founding of Slovak secondary schools (**28 August 1869**) and the amendment and observance of the **Nationality Law**. At the beginning of the 1870s, its orientation towards Budapest appeared unrealistic and divergent views led to a crisis in the party and, in 1875, to its dissolution. Some of its representatives began to work in the **Slovak National Party**, some withdrew from politics, and others, especially the more propertied and influential, joined Hungarian political parties. /DŠ/

NINTH – a tax serfs paid in kind (*naturalia*) to the landlords. It was introduced by King Louis of Anjou on **11 December 1351** and was a continuation of older customs since previously serfs had to turn over to their landlords various gifts in kind. As a form of **feudal rent,** the ninth was paid in agricultural products and wine. This obligation was extended by law 49/1492 to the vineyards that serfs had rented from other landlords. The royal free cities enclosed within defensive walls were exempt from the ninth. The collection of the ninth and the **tenth** followed the practice that the harvest was left in the fields and the ecclesiastical tenth collected first. From what remained the landlord took the ninth. Thus, the serfs turned over two-tenths or 20 per cent of the whole harvest. The ninth and the tenth were collected for a specific time during the harvest. Originally this term was rather long and crops were exposed to considerable damage in the field. During the first half of the 19th century it was shortened to eight and then to three days. During earlier periods the feudal landowners attempted to collect the ninth in money, which imposed heavier burdens upon the serfs and forced them to sell their products at city **markets,** which was not advantageous for them. The **Theresian** *urbár* (1772) made possible the substitution of monetary forms in paying the ninth on the basis of an agreement of the landlord and the serf. Originally the ninth was collected on the feast of St Stephen the King and from 1622 on the feast of St Giles (St Egidius). The payment of the ninth was abolished with other obligations of the serfs in March 1848. The ninth was replaced by a state land tax. /JB/

NITRA APPANAGE DUCHY – a territorial-administrative unit in Slovakia after the dissolution of the **Great Moravian Empire** and in the first century of the Kingdom of Hungary. After the fall of Great Moravia the fate of Nitra is unclear until 970 when the Archduke Géza turned over the government of Nitra to his brother Michael, who was murdered in 976 – 978. Géza then entrusted the Nitra appanage duchy to his nephew, Ladislas the Bald, whom he removed in 995, when Géza's son Stephen-Vajk (995 – 997) became duke. After Géza's death, Stephen became the sovereign prince and Nitra was again entrusted to his cousin Ladislas the Bald and later to Vazul, the younger brother of Ladislas. After the sudden death of his son Imrich (1031), Stephen had Vazul blinded so that he could not claim the succession. After the death of Stephen I (1038) the sons of Vazul returned from exile, and in **1048** Andrew I, as king of Hungary, bestowed this territory upon his younger brother Béla who later became king. It became the accepted custom for the Hungarian king to entrust the younger members of the Árpád family with the Nitra border duchy, to which Slovakia and the upper Tisza region belonged. As duke of Nitra (1048 to 1060), Béla struck his own coins, *denars*, had his own army and installed county administrators in his domains. Under King Solomon, the duke of Nitra (1064 – 1074) was Géza, who later became king. His younger brother, Ladislas (1074 – 1077), succeeded him as duke. When Ladislas obtained the royal title, he entrusted the Nitra appanage duchy to his youngest brother Lampert, but significantly limited his authority, so that the duke could not threaten his position as sovereign. The institution of a border duchy was transferred to Slavonia. Under King Coloman, Nitra was administered by his younger brother Álmos up to **1105**, when Coloman seized it from him. With this the border duchy officially ceased to exist. During the 11th century the dukes of Nitra had almost unlimited power in their territory, maintained their own army, struck coins and conducted an independent foreign policy (for instance, they maintained contacts with By-zantium). The coat of arms of the duchy displayed the two-armed cross that was absorbed into the Hungarian state emblem as a symbol for upper Hungary (Slovakia). /JB/

NITRA DEMANDS (the precise title is the Demands of the Slovak Nation in the County of Nitra) – the most important Slovak regional program which developed in the spring of 1848. It was prepared by a group of patriots led by Jozef Miloslav Hurban and was accepted on **28 April 1848** at an assembly of three thousand people in Brezová pod Bradlom, which was attended by representatives of 23 surrounding communities. This was the culmination of the popular movement in south-western Slovakia led by Jozef Miloslav Hurban. They responded to the threat of **Magyarization** and the inconsistency of the **March Laws** with a call for equality and the brotherhood of the nations of Hungary. They adopted several points from the **Liptov Demands** (Slovak in offices and courts, proportional representation of the Slovaks in the Hungarian diet, the legal prohibition of national oppression) and demanded in addition the teaching of Slovak in higher schools, a Slovak flag and the release of the revolutionaries Janko Kráľ and Ján Rotarides from prison. The teaching of Slovak at Hungarian schools and Hungarian at Slovak schools was to help introduce Slovak as one of the deliberative languages in the diet. The demands were also a response to social issues, especially the desire of remote village farmers from mountain areas to be freed from serfdom. They demanded its abolition and the return of woods, pastures and fields that the nobles had previously taken from them. The Hungarian power characterized this legal petition campaign as rebellion and sent an army into the area. Several of its organizers were imprisoned, as well as Daniel Bórik and Ľudovít Šulek, the emissaries of the assembly, who wanted to present the demands to a county session in Nitra. The violence of the authorities led to a rise in the level of popular defiance in south-western Slovakia. Some points of the petition were used in the **Demands of the Slovak Nation**. /DŠ/

NITRA PRINCIPALITY – the oldest known state of the Slovaks, which is associated with the name of Prince Pribina. During his reign it reached the Slovak-Moravia borderland in the west, in the south its border followed the Danube, in the north Turiec belonged to it (its other territory is unknown) and in the east its border was the Hron and Ipeľ rivers and it probably included the Štiavnické vrchy. After the expulsion of Pribina (**833**), the Nitra principality became a part of Great Moravia and the domain of younger members of the family of Mojmír. Svätopluk settled in Nitra as duke prior to 870. The only bishopric in Great Moravia was established there in **880**, as is documented by historical sources. At the end of the 9th and the beginning of the 10th century, Svätopluk II was the prince of Nitra and fought with his brother Mojmír for the rule of Great Moravia. Fighting on the side of Svätopluk, an army from the German empire burned Nitra (898 – 899). The fate of the Nitra principality after the disintegration of the Great Moravian Empire is not known. The further development of this territory is documented as the **Nitra appanage duchy.** /JB/

NOBILITY – a privileged, ruling class and estate in feudal society. Its power and privileged position derived from high birth (noble origin) and land ownership. It was created during the period when clan organizations disintegrated and **feudalism** was established by an hereditary aristocracy, the chiefs of tribes or clans and their leading retainers. As early as the era of the **Nitra principality** and the **Great Moravian Empire** groups existed whose property and privileged position differentiated them from the remainder of the population. After the Hungarian monarchy was established, the nobility was formed from the leaders of the Magyar warrior bands and from a remnant of native **magnates**, who were loyal to the Árpád dynasty. In the following centuries, alongside hereditary nobles, noble status was granted to many members of the *servienti* and *jobaggi* classes, in particular for their military service. In the Middle Ages some of the foreign knights, nobles, or courtiers who arrived in Hungary in the entourage of non-Hungarian queens or later rulers of non-Hungarian dynasties (Anjous, Luxemburgs, Habsburgs, Jagiellons) also became members of the Hungarian nobility. The privileged position of Hungarian nobles was legally anchored in the **Golden Bull** of Andrew II from 1222 and the decree of Louis I from **1351** which, like the **Tripartitum** of Stephen Werbőczy of 1514, declared the equality of all nobles. Later legal provisions confirmed the long-existing fact that a higher (**magnates**) and lower nobility had emerged. According to the law 1/1608, **dukes**, **counts, barons** and **magnates,** including the **prelates,** belonged to the higher nobility. The **yeomen** (*zemania*), **predialists** and armalists made up the lower nobility. Nobles had several **privileges,** the most important of which were personal freedom, legal exemptions (the nobility were subject only to the authority and the court of the king) and exemption from taxes and customs duties. The basic and really the only obligation of the nobility was military service (the so-called blood tax) and loyalty to the **king**. Nobility was hereditary through the male line and only exceptionally through the female. The Hungarian nobility was heterogeneous in nationality (ethnic origin), but was unified by its privileged position within the so-called **Hungarian nation** (*natio hungarica*). The main pillars of the nobility were, in particular, the **Hungarian diet** and the **county** (*stolica*), through which it was able to resist the centralizing efforts of **absolutism** and to preserve a high degree of autonomy in contrast with the nobility in other countries or other parts of the monarchy. The nobility lost its exclusive and privileged position with the **March laws** of 1848 as other classes and social groups in the Kingdom of Hungary obtained legal equality. However, it retained economic, political and social hegemony up to the dissolution of **Austria-Hungary** in 1918. /VS/

NORMALIZATION – the aggregate of political steps taken after the intervention of the armies of the Warsaw pact in August 1968. It reversed the achievements of the social renewal process from the spring of 1968. The term "normalization" appeared for the first time at the **Moscow negotiations of 23 – 26 August 1968**. The negotiations produced the Moscow protocols which stated that length of time Soviet troops would be in Czecho-Slovakia depended upon the "normalization of the situation". The Soviet side understood normalization to be the complete reversal of the developments in society from April 1968 to August 1968 (extensive personnel changes in the communist party and state functions, an explicit change of the political direction). Support for the policy of normalization was found first in the "realist group" made up of Ludvík Svoboda, Gustáv Husák and Oldřich Černík. They were originally among the defenders of the process of renewal but they made political concessions in order to prevent still greater damage. Support was also found in the conservative wing of the Communist Party of Czechoslovakia (Vasil Biľak, Alois Indra, Jozef Lenárt). Alexander Dubček also approved normalization but, as a symbol of the process of renewal, he was gradually forced from political life. Gustáv Husák replaced him in the highest office of the Communist Party on **17 April 1969**. The normalization policy lasted in fact until 1989 but was most severe in the 1970s. For passivity in political life, the state offered the citizen a "reasonable material existence". A policy of social corruption and an artificial rise in the living standard were the main pillars of normalization. The Soviet Union was aware of this and therefore, in the years 1971 – 1972, offered Czecho-Slovakia favorable loans in convertible currencies and delivered cheap raw materials, oil and natural gas. Industrial products from Czecho-Slovakia were assured outlets in the Soviet market and in the countries of "the Third World". The leadership of the Communist Party of Czechoslovakia fostered an increase in personal consumption, increased maternity and family allowances and introduced loans for newly married couples. A generous social policy led to a plundering of natural resources at the expense of future generations. Citizens who dared to express political dissatisfaction with the absence of liberty were punished as examples. Opposition to state policy was ex-

pressed primarily by the **dissidents** and the thousands of people who chose emigration (**December 1968**). /RL/

NOTITIA – the most significant encyclopedic work on the history and geography of Hungary in the 18th century. The author of the multi-volume work *Historical-Geographic Knowledge about New Hungary (Notitia Hungariae novae historico-geographica)*, Matej Bel, was a native of Očová and rector of the Bratislava Evangelical lyceum. The goal of the work was to describe all of the 48 counties of the Kingdom of Hungary at that time. The parts dealing with several, mostly Slovak, counties were printed but a substantial proportion of the work remained in manuscript. The first volume appeared in 1735 and was financially supported by the monarch, Charles III (VI). It contained a description of Bratislava as the capital city of Hungary. The second volume (1736) was dedicated to the counties of Bratislava, Turiec, Zvolen and Liptov. The third volume (1737) described several counties in Transdanubia: Pest, Pilis and Solt. The fourth volume (1742) contained material on Novohrad, Tekov, Nitra and Hont counties. The fifth and last volume from 1792 dealt with Moson county. The presentation of factual and descriptive material, rather than generalizations, predominated in the work. All counties were presented according to the same structural model. The basic chapters deal with the natural-geographic characteristics of the county, including an analysis of its name, a description of the borders, fields, hills, rivers, fauna and natural resources. In later chapters the political conditions in the county, its ancient and modern population, offices and institutions and important noble families were described. A special section was dedicated to the royal free cities, towns, fortresses and castles, and even the topography of communities. At the end of the presentation of each county was a map showing its roads. In preparing the materials for the work, Bel was helped by a wide circle of co-workers, such as Štefan Berzevici, Juraj Bohuš, Juraj Buchholtz, Andrej Hermann, Pavol Krai, Ján Matolai and Ján Tomka-Sásky. Samuel Mikovíni prepared the maps of the counties included in the work as well as engravings of several cities and castles. Like Ján Baltazár Magin's *Apology*, Matej Bel praises the Slovaks at several places in the *Notitia*, defends their autochthony and equality in Hungary, but also adopts the concept of the period that viewed the Hungarian nobility as the representatives of the political nation (**natio hungarica**). The *Notitia* met with an immediate and extraordinarily positive reaction. Soon after the first volume was issued, Pope Clement XII bestowed a medal upon Matej Bel. Bel became an internationally recognized scholar and was honored with the epithet "the great jewel of Hungary". Only an insignificant part of the *Notitia* has appeared in Slovak translation: Turiec County (*Turčianska stolica – 1989*), Bratislava (1984) and *About the wine of Svätý Jur* (*O svätojurskom víne - 1984*). /VS/

NUREMBERG LAW see **German law**

OBČINA (commune) – a collective right to use land. Its beginnings date back perhaps to the Neolithic Era. The original form was a family commune (*občina*) with collective family ownership. The existence of village or neighbor communes is thought to have existed among the Slavs in the 6th – 8th centuries. During feudalism individual members of a commune used an allotted parcel of land that was changed each year by lot. However, they did not own or have the right to sell it. Traces of the neighbor commune were evident in the common use of forests, meadows and pastures during the later feudal era and have continued until the present. /JB/

OCTOBER DIPLOMA – a law of Emperor Francis Josef I (**20 October 1860**). It was the consequence of the international isolation and military defeats of the Habsburg Empire in Italy as well as of its financial difficulties. These forced Vienna gradually to abandon neo-**absolutism** and open the way to reforms. By the October Diploma the Habsburg court renounced absolutism forever, renewed a **constitutional monarchy** and a system of representation and established the principles for the re-organization of the empire. The diploma defined the relationship between central power and local autonomy. The unity of the empire was to be maintained in common matters (especially defense, foreign policy, finance, the postal system and transportation). They were to be dealt with by the legislative activity of the imperial council (the assembly of the whole empire), in which all of the lands of the monarchy participated. Other questions were to be within the competence of the crown countries. The diploma allowed the restoration of their diets and other organs. It respected the unique constitutional position of the Kingdom of Hungary. By renewing its diet, county organizations and the vice-regency council, it recognized the pre-1848 constitution. The federalization of the monarchy was limited to the rights of historic entities and completely neglected the ambitions and potential strength of the nations that did not have a tradition of their own statehood. These rightly feared for their fate. However, neither the majority of the Austrian-German politicians, who feared the Slavic majority in the empire, nor the Magyar constitutional opposition that had demanded a free federation of Hungary with the empire since 1848 were satisfied. The February Constitution corrected the October Diploma. /DŠ/

OLD SCHOOL – the main stream of the Slovak national movement in the 60s – 70s of the 19th century. It began to form at the **Slovak national assembly**. It had its center in Martin, published the *Pest and Buda News* (*Pešťbudínske vedomosti*) and from 1870 the *National news* (*Národnie noviny*). Its chief representatives were Ján Francisci, Štefan Marko Daxner, Jozef Miloslav Hurban, Martin Čulen and Viliam Pauliny-Tóth. In contrast to the opposing **New School**, it did not trust the Magyar politicians and the "Slovak" nobility, it acknowledged the heritage of the **Štúr's group**, was oriented towards cooperation with imperial Vienna, refused any kind of expressions of Magyar supremacy, demanded a consistent national equality, and declared its adherence to **Slavic mutuality**. Its program was the **Memorandum of the Slovak Nation** and the idea of a territory (the autonomy of Slovakia within the framework of the Kingdom of Hungary). After the Austrian-Hungarian Compromise it found itself on the defensive and was not able to develop an attractive program against radical **Magyarization** or to express a day-to-day fighting spirit in the interests of defending the socially weaker classes. It anticipated help from other Slavs, especially from Czarist Russia. The Magyar side often characterized its representatives as traitors to the fatherland and pan-Slavists. At the beginning of the 1870s it began to be called the **Slovak National Party**. /DŠ/

ÓNOD DIET – an assembly, diet, of the insurgent Hungarian nobles. During the **Insurrection of Francis II Rákoczi,** the taxes demanded from the Slovak counties (*stolice*) by the insurgents grew immoderately. In addition to money they had to provide *naturalia* and housing for soldiers. With a view to approaching the diet summoned by the insurgents to meet in Ónod in Borsod county where, at that time, they had their main military camp, the citizens of Turiec county prepared a memorandum and a circular on **1 January 1707**. They called attention to the injustices that the counties had had to bear from the insurgents and urged that a peace be concluded quickly. They also sent these documents to Liptov, Nitra, Orava, Trenčín and Tekov counties to obtain their views. Some of them sent these directly to Rákoczi, who considered them to be a personal insult. The diet began on **31 May 1707** and the matter of Turiec county was discussed on 6 June. The memorandum was read by the viscount (podžupan) Krištof Okoličáni and his deputy Melchior Rakovský. The closest colaborators of Rákoczi attacked them with arms. Melchior Rakovský was killed where he stood and the severely wounded Krištof Okoličáni was condemned to death and beheaded on 9 June. Before his execution he was tortured. Other deputies to the diet

from Turiec were imprisoned, the county flag was shredded and its official seal was smashed. While the county was able to procure a new flag and seal shortly thereafter, it had to bear even greater burdens than before the diet. /MK/

PALATINE – the highest state official in the Kingdom of Hungary. In Slovak he was originally referred to as the *"nádvorný špán"* (court administrator) which was taken over into Hungarian as *"nádorispán"*. It is known that this office already functioned at the court of the rulers of Great Moravia. The first direct reports date back to the beginnings of the Kingdom of Hungary. Originally the Palatine was the administrator of the royal court, responsible for its operation, economic management and internal order. From the end of the 12th century he represented the **king** outside the cities as the chief justice. As the highest state official and **magnate**, he represented the king in various matters. From the time of King Sigismund he also functioned as the viceroy. He commanded the royal troops and presided at the diet of the country. Initially he was named to this office by the king for a specific term, with the consent of the diet. After 1526 the office of palatine was held for life. In the 16th to 18th centuries he presided at the diet of the country and its table of magnates, in the vice-regency council and at the table of the seven lords. After 1848 this office had only a symbolic significance and it legally ceased to exist in 1918. /VS/

PAN-SLAVISM – a movement pursuing the political unification of the Slavs, especially under the leadership of Czarist Russia. It spread during the 19th century among some of the adherents of **Slavic mutuality** and represented its extreme current. It was espoused mainly by conservative Russian intellectuals and was used by Russian diplomacy in the second half of the 19th century, primarily in the Balkan question. In Slovakia it appeared prior to 1848 only in the form of an indefinite conception of a federation of Slavic nations that was sketched out by the younger members of **Štúr's group**. Portents of pan-Slavism can be observed also in the emphasis of Kollár and Štúr upon the unique historical mission of the Slavs and their specific spiritual character. In 1848 – 1849 the Austrian Slavs appealed to **Austro-Slavism** and after the revolution a disappointed Ľudovít Štúr identified with pan-Slavism. In his work *Slavdom and the World of the Future (Slovanstvo a svet budúcnosti)*, he sketched a vision of the Slavs united under the leadership of Russia and he associated their future with czarism, orthodoxy, the Russian language and the communes. At the end of the 19th and the beginning of the 20th century certain elements of pan-Slavism appeared in the work of Svetozár Hurban Vajanský and that of some personalities of the so-called Martin center, who espoused Russophilia, messianism, and the liberating mission of Russia. After the First World War it became irrelevant. After 1945 this tradition was connected with the expansionist policy of the Soviet Union. During the 19th century practically every Slavic or Slovak public activity, even the most modest, was maliciously characterized as pan-Slavism, especially in Magyar and German circles. /DŠ/

PASHALIK see **Ejálet**

PATRICIATE (from the Latin *patricius* – highborn, noble) – a designation of the wealthiest class in the medieval cities of western Europe in the 12th – 13th centuries and in Slovakia from the 14th century. They were the wealthiest townsmen and representatives of financial capital. The majority belonged to the German nationality. Among the patricians in Buda were also Italians and members of other nations. In Slovakia there were patricians in the most significant and wealthiest cities, such as Bratislava, Trnava, Kremnica, Banská Bystrica, Banská Štiavnica, Levoča, Košice, Prešov and Bardejov. Patricians filled the majority of offices in the cities and were connected by the bonds of family relationships. /JB/

PEACE OF SATU MARE – the peace between representatives of the insurgent Hungarian estates and the newly elected king Charles III (VI). It was signed in Satu Mare on **30 April 1711** and concluded the last armed uprising of the estates, the **Insurrection of Francis II Rákoczi**. The peace treaty promised the leader of the insurrection, Francis II Rákoczi, that if he took an oath of fidelity to the ruler within three weeks, he and his supporters would have their property restored. Further, it proclaimed a general amnesty for the participants in the insurrection and the immutable validity of religious laws. The king obligated himself to respect the rights and liberties of the Kingdom of Hungary and Transylvania. The estates were to present their grievances to the sovereign in a legal manner. If the leader of the insurrection did not return to the country or swear an oath of fidelity, this would not hinder the peace treaty from going into effect. On 1 May, 12,000 *kuruc* soldiers under the command of Alexander Károlyi laid down their arms before the imperial generals John Pálffy and Karl Locher. At the end of July 1712 the **diet** in Bratislava accepted the suggested law by which Francis II Rákoczi and his emigrés were declared traitors. At the same time the regulations and laws accepted at the insurgent diets in Sečany, Ónod and Sárospatak were nullified. The peace treaty was a compromise between the ruler and the Hungarian **nobility**. The Habsburgs preserved their rule in Hungary and the Hungarian estates retained their prerogatives and **privileges**. /VČ/

PEASANTS – the more propertied serfs settled on the lands of a landlord. In the 16th century they still made up the most numerous category of the serf population. Later their number was reduced as a result of the growth in the class of propertyless **cotters** (tenant farmers) and subtenants in the 18th and 19th centuries. As a rule peasants held one **farmstead** (*sessia*) but they may have farmed more. Already in the 15th century the peasant farmsteads were divided into halves, later into quarters and even smaller parts. Their obligations to the landlord were commensurate with the size of the farmstead. The peasants paid the landlord **feudal rent** and also paid the state taxes and the church **tenth**. The law from 1514 and the *Tripartitum*, the collection of Hungarian customary rights, set the obligation of compulsory labor at 52 days per year for a settlement. Feudal landowners later arbitrarily increased this obligation. During the wars against the Turks, the peasants had to perform unpaid work to repair or build fortresses or county castles (*gratuitus labor, robota)* and make various extraordinary payments. Later the landlords demanded feudal rent in money instead of *naturalia.* The **Theresian urbár** (1772) defined the labor obligations (*robota*) as 52 days per year with draft animals or 104 days on foot. After the abolition of serfdom in 1848 the term peasant designated a wealthy farmer owning real estate. /JB/

PETITION MOVEMENT IN THE FALL OF 1849 – an initiative of the Slovak national movement. It started after the capitulation of the Magyar army, when a conference of the leading politicians began to negotiate, in Vienna, the future of the Kingdom of Hungary and the status of its nations. This definitely confirmed that imperial Vienna was unwilling to partition Hungary and detach Slovakia from it as a territorial-political entity, as demanded in the **March Petition**. Vienna was under the strong influence of the Magyar noble conservatives, who again controlled public administration in Slovakia, belittled Slovak constitutional efforts and the support for the Slovak movement and declared that Slovaks would be satisfied in Hungary if Magyarization was halted and their language demands satisfied. Slovak politicians decided to prove to a poorly informed Vienna that they were not a small group of radicals and that behind their demands stood the broad public. At the instigation of the editors of *Slovak News (Slovenské noviny)*, published in Vienna, and Ľudovít Štúr, a petition movement was established in western and central Slovakia in September and October 1849. Despite the opposition of the noble bureaucrats, assemblies and meetings took place that sent delegations to Vienna in the name of communities, districts and counties. Their members were drawn from the general public

to show the mass support for the Slovak constitutional program. The delegations were received by the emperor, the members of the government and general officers of the army. Only a few of them demanded the detachment of Slovakia from the Kingdom of Hungary and the establishment of a Slovak crown land. The remainder allowed this question to remain open and were satisfied to present demands for language and cultural rights. This impaired the credibility of the whole action. This discrepancy was rectified by a joint petition of the delegations that arrived in Vienna on **7 October 1849**. However, the imperial politicians had already decided that Slovakia would remain in the Kingdom of Hungary. The question of Slovakia thus continued to be a problem that awaited resolution in future decades. /DŠ/

PITTSBURGH AGREEMENT – a document signed by the representatives of Slovaks and Czechs in the United States of America and Tomáš Garrigue Masaryk. It was concluded on **31 May 1918** in Pittsburgh by representatives of the Slovak League in America and the Czech National Society with the chairman of the **Czechoslovak National Council**, Tomáš Garrigue Masaryk, who also composed the text. In it the compatriot societies expressed their approval for the program of the national council in Paris, which had proposed the creation of a common state of the Czechs and the Slovaks. According to this agreement, it was to be a republic and have a democratic constitution. Slovakia was to have an autonomous position, its own administration, diet and judiciary and Slovak was to be used as the official language. In contrast to the **Cleveland Agreement**, which it replaced, the Pittsburgh Agreement forsook a consistent federalism and inclined towards an asymmetrical autonomy. After the new state was established, the lawfully elected representatives of the Czechs and Slovaks at home were to draw up detailed principles for its organization. The constitutional principles of the agreement were not put into effect and Czecho-Slovakia was developed as a strictly unitary state with the ideology of **Czechoslovakism**. The Slovak autonomists cited the Pittsburgh Agreement in their arguments, but their opponents belittled its legal validity. The original copy of the agreement was brought to Slovakia by its signatories on **5 June 1938**. /DŠ/

PLACETUM REGIUM (Latin) – royal approval, agreement. On **6 April 1404** King Sigismund decreed that papal bulls were valid in Hungary only when they had been approved by the king. This was during a period of struggle with Ladislas of Naples, who was supported by Pope Boniface IX, an enemy of King Sigismund. At the same time Sigismund proclaimed that the king of Hungary had full patronage right over church offices and property. The papal curia could not fill ecclesiastical offices or dispose of land without the consent of the ruler. This sanction was renewed in 1440, 1486, 1715, 1723 and 1729. In 1765 Maria Theresa extended the *placetum regium* also to papal briefs (*breve*), letters about less weighty church questions. Joseph II extended it to include all papal and episcopal acts. The *placetum regium* was abolished by a decree of 1850 and the concordat of Austria with the Holy See in **1855**. /JB/

POPE – head of the Roman Catholic Church and, since 1929, the Vatican state. The name comes from the word *papa* – father. The popes were the Roman **bishops** upon whom devolved from the 3rd – 4th century the supreme ecclesiastical power, based on a succession from the apostle Peter. The position of the popes gradually became unlimited in questions of faith, legislative activity, as the highest judicial and penal power, in the administration of the Papal States and the Roman Catholic Church, as well as its supreme supervisory power. Today the pope is elected for life by cardinals less than eighty years old. Until the present, 262 popes, of whom 214 were of Italian origin, have occupied the papal see. In 1870 at the First Vatican Ecumenical Council, the pope was declared infallible in matters of faith. The advisory organs of the pope are church **councils**, the college of **cardinals** and the synod of bishops. The insignia of the popes are the triple tiara (triple crown), the pallium, the Ring of the Fisherman (recalling St. Peter), the staff with a cross (which, in distinction to that of the other bishops, is not curved), Roman purple (actually red) slippers (inherited from the later Roman emperors and symbolic of universal dominion), a white cassock and sash and gold pectoral cross. The external symbol of the papal dignity is the papal throne. With the exception of the triple tiara, the majority of these insignia are presently still used. /JB/

PORTAL (from the Latin *porta* – gate, portal) – the basic tax unit in the Kingdom of Hungary during the period of **feudalism**. The *port* or portal tax is first mentioned in a decree of Charles Robert from 1323. In 1338 it amounted to 18 *denars* for each port. The extent of a portal was changed during feudalism. It was understood as a peasant's household in which several families lived, or a gate through which a fully loaded wagon could pass. Until the 16th century a portal was identical with a farmstead (*sessia*). In the 17th century it comprised four peasant families or 12 cotter (sub-tenant) households, according to a decision of the diet approved by Matthias II Habsburg on **23 January 1610**. In the period of late feudalism the portals were divided into large portals and small portals; the tax levied on the latter was half that of the former. In the 18th century the portal was the specific monetary obligation prescribed for an individual community. Portal lists preserved from the 15th century are a valuable source for demographic and settlement investigations. /JB/

PRAGMATIC SANCTION – an extraordinary order of succession. It was proclaimed by the Emperor Charles VI (Charles III as Hungarian **king**) in Vienna on 19 April 1713. It declared the indivisibility of the rule over all countries of the **Habsburg Monarchy** and at the same time regulated the succession to the throne. Charles VI enacted the Pragmatic Sanction after the experience of the War of the Spanish Succession when, following the death of the childless Spanish king Charles II, the Austrian branch of the Habsburgs failed to secure the Spanish crown for a member of the family, namely Charles III (VI). According to the Pragmatic Sanction the rule of the Habsburg Empire devolved first upon male descendants of the sovereign. If there were no male descendants, the crown might also be inherited by female descendants in the following order: first the daughters of Charles and then the daughters of his predecessors Joseph I and Leopold I. Since no male heir was born to Charles VI after his son Leopold died in 1716 at the age of six months, after his death in 1740 he was succeeded by his daughter, Maria Theresa. The whole policy of Charles VI was directed towards obtaining the recognition of the Pragmatic Sanction by the individual countries of the monarchy and by the Great Powers of Europe. The **diet** of the Austrian lands accepted it in the years 1717 – 1720 and the Czech estates in 1720. The Hungarian **estates** accepted the Pragmatic Sanction by law at a diet in Bratislava on 19 June 1723. As consideration, the ruler had to confirm their rights and **privileges**. /VČ/

PREDIALISTS – a special privileged group in the service of the **magnates** and high church dignitaries. Legally and socially they belonged to the lowest level of the Hungarian **nobility**. Their emergence is dated to the second half of the 13th century and is connected with the right (later the obligation) of **prelates** and magnates to maintain *banderia*, private military units, at their own expense. Predialists came from the serfs and the free population that the magnates and prelates had settled on their lands or in **castles**. As a reward for military service they might even obtain a small part of the allodial (hereditary) land of the landlord, which was called *praedium* (estate). The peculiarity of this property was that its ownership and the right to inherit it were bound to the performance of the military (or other) obligations connected with the land. The predialists were normally freed from all public taxes and dues and paid only county taxes. The noble courts did not have jurisdiction in cases between the predialists, for they were subject to their own judiciary and administration. Such an organ was, for example, the seat (*stolica*) of the predialists of the archbishop of Esztergom located in Vojka nad Dunajom (from 1424 in Vráble). The predialists

were originally a numerous noble category; later their number significantly declined. From the 16th century only a few prelates retained the right to maintain predialists. At the transition from the 18th to the 19th centuries predialists disappeared completely. They were formally abolished as a specific privileged class by a patent of 3 February 1853. /VS/

PRELATES – high church dignitaries. They were a part of the Hungarian **estates**. **Archbishops**, **bishops**, titular bishops and dignitaries without ecclesiastical benefices, abbots, deans and priors of cathedral and collegial **chapters**, including titular priors, belonged to this group. The basic **privileges** of the clerical estates were confirmed by the second (ecclesiastical) **Golden Bull** of Andrew II of 1222. These were, in particular, the exemption from taxes and **tolls** and the special protection of the clergy, including their own ecclesiastical courts. According to this bull, the archbishop of Esztergom could even excommunicate a king who violated its provisions (shortly thereafter this provision was rescinded). The prelates enjoyed privileges similar to those of secular **magnates** and could even organize their own *banderia* (private armies). They did not have to take an oath when giving testimony in court, only exceptionally was the death penalty imposed upon them and their ecclesiastical income was not liable to confiscation for debt. The oath of a prelate was deemed to have the value of the oaths of ten nobles. The prelates were members of the royal council and filled many high offices of the country (for example, traditionally the office of chief chancellor) and had the right to participate personally in the **diet**, in which they comprised the first estate. From **1608** archbishops and bishops were automatically members of the upper table, while the remaining (lower) prelates were members of the lower table of the diet. From 1792 the metropolitans and bishops of the Orthodox Church (in contrast to the dignitaries of the Protestant churches, who never were recognized as prelates *de iure*) were also included in the estate of the prelates. In addition to holding significant political positions, the prelates also had extensive property and income at their disposal. A particularly important source of income was the ecclesiastical **tenth** that the serfs and, until the 15th century, even the nobility had to pay. /VS/

PREŠOV COLLEGE – a higher Evangelical school. The absence of a university for the Evangelicals in Hungary forced the convention of the eastern Slovak cities in 1665 to establish a ten-class scholastic college (*collegium scholasticum*) at which there would be lectures in the subjects of higher science, philosophy and theology. It was formally opened on **18 October 1667** in Prešov. Professor Samuel Pomarius from Wittenberg became its rector and 13 teachers worked there. In the final year of the course there were lectures on theology, philosophy and oriental languages. The significant Slovak philosophers, the atomist Izák Caban and the logician Johann Schwartz also taught here. After a promising beginning, the college began to stagnate as the result of the insurgencies of the estates and the pressure of the **Counter-Reformation**. In 1673 it was obtained and administered by the Jesuits until the **Thököly Insurrection** erupted, when it was again taken over by the Evangelicals. The rectors Eliáš Ladiver, Jr., Ján Rezik and Samuel Matthaeides initiated noteworthy pedagogical and cultural activity. Public disputations in theology, logic, geography, homiletics and other subjects took place. After the suppression of the **Insurrection of Francis II Rákoczi** in 1711 the college and its property was transferred to Catholic hands and placed under the administration of the Jesuits. In 1750 Maria Theresa allowed the Evangelicals to institute philosophical and theological courses and in 1815 lectures also began in law. Later the college was transformed into a theological school and in 1873 a teachers' institute. In the 19th century several famous revivers of the nation studied there (Jonáš Záborský, Pavol Országh Hviezdoslav, Michal Miloslav Hodža, Ján Francisci and others). /VČ/

PREŠOV SLAUGHTERHOUSE (also Caraffa's slaughterhouse) – the name given to the execution in Prešov of supporters of the **Thököly Insurrection**. After the insurrection had been suppressed, it was forbidden to have any kind of contact with the remnant of the insurgents who, under the command of Thököly's wife, Helena Zrínyi, defended the castle of Mukačevo. Many of the citizens of Prešov had enthusiastically supported the insurrection. The disclosure of correspondence between the citizens of Prešov and the supporters of Thököly, as well as the devastation of the Franciscan church in Prešov, preceded the executions. The first to be arrested was the notary Friedrich Weber who betrayed other persons. From **5 March 1687** to 12 September a military court led by General Anton Caraffa, after cruel torture, condemned to death and publicly executed 24 persons of the Evangelical faith, in particular townspeople and nobles. In addition to Friedrich Weber, David Feja, Sigmund Zimmermann, Andrew and Gabriel Keczer and others were executed. The court and executions were intended to intimidate the dissident nobility and the citizenry of the Protestant faith. /VČ/

PRIVILEGES – special rights giving preference to a certain group of the population, especially the **estates** (nobility, clerics and townspeople). The collective privileges of the **nobility** were anchored in the **Golden Bull** of Andrew II from **1222**, the decree of Louis (**1351**) and those of other rulers. The collective privileges of the townspeople were contained in the so-called minor decree (*Decretum minus*) of Sigismund from **1405**. There also existed privileges for specific individuals, especially nobles, by which they obtained property grants, dignities, offices, coats of arms (*armalia*), elevation to the noble estate or other rights. A special group of collective privileges was made up of privileges defined for individual cities. Although they emanated from **city laws** of a certain legal system, their wording varied from city to city. Only rarely did serfs obtain privileges. These were collective privileges for the royal villages, privileges for the Walachians (**Walachian Law**) or privileges for individual **freemen**. Special charters were issued to bestow privileges which, depending on the importance of the content, were so-called solemn (*privilegia maiora)* or simple (*privilegia minora*). Thus, the word privilege as used had two meanings: the charter itself and the right it granted to individuals or groups. The equality of citizens before the law was most explicitly proclaimed by the French revolution in 1789 but also in other revolutions that overthrew the feudal system. In Hungary it was the **revolution of 1848/1849** that eliminated feudal privileges. However, several were preserved up to 1918. /JB/

PROTESTANT PATENT – the legal decree that regulated the administration of the Evangelical and the Calvinist churches. Its chief author was Karol Kuzmány and it was issued by the ruler on 1 September 1859. It was intended to secure the decisive influence of Slovak Evangelicals in the congregations in which they had a majority, as well as to protect against the repetition of **Magyarization** in the Evangelical church, which had started at the beginning of the 1840s. At that time, the initiators of Magyarization were the noble secular dignitaries and the patrons of the church. The patent sought to free the Slovak congregations from their tutelage. It limited their authority and strengthened the rights of individual congregations and their members (for example, the election of clerical teachers and church administrators). It preserved the autonomous position of the Protestant churches, but subjected them to state supervision (the agreement of the ruler and the state to important decisions). It changed the territorial organization of the Evangelical Church where, instead of the four old superintendencies (bishoprics), it established five. The Prešov and Bratislava superintendencies were on the territory of Slovakia and in them the independence of the Slovak Evangelicals was particularly strengthened. In April 1860 Karol Kuzmány was elected as the bishop (superintendent) of the Slovak patent congregations in the Bratislava district. The Slovak believers welcomed the patent; the Magyar side resisted it. Anti-patent conventions characterized it as an anti-constitutional act of absolutism, a restriction of the autonomous rights of the Protestant churches by the state. Under the

pressure of the Magyar constitutional opposition, it gradually lost support even in Vienna. In May 1860 the ruler agreed that congregations could decide for themselves whether they would implement the patent or revert to the old order. After 1867 the Magyar side in Protestantism rejected the terms of the patent. Even if it did not fulfill expectations, the patent contributed to the revival of Slovak activity that culminated in the declaration of the **Memorandum of the Slovak Nation**. /DŠ/

PROTESTANTISM – the aggregate of several independent Protestant streams of thought and religious organizations. It developed during the era of the **Reformation** in the 16th century as the third basic variant of Christianity alongside Catholicism and Orthodoxy. Its name is derived from the protest of German princes in 1529 against the attempt of Emperor Charles V to abolish their right to decide the religious confession of their subjects. In the era of the Reformation individual forms of Protestantism developed: Lutheranism, Zwinglianism, the Anglican Church, Calvinism, Anabaptism and others. In the 18th and 19th centuries new forms were added: Methodism, Adventism, the Jehovah's Witnesses etc. Protestantism is based upon a doctrinal demand for the renewal of Christianity on the basis of the Bible, the abolition of the privileged position of the clergy and much ceremonial. It taught an immediate connection of man with God without the mediation of the church and the clergy, according to which each believer might conduct divine services. It did not recognize the cult of Virgin Mary and the saints and repudiated monasticism and the **celibacy** of the clergy. Protestantism limited and simplified the religious cult, preserved fewer holy days and reduced the numerous sacraments to baptism and the eucharist (communion). The divine services focused on preaching, common prayer and the singing of psalms. The churches did not have elaborate ornamentation, magnificent pictures and the like. The basis of doctrine was the Bible alone. However, individual forms of Protestantism have their own particular confessions of faith by which they differentiate themselves from one another. Protestantism penetrated the territory of Slovakia during the 16th century and the majority of the population adhered to the Evangelical Church of Augsburg Confession (**Synod of Žilina**). /VČ/

PROVISIONAL GOVERNMENT (PROVISORIUM) – a temporary political arrangement. It appears most frequently after great political, military or social crises when the old norms are already no longer valid and the new are not yet established. It is characterized by martial or semi-martial law, special authority for the army, the operation of extraordinary courts and the validity of temporary regulations. In Hungary it was clearly implemented for the first time in the 19th century after the imposition of the **dictated constitution**. Alexander Bach officially introduced it on **13 September 1850**. He renewed the **vice-regency council** headed by the Viceroy Karl Geringer and then, from April 1852, by the Archduke Albrecht. The Kingdom of Hungary was divided into 5 regions (*kraje*) and 45 counties (*župy*). Two of the regions, Košice and Bratislava, were on the territory of Slovakia. German was used in the higher offices and the language of the population in the lower offices. On **19 January 1853** the ruler introduced a definitive administration in the Kingdom of Hungary. However, it did not differ much from the provisional one. In the first half of the 1860s a provisional government was applied in Hungary for the second time. The principles of a **constitutional monarchy**, civic rights and a system of representation were restored with the promulgation of the **February Constitution**. There developed a strong Magyar constitutional opposition in the **Hungarian diet**, which was distinguished by an anti-Vienna radicalism. It maintained contacts with the Kossuth emigration, while in the counties it boycotted the decrees of the ruler and the vice-regency council. In an attempt to counter this destabilization, Francis Joseph suspended the restoration of constitutional forms in Hungary (in contrast to the western part of the monarchy). On **22 August 1861** he dissolved the diet, county and city self-administration, named commissioners for the counties and established special military courts. He convened the Hungarian diet, dissolved the government of bureaucrats, revoked the state of semi-martial law on 17 September 1865 and, three days later, withdrew even the **February Constitution**. /DŠ/

RATIO EDUCATIONIS – the school reform of Maria Theresa. Attempts to reorganize the system of education took place within the framework of enlightenment reforms, which were intended to raise the level of popular education as the basic non-material resource of the state. The ruler entrusted the task of preparing a new curriculum for Catholic schools in Hungary to a special commission. After ten years of work it presented a suggestion for reorganization to Maria Theresa, who approved it on **22 August 1777**. The reform established a unified school system from primary schools up to university. The system contained study and disciplinary regulations, as well as norms for physical, intellectual and moral training. The goal of instruction was to produce an individual, educated in practical matters to a level commensurate with his social position. Schools were divided into elementary and Latin schools. Three types of elementary schools offered basic education, the fourth type served to educate teachers for the elementary schools. Latin schools had three levels. The first were the grammar classes, the second level were the humanities classes that, together with the grammar classes, comprised the gymnasium. In the third level were the academies at which noble youths were to complete their studies. The state had ultimate supervision over schools. The towns had to maintain the school buildings and to pay the teachers. In the restructured school system of 4 November 1806 (the so-called second *Ratio educationis*) gymnasia, called lyceums, were established with higher courses of philosophy. Legal studies at academies lasted three years and a gymnasium had 6 classes. Protestant schools continued to have their own order and administration. /MK/

REALISM – an artistic movement that began in the 1830s in England and France. It found its expression especially in literature and the visual arts. Positivism corresponded to it in philosophy. In Slovakia it was dominant in the second half of the 19th and the beginning of the 20th century. It sought to capture reality, the environment and personalities truthfully and often critically. Among the first generation of Slovak literary realists elements of **Romanticism** were still manifested in the idealization of the nation and people (Svetozár Hurban Vajanský, Pavol Országh Hviezdoslav, Jaroslav Vlček, Jozef Škultéty). The second generation was already characterized by typically critical and even ironic attitudes, not only towards **Magyarization** but also towards the dark side of societal and national life (Timrava, Martin Kukučín, Jozef Gregor Tajovský, Janko Jesenský). Painters also were inspired by the commonplace and every day life instead of the sacred and exceptional life. While marks of a national idealization were evident in the pictures of Jozef Hanula, Ladislav Medňanský opened the way to psychological and Dominik Skutecký to social criticism. In sculpture it was evident in the works of the founder of the modern Slovak tradition of sculpture, Ján Koniarek, as well as in those of Ján Fadrusz. /DŠ/

RE-CATHOLICIZATION – in the era of the **Counter-Reformation** the process of re-converting the population of Protestant confession to the Catholic faith, resorting, alongside predominantly missionary methods, to the use of force. The process of re-Catholicization started at the beginning of the 17th century when the royal authorities and landlords joined the Counter-Reformation and, according to the asserted right of *cuius regio, eius religio* (whose rule, his religion), wanted to compel their subjects to convert to the faith of the ruler. They seized churches from the Protestants by force, exiled their teachers and preachers

and forbade them access to schools, offices and the professional guilds. This discontent of the Protestant population (nobles, townspeople and serfs) was often the pretext for an armed insurrection that the Hungarian nobility was always willing to lead. Under the slogan of religious freedom, they attempted to preserve their prerogatives and **privileges**. Insurrections led to new violence and often to the physical elimination of religious opponents (**Prešov Slaughterhouse**, **Bratislava Court**). The re-Catholicization reached its apogée in the second half of the 17th century when, from 1659 to 1681, 888 churches were taken from the Protestants and numerous church congregations were dissolved. The diet of Sopron (1681) resolved that the landlord determined the faith of his subjects and that the Protestants could conduct their devotions only in two designated (*articular*) places in each county where they could erect churches. They were compelled by force to participate in Catholic ceremonies, processions and the like. The Protestant clergy were subordinated to the Catholic clergy and had to pay to them the **tenth** and the stole fee (*štóla* – fees for baptism, burials etc.). /VČ/

REFORMATION – an ecclesiastical movement in Europe in the 16th and 17th centuries directed against the authority of the Catholic Church and the pope in the spiritual matters. It also contained social and political elements. Originally it was a movement of townspeople, farmers and the urban poor. Later the nobility, who wanted to secularize or appropriate church property, also adhered to it. The Reformation had the character of a religious struggle; it wished to renew the church on new principles. It laid the foundations for **Protestantism** (Lutheranism, Zwinglianism, Calvinism and the Anglican Church) through the activity of Martin Luther in Germany in 1517. The ideas of the Reformation were brought to Slovakia in the first half of the 16th century by students, teachers and scholars from Germany, Czechia and Moravia. They spread especially among the townspeople, but many secular feudal landowners also supported them. In September **1549** the five royal free cities of eastern Slovakia issued their confession of faith, the *Confessio Pentapolitana*, which was compiled by the rector of Bardejov, Leonard Stöckel. It indicated differences from the Catholic faith and, above all, differences from the teaching of radical Protestant sects. The mining cities of central Slovakia and the cities of the Spiš region took a similar step. The Calvinist Reformation spread among the Magyar population, while in western Slovakia and Spiš followers of radical sects – Anabaptists, later called Habaner – also settled. At the end of the 16th century, the moderate reformation of the Augsburg Confession, to which most of the population adhered, predominated (**Synod of Žilina, 22 January 1614**). The Reformation movement called forth in the Catholic camp the **Counter-Reformation**. /VČ/

REGIONAL SYSTEM – a type of organization of state administration for a certain territory. The regional system was preceded in Slovakia by the county (*župa*). The county, as an independent unit, had a tradition extending deep into the past of the Kingdom of Hungary. The 1920 law on districts was valid only in Slovakia; in Czechia the original regional system (*krajinské zriadenie*) was preserved. The new districts were neither territorially nor objectively the continuation of the old Hungarian counties and sheriffs' districts (which were transformed into political districts headed by a district chief). The authority of the district council was limited to economic and social matters. The administrator and the district chief had the right to appeal any of the council's decisions if, according to them, they exceeded its authority. The intended federation of the districts, which could have fulfilled the function of a unifying and coordinating organ, was not achieved. From this perspective Slovakia did not become a single whole. The acceptance of the law concerning the organization of political administration of **14 July 1927** redressed certain problems. The law was drafted, in particular, by the National Democratic Party of Karol Kramář. Hlinka's Slovak People's Party, a member of the ruling coalition, also contributed to its acceptance, for it viewed the regional system as a step in the direction of the **autonomy of Slovakia**. By a new law of 1 July 1928 Slovakia became a single administrative unit under the title Slovak region (*krajina*). Thus, Czecho-Slovakia was comprised of four regions, Czechia, Moravia-Silesia, Slovakia and Sub-Carpathian Ruthenia. The organs of the regional system were the regional councils, which elected regional committees from their midst. Two-thirds of the members of the council were elected and one-third were named by the government. In Slovakia the council had 54 members. It was presided over by a regional president named by the president of the state and subordinated to the ministry of the interior. The government could exclude any kind of issue from the jurisdiction of the council. The influence of the regional council was limited to culture, health and social matters, the building of communications and the like. In economic and social questions it had an advisory function. The first election to the regional council took place in Slovakia on 2 December 1928 and Hlinka's Slovak People's Party was victorious. Jozef Drobný (1928 – 1929), an autonomist, became the first regional president. He was followed by Jozef Országh (1929 – 1938). The last was Julián Šimko (1938 – 1939). The regional administration was part of the centralist model of the administration of the first Czechoslovak Republic. /RL/

RENAISSANCE – an intellectual and artistic movement between the **Gothic** and the **baroque** eras, from the 14th to the end of the 16th and the beginning of the 17th century. The ideological basis was the idea of **humanism** and the attempt to recover and revive the legacy of antiquity. It originated in the 14th century in Italy, from where it spread into the transalpine countries and also, during the reign of Matthias Corvinus, to Hungary. In art it reflected especially the ideal of an affluent citizenry, a joyful and natural life, as well as a desire for beauty proceeding from the emotional rather than the rational. It was most expressively manifested in architecture, especially in a logical and consistent floor-plan, balanced space and effective exteriors. In Slovakia the Renaissance and late Gothic styles dovetailed to create an individual transitional style. In the seventeenth century Renaissance stylistic elements merged into Mannerism. The development of domestic Renaissance architecture is represented especially in the town halls of Bratislava, Bardejov and Levoča, the building of the **Academia Istropolitana** in Bratislava, castles in Levice and Komárno, the fortress in Vráble, the fortified castle and city of Nové Zámky and in numerous other castles. Renaissance painting was concentrated primarily in Spiš County and it focused on ornamental embellishments. Renaissance literature was written almost exclusively in the national language, used simple stylistic elements that brought the language of literary works closer to that of popular speech. The poetry of the Slovak Renaissance is represented mostly by anonymous historical songs from the 16th – 17th centuries, amorous poetry and, to some extent, by the religious spiritual songs of Ján Silván and Eliáš Láni. The works of Pavol Kyrmezer and Juraj Tesák-Mošovský are representative of Renaissance drama. Renaissance prose has been preserved only in fragments – in small anecdotal tales, the so-called *facetiae*. In music the Renaissance was expressed especially in the development of vocal polyphony. /VS/

REPUBLICAN PARTY OF AGRICULTURAL AND SMALL FARM PEOPLE see **Agrarian Party**

RESOLUTIO CAROLINA – regulations concerning the arrangement of religious relations in Hungary. It was issued by Charles III on **21 March 1731**. It was based upon the laws of 1681 and 1687 and confirmed the Roman Catholic religion as the state religion. Protestants were allowed to practise their religion freely only in places designated in the articles and to elect superintendents who were to ordain pastors and to issue regulations in questions of doctrine and morals. Baptisms were subject to the supervision of the Catholic clergy. The **Toleration Patent** (1781) abolished the provisions of the *Resolutio Carolina*. /MK/

RETAINERS (*Familiari* – in general servants, companions, members of a family.) In the medieval Kingdom of Hungary, the institution of *familiari* (retainers or household), which developed from the 13th century, represented a special form of vassal dependency or a feudal relationship. The minor nobles (and to a lesser degree also non-nobles) entered the household, that is, the service, of nobles of higher status, **magnates**, **prelates** and **kings**, as their retainers. Their legal status was that of a servant in a master-servant relationship that, as a rule, was contracted by an oral agreement. For the performance of services, the lord (*dominus, seigneur*) offered the retainer not only social and legal protection but also a livelihood and often even land. The retainers were mostly administrators and officials on the property of the lord, served as heavily-armored cavalry in the lord's military entourage or as lower-level commanders of his *banderium*. Retainers could receive into service their own retainers and these again still others. Thus, in the 14th and 15th centuries a stratified network of subordination existed in Hungary, at the head of which was the king. This was similar to the feudal system among the lords and vassals in western Europe (*feudum*). The retainers' obligations were not life-long and they could go to serve other lords and thus the institution of the household was characterized by considerable mobility. This enabled the lower nobility to ascend to the higher rungs of Hungarian society. Many retainers of non-noble origin were able to achieve noble **estate** or status. During the reign of the Habsburgs the significance of the retainers gradually declined. An imperial patent of 1855 formally abolished them. /VS/

RETRIBUTION (from the Latin *retributio* – to pay back, to return as due) – a type of extraordinary courts. Immediately after the conclusion of the **Second World War**, on **15 May 1945** the **Slovak National Council (1945)** promulgated law number 33 that established a retributive judiciary. It created extraordinary, so-called people's courts that were to try all who had contributed to the declaration of the **autonomy of Slovakia** in 1938 and the first **Slovak Republic** in 1939, as well as those who had committed "a betrayal of the Uprising" (**1944**) and had actively taken part in the struggle against the Uprising, the Soviet Union and the allies and in the persecution of the Jews. Retributive courts proceeded on the principle of retroactivity – actions considered legal in the past were declared illegal. The institution of the people's court had three levels, local and district courts and the so-called national court. While the first two dealt with cases of local significance, the national court tried the most important political, economic and military representatives of the first Slovak Republic. Of 20,550 indicted for acts from 1938 to 1945, the people's courts in Slovakia condemned 8,058 persons, 55 of these to death (carried out in 29 cases), while the remainder were freed. The largest retributive trial before the so-called national court was the trial of the president of the Slovak Republic, Jozef Tiso, who was condemned to death on **15 April 1947** and executed three days later. The decisions of the people's court often affected the innocent and some of the sentences were disproportionate. For the leadership of the Communist Party of Czechoslovakia the retributive courts were a suitable means to weaken "the bourgeoisie" under the pretense of struggling against "collaborators and fascists". /RL/

REVOLUTION OF 1848/1849 – a chain of revolutions in western and central Europe. Their goal was to abolish **absolutism** and **serfdom**, enact equality before the law, introduce a constitutional political system, assure the representation of the people and secure freedom for nations. From France and the German states the revolutionary wave spread to Vienna where, on 13 March 1848, an uprising overthrew **Metternichian absolutism**. The ruler proclaimed basic civil liberties and a new constitution. Soon the whole monarchy was affected. In the Kingdom of Hungary it resulted in the **March laws**. However, instead of recognizing the national rights of the non-Magyars, these opened the way to a radical **Magyarization**. This resulted in the emergence of national movements that demanded the territorial-political secession of their ethnic lands. The Slovak national movement, led by the followers of Štúr (**Štúr's group**), convened petition assemblies in the regions that resulted in the **Liptov Demands** and the **Nitra Demands**. The Slovak movement climaxed in the spring of 1848 with the declaration of the **Demands of the Slovak Nation** and the appearance of its representatives at the **Slavic Congress**. The subsequent power struggles between the Hungarian forces led by representatives of the **Magyar Reform Movement,** on the one hand, and, on the other hand, the forces of Vienna and the non-Magyar movements came to a head and resulted in civil war and the campaigns of the imperial army in Hungary. The **September Insurrection**, the **Winter Campaign** and the **Summer Campaign** were a part of these armed conflicts. Since the Vienna government and the Habsburgs had promised to preserve the achievements of the revolution, to secure the equality of nations and to transform the empire into a federal state, they were supported by Slovak politicians. They identified with the principles of **Austro-Slavism** and officially presented their new program to the ruler in the **March Petition**. Other proposals and programs suggested the detachment of Slovakia from Hungary and its establishment as an autonomous entity within the empire. After the **dictated constitution** was proclaimed and especially after the capitulation of the Hungarian army near Világos, the Vienna authorities followed a centrist course that led to the introduction of **neo-absolutism**. Therefore, even the **petition movement** in the fall of **1849** was unsuccessful. The revolution brought meager results in the resolution of the Slovak question. Slovakia remained a part of Hungary, several dozen Slovaks obtained official posts, a Slovak newspaper began to be published, Slovak was to be used as the language of instruction at elementary and especially secondary schools and Magyarization was temporarily slowed. /DŠ/

RIGHT OF THE SWORD (Latin *ius gladii* – right of the sword) – capital punishment, the right to punish serious crimes with the death penalty. The oldest Hungarian laws still allowed blood revenge, that is, private individuals we-

re able to kill in retaliation. On the intervention of the church, the laws of St Stephen already conceded the possibility that a trans-
gressor could be redeemed. From the 13th
century the right of the sword was excercised
on the basis of a special royal **privilege**. In
the 13th – 15th centuries the right of the
sword was obtained not only by the most influential fief-holders (**magnates**) but also by
the royal cities. The towns of landlords were
subordinate to the judicial authority of the
fief-holder. The middle and lower **nobility**
exercised the right of the sword through county judicial organs (tribunals) under the presidency of the vice county administrator (*podžupan*) sitting with four officials. Until the
18th century there were great differences in
the exercise of the right of the sword, insofar
as it concerned the nature of the crimes and
penalties. Torture was used in investigations.
The courts gradually began to take into account extenuating circumstances. Under the
influence of enlightenment ideas, during the
reigns of Maria Theresa and Joseph II, torture
ceased to be used in investigations and the
death penalty was imposed only for the most
serious crimes and was carried out more hu-
manely. As a remnant of feudal justice the
right of the sword was abolished in 1848 and
replaced with capital punishment carried out
by the state. /JB/

RIGHT TO VOTE IN HUNGARY – a basic right of
citizenship. Until 1848 it belonged almost exclusively to the privileged classes. The **March
laws** of 1848, which made people equal before the law, extended it also to other levels of
society. However, property and education
qualifications limited it and it was therefore
really extended only to a small segment of society. Even the law from **26 November 1874**,
which defined the right to vote in Hungary
during **dualism**, preserved these qualifications. The right to vote was limited to men
with an income of 500 – 700 florins annually,
over 20 years of age; moreover, candidates
had to master Hungarian. Thus, it remained
reserved for the old and new propertied classes, the smaller entrepreneurs, bureaucrats,
graduates of universities and propertied far-

mers. In fact, only five to seven per cent of
the male population could vote. Moreover,
elections to the **Hungarian diet** and in the
counties (*župy*) in Hungary were not secret,
but public, and they were accompanied by
so-called electioneering for which Hungary
became "famous" throughout Europe (buying
votes with money, spirits, or goulash). Government candidates were not averse to
fraud, open pressure on the voters, violence
against opposition candidates of the non-Magyar movements, especially Slovaks. The representative system was not democratized before 1918, which facilitated the preservation
of the spirit of aristocracy, Magyar hegemony
and radical **Magyarization** in Hungary. The
inability of the non-propertied classes and
non-Magyar movements to share in power
placed them on the periphery of political
events. From the end of the 19th century the
workers movement, the Magyar left, the movements of non-Magyar nations including all
Slovak currents, struggled for the general right
to vote. It was enacted into law only in democratic Czecho-Slovakia in 1918. /DŠ/

ROMANESQUE STYLE – an artistic and cultural
style prevailing from the end of the 10th to
the late 12th century in western Europe and
in the regions into which western Christianity
spread. It adopted several elements of ancient
Roman building (the arch, column, apse etc.).
In architecture it utilized the barrel vault and
masonry or stone walls. Curved friezes were
among the typical decoration. The buildings
are massive, seldom segmented, and often
fulfilled a defensive function. A new style of
architecture developed in the Benedictine abbey of Cluny and spread throughout all of Europe. Typical Romanesque buildings are basilicas with an elevated central nave and towers
on the facades, small churches with a single
nave and rotundas with a circular floor-plan.
In Slovakia, Romanesque architecture appeared in the 11th century and was based upon
the Great Moravian tradition (Kostoľany pod
Tribečom). Romanesque rotundas from this
period are preserved in Skalica, Bíňa and elsewhere. Small village churches were built at
Hamuliakovo and Štvrtok na Ostrove. Some

Romanesque buildings, documented in writing from the 11th century, were destroyed or hidden under newer architectural elements (for example, the cloister of St Hypolitus on Zobor, the basilica of St Emmeramus in the castle of Nitra, the church of St Savior in the Bratislava castle were built on Great Moravian structures, the Romanesque church under the present Gothic monastery church in Sv. Beňadik and the church of St Stephen in Nitra-Párovce). It is possible to trace the construction of the royal castles in Bratislava, Hlohovec, Šintava, Beckov and Trenčín back to the 11th century and several have Great Moravian origins. It is assumed that Spiš Castle was also built before the 13th century. At the end of the 11th and the beginning of the 12th centuries the Benedictines erected a three-nave basilica in Diakovce. In the 12th century other monastery and parish churches were built, the most noteworthy of which is the small church in Dražovce from the beginning of the 13th century. The **Benedictine**, Premonstratensian and Cistercian **religious orders** generated the greatest building activity. Examples of Romanesque painting and sculpture are scarce in Slovakia; documented are fragments of plaster in Nitra (Martinský vrch) and in Bratislava (the basilica at the castle). Among the most significant are the preserved wall paintings in Kostoľany pod Tribečom, Šivetice and Dravce. Romanesque sculptures have only rarely been found in Slovakia (the figure of a lion, *leo albus,* in Spišská Kapitula). From the mid 12th century elements of the **Gothic** style began to replace Romanesque characteristics. /JB/

ROMANTICISM – an artistic current and intellectual movement. It developed at the end of the 18th century in Germany, caught on in Slovakia in the 1830s and continued until the end of the 19th century. It was manifested especially in philosophy, literature, the visual arts and architecture. It was based on the feelings of people who were being liberated from feudal bondage and who, at the same time, were exposed to the new pressures of civilization (industrialization, alienation in the cities and a new human, social and national bonda-

ge). It emphasized the will and the sense of individuality. It often found a defense against division, hypersensitivity, and isolation in national patriotism, in the elevation and even the idealization of the common people as well as their culture and language. In Slovakia, these principles were most creatively expressed by **Štúr's group,** which contributed substantially to hastening the process of Slovak national emancipation and the development of a literary language. Their Romantic creativity, inspired by popular oral tradition, was expressed especially in poetry. Romanticism condemned social and national oppression, sought to improve the world, and extolled the value of the nation and the ideals of liberty and justice (Janko Kráľ, Ján Botto, Pavol Dobšinský). The heroes of their epic works have genuine personalities and a willingness to fight and die for freedom (Samo Chalupka), others prefer messianic expectations (Samo Bohdan Hroboň). Lyrical works expressed the inner world of man, his emotional disposition (Andrej Sládkovič). In painting, landscape and historical themes were characterized by tension and drama (Karol Marko, Jozef Božetech Klemens, Karol Tibelly) or idealized pathos (Peter Michal Bohúň). Romanticism influenced also the compositions of the author of the first Slovak opera, Ján Levoslav Bella. Architecture mimicked historical styles (pseudo-historicism, neo-historicism). A distinct variant of Romanticism was the **Biedermeier**. /DŠ/

ROTUNDA see **Romanesque style**

ROYAL COUNCIL – the highest advisory council and later organ of the estates in medieval Hungary. It developed contemporaneously with the Kingdom of Hungary. Originally it was only an advisory body for the **king**, who formed it from his confidants and court and ecclesiastical dignitaries without any limitation. From the first half of the 13th century, the **nobility** also tried to obtain influence in the royal council. The first legal provisions which designated the permanent members of the council and bound the king to hear their views were accepted by the Hungarian **Diet** in 1298. During the 14th century the kings controlled the royal council again. They used it especially for judicial matters as the so-called law court of the royal court. King Charles Robert also established another broader royal council. He attempted to use it as a replacement for the diet and invited to it the highest officials of the country and the wealthiest **magnates**. The importance of the original (the so-called narrow) royal council grew in 1446 when a law was adopted that required the regent of the kingdom, John Hunyady, to share power with it. In the second half of the 15th century, the royal council was reshaped into a central institution of state administration and a court of law by King Matthias Corvinus. Its members were the highest state and church dignitaries (for example, the **palatine**, **chief justice** and **treasurer**), as well as officials from the royal chancellery who represented the interests of the middle and lower nobility. Under the Jagiellons (from the end of the 15th to the beginning of the 16th century) the royal council was controlled by the nobility and the diet. They determined its composition in relation to the views of the estates representing the **prelates**, magnates and the other nobility. It obtained formal status in public law and began to be called the Hungarian council. The importance of the Hungarian council declined after 1526 with the accession of the Habsburgs to the Hungarian throne. The bulk of its jurisdiction was gradually assumed by other institutions, especially the **vice-regency council**. /VS/

ROYAL RIGHTS – (Latin *ius regale* – royal right) – the collection of customary prerogatives belonging to the king. They are called royal rights (*regál*). From the establishment of the Hungarian feudal state, they formed an integral part of the income of the royal treasury. The royal rights were divided into the major (*iura regalia maiora*) and minor (*iura regalia minora*) rights. The major rights were included the income from the exchange and minting of coins (mint right) and mining rights, which were transformed into a mining tax (*urbura*) after the introduction of the mining right on 17 May 1327. A significant portion of mining activities remained in the hands of the

royal chamber. The salt right (the right to mine and distribute salt) and the right to collect duties (**thirtieth**) also belonged among the major royal rights. The major rights of the ruler were excercised by means of various chambers (mint, mining, salt and thirtieth). Sometimes these incomes were leased without permanent grants being made. The minor rights were bestowed by the king in the form of privileges to nobles, the church and cities. The right to sell alcoholic beverages, to brew beer, to butcher meat, to operate a mill, to hold annual and weekly **markets**, to collect **tolls**, to operate ferries across rivers and others belonged among the minor royal rights. These rights could be sublet for prescribed payments to townspeople or other subjects by the nobles, church institutions and cities. The royal rights or prerogatives were a substantial source of income for those who held them. However, they limited free trade, production and competition. For instance, they required the holder of the milling right to mill grain only in his own mill, while the sale of alcohol and the butchering of meat were reserved to a specific group of the population. The majority of the royal rights were abolished in the **revolution of 1848/1849**. /JB/

SALZBURG NEGOTIATIONS – negotiations between representatives of Germany and the first Slovak Republic. It brought about a change in Slovak foreign and domestic policy. From January 1940, the relationships in it between moderate (Jozef Tiso, Ferdinand Ďurčanský) and radical elements (Vojtech Tuka, Alexander Mach) deteriorated. The radicals reproached the moderates for their contacts with representatives of the former centralist parties and a lack of interest in serious social changes (the Jewish question, the presence of Czechs in Slovakia), for an insufficiently pro-German foreign policy and for limiting the authority of the **Hlinka Guard**. They reckoned that German intervention would strengthen their position. After several months of controversy, Jozef Tiso accepted the resignation of Alexander Mach as supreme commander of the Hlinka Guard on 21 May 1940, following a meeting of the district and county commanders of the guard in Ružomberok which approved a resolution directed against Tiso and Ďurčanský. Tiso named František Galan, one of his supporters, as the supreme commander of the Hlinka Guard. Germany, until then occupied with the war against France, decided to intervene. The German ambassador, Hans Bernard, left Bratislava on 28 May and on 22 July 1940 placed before the minister of foreign affairs, Joachim von Ribbentrop, a plan to resolve the Slovak government crisis. Ferdinand Ďurčanský, the minister of foreign affairs and of the interior, was to be removed from public life, the new government was to provide assurances of friendship to Germany, and Slovakia was to accommodate its economic and social policy to Germany and accept German advisors. At the invitation of Germany, an official Slovak delegation (Jozef Tiso, Vojtech Tuka and Alexander Mach) negotiated with Joachim von Ribbentrop and Adolf Hitler in Salzburg on **27 – 28 July 1940**. Pressured by the Slovak radicals and Germany, Tiso accepted the conditions of the German ultimatum. After the delegation returned to Bratislava, Jozef Tiso accepted the resignation of Ferdinand Ďurčanský and reshuffled the government. Vojtech Tuka became the prime minister and the minister of foreign affairs; Alexander Mach became the first deputy prime minister, the minister of the interior and the supreme commander of the Hlinka Guard. Jozef Tiso prevented further changes in the government. The Salzburg Negotiations were a gross encroachment upon the sovereignty of the **Slovak Republic** and strengthened the position of the radicals in it. This led to an increase in the political and economic subservience of Slovakia to Germany, as well as changing the approach towards the so-called Jewish question (**Jewish code**). The struggle with the moderate group continued for years. The power of the radicals was limited, in particular with the help of the leadership of **Hlinka's Slovak People's Party**, within which the position of Jozef Tiso and of some of the moderate ministers was strengthened. /RL/

SANDJAK (or *liva*) – a district of the Turkish imperial administration. It was administered by an official with the title of *sandjakbeg* or *míri-liva*. He not only supervised its administration but also commanded its garrison. He was subordinate to the *beglerbeg*. In the 17th century some *sandjakbegs* also used the title *pasha*. But this was only an honorary title bestowed upon them by the sultan for extraordinary military and administrative service. Unlike the *sandjaks* in the inner lands of the Ottoman Empire, the *sandjaks* in southern Slovakia (or on the northern border of conquered Hungary) had the character of frontier districts. This also affected the primary roles of the *sandjakbegs* and their subordinates. They defended the conquered lands from attacks by enemies (especially the imperial army and the Hungarian home guard) but also organized and undertook predatory and punitive raids into nearby areas. The *sandjakbeg* granted temporary military tenure of some of the agricultural land of the conquered territory to his subordinates. Like the *beglerbeg*, the *sandjakbeg* also had his own advisory body (*divan*). Senior administrative officials and military commanders, as well as the *kadi* (*qadi*), the Islamic judge, participated in its meetings. The first *sandjak* to encroach upon Slovakia was the Esztergom *sandjak,* which was formed in 1545 – 1546. According to a *deftera* from 1570, more than 420 Slovak communities and villages belonged to it. Among the other *sandjaks* incorporating some of the territory of Slovakia prior to the so-called Fifteen Years' War (1593 – 1606) were the Novohrad, Sečany and especially the Fiľakovo *sandjak* (1554 – 1593), to which belonged a greater part of Gemer, Hont and Novohrad counties. When the Turks conquered Nové Zámky (**1663**), they established three other *sandjaks* within the Nové Zámky *ejálet,* Nitra, Levice and Novohrad. /VS/

SCRIPTORIA see **Codex**

SECOND WORLD WAR – the second world-wide armed conflict between two blocs of states (Germany, Italy, Japan and their allies, against the Soviet Union, the United States of America, Great Britain and their allies). It began on **1 September 1939** with the attack on Poland by Germany. Germany sought to involve Slovakia in this war in the summer of 1939. On 24 August 1939 the German ambassador Hans Bernard informed the Slovak government that Germany would invade Poland. Under the pretext of a possible Polish attack on Slovakia, he demanded the subordination of the Slovak army to German leadership. The German side gave assurances that the Slovak army would not be used outside the territory of Slovakia. In return for a loyal attitude, the Polish lands inhabited by Slovaks would be restored to Slovakia. Despite assurances, Germany moved the Slovak army onto Polish territory on **1 September 1939**. After the victory over Poland, Germany focused its attention to the west. Slovakia attempted to follow a neutral foreign policy. This course of action lasted until the **Salzburg Negotiations** of **27 – 28 July 1940**. On **22 June 1941**, on the initiative of the prime minister, Vojtech Tuka, Slovakia was drawn into the war against the Soviet Union. Two Slovak divisions took part in battles on the eastern front and helped to occupy Kiev and Rostov. Due to the policy of the minister of national defense, Ferdinand Čatloš and President Jozef Tiso it was possible to reduce gradually the numerical strength of the army on the eastern front from 50,000 to 13,000 men. From 26 June 1941 to 20 March 1944, the losses of the Slovak army on the eastern front were 1,179 dead, 2,969 wounded and 2,719 missing in action, some of whom deserted to the Soviet side. In the Crimea, 2,700 Slovak soldiers and 50 officers were captured on 30 October 1943. The Slovak army did not recover from this blow. Part of it was transferred to fortification work in Italy and Romania. After the eruption of the armed **Insurrection of 1944**

two divisions of the Slovak army in eastern Slovakia were disarmed. A reorganization of the army was entrusted to the new minister of national defense, Štefan Haššík. In September 1944 the first regiment of the Home Guard was formed and in January 1945 the Slovak army had 41,533 soldiers and officers, of which 12,287 were stationed outside of Slovakia. On the territory of the insurgents the 1st Czechoslovak army in Slovakia was formed. It was led by General Ján Golian and later by Rudolf Viest. Slovaks also fought in other armies. Under an agreement between the Czecho-Slovak government in exile and the Soviet government, the Soviet Union permitted Czecho-Slovak army units to be formed on its territory. A further impulse was the Czecho-Slovak – Soviet agreement of **12 December 1943**, under which the first Czecho-Slovak army corps was created on 10 April 1944. By the beginning of September 1944 it mustered 16,451 troops (44 per cent Czechs, 24.5 per cent Ruthenians and Ukrainians, and 20 per cent Slovaks). Under the leadership of General Ludvík Svoboda, the 1st Czecho-Slovak army corps took part in the Carpathian-Dukla operation (**8 September 1944**) as part of the 38th Soviet army. Breaking through the German defense in the Carpathians and the entry into Slovak territory on **6 October 1944** resulted in the loss of 80,000 Soviet soldiers (19,000 were killed) and 6,500 men of the 1st Czecho-Slovak army corps (1,800 were killed). From November 1944 the 1st Czecho-Slovak army corps was reinforced by newly mobilized Slovaks, often without training. During a period of three months, it lost 6,318 men in battles at Liptovský Sv. Mikuláš and in the Small and High Fatras. In May 1945 the corps numbered 95,047 men, 73,412 of which were Slovaks. The 11th Czecho-Slovak battalion and later the 200th Czecho-Slovak light anti-aircraft regiment fought in the British army in the battle for Tobruk. After the allies landed in Normandy in 1944 the Czecho-Slovak armored brigade laid siege to the city of Dunkerque (Dunkirk). About 20 per cent of those who fought in Czecho-Slovak units based in Great

Britain were Slovaks such as the outstanding pilot Otto Smik. In the American army Slovaks fought in western Europe and in the Pacific against Japan (one of the six Marines who raised the American flag on Mount Suribachi on the Japanese island of Iwo Jima was Sergeant Michael Strang; this act is depicted in the statue on the famous monument in Washington). In the French army the Czecho-Slovak Legion fought against Germany in 1940 (551 Slovaks were members in April 1940). Unlike the **First World War,** the Second World War affected Slovakia in two destructive waves. The first was the German occupation and the **Insurrection of 1944** (September – October 1944) and the second was the German-Soviet front (October 1944 to April 1945). Damage during the war amounted to more than 114 billion crowns. /RL/

SENIORAT – an association of church congregations (parishes) in the Evangelical Church of the Augsburg Confession and the Reformed Christian Church. They were called *contubernia* until 1735. It was headed by an elected senior, who at the same time was the pastor of a church congregation and a lay supervisor. The *seniorats* are associated into districts, originally superintendencies. This organization of the Protestant churches has been preserved until today. /JB/

SEPTEMBER UPRISING – the first armed uprising of Slovaks in modern history. It was a reaction to the neglect of the Slovak question by the Hungarian government and was an integral part of both the armed resistance of non-Magyars against the policy of Pest and the jurisdictional struggle between Vienna and Pest. It was planned in Vienna by the **Slovak National Council (1848)**, which became its supreme military and political organ, with the assistance of the Czechs and Croatians. The corps led by the Czech Bedřich Bloudek was originally comprised of about 500 volunteers, in particular Czechs and Slovaks. The original plan of the uprising was grandiose. The corps was to be quickly transferred from the sub-Javorina region to central Slovakia, where the Slovak National Council was to declare a nation-wide uprising. The organizers believed that, under pressure from the Croatians, Serbians and Romanians and from Vienna, the Hungarian government would accept Slovak demands. During the uprising, which began on **18 September 1848,** the Slovak National Council declared the autonomy of Slovakia within Hungary, dismissed the unpopular officials of Kossuth's administration and laid the foundations for an autonomous public administration. The uprising was supported especially by the hill farmers who believed that they would be freed from the obligations of serfdom. They actually predominated among the forces of the uprising, which numbered almost 10,000 men. The uprising also acquired sympathizers in the Záhorie, Turiec, Gemer and Liptov regions who were prepared to help it. The insurgents defeated the Kossuth Guard several times. However, the Slovak National Council abandoned the offensive plan, because its units were poorly armed and equipped and had minimal military experience and because of spreading anti-insurgency propaganda. Moreover, the attitude of the imperial army towards the insurgents and the manifesto of the sovereign, who ordered the pacification of the uprising, sidelined it. Therefore it remained limited to the small territory below the Javorina and Bradlo and the Slovak National Council declared it to be at an end on 28 September. The Hungarian administration cruelly took its revenge on the uprising's participants and sympathizers. After its failure, Slovak politicians began to cooperate with the imperial government to prepare the **Winter Campaign** and to defend the program of **Austro-Slavism**. /DŠ/

SERFDOM – the relationship between the owners of the land (feudal landlords) and the farmers settled on their soil who were personally dependent on the landlord. All the land was the property of the feudal landlord and the serfs farming this soil only had usufruct. Their right to ownership of moveable property (chattels) (household furnishings, clothing, domestic animals) was respected. For the right to use the soil the serfs paid **feudal rent** to their lord. The class of serfs was made up of free peasants, non-free subjects, servants (**courtiers** – *dvorníci*) and some of the castle *jobaggi*, who were obligated to perform military service in royal fortresses. They became dependent upon the feudal lords when the castle domain passed to the nobility in the form of a grant. In the various countries of Europe serfdom took different forms. In the period of the high Middle Ages it had rather a free form: the serfs had almost complete personal freedom and could move to other estates or to cities if they fulfilled their tax obligations towards their previous landlord. The class of serfs was internally differentiated. Alongside **peasants** who owned a whole or half a farmstead (*sessia*), there were tenant **cotters** (*želiari*) or sub-tenants (*podželiari*). These did not hold land or only a very small plot and sometimes not even a house. They worked on the farmsteads of the peasants or had specific obligations (especially the *robota*) to the landlord. While in western Europe the obligations of the serfs were gradually lessened and finally abolished during later **feudalism** (the Early Modern Era), in central Europe serfdom was strengthened in the form of **servitude**. Serfdom was abolished by the **March laws** of 1848. /JB/

SERVIENTI (SERVANTS) – in general servants. During the period of early feudalism this term was used in Hungary to characterize the immediate vassals of the king who performed military service in the royal army. In the 11th – 13th centuries, the servants (*servienti*) of the king formed a privileged part of Hungarian society. Most of them owned land worked by **serfs** and stood higher in the hierarchy than the castle servants (*iobagiones castri* or *jobbagi*), since they were subordinated only to the **king** and not to the castle administrator. The *servienti* were personally free and were the real initiators of the **Golden Bull** of Andrew II (1222) since their privileged position was threatened by the self-aggrandizement of the **magnates** and the autocratic royal bureaucrats. The bull guaranteed a judicial exemption to the *servienti*. Only the king or a judge commissioned by him was able to judge them (minor cases were adjudicated by a sheriff,

slúžny, whom they elected). The *servienti* did not pay the extraordinary military tax (*colecta*) on their own property or the so-called *denars* of the freemen. They fought only under the king's banner (*banderium*): in the case of the defense of the country, at their own expense; in the case of a military expedition abroad, only if the ruler bore the expense. The provisions concerning inheritance rights enabled the *servienti*, to a certain extent, to acquire and dispose of property freely. From the end of the 13th century all royal *servienti* were considered nobles (**yeoman**, *zeman*). In a later period (14th – 18th centuries) other servants, especially the constables (*drábi*) of the lords, were also called *servienti*. However, in the 14th century the term *servienti* was sometimes synonymous with the designation *familiari* (**retainers** or members of the household). /VS/

SERVITUDE (bondage) – the economic, social, and legal position of serfs in the period of early **feudalism** (9th – 12th centuries) and late feudalism (16th – 18th centuries), especially in the countries of central and eastern Europe. In the first phase of servitude the farmers settled on the land naturally as a part of feudal property. Without the prior approval of their landlord they could not change their place of residence, take up a trade or change other facets of their life or the life of their children. The class of serfs was a conglomeration of former slaves, captives, servants and others. The development of a monetary system in the 13th – 15th centuries gradually lessened the attachment of the serfs to the soil. In western countries it disappeared completely. In Slovakia the introduction of the **German Law** (emphyteutic) contributed to the termination of servitude and was accepted by the domestic population since it was more advantageous for them. In central and eastern Europe, the nobility defended the extensive prerogatives of the **estates** and the consequent strengthening of the dependency of the serfs was so great that it is possible consider it a second servitude. After the suppression of the **Dózsa Insurrection** (1514) in Hungary, resolutions of the **diet** bound the serfs to the soil, proclaimed their eternal servitude, abolished the right to emigrate and set the minimum extent of the compulsory labor (*robota*) at 52 days a year. This was further increased on individual estates, especially as landlords established farmsteads. The suppression of the serfs moderated only after Joseph II issued decrees for the **abolition of servitude** (1781 in the Austrian part of the monarchy, including the Czech kingdom, and 1785 in the Kingdom of Hungary). /JB/

SCHISM – ecclesiastical cleavage, the disintegration of the unity of the church. The word comes from the Greek *schismos*. The first great schism in the history of Christianity was the separation of the eastern Greek Orthodox Church and the western Roman Catholic Church in 1054. It was a result of the divergent development of Christianity in Byzantine Empire and in the countries of western Europe. There was a long schism in the history of the western Christianity in the years 1378 – 1417 and 1439 – 1449. The popes, who since 1309 had resided in Avignon, returned to Rome beginning with Urban VI. In 1378 the dissatisfied French cardinals elected an anti-pope and the **Council** of Pisa in 1409 elected a third pope. The two preceding popes refused to relinquish their office. The schism was ended by the Council of Constance and the deposition or abdication of the preceding three popes and the election of a new one (1417). At the Council of Basle in 1439 some of the participants rejected its dissolution and elected the anti-pope Felix V. After his death (1449) his supporters returned to the legal pope, Nicholas V. The disorder in the church also called forth the development of the Hussite movement. The moderate **Hussites** (Calixtines) were reconciled with the Catholic Church on **5 July 1436** with the acceptance of the Basle *Compacta*. The greatest schism in the history of western Christianity began in 1517 with the appearance of Martin Luther. The Protestant churches (Lutheran, Calvinist, Anglican churches) that were established separated completely from Catholicism and rejected the pope as the supreme head of the church (**Reformation**). /JB/

SCHOOLS – developed on the territory of Slovakia early in the Middle Ages. The existence of a Great Moravian school for priests, founded by Methodius, is presumed; it ceased to exist after his pupils were expelled. The first indirect reference to a school (at the Nitra chapter) dates from 1111. The oldest schools in Slovakia were established at the seats of bishops, **chapters** and **cloisters**. Information about city schools comes from the 14th century. A few village schools also appear (Diviaky na Nitricou, 1342) at this time. The network of city and village schools spread during the Reformation and during the **Counter-Reformation**, which also emphasized education. The main content of instruction was Latin and basic Christian teachings. The city schools also provided instruction about the natural world and society. For their highest education students went to universities abroad, especially to Prague (founded 1348), Cracow (1364) and Vienna (1365). The first university in Slovakia, the **Academia Istropolitana,** was established only in 1467, but ceased to function after several years. In the universities the course for the Bachelor's degree consisted of the **trivium** and the **quadrivium**. The so-called *trivium* was comprised of grammar, rhetoric and dialectics, while arithmetic, geometry, astronomy and music made up the *quadrivium*. From the 16th century there existed higher schools, gymnasia and colleges and, alongside these, elementary popular schools. They were established by both Catholics and Protestants. The **Jesuits** founded **Trnava University** in 1635 and **Košice University** in 1657. The Jesuit schools were regulated by the provisions of the *Order of Studies (Ratio studiorum)* of 1599. The Protestants were not able to establish a university because of the opposition of the imperial court. The ten-class **Prešov College** (1667) was originally an Evangelical secondary school. As a result of political conflicts at the end of the 17th and the beginning of the 18th century, it was alternately in the hands of the Protestants and the Catholics. A **mining academy,** the first technical university in the world, was founded in Banská Štiavnica in 1763. A specialized higher economic school (*Collegium oeconomicum*) functioned in Senec. The enlightenment and the absolutist efforts of Maria Theresa and her son Joseph II sought to impose state control of schooling and its subordination to the interests of the court. The reform *Ratio educationis (Order of Education)* of 1777 affected all types of schools. It resulted in the transfer of the Trnava University to Buda. Academies in Bratislava and Košice, which like the lyceums, offered basic philosophical, theological and legal education, replaced the two universities that had existed in Slovakia. In the second half of the 19th century other reforms of the school system were implemented. Eight-class classical and *real* (natural sciences and modern languages) gymnasia were established. The law of 1868 imposing the obligation of school attendance for six years made possible the development of elementary schools. City schools developed as a superior type of elementary school. At the end of the 19th and the beginning of the 20th century the education of a broad spectrum of the Slovak population was held back by the growing **Magyarization** that, after the Apponyi school laws of 2 June 1907, was extended also to the lowest classes of elementary schools. At the Elizabeth University, established in Bratislava in 1912, instruction took place only in Hungarian, which served denationalization. After the **Slovak gymnasia** had been closed, the Slovaks did not have their own national schools until 1918. After the **Czechoslovak Republic** was established (1918), the development of Slovak schools ensued. An obligatory eight-year school attendance was introduced and new schools of all levels and types were established. Comenius University was founded in Bratislava on **27 June 1919**. However, the development of schools in 1918 – 1939 did not sufficiently satisfy the real needs of the population. In particular, many Czech teachers worked at Comenius University and many secondary schools. Despite their unquestionable service, they usually did not teach in Slovak and they injected a non-Slovak spirit into the instruction. A Slovak technical university was founded on **25 June 1937**

only after a long political struggle. The development of schools continued in the first **Slovak Republic**. The law instituting a Slovak University (the renamed Comenius University) was approved on **3 July 1940** and the university obtained new faculties. A business college was established on **4 October 1940**. A gradual process of centralizing the administration and state control of the schools ensued after the Czechoslovak Republic was restored in 1945. Church schools had already been abolished in 1944 by the **Slovak National Council (1944)**. In 1946 an agricultural and forestry college was established in Košice (after 1952 it was located in Nitra). The unified school system after the **Communist state coup** dissolved the classical gymnasia. A system of unified schools enabled pupils to be regimented and controlled in the spirit of communist ideology, which set them against citizen, national and Christian values. Thousands of "unreliable" pedagogues had to leave schools, while students were excluded from universities on a large scale. The Soviet Union served as a model for the school system. Russian was a required subject and the teaching of other languages was limited. However, new colleges also were established: the College of the Visual Arts and the College of Music and Theater Arts (1949), a Veterinary School (1949) and the College of Transportation and Communication (1960). The so-called system of socialist schooling went through frequent reforms and changes. The cadre question, i.e. membership in the **Communist Party of Czechoslovakia** and working-class origin, was used to screen students for further study at secondary schools and universities. From the 1950s to the 1980s many school buildings and dormitories were erected, especially in the cities. Significant changes took place after 1989 when schooling began to be democratized. Emphasis was placed upon the teaching of languages and an encounter with knowledge from the whole world. New universities were established: Trnava University, the University of Matej Bel in Banská Bystrica, the University of Constantine Philosopher in Nitra, the University of Saints Cyril and Methodius in Trnava, the University of Trenčín and the University of Prešov. /JB, RL/

SLAVIC CONGRESS – the assembly of representatives of the Slavs in the Habsburg monarchy. The Croatian Ivan Kukuljevič-Sakcinskij and Ľudovít Štúr provided an impetus for it at the April meetings of Slavs in Vienna. The congress took place on 2 – 12 June 1848 in Prague with 340 delegates participating, about 20 of which were Slovaks. The Russian anarchist Michael Bakunin and several Poles were the only Slavs not from the Austrian Empire to participate in it. The chairman of the congress was the Czech, František Palacký. Discussions took place in Czecho-Slovak (247 delegates), Polish-Ruthenian (61) and Yugoslavian (42) sections. It counter-balanced the all-German parliament in Frankfurt am Main. It declared its opposition to the incorporation of Slavic territory into the new Germany, to Magyar supremacy in the Kingdom of Hungary and to Russian expansion. It sought a common approach by the Austrian Slavs that would assure their freedom and establish a union. It attempted to define their relationship to the non-Slavic nations of Europe and the empire, to the empire itself and to other Slavs. It was dominated by Austro-Slavism; radical pan-Slavic currents and the criticism of Austria (Bakunin, Libelt and Štúr) were pushed into the background. The Slovaks linked their future to the Kingdom of Hungary and presented a solution to the Slovak question in the **Demands of the Slovaks and Ruthenians of the Kingdom of Hungary**. They discussed with the Croatians and the Czechs the possibility of armed action against the Hungarian government, if it did not change its assimilation policy and halt the persecution of Slovak patriots. Before the congress could achieve some objectives and after the unexpected eruption of the Prague uprising, in which some Slovaks participated, its discussions were suspended. It never convened again and the Austrian Slavs were not able to establish a common representative organ. After the Prague uprising was quelled, hope for an agreement with the Magyars practically disappeared. The nucleus of the Slovak national movement left for Vienna, where it prepared the armed **September Uprising**. /DŠ/

SLAVIC MUTUALITY – the concept and expression of the ethnic propinquity and cooperation of the Slavs. As modern nationalism developed at the end of the 18th and the beginning of the 19th century, the theoretical justification for the traditional consciousness of Slavic affinity began to take shape. This theory was a form of defense against the oppression of the Turks and the threats of Germanization and **Magyarization**. Its creators were, therefore, representatives of small nations, primarily the Slovaks Ján Kollár, Pavol Jozef Šafárik, Ján Koiš and Ján Herkeľ. Inspired by the German philosopher Johann Gottfried Herder, Kollár's work inspired the Slavic intellectuals and remained attractive to them during the whole of the 19th century. The emphasis upon a great Slavic community, its common and positive spiritual characteristics and the humanistic mission of the Slavs in world history raised their self-awareness. Ján Kollár considered the Slavs to be one nation made up of four tribes (Russian, Polish, Czechoslovak and Illyrian). Therefore he recognized only four literary languages and rejected a literary Slovak as well as the concept of Slovak national particularity. He appealed for the cultural and literary cooperation of the Slavs and for the establishment of societies. However, he refused to identify his theory with **pan-Slavism**. Ľudovít Štúr further developed Kollár's concept of Slavic mutuality. He considered the division of the Slavs into four tribes to be artificial and cast doubt upon the national unity of the Czechs and the Slovaks by justifying their particularity. Slavic mutuality was associated with political questions, the reform of society and a constitutional reconstruction. He demonstrated this at the Vienna assemblies during the **Revolution of 1848/1849**, when **Austro-Slavism** dominated Slavic mutuality. After 1867, as Magyarization quickly intensified, Slavic mutuality became one of the fundamental ideas of the **Slovak National Party**. It uncritically adhered to Russophilism. With Svetozár Hurban Vajanský, in particular, the vision of the liberating mission of Russia grew into a political messianism masked as pan-Slavism. It assumed a practical form in cooperation with the Czechs (**Czechoslavic Union**) and the nations of Hungary (**Congress of non-Magyar nationalities**). During the First World War the idea of Slavic mutuality served the politicians of the suppressed nations as an argument for the creation of new states. After the Second World War it was deformed and misused by the Communist regimes. /DŠ/

SLOVAK AUTONOMY see **Autonomy of Slovakia**

SLOVAK COURT CONFIDANTS – representatives of the Slovaks in the central imperial organs. In March 1849 the government named them as its advisors. They created a kind of first Slovak lobby in the center of Viennese politics. They functioned alongside the representatives of the Magyars, Romanians, Serbs and Germans. Their task was to seek new arrangements for the monarchy and ways to guarantee the rights of its nations. Among the confidants were Ján Kollár, Ján Hlaváč and František Hánrich. Their activity was coordinated by Count John Majláth, who was favorably inclined towards the resolution of the Slovak question. They pushed for the linguistic, cultural and educational rights of the Slovaks and the gradual construction of their autonomous administration. However, the possibility of secession from the Kingdom of Hungary was long considered unrealistic and therefore they did not support even the **March Petition**. They agreed with the government that the Slovak question could be definitively resolved only after the defeat of the Magyar army. The court confidants weakened the prestige and influence of **Štúr's group** in government circles. However, they did push the government to make some concessions (Slovak newspapers, use of Slovak in the lower offices) and they informed it about the behavior of the Magyar noble old conservative officials in Slovakia. It was precisely this situation that convinced the confidants of the need to separate Slovakia from Hungary and to establish a Slovak crown land (**10 September 1849**).

The government rejected these arguments and abolished the function of confidant at the end of 1849. /DŠ/

SLOVAK GYMNASIA IN THE 19th CENTURY – educational institutions with Slovak as the language of instruction. Until 1848 instruction at gymnasia was conducted primarily in Latin and to a lesser extent in German and Hungarian. **Neo-absolutism** modernized secondary schools after 1849 and in 1851 the government issued regulations that instruction would be in the native language at secondary schools. Because of this, eight of the 27 gymnasia in Slovakia began to teach in Czech, in three Czech was one of the languages of instruction and in the others it was taught as a subject. During the 1850s and 60s the gymnasium in Banská Bystrica was especially significant. Due to the initiative of Bishop Štefan Moyzes, outstanding Slovak and Czech professors lectured there and strengthened Slovak national consciousness. During the 1850s, Hungarian and German replaced Slovak or Czech at most of the state gymnasia and in the 1870s it had completely displaced them. During the 1860s Slovak patriots founded non-state church schools, so-called patronage gymnasia, which were to thwart the spread of Magyar in the state gymnasia. An Evangelical higher gymnasium was founded in Revúca in 1862; its director was Augustín Horislav Škultéty. An Evangelical lower gymnasium in Martin and in 1869 a Catholic lower gymnasium in Kláštor pod Znievom was established in 1867 and 1869 respectively. The director at the latter was Martin Čulen. A total of about 30 professors taught in these schools, which were attended by approximately 1900 students. They obtained financial support from benefactors and collections from church members. Instruction was conducted in Slovak and it attained high quality in the subjects of natural science, languages and physical education. Students who were inculcated with national pride founded cultural societies. A generation of strong cultural leaders, entrepreneurs and politicians were trained in them. Together with the **Matica slovenská**, they represented a bastion of Slovak national life.

Therefore, some of the Magyar public, press (**8 April 1873**) and politicians exerted pressure upon them, which ultimately resulted in their dissolution (**20 August 1874**). After this there was not a single Slovak secondary school in the Kingdom of Hungary until 1918. /DŠ/

SLOVAK LEARNED SOCIETY – the first cultural society with a national orientation and mass support. It was established in the first half of 1792; its chairman was Anton Bernolák and Juraj Fándly its treasurer. Headquartered in Trnava, it founded branches led by trustees (Nitra, Veľké Rovné, Solivar, Rožňava, Banská Bystrica, Spišská Kapitula, Eger, Esztergom and Vienna). It had 450 members, of which 355 were Catholic clerics (including eight bishops) and several high officials and businessmen also were members. The society propagated the new literary language of Bernolák in the literature they published and distributed and thus strengthened national consciousness. Books and magazines were printed at the newly established printery of Václav Jelínek in Trnava. It published eleven educational and religious works, in particular by Juraj Fándly, in twenty volumes. The society was the organizational core of **Bernolák's group** and was the largest cultural society in Hungary in the 1790s. It ceased to exist at the beginning of the 19th century. /DŠ/

SLOVAK MUSEUM SOCIETY – a cultural institution. It was established on 24 April 1893 and its activity began on 22 August 1895. Its goal was to collect artifacts and preserve and promote values connected with Slovak culture and the Slovak territory, as well as to develop disciplines connected with the study of the country. It considered itself to be a continuation of the **Matica slovenská**. Before 1918 it rendered great service to collecting activity and museology and the organization of scholarly, especially archaeological, research in Slovakia. Its highest organ was the general assembly. It was located in Martin and its chairman was the tireless collector and organizer of research Andrej Kmeť and, after his death (1909), Štefan Mišík. In 1918 it had 1,677 members. The collections of the society grew quickly and in 1918 it contained 22,000 archaeological, ethnographic and scientific exhibits and 70,000 books and manuscripts. It obtained them as gifts, by exchanges and through its own research. Among the most interesting exhibits are the bones of a mammoth from Beča, Kmeť's herbarium of 70,000 plants, which even today represents more than 10 per cent of the collections of Slovak herbaria and a relief map of Slovakia, the gift of American Slovaks. In 1908, helped by *grajciar* ("penny") collections, Slovaks living in the United States and many other compatriots, the Slovak Museum Society constructed a building in Martin containing a museum that was able to display the exhibits publicly. It established four scientific sections and published the *Annual of the SMS (Zborník MSS)* and the *Journal of the SMS (Časopis MSS)*. Moreover, in the period of forced **Magyarization** it clearly represented Slovak particularity. The society was active until 1960 when it was banned. After 1989 it renewed its activity. /DŠ/

SLOVAK NATIONAL ASSEMBLY (also the Memorandum Assembly) – assembly of the Slovak political representatives and the public. It took place on 6 and 7 June 1861 in Martin and was initiated especially by Štefan Marko Daxner and Ján Francisci, who presided over it. It was opened by the **magistrate** (*richtár*) of Martin, Ondrej Koša. The program of the first day was the discussion of the new political program, prepared by Štefan Marko Daxner, by more than 200 leading personalities. It was based upon the principles of self-determination, the equality of nations and the national particularity of the Slovaks, which would be expressed and secured in an autonomous territorial unit. Two currents of thought emerged on the question of autonomy and the orientation of Slovak policy. From these ideological embryos the **Old School** and the **New School** developed. The result of these lively discussions was the **Memorandum of the Slovak Nation**. On the second day this new program was enthusiastically accepted by an assembly of about 5,000 people. A delegation to present the memorandum to the **Hungarian diet** and a standing national committee of 23 members were elected. Ján Francisci presided over the latter and was to become a leading figure in Slovak politics. The assembly also approved the establishment of the **Matica slovenská**. /DŠ/

SLOVAK NATIONAL COUNCIL (1848) – the first Slovak political organ in modern history. It was founded in Vienna on **16 September 1848** by about 200 organizers of and participants in the **September Uprising**. The authority to make decisions was held by its political members, Ľudovít Štúr, Jozef Miloslav Hurban and Michal Miloslav Hodža; other members were the Czech military commanders Bedřich Bloudek, František Zach and Bernard Janeček and the secretaries Bohuš Nosák and Daniel Bórik. It was the supreme military and political organ of the uprising, repudiated allegiance to the Hungarian government and its subordinate organs and declared an independent Slovakia (autonomy) within the Kingdom of Hungary. It governed in the small territory of the uprising by means of decrees, dismissed from local offices the unpopular administrators appointed by Kossuth and replaced them with men of Slovak and social consciousness. By means of the revolution it attempted to create the basis for a new autonomous public administration, in which the nobles would not have the main role. It respected the principles of humanity and therefore did not condemn the opponents of the uprising punitively, but only morally. It viewed its power as temporary and, after the eruption of a nation-wide uprising, the Slovak public would choose their own representatives themselves. The political indecision and the lack of the military experience of its members contributed to the bogging down of the uprising in the small Javorina region, which ended after less than two weeks. After its failure, Slovak politicians were dependant upon the decisions of Vienna. They organized the **Winter Campaign** and within its framework some of them founded town and county national councils to serve as political advisory bodies to the imperial commanders. However, they were not able to preserve the Slovak

National Council as the representative organ of the Slovaks. /DŠ/

SLOVAK NATIONAL COUNCIL (1918 – 1919) – a nation-wide representative organ. On the initiative of the chairman of the **Slovak National Party**, Matúš Dula, representatives of Slovak political movements met in Budapest on **26 May 1914** and proposed a body that would coordinate Slovak political, economic and cultural activities under the name Slovak National Council. The **First World War** postponed the realization of this idea. Candidates for the Slovak National Council were finally proposed at a consultation of leading figures of the Slovak National Party in Budapest on 12 September 1918. Matúš Dula was entrusted with the founding of the Council, which took place on **30 October 1918** when the participants in the founding assembly in Martin elected its 20 members. In the name of the Slovak National Council, the founding assembly accepted the **Declaration of the Slovak Nation**. The Slovak National Council became the definitively authorized representative of the Slovak nation and declared itself in favor of a common state with the Czechs. In the regions local national councils were established. However, its position was respected neither by the Prague National Committee nor by some Slovak politicians led by Vavro Šrobár. On **4 November 1918** the National Committee, without the consent of the Slovak National Council, named a "temporary Slovak government" led by Vavro Šrobár, who was named by the Czecho-Slovak government as the plenipotentiary minister for the administration of Slovakia on **7 December 1918**. Šrobár, charged with the incorporation of Slovakia into a centralist Czechoslovak Republic, abolished the Slovak National Council. Under his regulation number 6/1919 **8 January 1919**, all local national councils and committees, including the central Slovak National Council in Martin, were dissolved on 23 January. /RL/

SLOVAK NATIONAL COUNCIL (1929, 1933) – an organ of the political emigrants grouped around František Jehlička, a Catholic priest and professor. It was established by Jehlička, who also was one of the founders of the **Slovak People's Party**. Together with Andrej Hlinka, he left secretly for the peace conference in Paris (**27 August 1919**) and remained abroad. His political views varied from the founding of an independent Slovak state through a Slovak-Magyar federation to the cultural autonomy of Slovakia within the context of the Kingdom of Hungary. At first he worked in Hungary, from 1920 in Poland and later in Austria. Together with V. Dvorcsák, he founded a Slovak National Council in 1920 in Warsaw in which Jehlička was elected chairman. Originally they reckoned that the Slovak National Council would assume power in Slovakia after it was occupied by the Magyar army and the Slovak legions forming in Poland. Disagreement with the Magyar politicians led to the declaration of an independent Slovak Republic on **25 May 1921** in Cracow. František Jehlička became the prime minister and František Unger the minister of foreign affairs. František Jehlička revived the activity of the Slovak National Council in 1933 in Geneva, the seat of the League of Nations. The goal of both of the Slovak National Councils led by Jehlička was to provide information abroad about the situation in Slovakia and the status of the Slovak nation. František Jehlička implemented his plans in cooperation with the Magyar, Polish, German and Italian politicians who sought a revision of the borders from 1920. /RL/

SLOVAK NATIONAL COUNCIL (1939 – 1940) – an organ of the politicians grouped around Milan Hodža. The former prime minister of Czecho-Slovakia, Milan Hodža created it on **22 November 1939** after he emigrated. Its development was preceded by long negotiations with a group of emigrants around the former president of Czecho-Slovakia, Edvard Beneš. Since Edvard Beneš generally refused to have Hodža and the Slovaks play an important role in the yet-to-be-established Czecho-Slovak National Committee and because this organ was created without him on **13 November 1939**, Milan Hodža founded the Slovak National Council and became its chairman. Its secretary was Peter Prídavok; Ján Paulíny-

Tóth and Milan Janota were members. The program of the Slovak National Council was the renewal of the Czecho-Slovak state based upon the equality of the Czechs and the Slovaks and representational parity. In the new Czecho-Slovak state the **Žilina Agreement** and the revised law on the **autonomy of Slovakia** were, with some concessions, to be preserved. This effort was welcomed by some of the Czech emigrants who opposed Edvard Beneš and had prepared for the establishment of a Czech National Council. After a joint consultation, the Czecho-Slovak National Council was established in Paris on 28 January 1940. Milan Hodža became its chairman; its vice-chairman was the former national democrat František Schwarz and the secretaries were Peter Prídavok and the journalist Vladimír Ležák-Borin. The new organization criticized the work of the Czecho-Slovak National Committee of Beneš. It declared its support for democracy in the future democratic Czecho-Slovak Republic, respect for Slovak national individuality, the autonomy of Slovakia and close relations with neighboring countries, especially Poland. It also was sympathetic to the idea of a central European federation. With the occupation of the France by the German army, Paris, the seat of the Czecho-Slovak National Council, was lost. On the initiative of the Czech espionage service led by František Moravec, who worked for Beneš, some of its members were arrested by British security. Milan Hodža capitulated and, after the recognition of the provisional Czecho-Slovak government by Great Britain on 21 July 1940, accepted a subordinate function in the State Council from Edvard Beneš. /RL/

SLOVAK NATIONAL COUNCIL (1943 – 1960) – an organ of some of the Slovak emigrants. Its founder was the journalist Peter Prídavok, who emigrated from Slovakia in September 1939. After the dissolution of the Czecho-Slovak National Council (1940), he first created the Slovak National Union in London in 1942, which he transformed into the Slovak National Council in London on 31 December 1943. Peter Prídavok became its chairman and Karol Vychodil was its secretary. The increase in Prídavok's activity from the end of 1943 was connected with the signing of a Czecho-Slovak – Soviet treaty of friendship, mutual assistance and post-war cooperation and the approach of the strategic front. The program of the Slovak National Council was a democratic Slovak state in a federated central Europe. Peter Prídavok demanded from the British-American allies the international control of Slovak territory and the participation of Slovakia in the post-war peace conference as an independent entity. After the war, the Slovak National Council of Prídavok was to unite all the Slovak political emigrants who supported the existence of the Slovak state. This did not happen. In January 1946 the former Slovak minister of foreign affairs, Ferdinand Ďurčanský, founded the Slovak Action Committee in Rome (later renamed the Slovak Liberation Committee), which became its competing organization. On 12 September 1948 the Slovak National Council in London was renamed the Slovak National Council Abroad. Karol Sidor, the former Slovak ambassador to the Vatican, became its chairman and Peter Prídavok became the general secretary. The program of the Slovak National Council Abroad was to extract Slovakia from a Communist dictatorship and to create a democratic Slovak state in a federated Europe. It was made up of representatives of the former Hlinka's Slovak People's Party, the Slovak National Party, the Agrarian Party, the Democratic Party, and the Liberty Party. On 28 – 29 May 1960 in New York, the Slovak National Council Abroad and the Slovak Liberation Committee merged and formed the Slovak Liberation Council. The anticipated broad integration was achieved only with the founding of the Slovak World Congress (**19 – 21 June 1970**). /RL/

SLOVAK NATIONAL COUNCIL (1944) – an underground resistance organ and the highest leadership body in the **Uprising of 1944**. It was created in embryonic form in September 1943 at regular meetings of the representatives of the former civic parties, Ján Ursíny, Jozef Lettrich (both from the **Agrarian Party**), Matej Josko (national socialist) and the com-

munists Gustáv Husák, Ladislav Novomeský and Karol Šmidke. The first fundamental program document, which declared the formation of the Slovak National Council, was the **Christmas Agreement** of **25 December 1943**. At the beginning of 1944 the Slovak National Council was supplemented with new members, the writer Ivan Horváth (a social democrat) and the representative of the Slovak parliament and inspector of the Evangelical Church of the Augsburg Confession, Peter Zaťko. The aim of the Slovak National Council was a coordinated policy for the resistance groups directed against the first Slovak Republic and its political system, the preparation of an armed uprising and the assumption of power. After the Uprising was declared on **29 August 1944** a struggle over jurisdiction developed between the Slovak National Council and the "revolutionary national committee in Banská Bystrica" that included Vavro Šrobár. The council officially assumed legislative and executive power in Slovakia by the declaration of **1 September 1944**. It was comprised of a presidium, a plenary assembly and a board of commissioners. It was located in Banská Bystrica. The number of the members of the Slovak National Council gradually increased from 13 at the beginning of September 1944 to 50 at the end of October 1944. In the organs of the council parity was maintained between the citizen block and the Communist Party of Slovakia. The functioning of the insurgent Slovak National Council legally ended on 23 October 1944, five days before the occupation of Banská Bystrica by the German army. /RL/

SLOVAK NATIONAL COUNCIL (1945) – a body representative of the national sovereignty and independence of the Slovaks. It was formed after the arrival of the Soviet army on the territory of Slovakia and replaced the insurgent **Slovak National Council (1944)**. Some members of the insurgent Slovak National Council began to work with the office of the Czecho-Slovak governmental delegation located in the Ukrainian city of Chust. The council renewed its activity in Trebišov on 21 January 1945 under the name "Declaration of the Slovak National Council for the liberated territory". However, the real power was held by the Soviet army and its NKVD security service. From 21 February 1945 the Slovak National Council worked at Košice. Vavro Šrobár, Gustáv Husák, Ladislav Novomeský, Jozef Styk and Ján Ursíny made up its presidium. At mid-May 1945 it moved to Bratislava. The authority of the Council vis-à-vis the central organs of the Czecho-Slovak state was limited by the so-called three Prague Agreements (**2 June 1945, 11 April 1946, 27 June 1946**), which gradually stripped it of its original sovereignty and subordinated it to the central offices in Prague. Up to 1968 the Slovak National Council represented an asymmetrical political arrangement, since it did not have a counterpart in the Czech part of the state. The constitution of **11 July 1950** even abolished the board of commissioners. The Slovak National Council was established on a new basis with constitutional law number 143 of **27 October 1968** on the **federation**, which defined it as the representative of the national sovereignty and particularity of the Slovak nation as well as the supreme organ of state power in the Slovak Socialist Republic. It was composed of 150 commissioners. This law also created a Czech National Council. The socialist character of the federation and the monopolistic position of the Communist Party limited the area of operations of the council. The presidium of the Slovak National Council had disproportionately great authority. After the victory of democratic forces (**16 – 17 November 1989**), the gradual transformation of the Slovak National Council into a democratic parliament occurred. On **17 July 1992** it declared state sovereignty and on **1 September 1992** it accepted the constitution of the Slovak Republic and changed its name to the National Council of the Slovak Republic. Since **1 January 1993** it has been the parliament of the independent Slovak Republic. /RL/

SLOVAK NATIONAL NEWS (SLOVENSKJE NÁRODŇJE NOVINI) – first Slovak political newspaper. Unofficially it was the organ of the Slovak national movement and expressed, in particular, the views of **Štúr's group**. Ľudovít

Štúr published it in Bratislava with a literary supplement, *Tatra Eagle (Orol tatransk)*, from 1 August 1845. It was published twice each week using the literary Slovak of Štúr. It called for social reforms, the modernization of life, education, national liberty and equality. It focused especially on the life of non-privileged groups and sought their advancement through the promoting modern business methods, the improvement of schools and education and **temperance societies** or **Sunday schools**. It presented reports from abroad and the rest of the monarchy and devoted space to life in Slovak regions where it had a network of correspondents. Initially it encouraged patient, everyday educational work and later became critical of the feudal system and serfdom, which it viewed as the cause of the miserable social and economic position of the greater part of Slovak society. It was devoted to the national movement, defended the idea of Slovak national particularity and valued the rapprochement of the groups of Štúr and Bernolák who contributed articles to the newspaper. The articles of Ľudovít Štúr, in particular *Where our misery lies (Kde leží naša bieda)* and *Our hope for the forthcoming diet (Naše nádeje k nastávajúcemu snemu)*, which demanded social reforms in the spirit of human dignity and national justice, contributed to the formation of the Slovak political program. It ceased publication on 9 June 1848 as a result of the pressure exerted by the followers of Kossuth. /DŠ/

SLOVAK NATIONAL PARTY – the main Slovak political force during the period of **dualism**. It was based on the **Old School** and the ideological legacy of **Štúr's group** and was established as an organization on **6 June 1871**, with its seat in Martin. Its chairman was Viliam Paulíny-Tóth, from 1877 Pavol Mudroň and, from 1914, Matúš Dula. Martin Čulen, Andrej Halaša, Ján Francisci, Miloš Štefanovič, Ambro Pietor and Svetozár Hurban Vajanský were among its leading personalities. Its press organ was the *National News (Národnie noviny)*. Its leadership was in Martin (the so-called Martin center) and it had supporters in throughout the country. It constantly opposed the Hungarian government and powers that did not respect the national individuality of the Slovaks and the equality of nations. It not only repudiated the Austrian-Hungarian Compromise, the idea of a single Hungarian nation and the **Nationality Law**, but also criticized the failure to adhere to it. The permanent basis of its policy was the **Memorandum of the Slovak Nation** with its demand for an "Upper-Hungarian Slovak Territory". In the milieu of an intensive **Magyarization** it was not able to develop activities that could obtain the broad support of the public and it therefore felt isolated. It expressed opposition to the aristocratic regime, to the **right to vote in Hungary,** and to social injustice, especially through propaganda and the declaration of electoral passivity (1878, 1884 – 1901). Its Martin center uniquely combined traditionalism, humanism and democracy. Its hope for a resolution of the Slovak question was associated with **Slavic mutuality**, primarily with the help of Russia. Its Russophilism even grew into a messianism. At the turn of the century the Slovak National Party began to be more active. It cooperated with representatives of the Serbs and Romanians (**Congress of non-Magyar Nationalities**) and the Czechs and welcomed the activity of the **Czechoslavic Union**. It also built up its organization and in 1912 Jozef Gregor Tajovský, as its secretary, became its first paid employee. It secured support in the regions that resulted in the development of other Slovak political centers (for example, Ružomberok, Zvolen, Trnava, Liptovský Mikuláš and Myjava). It organized public and electoral assemblies and demanded a general suffrage right (in 1913 also for women). Several currents of thought developed within the party that criticized its leadership for an insufficiently aggressive policy (Milan Hodža, **Hlasists**, Slovak People's Party). The only other party functioning at the time was the **Slovak Social Democratic Party of Hungary**. Representatives of the party were in contact with Czech politicians during the war and on **24 May 1918** its leaders expressed their support for a state union with the Czechs. It initiated the founding of the **Slovak National Council (1918)** and supported the acceptance of the **Declaration of the Slovak Nation** by which the Slovaks declared their support for Czecho-Slovakia. After the Czechoslovak Republic was established, it merged with the agrarians to form the Slovak National and Agrarian Party. It became independent again on 30 March 1921 because it wanted to achieve the effective **autonomy of Slovakia**. In the inter-war period the chairmen of the Slovak National Party included Emil Stodola, Martin Rázus and Ján Paulíny-Tóth. In elections an average of 2.5 per cent of the voters, mainly Evangelicals, voted for the Slovak National Party. In order to obtain a seat in parliament it had to depend upon cooperation with other parties, first with the Czechoslovak National Democrats and from 1932 with Hlinka's Slovak People's Party (**16 October 1932**). A dispute with Hlinka's Slovak People's Party over a parliamentary seat after the elections of 1935 led to the decline of the autonomist bloc. The Slovak National Party accepted the **Žilina Agreement** of **6 October 1938**. The controversial question of merging with Hlinka's Slovak People's Party provoked a dispute among its leaders. On 23 November 1938 the majority of members of the executive committee declared that they were opposed to a merger and on 24 November 1938 its activity officially ceased. After negotiations with Hlinka's Slovak People's Party on 15 December 1938 in Žilina it voted for a merger. /RL, DŠ/

SLOVAK NATIONAL UPRISING see **Uprising of 1944**

SLOVAK PEOPLE'S PARTY see **Hlinka's Slovak People's Party**

SLOVAK PETITION TO THE THRONE – a programmatic document of the Slovak national movement. It reacted to the intensified **Magyarization** after Count Karol Zay became the general inspector of the Evangelical Church on **8 – 10 September 1840**. Although it was presented only in the name of the Evangelicals, of whom 200 signed it, it can be considered the first representative political action of the Slovaks. The signatories, mostly from **Štúr's group**, addressed it to King Ferdinand V and presented it to him in Vienna on **5 June 1842**. The petition protested against the introduction of Hungarian as the official language in Hungary, the spread of Magyarization, demanded the naming of censors of Slovak books in Bratislava and Pest, the confirmation of the Department of the Czechoslavonic Language at the lyceum in Bratislava, the organization of like departments at other Evangelical schools, the preservation of Latin in maintaining church registers and the use of Czech in the worship services of the Evangelicals. Although it contained only modest language and cultural demands, the leadership of the Evangelical Church and the Magyar press accused its signatories of high treason and **pan-Slavism**. To these attacks the Slovak side responded with a second petition, which was delivered on **19 May 1844** by Ľudovít Štúr, Jozef Miloslav Hurban, Michal Miloslav Hodža and Ján Čaplovič. Although Vienna did not satisfy all the requests, on its intervention Karol Zay curbed Magyarization in the Evangelical Church and the anti-Slovak attacks from the Magyar side. /DŠ/

SLOVAK REPUBLIC (SR) – state entity. The first Slovak Republic was established on **14 March 1939** in a complicated situation marked by a crisis of the European democracies, when Nazi Germany had a dominant influence in central Europe. German interest in the final elimination of the remnant of **Czecho-Slovakia** hastened its foundation. Despite German pressure at the negotiations in Berlin on **13 March 1939,** constitutional procedure was observed and the Slovak state was declared by a decision of the Slovak autonomous assembly (**14 March 1939**) and not by a group of individuals. Its establishment realized the idea of Slovak national and state sovereignty. The Slovak state – from the acceptance of its constitution on **21 July 1939** the Slovak Republic – was recognized by 27 states (among them Great Britain, France and the Soviet Union) during its existence. It was set up as a state with an authoritarian political system (emphasis upon the unity of the nation, the suppression of parliamentarianism and the elimination of the activity of the political left,

especially the communists etc.). The original function of political parties was to be replaced by six estates of employers and employees. Because of unfavorable conditions (the **Second World War**, German pressure and domestic political controversies), this model was not implemented. Instead, the influence in the political life of the first Slovak Republic of Hlinka's Slovak People's Party, the only party representing Slovaks on a national basis, increased. In addition to it there existed parties for the German and Magyar minorities. By means of the Hlinka's Slovak People's Party, a moderate group of politicians (Jozef Tiso, Gejza Medrický, Július Stano) weakened the influence of the radicals (Vojtech Tuka, Alexander Mach) concentrated in the government and in the **Hlinka Guard**, which grew artificially after the **Salzburg Negotiations**. The Salzburg Negotiations, together with the treaty concerning the protective relationship with Germany of **23 March 1939**, limited the sovereignty of the Slovak Republic, which had achieved good results in the economic and cultural spheres and in social policy. Against its will it was drawn by Germany into the war against Poland on **2 September 1939** and on **23 June 1941**, at the initiative of Vojtech Tuka, against the Soviet Union. On 12 December 1941 Vojtech Tuka declared war also on the United States and Great Britain. Through its laws and government regulations the Slovak Republic gradually excluded the Jews (**Jewish code**) from economic and public life and on **25 March 1942** started their deportation to German concentration camps on the former territory of Poland. It politically persecuted Communists and the representatives of the former political parties. In contrast with the surrounding countries, however, the intensity of the persecution and the level of punishment reached only a moderate level. The first Slovak Republic experienced its most severe political crisis with the arrival of German occupation troops and the declaration of the **Uprising of 1944**. In this period the existence of the Slovak Republic was guaranteed only by one great power, Germany; the other great powers recognized the Czecho-Slovak government in exile in London. The Slovak president, government, and some of the military leaders and officials emigrated. With the act of capitulation on **8 May 1945** the first Slovak Republic ceased to exist. Slovakia was incorporated into the renewed Czechoslovak Republic as an autonomous unit. In 1968 the Slovak Socialist Republic was created as part of the Czecho-Slovak Federation. On **1 January 1993** the second independent Slovak Republic was created which is a parliamentary democracy. /RL/

SLOVAK SOCIAL DEMOCRATIC PARTY OF THE KINGDOM OF HUNGARY – a workers political party. It began to be formed in 1904 but was established as an independent party on 11 – 12 June 1905. On 18 June 1906 it became an autonomous unit of the Social Democratic Party of the Kingdom of Hungary. Its chairman was Emanuel Lehocký. The party issued the *Slovak Workers' News* (*Slovenské robotnícke noviny*) and its mainstay was the Bratislava organization. With the founding of an independent party, the Slovak workers, activists and unionists expressed dissatisfaction with the lack of attention of the leadership of the Hungarian social democrats to the national oppression of the Slovaks and their minimal interest in the needs of the Slovak workers (Slovak press, the use of Slovak etc.). It cooperated with the Czech Social Democrats in Vienna and obtained from them financial and moral support. It viewed social questions and policy in the spirit of the Second International, spread the idea of socialism and organized assemblies on 1 May, educational courses and lectures for workers. It criticized the government for its oppression, demanded the democratization of the regime in Hungary, universal suffrage, the improvement of social conditions, expressed solidarity with striking workers of other nations, demanded the resolution of the Slovak question in the spirit of national toleration and equality and advocated the idea of a united states of Europe. Among the Slovak political currents, it cooperated especially with the **hlasists** and Milan Hodža. After the **First World War** broke out, it halted its activity and renewed it in 1918

when the first public Slovak proclamation favoring a political alliance of the Czechs and the Slovaks (**Mikuláš Resolution**) took place on its premises. On 15 December 1918 it joined with the Czech social democrats to form the **Czecho-Slovak Social-Democratic Party of Workers**. /DŠ/

SLOVAK STATE see **Slovak Republic**

SOCIALIST REALISM – artistic movement. It was introduced in literature and the Soviet author Maxim Gorkij defined its ideology in his works. It later took hold also in the visual arts, film, theater and architecture. It was based upon a Marxist world view and fulfilled the **Communist Party of Czechoslovakia's** conception of art. The endeavor to depict life and the world in a faithful manner was replaced by a class approach. It concentrated on social problems, which were often artificially placed in the foreground and vulgarized. It was marked by a pathetic heroism and monumentality, by an emphasis upon so-called revolutionary traditions and by admiration for the first socialist country, the Soviet Union. In countries with communist regimes, it was the only artistic movement officially allowed. In Slovak literature it was expressed in the works of Václav Chlumecký, Ján Poničan, Eduard Urx, Fraňo Kráľ, Ladislav Novomeský, Peter Jilemnický, Miroslav Válek, Pavol Horov, Vojtech Mihálik, Andrej Plávka, Miloš Krno, Alfonz Bednár and many others. In the visual arts socialist realism is seen in the works of Konštantín Bauer, Edmund Gwerk, Štefan Bednár, Ladislav Čemický, Ján Želibský, Július Lörincz, Rudolf Pribiš and Ján Kulich among others. From 1948 to 1989 it was necessary for artists to conform, at least outwardly, to the official line. /RL/

SOCIETY OF THE DEVOTEES OF THE SLOVAK LANGUAGE AND LITERATURE (*Spolok milovníkov reči a literatúry Slovenskej*) – a cultural and publishing institution. It was founded on 1 August 1834 by members of **Bernolák's group** working in Pest and Buda. Its first chairman was Ján Kollár and the secretary was Martin Hamuljak. The society resolved to cultivate the mother tongue and to overcome the different concepts of the nation espoused by the defenders of Slovak national particularity (Bernolák's group) and those favoring a Czechoslovak tribal unity (followers of Kollár). It published four volumes of the almanac *Aurora (Zora)*, in which contributions from authors of both traditions were published in the literary Slovak of Bernolák and in Czech. The difference between the points of view concerning the basic understanding of the nation were so great that Ján Kollár and his followers withdrew from the society after a year. It remained exclusively a society of Bernolák's group. The society published Hollý's *Catholic Hymnal (Katolícky spevňík)* in **1842** and four volumes of his collected works (1841 – 1842), but was not able to develop any other significant activity and ceased to function in 1850. Despite lack of success, it was the first important attempt at bringing closer together and ultimately uniting the Catholic and Evangelical streams of the national movement. /DŠ/

SOLIDUS (also schilling) – Byzantine gold coin. During feudalism it also was in circulation in Slovakia. Eight *solida* were equal to one Rheinish florin, ten *solida* were equal to one Hungarian florin or **gold piece**. This ratio was maintained until about 1620. The *solidus* was understood also as a unit of metallic content used in the Hungarian minting. One gold *solidus* with a content of 4.4 grams of gold was equal to 30 *denarii* (with a content of 51 grams of silver) or 1 pound (*funt*), that is, 250 *denarii* with a content of 408 grams. In the 16th and 17th centuries a small Polish coin also called a *solidus* circulated in Slovakia. /JB/

SPIŠ CHAMBER – a financial and economic-legal institution with jurisdiction for north-eastern Hungary. Despite the transfer of the seat of the **Hungarian chamber** to Bratislava, the eastern lands of Habsburg Hungary at that time could be visited by chamber officials only with difficulty due to poor roads and frequent Turkish raids. Therefore, in 1539 the ruler decided to establish a branch which was named the Spiš chamber, after the then most significant economic region of eastern Slovakia (Upper Hungary). It definitively became inde-

pendent by a mandate of the ruler of 1 April 1563. It administered finances, tolls, the **thirtieth**, taxes and contributions, as well as provided funds for the army and the building of fortresses. Its seat was in Košice but during the anti-Habsburg insurrections of the estates, when the city was occupied by the insurgents, it was forced to transfer several times to Prešov. As a collective organ it was composed of a prefect and three, later six, advisors. Various changes were also implemented in the administration of the chamber. Its office structure was stabilized at the end of the 17th century and it included the chancellery, the shipping office, registry, accounting office and an archive. Of the territory of today's Slovakia the counties of Spiš, Šariš, Zemplín, Uh, Abov, Turňa and Gemer, the free royal cities of Košice, Prešov, Bardejov, Sabinov and Levoča, as well as the royal feudal estates lying within their borders and the thirtieth (customs) stations, were within the area of jurisdiction of the Spiš chamber. Its activity ended together with that of the Hungarian chamber in 1848. /VS/

SPIŠ PRAYERS – the oldest complex literary monument in the Slovak language. They are recorded as a draft in a codex, which was written in the cathedral church in Spišská Kapitula, later belonged to the Carthusian cloister in Spiš and from the 16th century was preserved in Olomouc. The most likely author is Gašpar Bak, the provost of Spiš, who wrote them in 1464 – 1493. He obtained his office for service in the **Black Army** of King Matthias. On the anniversary of his priestly ordination, on 25 October 1479, he dedicated the completed cathedral in Spišská Kapitula and preached a sermon. It contained short prayers recited before and after the Gospel, before and after the sermon and basic Christian prayers such as the Lord's Prayer, the Hail Mary and the Apostles' Creed. The prayers are for the authorities, for King Matthias Corvinus, for peace, good weather, pilgrims, the dead, the lonely, the sick and the donors to the church. The prayers are characterized by Eastern Slovak, Czech and Polish linguistic elements, and it has been held that their texts reflect an older form of the language when the domestic language was still used in non-liturgical devotions. /VS/

SUB-TENANTS (PODŽELIARI) see **Cotters (želiari)**

SUDNYJ LJUDEM LAW (judicial law for secular people) – the oldest Slavic legal writing. It developed at the middle of the 9th century. Originally it was presumed to be an old Bulgarian or old Russian legal monument. Newer linguistic research has shown that it is connected with the mission of Cyril and Methodius to Great Moravia. It is an Old Slavonic translation of Byzantine legal norms, the so-called *Eclogy* from the 8th century, with changes and additions of a western Roman and Slavic character. In 32 articles it contains in particular penal regulations relating to crimes against the faith and morality (lewdness, rape) and crimes against property (thieft and arson), as well as regulations relating to the right of asylum and the division of the spoils of war. An important portion (eleven articles) is made up of family law provisions relating to marriage and its impediments, separation, divorce, conjugal infidelity and the like. This code was probably not utilized for very long in the **Great Moravian Empire** or was used alongside domestic customary law. Through Methodius Pope John VIII sent a law code, the so-called expanded *Dionysia*, to Svätopluk. Related to it is a Greek collection of canon law, the so-called *Synagoga* (from the 6th century), which became the basis of the Old Slavonic *Nomokánon* of Methodius. From Great Moravia the *sudnyj ljudem* law, with the Old Slavonic translation of the *Nomokánon*, was taken to Bulgaria and from there to Kiev. /JB/

SUMMER CAMPAIGN – the third Slovak armed intervention in the **revolution of 1848/1849**. It was planned by leading Slovak personalities from May 1849 and supported by the imperial ministry of defense. A corps was formed in Skalica and near Bratislava (Stupava, Rača). Its commander was Major Henrich Lewartowski and companies were led by members of **Štúr's group** (for example, Ján Francisci, Štefan Marko Daxner, Samuel Štefanovič, Ján

Kučera). It did not take part in the campaign against the Magyar army. The Magyars capitulated on 13 August and the corps was transferred to the mining region of central Slovakia after 20 August. It covered the rear of the Russian and imperial armies and disarmed the Hungarian guerrillas (partisan units), which had assembled in the mountains of central Slovakia (especially in the Slovak Ore Mountains). The command had its headquarters in Banská Bystrica and Banská Štiavnica. The corps was made up of about 2,000 volunteers and was supported by 4,000 home guards, mainly in the areas of the upper Hron, Liptov and Turiec. It had more of a political than a military significance. Its officers restored public order and a provisional administration that conducted business in Slovak. They informed the public about the program to split Slovakia from Hungary and obtained support for it. Their activity was attacked by the Magyar noble old conservatives who took control of political life in Slovakia. They accused the participants in the Summer Campaign of inciting disorder and intervened to dissolve the corps. This occurred on **21 November 1849** in Bratislava. Slovakia was occupied by imperial units. The Slovak national movement lost the only power supporting its constitutional ambitions. This made it easier for the imperial power to avoid almost completely a resolution of the question of Slovakia. /DŠ/

SUNDAY SCHOOLS – educational and training institutions in the 19th century. They helped to eliminate the illiteracy and cultural backwardness of the poorer classes and compensated for the lack of schools and teachers. Even the state supported their activity. They were founded and led by pastors, teachers and students and attended primarily by adults, especially craftsmen, merchants and farmers. The first Sunday school in Slovakia was founded in Horná Súča by Pastor Michal Rešetka (1834) and others were established in the 1840s, especially with the help of **Štúr's group**. They were divided into two types. The lower type was aimed at eliminating the illiteracy of the young people and adults, while the higher offered basic instruction in the natural sciences, technology, health, agriculture, history and higher arithmetic. Some even prepared assistant teachers who worked in remote settlements. Libraries formed a part of the Sunday schools. Štúr's group considered Sunday schools and **temperance societies** as both important instruments for education and for strengthening the national and civic spirit. In the revolutionary years (1848-49) the majority of them ceased to function. Only a small proportion of them were later renewed, since the state itself assumed most of the responsibility for education. /DŠ/

SURREALISM (from the French *surréalisme*) – artistic movement. It originated in France at the beginning of the 20th century and affected the visual arts and literature. It was based on Dadaism from which it took over an anarchistic disposition to topple the cult of the rational and a strong opposition to logical, moral and esthetic values. The manifesto of the surrealists was issued in France in 1924 by André Breton. The goal of the new movement was to replace a rational view of things with an irrational. It drew inspiration from uninvestigated regions of the human mind. The desire to uncover the source of creative interpretation led the surrealists to investigate the subconscious and dreams and they were inspired by hallucinations, raptures and even madness. They devoted special attention to the spontaneity of the experiences of children, enchantments and miracles and mythological and magical pictures. In this way they satisfied the growing interest in the irrational. Representatives of surrealism in literature were, in particular, Louis Aragon and Robert Desnos and in the visual arts Max Ernst, Salvador Dalí, and André Masson. Slovak surrealists emerged in the 1920s and were active in Slovak artistic life until the 1940s. They were also inspired by folklore motifs, especially from the works of Janko Kráľ and Baroque literature. Surrealist writers and poets were Rudolf Fabry, Vladimír Reisel, Štefan Žáry, Július Lenko, Pavol Bunčák, Michal Považan and Mikuláš Bakoš, while Imrich Weiner-Kráľ was especially important in painting. Other painters influenced by surrealism included Ján Mudroch, Cyprián Majerník, Ester Šimerová-Martinčeková and Ladislav Guderna. Surrealism was the first artistic movement in Slovakia in which poets, literary theoreticians, painters and sculptors exhibited jointly. /RL/

SVÄTOPLUK'S EMPIRE see **Great Moravian Empire**

SYLVESTER PATENTS – documents of the emperor from **31 December 1851**. They confirmed the previous development that negated constitutional forms of government and were directed towards absolutism. The first patent revoked the **dictated constitution** because of "unsuitable" conditions and its "inappropriateness". The second confirmed the abolition of serfdom, the equality of people before the law and the protection of the churches recognized by the state, but abolished civil rights. The third one (a cabinet letter) was formulated by Alexander Bach, the minister of the interior, and was addressed to Prime Minister Prince Felix Schwarzenberg. It set out the principles of a new administrative organization and the structure of the monarchy. It established judicial authority on three levels, excluded the public from trials and introduced a common civil and criminal code for the whole empire. The Sylvester patents showed that renewal of the **constitutional monarchy** was not possible and established the legal foundations for **neo-absolutism**. Its ideal was an effectively functioning state mechanism, the indivisibility of the power of the sovereign, a loyal bureaucracy and a disciplined police and army. The autonomy of communities was abolished and the public was excluded from participation in political power. This was concentrated in the hands of Francis Joseph I and his "enlightened" co-workers (the emperor's mother Sophia, Alexander Bach, the chairman of the imperial council, Charles Kübeck, the minister of police, Johann Kempen, and Cardinal Otmar Rauscher). /DŠ/

ŠOLTÝSI see **Magistrate** (*richtár*)

ŠTÚR'S GROUP – representatives of the main stream of the Slovak national movement of the mid 19th century that gathered around its most significant personality, Ľudovít Štúr. It was formed in the 1830s, in particular at the Evangelical lyceum in Bratislava, where the **Czechoslavic Society** and the society **Mutuality** were active. Its members rejected feudalism, absolutism, the privileges of the estates and **Magyarization** and professed modern political ideas such as constitutionalism, representationalism, the equality of nations, **romanticism** and **Slavic mutuality**, admired folk culture and the non-privileged classes. In the 1840s they preferred (especially due to Štúr) patient daily work and education to radical attitudes. They promoted modern entrepreneurship (insurance companies, cooperatives), the importance of education, especially technical education, agricultural knowledge, founded **Sunday schools**, libraries and **temperance societies,** and appealed for the cultivation of the national arts (theater, poetry). By means of gradual changes they wanted to improve social and cultural relations, strengthen the feeling of human dignity and self-awareness of the non-privileged classes, stimulate their interest in public matters and thus establish the foundations of a civil society. Alongside this, they strengthened national solidarity and pride. They formed the modern Slovak nation not by political decisions but from below, by emancipating the common people. Gradually they forsook the traditional conception of the Evangelicals about a Czechoslovak tribal unity and identified with the idea of Slovak national particularity. The result was the new literary language of Štúr (*štúrovčina, 14 February 1843*, **11 – 16 July 1843**), a rapprochement with the views of **Bernolák's group** and a general strengthening of national unity. By founding the society *Tatrín* and the *Slovak National News* (*Slovenskje národňje*

novini) Štúr's group elicited an unusual public exchange of views. At the same time they prepared to enter higher politics. They initiated the **Slovak Petition to the Throne** and finished shaping a political program. Like the **Magyar reform movement**, they demanded the abolition of serfdom, noble privileges and courts, the securing of the equality of citizens and, in contrast to it, demanded a halt to Magyarization, the recognition of the Slovaks as a nation, the use of Slovak in lower schools, offices and in the church. During the **revolution of 1848/49** they initiated all the important Slovak activities and in the 1860s became the nucleus of the **Old School**. /DŠ/

TATRÍN – the most significant nation-wide cultural society of the Slovaks in the first half of the 19th century. It represented the main organizational support of the Slovak national movement. It was founded on **26 – 28 August 1844** in Liptovský Mikuláš, where it had its headquarters. Michal Miloslav Hodža was its president and the members of its committee were from **Štúr's group** (for example, Ľudovít Štúr, Jozef Miloslav Hurban, Ctibor Zoch and Samo Chalupka), younger members of Bernolák's group (Matej Tučko, Štefan Závodník and Jozef Ščasný) and other streams (Gašpar Féjérpataky-Belopotocký and Karol Kuzmány). In addition to the Evangelical and Catholic clergy, students, teachers, doctors, bureaucrats, artisans and merchants were members. It supported the grandiose plans of Štúr's group, the goals of the **Sunday schools**, **temperance societies**, associations of farmers and youth, published textbooks, educational and ethnographic literature, laid the foundations of national museum collections and financially supported talented students. In the numerous and impressive events organized by Tatrín, members of Štúr's group and **Bernolák's group** met for the first time. A turning point was, in particular, the general assembly in Čachtice on **10 August 1847**, in which more than 70 leading personalities took part. They agreed that, after some modifications, the literary language of Štúr would also be accepted by the Bernolákians and thus become the literary language of the whole nation. The achievement of linguistic unification definitively completed the foundations for the national unity of the Slovaks on the basis of particularity. Tatrín realized only a small part of its grandiose plans since the Hungarian authorities did not approve its constitution. After the **revolution 1848/1849** erupted it disbanded. The **Matica slovenská** later continued its activities. /DŠ/

TAVERNÍK (TREASURER) – a high royal dignitary of the Kingdom of Hungary. The title is derived from the Slavic *tovor* (chest). Originally he was the administrator of the princely treasury and, after the establishment of the Kingdom of Hungary, the royal treasury. In the 12th – 13th centuries he gradually took over the administration not only of the revenue of the court but also of other property of the **king**. He became the superior of lower economic officers including the tax collectors, customs (**thirtieth**) collectors, money changers and the collectors of salt taxes. He also supervised the rights and obligations of the royal cities. Due to their development in the 14th – 15th centuries, the importance of the treasurer grew. He became an independent judge with the authority of a court of appeal for the most important royal cities; in Slovakia these were, for example, Bratislava, Bardejov, Košice, Prešov and Trnava. The treasurer was a member of the **royal council** and later of the **vice-regency** council. His influence diminished after the establishment of the **Hungarian chamber** that, from 1528, assumed much of his jurisdiction. The office of *taverník* and the court of the *taverník* were abolished in 1848. /VS/

TEMPERANCE SOCIETIES (also abstinence societies) – societies with an educational mission. They were part of the struggle of the Slovak national movement against feudalism and the backwardness of the peasants and agricultural workers. They were established in the 1840s by **Štúr's group** and Catholic priests on the basis of foreign, especially Irish, experience. Their mission was to point out the danger of alcoholism among the poorest people, who were being devasted by it, and to strengthen a consciousness of their own dignity. They were voluntary associations of people who pledged to renounce alcohol. The first society was established in 1840 in Bobrovec. They soon achieved a broad social scope and mass support. In the mid 1840s there were about 500 societies. In Orava they had more than 20,000 members and in the larger villages of Kysuce up to several thousand members. The first congress of the founders of the temperance societies took place on **12 August 1847**. It elected a central committee that, under the presidency of Štefan Závodník, prepared a petition to the **Hungarian diet**. After the revolution of 1848/49 the previous significance and scope of the societies was not regained. /DŠ/

TENTH (tithe, from the Latin *decima* – tenth) – a church tax in the amount of one tenth of the yield of agricultural products. In antiquity, the Jews paid a tithe and this was adopted by the Christians. In medieval Hungary the ecclesiastical tenth is already found in the first laws of the kings Stephen I (before **1031**), Ladislas I and Coloman. The tenth belonged to the **bishop** who could assign it to subordinate ecclesiastical institutions. The nobility and property intended for church or school purposes were exempt from the tenth. The tenth was also not paid by adherents to the eastern churches, unbelievers and heretics or schismatics (e.g. Serbians, Ruthenians, Jazygs, Cumans, Hajduks and Walachians). Representatives of the church did not always respect this and collected the tenth from adherents to other churches and, during the Reformation of the 16th century, even from the Protestants. The so-called large tenth was paid on grain and wine, the small tenth on sheep, goats and other agricultural animals (even bees). With the development of agriculture and the cultivation of other sorts of plants, the payment of the tenth was extended to them also.

The tenth had to be paid at the same time as the **ninth** that belonged to the landlord. It was collected in kind (naturalia) but sometimes it was also paid in money. The income from the tenth was leased for a previously agreed amount to lessees who then had to collect it at their own expense. Even the royal chamber operated in this manner. For example, during the 16th century, the income from the tenth was used to finance anti-Turkish defenses. The rulers used situations when high church offices were not occupied (*sedis vacancia,* vacant see) and kept for themselves the income collected from the tenth. The payment of the tenth and other obligations of the serfs towards the authorities in 1848 ended with the abolition of **serfdom**. /JB/

TEUTONIC ORDER see **Orders**

THERESIAN REFORMS – collection of reforms of Maria Theresa. With them Maria Theresa sought to overcome the economic backwardness of the Kingdom of Hungary. They concerned the position of the serfs, the school system, agriculture, the production of craftsmen, the judiciary, the churches and health care. The country-wide **Theresian urbár** was intended to improve the position of the serfs. Other reforms were introduced favoring the cultivation of new produce and feed crops, the raising of new breeds of horses and cattle and the publication of literature popularizing agriculture. The development of production was influenced by the reform of the guild organization (**guilds**). By the reform of the school system, the state determined the main direction of school instruction (*Ratio educationis*). Among the reforms affecting the church, the sovereign established three new bishoprics in the province of the archbishopric of Esztergom (Banská Bystrica, Rožňava and Spiš), reduced the number of obligatory church holidays, revised the stole fees (*štóla*), the payments for the performance of religious ceremonies (baptism, marriage, burial etc.), renewed the prohibition against the publication of papal bulls without the approval of the government (*placetum regium*). In the judicial area she forbade trials for witchcraft and magic. In health care she sought to protect the

population from plague epidemics and other diseases by establishing a commission which supervised the activity of health workers and the regulations connected with public hygiene. The propagation of measures to protect against fires and the prohibition of superstition, magic and irrational forms of folk healing and some folk customs also were included in the reforms. The provisions of Maria Theresa, which corresponded with the goals of **enlightenment absolutism**, were intensified by the **Josephinian reforms**. /MK/

THERESIAN URBÁR – the most important reform of Maria Theresa. It was part of the **Theresian reforms** and the policy of **enlightenment absolutism**. It established a uniform system of recording serf obligations in the Kingdom of Hungary. Its goals were to protect the serfs from the excessive exploitation by the landlords, increase their ability to pay taxes and to assure the preservation or the growth of the productivity of the serfs in agriculture. The reform began in **1767** with the issuing of the urbarial patent and concluded in the years 1770 – 1772 with the introduction of a country-wide land register (*urbár*). In an attempt to adapt the obligations of the serfs to the extent and quality of soil that they farmed, officials ascertained their existing status by means of answers to nine questions and carried out an inventory of land and of serfs. The area of serf farmsteads and the obligations of the serfs were determined on the basis of this. The average settlement in Slovak counties had an area of 19 – 25 Bratislava *jutro* (acres) of arable fields and 7 – 8 wagons of hay in the meadows. (On higher quality soil the settlements were smaller). The *urbár* defined also the work, monetary and *naturalia* obligations of the serfs. The urbarial regulations did not change the principles of the relationship of the serfs to the soil. The serfs obtained personal freedom only with the **abolition of servitude** . /MK/

THIRTIETH – a type of border toll (customs duty), a payment for the import and export of goods. In the laws of King Coloman, the toll collectors of border county administrators and border tolls without further specification are mentioned. The first toll station in Slovakia documented in writing was in Tvrdošín (1265). From the end of the 12th to the end of the 13th century the border customs duty was an eightieth. It was used to maintain the court of the queen. The income from it was lower than the income from **tolls**. In 1336 Charles Robert ordered the collection of a thirtieth instead of a eightieth. Even then, this did not represent a thirtieth of the value of goods but only one per cent. The decree of Sigismund of Luxemburg of 1405 set the level of the thirtieth at 3.33 per cent; after 1526 it reached 5 per cent of the value of goods. Originally the thirtieth was collected only for imported goods. In 1370 King Louis ordered the collection of the thirtieth also from exports. The rulers did not grant permanent exemption from the thirtieth, unlike tolls, but only for a specific time or for some types of goods specifically named. Some wealthy cities, for example Bratislava, leased the thirtieth from the royal chamber and then collected it under their own management. Charles Robert began to build a system of thirtieth stations. The law of Vladislav II (1498) enumerated the main thirtieth stations on the territory of Slovakia: Orava (Tvrdošín), Trenčín, Bratislava and Košice which had their own branches with barriers on the network of roads leading to the main stations. The building of the thirtieth network was completed in the last third of the 17th century and then subordinated to the two royal chambers (in Bratislava and Košice). The thirtieth, as a medieval border duty, was unable to protect domestic productions and neither impeded nor motivated international trade, as is the case with modern customs duties. In 1755 the thirtieth was abolished and replaced by a new customs duty which differentiated the level of duties applied to foreign countries and the Austrian and Hungarian parts of the monarchy. /JB/

THÖKÖLY INSURRECTION – insurrection of the estates. After the disclosure of the **Conspiracy of Francis Wesselényi,** some of the nobility fled from prosecution to Transylvania. Here assembled also the *kuruci* soldiers who had been dismissed from service in the border for-

tresses at the end of 1671. With the support of Transylvania and the Oradea pasha, they undertook raids into eastern Slovakia where they occupied several cities. The Protestant population of the cities used this opportunity to expel the Catholic priests. Even Transylvanian magnates attempted to use these armed forces for their own goals. Prince Michael Apafi and his chancellor, Michael Teleki, in alliance with the French, created a large army that invaded the royal lands in **1678** and occupied eastern Slovakia, the upper Váh valley, the Nitra valley, Turiec, and the area of the central Slovak mining cities up to Levice. The Kežmarok magnate Imrich Thököly, whom the *kuruci* elected as supreme commander, then obtained the leadership of the insurgents. The Viennese court offered him a truce which did not last long. With Turkish assistance, he took possession of the greater part of Slovakia in the fall of 1682 and, on **16 September 1682**, in the captured city of Fiľakovo, Thököly was crowned the king of central Hungary by the governor of Buda, Ibrahim pasha, and thus became a Turkish vassal. At the beginning of **1683** the Ottomans declared war on Vienna. The imperial army began to withdraw from eastern and central Slovakia to the Danube and Váh rivers, and Thököly occupied the vacated territory. Imperial garrisons remained only at the Spiš, Muráň, Orava, Trenčín, Leopoldov and Bratislava castles. Throughout the whole of Slovakia the commissioners of Thököly confiscated the property of his enemies, collected tribute from the towns and assembled troops. After an unsuccessful two-month siege of Vienna, the Ottomans suffered a decisive defeat on **12 September 1683**. This meant the beginning of the end of their dominion in Hungary. The Ottomans imprisoned Imrich Thököly in 1685, since they believed he stood in the way of concluding an agreement with the emperor. In 1686 Prince Apafi accepted the protection of the emperor in Vienna, which meant the war was over. Thököly left for Turkey. An aftermath of the insurrection was the **Prešov Slaughterhouse**. /MK/

THURZO-FUGGER COMPANY – the most significant commercial and mining company in copper-ore mining, with European-wide operations, at the end of the Middle Ages and the beginning of the modern era. It really represents the first proto-company undertaking of its type. Copper-bearing ore mines in the region around Banská Bystrica were in decline in the second half of the 15th century and John Thurzo gradually took possession of them. He was a citizen of Cracow and a native of Levoča, where he was born into a family that originally came from Betlanovce in Spiš County. The mines were flooded with ground water and the realization of projects to revive mining demanded a substantial investment. Therefore the Thurzos joined with the banking family of the Fuggers of Augsburg. On the basis of contracts of **15 November 1494** and **16 March 1495** they created an entrepreneurial company, Hungarian Trade (*Ungarischer Handel*), also called *Neusohler Kupferhandel* (Banská Bystrica Copper Trade). The company modernized mining production, consolidated the extraction and transportation of ore and built two large smelting centers (Staré Hory and Harmanec). For the purification of copper a smelter was established in Tajov and a puddling smelter in Moštenica. A large copper forge was built in Banská Bystrica, in which copper was hammered into plates and various containers produced. In 1495 – 1504 more than a million **florins** were expended for the building of the copper business and the purchase of raw copper. In 1498 John Thurzo also leased the Kremnica mint. Several mine operators, the Hungarian **nobility** and the patricians of Banská Bystrica became opponents of the company. The controversy culminated in the **insurrection of the miners** of 1525, when the company was expropriated by the royal treasury. However, the treasury was not able to secure its full production. Another contract for the leasing of the copper company was concluded by the royal treasury on 15 April 1526, but only with the Fuggers, who leased the company until **1546**, when it was taken over and administered by the treasury (Lower Austrian Chamber). Almost all of the production of copper and sil-ver from the Banská Bystrica area was exported by means of agents (factors) at markets in Antwerp, Nuremberg and Venice, from which it circulated further in Europe. Between 1494 and 1546 about 600,000 metric hundredweight of copper and 115 tons of silver were extracted. The net profit of the company was more than two and a half million florins. /VS/

TOLERATION PATENT – reform of Joseph II that removed discrimination against the Evangelicals (Lutherans), Calvinists and Orthodox believers. The ruler issued it on 29 October 1781. Non-Catholics were allowed to conduct religious services freely, and, in communities where at least one hundred families belonged to these confessions, they were able to organize religious congregations and to have their own preachers and teachers. They were able to establish houses of prayer which, however, could not have their main entrance on the street, or possess a tower or bells. The patent abolished their obligation to participate in Catholic ceremonies (for example, pilgrimages) and, in the case of religious mixed marriages, to raise children in the Catholic faith. It denied to the Catholic bishops the right to certify the qualifications of the Protestant preachers. From the religious point of view, the toleration patent did not as yet provide full equality for these churches with Catholicism, which still preserved its position as the state church. Indirectly, however, it concluded a long period of religious polarization and intolerance. From the viewpoint of civil rights, it made the Protestants and Orthodox fully equal with the Catholics. They were allowed to fill public offices, serve the state, receive academic degrees, obtain the right of domicile, to become masters in guilds and to freely dispose of property. This patent, one of the most radical of the **Josephinian reforms,** met with the incomprehension of many contemporaries. Nevertheless, Joseph II wished to intensify it. In 1790 – 1791, after his death, the **Hungarian diet** and Emperor Leopold II declared the three above-mentioned non-Catholic churches recognized by the state. They thus obtained complete freedom.

The reforms contributed to the educational and civic progress of the Protestants and to their active participation in the national movements. /DŠ/

TOLL – payment for the goods transported within a country. In the sources they are referred to as *telonium* or *tributum*. The latter term signifies a payment in general. Tolls belonged among the so-called lesser **royal rights**. The earliest law of King Ladislas I already regulated commerce at **markets** and under Coloman, his successor, a third of the receipts from tolls belonged to the county administrator (*župan*) and a tenth to the **bishop**. The oldest were market tolls (*tributum fori*), from which road (*suché*, dry) and passage tolls developed. They were collected especially at bridges or fords across rivers. The income from tolls was used to maintain roads and support the construction and repair of bridges and the like. From the tolls collected on entry or departure from the country there developed the border toll, the **thirtieth**. From the 12th century tolls were in the hands of ecclesiastical and secular lords (fief-holders) and, later, also the cities. The right to collect a toll was connected with the ownership of land but did not result directly from it. It was necessary for the **king** to bestow the right to collect a toll by a special privilege. The oldest toll tariffs, a list of the types of goods and the payments for each, come from the 13th century. The ruler bestowed upon market settlements and developing cities not only the right to conduct markets but also the right to collect the income from them that originally belonged to the king. Another large group of privileges was the freedom from tolls. The nobles and high clergy as privileged Hungarian **estates** did not pay tolls. The cities obtained the freedom from tolls in the oldest charters of privileges. For example, exemption from the payment of tolls on the territory of the whole country was a part of the Buda privilege, which was adopted by several Slovak cities. Serfs were freed from tolls to a limited extent and under special circumstances (e.g., when a wedding procession went through the toll station, for carting grain or flour to a mill, for public works, or for the transport of military materials and the like). The ownership and payment of tolls declined with feudal obligations in the 19th century. A relic of the tolls were payments for places at city markets in the 19th and 20th centuries, which were extended to bourses and other occasional forms of buying and selling in Slovakia after 1989. The payment by automobile drivers on highways can be considered a modern type of road toll. /JB/

TRILINGUALS – Christian priests declaring that only the Hebrew, Greek and Latin languages may be used in ecclesiastical liturgies. This concept appeared in a dispute of Constantine with opponents of the Slavic liturgy in Venice in **867** when he, together with his brother Methodius and a group of disciples, departed for Rome in order to be ordained there as priests. /JB/

TRIPARTITUM – the short title of the law-book *Three Part Compilation of the Customary Laws of the Glorious Hungarian Monarchy and Attached Countries*. Stephen Werbőczy compiled and completed it in 1514. This is a collection of valid medieval Hungarian private and public customary laws. It contains also a theoretical explanation of the fundamental principles of noble rights. The work is divided into an introduction and three parts; the first part has 134 articles (titles) and contains noble private law (grants, obligations, inheritance, material and others); the second part with 84 articles deals especially with the sources of law and legal process; in 36 articles the third part deals with the particular Croatian, Transylvanian, municipal and serf laws, and also contains criminal laws. The work of Werböczy was examined by a special royal commission, which acknowledged that it faithfully depicted valid customary law. The **Hungarian diet** approved the *Tripartitum* by law article 63 of **1514**. On 19 November 1514 King Vladislav II also signed it, but since it lacked the royal seal, it did not obtain the formal validity of a law. Despite this, it was used as a legal manual, recognized and applied in judicial and legislative practice and in legal study, up to the collapse of the monarchy in 1918. Some of its provisions were valid in Slovakia up to 1950. Proceeding from the serf laws of 1514 the *Tripartitum* laid down the perpetual attachment of the serfs to the soil and thus contributed to the formation of the so-called second **servitude**. /VS/

TRNAVA UNIVERSITY – Jesuit university. In **May 1635** the archbishop of Esztergom, Peter Pázmány, obtained from the ruler, Ferdinand II, a founding charter for a Catholic university in Trnava. Instruction began on **13 November 1635** in the philosophical and theological faculties. The university was administered by the **Jesuits** and Thomas Jászberényi was the first dean of the philosophical faculty. In 1637 it bestowed the degree of bachelor on 26 graduates and one year later the degree of master on 14 graduates of the philosophical faculty. In the 1667/1668 academic year, instruction began also in the law faculty that was established with the support of the archbishops Imrich Lósy and George Lippay. Lectures were given in the departments of civil, canon and Hungarian law. Twenty professors worked at the university and it had about 4900 students. With the founding of a medical faculty (1770) about one hundred years later, the structure of the university was complete. At this time a reorganization of university studies in the spirit of the enlightenment was implemented and the university became a modern higher educational institution. It was taken over by the state and non-Jesuit professors could also teach at the university. A university press, observatory, and botanical garden were established. Many important scholars were representative of its pedagogical and scientific activity: Martin Palkovič, Martin Szentiványi, Andrew Adányi, Anton Revický, Andrej Jaslinský, Ján Krstiteľ Horvát, Jakub Winterl and others. The university was also a cultural center that, together with **Košice University**, significantly contributed to the development of Slovak national awareness. In **1777** it was moved to Buda. /VČ/

TURKISH ADMINISTRATION – from the 1540s to the mid 1680s part of southern and central Slovakia was under Turkish rule. In this territory, as also in Turkish-occupied Hungary, the administrative system of the Ottoman em-

pire was introduced. In the structure of Turkish administration the highest territorial unit was the *ejálet* (*vilayet* or pashalik), the province of a viceroy. The *ejálet* was governed by a pasha or *beglerbeg* (*beylerbey*) or *beg* of *begs* and was divided into several districts or *sandjaks,* where designated *begs* represented military and administrative authority. The smallest territorial-administrative unit was the *náhije.* A certain individuality characterized the Turkish judicial administration that was closely connected with the Muslim religion. In each *ejálet* the *kádi* functioned as the judge of Islamic law (*sharia*), which being of a religious character was not subject to the authority of the pasha. For example, the *kádi* of Buda was subject to the advice of the Rumelian assembly of the *kádi* (*kádiasker*). The competence of the *kádi* extended to implementing some public law provisions and decisions (for example, supplying the army and the control of markets) or their sanctions (e.g. the assignment and collection of taxes). The function of legal expert and advisor in the judicial administration was filled by the *mufti,* who did not make judicial judgments but issued authoritative opinions in controversial cases. The main task of the Turkish occupational administration was the steady and regular collection of state and military taxes from the population of the conquered territory. Therefore they maintained very precise tax registers, *deftera.* In times of peace the representatives of the Turkish administration did not directly or significantly intervene in local self-administration or in the religion of the "unbelievers" (that is, the Christians). /VS/

UPRISING OF 1944 – SLOVAK NATIONAL UPRISING – an armed uprising against the occupation of Slovakia by the German army and the political system in Slovakia. Already in 1939 several underground groups had been created that were not satisfied with the existence of the Slovak Republic and its political system and relations. They were oriented either towards the Czechoslovak government in exile in London or the leadership of the Communist Party of Czechoslovakia in Moscow, but did not obtain great popular support. The signing of an agreement between the Czechoslovak government in London and the Soviet government on **12 December 1943** and the success of the Soviet army on the Russian front brought about a unification of the opposition political forces. This led to the signing of the **Christmas Agreement** that declared the establishment of the **Slovak National Council (1944)**. The seizure of power by the army was planned by Lieutenant Colonel Ján Golian of the General Staff. The army respected Edvard Beneš more than the Slovak National Council. The uprising was to be coordinated with the Soviet army and intended to secure its advance across the Carpathians. An emergency provision dealt with the declaration of an uprising in the event of the arrival of the German army in Slovakia, irrespective of external circumstances. The military plan for the uprising was approved at the end of June 1944 by the underground Slovak National Council and later by the Czechoslovak government in London. The economic basis for the uprising was provided by the governor of the Slovak National Bank, Imrich Karvaš, and director of the Supreme Supply Office, Peter Zaťko and Dalibor Miloš Krno from the Grain Company of Slovakia. The problem for the conspiracy, especially for some of the non-Communist resistance, was the question of the national particularity of the Slovaks and Slovak statehood. From 1943 the domestic partisan movement grew in strength, supported by Soviet escapees from German captivity. In the summer of 1944 it was directly supported by paratroopers from Soviet territory. It was practically no longer under the control of the underground Slovak National Council: in July 1944 the minister of national defense, General Ferdinand Čatloš, hatched a plan that became known to the commander of the two Slovak divisions stationed in ea-

stern Slovakia, General Augustín Malár, and a group of his officers. The possibility cannot be excluded that even Jozef Tiso knew about this plan. The memorandum of Čatloš reckoned on cooperation from the Soviet army. After the arrival of the Soviets in Cracow, the two Slovak divisions designated for the defense of the Carpathians were to open a way for them through Slovakia to the south and west. A planned state coup would install a military dictatorship in Slovakia. The result would be the rapid progress of the Soviet army and Slovakia would be spared greater military devastation. The plan of Čatloš, in contrast to the plan of the general staff, was aimed at the preservation of Slovak statehood. Čatloš established contact with the Slovak National Council. Its delegation flew to the Soviet Union on 4 August 1944 with the memorandum of Čatloš. The Soviet side was well informed about the preparations for the uprising. In the meantime, sabotage instigated by the Soviet partisan commanders increased in Slovakia. This turned the attention of the Germans towards the Slovak territory, and intervention by the German army became a real danger. The warnings of the underground Slovak National Council were not heeded. Partisans shot a group of German officers, soldiers and civilians on **28 August 1944**. For Hitler's Germany this was proof that the Slovak government was not able to maintain order in its own territory and the German army subsequently occupied Slovakia. President Tiso, who until then had vigorously rejected the entry of the German army, and the government were forced to agree to this. The uprising thus took place (as anticipated in the "worse case scenario") as a reaction to German occupation. It was proclaimed by Lieutenant Colonel Golian in Banská Bystrica on **29 August 1944** when he gave the password "begin the emigration". Golian was the only member of the Slovak National Council in Banská Bystrica on 29 August. On **31 August** the German army disarmed the two Slovak divisions in eastern Slovakia that were to have been the basis of the uprising. After a short controversy, the Slovak National Council took command of the insurgents and declared the renewal of the Czechoslovak Republic on **1 September 1944**. The foundations of a new political structure were set in place on the territory of the uprising. The **Democratic Party** was established, the Social Democrats merged with the Communist Party of Slovakia and, at the lower levels, power was assumed by revolutionary national committees. Two governments thus existed in Slovakia, since the president and government continued to function in Bratislava. The insurgents conducted two mobilizations on the territory of central Slovakia which they controlled. The main burden of the fighting fell upon the insurgent army (50 – 60,000 men). 12,000 partisans fought alongside it on the territory of the insurgency and a further 5,500 fought in the German rear – a total of 17,500 partisans, of whom 11,700 were Slovaks. The main military units that fought against the insurgents were two divisions of the German SS, units of the Home Guard and paramilitary units of the **Hlinka Guard**. The heaviest fighting took place near Strečno, in Martin – Priekopa, Telgárt and in the Rajecká dolina Valley (35,000 – 40,000 men, units of the Home Guard and the paramilitary units of the **Hlinka Guard**). Despite the tenacious resistance of the insurgents, the uprising was doomed to failure from the beginning. The Soviet Union did not offer it effective military assistance or allow their British-American allies to help it, because the territory of the uprising belonged to its operational zone. It was not the fault of the insurgents that they did not attain their original aim. Moscow had its own plans for central Europe. Most of the insurgents fought against German occupation, not the Slovak state. The uprising ended with a military defeat on **27 October 1944** and the occupation of Banská Bystrica. The military operations of the uprising claimed 20,000 casualties on the Slovak side. Both the insurgents and the counter-insurgents committed individual and mass murders of prisoners, refugees and civilians accused of favoring one side or the other. Several names have been used for the Uprising of 1944 (Slovak Uprising, the Uprising, Ban-ská Bystrica Uprising, the Slovak National Uprising). The Slovak government in Bratislava and later some of the emigrants after 1945 called it a putsch. On 23 July 1948 the communist presidium of the Slovak National Council decided to use exclusively the title Slovak National Uprising, abbreviated as the Uprising. /RL/

URBÁR – inventory of landed property and the obligations of subjects (serfs). This term originally meant a municipal land (*cadastral*) book. In the period of the early Middle Ages so-called traditional books were maintained in **cloisters.** They recorded the properties which the cloister had obtained. In Germany and Czechia land registers existed already in the 13th century. In Slovakia the first urbarial registers preserved data from the second half of the 15th century and they were regularly kept from the 16th century. Several were only brief registers, others contained detailed data about the obligations of payments, taxes in kind, obligatory labor (*robota*) and the demarcation of property. The registers were maintained for a whole estate by individual villages and sometimes also contained a list of the landlord's property, farmsteads, fish-ponds, woods and the like. Others also contain instructions for the officials of the landlords. Up to the second half of the 18th century local variations and different degrees of serf obligations were prevalent in the registers. The **Theresian urbár** brought uniformity to the registers (1772). The *urbár* lost validity with the **March laws** of 1848, concerning the abolition of **serfdom** and the urbarial patent from 1853. It is a valuable source for the investigation of demographic, social and economic developments under **feudalism**. /JB/

URBURA – mining tax. It was paid to the ruler through the mining chambers either in the form of mined ore, processed metal or money deducted at the exchange of metals in the mining chambers. It was paid only on metals designated as reserved to the king (gold, silver, copper, lead). The oldest document on *urbura* is included in the privilege for Banská Bystrica (**1255**). On **17 May 1327** Charles Robert decreed that the **nobility** and **prelates**, who mined ore on their property, were to pay one twelfth for gold and silver and one fifteenth for less valuable metals. This value was later changed. Under **Maximilian's mining order** of 1570 one tenth of the mined ore was to be collected as a tax. Later, for copper, only one seventeenth was collected. In 1782 Joseph II introduced the payment of a mining tax for iron in the amount of one twentieth of the iron produced. In 1862 the *urbura* was replaced by a revenue tax. /JB/

VASSALAGE – VASSAL see **Feudum, Feudalism, Retainers**

VESNÍK see **Magistrate (*richtár*)**

VICE-REGENCY COUNCIL – council of the Hungarian palatine or the viceroy. The institution of the viceroy in the Kingdom of Hungary was mentioned for the first time during the reign of King Sigismund of Luxemburg. The law of 1485 stated that when the king was absent from the country, the **palatine** would be his representative (viceroy or regent) because of his function. The viceroy began to function permanently in Hungary after 1526, since the Hungarian kings of the Habsburg dynasty resided outside the kingdom. At first this role was performed by the widowed Queen Mary together with the Hungarian council. In 1527 a new vice-regency council was made up of the Palatine Stephen Báthory, five of the highest dignitaries of the country and other representatives of the estates. To its jurisdiction belonged public administration, the judiciary and finance and it was institutionally superior to the **counties** as well as to the royal free and mining cities. After the death of Stephen Báthory (1530), the **king** did not fill the office of palatine and the vice-regency council disappeared for a time. It was organized again in 1535. In addition to the palatine as viceroy, a further seven, later up to 10, councilors representing the **prelates**, **magnates** and other **nobility** were nominated to it. From 1549 the vice-regency council functioned as a permanent body and decided property grants and military matters. In 1608 the offices of viceroy and palatine were formally separated. After the supression of the Conspiracy of Francis Wesselényi in **1673** the vice-regency council was abolished. Charles III (VI) renewed it by law number 97/1723, only after the **Hungarian diet** accepted the **Pragmatic Sanction** and it was named the Hungarian vice-regency council. Its seat was in Bratislava and later, from **1784** to 1848, in Buda. After 1849 a reorganized vice-regency royal office became part of the bureaucratic structure of the neo-absolutist government. It was abolished after the Austrian-Hungarian (Magyar) Compromise (1867). /VS/

VIENNA ARBITRAGE (from the Latin *arbiter* – referee, conciliating judge, mediator) – a decision of the great powers concerning the territorial trimming of Slovakia in favor of Hungary. The **Munich Agreement** of the four great powers, **29 – 30 September 1938,** was to detach from the Czecho-Slovak state and give to Germany the territory in which the preponderate majority of the inhabitants was German. It contained an appendix under which the Czechoslovak Republic would obtain an international guarantee of its borders, but only when it had also satisfied the territorial claims of Poland and Hungary. The negotiations between the Czecho-Slovak and Hungarian delegations took place in Komárno from **9 October 1938**. In accordance with a commission of the government in Prague, the Czecho-Slovak delegation was led by the president of the autonomous government of Slovakia, Jozef Tiso, and its members were the minister of justice, Ferdinand Ďurčanský, General Rudolf Viest and Ivan Krno, while I. Parkányi represented sub-Carpathian Russia. Charles de Kánya, the minister of foreign affairs, and Paul Teleki led the Hungarian delegation. The Hungarian government viewed the revision of the borders as an "expiation of the injustice" inflicted upon Hungary by the peace treaty of Trianon of **4 June 1920**. It demanded that **Czecho-Slovakia** withdraw from a territory in southern Slovakia with an area of 12,124 km^2 and a population of 1,360 000 (according to a census of 1930, 549,376 people of Magyar and 431,545 of Slovak nationality lived there). This was based on older statistics from 1910, which reflected the period of the most severe **Magyarization**. Since the participating parties could not reach agreement, the arbiters, Germany and Italy, had the last word. Their ministers of foreign affairs, Joachim von Ribbentrop and Galeazzo Ciano, decided the modifications of the borders between the **Czechoslovak Republic** and Hungary on **2 November 1938** at the Belvedere palace in Vienna. Slovakia had to cede 10,390 km^2 of its territory, with 859,643 inhabitants to Hungary. According to the census of of 1930, this included 503,980 people of Magyar and 272,145 of Slovak and Czech nationality. Of the 776 communities ceded, 175 had a Slovak majority. Slovakia lost Košice, Rožňava, Rimavská Sobota, Lučenec, Levice, Komárno, Nové Zámky, Štúrovo and Dunajská Streda. This territory was occupied by Hungary between 5 and 10 November 1938. The decision of the arbitrage was a further attempt to resolve the burning question of national minorities in central Europe by changing state borders. But this only contributed to a deterioration in the relationships between the nations of this region. After the annexation of southern Slovakia to Hungary, the so-called second Vienna arbitrage followed on 30 August 1940, in which Hungary obtained Transylvania from Romania. Both Vienna arbitrages were declared invalid by the terms of the truce between Hungary and the allies of January 1945. This decision was confirmed by the peace treaty with Hungary concluded on 10 February 1947 at the peace conference in Paris. /RL/

VIENNA CONGRESS see **Congress of Vienna**

VIENNA SLOVAK MEMORANDUM – a program document of the Slovak national movement. It made more precise and supplemented the **Memorandum of the Slovak Nation**. After the dissolution of the **Hungarian diet** and the proclamation of the **provisional government**, Slovak politicians turned directly to Francis Joseph I as king of Hungary with their demands. About 50 leading figures prepared the document on 3 December 1861, which they presented to the ruler on **12 December 1861**. Štefan Moyzes led the eight-member delegation. The Vienna Memorandum was made up of two documents, a revision of the Memorandum of the Slovak Nation and a draft for a charter of privilege for the establishment and organization of a Slovak province (*Slovenské okolie*). It precisely delimited the authority and organs of the province and the authority of the king and the Hungarian officials. The province would be made up of five purely Slovak counties (*župy*), and the nine counties in which Slovaks and Magyars lived would be divided by a special commission. The province would be divided into 16 districts and each would be led by a district chief named by the ruler. The supreme organ of the self-government of the province would be a provincial diet, while a standing committee would exercise executive power. Its center was to be Banská Bystrica. Alongside educational, cultural and judicial questions, the autonomous Slovakia would have authority also in some economic and taxation matters. Saints Cyril and Methodius would be named the patrons of the province and its coat-of-arms would be a two-headed eagle with a white cross on three blue peaks. The ruler turned the memorandum over to the Hungarian court chancellery and the **vice-regency council**. Under pressure from the Magyar opposition, they rejected it and promised to excerpt from it only suggestions for the preparation of a **Nationality Law**. /DŠ/

VOJVODA see **Duke**

WALACHIAN COLONIZATION see **Walachian law**, **Colonization**

WALACHIAN LAW – a collection of legal norms and customs regulating the Walachian population. It developed as part of the Walachian colonization at the beginning of the 14th century, when the first groups of the Walachian-Ruthenian population came to Slovakia. This law is considered substantially emphyteutic. Unlike the **German Law**, however, only the representatives of the Walachian self-administration were allowed to deal with the land freely. The Walachians elected, from among the leaders of the Walachian community, the Walachian duke, who had to be confirmed in this function by the landlord. The Walachian duke represented the Walachians before the authorities, presided at the Walachian court, from which he collected a part of the fines, gathered the prescribed payments and turned them over to the estate. From the landlord he obtained in hereditary tenure the land designated for the grazing of sheep or for cultivation. When the Walachians arrived in the territory of Slovakia, their law had already been influenced by norms and customs that had spread among them in the Balkans (Walachian, Moldavian), as well as in the Ukraine and southeastern Poland, which had been affected by the Walachian colonization. In the 16th and 17th centuries Slovaks and other elements of the domestic population, who fled from serf obligations, were added to the original Walachian ethnic group that also included Ruthenians. This was because the Walachians had greater legal freedom. The best-known and most complete Walachian privileges are the privileges of the Orava and Liptov Walachians issued by Matthias Corvinus in 1474. The Walachians were generally exempted from all obligations for six to twenty years. Then they turned over to the landlord a twentieth (exceptionally a fiftieth) part of their cattle, a tenth of the swine and bees, horse harnesses, Walachian cheese, sheepskin coats, martin pelts and the like. They guarded the roads, the country barricades and forests and performed military service. They did not pay tax to the state or the church **tenth** because most were Orthodox Christians. They were also exempted from compulsory labor (*robota*). The last settlements with the Walachian law were established at the beginning

of the 17th century, when the landlords had already significantly limited their privileges. By the reforms of Maria Theresa in 1773 the Walachians lost their privileged position and fell to the level of the other serfs. They preserved their individual customs and way of life up to the 19th century. /JB/

WALDENSIANS – medieval sect. Its founder was the Lyon merchant Peter Waldo (Valdes), who, in the second half of the 12th century, relinquished all of his property and began to call for a return to the original teachings of the church. His followers were governed by the New Testament and repudiated the organizational structure of the church and church dignitaries and adhered to poverty. The Third Lateran Council of 1179 condemned their teachings and the Waldensians were excommunicated from the church. The **inquisition** and the new **religious orders** of the **Dominicans** and **Franciscans** proceeded against them severely, as well as against other sects (for example, the Albigensians). From the end of the 12th century, Waldensian views spread into southern France (Burgundy, Provence) and northern Italy (Lombardy) and, in later centuries, also into Germany, Austria and Czechia. In Czechia and Austria the Waldensians influenced the beginnings of Hussitism at the end of the 14th century. At the beginning of the 15th century they created their best-known community in Slovakia in Trnava. /JB/

WAREHOUSING RIGHT – the obligation of merchants to store and, for the appointed term, to sell their goods in a city that had this right. It developed from the **thirtieth** collected at the borders of the country. Cities obtained the warehousing right on the basis of royal **privileges**, which in some cases were only a confirmation of older customs. Its goal was to limit competition of foreign merchants and to exclude them from the inland retail sale since, by the warehousing right, some of the privileged cities prescribed the sale of goods only in wholesale, and foreign merchants were allowed to continue on the way to the interior of the country only after a certain period of time. The inhabitants of the towns with the warehousing right were freed from this obligation in other cities that had this right. Foreign merchants or people from other cities, so that they would not be encumbered by the provisions of the warehousing right, bought houses in these cities by means of which they obtained the rights of townsmen and indeed became full-fledged townsmen. The provisions of the warehousing right forbade the native townspeople to form companies with foreigners in order to transport foreign goods under their own name and thus circumvent this right. The oldest warehousing rights in Hungary was obtained by Buda (1244), Győr (1271), Podolínec (1292) and in the 1320s Levoča and Košice (1347). In 1402 King Sigismund bestowed the warehousing right upon Sopron, Bratislava, Trnava, Trenčín and Bardejov and renewed it for Levoča. Later Levoča fought with Kežmarok over the warehousing right that the latter had usurped in 1435. The warehousing right related either to all goods or only to selected types. /JB/

WASHINGTON DECLARATION – political document of the Czecho-Slovak foreign resistance. Tomáš Garrigue Masaryk drafted it on 13 – 16 October 1918 in Washington and, in the name of the newly created provisional Czecho-Slovak government, personally presented it to the American government on 17 October. On 18 October it was published in the press. The declaration reacted to concerns that the United States would open peace negotiations with Austria-Hungary and support its preservation. This could have thwarted efforts for the creation of an independent Czecho-Slovak state. It declared the independence of Czecho-Slovakia and the main principles of its organization and foreign policy were conceived in the spirit of the American democratic tradition. The new state would be a republic with a democratic constitution. It would incorporate into its law basic liberal principles such as universal suffrage, freedom of conscience, religion, culture, speech, the press, and assembly, the right of petition, the replacement of a standing army by a militia, the abolition of noble titles and the separation of church and state, and minorities would ha-

ve the same rights as the majority nation in the state. The document referred to a Czechoslovak nation and did not recognize the national particularity of the Slovaks. At the very same time, on 18 October, and unconnected with the declaration, in a note to Austria-Hungary the American government emphasized that it recognized the **Czechoslovak National Council** as a provisional government and stated that the nations of the monarchy had the right to decide their own future freely. /DŠ/

WHITE LEGION – the largest organized and individual form of the anti-communist struggle in Slovakia from 1948 to 1955. After the **Communist state coup** in 1948, Anton Tunega, a student at the Slovak Technical University, had the idea of creating a basis for consolidating the anti-communist resistance regardless of divergent views. The name White Legion was provided by Jozef Vicen who emigrated in 1945 and lived abroad. Its goal was to resist by non-violent means the communist dictatorship and its violent manifestations and propaganda. It defined itself as "a self-help movement of the population to defend human rights against communist state terror". Because of the closed, impermeable borders and the climate of fear and uncertainty, the movement spread with great difficulty. With the aid of provocateurs, state security captured Albert Púčik, Eduard Tesár and Anton Tunega. A total of more than 70 persons were arrested. The prosecutor Anton Rašla laid charges against 63 persons: 12 of the accused were freed, the rest received sentences from six months to life. After an appeal to the supreme court in Prague, the life sentences of Albert Púčik, Eduard Tesár and Anton Tunega were changed to the death sentence on **11 July 1949**. On 20 February 1951 they were executed in Bratislava. However, the White Legion was not completely liquidated. From April 1950 until 1955 the radio station White Legion transmitted from Austria. If we do not take into account the Slovak station Radio Barcelona that transmitted from northern Italy in 1947 (the station Radio Free Europe began transmissions only in 1951), this was the very first radio station broadcasting to the countries of the so-called eastern block. The transmitter of the White Legion was constructed by Dezider Murgaš (a relative of the inventor Jozef Murgaš). This station ideologically and organizationally shaped the anti-communist resistance in Slovakia. Each person who "in whatever way possible thwarted actions of communists directed against fundamental human and citizen rights" was considered a member of the White Legion. The name White Legion was not allowed to appear in newspapers, so that it would not be indirectly promoted. With the help of provocateurs, state security created counterfeit groups of this organization in order to discredit the whole movement and stamp it as a terrorist group. /RL/

WINTER CAMPAIGN – the second Slovak armed insurrection during the **revolution of 1848/1849.** With the **September Uprising** the civil war in Hungary intensified. Because Vienna promised to assure the equality of nations, Slovak politicians joined its side. This made a new armed uprising easier. The Winter Campaign was conducted by two volunteer corps. They fought as special units within the imperial army. The larger and more important corps was formed in Silesian Těšín and led by Bedřich Bloudek. From the end of 1848 it helped imperial troops expel the Magyar army of General Arthur Görgey and the volunteers of Ľudovít Beniczky from Slovakia. After the occupation of northern and central Slovakia, it was active in eastern Slovakia until April 1849. The staff of the corps, which had about 2,000 volunteers, was based for the longest time in Prešov. A smaller unit with a thousand men was formed in the Myjava area. It was initially led by Bernard Janeček and, from March 1849, by Ján Francisci. It was poorly supplied and armed, since the imperial general, Baltazár Šimunič, tolerated it only out of necessity. It performed auxiliary, sentry, supply and garrison duty at the sieges of Lepoldov and Komárno. During the offensive of the Magyar army at the **end of March 1849**, both corps retreated with the imperial units. The first moved through the Váh River valley to Moravia, the second to Bratislava. The volunteers were the only official representatives of Slovak national ambitions and therefore political figures (Ľudovít Štúr, Jozef Miloslav Hurban, Michal Miloslav Hodža, Štefan Marko Daxner and others) were active in the corps and agitated for the detachment of Slovakia from Hungary. This program was presented to Emperor Francis Joseph as the **March Petition**. At the same time, they removed the officials of the Kossuth administration and founded national councils (**13 January 1849**). The Winter Campaign strengthened the self-awareness of the Slovak politicians and the interest of the broader public in their constitutional program. Some of its participants also joined the **Summer Campaign.** /DS/

YEOMEN (*zemania*) – in the broadest sense of the word all nobles except the **magnates**, that is the middle, lower and minor **nobility**. The yeomen developed from a part of the free servant population, that is, from the *jobaggi* and the royal *servienti*, from the petty free holders of landed property that the **king** bestowed upon them in particular for military service. Other classes of the serf, country and city population also became yeomen for service of various sorts. From the 13th century, when the yeomanry was specified as a noble estate, it was possible to obtain membership in this privileged stratum exclusively by being ennobled, that is, being elevated to the noble estate by the king. The basic privileges and rights of this estate emanated especially from the provisions of the **Golden Bull** of Andrew II of **1222** and the decree of King Louis I of **1351** and were anchored in the *Tripartitum* (1514). These privileges were namely that the nobility could not be imprisoned without the verdict of a court (except where a noble committed murder, arson, robbery and was apprehended in the act); the nobility was judicially subject only to the king; it was exempt from taxation and had the right of armed resistance against the king (only to 1687). The principle of the equality and unity of the nobility declared by the *Tripartitum* did not correspond, however, with reality, for the yeomen could not be compared with the magnates (with whom they formally made up a common estate until **1608**) as regards property, influence and even participation in power, although they had the right to vote. The yeomanry was employed in the **county** (*stolica*) administration as lower officials of the state administration and sometimes served as **retainers** of the magnates. They were the most numerous and most differentiated estate and comprised the middle and lower nobility as well as the minor or even non-propertied nobility, poorer than landed **peasants** or **serfs**. The lowest rank of the yeoman class were the *curialists* (**curial villages**), *armalists* and *predialists*. The majority of Slovak counties were characterized by a high concentration of yeomen. /VS/

YEOMEN COLONIZATION see **Colonization**

YOUNG SLOVAKS (mladoslováci) see **Štúr's group**

ŽILINA AGREEMENT – the document in which, on the initiative of **Hlinka's Slovak People's Party**, other political parties also supported the **autonomy of Slovakia** within the **Czechoslovak Republic**. It was prepared after the **Munich Agreement** of 29 – 30 September 1939 in the context of a weakened centralist state and the threat of the loss of southern Slovakia to Hungary. The agreement was accepted on **6 October 1938** after the declaration of the **Žilina Manifesto**. Representatives of the second strongest political party, the **Agrarian Party**, made comments on its draft. They demanded that Jozef Tiso, the vice-chairman and deputy of Hlinka's Slovak People's Party, be entrusted with the formation of a government after agreement with other political parties and that the autonomy of Slovakia be ac-

cepted as the definitive solution. Jozef Tiso accepted the proposal. The Agrarians secured two ministrial portfolios in the first government of autonomous Slovakia. With the Žilina Agreement, the representatives of the political parties accepted the proposal of Hlinka's Slovak People's Party concerning the promulgation of a constitutional law on the autonomy of Slovakia, as presented in the Prague parliament and published in the newspaper *Slovák* on **5 June 1938**. The government and executive power in Slovakia was to be placed immediately into the hands of the autonomous Slovak government. Pavol Teplanský, Ján Ursíny, Ján S. Vančo, Ján Petrovič, Ján Lichner, Karol Rybárik, Ondrej Devečka, Kornel Stodola, Adolf Šelmec, Jozef Styk and Milan Polák signed the agreement for the Agrarians, Ján Liška for the Tradesmen Party, Emil Boleslav Lukáč for the Czechoslovak National Socialist Party, Ján Ivák for the Fascist Party, Miloš Vančo and Ján Paulíny-Tóth for the **Slovak National Party** and Jozef Tiso, Karol Sidor, Jozef Buday, Jozef Sivák, Martin Sokol and Karol Mederly for Hlinka's Slovak People's Party. Parties with Marxist ideology, the Communist Party of Czechoslovakia and the social democrats were excluded from the Žilina agreement. /RL/

ŽILINA CITY BOOK – the oldest preserved city book in Slovakia and, at the same time, the oldest legal monument in the native official language (Slovakized Czech). It is made up of three parts. Its basis is a transcription of the German text of the Magdeburg or **German Law** that was copied in 1378 by the Žilina official Mikuláš of Litovel (de Lutovia), not far from Olomouc (and not Mikuláš of Lukovské near Zvolen, as was presumed up to 1985). This law, also called the *Sachsenspiegel* (Saxon Mirror), was used in Krupina, which was for Žilina an appellate city, that is, a higher legal institution. Alongside the introduction and register of titles, it contains exactly 480 provisions legally regulating a broad range of relations in daily life. A copy of a 23-article German text of the city and mining law of the Transylvanian city of Rudnava (also from 1378) is likewise considered part of the first section. From the viewpoint of the Slovak language, the most important section is the second part of the book, which is a translation of the Magdeburg law into Slovakized Czech. The Žilina *fojt,* Václav Pangrác and scribe Václav of Kroměříž prepared the bulk of the translation of **1473**, which in some places is a word for word translation, in other places a free and even, occasionally, incomprehensible or incomplete paraphrase. It contains 363 legal regulations. The third part was made up of 117 different civil law notations and charters from 1380 to 1524 (including two cases from 1561). The notations were initially written in Latin and German, but from 1451 almost exclusively in Slovakized Czech (in total 70). They primarily concern property issues of Žilina citizens, the verification of debts, inheritance, the pawning of property, testaments and the transfer of houses. There are also records of direct legal proceedings, the evidence for the populations of the small towns and villages belonging to the system of the Žilina law and there is even a record of the immoral behavior of a certain inhabitant of Žilina. The Slovakized notations are evidence for the use of the native language in oral public declarations and in the deliberations of the city council in the 15th century. An analogous legal custom was prevalent in the 14th century and reflected the situation when these legal proceedings were conducted only orally, and in Slovak, and the notations were only complementary to oral declarations. The Slovakisms of the Žilina notations are evidence for the supra-dialect use of Slovak in official communications and are considered the beginning of cultured Slovak. /VS/

ŽILINA MANIFESTO – a document about the self-determination of the Slovak nation. In the period of the first **Czechoslovak Republic** the official ruling circles considered the Slovaks part of a single Czechoslovak nation (Czechoslovakism) and therefore it was then practically impossible to achieve the **autonomy of Slovakia**. The government expressed a willingness to consent to autonomy only after the signing of the **Munich Agreement**. In Žilina, on 5 October 1938, the presidium of

Hlinka's Slovak People's Party prepared a draft of the Manifesto of the Slovak Nation, which was unanimously approved by its executive committee on **6 October 1938**. According to the manifesto, the Slovaks, as a distinct nation, asserted their right to self-determination and claimed an international guarantee for the indivisibility of their national unity and the territory they occupied. They expressed the will to determine freely and fully their own future in fraternal co-existence with all surrounding nations, and to contribute in a Christian spirit to the settlement of relations in central Europe. The manifesto demanded that, in Slovakia, the Slovaks immediately assume executive and ruling power. It supported the struggle against the "Marxist-Jewish ideology of subversion and violence", demanded a rapid demobilization, the peaceful resolution of the problems in central Europe, the international protection of the Slovak minority abroad and protested against deciding the borders of Slovakia without plenipotentiary representatives of the Slovak nation. Representatives of other political parties, including the **Agrarian Party**, the **Slovak National Party**, the Tradesmen, Fascist and National Socialist parties expressed agreement with the memorandum. Since the Žilina Manifesto positioned itself against Marxists ideology, the Communist Party of Czechoslovakia and the Social Democratic Party were not invited to the discussions (**Žilina Agreement**). /RL/

ŽILINA SYNOD – the assembly that organized the Evangelical Church. It was called by the Palatine George Thurzo in the spirit of the resolution of the Bratislava **diet** and took place on **28 – 30 March 1610** in Žilina. Representatives from Evangelical congregations from ten Cisdanubian counties (central and western Slovakia) participated in it. They established an independent ecclesiastical organization for the Evangelicals, who thus freed themselves from the authority of the Catholic hierarchy. Three superintendencies were established: 1. Bytča for Liptov, Trenčín and Orava counties (Superintendent Eliáš Láni); 2. Brezno for Turiec, Novohrad, Zvolen and

Hont counties (Superintendent Samuel Melík); 3. Bojnice for Tekov, Nitra and Bratislava counties (Superintendent Izák Abrahamides). For the German and Hungarian population of the Evangelical confession, three inspectors were elected (2 for the Germans, 1 for the Magyars). At the synod of **22 January 1614** in Spišské Podhradie the organization for the Evangelicals in eastern Slovakia was put in place by establishing the Spiš-Šariš superintendency (Superintendent Štefan Xylander) and a superintendency for the five royal free cities (Košice, Prešov, Levoča, Bardejov, Sabinov) with Superintendent Peter Zabler. The ecclesiastical relations of the Evangelicals in Gemer were regulated by the palatine through a special charter. /VČ/

ŽUPA (COUNTY-DISTRICT) – administrative-territorial unit of state administration in the Kingdom of Hungary in 1849 – 1918 and in Slovakia in 1918 – 1828 and 1940 – 1945. In Hungary the counties replaced a system of noble seats (*stolice*, **counties**). Their supreme organ was the county (*župný, municipálny*) committee. Half of their members were made up of the so-called *virilists* (the citizens paying the highest taxes), the other half was comprised of elected members (**right to vote in Hun-**

gary). After 1918 the counties were transferred to the administrative system of the newly developed state, the Czechoslovak Republic. From 1 January 1923 Slovakia was made up of six counties (unofficially also called large counties, *veľžupy*): Bratislava, Nitra, Považská, Zvolen, Podtatranská and Košice. The county was headed by a state official, the county administrator (*župan*). The county representative organ and county committee exercised limited self-government. The work of the administrator and the other units of the county was performed by a county office. These counties were abolished on 1 July 1928 when they were replaced by a **regional system**. Six counties were again established in 1939: Bratislava, Nitra, Trenčín, Tatra, Pohronie and Šariš-Zemplín. However, their character was different from those existing in 1923 – 1928. Each was administered by an administrator named by the government and an office subordinated to him. Certain self-government tasks in the communal area were carried out by a county committee. The county administration of the first **Slovak Republic** was abolished after the renewal of the Czechoslovak Republic in 1945 and replaced by regions (*kraje*). /VS/

THE ARPÁD DYNASTY

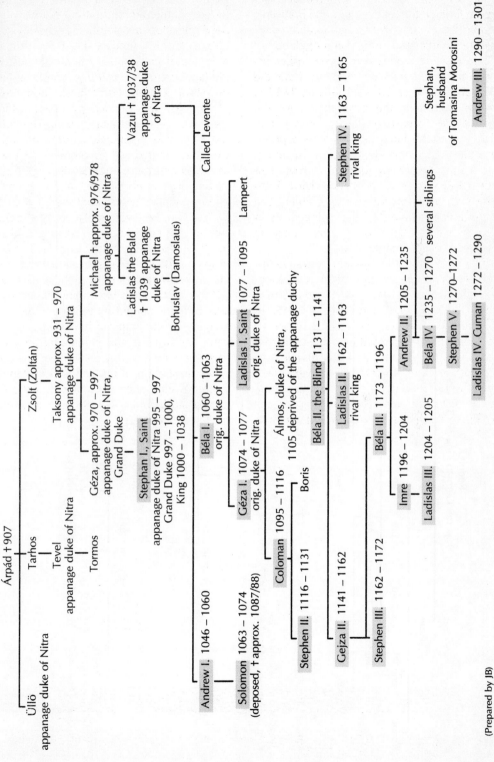

Árpád † 907

Üllő
appanage duke of Nitra

Tarhos

Tevel
appanage duke of Nitra

Zsolt (Zoltán)

Taksony approx. 931 – 970
appanage duke of Nitra

Tormos

Géza, approx. 970 – 997
appanage duke of Nitra,
Grand Duke

Michael † approx. 976/978
appanage duke of Nitra

Vazul † 1037/38
appanage duke
of Nitra

Stephan I., Saint
appanage duke of Nitra 995 – 997
Grand Duke 997 – 1000,
King 1000 – 1038

Ladislas the Bald
† 1039 appanage
duke of Nitra

Bohuslav (Damoslaus)

Called Levente

Andrew I. 1046 – 1060

Béla I. 1060 – 1063
orig. duke of Nitra

Lampert

Solomon 1063 – 1074
(deposed, † approx. 1087/88)

Géza I. 1074 – 1077
orig. duke of Nitra

Ladislas I. Saint 1077 – 1095
orig. duke of Nitra

Coloman 1095 – 1116

Álmos, duke of Nitra,
1105 deprived of the appanage duchy

Stephen II. 1116 – 1131

Boris

Béla II. the Blind 1131 – 1141

Gejza II. 1141 –1162

Ladislas II. 1162 – 1163
rival king

Stephen IV. 1163 – 1165
rival king

Stephen III. 1162 –1172

Béla III. 1173 – 1196

Imre 1196 – 1204

Andrew II. 1205 – 1235

Stephan,
husband
of Tomasina Morosini

Ladislas III. 1204 – 1205

Béla IV. 1235 – 1270   several siblings

Stephen V. 1270–1272

Andrew III. 1290 – 1301

Ladislas IV. Cuman 1272 – 1290

(Prepared by JB)

HABSBURG DYNASTY

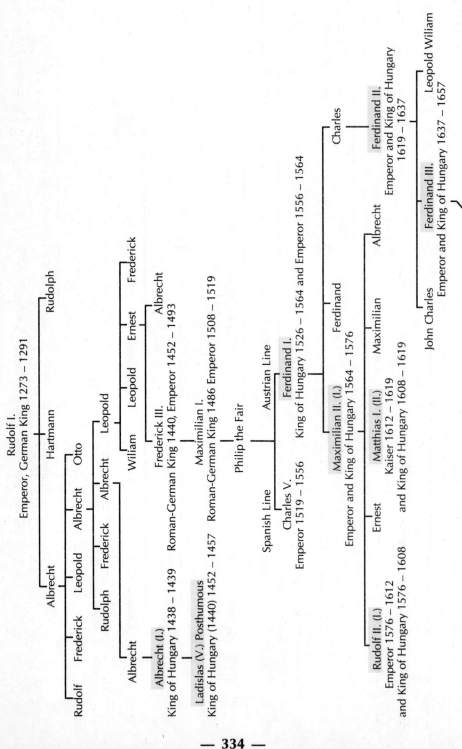

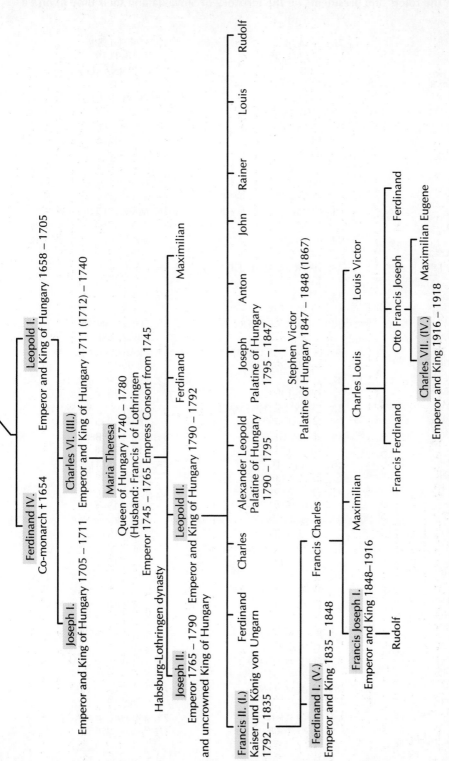

The family tree depicts the Habsburg Dynasty from the viewpoint of the Hungarian royal succession, including:

- **Leopold I.** Emperor and King of Hungary 1658 – 1705
- **Ferdinand IV.** Co-monarch † 1654
- **Joseph I.** Emperor and King of Hungary 1705 – 1711
- **Charles VI. (III.)** Emperor and King of Hungary 1711 (1712) – 1740
- **Maria Theresa** Queen of Hungary 1740 – 1780 (Husband: Francis I of Lothringen) Emperor 1745 – 1765 Empress Consort from 1745
- Habsburg-Lothringen dynasty
- **Joseph II.** Emperor 1765 – 1790 Emperor and King of Hungary and uncrowned King of Hungary
- **Leopold II.** Emperor and King of Hungary 1790 – 1792
- Ferdinand
- Maximilian
- Charles
- Alexander Leopold Palatine of Hungary 1790 – 1795
- Joseph Palatine of Hungary 1795 – 1847
- Anton
- John
- Rainer
- Louis
- Rudolf
- **Francis II. (I.)** Kaiser und König von Ungarn 1792 – 1835
- Ferdinand
- Francis Charles
- Stephen Victor Palatine of Hungary 1847 – 1848 (1867)
- **Ferdinand I. (V.)** Emperor and King 1835 – 1848
- Maximilian
- Charles Louis
- Louis Victor
- Rudolf
- **Francis Joseph I.** Emperor and King 1848–1916
- Francis Ferdinand
- Otto Francis Joseph
- Ferdinand
- Maximilian Eugene
- **Charles VII. (IV.)** Emperor and King 1916 – 1918

Included in the table are all male descendants in the line of succession or descendents essential from the viewpoint of the throne of Hungary. The number following the name refers to the imperial title while the number in brackets refers to the Hungarian royal title. The dates indicate the actual years of rule. (Prepared by VS)

List of the rulers and presidents on the territory of Slovakia and their time in office

1. SAMO
623/4–658/9

2. PRIBINA
beginning of 9th century – 833

3. MOJMÍR I
833–846

4. RASTISLAV
846–870

5. SVÄTOPLUK
870–871
871–894

6. SLAVOMÍR
871

7. MOJMÍR II
894–907

8. SVÄTOPLUK II
end of 9th cent. – beg. of 10th century

9. GÉZA
940–997

10. STEPHEN I
997–1038

11. PETER
1038–1041
1044–1046

12. SAMUEL ABA
1041–1044

13. ANDREW I
1046–1060

14. BÉLA I
1060–1063

15. SOLOMON
1063–1074

16. GÉZA I
1074–1077

17. LADISLAS I
1077–1095

18. COLOMAN
1095–1116

19. STEPHEN II
1116–1131

20. BÉLA II THE BLIND
1131–1141

21. GÉZA II
1141–1162

22. STEPHEN III
1162–1172

23. LADISLAS II
1162–1163 rival king

24. STEPHEN IV
1163–1165 rival king

25. BÉLA III
1173–1196

26. IMRE
1196–1204

27. LADISLAS III
1204–1205

28. ANDREW II
1205–1235

29. BÉLA IV
1235–1270

30. STEPHEN V
1270–1272

31. LADISLAS IV CUMAN
1272–1290

32. ANDREW III
1290–1301

33. WENCESLAS (LADISLAS)
1301–1305

34. OTTO
1305–1307

35. CHARLES ROBERT
1308–1342

36. LOUIS THE GREAT
1342–1382

37. MARIA
1382–1395

38. CHARLES THE SMALL
1385–1386

39. SIGISMUND
1387–1437

40. ALBRECHT
1438–1439

41. VLADISLAV I
1440–1444

42. LADISLAV V
1453–1457

43. MATTHIAS CORVINUS
1458–1490

44. VLADISLAV II
1490–1516

45. LOUIS II
1516–1526

46. JOHN ZÁPOLYA
1526–1540

47. FERDINAND I
1527–1564

48. MAXIMILIAN I
1564–1576

49. RUDOLF I
1576–1608

50. MATTHIAS II
1608–1619

51. FERDINAND II
1619–1637

52. FERDINAND III
1637–1657

53. LEOPOLD I
1657–1705

54. JOSEPH I
1705–1711

55. CHARLES III
1711–1740

56. MARIA THERESA
1740–1780

57. JOSEPH II
1780–1790

58. LEOPOLD II
1790–1792

59. FRANCIS I
1792–1835

60. FERDINAND V
1835–1848

61. FRANCIS JOSEPH I
1848–1916

62. CHARLES IV
1916–1918

63. TOMÁŠ G. MASARYK
1918–1935

64. EDVARD BENEŠ
1935–1938

65. EMIL HÁCHA
1938–1939

66. JOZEF TISO
1939–1945
EDVARD BENEŠ
1945–1948

67. KLEMENT GOTTWALD
1948–1953

68. ANTONÍN ZÁPOTOCKÝ
1953–1957

69. ANTONÍN NOVOTNÝ
1957–1968

70. LUDVÍK SVOBODA
1968–1975

71. GUSTÁV HUSÁK
1975–1989

72. VÁCLAV HAVEL
1989–1992

73. MICHAL KOVÁČ
1993–1998

A magyarok krónikája Glatz, F. (ed) Officina Nova 1995. [B. m. v. 1995]

Bartl, J. – Kamenický, M. – Valachovič, P.: Dejepis pre 1. ročník gymnázií. Bratislava 2000.

Benčík, A. – Domaňský, J. – Hájek, J. – Kural, V. – Mencl, V.: Osem mesiacov pražskej jari. Martin 1990.

Beneš, E.: Mnichovské dny. Paměti. Praha 1968.

Beneš, E.: Od Mnichova k nové válce a k novému vítězství. Paměti. Praha 1948.

Bokes, F.: Dejiny Slovákov a Slovenska od najstarších čias až po prítomnosť. Bratislava 1946.

Braxátor, F.: Slovenský exil 68. Bratislava 1992.

Brock, P.: The Slovan National Awakening. University of Toronto Press, Toronto 1976.

Burák, P. – Miškufová H. a kol.: Slovensko vo vede a svet na Slovensku. Košice 1993.

Butvin, J.: Slovenské národnozjednocovacie hnutie (1780 – 1848). Bratislava 1965.

Čarnogurský, P.: 14. marec 1939. Bratislava 1992.

Československé dějiny v datech. Praha 1986.

Čičaj, V.: Knižná kultúra na strednom Slovensku v 16. – 18. storočí. Bratislava 1985.

Dangl, V. – Kopčan, V.: Vojenské dejiny Slovenska II. 1526 – 1711. Bratislava 1995.

Dangl, V. – Segeš, V.: Vojenské dejiny Slovenska III. 1711 – 1914. Bratislava 1996.

Daniel, D. P.: The Reformation and Eastern Slovakia. *Human Affairs* 1, no. 2 (1991), pp 17 – 86.

Dejiny Slovenska I. Od najstarších čias do roku 1848. Eds.: Ľ. Holotík a J. Tibenský. Bratislava 1961.

Dejiny Slovenska I. (do roku 1526). Ed.: R. Marsina. Bratislava 1986.

Dejiny slovenského národného povstania 1944 I – V. Bratislava 1984.

Dejiny Spoločnosti Ježišovej na Slovensku. 1561 – 1988. Cambridge 1990.

Dejiny štátu a práva 2. zv. Ed.: L. Bianchi. Bratislava 1973.

Dejiny Trnavy. Trnava 1989.

Dokumenty k slovenskému národnému hnutiu v rokoch 1848 – 1914. I. zv. Ed.: F. Bokes, Bratislava 1962.

Dvorník, F.: The Making of central and Eastern Europe. Academic International Press, Gulf Breeze, FL, 1974.

Ďurica, M. S.: Dejiny Slovenska a Slovákov. Bratislava 1996.

Encyklopédia Slovenska I. – VI. Bratislava 1977 – 1982.

Golan, G.: The Czechoslovak Reform Movement, Communism in Crisis 1962 – 1968. Cambridge University Press, Cambridge 1971.

Historická revue, 1990 – 1996.

Hodza, M.: Federation in Central Europe, Jarrolds Publishers, London 1942.

Horváth, P.: Poddaný ľud na Slovensku v prvej polovici XVIII. storočia. Bratislava 1963.

Horváth, P. – Kopčan, V.: Turci na Slovensku. Bratislava 1971.

Hronský, M.: Slovensko pri zrode Československa. Bratislava 1987.

Hrubý, P.: Fools and Heroes, The Changing Role of Communist Intellectuals in Czechoslovakia. Pergamon Press, Oxford 1980.

Hrušovský, F.: Slovenské dejiny. Turčiansky Sv. Martin 1939.

Hučko, J. a kol.: Bratislava a počiatky slovenského národného obrodenia. Dokumenty. Bratislava 1992.

Jablonický, J.: Povstanie bez legiend. Bratislava 1990.

Jelinek, A.: The Lust for Power: Nationalism, Slovakia and the Communists 1918 – 1948. East European Monographs, Boulder, Co 1976.

Johnson, O. V.: Slovakia 1918 – 1938. Education and the Making of a Nation. Columbia University Press, New York 1985.

K počiatkom slovenského národného obrodenia. Ed.: J. Tibenský. Bratislava 1964.

Kaplan, K.: Nekrvavá revoluce. Praha 1993.

Kaplan, K.: Stát a církev v Československu 1948 – 1953. Brno 1993.

Kamenec, I.: Po stopách tragédie. Bratislava 1991.

Kirschbaum, S. J.: A History of Slovakia: The Struggle for Survival. St. Martin's Griffen, New York 1995.

Klein, B. – Ruttkay, A. – Marsina, R.: Vojenské dejiny Slovenska I. Do 1526. Bratislava 1993.

Kopčan, V.: Turecké nebezpečenstvo a Slovensko. Bratislava 1986.

Kopčan, V. – Krajčovičová, K.: Slovensko v tieni polmesiaca. Martin 1983.

Korec, J. Ch.: Cirkev v dejinách Slovenska. Bratislava 1994.

Kowalská, E.: Štátne ľudové školstvo na Slovensku na prelome 18. a 19. stor. Bratislava 1987.

Kružliak, I. – Okáľ, J.: Svedectvo jednej generácie. Cambridge-Ontario 1990.

Kubín, Ľ. – Velšic, M. – Daňo, R. – Juhás, B. – Balko, D. – Stupňan, I.: Dva roky politickej slobody. Bratislava 1992.

Kučera, M. – Kostický, B.: Slovensko v obrazoch. *História*. Bratislava 1990.

Kvačala, J.: Dejiny reformácie na Slovenku. 1517 – 1711. Liptovský Sv. Mikuláš 1935.

Letz, J.: Historické udalosti Slovenska v rokoch 1938 – 1950. Bratislava (samizdat) 1987.

Letz, R.: Slovensko v rokoch 1945 – 1948. Bratislava 1994.

Lipscher L.: Židia v Slovenskom štáte (1939 – 1945). Bratislava 1992.

Lukes, I.: Czechoslovakia between Stalin and Hitler: The Diplomacy of Edvard Benes in the 1930s., Oxford University Press, New York 1996.

Macartney, C. A.: The Habsburg Empire 1790 – 1918. Weidenfeld and Nicolson, London 1969.

Magyarország történeti kronológiája. I. – III. zv. Ed.: K. Benda. Budapest 1983, 1986, 1989.

Majtán, M.: Názvy obcí na Slovensku za ostatných dvesto rokov. Bratislava 1972.

Malá vojna. Zost. L. Deák. Bratislava 1983.

Malý, K. – Sivák, F.: Dejiny štátu a práva v Česko-Slovensku do roku 1918. Bratislava 1992.

Mamatey, S. – Luza, R. eds.: A History of the Czechoslovak Republic, 1918 – 1949. Princeton University Press, Princeton 1973.

Marsina, R. – Čičaj, V. – Kováč, D. – Lipták, Ľ.: Slovenské dejiny. Martin 1992.

Matej Bel. Doba. Život. Dielo. Bratislava 1987.

McGuigan D. G.: Die Habsburger, Aufstieg und Fall einer europäischen Dynastie. Wien 1995.

Medrický, G.: Minister spomína. Bratislava 1993.

Mésároš, J. a kol.: Dejiny Slovenska II. Bratislava 1968.

Minárik, J. a kol.: Dejiny staršej slovenskej literatúry. Bratislava 1964.

Minárik, J.: Baroková literatúra. Svetová, česká, slovenská. Bratislava 1984.

Národohospodár Peter Zaťko spomína. Ed.: Š. Teren. Liptovský Mikuláš 1994.

Naše dejiny v plameňoch. Bratislava 1971.

Pauliny, E.: Dejiny spisovnej slovenčiny od začiatkov po súčasnosť. Bratislava 1983.

Petruf, P. – Štefanský, M. – Uher, J. – Žatkuliak, J.: Slovenská spoločnosť v krízových rokoch 1967 – 1970. Bratislava 1993.

Podrimavský, M.: Slovenská národná strana v druhej polovici XIX. storočia. Bratislava 1983.

Polakovič, Š. – Vnuk, F.: Zahraničné akcie na záchranu a obnovenie slovenskej samostatnosti 1943 – 1948. Lakewood-Hamilton 1988.

Politické strany na Slovensku 1860 – 1989. Ed.: Ľ. Lipták. Bratislava 1992.

Pražák, R. a kol.: Dějiny Maďarska. Brno 1993.

Přehled dějin Československa (do roku 1526) I/1. Eds.: J. Purš, M. Kropilák. Praha 1980.

Prešovské kolégium v slovenských dejinách. Košice 1967.

Rapant, D.: Ilegálna maďarizácia 1790 – 1840. Turčiansky Sv. Martin 1947.

Rapant, D.: K počiatkom maďarizácie. I. – II. Bratislava 1927, 1931.

Rapant, D.: Slovenské povstanie 1848 – 49. I. – V. zv. Turčiansky Sv. Martin – Bratislava 1937 – 1972.

Ratkoš, P. – Butvin, J. – Kropilák, M.: Naše dejiny v plameňoch, Bratislava 1971.

Rebro, K.: Urbárska regulácia Márie Terézie a poddanské úpravy Jozefa II. Bratislava 1959.

Rozloučení s Československem. Eds.: R. Kipke a K. Vodička. Praha 1993.

Ružička, V.: Školstvo na Slovensku v období neskorého feudalizmu. Bratislava 1974.

Rychlik, J., Marzik, T. D. – Bielik, M.: R. W. Seton-Watson: Documents 2 vols, Martin (SR) 1995.

Sidor, K.: Andrej Hlinka 1864 – 1926. Bratislava 1934.

Sidor, K.: Slovenská politika na pôde pražského snemu 1918 – 1938. Bratislava 1943.

Sidor, K.: Takto vznikol Slovenský štát. Bratislava 1991.

Siracký, J.: Sťahovanie Slovákov na Dolnú zem v 18. a 19. storočí. Bratislava 1966.

Slováci a ich národný vývin. Bratislava 1969.

Slovensko I. Dejiny. Ed.: J. Tibenský. Bratislava 1971, 1987.

Slovenský biografický slovník I. – VI. Martin, MS 1986 – 1994.

Sokolovský, L.: Prehľad dejín verejnej správy na území Slovenska, I. – III. časť, Bratislava 1995.

Spiesz, A., – Votruba, M.: Slovak History: The Road to Self-Awareness: Bolchazy-Carducci Publishers, Wauconda, IL 2000.

Stolarik, M. M.: The Role of American Slovaks in the Creation of Czecho-Slovakia. *Slovak Studies* 8 (1968), pp. 7 – 82.

Suchý, M.: Dejiny Levoče I. Košice 1975.

Sutherland, A.: The Fathers of the Slovak Nation: From Juraj Tranovský to Karol Salva or From the Reformation to the Rise of the Populists. *Slovak Studies* 21 (1981), pp. 5 – 187.

Šimončič, J.: Ohlasy francúzskej revolúcie na Slovensku. Košice 1982.

Špetko, J.: Slovenská politická emigrácia v 20. storočí. Praha 1994.

Špiesz, A.: Slobodné kráľovské mestá na Slovensku v rokoch 1680 – 1780. Košice 1983.

Špiesz, A.: Manufaktúrne obdobie na Slovensku 1725 – 1825. Bratislava 1961.

Špiesz, A.: Remeslá, cechy, manufaktúry na Slovensku. Martin 1983.

Táborský, E.: Prezident Beneš mezi Západem a Východem. Praha 1993.

Tibenský, J.: Dejiny vied a techniky na Slovensku. Martin 1979.

Tibenský, J.: Dejiny Slovenska slovom i obrazom I. Martin 1981.

Tibenský, J.: Veľká ozdoba Uhorska. Dielo, život a doba Mateja Bela. Bratislava 1984.

Tibenský, J.: Slovenský Sokrates. Bratislava 1983.

Tibenský, J. a kol.: Priekopníci vedy a techniky na Slovensku. I. – II. Bratislava 1986 – 1988.

Tomášek, D.: Deník druhé republiky. Praha 1988.

Trnavská univerzita v slovenských dejinách. Bratislava 1987.

Udvari, I.: A Mária Terézia-féle úrbérrendezés szlovák nyelvü dokumentumai. Slovenské dokumenty urbárskej regulácie Márie Terézie. Nyíregyháza 1991.

Vajda, S.: Felix Austria. Eine Geschichte Österreichs. Wien 1980.

Vaško, V.: Neumlčaná. Kronika katolíckej cirkvi v Československu po druhé světové válce. Zv. 2. Praha 1990.

Viedenská arbitráž. Ed.: L. Deák. Bratislava 1993.

Vlastivedný slovník obcí na Slovensku I. – III. Ed.: M. Kropilák. Bratislava 1977 – 1978.

Vnuk, F.: Slovakia's Six Eventful Months (October 1938 – March 1939). *Slovak Studies* 4 (1964), pp. 7 – 164.

Vnuk, F.: Mať svoj štát znamená život. Bratislava 1991.

Vnuk, F.: Pokus o schizmu. Bratislava 1995.

Vnuk, F.: Akcie K a R. Bratislava 1995.

Vojenské dějiny Československa I. – III. Praha 1985 – 1987.

Vykoupil, L.: Slovník českých dějin. Brno 1994.

Zlatá kniha banícka. Ed.: J. Vozár. Bratislava 1983.

Žudel, J.: Stolice na Slovensku. Bratislava 1984.

CONTENTS

Július Bartl   Viliam Čičaj   Mária Kohútová
Róbert Letz   Vladimír Segeš   Dušan Škvarna

SLOVAK HISTORY
CHRONOLOGY & LEXICON

Editor *Mgr. Soňa Stušková*
Text Editors *Anton Šteffek, Ph.D. and Albert M. Devine, Ph.D., LL.B.*
Technical Editor *Eva Onderčinová*
Cover *Pavol Čisárik*

Published by MEDIA TRADE, spol. s r. o. – Slovenské pedagogické nakladateľstvo,
Sasinkova 5, 815 60 Bratislava 1, Slovak Republic

BOLCHAZY-CARDUCCI Publishers, Inc.
1000 Brown Street, Wauconda, Illinois 60084, USA

Printed in Slovak Republic

ISBN 80-08-00400-2
ISBN 0-86516-444-4

Slovak Educational Publishing House has already published

Lexikón slovenských dejín

(Original version in Slovak)

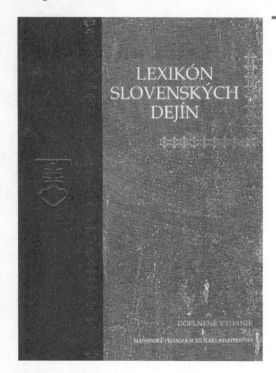

Lexikon der Slowakischen Geschichte

(German translantion of the original Slovak version)